International Harmonization of Accounting

The Library of International Accounting

Series Editor: Christopher W. Nobes
Coopers & Lybrand Professor of Accounting
Department of Economics, University of Reading, UK

1. International Accounting – General Issues and Classification
   Christopher W. Nobes

2. Country Studies in International Accounting – Europe
   Peter J. Walton

3. Country Studies in International Accounting – Americas and the Far East
   Gary K. Meek

4. International Harmonization of Accounting
   Christopher W. Nobes

5. Financial Reporting by Multinationals
   Carol A. Adams and Clare B. Roberts

International Harmonization of Accounting

Edited by

Christopher W. Nobes

Coopers & Lybrand Professor of Accounting
University of Reading, UK

THE LIBRARY OF INTERNATIONAL ACCOUNTING

An Elgar Reference Collection
Cheltenham, UK • Brookfield, US

Published by
Edward Elgar Publishing Limited
8 Lansdown Place
Cheltenham
Glos GL50 2HU
UK

Edward Elgar Publishing Company
Old Post Road
Brookfield
Vermont 05036
US

British Library Cataloguing in Publication Data
International harmonization of accounting. (The library of international accounting; v. 4)
1. Accounting – Standards
I. Nobes, Christopher W.
657'.0218

Library of Congress Cataloguing in Publication Data
International harmonization of accounting / edited by Christopher W. Nobes.
p. cm. — (The library of international accounting : v.4)
Includes bibliographical references and index.
1. Accounting—Standards. 2. Financial statements—Standards.
3. Comparative accounting. I. Nobes, Christopher. II. Series.
HF5626.I584 1996
657—dc20 96-2503
CIP

ISBN 1 85898 147 6

Printed in Great Britain by Galliard (Printers) Ltd, Great Yarmouth

Contents

Acknowledgements

The editor and publishers wish to thank the authors and the following publishers who have kindly given permission for the use of copyright material.

American Accounting Association for article: R.S. Olusegun Wallace (1990), 'Survival Strategies of a Global Organization: The Case of the International Accounting Standards Committee', *Accounting Horizons*, **4** (2), June, 1–22.

Basil Blackwell Ltd for articles: J.S.W. Tay and R.H. Parker (1990), 'Measuring International Harmonization and Standardization', *Abacus*, **26** (1), March, 71–88; Leo G. van der Tas (1992), 'Measuring International Harmonization and Standardization: A Comment', *Abacus*, **28** (2), September, 211–16; J.S.W. Tay and R.H. Parker (1992), 'Measuring International Harmonization and Standardization: A Reply', *Abacus*, **28** (2), September, 217–20.

Betriebswirtschaftlicher Verlag Dr. Th. Gabler GmbH for articles: S. Doupnik and M.E. Taylor (1985), 'An Empirical Investigation of the Observance of IASC Standards in Western Europe', *Management International Review*, **25** (1), 27–33; C.W. Nobes (1987), 'An Empirical Investigation of the Observance of IASC Standards in Western Europe: A Comment', *Management International Review*, **27** (4), 78–9.

Dieter Ordelheide for his own excerpt: (1990), 'Soft-Transformations of Accounting Rules of the 4th Directive in Germany', *Les Cahiers Internationaux de la Compatabilité*, **3**, 1–15.

Graham Diggle, Christopher Nobes and Accountancy Magazines for article: Graham Diggle and Christopher Nobes (1994), 'European Rule-making in Accounting: The Seventh Directive as a Case Study', *Accounting and Business Research*, **24** (96), Autumn, 319–33.

Elsevier Science B.V. for excerpt: Robert Coleman (1984), 'The Aims of EEC Company Law Harmonisation: Corporate Accounting and Disclosure Issues', in S.J. Gray and A.G. Coenenberg (eds), *EEC Accounting Harmonisation: Implementation and Impact of the Fourth Directive*, 3–8.

Emmanuel N. Emenyonu, Sidney J. Gray and Accountancy Magazines for article: Emmanuel N. Emenyonu and Sidney J. Gray (1992), 'EC Accounting Harmonisation: An Empirical Study of Measurement Practices in France, Germany and the UK', *Accounting and Business Research*, **23** (89), Winter, 49–58.

European Accounting Association and Routledge for articles: Leo G. van der Tas (1992), 'Evidence of EC Financial Reporting Practice Harmonization: The Case of Deferred Taxation',

European Accounting Review, **1** (1), May, 69–104; K. Van Hulle (1992), 'Harmonization of Accounting Standards: A View from the European Community', *European Accounting Review*, **1** (1), May, 161–72; K. Van Hulle (1993), 'Harmonization of Accounting Standards in the EC: Is it the Beginning or is it the End?', *European Accounting Review*, **2** (2), September, 387–96; Sara York Kenny and Robert K. Larson (1993), 'Lobbying Behaviour and the Development of International Accounting Standards: The Case of the IASC's Joint Venture Project', *European Accounting Review*, **2** (3), December, 531–54.

International Accounting Standards Committee for articles: 'Preface to Statements of International Accounting Standards'; 'IASC's Framework for the Preparation and Presentation of Financial Statements'.

Christopher W. Nobes and Accountancy Magazines for articles: C.W. Nobes (1983), 'The Evolution of the Harmonising Provisions of the 1980 and 1981 Companies Acts', *Accounting and Business Research*, **14** (53), Winter, 43–53; Christopher Nobes (1993), 'The True and Fair View Requirement: Impact on and of the Fourth Directive', *Accounting and Business Research*, **24** (93), Winter, 35–48.

Springer Verlag GmbH & Co. for articles: R.D. Nair and Werner G. Frank (1981), 'The Harmonization of International Accounting Standards, 1973–1979', *International Journal of Accounting, Education and Research*, Fall, 61–77; Thomas G. Evans and Martin E. Taylor (1982), '"Bottom Line Compliance" with the IASC: A Comparative Analysis', *International Journal of Accounting, Education and Research*, Fall, 115–28; William J. Violet (1983), 'A Philosophical Perspective on the Development of International Accounting Standards', *International Journal of Accounting, Education and Research*, Spring, 1–13; S.M. McKinnon and Paul Janell (1984), 'The International Accounting Standards Committee: A Performance Evaluation', *International Journal of Accounting, Education and Research*, Spring, 19–34; Richard Vangermeersch (1985), 'The Route of the Seventh Directive of the EEC on Consolidated Accounts – Slow, Steady, Studied, and Successful', *International Journal of Accounting, Education and Research*, Spring, 103–18; Juan M. Rivera (1989), 'The Internationalization of Accounting Standards: Past Problems and Current Prospects', *International Journal of Accounting, Education and Research*, **24** (4), 320–41.

Leo G. van der Tas and Accountancy Magazines for article: Leo G. van der Tas (1988), 'Measuring Harmonisation of Financial Reporting Practice', *Accounting and Business Research*, **18** (70), Spring, 157–69.

Every effort has been made to trace all the copyright holders but if any have been inadvertently overlooked the publishers will be pleased to make the necessary arrangement at the first opportunity.

In addition the publishers wish to thank the Library of the London School of Economics and Political Science and the Marshall Library, Cambridge University, for their assistance in obtaining these articles.

Introduction

Christopher W. Nobes

Context

Harmonization is a fairly recent topic for discussion, at least in English. This is partly because the whole field of international accounting is fairly new, as examined in other volumes of this series, and partly because the mechanisms for harmonization are also relatively recent: (i) the International Accounting Standards Committee (IASC) was founded in 1973 and (ii) the UK joined the 'Common Market' in that year, two years after the first draft of the Fourth Directive had been published.

The 1970s saw a spate of articles on these new harmonizing agencies, particularly in the professional accountancy press. One of the earliest substantial works was by Mason (1978), and there were collections of papers, such as Brennan (1979). By the end of the 1970s (after the Fourth Directive had been adopted by the Council of Ministers in 1978), there were detailed discussions of European harmonization (for example Watts, 1979). The early textbooks also took up the harmonization topic (for example Choi and Mueller, 1978, Chapters 5 and 6; and Nobes and Parker, 1981, Chapter 12).

The Measurement of Harmonization

Part I contains papers which construct or examine (or both) methods of measuring harmonization. Others which use relatively straightforward statistics to examine compliance with International Accounting Standards (IASs) are looked at in Part II of this volume, but the first paper to construct a reasonably sophisticated measure of harmonization was that by van der Tas (Chapter 1), who uses the Herfindahl index and then two variants of it. These techniques are applied to five examples of national practices, for example deferred tax practices in the UK and the investment tax credit in the Netherlands. Van der Tas then examines international harmonization of investment tax credit practices in the Netherlands and the US. Although he found increasing uniformity within the Netherlands and within the US, the international picture showed decreasing uniformity because the two countries were concentrating on two different methods.

Tay and Parker (Chapter 2) begin by looking at terminology. They set out some distinctions:

> Harmonization (a *process*) is a movement away from total diversity of practice. Harmony (a *state*) is therefore indicated by a 'clustering' of companies around one or a few of the available methods. Standardization (a process) is a movement towards uniformity (a state). ... both states and processes may be either *de jure* or *de facto*. The former refers to harmony or uniformity of accounting regulations (which may be contained in the law and/or professional accounting standards). The latter refers to the actual practices of companies.

Tay and Parker then examine six papers. Two of these are the van der Tas paper, discussed above, and Nobes (1990), which briefly examines *de facto* uniformity by US companies with IASs, and finds no evidence of deliberate compliance. The other four papers are included in Part II of this volume: Nair and Frank (Chapter 7), Evans and Taylor (Chapter 8), McKinnon and Janell (Chapter 10), Doupnik and Taylor (Chapter 11). Tay and Parker make criticisms of these papers, some of which are mentioned below. They also question whether van der Tas's indices (drawn from industrial economics) are fully suitable. This gave rise to the exchange of views in the two short papers by van der Tas (Chapter 3) and Tay and Parker (Chapter 4) included here.

In Chapter 5 van der Tas, after further discussion of appropriate indices, concentrates on EC harmonization in the case of deferred tax. He finds that European harmony is low when considering the primary financial statements but higher and increasing when including the note disclosures. Emenyonu and Gray (Chapter 6) use the chi-square test and a variant of the Herfindahl index to study six major accounting topics for France, Germany and the UK. They look at the practices in a sample of annual reports relating to 1989. They find low levels of harmony.

Further papers which could have been included in Part I (or in Part III below) are those by (i) Walton (1992) which looks at harmonization between (and within) Britain and France in eight accounting areas; and (ii) Biener (1994) which asks whether mutual recognition might be a substitute for international standardization. These two papers are included in Volume 2 of this series (Walton, *Country Studies in International Accounting – Europe*). A further relevant paper, which was published too late to be included in this volume, is by Archer *et al.* (1995). The authors separate the van der Tas index into intra-national and inter-national effects, and apply this to goodwill and deferred tax in Europe.

The International Accounting Standards Committee

Part II of this volume contains nine papers on the subject of the IASC, four of which were mentioned above. In Tay and Parker's terms, Evans and Taylor (Chapter 8) study *de facto* standardization with certain IASs, whereas Nair and Frank (Chapter 7), McKinnon and Janell (Chapter 10) and Doupnik and Taylor (Chapter 11) study *de jure* uniformity or standardization. Generally, the papers find little uniformity.

In Chapter 8 Evans and Taylor study compliance by large corporations in five countries with the main requirements of five IASs over six years. This paper illustrates some typical problems with some research in international accounting. For example, the first IAS examined is that on inventory valuation. Evans and Taylor impute the 100 per cent use of the 'lower of cost and net realisable value' rule in the UK to a change of UK accounting standards (SSAP 9) to conform to IAS 2. However, there is little evidence that this was the motivation for the content of SSAP 9, rather than the formalization of long-standing UK practice. Evans and Taylor then say that US compliance was weak because the popular US method of LIFO was unacceptable in IAS 2. Of course, this was (and is) untrue. However, even if it were true it would anyway be irrelevant because LIFO is merely a way of measuring 'cost', so it fits happily into the general rule, and does not mean that US compliance is low.

Readers of this who are students or young researchers may be surprised that such blatant errors can be invented by authors, are not filtered out by comments from colleagues on draft versions of the paper, and can survive scrutiny by journal referees and editors. However, more experienced researchers are used to the weaknesses of some international accounting research and they sometimes complain about them (for example Gray, 1983; Wallace and Gernon, 1991), as reprinted in Volume 1: Nobes, *International Accounting – General Issues and Classification*). As in all fields of enquiry, alert scepticism for the written word is a useful attitude.

Nair and Frank (Chapter 7) look at standardization over three periods, using Price Waterhouse (PW) survey data which seems more concerned with accounting requirements rather than accounting practices (that is they look at *de jure* standardization). McKinnon and Janell (Chapter 10) look at three topics contained in IASC rules: depreciation, the equity method and currency translation. They use PW data of 1979 for the 64 countries surveyed. The authors are fairly circumspect but even they do not give full weight to the fact that many PW answers refer to an IAS as the source of authority in a particular country (irrespective of whether the practice is widespread). So, the use of PW data to check compliance with IASs is circular for many countries.

Doupnik and Taylor (Chapter 11) performed their own up-date of the PW survey in 1983 for questions relating to the first eight IASs, and they received answers for 50 countries. They, too, do not notice the circularity problem, so they are impressed that France seemed to 'comply' with all relevant IAS rules in the original 1979 survey. This and other problems are examined in the comment paper by Nobes (Chapter 12).

As may be inferred, the inclusion of these papers in this volume should not be taken as a suggestion that they are flawless. However, when taken as a package, they illustrate the development of the subject.

The remaining four papers in Part II study background or institutional aspects of the IASC. Violet (Chapter 9) takes a 'philosophical perspective'. An earlier paper (Violet, 1983) took an 'anthropological perspective'. Rivera (Chapter 13) looks at the problems of harmonization and the prospects for its success. Wallace (Chapter 14) looks at the institutional legitimacy of the IASC, then at its survival strategies in relation to its management of resources and its procedural process. He concludes that the IASC will survive, partly because of increasing globalization of markets and partly because it has no competitor.

In Chapter 15 York Kenny and Larson study lobbying behaviour in relation to IAS 31 (accounting for interests in joint ventures). It is a compliment relating to the increasing respectability of the IASC that this issue should be studied, and by US researchers.

Another paper which could have been included here (but is in Volume 5: Roberts and Adams, *Financial Reporting by Multinationals*) is that by Brunovs and Kirsch (1991) who look at the harmonization of accounting in the context of IAS 22 on goodwill.

Forthcoming papers (which are no doubt in gestation as I write) will concern the outcome of the IASC's improvements project, which led to ten revised standards in 1993. These came into force in 1995 and, if obeyed, may lead to noticeable increases in uniformity. It will also be possible to study any effects of the IASC on China and Eastern Europe. There are also the ongoing negotiations with the International Organization of Securities Commissions (IOSCO) concerning the possible use of IASs for cross-border listings. These have led to a joint announcement in 1995 by IOSCO and the IASC agreeing a four-year programme of work aimed at achieving a set of core accounting standards for cross-border listings.

European Harmonization

The eight papers in Part III concentrate on European harmonization. Chapter 16 by Coleman and Chapters 20 and 21 by van Hulle are concerned with the purposes and processes of European harmonization. Such issues as mutual recognition, equivalence and the Accounting Advisory Forum are examined here. There is also examination of the options for further harmonization in Europe; for example, leave everything to the IASC or to the US standard setters.

There are three papers on the Fourth Directive. Nobes (Chapter 17) looks at some of the major changes produced in the UK by the 1980 and 1981 Companies Acts. The origins of these changes are traced back, through the Second and Fourth Directives, to precedents in German law. Ordelheide (Chapter 19) looks at the ways in which Germany avoided changes to its laws when implementing the Fourth Directive. This involves: (i) the choice of options; (ii) the clever implementation of requirements in a way probably not intended by the drafters; (iii) the addition of definitions or interpretations which limit change; and (iv) the downright ignoring of a requirement. It seems to be the conclusion of these and other writers that a country's accounting practices are quite good at surviving foreign influences when these come through governmental instructions.

In Chapter 22 Nobes examines the origins of the signifiers of the true and fair view requirement in the various language versions of the Fourth Directive. The signifiers are traced through to national laws. The signified is also examined, as is the degree of effect that the requirement seems to have in different member states. It is concluded that the true and fair view requirement is of considerable significance in its home country (the UK) but of little importance in some other countries (for example Germany). Other papers of relevance in this area can be found in Volume 2: Ordelheide (1993), Walton (1993) and Zeff (1990).

A further two chapters in Part III concern the Seventh Directive. Vangermeersch (Chapter 18) looks at the process whereby the Directive evolved. There are descriptions of various documents and stages involved. Diggle and Nobes (Chapter 23) create a model of the creation of a Directive involving three stages, with different mixes of influences. They then look at 19 areas of consolidation rules and trace the changes in Seventh Directive documents from the early 1970s to adoption in 1983. A move from German to UK rules is observed.

As no more Directives on accounting are presently planned, the attention of researchers may shift to the results of implementation in such countries as Italy (where the Seventh Directive came into force for 1994 year ends), and then to implementation in new European Union members (Austria, Finland and Sweden) and possibly elsewhere (for example Norway, the Czech Republic, Hungary and Poland).

Meanwhile, considerable amounts of data are being generated on *de jure* implementation of Directives (for example FEE, 1993) and on *de facto* practices of European companies (for example FEE, 1991). Further books which discuss the implementation of the Fourth and Seventh Directives, respectively, are by Gray and Coenenberg (1984) and Gray, Coenenberg and Gordon (1993).

Official Material

In Part IV four official documents are reproduced which are frequently referenced by academics and which therefore often need to be consulted by researchers and students. These are the IASC's Preface and Conceptual Framework, and the Fourth and Seventh Directives.

References

Archer, S., P. Delvaille and S. McLeay (1995), 'The Measurement of Harmonisation and the Comparability of Financial Statement Items: Within-country and Between-country Effects', *Accounting and Business Research*, **25, Spring**, 67–80.

Biener, H. (1994), 'What is the Future of Mutual Recognition of Financial Satements and is Comparability Really Necessary?', *European Accounting Review*, **3** (2), 335–42.

Brennan, W.J. (ed.) (1979), *The Internationalization of the Accountancy Profession*, Toronto: CICA.

Brunovs, R. and R.J. Kirsch (1991), 'Goodwill Accounting in Selected Countries and the Harmonisation of International Accounting Standards', *Abacus*, **27** (2), 135–61.

Choi, F.D.S. and G.G. Mueller (1978), *An Introduction to Multinational Accounting*, London: Prentice Hall.

FEE (1991), *European Survey of Published Accounts 1991*, London: Routledge.

FEE (1993), *Seventh Directive Options and Their Implementation*, London: Routledge.

Gray, S.J. (1983), 'International Accounting: A Review of Academic Research in the United Kingdom', *International Journal of Accounting Education and Research*, Fall, 15–42.

Gray, S.J. and A.G. Coenenberg (1984), *EEC Accounting Harmonisation: Implementation and Impact of the Fourth Directive*, North Holland.

Gray, S.J., A.G. Coenenberg and P.D. Gordon (1993), *International Group Accounting*, London: Routledge.

Mason, A.K. (1978), *The Development of International Financial Reporting Standards*, Lancaster University, UK: International Centre for Research in Accounting, Chapter 6.

Nobes, C.W. (1990), 'A Note on Compliance by US Corporations with IASC Standards', *British Accounting Review*, **22** (1), March, 41–9.

Nobes, C.W. and R.H. Parker (1981), *Comparative International Accounting*, London: Philip Allan.

Ordelheide, D. (1993), 'True and Fair View: a European and a German Perspective', *European Accounting Review*, **2** (1), 81–90.

Violet, W.J. (1983), 'The Development of International Accounting Standards: An Anthropological Perspective', *International Journal of Accounting Education and Research*, Fall, 1–13.

Wallace, R.S.O. and H. Gernon (1991), 'Frameworks for International Comparative Accounting', *Journal of Accounting Literature*, **10**, 209–64.

Walton, P. (1992), 'Harmonization of Accounting in Britain and France: Some Evidence', *Abacus*, **28** (2), September, 186–99.

Walton, P. (1993), 'The True and Fair View in British Accounting', *European Accounting Review*, **2** (1), 49–58.

Watts, T.R. (1979), *Handbook on the EEC Fourth Directive*, London: ICAEW.

Zeff, S.A. (1990), 'The English Language Equivalent of "Geeft Een Getrouw Beeld"', *De Accountant*, **2**, October, 83.

Part I
The Measurement of Harmonization

[1]

Accounting and Business Research. Vol. 18. No. 70. pp. 157-169. 1988

Measuring Harmonisation of Financial Reporting Practice*

Leo G. van der Tas

Abstract—Many organisations are currently engaged in the process of national and international harmonisation of financial reporting. This paper examines the nature of the harmonisation problem and the possibility of developing a method to quantify the degree of harmony of financial reporting practice. This quantification can be useful in determining problem areas where the degree of harmony is low, and the impact of standards on financial reporting harmony and spontaneous harmonisation, i.e. harmonisation that cannot be attributed to laws, standards or guidelines. Standard setters might use the method to set goals in respect of the required degree of harmony when issuing a standard, guideline or opinion.

Introduction

Many national and international organisations, such as the Accounting Standards Committee, the Financial Accounting Standards Board (FASB), the International Accounting Standards Committee (IASC) and the European Community (EC), and also governments, are currently engaged in the process of national and international harmonisation of financial reporting. They issue guidelines, standards and laws aiming, among other things, at the harmonisation of financial reporting practice. However, it is not always clear what harmonisation is and how to measure the impact that these organisations have on the degree of harmony.

This paper tries to quantify degrees of harmonisation. First, a framework will be developed to define harmonisation, identify the various harmonisation objects and state the object to be measured. Subsequently a method will be developed that quantifies the degree of harmony of financial reporting practice for each item in the annual accounts. This method can be used by the organisations mentioned above to identify problem areas requiring harmonisation. Second, it is possible with the aid of this method to determine when and to what extent harmonisation has taken place. Third, the method can be used to measure what impact the above-mentioned organisations have on the harmonisation of financial reporting practice by attributing changes in the degree of harmony to three factors:

1. the introduction or amendment of mandatory provisions;
2. the introduction or amendment of non-mandatory provisions;
3. spontaneous harmonisation, for example as a consequence of developments abroad or evolution of practice.

*This paper is a revision of one presented at the Ninth Annual Congress of the European Accounting Association in Stockholm, March 1986. The author would like to thank Professors M. A. van Hoepen and F. Krens for their valuable comments on a previous draft.

Definition of harmonisation

Financial reporting is a communication process. A company translates the events that influence its financial position and affairs into its financial report so as to provide users with information about its financial position and affairs. The translation process is based upon the company's accounting policies. As part of these policies, a company decides whether to translate a particular event in its financial report (the decision between alternative degrees of disclosure) and which accounting method to apply (the choice between alternative methods of valuation, profit determination, consolidation and presentation). For example, the company must decide whether to provide segmental information and forecasts, and whether to use historical cost or current value.

When formulating an accounting policy the company's choice between alternative degrees of disclosure and alternative accounting methods is restricted by standards. Standards will be defined as any financial reporting rule published by either the government or a private standard setting body. These standards can refer either to the degree of disclosure or to the accounting method to be applied.

Harmonisation is a coordination, a tuning of two or more objects. Users are confronted with several financial reports. It would be useful for them if these financial reports were more in harmony. Therefore, financial reports are a target of harmonisation. One way to harmonise financial reports is by formulating standards, thus setting limits to the difference between financial reports. Standards are not only a means of achieving the harmonisation of financial reports. They are also an object of harmonisation themselves. Companies, notably multinationals, are confronted with differing and sometimes conflicting national standards. For them harmonisation of standards is presumed to be useful.

Harmonisation of financial reports will be called *material harmonisation* while harmonisation of standards will be called *formal harmonisation*. This paper is confined to material harmonisation. When measuring the degree of material harmony it is possible to determine the impact of standards and formal harmonisation on material harmonisation. Since they limit the company's choice between alternatives, standards lead towards harmonisation. Formal harmonisation is not only an end in itself but also a means of accomplishing material harmonisation by coordinating the national standards. However, formal harmonisation may be accompanied by disharmonisation if the coordination of standards leads to more options for companies in one country. It should also be noted that material harmonisation can take place without being initiated by standard setting. This will be referred to as spontaneous harmonisation. The harmonisation of financial reports or standards can refer either to the degree of disclosure or to the accounting method to be applied. Harmonisation of the extent of disclosure will be called *disclosure harmonisation*, while harmonisation of the applied accounting methods will be called *measurement harmonisation*. This paper is confined to measurement harmonisation.

Thus, this paper is concerned with the harmonisation of financial reports in respect of the accounting method applied (material measurement harmonisation), which implies an increase in the degree of comparability of financial reports. Two financial reports are comparable in respect of one specific event if under the same circumstances this event is accounted for in the same way in both reports or if multiple reporting takes place. Multiple reporting means that a company gives additional information based on an accounting method other than its primary accounting method. There are three forms of multiple reporting:

1. A company provides two financial reports, each based on a different accounting method.
2. A company provides one financial report with two sets of annual accounts based on two different accounting methods.
3. A company provides one financial report with one set of annual accounts, but gives additional information so that the primary accounts can be transformed into secondary accounts based on another accounting method. For example, a company defers research and development (R&D) costs and writes them off in subsequent years. In order to make the accounts comparable with the accounts of a company which writes off R&D costs immediately, this company gives additional information, specifically the level of R&D costs deferred and the level of R&D costs written off in the current year.

In conclusion we reach the following definition:

> Material measurement harmonisation is an increase in the degree of comparability and means that more companies in the same circumstances apply the same accounting method to an event or give additional information in such a way that the financial reports of more companies can be made comparable.

The words 'comparability' and 'harmony' will be used as synonyms for 'material measurement harmony'.

Another problem to be addressed is the question of when circumstances are the same. A distinction can be made between the circumstances of the company itself and the circumstances in which an event to be accounted for occurs. In the first case, the nature of the firm is involved. Taking a narrow point of view one could state that every firm operates under unique circumstances, and that consequently each firm can set up its financial reports in the way it thinks is best in line with these unique circumstances. Taking a broader point of view, companies can be grouped into categories of the same industry or the same product groups. However, most of the organisations engaged in the process of harmonisation of financial reporting use an even coarser division. In general, only companies in a limited number of sectors (such as banking and insurance) are thought to be in a position which is so special that separate provisions are necessary. This latter view is taken in this paper.

In the second case, the nature of the event is involved. We should guard against unlike events being accounted for in the same way simply for the sake of harmonisation. For example, it might be argued that the choice of depreciation method should not be imposed on the companies. This choice depends upon the situation within the company, such as the expected useful lifetime of the asset and the production process.

Measurement methods

National Harmonisation

In this section a method is developed to measure the degree of comparability for each item in the financial reports, based upon the number of financial reports which are comparable in respect of an item: for example, acquisitions of fixed assets, treatment of foreign currencies. It is presumed here that two financial reports are either comparable or not comparable in respect of one item. Thus, there is no gradation in comparability when only one item is taken into account. First, a method is developed without taking multiple reporting into account. Subsequently this method is modified to make allowance for multiple reporting.

Comparability increases when the result of the choice that companies make between alternative accounting methods becomes concentrated on one or on only a limited number of accounting methods, even where the number of available methods remains the same. Thus, comparability can be considered as an increase in the degree of consensus concerning the choice between the alternative methods of accounting for an item in financial reports. Kirkpatrick (1985) suggests that a reduction in the number of alternative accounting practices contributes to harmonisation. However, the degree of harmony depends not only on the number of alternative accounting methods used, but also on the extent to which each method is applied.

The increase in the degree of consensus can be forced or stimulated, or it may be spontaneous. In the first case mandatory provisions prescribe or forbid one or more accounting methods. In the second case non-mandatory guidelines recommend or discourage the application of one or more accounting methods. In the third case the increase of the degree of consensus cannot be attributed to the introduction or amendment of mandatory or non-mandatory provisions. This spontaneous harmonisation may be caused by developments in theory, experimentation or developments in other countries.

Harmony should not be seen as synonymous with rigid uniformity. As stated in the preceding section, one should take account of differences in circumstances. The companies included in the sample to which the method is applied should be chosen carefully. They should be operating under like circumstances. It is also possible to apply the method only to companies operating in a specific industry.

Stâtistical methods have been developed to measure the degree of concentration. One of these concentration indices is the Herfindahl index (Theil, 1973, pp. 42–43), which is calculated by weighting the relative frequencies of the alternative opinions against each other. This means that high relative frequencies have a higher weighting than low relative frequencies. As a consequence, the Herfindahl index (H index) rises when the methods of the parties involved concentrate more on one or only a limited number of alternative methods. In this context the frequency of a method means the number of parties choosing this particular method. The relative frequency is the number of parties choosing this particular method divided by the total number of parties.

An example may serve to illustrate the H index. A particular item can be accounted for by two different methods, A and B. Fifty companies from a group of 100 companies apply method A in period 1. The other 50 apply method B. In period 2, 70 companies apply method A and 30 companies method B. In period 3 the ratio is 90:10. The relative frequencies and the H index derived from these data are given below:

	Method		
Period	A	B	*H Index*
1	0.5	0.5	$0.5^2 + 0.5^2 = 0.5$
2	0.7	0.3	$0.7^2 + 0.3^2 = 0.58$
3	0.9	0.1	$0.9^2 + 0.1^2 = 0.82$

This is only a trivial example but it clearly shows that the H index increased, indicating an increase in the concentration of opinions and a growth in the degree of consensus. Thus, in this case the degree of harmony rose, which means that harmonisation took place. This method can also be applied in cases involving more than two different methods. The formula of the Herfindahl index is:

$$H = \sum_{i=1}^{n} p_i^2 \qquad (1)$$

where:

H = Herfindahl index.
n = number of alternative accounting methods.
p_i = the relative frequency of accounting method i.

The H index fluctuates between 0 (no harmony, with an infinite number of alternative methods all with the same frequency) and 1 (all companies using the same method). The movements of this index indicate the degree of (dis-) harmonisation. The number of different opinions is, in this case, the number of accounting methods applied in practice. However, if all theoretically possible accounting methods are taken into account, this leads to the same H value because the H index does not change when accounting methods with a frequency of 0 are added.

The Herfindahl index is only one of many concentration measures. The advantage of this method is that it is simple but on the other hand gives more information than the rough method of taking as a measure the relative frequency of the accounting method most applied by the examined companies or the sum of the relative frequencies of the two or three accounting methods most applied, especially when many alternative accounting methods are applied. If only two accounting methods are differentiated as is the case in the simple illustration above, the rough method of only taking into account the relative frequency of the accounting method most applied leads to the same conclusion as the application of the H index. But if more than two alternative accounting methods can be distinguished the H index is a more refined method of measuring harmony/harmonisation. The following examples illustrate the application possibilities of the Herfindahl index.

Example I. Deferred Tax in the UK

In the *Survey of Published Accounts* (ICAEW, 1968–1981) the following ways of presenting deferred tax were found:

1. As a separate heading or grouped with deferred liabilities.
2. Grouped with current liabilities.
3. Grouped with reserves.
4. As a deduction from assets less current liabilities.
5. Not identifiable in balance sheet, but transfer shown in profit and loss account.

The following regulations relate to how deferred tax should be presented in the balance sheet:

Companies Act 1967: not as a reserve.
Recommendation N27 of the ICAEW, July 1968: not as a reserve, nor as a current liability.
Exposure Draft 11, May 1973: not as a reserve, nor as a current asset or current liability.
SSAP 11, August 1975: same as ED 11.
Exposure Draft 19, May 1977: not as a reserve, but presentation as a current asset or current liability is allowed again.
SSAP 15, October 1978: same as ED 19.
Companies Act 1981: as a provision.

As can be seen, method III was rejected in 1967. Method II was rejected in 1968, but allowed again in 1977 (proposal) and 1978 (definitive).

Table 1 shows the application frequencies of these five methods in the period from 1968 to 1980. The ICAEW Surveys in respect of deferred tax only covered this period, so one cannot examine the impact of the Companies Act 1967, of N 27 or of the Companies Act 1981. This table also contains the relative frequencies and the H indices. Figure 1 is a graph of the fluctuations of the H index and the periods in which the provisions concerning deferred tax mentioned above were issued.

The figure shows a gradually rising trend until 1978, indicating an increase in the degree of harmony. In 1971 the H index shows a fall which cannot be explained here. In 1978 the rising trend changed into a declining one. This was caused by the fact that SSAP 15 (October 1978) gave companies more freedom in the presentation of deferred tax by allowing them to be presented as a current asset of current liability.

The following conclusions can be drawn from this example:

—The H index of the presentation of Deferred Tax shows a gradual increase in the 1968–1978 period which cannot be attributed to the introduction or amendment of mandatory or non-mandatory provisions. In other words, spontaneous harmonisation took place.

—The impact of the introduction or amendment of provisions can be measured by the H index (see, for example, the change after SSAP 15 was introduced).

Table 1
Frequencies and, in brackets, relative frequencies of deferred tax methods

Period	Method I	II	III	IV	V	Total	H Index
1968	161 (0.809)	6 (0.03)	6 (0.03)	26 (0.131)	—(—)	199	0.673
1969	169 (0.849)	3 (0.015)	4 (0.02)	23 (0.116)	—(—)	199	0.735
1970	176 (0.871)	3 (0.015)	2 (0.01)	20 (0.099)	1 (0.005)	202	0.769
1971	205 (0.833)	3 (0.012)	8 (0.033)	29 (0.118)	1 (0.004)	246	0.709
1972	241 (0.92)	—(—)	4 (0.015)	17 (0.065)	—(—)	262	0.851
1973	248 (0.915)	1 (0.004)	2 (0.007)	20 (0.074)	—(—)	271	0.843
1974	254 (0.907)	—(—)	1 (0.004)	25 (0.089)	—(—)	280	0.831
1975	266 (0.908)	—(—)	—(—)	27 (0.092)	—(—)	293	0.833
1976	275 (0.945)	—(—)	—(—)	16 (0.055)	—(—)	291	0.896
1977	252 (0.962)	2 (0.008)	1 (0.004)	7 (0.027)	—(—)	262	0.926
1978	237 (1)	—(—)	—(—)	—(—)	—(—)	237	1
1979	239 (0.992)	2 (0.008)	—(—)	—(—)	—(—)	241	0.984
1980	213 (0.943)	13 (0.058)	—(—)	—(—)	—(—)	226	0.892

Source: *Survey of Published Accounts*, Institute of Chartered Accountants in England and Wales.

Figure 1
H Index for deferred tax in the UK

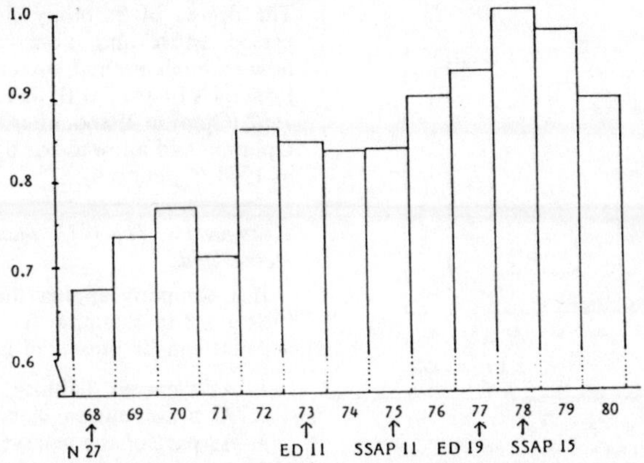

Table 2
Frequencies and, in brackets, relative frequencies of WIR methods

Period	Method 1	Method 2	Method 3	Total	H Index
1978	5 (0.062)	21 (0.259)	55 (0.679)	81	0.532
1979	3 (0.032)	19 (0.204)	71 (0.763)	93	0.625
1980	1 (0.011)	17 (0.181)	76 (0.809)	94	0.687
1981	1 (0.011)	15 (0.158)	79 (0.832)	95	0.717
1982	1 (0.011)	13 (0.139)	80 (0.851)	94	0.744
1983	2 (0.017)	15 (0.13)	98 (0.852)	115	0.743
1984	2 (0.017)	14 (0.121)	100 (0.862)	116	0.758

Sources: 1978–1982: Beckman (1980) and Noordzij (1984); 1983–1984: Van der Tas (1986).

Example II. Accounting for the WIR (Investment Tax Credit) in the Netherlands

In 1978 an investment stimulation plan was introduced. This involved an investment tax credit (WIR), comparable to the investment tax credit in the United States before it was abolished by the Tax Reform Act in 1986. There are three ways of accounting for the WIR:

1. The credit is recognised directly in the Profit and Loss Account or in Equity in the year it is awarded (flow-through method).
2. The credit is deducted from the investment, thus leading to lower depreciation in subsequent years (deduction method).
3. The credit is charged to an equalisation account on the credit side of the balance sheet and expensed during subsequent years (equalisation method).

In 1983 the Dutch Council for Annual Reporting (Raad voor de Jaarverslaggeving, 1983) issued a draft guideline stating its preferrence for methods 2 and 3.

Table 2 contains the application frequencies of these three methods for the surveyed companies in the period 1978 to 1984. In the same table the relative frequencies and the H indices are given. In Figure 2 fluctuations in the H index are plotted and the period in which the draft guideline was issued is indicated. The figure shows clearly a strong increase in the H index. The draft guideline had a slight impact on the degree of harmony at the very time when the process of harmonisation stopped.

Figure 2
H Index for the WIR in the Netherlands

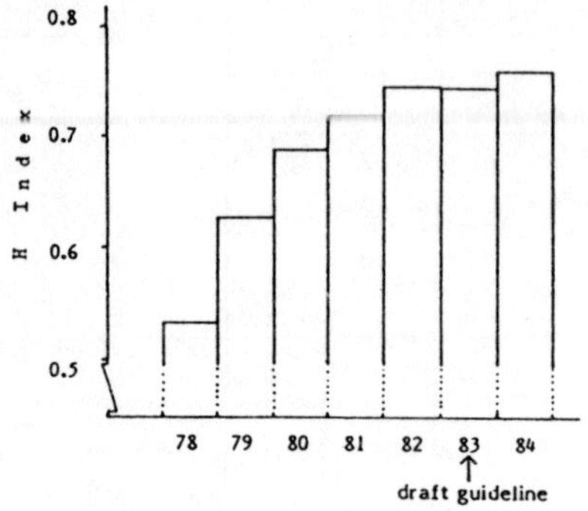

Example III. Accounting for the Investment Tax Credit (ITC) in the US

In *Accounting Trends and Techniques* (AICPA, various years) two different methods were found to account for the ITC:

1. Flow-through method, comparable to method 1 in Example II;
2. Deferral method, comparable to methods 2 and 3 in Example II.

Table 3 gives the application frequencies of the two methods in the 1965–1982 period based on data from *Accounting Trends and Techniques.* In Figure 3 the H index is plotted against time. The degree of harmony clearly rose during this period. More and more companies applied the flow-through method, even though the Accounting Principles Board (APB) had rejected this method in 1962 (Opinion 2) and, after Congress overrode this Opinion, had allowed but discouraged the method in 1964 (Opinion 4).

Example IV. The WIR equalisation account in the Netherlands

If a company applies the equalisation method (method 3 in Example II), the WIR equalisation account can be presented in five ways:

1. As a current liability;
2. As a non-current liability or as a provision;
3. As part of the reserves;
4. As a separate item between debt and equity (deferred income);
5. As a separate deduction from fixed assets.

In a 1983 draft guideline the Council for Annual Reporting discouraged presentation as part of the reserves or as a provision. In 1984 the EC Fourth Directive was implemented in Book 2 of the Dutch Civil Code as a new Title 8. This makes it clear that a WIR equalisation account cannot be presented as a provision.

Table 3
Frequencies and, in brackets, relative frequencies of ITC methods

Period	*Method* 1	2	*Total*	*H Index*
1965	226 (0.787)	61 (0.213)	287	0.665
1967	257 (0.793)	67 (0.207)	324	0.672
1968	290 (0.815)	66 (0.185)	356	0.698
1969	300 (0.831)	61 (0.169)	361	0.719
1970	245 (0.819)	54 (0.181)	299	0.704
1971	329 (0.801)	82 (0.199)	411	0.681
1972	489 (0.864)	77 (0.136)	566	0.765
1973	496 (0.864)	78 (0.136)	574	0.765
1974	504 (0.875)	72 (0.125)	576	0.781
1975	518 (0.896)	60 (0.104)	578	0.814
1976	502 (0.869)	76 (0.131)	578	0.772
1977	504 (0.871)	75 (0.129)	579	0.775
1978	521 (0.88)	71 (0.12)	592	0.789
1979	529 (0.888)	67 (0.112)	596	0.801
1980	528 (0.887)	67 (0.113)	595	0.8
1981	531 (0.895)	62 (0.105)	593	0.813
1982	537 (0.909)	54 (0.091)	591	0.834
1983	541 (0.915)	50 (0.085)	591	0.844
1984	543 (0.919)	48 (0.081)	591	0.851

Source: *Accounting Trends and Techniques.*

Figure 3
H Index for the ITC in the US

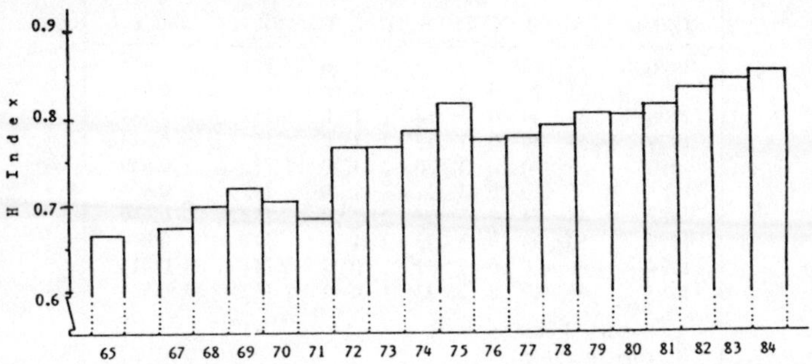

Table 4 shows the application frequencies of these five methods in the examined financial reports. In Figure 4 the fluctuations of the H index are plotted, showing a slight increase from 1978 to 1983 and a big increase in 1984, caused by the new legislation.

Multiple Reporting

The advantage of the H index is that it is simple and easy to calculate. However, a disadvantage is its inability to take account of multiple reporting, because each company can only be assigned to one of the alternative accounting methods. Here a method will be developed which does take multiple reporting into account.

The degree of comparability of financial reports in a country can be measured by relating the number of 'compatible' pairs of companies to the number of pairings possible. The financial reports of two companies are compatible if both companies apply the same accounting method or if one or both of the companies give additional information to enable comparison. For example, if there

Figure 4
H Index for the WIR equalisation account in the Netherlands

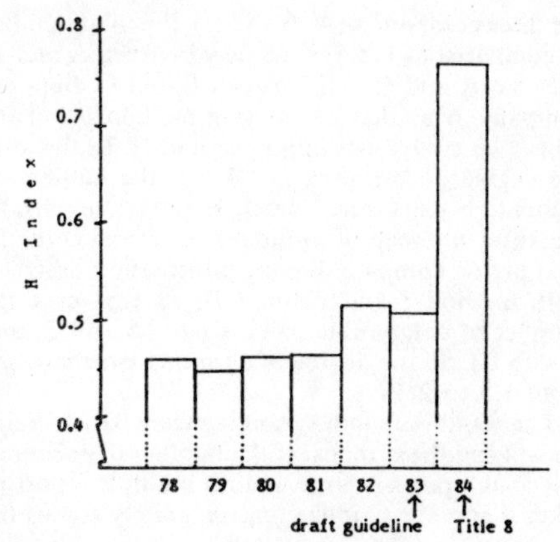

Table 4
Frequencies and, in brackets, relative frequencies of the WIR equalisation account

	Method						*H*
Period	1	2	3	4	5	*Total*	*Index*
1978	2 (0.036)	30 (0.546)	1 (0.018)	22 (0.4)	—(—)	55	0.459
1979	2 (0.028)	35 (0.493)	2 (0.028)	32 (0.451)	—(—)	71	0.448
1980	1 (0.013)	37 (0.487)	2 (0.026)	36 (0.474)	—(—)	76	0.462
1981	1 (0.013)	36 (0.456)	2 (0.025)	40 (0.506)	—(—)	79	0.465
1982	—(—)	30 (0.375)	1 (0.013)	49 (0.613)	—(—)	80	0.516
1983	—(—)	35 (0.358)	—(—)	61 (0.617)	2 (0.025)	98	0.51
1984	—(—)	10 (0.107)	—(—)	88 (0.869)	2 (0.024)	100	0.767

Sources: 1978–1982: Beckman (1980) and Noordzij (1984); 1983–1984: Van der Tas (1986).

Table 5
Frequencies of valuation methods, and C Index

Period	Method A	B	C	D	E	F	G	H	*Total*	*C Index*
1976	73	26	0	2	7	2	1	0	111	0.633
1977	71	29	0	2	7	1	1	0	111	0.611
1978	63	29	0	3	14	2	1	0	112	0.634
1979	59	30	0	3	17	2	1	0	112	0.644
1980	56	30	0	3	20	2	1	0	112	0.659
1981	55	30	0	3	21	2	1	0	112	0.664
1982	54	31	0	3	21	2	1	0	112	0.660
1983	53	30	0	3	23	2	1	0	112	0.674
1984	46	20	0	2	41	1	0	1	111	0.811
1985	46	19	0	2	43	1	0	1	112	0.821

A. historical cost
B. current value
C. land at current value, buildings at historical cost
D. land at historcal cost, buildings at current value
E. both A and B
F. both A and C
G. both B and D
H. both A, B and D

} by way of additional information in the notes

are three companies (A, B and C), the total number of comparisons is three, namely between A and B, between A and C and between B and C. Suppose company A applies accounting method I and the other two companies apply method II. In this case the degree of harmony is 1/3, i.e. the number of compatible pairs (one, namely B and C), divided by the total number of comparisons (three). In the next period company B gives information based on both method I and method II. In that case the number of compatible pairs is two (A and B, and B with C). So the degree of harmony has increased from 1/3 to 2/3.

The result is an index, ranging from 0 to 1, which we will call the C index. If the number of examined financial reports is large and no multiple reporting takes place, the C index approximately equals the H index discussed above. The advantage of the C index, however, is its ability to take account of multiple reporting. The derivation of the formula of the C index is shown in Appendix 1. The same applies to the proof of the statement that the C index and the H index are approximately equal when a large number of companies is examined and no multiple reporting takes place. An example of the application of the C index follows.

Example V. Valuation of Land and Buildings in the Netherlands

Both historical cost and current value are allowed as valuation methods for land and buildings. Many companies, when applying one of these methods, provide additional information based upon the other. Table 5 shows the findings of an

Figure 5
C Index of valuation methods in the Netherlands

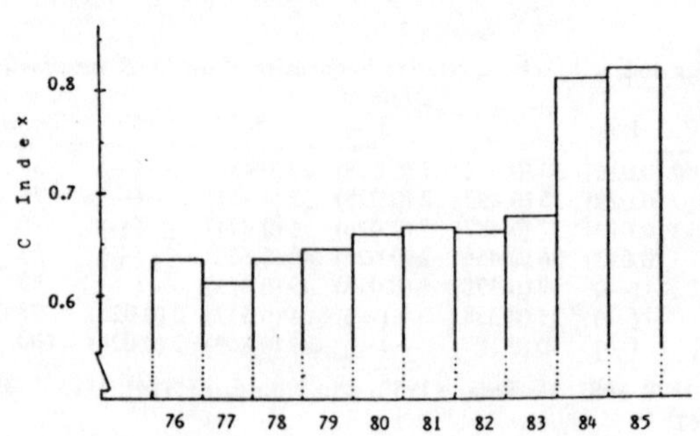

examination of how many companies listed on the Amsterdam Stock Exchange provide additional information on the value of land and buildings based upon the method not used in the main financial statements. The fluctuations in the C index are shown in Figure 5.

The increase in the C index in 1984 was caused by the new Title 8 of the Dutch Civil Code which encouraged companies applying historical cost to give additional information about the current value of these assets.

International Harmonisation

There are two ways of looking at international material harmonisation. From the first point of view international harmony is the degree of comparability of financial reports of companies irrespective of the country in which they are established. This could be the point of view of an international investor who wants to compare financial reports irrespective of the home country of the companies. From the second point of view international harmonisation takes place when there is a convergence of opinions in two or more countries on the way in which a specific item should be accounted for. This could be the point of view of a standard setting body that wants to know what differences exist between the countries in respect of the way in which a particular item is accounted for.

From the first point of view international harmony is measured in the same way as national harmony, except that the area of examination consists of more than one country. The two indices developed above can be applied accordingly. However, it should be borne in mind that, in this case, countries with many companies have a larger weighting than countries with fewer companies. From the second point of view the degree of international material harmony indicates the degree to which the companies in one country apply the same or only a limited number of alternative accounting methods, compared to the companies in another country. It can be measured in the following way. If the companies in two countries apply the same method to a large extent this means that the relative frequencies with which this method is applied in the two countries reinforce each other. So we can measure the degree of international material harmony by multiplying the relative application frequency of a method in country A by the relative application frequency of the same method in country B and subsequently by adding the results of all alternative methods. This sum will be called the I index.

As an example of the use of the I index, assume that the relative frequencies of the alternative accounting methods 1 and 2 in countries A and B are as follows:

		Country A	B	*I index*
Time 1:				
Method	1	1	0	$1 \times 0 + 0 \times 1 = \underline{0}$
	2	0	1	
Time 2:				
Method	1	0.6	0.3	$0.6 \times 0.3 + 0.4 \times 0.7 = 0.46$
	2	0.4	0.7	

The result is an index ranging from 0 to 1, indicating the degree of international material harmony. The formula of the I index is:

$$I = \sum_{i=1}^{n} (f_i^1 \times f_i^2) \qquad (2)$$

where

f_i^1 = the relative application frequency of method i in country 1.

n = the number of alternative accounting methods.

Example VI. I Index for the ITC in the US and the Netherlands

In the previous section, we saw an increasing application of the flow-through method in the US, while in the Netherlands the deferral method received greater support. The frequencies and relative frequencies in the USA and the Netherlands as well as the I indices are given in Table 6, which

Table 6
I Index for ITC

	Netherlands		*US*		*I*
Period	*deferral*	*flow-through*	*deferral*	*flow-through*	*Index*
1978	0.938	0.062	0.12	0.88	0.167
1979	0.968	0.032	0.112	0.888	0.137
1980	0.989	0.011	0.113	0.887	0.122
1981	0.989	0.011	0.105	0.895	0.113
1982	0.989	0.011	0.091	0.909	0.1
1983	0.983	0.017	0.085	0.915	0.099
1984	0.983	0.017	0.081	0.919	0.095

The I index for 1978, for example, is calculated as:
$0.938 \times 0.12 + 0.062 \times 0.88 = 0.167$

shows that the degree of international harmony decreased, while the two countries concentrated on a different method. They moved in opposite directions.

This method is also applicable to more than two countries. In that case, however, a correction factor should be built in, as otherwise the I index would be very unequally distributed over the interval 0 to 1. The resulting formula and the statistical motivation for the correction factor can be found in Appendix 2.

Application possibilities

The potential applications of such a quantification of the degree of material measurement harmony/comparability are:

1. It gives an indication of the degree of harmony in respect of the accounting treatment of a specific item at a particular moment.
2. Fluctuations in the degree of harmony indicate when and to what extent harmonisation has taken place.
3. Fluctuations in the degree of harmony can be attributed to:
   —the introduction or amendment of mandatory provisions concerning financial reporting;
   —the introduction or amendment of non-mandatory provisions concerning financial reporting;
   —spontaneous harmonisation caused, for example, by developments in accounting theory or developments abroad.
4. It can be used to identify problem areas in financial reporting; these are the items with a low degree of harmony.
5. Organisations concerned with the harmonisation of financial reporting might use the measurement method to set goals in respect of the desired degree of harmony for a certain item in the financial report. In that case the degree of harmony achieved by a standard or by harmonisation of standards can be compared with the goal being pursued.

As mentioned earlier, comparability of financial reporting is related to the circumstances of the reporting companies as well as to the circumstances under which an event to be accounted for takes place. Harmonisation should not lead to unlike circumstances being accounted for in the same way. This means that, when applying the developed measurement methods, the sample of companies to be examined should be chosen carefully. What exactly is meant by 'like curcumstances' is open to discussion but is independent of the measurement method. It influences only the sample of companies to be examined.

The problem of like circumstances also has an impact on the question of whether there is any purpose in calculating the degree of harmony in respect of a specific item. For example, the choice of the depreciation period depends on the specific circumstances within the company such as the production process and the expected useful lifetime of the assets. Thus, calculating the degree of harmony in respect of the depreciation period applied to specific assets is of hardly any use.

A practical problem is that it is not always possible to determine the way in which a company has chosen to account for an item, for example because of insufficient explanation. Moreover it can prove difficult to determine whether a company did not account for a particular item because it was not applicable or because the company opted not to take the item into account. For example if a company presents no deferred tax in its balance sheet, there are two possibilities:

—there is no deferred tax; or
—there is deferred tax, but the company applied the flow-through method, which does not take deferred tax into account.

These practical problems may hamper the application of the described measurement methods.

However, there is a third limitation of a more fundamental character. The measurement indices presuppose that the differences between the alternative accounting methods are of about the same size. If three alternative methods are distinguished (A, B and C) the measurement indices presuppose that the magnitude of the differences between A and B, B and C and between B and C are about the same. This is not always true, as we saw in Examples II and III concerning accounting for the ITC. The difference between the flow-through method and the other two methods is larger than the difference between the deduction method and the equalisation method. This problem arises at the time when the alternative accounting methods are distinguished, even before collecting the data. This might impose a limitation on judging the degree of material harmony. On this subject, three remarks should be made here:

—It was assumed that financial reports are not comparable if they are each based on a different accounting principle, regardless of the extent of the difference between the methods. Two financial reports are either comparable or not; there is no gradation in comparability when only one item is taken into account.
—The most important advantage of the described methods is the possibility of quantifying the degree of harmonisation. This means that *fluctuations* in the degree of harmony are more important than the level of harmony. Thus, once a particular classification of alternative account-

ing methods is chosen, the problem of unequal differences is of minor importance. In any case it is possible to determine whether and when (dis-) harmonisation took place. Only the determination of the extent to which harmonisation took place might cause some difficulties.

—A solution to the problem of unequal differences between the alternative accounting methods could be found by applying a more sophisticated measurement method that weights the differences between the alternative accounting methods. Further research should determine how this could be realised.

Conclusion

In this paper there is an attempt to identify ways of quantifying the degree of harmony in financial reporting practice. First, it was concluded that harmonisation is a process whereas harmony is a state. Harmonisation is an increase in the degree of harmony. Subsequently, a distinction was made between formal and material harmonisation. *Formal harmonisation* is harmonisation of the provisions concerning financial reporting. *Material harmonisation* is harmonisation of financial reporting practice itself. A second distinction was made between *disclosure harmonisation* (harmonisation of the extent of information disclosure) and *measurement harmonisation* (harmonisation of the nature of information disclosed). This paper is confined to material measurement harmony, which is an increase in the degree of comparability of financial reporting practice. More specifically:

> Material measurement harmonisation means that more companies in the same circumstances apply the same accounting method to an event or give additional information in such a way that the financial reports of more companies can be made comparable.

Based on this definition, a statistical concentration index was used to develop a method that quantifies the degree of comparability (the H index). This method could not, however, take account of multiple reporting (supplying information based on more than one accounting method). So the next step was to develop a method that could take account of multiple reporting (the C index). These two methods can be used to measure national comparability. They can also be used to measure international comparability from the point of view of an international investor or creditor but are less suited for measuring international comparability from the point of view of an international standard setter, for which a third method was described which is more suitable (the I index).

These methods were illustrated by applying them to some items in financial reporting, with the conclusions that it is possible to quantify the degree of harmony and harmonisation of financial reporting. It also proved possible to measure the influence of mandatory and non-mandatory provisions concerning financial reporting and the degree of spontaneous harmonisation.

Organisations engaged in the process of harmonisation of financial reporting might use the developed measurement methods to set goals in respect of the degree of harmony of a particular item in financial reporting. In this way the realised degree of harmony can be compared with the desired degree of harmony in order to evaluate the impact of a specific standard, guideline or law.

Appendix 1. Formula for the C Index

The C index divides the number of compatible pairs of financial reports by the total number of possible comparisons. The number of pairs of financial reports out of a sample of n financial reports is:

$$0.5 \times (n^2 - n). \qquad (3)$$

Two financial reports are comparable if they are based on the same accounting method. This means that, if no multiple reporting takes place, the total number of financial reports must be subdivided into classes of financial reports with the same accounting method in respect of a specific item. *Within* these classes it is possible to compare the financial reports. However it is not possible to make comparisons *between* financial reports in different classes. The number of possible comparisons within such a class is $0.5\,(a_i^2 - a_i)$ where a_i is the number of financial reports within this class. This means that the total number of compatible pairs is:

$$0.5(a_1^2 - a_1) + 0.5(a_2^2 - a_2) + \cdots + 0.5(a_i^2 - a_i)$$

where

a_i = the number of companies applying accounting method i.

i = the number of alternative accounting methods.

This sum must be divided by the total number of possible comparisons. So the formula for the C index is:

$$C = \frac{0.5(a_1^2 - a_1) + 0.5(a_2^2 - a_2) + \cdots + 0.5(a_i^2 - a_i)}{0.5(n^2 - n)} = \frac{\left(\sum_{i=1}^{i} a_i^2\right) - n}{n^2 - n} \qquad (4)$$

where:

a_i = the number of companies applying accounting method i.
i = the number of alternative accounting methods.
n = the total number of companies.

Applying the formula to the example in the sub-section 'Multiple Reporting' in the situation without multiple reporting gives the following result:

$$C = \frac{1^2 + 2^2 - 3}{3^2 - 3} = 1/3$$

It is possible to relate the C index to the H index, because the latter can be stated as:

$$H = \frac{\sum_{i=1}^{i} a_i^2}{n^2} \qquad (6)$$

So

$$C = \frac{H \times n^2 - n}{n^2 - n} = \frac{H - 1/n}{1 - 1/n} \qquad (7)$$

When n reaches infinity: $C = H$.

If a financial report provides information based on more than one accounting method (multiple reporting), this financial report has to be subdivided into more than one class of financial reports. However, this means that the comparison between two financial reports which both supply information based on the same two or more accounting methods is counted double, triple or more because the comparison is counted in more than one class of financial reports. To avoid this double counting the number of comparisons between two financial reports based on the same two or more accounting methods should be deducted. The result is that the total number of compatible pairs is the same as described above in the case of no multiple reporting, except that a deduction is made to avoid double counting (analogous to Mood, Graybill and Boes, 1974, p. 24):

$$0.5 \sum_{j=1}^{i} (a_j^2 - a_j) - 0.5\left(\sum_{j=1}^{i-1} \sum_{k=j+1}^{i} (a_{jk}^2 - a_{jk}) + \sum_{j=1}^{i-2} \sum_{k=j+1}^{i-1} \sum_{l=k+1}^{i} (a_{jkl}^2 - a_{jkl}) \ldots + (-1)^{i+1} \sum \ldots \sum (a_{j..}^2 - a_{j..}) \right)$$

where $a_{jkl..}$ is the number of companies supplying information based on accounting methods j, k, l, et cetera and j, k and l are parameters fluctuating between 1 and i. This sum must be divided by the total number of possible comparisons $(0.5(n^2 - n))$. The result is:

Applying this formula to the earlier example with multiple reporting gives:

$$C = \frac{2^2 - 2 + 2^2 - 2 - 0}{3^2 - 3} = 2/3$$

Appendix 2: The I Index in the case of more than two countries

On p. 165 above the situation was described where two countries were compared. The I index is also applicable when more than two countries are compared. However, in this case the I index becomes very small because a large number of fractions are multiplied. This leads to a very unequal distribution of the I index over the interval 0 – 1.

To improve the possible application of the I index a correction factor should be built in, perhaps as follows. Where all accounting methods are applied with the same relative frequencies in every country, the addition of another similar country only leads to a small change in the I index. For example:

	Country A	B	
Method I	0.5	0.5	I = 0.5 × 0.5 + 0.5 × 0.5
Method II	0.5	0.5	= 0.5

After the addition of country C (where half of the companies apply method I and the rest apply method II) the calculation of the uncorrected I index leads to:

	Country A	B	C	
Method I	0.5	0.5	0.5	I = 0.5 × 0.5 × 0.5
Method II	0.5	0.5	0.5	+ 0.5 × 0.5 × 0.5
				= 0.25

The I Index with correction factor is: $I^x = I^{1/(m-1)}$ where m = the number of examined countries. In the example above the corrected I index would be: $I^x = 0.25^{1/2} = 0.5$. The addition of country C does not therefore lead to a change in the corrected I index.

The general formula of the I index is as follows:

$$I^x = \left(\sum_{i=1}^{n} (f_i^1 \times f_i^2 x \ldots x f_i^m) \right)^{1/(m-1)} \qquad (9)$$

where

f_i = relative frequency of method i in country m.
m = number of countries.
n = number of alternative accounting methods.

$$C = \frac{\sum_{j=1}^{i} (a_j^2 - a_j) - \sum\sum_{j<k} (a_{jk}^2 - a_{jk}) + \sum\sum\sum_{j<k<l} (a_{jkl}^2 - a_{jkl}) - \cdots + (-1)^{i+1} \sum \ldots \sum (a_{j..}^2 - a_{j...})}{n^2 - n} \qquad (8)$$

References

AICPA, *Accounting Trends and Techniques*, annual publication.

Beckman, H. (1980), *Verwerking van WIR-premies, voorontwerp van Beschouwingen en de praktijk van de jaarverslaggeving*, Rapport 8014/Acc, Centrum voor Bedrijfseconomisch Onderzoek, Erasmus Universiteit, Rotterdam.

ICAEW, *Survey of Published Accounts*, editions 1968 to 1981, Institute of Chartered Accountants in England and Wales.

Kirkpatrick, J. L. (1985), *Proceedings of the OECD Congress on Harmonization of Accounting Standards*, Paris, April 1985.

Mood, A. M., F. A. Graybill and D. C. Boes (1974), *Introduction to the Theory of Statistics*, Tokyo.

Noordzij, M. W. (1984), *De verwerking van WIR-premies in de jaarrekening van 100 ondernemingen over de periode 1979 tot en met 1982*, Centrum voor Bedrijfseconomisch Onderzoek, Erasmus Universiteit, Rotterdam.

Raad voor de Jaarverslaggeving (1983), *Ontwerp-richtlijn 'Voorzieningen voor latente belastingen'*.

Theil, H. (1973), *Statistical Decomposition Analyses*, Amsterdam.

Van der Tas, L. G. (1986), 'Belastingen naar de winst', *Jaar in/Jaar uit*, J. Dijksma (ed.), Groningen.

[2]

ABACUS, Vol. 26, No. 1, 1990

J. S. W. TAY AND R. H. PARKER

Measuring International Harmonization and Standardization

This paper analyses six recent studies dealing with the measurement of international harmonization of financial reporting. Methodological issues and problems relating to the definition and operationalization of terms, sources of data, statistical methods and causation are discussed, and an alternative methodology for measuring harmonization suggested.

Key words: Accounting policies; Standardization; Uniform systems of accounts.

The purpose of this paper is to discuss the problems involved in the measurement of the concepts of 'harmonization' and 'standardization'. We do so by analysing six recent empirical attempts to measure those concepts in the context of international accounting. These harmonization measurement studies may differ from studies which appraise the extent of disclosure in company accounts (e.g., Singhvi and Desai, 1971; Buzby, 1974; Barrett, 1976). Such disclosure studies are ultimately concerned with the quality of information contained in company accounts. Harmonization measurement studies are, more simply, concerned with the similarity or otherwise of accounting practices and regulations. Table 1 summarizes the six studies in terms of their objectives, the data sources used, the countries surveyed, their general methodology, the statistical methods employed, and their main conclusions. These studies used different data sources and methodologies and, perhaps unsurprisingly, arrived at somewhat different conclusions.

SOME TERMINOLOGICAL DISTINCTIONS

Both 'harmonization' and 'standardization' are used rather loosely in accounting practice and in the literature. This paper therefore begins with an attempt to clarify the distinction between them, and the related concepts of 'harmony' and 'uniformity'. The suggested terminology is intended for both national and international contexts. The use of the term 'harmonization' is not restricted to the latter.

J. S. W. Tay is a Senior Tutor in the School of Accountancy and Commerce, Nanyang Technological Institute, Singapore, and R. H. Parker is Professor of Accountancy, Department of Economics, University of Exeter, England.

The authors acknowledge the helpful comments of C. W. Nobes, R. S. O. Wallace and the anonymous referees of earlier versions of this paper. One of the earlier versions was presented at the Tenth Congress of the European Accounting Association, London, March 1987.

TABLE 1

MEASUREMENT STUDIES SURVEYED

	Nair and Frank (1981)	Evans and Taylor (1982)	McKinnon and Janell (1984)	Doupnik and Taylor (1985)	Nobes (1987b)	van der Tas (1988)
Objectives	To assess the success of 'formal' harmonization efforts by the IASC	'To determine the impact of IASC standards on the financial reporting in member nations' (p. 119)	To analyse the direct and indirect influence of the IASC on accounting standards and requirements	To assess conformity of Western European countries to a 'basic core of accounting practice' (p. 27), and changes in conformity over time	To test the hypothesis that U.S. and U.K. companies do not obey IASC standards	To quantify harmony, determine when and to what extent harmonization has taken place, and the impact of standard-setting bodies
Countries surveyed	37 countries common to the 3 PW surveys	France, Japan, U.K., U.S. and West Germany	64 countries covered by the 1979 PW survey	16 Western European countries	The U.K. and the U.S.	The Netherlands, the U.K. and the U.S.
Scope	IASs 1–10	IASs 2–4, 6 and 7	IASs 3 and 4, ED 11 (IAS21)	IASs 1–8	IASs 3, 4 and 22 (U.S.) and IASs 9, 14 and 19 (U.K.)	Accounting for deferred tax and investment tax credit; valuation of land and buildings
Data sources	PW surveys 1973, 1975 and 1979	9–10 financial reports from each country surveyed, for the period 1975–88	PW 1979 survey	PW 1979 survey and own questionnaire	Published 1985 accounts for separate random samples of listed companies	National surveys
Methodology	Changes in the distribution of countries among requirement categories tested for significance with Friedman's ANOVA	Reports examined for evidence of compliance with IASs. Results given as percentage compliance rates per country for each year	Descriptive analysis of accounting regulations of IASC members. Discussion of IASC influence on ASC and FASB statements on foreign exchange translation	Response categories weighted. Average scores calculated for regions and countries. Nonparametric tests used to differentiate regions and groups	Differences of content or timing identified between national standards and IASs. Compliance rates inspected for signs of obedience to IASs	3 indices developed to measure harmony and comparability, used for different countries. Changes in values related to legal and professional regulation
Main conclusions	'the period of the IASC's existence has coincided with a growing harmonization of accounting standards' (p. 77)	'the IASC has had very little impact on the accounting practices of the countries surveyed' (p. 126)	'the IASC has not succeeded in changing existing standards or setting new standards' (p. 33)	'much diversity continues . . . to exist among the countries of Western Europe' (p. 33)	that 'IASs are not obeyed may be accepted' (p. 13)	'it is possible to measure the influence of mandatory and non-mandatory provisions' (p. 167)

HARMONIZATION AND STANDARDIZATION

Harmonization and Standardization

Harmonization (a *process*) is a movement away from total diversity of practice. Harmony (a *state*) is therefore indicated by a 'clustering' of companies around one or a few of the available methods. Standardization (a process) is a movement towards uniformity (a state). It includes the clustering associated with harmony, and reduction in the number of available methods. (As it is difficult to measure a process, the six studies have tried to measure harmony or uniformity at different points in time.) Harmony and uniformity are therefore not dichotomous. The former is any point on the continuum between the two states of total diversity and uniformity, excluding these extreme states, as illustrated in Figure 1.

FIGURE 1

HARMONIZATION AND STANDARDIZATION

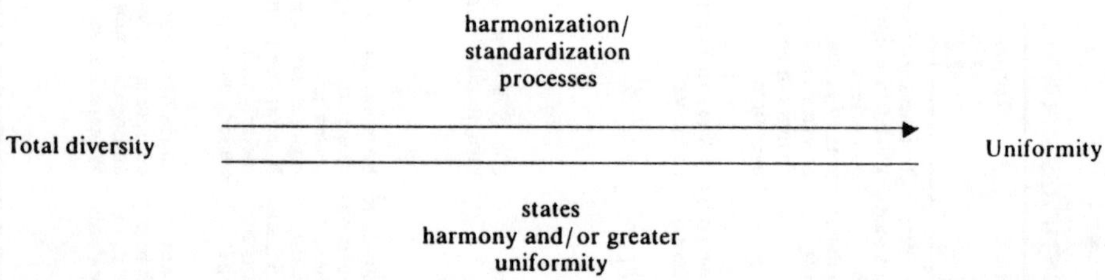

Regulation and Practice

Harmonization, harmony, standardization and uniformity exist at the levels of concepts, principles, regulations and practice. This paper is concerned with the last two, which have the most immediate impact on company accounts. In this context, both states and processes may be either *de jure* or *de facto*. The former refers to harmony or uniformity of accounting regulations (which may be contained in the law and/or professional accounting standards). The latter refers to the actual practices of companies.

Strict and Less Strict Regulation

Accounting regulations may be strict or less strict in three different senses. First, a regulation may apply to all companies (strict) or only to some companies (less strict). Second, a regulation may be contained in the law (strict) or in a professional accounting standard (less strict). Compliance with a legal regulation may be expected to be higher than compliance with a standard. Third, a regulation may contain a precise definition (strict) or a discretionary one (less strict). All three senses of the terms 'strict' and 'less strict' imply that the former is associated with uniformity, the latter with harmony.

Figure 2

TERMINOLOGY OF HARMONIZATION AND STANDARDIZATION

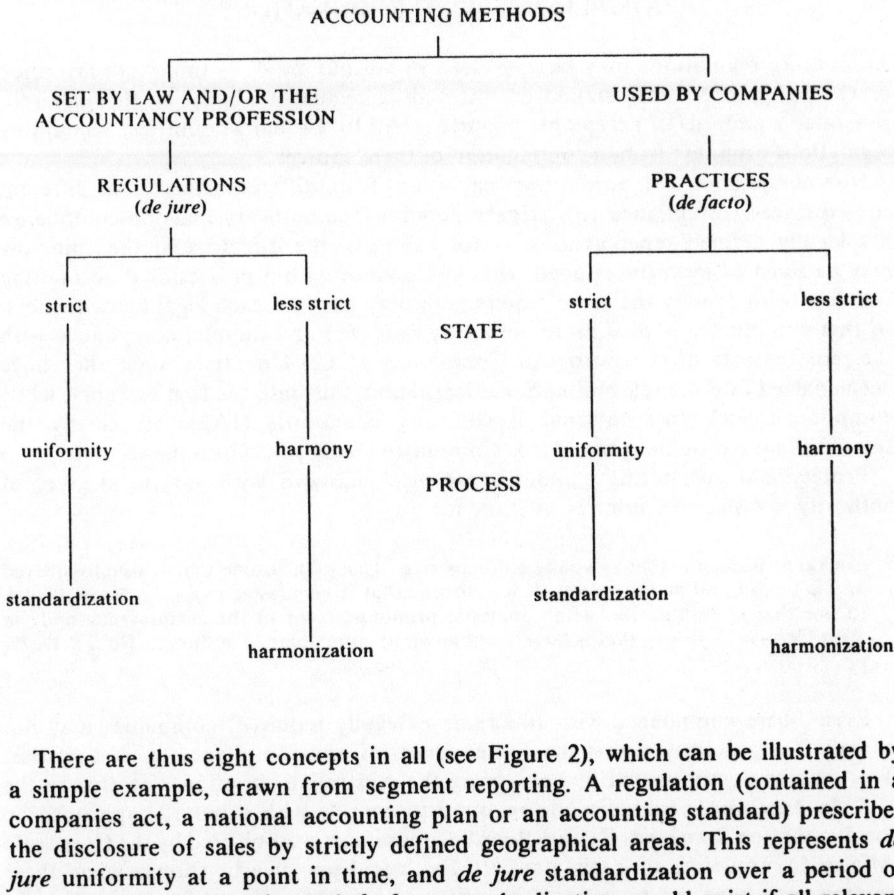

There are thus eight concepts in all (see Figure 2), which can be illustrated by a simple example, drawn from segment reporting. A regulation (contained in a companies act, a national accounting plan or an accounting standard) prescribes the disclosure of sales by strictly defined geographical areas. This represents *de jure* uniformity at a point in time, and *de jure* standardization over a period of time. *De facto* uniformity and *de facto* standardization would exist if all relevant companies actually disclosed sales as required, by strictly defined geographical areas. (Uniformity and standardization can exist *de facto* with or without concurrent *de jure* uniformity and standardization, as it may be in the interest of all companies to make such disclosures even if there are no formal regulations.) If, however, regulation or practice result in disclosure of sales by geographical areas which are not strictly defined but left to the discretion of the company, the result is *de jure* harmony, *de jure* harmonization, *de facto* harmony and *de facto* harmonization respectively.

Taking account of both the desirability of international comparability of financial statements, and the operational difficulties involved in measuring processes rather than states, the most suitable concept for measurement appears to be *de facto* harmonization, in the form of studies of *de facto* harmony over time.

COMPLIANCE WITH REGULATIONS

Accounting regulations may be expressed in various ways — in statute law and/or through professional standards, through a regulatory body or through self-generated standards of acceptable practice (GAAP). In many countries, accounting regulations originate from a combination of these sources.

Non-compliance with accounting regulations from different sources has different consequences. Compliance with a legal regulation is compulsory, and non-compliance has legally defined repercussions — for example, the directors of the company may be fined or even imprisoned. Non-compliance with a professional accounting standard with exactly the same requirement may have no such legal consequences, so that compliance is of a more voluntary nature. For example, compliance with the requirements of the European Community (E.C.) Directives, once they have been enacted into the relevant national legislation, falls into the first category, while compliance with International Accounting Standards (IASs) issued by the International Accounting Standards Committee (IASC) falls into the second.

Professional accounting standards are also endowed with varying degrees of authority in different countries. A standard

> can range from one that is legally enforced (e.g., Canada), to one that is usually obeyed and is binding on auditors (e.g., U.K.), to one that is persuasive (e.g., the Netherlands), to one that is unimportant (e.g., domestic pronouncement of the accountancy body in West Germany), to one that is largely unknown to companies or auditors. (Nobes, 1987b, pp. 78–9)

Even where compliance with standards is legally required, companies may not comply if it is perceived that the consequences of non-compliance are not serious. This may be demonstrated by comparing the Australian situation with that in the U.S. In Australia, companies are required to comply with standards approved by the Accounting Standards Review Board. Compliance is monitored by the Corporate Affairs Commission of each state. It has not been clearly shown what these commissions have the power (or the will) to do to non-complying companies. In the U.S., the SEC has the power, and the will, to refuse to register financial statements.

Both legal and professional regulations may apply to all companies, or only to a certain specified sub-set of companies, such as publicly listed companies. Thus, when seeking to measure compliance, the different types of regulations, and the different types of companies to which they relate, must be distinguished.

In the sections which follow, the distinctions which have been made here are used to indicate more clearly what each study has tried to measure and whether or not concepts have been confused. Attention is also drawn to what researchers have *not* tried to measure.

MEASUREMENT STUDIES REVIEWED

In terms of Figure 2, the studies may be categorized as follows:

1. Nair and Frank (NF; 1981): *de jure* uniformity in three different periods. The study used survey data based on accounting requirements.
2. Evans and Taylor (ET; 1982): *de facto* uniformity over a six-year period. The accounts of companies were examined for compliance with certain IASs.
3. McKinnon and Janell (MJ; 1984): *de jure* uniformity. This is a non-statistical analysis of the IASC's influence on accounting standards in various countries.
4. Doupnik and Taylor (DT; 1985): *de jure* uniformity in two different years. Accounting requirements in various countries were ranked in terms of compliance with IASs.
5. Nobes (N; 1987b): *de facto* uniformity. Accounts of companies were examined for compliance with certain IASs.
6. van der Tas (VDT; 1988): *de facto* harmony over periods of time. The study developed a cardinal measurement method, which was used on national survey data of company reporting practices.

It must be noted that NF, ET and DT all believed that they were measuring *de facto* harmonization. However, this was not the case. NF and DT assumed erroneously that the accounting requirements provided by their data sources were strictly adhered to. All three studies defined harmonization in terms which actually defined standardization. These problems are discussed in later sections of this paper.

To summarize, despite the authors' claims to the contrary, two of the six studies are concerned with states: MJ (*de jure* uniformity) and N (*de facto* uniformity). The other four are concerned with the processes of harmonization and standardization, represented by studies of harmony and uniformity at different points in time. Of the eight concepts outlined in Figure 2, it appears that only five have been covered by the six studies: *de jure* uniformity (MJ); *de jure* standardization (NF, DT); *de facto* uniformity (N); *de facto* standardization (ET); and *de facto* harmonization (VDT). There has not been any comprehensive measurement study of the concept of *de facto* harmonization. Thus, evaluations of the work of the IASC and the E.C. in achieving greater comparability of financial statements produced by companies in different countries have been incomplete.

PROBLEMS ARISING

Several important questions arise in relation to the measurement of harmony, harmonization, uniformity and standardization:

1. What data sources should be used?
2. How should the concepts be operationalized?
3. What statistical methods should be used?
4. How can changes in accounting practice due to compliance with a standard be distinguished from changes due to other reasons?

Each of these questions is discussed below, in the context of the six studies surveyed.

HARMONIZATION AND STANDARDIZATION

POSSIBLE DATA SOURCES

The six studies under review made use of three types of data sources: international or multi-country surveys (NF, DT and MJ), original financial statements (ET and N), and national surveys (VDT). The choice of data source has important repercussions for the overall research design, as there are advantages and difficulties involved with using each of them.

Surveys

The international surveys used were those prepared by Price Waterhouse International (hereafter referred to as 'the PW surveys'), reflecting reporting requirements in 1973, 1975 and 1979 in a varying number of countries. The national surveys used by VDT were those published by the professional accounting bodies in the U.S., the U.K. and the Netherlands. A list of international and national surveys available is given in Appendix A.

There are obvious advantages involved in using survey data, whether national or international — someone else has already done all the difficult and tedious work of collecting the data, which relate to a large number of countries and/or companies, cover a wide range of accounting topics and are available in a language which the researcher can understand (the PW surveys, for example, are available in five major languages). However, the difficulties involved with using survey material are also well known, and perhaps best summarized by Nobes (1981).

Probably the main difficulty involved with using surveys is the appropriateness (and hence the validity) of the data collected. Often, the questions were not asked for the purposes to which researchers subsequently put them. In the PW surveys, respondents were asked to fit their country's requirements in relation to an accounting practice into one of several categories, ranging from Required to Not Permitted. However, both these extreme categories imply the same degree of *uniformity*. Moreover, all the questions may not be of the same relative importance in capturing the variable in which the researcher is interested.

Survey data may not be provided in the way in which the researcher needs them. This is a particular problem when using data from more than one survey. NF found that only 37 countries and 131 accounting practices were common to the three PW surveys, and that the response categories had changed over time (pp. 66–7). It would obviously be even more difficult to compare data from surveys carried out by different organizations.

Furthermore, surveys (especially international surveys) may not contain sufficient detail. The PW survey (1979) contains a warning to this effect:

> given the necessity for a brief description of a principle or practice, it is not possible to indicate variations that may be of importance in a particular country. The reader is therefore cautioned against drawing too precise an interpretation on specific matters or in relation to specific countries. (p. 3)

Survey data may also be unreliable. Nobes (1981) has pointed out several inaccuracies in the 1979 PW survey, relating to the responses given about practice in the U.K. (p. 268). It is probable that there were similar inaccuracies involved in the responses given for other countries; inaccuracies which the researcher may not be aware of through unfamiliarity with different accounting systems.

Such unfamiliarity may also lead researchers to misinterpret survey data. Both NF and DT assumed that practices which are categorized as Required or Recommended in countries are complied with by all relevant companies. This assumption may be due to the authority of FASB standards for SEC-listed companies in the U.S. However, it ignores the 'hierarchy of sources' (i.e., different sources of regulations have differing degrees of authority in different countries).

A copy of the DT questionnaire (kindly provided by Doupnik) showed that, in all cases, the source of regulations for various accounting practices in France was an IAS. However, although IASs are recommended by the *Commission des Operations de Bourse* (COB), they are not uniformly practised, even by listed companies. COB data quoted by Nobes (1987b) 'show that only about half of even the listed French companies prepared consolidated accounts (as required by IAS3) in 1979' (p. 78). However, the assumption that regulations are complied with led to DT's conclusions that France was in complete compliance with the requirements of IASs 1–8 in 1979.

The possibility of similar misinterpretation is lessened in a more recent international survey carried out by Gray, Campbell and Shaw (1984; hereafter referred to as 'the Gray survey'), in conjunction with Deloitte Haskins & Sells. This gives information on the (estimated) level of compliance as well as requirements for 1982. A comparison of the 1979 PW survey and the Gray survey is contained in Appendix B.

The researcher must also consider the sample of companies and/or countries involved in each survey. At least ten IASC member countries are excluded from the 1979 PW survey, and there is no information on the type of companies (either by size or by industry) whose reporting practices are assessed. The Netherlands is noticeably absent from the Gray survey, although it is revealed that the sample consists of about fifty large companies in developed countries, and twenty large companies in less developed or smaller countries (Gray *et al.*, 1984, p. 4). It is obviously important for researchers to be aware of the sample on which their data are based, as this could affect the suitability of the data for their particular research purposes. Both NF and MJ, who used PW survey data, expressed reservations about the data (NF, p. 65; MJ, p. 22); whereas neither DT (who used the 1979 PW survey) nor VDT (who used three national surveys) gave any evidence of having considered the shortcomings of their data sources and the effects which these might have on their conclusions.

One final drawback with using survey data is that there is a time-lag between the publication of the survey and the period surveyed. In some cases this is not a problem: the 1979 PW survey, published in 1980, is based 'on the position at January 1, 1979, in all cases' (PW, 1979, p. 7); the Gray survey, published in 1984, is based on 'relevant current pronouncements as at 1 January 1982' (Gray *et al.*, 1984, p. 3). Some national surveys (e.g., France) may relate to financial statements issued either two or even three years earlier. Moreover, there may also be a small time-lag between the date at which requirements were current and the period to which the surveyed financial statements relate (Gray *et al.*, 1984, pp. 3–4).

National surveys are generally more detailed and more reliable than international surveys, simply because their scope is smaller. However, they are not carried out in many countries, or may only be produced sporadically. Moreover, the bases on which each national survey is compiled may render comparisons between countries difficult and even invalid. Finally, they may not be available in a language which the researcher can understand.

Financial Statements

The use of financial statements is not without its own difficulties. While the data are 'raw' and may be manipulated in any way the researcher wishes, the collection of these data is often a tedious, time-consuming process. This may be a problem especially if the researcher wishes to obtain reports from countries other than his or her own. First, companies in that country may not be in the practice of sending their annual reports to anyone apart from their shareholders. Second, the reports may not be available in a language which the researcher can understand (translation is sometimes difficult, and always expensive). Third, even when, say, English-language versions are available, other problems may arise (McLeay, 1988). These may be either abridged (one has only to compare the English and French versions of the annual reports of some French companies to appreciate this), or the financial statements may be restated on bases other than those used in the original statements. Campbell (1985) points out that in Japan, for example, some companies produce 'convenience translations' which 'may include additional disclosure items that are not required by Japanese GAAP, and may reclassify some financial statements into a form that is more familiar to non-Japanese readers' (p. 153). Thus, while such translations may provide useful insights for the researcher, 'they do not provide a completely accurate picture of financial reporting in Japan' (p. 154). N used original statements of U.S. and U.K. companies, which presented no language problems. However, ET used Japanese, French and German reports, of which 'all the Japanese and part of the French and West German statements were English-language versions' (p. 121). It is therefore possible that their data are either incomplete, or presented in a different form from the original statements.

The choice of countries and/or companies sampled is also important when using financial statements. ET was the only study of the six which used such a sample, but little attempt was made to justify their choice:

> The countries selected . . . are France, Japan, the United Kingdom, the United States and West Germany. All these nations are founding members of the IASC . . . the published financial statements of a sample of corporations in each country were examined . . . in general, nine or ten financial statements were examined in each country. (pp. 120–1)

However, there are four other founding members of the IASC, and the inclusion of one more of them, the Netherlands, would have enabled ET to justify the countries selected as being those identified as 'vital countries' by Mason (1978). Moreover, an examination of the companies surveyed (ET, pp. 127–8) does not give any evidence that they have been matched. Given the shortcomings of the sample, it is therefore surprising that the authors extended their results to conclude that 'the IASC has had very little impact on the accounting practices of countries involved' (ET, p. 126).

OPERATIONAL DEFINITIONS

The operationalization of the concepts of harmony, harmonization, uniformity and standardization is necessarily linked with the type of data used. NF, MJ and DT used the PW survey, where regulations were categorized as Required, Recommended, etc. (see Appendix B). This has two effects on operationalization. First, it is assumed that companies comply 100 per cent with the requirements, whatever they might be. As pointed out above, this is a somewhat naive assumption. Second, harmonization is viewed in terms of movements of countries from category to category. NF 'looked for those practices on which more than half of the thirty-seven countries [common to the three PW surveys] . . . were to be found in either the Required or Not Permitted categories by 1979' (p. 68). This is perhaps too strict a definition of harmonization, as the categories selected imply uniformity rather than harmony. More appropriately, harmonization would merely involve looking for changes, over the period surveyed, in the *clustering* of companies within any of the categories, that is, whether *more* countries were grouped into particular categories at the end of the period than at the beginning.

DT assigned 'weights' to the PW categories, and assessed the level of harmony by calculating weighted average scores. The use of weights implies that there is some quantifiable relationship among the response categories. For example Majority Practice, weighted as 3, represents three times more harmony than Rarely or Not Found, which is weighted as 1. This implication was strengthened in their analysis by frequent references to percentage changes in the weighted average scores over time. However, such relationships would be difficult to support, given the form of the PW data.

The other three studies used sources which give actual compliance rates, although VDT's rates are based on national surveys, while those of N and ET are based on samples of financial statements. Harmony was a function of the observed compliance rate, with a higher rate indicating a greater degree of harmony. However, one could argue that compliance with strictly defined disclosure requirements is more an indication of uniformity than of harmony.

STATISTICAL METHODS

The six studies used three different statistical methods to measure harmonization and standardization. These may be broadly described as descriptive statistics, nonparametric statistics and indices.

Descriptive Statistics
This was the simplest and the most common method employed (used by ET, MJ and N), involving the calculation of the number or percentage of companies within the sample which complied with specified regulations. The size of the percentage described the degree of uniformity.

These studies fall short of providing useful insight into the overall degree of harmony, either among countries or across time. ET showed the level of compliance per country, per year, but there was no summary of the overall level of compliance for any one country over the period surveyed, or of compliance among the group of countries for any particular year. MJ summarized the requirements of IASC member countries in relation to IAS4 (p. 24), but were unable, given the non-quantitative nature of their analysis, to comment on the level of uniformity involved. N's results were shown in terms of both the numbers and percentages of companies displaying different levels of disclosure. This was extrapolated to apply to the populations of large U.S. and U.K. corporations from which the two random samples were drawn. However, given the emphasis on compliance with very narrowly defined IAS requirements, the result does not reflect general standardization of accounting practice so much as uniformity of compliance with these IAS requirements.

Nonparametric Statistics
NF and DT employed PW survey data, which place countries into requirement categories. These categories may be regarded as ordinal in nature, except that the extreme categories (Required and Not Permitted) imply the same degree of uniformity.

NF assigned ranks to the survey categories, and tested changes in these rankings with Friedman's ANOVA (appropriate 'when the data from *k* matched samples are in at least an ordinal scale', Siegel, 1956, p. 166). Of the five response categories (NF, p. 67), it is obvious that movements from 3 (Minority Practice) to 2 (Predominant Practice) to 1 (Required Practice) would indicate increasing uniformity, as would movements from 3 to 4 (No Application), and from 3 to 5 (Not Permitted). (What movements from 4 to 5 would indicate is not clear.) In a small example (p. 69), it is not apparent that this fact has been appreciated. For country A, increasing harmonization is shown as a movement from 1 to 3; for B, the same movement is given the opposite ranking. It is possible that this inconsistency affected the analysis, as the Friedman ANOVA test is based on the simple idea that 'under *Ho* [i.e. the three matched samples have been drawn from the same population] the mean ranks of the various columns would be about equal' (Siegel, 1956, p. 168). Thus the actual *numbers* assigned by NF to indicate varying degrees of harmonization would affect the analysis.

DT assigned weights to the PW categories, calculated weighted average scores for countries, ranked the scores, and tested these rankings for significant changes. The Kruskal–Wallis test was applied to data from five regions differentiated by DT, to ascertain whether they could be said to have been drawn from different populations (see Siegel, 1956, p. 184). (However, DT had no statistical basis for differentiating these five regions, which appear to have been rather arbitrarily drawn.)

The Mann–Whitney *U* test, which shows 'whether two independent groups have been drawn from the same population' (Siegel, 1956, p. 116), was used to see if there was a significant difference between the mean scores of the E.C. and non-E.C. groups of countries.

These two studies show that nonparametric statistics may be useful in testing for evidence of harmony when data are ordinal in nature. However, they also show that the concept must be properly defined and operationalized, and data properly interpreted and appropriately categorized.

Indices

VDT's study is based on the calculation of three indices, the H-index, the I index and the C index. The first two are used for calculating national and international harmony. The third calculates comparability of accounts when different accounting methods are used but sufficient information is provided to show the effect of using alternative methods.

The H-index, from which the I index is developed, is one of many measures developed by industrial economists to quantify industrial concentration. Its use in the context of financial reporting harmonization implies an analogy between accounting harmonization and industrial concentration. The validity of this analogy is worthy of some discussion.

Industrial concentration deals with measuring actual market structures in relation to the two extremes of monopoly and perfect competition. The former is a situation in which one firm generates all the sales in a particular market. The accounting counterpart of this would be a situation in which one strictly defined accounting method is used by all companies, that is, there is *uniformity* in accounting practice. Perfect competition could be regarded as a situation in which every company was free to use a different accounting method. This may be difficult to envisage for accounting for a particular item within a set of financial statements, but it is something which is possible for the financial statements as a whole — very few companies use identical combinations of accounting methods in producing their financial statements. The 'real world' of accounting lies somewhere between these two extremes, that is, there is some degree of uniformity in some areas. Harmony is thus the counterpart of imperfect competition.

This analogy has intuitive appeal, but may be difficult to operationalize. In measuring industrial concentration, the variables measured are the number of firms, and their market share, share of labour or capital employed, or share of value-added. Industrial economists complain that it is difficult to ascertain how many firms there are in a particular industry. In accounting harmonization, the relevant variables would be the number of accounting methods, and the number of companies using each method. The following questions would have to be answered: How many accounting methods are there for any particular topic? Should we consider only the ones which are allowed by law or professional standards, or should we include all methods which are used? Do we know what all the methods actually in use are? How do we identify the companies which are affected by accounting for this particular topic?

Such questions may be satisfactorily answered in relation to *samples* of companies. The results obtained can then be generalized if the sample used is representative of a certain type of company.

Different methods of calculating concentration are described and compared in a comprehensive survey by Curry and George (1983), who discuss in detail the five most widely used methods: the concentration ratio (CR); the Herfindahl index (VDT's H-index); entropy/relative entropy; the variance of logarithms; and the Hannah-Kay index, which is a generalized version of the Herfindahl index). Curry and George also provide a useful worked example, showing how different measurement methods give different results for industries with different structures (p. 212). Although they conclude that

> the literature which considers the mathematical properties of concentration measures has not resolved the question of which is the best measure to use . . . [and] the complexity of business life is such that in practice it is unlikely that there is one concentration measure which will clearly be superior in all circumstances (p. 215)

this does not detract from the approach suggested by VDT. The use of a concentration index seems to be a useful way to evaluate the level of harmony, and track movements in harmonization over time.

The main problem with concentration indices is that no significance tests have been devised to indicate how trivial or significant (statistically) variations in index values are.

CAUSES OF CHANGES IN COMPLIANCE

Causation poses a difficult problem in the social and management sciences, because of the inability to conduct controlled laboratory experiments. However, it is easier to show causation between legal regulations and the use of accounting methods and/or the disclosure of certain information, than between professional regulations and accounting practices. This is because compliance with legal regulations is compulsory, whereas compliance with professional regulations is not, and it is thus often assumed that compliance with the former is greater than compliance with the latter. Taking the example of consolidation accounting in France again, the proportion of companies producing consolidated accounts will rise now that the Seventh Directive has been partially implemented in France.

Five of the six studies surveyed examined compliance with IASC standards, which are not mandatory. VDT alone looked at legal regulations as a possible explanation for some observed changes in practice. All six studies looked for direct links between IASC activities and accounting practices. MJ and N also pointed out that the IASC may also have indirect influence on practice.

NF's conclusion reflects the difficulty of establishing direct causation:

> The period of the IASC's existence has *coincided* with a growing harmonization of accounting standards. This association between the two is *strengthened* by the fact that many of the topics on which the IASC has issued pronouncements are those on which the authors observe harmonization. (NF, p. 77, emphasis added)

However, this conclusion, cautious as it is, does not appear to be fully supported by NF's results. The study identified 37 countries and 131 accounting practices common to the three PW surveys, and 49 practices which showed evidence of harmonization as defined in the study. These 49 practices were tested for statistically significant changes in the distribution of ranked groupings over the time period, and 29 practices showed changes significant at the 5% level. These 29 practices were then related to the requirements of IASs 1–10, and formed the basis of NF's conclusion. However, this does not take into account the 102 practices for which there was no evidence of harmonization as defined by the study, nor how these practices relate to the ten IASs. NF's conclusion would be more defensible if it had been based on a study of the changes in the distribution of country groupings over all the 131 common practices (or at least all of those which related to the relevant IASs).

MJ postulate that even the degree of compliance observed may be due to reasons other than the conscious desire to comply with IASs. For example, 'France, which credits the IASC standard [on depreciation], is actually strictly governed by its uniform *Plan Comptable*' (p. 24); similarly, the fact that Japanese companies now practice equity accounting on a wider scale than before is 'not in response to IAS No. 3 but to new securities legislation' (p. 26). Their conclusion is that 'the IASC has not succeeded in changing existing standards or setting new standards' (p. 32).

However, MJ's analysis leads to the comment that the IASC is

> most effective when it has been able to obtain endorsements for its opinions by parties having greater enforcement powers . . . [it] lobbies to have its standards considered by the FASB and the ASC, and its power to influence EEC law directives is considerable. (pp. 32–3)

Similarly, N's results suggest that, while IASs 'are not generally obeyed . . . there is some doubt [that] IASs have no direct impact' (p. 13)

VDT graphs fluctuations in the H-index over time (VDT, pp. 161–4). These indicate a rising trend in the level of harmony, as measured by the H-index, with year-to-year fluctuations. Some of these fluctuations are ascribed to particular events (e.g., p. 163, the effect of new legislation on the presentation of the investment tax credit equalization account in the Netherlands); but others appear to have no particular cause (e.g., p. 160, the presentation of deferred taxation in the U.K. in 1971). The analysis shows that, while it may be possible to measure the degree of harmony, it is difficult to distinguish trend movements from random movements. It also reflects our view that little is known about causation.

AN ALTERNATIVE APPROACH TO HARMONIZATION MEASUREMENT

Based on the discussion above, the following approach to measuring harmonization is suggested.

First, if harmonization activities are the result of concern about the comparability of accounts produced by companies from different countries, then a measurement study should focus on actual reporting practices rather than regulations, that is, on *de facto* rather than *de jure* harmonization.

Second, actual reporting practices may be assessed most accurately from annual accounts, or detailed surveys of such accounts. Thus the appropriate data sources would be published accounts, or national surveys based on samples of company accounts (if the companies in the sample are appropriate to the research objective), rather than surveys of legal and professional accounting regulation.

Third, given the sources suggested, data on proportions of companies using different accounting methods can be obtained. An operational definition of harmony could then take the form of comparing the observed distribution of companies among different methods with either a random distribution or some expected distribution. A suitable proxy for the former could be a uniform/equal/rectangular distribution, that is, a distribution in which equal numbers of companies would be expected to use each of the available alternatives. (This would represent no preference for, or bias towards, any one available method.) Evidence of harmony would then be the existence of a significant difference between the observed and expected distributions, as measured by some appropriate significance test, for example, chi-square.

Finally, the level of harmony could be quantified by using a concentration index, preferably one describing the entire distribution, rather than just a portion of it. Comparison of levels of harmony over different periods would yield evidence of harmonization or disharmonization.

SUMMARY

This paper has shown that insufficient research has been undertaken to date on the measurement of harmonization and standardization of financial reporting. The concepts involved have not been clearly defined, and this may explain the evidence of confusion in the methodology of some studies, and the inconsistent results between studies.

Two important points have emerged from this review: first, that none of the six studies reviewed involved a comprehensive measure of *de facto* harmonization, that is, the increasing comparability of financial statement produced by companies. This is a somewhat surprising result, as comparability would appear to be the *raison d'être* of harmonization activities.

Second, the studies suggest two useful measurement approaches — the use of concentration indices, which may be applied to cardinal data; and the use of nonparametric tests when data are only ordinal. Both approaches have been incorporated in a suggested methodology for measuring *de facto* harmony.

REFERENCES

Barrett, M. E., 'Financial Reporting Practices: Disclosure and Comprehensiveness in an International Setting', *Journal of Accounting Research*, Spring 1976.

Buzby, S. L., 'Selected Items of Information and their Disclosure in Annual Reports', *The Accounting Review*, July 1974.

Campbell, L. G., 'Financial Reporting in Japan', in C. W. Nobes and R. H. Parker (eds), *Comparative International Accounting*, Philip Allan, 1985.

Curry, B., and K. D. George, 'Industrial Concentration: A Survey', *Journal of Industrial Economics*, March 1983.

Doupnik, S., and M. E. Taylor, 'An Empirical Investigation of the Observance of IASC Standards in Western Europe', *Management International Review*, Spring 1985.

Evans, T. G., and M. E. Taylor, ' "Bottom-line Compliance" with the IASC: A Comparative Analysis', *International Journal of Accounting*, Fall 1982.

Gray, S. J., S. G. Campbell and J. C. Shaw, *International Financial Reporting: A Comparative Survey of Accounting Requirements and Practices in 30 Countries*, Macmillan, 1984.

McKinnon, S. M., and P. Janell, 'The International Accounting Standards Committee: A Performance Evaluation', *International Journal of Accounting*, Spring 1984.

McLeay, S., 'International Financial Analysis', in C. W. Nobes and R. H. Parker (eds), *Issues in Multinational Accounting*, Philip Allan, 1988.

Mason, A. K., *The Development of International Financial Reporting Standards*, International Centre for Research in Accounting, Lancaster University, 1978.

Nair, R. D., and W. G. Frank, 'The Harmonization of International Accounting Standards', *International Journal of Accounting*, Fall 1981.

Nobes, C. W., 'An Empirical Analysis of International Accounting Principles: A Comment', *Journal of Accounting Research*, Spring 1981.

——, 'Compliance by U.K. and U.S. Corporations with IASC Standards', paper presented at the Tenth Congress of the European Accounting Association, London, March 1987a.

——, 'An Empirical Investigation of the Observance of IASC Standards in Western Europe: A Comment', *Management International Review*, Winter 1987b.

Price Waterhouse International, *Survey of Accounting Principles and Reporting Practices in 38 countries* Institute of Chartered Accountants in England and Wales, 1973.

——, *A Survey in 46 Countries: Accounting Principles and Reporting Practices*, Institute of Chartered Accountants in England and Wales 1975.

——, *International Survey of Accounting Principles and Reporting Practices*, Butterworths, 1979.

Siegel, S., *Nonparametric Statistics for the Behavioral Sciences*, McGraw-Hill, 1956.

Singhvi, S. S., and H. B. Desai, 'An Empirical Analysis of the Quality of Corporate Financial Disclosure', *The Accounting Review*, January 1971.

van der Tas, L. G., 'Measuring Harmonisation of Financial Reporting Practice', *Accounting and Business Research*, Spring 1988.

APPENDIX A

POSSIBLE DATA SOURCES

International Surveys

Gray, S. J., L. G. Campbell and J. C. Shaw, *International Financial Reporting: A Comparative Survey of Accounting Requirements and Practices in 30 Countries*, Macmillan, 1984.

OECD, *Accounting Practices in OECD Member Countries*, OECD, 1980.

Price Waterhouse International, *Survey of Accounting Principles and Reporting Practices in 38 Countries*, The Institute of Chartered Accountants in England and Wales, 1973.

——, *A Survey in 46 Countries: Accounting Principles and Reporting Practices*, The Institute of Chartered Accountants in England and Wales, 1975.

——, *International Survey of Accounting Principles and Reporting Practices*, Butterworths, 1979.

SGV, *Comparative Accounting Practices in ASEAN*, Sycip, Gorres, Velayo and Co., 1984.

National Surveys

Australia: *Australian Financial Reporting*, based on 120 public companies. First survey published in 1972. Several surveys since, carried out by the Australian Accounting Research Foundation. Most recent based on 1980 accounts. No further surveys planned.

Canada: *Financial Reporting in Canada*, published bi-annually by the Canadian Institute of Chartered Accountants since 1955. Sixteenth edition (1985) relates to 1983 and 1984 accounts of 325 public companies; 1981 and 1982 data are also included.

France: *Les Rapports Annuels des Sociétés Françaises*, published bi-annually by l'Ordre des Experts Comptables et des Comptables Agréés. Based on a sample of 150 large French companies. Available in French only.

India: *Precedents in Published Accounts*, published by the Institute of Chartered Accountants of India in 1981. Relates to the 1979 accounts of 202 public and private-sector companies. Available in English.

Netherlands: *Onderzoek Jaarverslaggeving*, published by the Nederlands Instituut van Registeraccountants, based on the accounts of 120 companies. Editions relate to accounts published one to two years before. Available in Dutch only.

New Zealand: *New Zealand Company Financial Reporting*, published in 1982 and 1984 with financial support from universities. The latter contains information on annual reports of the 100 largest NZ companies for 1979, 1982 and 1983.

Sweden: *Survey of Accounting Practices*, most recently published in 1985 by the Swedish Institute of Authorised Public Accountants. Based on 100 companies listed on the Stockholm Stock Exchange, with year-ends between 1/3/83 and 29/2/84. Four earlier editions. English translations are available.

United Kingdom: *Financial Reporting* (called *Survey of Published Accounts* until the 1983 edition), published annually since 1970 by the Institute of Chartered Accountants in England and Wales. Editions relate to annual reports issued in the previous year, by a sample of 200 large and medium listed companies, and 100 large unlisted companies.

United States: *Accounting Trends and Techniques*, published annually by the American Institute of Certified Public Accountants since 1944. Covers 600 industrial and merchandising companies, about 90% of which are SEC-listed.

APPENDIX B

THE 1979 PW and GRAY SURVEYS COMPARED

	1979 PW	Gray
Publication date	1980	1984
Based on position at	1/1/79	1/1/82
Available in	English, French German, Spanish and Italian	English
No. of countries covered	64	30
No. of propositions/questions	267	430
Response categories	*Requirements* Required Insisted upon Predominant practice Minority practice Rarely or not found Not accepted Not permitted	*Requirements* Required Recommended Permitted Not permitted *Practice* A 91–100% B 76–90% C 51–75% D 26–50% E 11–25% F 1–10%

[3]

ABACUS, Vol. 28, No. 2, 1992

LEO G. VAN DER TAS

Measuring International Harmonization and Standardization: A Comment

Key words: Accounting policies; Standardization; Uniform systems of accounts.

In the March 1990 issue of this journal Tay and Parker (T&P) compared six studies in the field of international accounting. According to T&P, each of those studies deals with the measurement of international harmonization of financial reporting and they evaluate the advantages and disadvantages of those studies. Moreover, T&P suggest an alternative methodology for measuring harmonization. This comment is a reaction to the definitions and methodology applied and the suggested alternative method for measuring harmonization of financial reporting.

Although there is increasing interest in international accounting, little research has been done in the field of the measurement of (international) harmonization. That is why contributions like that of T&P are very important.

STUDIES EXAMINED

First of all, only two of the six studies T&P refer to are really trying to measure harmonization (Nair & Frank, 1981, and van der Tas, 1988). The other four are measuring the degree of compliance with or observance of the standards of the International Accounting Standards Committee (IASC). Although T&P argue that Evans and Taylor (1982) and Doupnik and Taylor (1985) believed they were measuring de facto harmonization, the articles of Evans and Taylor and Doupnik and Taylor provide no evidence of the fact that they did believe so. This makes a comparison of both categories of studies less appropriate. International harmonization on the one hand and compliance or observance with IASs on the other are related in the sense that setting international standards may further harmonization. But they are two very different phenomena.

1. When an IAS allows different methods to be applied and companies apply these different methods, compliance with the IAS may be high, but because different methods are applied, the degree of harmony may be low.

LEO G. VAN DER TAS is a Member of the Commission of the European Communities and of the Department of Finance and Management, Erasmus University, Rotterdam.

2. If all or a large number of companies apply the same method, the degree of harmony is high. The degree of compliance with IASs, however, may be low when that method is not allowed by the IAS. A comparable situation existed when APB-Opinion 2 on accounting for the Investment Tax Credit (ITC) in the United States of America prescribed the deferral method, but most of the companies applied the flow-through method (compliance is low, the degree of harmony is high).

One could argue that the first problem will be reduced after the adoption of IASC's Exposure Draft 32 on comparability (1989) and the related Statement of Intent (IASC, 1990) because the number of options offered by IASs will be reduced, but it will increase the second problem. That is, the degree of observance of or compliance with IASs is a poor proxy for the degree of harmony.

DEFINITIONS

I agree with T&P that a distinction must be made between harmonization of financial reporting regulation (defined by T&P as '*de jure* harmonization') and harmonization of accounting practice ('*de facto* harmonization'). I also agree that harmony and uniformity are states while (dis)harmonization is a process which reflects a decrease/an increase in the degree of harmony. Both distinctions were made in my earlier article (van der Tas, 1988). However, the distinction between standardization (strict rules) and harmonization (less strict rules) is less appropriate. What T&P are probably trying to say is that before we are able to measure harmonization, we will first have to define the level of detail at which we want to measure harmony. For example, when accounting for deferred taxation, a distinction can be made between the application of the tax payable method and the deferral method. We can measure the degree of harmony concerning the choice companies make between these two alternatives. This implies a low level of detail. However, we can also increase the level of detail at which we measure the degree of harmony when we distinguish between alternative types of the deferral method: net-of-tax method versus separate deferred taxes; liability versus deferred method; and partial versus comprehensive method. At this level of detail the companies' choice between two methods changes into a choice between nine methods and we measure the degree of harmony concerning the choice companies make between these nine alternative methods.

Therefore, instead of a distinction between harmonization and standardization we can speak of different levels of detail at which to measure the degree of harmony. The choice of the level of detail is at the discretion of the researcher and determined by the purposes of the study.

The distinction between measurement harmony and disclosure harmony is very important when seeking to measure harmonization. Measurement harmonization is concerned with the choice between alternative measurement methods. Disclosure harmonization is concerned with the amount and detail of information supplied in the financial report. To clarify the importance of this distinction we will consider the goals of harmonization. *De facto* measurement harmonization is aimed at an improvement in the comparability of financial reporting. To facilitate comparability, it is important that companies operating in comparable circumstances make the same choice between alternative accounting methods. This would eliminate one of the disturbing aspects causing differences between the figures in a financial report not originating from performance differences. But is it important that companies make the same choice in disclosure issues? Does the fact that one company is disclosing particular information while the other is not cause any problem? *De facto* disclosure harmonization is aimed at the disclosure of specified information with a specified degree of detail, which is regarded as the minimum required for all financial reports. In order to conform with this minimum disclosure, we will have to distinguish between items which form part of the minimum information to be disclosed and other items. In respect of items which belong to the minimum information, the degree of harmony increases when the percentage of companies disclosing that information increases. To assess *de facto* disclosure harmonization in respect of other items, the degree to which that information is disclosed is of no interest. If the degree of *de facto* disclosure harmony was measured the same way as *de facto* measurement harmonization, namely as the extent to which companies make the same choice between alternatives, harmony would increase when, instead of 60 per cent, 80 per cent of the companies do *not* disclose information concerning a particular item. This is a rather strange interpretation of *de facto* disclosure harmonization. Still this would be the outcome of T&P's method if they applied it to measure disclosure harmony.

Also in respect of *de jure* harmony, the distinction between measurement and disclosure harmony is important. Apart from improving *de facto* measurement harmony, one of the aims of measuring *de jure* harmony is the avoidance or removal of obstacles such as conflicting or substantially different standards. In disclosure issues, standards may differ substantially but will seldom conflict, because few standards will prohibit companies from disclosing particular information in the financial report. Differing from measurement issues, in *de jure* disclosure harmonization the introduction of minimum standards is important.

The conclusion reached from the argument presented above is that it is not possible to develop one method for measuring both *de jure* harmony and *de facto* harmony. Differing methods must be developed for measurement and disclosure issues respectively. T&P argue (pp. 84–5) that measurement studies should focus on actual reporting practices rather than regulation, that is, on *de facto* rather than *de jure* harmonization. These are, however, two different phenomena, each pursuing different goals.

SUGGESTED METHOD OF MEASURING HARMONIZATION

As pointed out above, only two of the studies in T&P's analysis provide methods for measuring harmonization. One of these studies (Nair and Frank, 1981) claims to be measuring *de jure* harmonization, both disclosure and measurement. Their idea is to classify countries into five categories with respect to each accounting method or disclosure issue. These five categories are: required (application of this accounting method or the disclosure of this particular information respectively is required in this country); predominant practice; minority practice; no application; not permitted.

According to Nair and Frank, the movement toward harmonization is defined as movement in the direction taken by a majority of countries toward requiring (or prohibiting) a given accounting practice. The Nair and Frank method is, however, not appropriate to measure either *de jure* measurement harmony/harmonization or *de jure* disclosure harmony/harmonization. Apart from the terminology and data problems already brought forward by T&P, their method mixes up accounting regulation and accounting practice. The five categories incorporate both regulation (required, not permitted) and practice (predominant practice, minority practice and no application) which implies that neither *de jure* harmony, nor *de facto* harmony is measured. Moreover, in disclosure issues they do not distinguish between items which can be considered part of the minimum information to be disclosed and other items. Furthermore, as far as *de jure* measurement harmony is concerned, their measurement harmony approach is incorrect. They start by looking at a particular measurement method, while the starting point for measuring measurement harmony should be a particular sort of transaction or event to be accounted for by alternative measurement methods. If, for example, all countries prohibit measurement method A, their conclusion would be that the degree of *de jure* measurement harmony is high. However, the degree of *de jure* measurement harmony may be very low, for example, when that sort of transaction must be accounted for by method B in country I, by method C in country II and by method D in country III. So we may conclude that the Nair and Frank method is inappropriate for *de jure* measurement harmony and is only applicable to measuring *de jure* disclosure harmony when it is modified.

The second study providing methods to measure harmony/harmonization is my earlier study (1988). I provide two methods to measure the degree of *de facto* measurement harmony, namely the H index and the C index. The H index is calculated as the square of the relative frequencies of each of the alternative measurement methods for a particular sort of transaction or event, applied by companies. In this way a concentration of the companies on one or only a few alternative measurement methods leads to a higher H index, indicating an increase in the degree of harmony. The criticism of T&P upon the H index concerns the fact that this index is a concentration index for which no significance tests have been derived to indicate how trivial or significant (statistically) variations in index values are. This is indeed a problem. Unfortunately T&P do not discuss the other *de facto* measurement harmony method (C index) because this index does not suffer from this problem, as shown below.

The C index is not a concentration index. It is a ratio, calculated as the number of comparable pairs of financial reports divided by the total number of pairs of financial reports. So there is no problem in applying the usual statistical significance tests. We are even able to apply regression analysis. The advantages of the C index are that:

1. The C index is able to include the effect on the degree of *de facto* measurement harmony of multiple reporting and the disclosure of additional information in the notes on the accounts enabling the reader to reconcile the financial report into a report based upon an alternative measurement method.
2. Movements in the C index can be tested for their significance and can be correlated with movements in explaining variables such as the introduction of a standard.

The alternative to the measurement harmonization approach suggested by T&P (p. 85) involves the following:

> [First] ... data on proportions of companies using different accounting methods can be obtained ... [Second,] ... the observed distribution of companies among different methods ... [is compared] ... with either a random distribution or some expected distribution. A suitable proxy for the former could be a uniform/equal/rectangular distribution, that is, a distribution in which equal numbers of companies would be expected to use each of the available alternatives. (This would represent no preference for, or bias towards, any one available method.) Evidence of harmony would then be the existence of a significant difference between the observed and expected distributions, as measured by some appropriate significance test, for example, chi-square. [Finally,] the level of harmony could then be quantified by using a concentration index, preferably one describing the entire distribution, rather than just a portion of it. Comparison of level of harmony over different periods would yield evidence of harmonization or disharmonization.

Unfortunately T&P did not illustrate their method and, by its description, it seems rather complicated and leaves some questions unanswered, such as what significance test and what concentration measure to apply and how to apply the method in disclosure issues. Moreover, the significance test included in their method is not used to test the significance of movements in the degree of harmony, as one would expect when looking at their criticism of the H index, but it is directed towards the significance of the degree of harmony itself. The significance of movements in the degree of harmony is not tested by their method either. That is, their method suffers from the same problem they raised against the H index.

Further disadvantages of the methodology of T&P are that it is not able to include the impact of multiple reporting or additional information in the notes on the accounts on the degree of *de facto* measurement harmony, because each financial report can only be allocated to one alternative measurement method.

The conclusion reached is that the methodology of Tay and Parker is certainly not a better method to measure *de facto* measurement harmony than the C index, and may even be worse.

REFERENCES

Doupnik, S., and M. E. Taylor, 'An Empirical Investigation of the Observance of IASC Standards in Western Europe', *Management International Review*, Spring 1985.

Evans, T. G., and M. E. Taylor, '"Bottom-Line Compliance" with the IASC: A Comparative Analysis', *International Journal of Accounting*, Fall 1982.

International Accounting Standards Committee, *Exposure Draft 32: Comparability of Financial Statements*, London, January 1989.

———, Statement of Intent: *Comparability of Financial Statements*, London, 1990.

Nair, R. D., and W. G. Frank, 'The Harmonization of International Accounting Standards, 1973–1979', *International Journal of Accounting*, Fall 1981.

Tay, J. S. W., and R. H. Parker, 'Measuring International Harmonization and Standardization', *Abacus*, March 1990.

van der Tas, L. G., 'Measuring Harmonisation of Financial Reporting Practice', *Accounting and Business Research*, Spring 1988.

[4]

ABACUS, Vol. 28, No. 2, 1992

J. S. W. TAY AND R. H. PARKER

Measuring International Harmonization and Standardization: A Reply

Key words: Accounting policies; Standardization; Uniform systems of accounts.

Van der Tas' comment (1992) on our article (Tay and Parker, 1990) is greatly appreciated for two reasons: first, as he points out, and as evidenced by our article, there is little research in the field of measuring international harmonization and standardization; second, because his original paper (van der Tas, 1988) was instrumental in beginning our evaluation of different measurement approaches.

We consider our article a preliminary examination of the issues involved in the measurement of harmonization and standardization. It did not include an example of the measurement approach we proposed, as we did not have what we had suggested were the necessary data, nor had we concluded which (if any) of the available concentration measures and tests of statistical significance to apply. These issues have been addressed in a more comprehensive work (Tay, 1989), and will be dealt with below.

STUDIES EXAMINED

Measuring Harmonization

Only two of the six studies we reviewed contained the word 'harmonization' in their title, and explicitly cited harmonization measurement as a formal objective. In the four other studies, however, compliance with IASC standards was more or less explicitly linked with harmonization, indicating, to our minds, that the authors of those studies had assumed that greater compliance with IASC standards would be equivalent to greater harmony of financial reporting.

Compliance with IASC Standards and Harmonization

We recognize, as does van der Tas, the difference between the two phenomena of compliance with IASC standards and accounting harmonization, hence the distinction we drew between *de jure* and *de facto* harmonization. The point which

---

J. S. W. Tay is a Senior Lecturer in the School of Accounting and Business, Nanyang Technological University, Singapore, and R. H. Parker is Professor of Accountancy, Department of Economics, University of Exeter.

was made was that some of the authors of these studies appeared not to be aware of this difference.

DEFINITIONS

Standardization and Harmonization

Van der Tas' point about differing levels of detail at which harmony may be measured is interesting, and conceptually important. However, it is not what we meant when discussing the differences between standardization and harmonization. The former we associated with regulation applying to all companies, legal regulation and/or regulation containing precise definitions; the latter with regulation affecting only certain subsets of companies, professional regulation and regulation containing discretionary definitions. In short, the concept of standardization appears to us to be associated with reduction or exclusion of choice; harmonization with a degree of flexibility and some choice.

Measuring Measurement and Disclosure Harmonization

One of our first statements about harmonization measurement was that it is simply concerned 'with the similarity or otherwise of accounting practices and regulations' (p. 71). We followed this with a general definition of harmony as 'a "clustering" of companies around one or a few of the available [accounting] methods' (p. 73). This implies that pure harmonization is, in a sense, value neutral, that is, not concerned with whether suitable or unsuitable accounting methods are being used, or more or less information is being disclosed. If one accepts this premise, then the same measure can be applied to measurement and disclosure harmony. Otherwise, we agree with van der Tas that strange results can be obtained in relation to disclosure harmony. However, incorporating some notion of more suitable accounting methods or higher levels of disclosure (such as the 'minimum information to be disclosed' suggested by van der Tas) will inevitably introduce value judgment — and subjectivity — to the measurement process. It will also, in our opinion, necessitate the use of a separate measure.

De jure *and* de facto *Harmony*

The measurement of *de jure* harmony was not explicitly addressed in our article, as our main concern was (and remains) with *de facto* harmony. We appreciate van der Tas' point about the different aims of *de jure* harmonization, although we do not agree with it completely. However, the measurement of *de jure* harmonization does not appear to us a very useful exercise in itself, if the ultimate concern of harmonization is to increase the comparability of financial reporting. In fact, focusing on *de facto* harmony when regulation changes would help to indicate the closeness (or otherwise) of the link between *de jure* and *de facto* harmonization. This would be important in terms of evaluating the effectiveness of, for example, the harmonization efforts of the IASC and the EC.

HARMONIZATION AND STANDARDIZATION

SUGGESTED METHOD OF MEASURING HARMONIZATION

Application

The methodology we proposed has since been applied in more or less the manner suggested (Tay, 1989). Briefly:

1. Data on accounting methods and disclosure levels were obtained from the financial statements of listed companies from five different countries.
2. For each accounting method or disclosure item, companies were grouped according to the practice followed.
3. The chi-square test was used to assess the significance of the actual degree of harmony demonstrated by the grouping, compared with a rectangular distribution.
4. Harmony was quantified using two different concentration measures — the H-index suggested by van der Tas, and the entropy measure (E) — in three different forms (absolute, numbers-equivalent and relative measures).
5. Improvements in the level of disclosure and superiority of accounting method were quantified using a disclosure index.
6. The effects of disclosure of information and accounting methods on comparability were quantified by calculating the C index.
7. Changes in the values of H, E, C and the disclosure index were tested for statistical significance by using nonparametric tests.

Problems Encountered with Harmony Measures

A general problem associated with using concentration measures to quantify harmony stems from their implicit weighting of clustering (c) of companies around one or two of a number of available alternatives, against the number (n) of those available alternatives. Intuitively, harmony should increase when c increases, and decrease when n increases. However, it is difficult to predict how a particular harmony measure will react when both c and n change at the same time, and in different directions.

A survey of common concentration measures suggested by the relevant literature suggested that the Herfindahl index (H) and the entropy measure (E) would be the best measures to test. In application, the latter proved to be unsatisfactory in two instances: first, it could not be calculated when the companies in the sample failed to use one of the available accounting methods; second, values of the relative E measure sometimes conflicted with values for the absolute and numbers-equivalent forms of E. H therefore proved to be a more reliable measure of harmonization, and appeared to be most meaningful in its numbers-equivalent form.

Problem with the Comparability Measure

The C-index value is affected by changes in either similarity of accounting methods used (i.e., harmony) or disclosure or both. Once again, there was a general problem of assessing how the index weights changes in harmony against changes in disclosure, which occur at the same time.

Statistical Significance of the Degree of Harmony and Harmonization

We believe that assessing the significance of the existing degree of harmony (compared to no preference or bias in favour of any one method) is an important part of measuring harmonization. For a start, it could indicate to standard-setters areas in which the existing situation is satisfactory. Also, given the lack of significance tests for the various measures used, comparing the significance of the degree of harmony at different points in time appears to be an acceptable substitute for evaluating the significance of harmonization. While van der Tas asserts that 'there is no problem in applying the usual statistical significance tests' to C, as it is not a concentration measure, he throws no light on exactly what tests he is referring to. It is our belief that more work should be conducted on the distribution of the measures used, and the distribution of companies among alternative accounting methods and levels of disclosure, and it is in these areas that our future efforts will be focused.

REFERENCES

Tay, J. S. W., 'Corporate Financial Reporting: Regulatory Systems and Comparability', PhD thesis, University of Exeter, June 1989.

Tay, J. S. W., and R. H. Parker, 'Measuring International Harmonization and Standardization', *Abacus*, March 1990.

van der Tas, L. G., 'Measuring Harmonization of Financial Reporting Practice', *Accounting and Business Research*, Spring 1988.

——, 'Measuring International Harmonization and Standardization — a Comment', *Abacus*, September 1992.

[5]

Evidence of EC financial reporting practice harmonization

The case of deferred taxation

Leo G. van der Tas
Erasmus University and Moret Ernst & Young, Rotterdam and EC Commission

1. INTRODUCTION

In literature on the subject of European financial reporting we frequently find expressions of doubts concerning the level of harmony of financial reporting in the European Community (EC), especially on topics such as deferred taxation. Most of these statements are based on a rather ad hoc (one year) and insufficiently detailed survey of either the national member state requirements in this respect or the accounting policies of European companies. However, a thorough and detailed analysis of the deferred taxation accounting policies of European companies, covering a long period of time, is necessary to make a balanced assessment of the degree of harmony, the extent of harmonization and the impact of harmonization efforts in the EC on this subject.

This paper provides the results of an empirical survey of the degree of harmony of the deferred taxation accounting policies of 154 European listed companies over the period 1978 to 1988. The companies were selected from the nine EC member states that implemented the Fourth EEC Directive before 1989. We examined both the individual and the consolidated accounts and took into account not only the accounting policy in the primary accounts, but also any data provided in the notes on the accounts that enable the reader to reconcile the financial report to a financial report based upon another method of accounting for deferred taxation.

The purpose of this empirical survey is to measure the degree of harmony in each year, to determine the extent to which harmonization took place during that period and the impact of EC harmonization efforts. This requires, first, a definition of harmony, second, a quantitative method to measure the degree of harmony and, third, a method to determine the

Address for correspondence
Commission of the European Communities, Directorate General XV: Financial Institutions and Company Law, Rue de la Loi 200, B-1049 Brussels, Belgique.

impact of harmonization efforts on the degree of harmony. We will address the first two questions in the second section. The third question will be examined in section 3. The fourth section contains the application of the methods developed in sections 2 and 3. Finally, the conclusions are outlined in section 5.

2. MEASURING FINANCIAL REPORTING PRACTICE HARMONIZATION

In general, harmony can be defined as a state in which a certain degree of co-ordination exists between two or more subjects. In applying this to financial reporting it is necessary to fill in which subjects are concerned and what degrees of co-ordination exist. As far as the subjects are concerned, we can distinguish between the financial reports themselves and the financial reporting standards. A particular degree of co-ordination of the *financial reports themselves* (financial reporting practice) might be important for those reading the financial reports of different companies and willing to compare them. I shall refer to this by the term 'material harmony'. A degree of co-ordination of *financial reporting standards* could be important not only to achieve harmony of financial reports, but also for companies with financial reporting obligations in more than one country. If financial reporting standards differ from one country to the next, companies with reporting obligations in both the countries might face difficulty, for example because they would have to satisfy conflicting requirements or because they would have to disclose more information compared to their local competitors. This will be called 'formal harmony'. The difference between material and formal harmony is important. Material harmony refers to the harmony of the accounting methods actually applied in the financial reports, the amount and detail of data actually provided in the financial report, etc. Formal harmony refers to the harmony of the financial reporting standards (legal or other requirements or guidelines). Formal harmonization would normally induce material harmonization, but this is not necessarily true. Material harmonization might take place without being furthered by formal harmonization. The measurement of each type of harmony shows very different characteristics (compare van der Tas, 1992, especially Chapter 6). In this survey I deal only with harmony of financial reports (material harmony).

A second distinction made here is between measurement issues and disclosure issues. *Measurement issues* concern the way in which transactions and events are reflected in the financial report and comprise the choice between alternative methods of recognition, valuation, income determination, consolidation, estimation and presentation. Examples are the choice between alternative methods of accounting for pension liabilities, lease-contracts, long-term construction contracts, alternative depreciation methods and alternative presentations of an item in the balance sheet. *Disclosure issues* concern the extent and detail of data provided in the financial report. Examples include whether or not to disclose segmental net turnover figures by geographical market and whether or not to disclose directors' remunerations. In this survey only measurement issues will be examined. Summarizing, this survey will cover only material measurement harmony, defined as the degree to which financial reports are co-ordinated with respect to the way in which transactions and events are reflected in the financial report.

Here the ways in which this degree of material measurement harmony can be measured quantitatively will be examined. This examination starts with an inventory of the methods developed so far, assessing their pros and cons, ultimately resulting in the method which best suits the purposes of this study.

The problem of measuring harmonization is addressed in three studies (Nair and Frank, 1981; Van der Tas, 1988; Tay and Parker, 1990). I shall discuss the pros and cons of these methods below and try to develop and illustrate a measurement method that avoids the disadvantages of these methods.

Although the title of Nair and Frank's article seems to suggest a focus on a measurement of formal harmony, their measurement method also contains material harmonization elements, measurement as well as disclosure. For each accounting practice or accounting concept, for each country, they examined whether the practice or concept was:

- required;
- majority practice;
- minority practice;
- not applied;
- not permitted.

'Required' and 'not permitted' refer to formal harmony, the other three refer to material harmony.

According to Nair and Frank harmonization takes place when either:

- a movement towards 'required' can be identified when the majority of the countries is in the category 'required'; or
- a movement towards 'not permitted' takes place when the majority of the countries belongs to the category 'not permitted'.

This method does not make a distinction between formal and material harmonization and between measurement and disclosure harmonization. When this method is applied to measure material measurement harmonization it assumes that 'required' means that all companies apply this accounting practice and that 'not permitted' means that none of the companies apply this accounting practice. This is the first problem encountered when using this method, because this is not necessarily true. Nobes (1987b) clearly explains the problem associated with this assumption. The second problem is more fundamental. The angle from which Nair and Frank approach harmonization is not appropriate to measure harmony. Nair and Frank measure harmony in respect of a particular accounting practice or accounting concept. This, however, denies the relationship between harmony and comparability. It is better to approach harmony from the angle of the sort of transaction or event. This can be illustrated by the following example. If a particular accounting practice is not permitted or not applied in each of the surveyed countries, Nair and Frank would conclude that the degree of harmony is maximal. However, it may well be that a number of other alternative methods is applied and/or permitted, which means that financial reports are hardly comparable. Thus, this method of measuring harmonization has no direct relationship with comparability, which is one of the main purposes of material harmonization. The third problem with this method is that the method is applicable only when either a majority of the countries belongs to the 'required' category or a majority of the countries belongs to the 'not permitted' category. This limits the applicability of the measurement method. The fourth limitation of this method is its inability to cope with multiple reporting or additional data in the notes on the accounts about the outcomes of alternative measurement methods.

In an earlier article (Van der Tas, 1988) I approached harmonization from the point of view of the sort of transaction or event and used the analogy between concentration and harmony to apply methods of measuring concentration to measure material measurement harmony. The idea is that 'comparability increases when the result of the choice that companies make between alternative accounting methods becomes concentrated on one or only a limited number of accounting methods, even where the number of available methods remains the same. Thus, comparability can be considered as an increase in the degree of consensus concerning the choice between the alternative methods of accounting for an item in the financial reports' (Van der Tas, 1988: 159). One concentration index, the Hirschman-Herfindahl index (H index), is chosen to measure harmony and harmonization. This index adds the square of the relative frequencies of each of the applied methods (number of companies applying a particular method divided by the total number of companies). Thus:

$$[1]\quad H = \sum_{i=1}^{m} p_i^2$$

Where
H = Hirschman-Herfindahl index.
m = Number of alternative accounting methods.
p_i = The relative frequency of accounting method i.

The limitations of this method are:

- the difficulties in calculating the significance of changes in the degree of harmony, measured by the H index. This limitation was brought forward by Tay and Parker. They conclude that 'the use of a concentration index seems to be a useful way to evaluate the level of harmony, and track movements in harmonization over time. The main problem with concentration indices is that no significance tests have been devised to indicate how trivial or significant (statistically) variations in index values are' (1990: 83). This is true for our H index, but is not true for the alternative method (C index) we proposed in the same article. We will elaborate on this method below.
- its inability to cope with multiple reporting or additional data in the notes about the outcomes of alternative measurement methods. Each company (or financial report) must be assigned to one and only one alternative measurement method. This limitation is recognized by the author and accounted for by suggesting another method (the C index) which will be discussed below.

Tay and Parker suggest an alternative method of measuring harmonization which is applicable to material measurement harmonization.

> [D]ata on proportions of companies using different accounting methods can be obtained. An operational definition of harmony could then take the form of comparing the observed distribution of companies among different methods with either a random distribution or some expected distribution. A suitable proxy for the former could be a uniform/equal/rectangular distribution, that is, a distribution in which equal number of companies would be expected to use each of the available alternatives. . . . Evidence of harmony would then be the existence of a significant difference between the observed and expected distributions, as measured by some appropriate significance test, for example, chi-square.
>
> (Tay and Parker 1990: 85)

It is unfortunate they do not illustrate their method because their proposals have some drawbacks. First, their significance test can be applied only to measure the degree of harmony, not to measure the significance of movements in the degree of harmony. This is rather peculiar because their criticism on our H index concerns the fact that it is not possible to measure the significance of movements in the H index. Second, the chi-square test is only a weak test of significance. Methods of measuring harmonization which are susceptible to stronger tests of significance would be preferred. Their further proposal to quantify the level of harmony by using a concentration index, preferably one describing the entire distribution, rather than just a portion of it, and then to compare the levels of harmony over different periods for evidence of harmonization or disharmonization describes exactly my procedure when introducing the H index.

Tay and Parker state that another type of research claims to be measuring harmonization. This research measures compliance with or observance of international standards. They give Evans and Taylor (1982), Doupnik and Taylor (1985) and Nobes (1987a) as examples. Firstly, I do not think that these researchers thought they were measuring harmonization. They do not say so and, moreover, they clearly claim to be measuring the impact of particular standards (in these three surveys the impact of the IASC standards on international financial reporting). Secondly, their methods are not applicable to the measurement of material measurement harmonization. If compliance with international standards is high, this does not necessarily mean that the degree of harmony is high, because the standard may leave many options, all of which are exercised by the companies. If compliance is low, the degree of harmony may be high if all companies apply the same method, not allowed by the standard. For example, APB-Opinion 2 on accounting for the Investment Tax Credit in the United States prescribed the deferral method, but most companies used the flow-through method. Compliance was very low, but the degree of harmony was high. Because of the difference between compliance and harmony, this method is not suitable for measuring material measurement harmony.

This leaves one method to be discussed: the C index introduced in my article of 1988 (Van der Tas, 1988). This method satisfies three criteria. Its quantification of the degree of harmony is directly related to comparability. It is able to take account of multiple reporting and reconciliation data in the notes on the accounts. And it makes it possible to calculate the significance of movements in the degree of harmony by a very powerful significance test, i.e. regression analysis. For these reasons I prefer this method, and will describe it in more detail below.

The C index measures the degree of comparability for each item in the financial reports, based upon the number of financial reports which are comparable in respect of this item: for example, the acquisition of fixed assets or the translation of foreign currencies. It is presumed that two financial reports are either comparable or not comparable as regards one sort of transaction or event. Thus, there is no gradation in comparability between two financial reports since only one sort of transaction or event is taken into account. This is of course a simplified model of reality, where the user is interested in a comparability of, for example, income and equity for two or more financial reports. However, there are several reasons for not measuring material measurement harmony for the aggregate of all sorts of transactions and events, but for each sort of transaction or event separately:

- Measuring separately gives more refined results because one is able to measure the degree of material measurement harmony for each sort of transaction or event accounted for in the financial report, whereas measuring harmony of the aggregate of all sorts of transactions or events gives only aggregate results, making it difficult to draw policy conclusions on the basis of these measurements.
- Measuring harmony of the aggregate of all sorts of transactions or events would require a complete list of sorts of transactions and events. It will be very difficult to make an exhaustive list because of the tremendous number of sorts of transactions and events and the fact that such a list would change in the course of time. So measuring material measurement harmony separately for each sort of transaction or event is more practical.

The method of measuring material measurement harmony developed is based upon this definition. The extent to which companies apply the same measurement method is measured by dividing the number of pairs of companies applying the same measurement method with respect to a particular sort of transaction or event by the total number of pairs of companies in the population. For example, if there are three companies (A, B and C), the total number of comparisons is three: between A and B, between A and C and between B and C. Suppose company A applies measurement method I and the other two companies apply method II. In this case the degree of harmony is 1/3, i.e. the number of comparable pairs (one, the pair B and C), divided by the total number of pairs (three). The result is an index, ranging from 0 to 1, which we call the C index. The number of pairs of financial reports out of a population of n financial reports is:

[2] $$0.5 \times (n^2 - n)$$

We do not have to check every pair individually. If we group those which use the same measurement method for a particular sort of transaction or event together, we will know that within each group all the financial reports will be comparable, and there will be no pairs of reports in different groups which are comparable. The sum of the number of possible comparisons within the groups is:

[3] $$0.5(a^2_1-a_1) + 0.5(a^2_2-a_2) + \dots + 0.5(a^2_m-a_m)$$

where

a_i = the number of companies applying measurement method i.
m = the number of alternative measurement methods.

This sum must be divided by the total number of possible comparisons. So the formula for the C index is:

$$[4] \quad C = \frac{0.5(a^2_1 - a_1) + 0.5(a^2_2 - a_2) + \ldots + 0.5(a^2_m - a_m)}{0.5\,(n^2 - n)}$$

$$= \frac{0.5\left(\sum_{t=1}^{m} a^2_t\right) - 0.5\left(\sum_{t=1}^{m} a_t\right)}{0.5\,(n^2 - n)}$$

$$[5] \quad = \frac{\left(\sum_{t=1}^{m} a^2_t\right) - n}{n^2 - n}$$

Applying the formula to the example mentioned above gives the following result:

$$C = \frac{1^2 + 2^2 - 3}{3^2 - 3} = 1/3$$

Harmony increases if the number of measurement methods applied decreases (Kirkpatrick, 1986). However, harmony also increases if more companies apply the same measurement method even though the number of alternative measurement methods applied remains the same or even increases. The C index takes account of both aspects.

The index ranges from 0 (no harmony, none of the pairs of financial reports is comparable with respect to the particular sort of transaction or event surveyed because they all apply a different measurement method) to 1 (maximum harmony, all pairs of financial reports are comparable with respect to this sort of transaction or event because all companies apply the same measurement method under the same circumstances). The number of different measurement methods is, in this case, the number of measurement methods applied in practice. However, if all theoretically possible measurement methods are taken into account, this does not alter the value of the C index because the C index does not change if measurement methods are added that are not applied (if a_i=0). The index is directly related to the degree of harmony as defined by the number of comparable pairs of financial reports related to the total number of pairs of companies.

The C index is not a concentration index, although a mathematical relationship exists between the C index and the H index (in Appendix 1 of my article in 1988 I described this relationship). The C index is a simple ratio with a 'natural' zero point where no pair of financial reports is comparable. It satisfies the criteria of a ratio scale. This makes it possible to apply regression analysis as a test of significance of movements in the degree of harmony.

The C index assigns each financial report to a particular measurement method, assuming that financial reports are comparable in respect of a particular item only if this item is accounted for using the same measurement method in the primary accounts. This does not allow for the possibility of readers reconciling financial reports based upon additional data available. This may be data provided by the company by way of multiple reporting or additional data in the notes on the accounts. In some cases it may even be possible to reconcile without any additional data as is the case with many of the presentation differences between financial reports. As long as the amount of a particular item is known, differences in presentation can be reconciled by the reader by subtracting this amount from the heading under which it is presented and adding it under the required heading.

One way to improve comparability of financial reports is to apply multiple reporting or to disclose additional data based upon an alternative measurement method in the notes on the accounts. Where this is done, or where reconciliation is possible without any additional data, the company can be assigned to more than one subset so that it is entered in all groups of companies to which its report, by one or other method, can be reconciled. A financial report may even be assigned to more than two subsets. This will create overlapping subsets within the population. An extension of the C index which takes account of these overlaps to the calculation of material measurement harmony is applied.

The derivation of the extended C index can be illustrated as follows. Suppose there are four companies, A, B, C and D. Company A applies method I, company B applies method II and companies C and D apply method I but give additional information in the notes enabling the user to reconcile the financial report to a report in which method II is applied. The number of pairs of financial reports is six (applying equation 2 with $n=4$). The number of comparable pairs of financial reports is five (A and C; A and D; B and C; B and D; and C and D). So the degree of harmony is five divided by six = 0.833. The C index as derived before in equation 5 does not allow us to assign a financial report to more than one measurement method. This would lead to the double-counting of pairs of financial reports. The solution to this problem is to assign financial reports to more than one measurement method and then deduct the resulting double-counted pairs. In the example used above this would mean that the subset of method I contains three financial reports (A, C and D) and the subset of method II also contains three financial reports (B, C and D). Within the subset of method I the number of financial reports is three, so the number of comparable pairs of financial reports is $0.5(3^2-3) = 3$ (A and C; A and D; and C and D). Within the subset of measurement method II the number of financial reports is also three, with three comparable pairs (B and C; B and D; and C and D). This adds up to six comparable pairs of financial reports. However, the comparison between C and D is counted in both subsets. So we must subtract the number of possible comparisons within the overlapping area. This contains two financial reports, so the number of pairs of financial reports is $0.5(2^2-2) = 1$. The result is $3+3-1=5$ comparable pairs. The C index becomes $(3+3-1)/6 = 0.833$.

The general formula of the number of comparable pairs of financial reports if some of the financial reports are assigned to two measurement methods becomes:

$$[6] \quad 0.5 \sum_{j=1}^{m} (a_j^2 - a_j) - 0.5 \left\{ \sum_{j=1}^{m-1} \sum_{k=j+1}^{m} (a_{jk}^2 - a_{jk}) \right.$$

Where: a_j = the number of companies applying method j
a_{jk} = the number of companies applying method j and k
m = the number of alternative measurement methods
jk = parameters, fluctuating between 1 and m.

Dividing equation 6 by the total number of pairs of financial reports $(0.5(n^2 - n))$ where n is the number of companies gives us an extended C index to apply where financial reports can be assigned to two measurement methods (but not to more than two):

$$[7] \quad C = \frac{\sum_{j=1}^{m} (a_j^2 - a_j) - \left\{ \sum_{j=1}^{m-1} \sum_{k=j+1}^{m} (a_{jk}^2 - a_{jk}) \right.}{n^2 - n}$$

If financial reports are assigned to more than two measurement methods the formula becomes more complex because in that case double-counting itself. The general formula of the number of comparable pairs of financial reports becomes (analogous to Mood, Graybill and Boes, 1974: 24):

$$[8] \quad 0.5 \sum_{j=1}^{m} (a_j^2 - a_j) - 0.5 \left\{ \sum_{j=1}^{m-1} \sum_{k=j+1}^{m} (a_{jk}^2 - a_{jk}) + \right.$$

$$\sum_{j=1}^{m-2} \sum_{k=j+1}^{m-1} \sum_{l=k+1}^{m} (a^2_{jkl} - a_{jkl}) \ldots \left. \begin{matrix} \\ + (-1)^{m+1} \Sigma \ldots \Sigma (a^2_{j..} - a_{j..}) \end{matrix} \right\}$$

Where:

$a_{jkl..}$ = the number of companies supplying data based on measurement methods j,k,l etc.

The last term refers to the pairs of companies that apply the m methods.

This sum must be divided by the total number of pairs of financial reports ($0.5(n^2 - n)$) to get the formula of the extended C index. The result is:

$$[9] \quad C = \frac{\sum_{j=1}^{m} (a^2_j - a_j) - \sum\sum_{j \leq k} (a^2_{jk} - a_{jk}) + \sum\sum\sum_{j \leq k \leq l} (a^2_{jkl} - a_{jkl}) \ldots + (-1)^{m+1} \Sigma .. \Sigma (a^2_{j..} - a_{j..})}{n^2 - n}$$

It is not always easy to determine whether a company provides data based on more than one measurement method or whether a financial report based upon one method can be reconciled to another without additional disclosure. Firstly, experts in financial reporting will be able to extract more information from the data provided and may be able to reconcile where less experienced people are not able to. Secondly, the situation may be less complex in one company compared to the other, making it easier to restate its financial report, possibly with fewer data. These problems have to be dealt with, case by case, when assigning financial reports to more than one group.

3. EXAMINING THE IMPACT OF HARMONIZATION EFFORTS

To measure the statistical significance of the impact of harmonization efforts (such as EEC Directives or International Accounting Standards) we can apply (multiple) regression analysis. If the effort has a significant impact we expect a trend break in the year of the effort and a graph of the degree of harmony against time would typically show something like Figure 1.

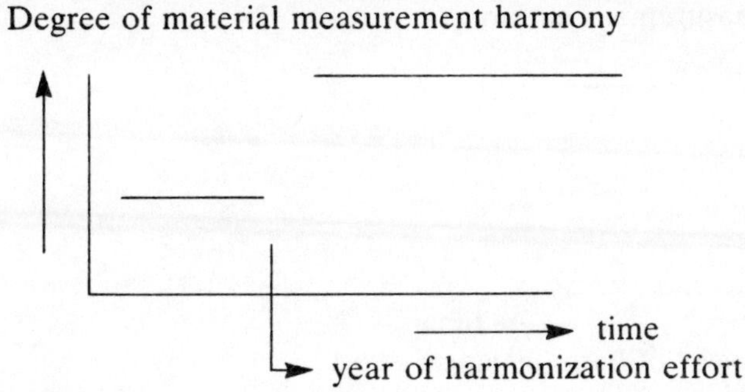

Figure 1

Regression analysis enables us to determine whether or not (or to what extent) the real data fit into this 'typical' picture. This may be done by taking the degree of harmony as the dependent variable. The independent, or explanatory, variable is the harmonization effort, represented by a dummy variable which is 0 in the years before the harmonization effort and 1 in the years after the effort. For example, in respect of the Fourth EEC Company Law Directive,[1] the dummy variable is 0 in the years in which the national provisions had not yet been brought into line with the directive or had been amended but were not yet applicable to companies. It is 1 in the years the national provisions were amended *and* applicable. The resulting regression equation is:

[10] $CINDEX_t = \alpha X4_t + C + \mu_t \qquad (t = 1,2, \ldots n)$

Where
$CINDEX_t$ = C index in year t
$X4_t$ = Dummy variable representing the harmonization effort, in this case the Fourth EEC Directive
C = Constant factor
μ = parameter
μ_t = residual in year t
n = number of years

Movements in the degree of harmony do not necessarily have to be caused by the harmonization effort focused upon, such as this directive. There may be some general trend, independent of the harmonization effort. In the case that a general rising trend exists, without any impact of the harmonization effort, the typical picture of the degree of material measurement harmony against time would be as in Figure 2.

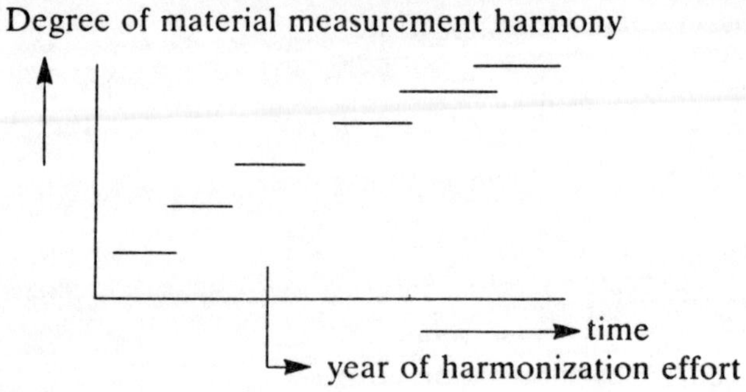

Figure 2

We can identify this situation by applying the simple regression equation 10, with variable YR as the explanatory variable where $YR_t = t$, for $t = 1 .. n$. This should show a significant correlation between YR and CINDEX.

If both a general increasing trend in the degree of harmony and a break in this trend caused by the harmonization effort exist, the 'typical' picture is like that in Figure 3.

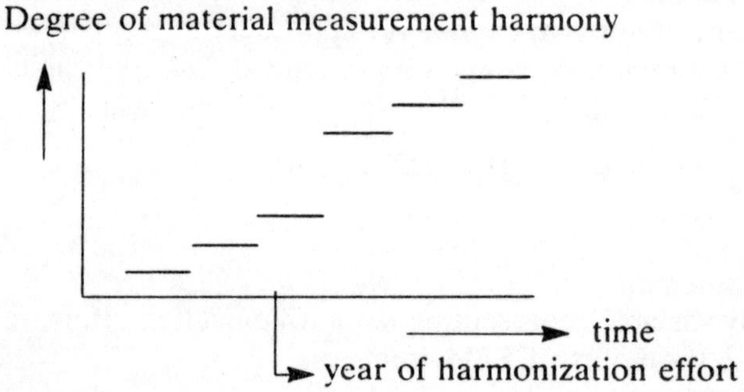

Figure 3

In that case application of multiple regression with the variable X4 and YR as explanatory variables would identify a significant impact of both explanatory variables on CINDEX.

Some companies may anticipate a harmonization effort such as a standard and others will lag. If there is no general trend this would lead to the 'typical' picture in Figure 4.

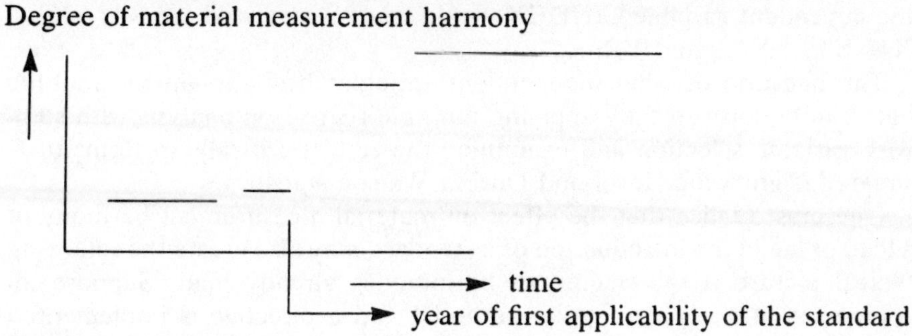

Figure 4

To examine whether and to what extent such an effect occurs, one has to introduce leads and lags. If this is confined to a maximum lead and lag of two years, the independent variables for which the association with the dependent variable CINDEX is tested are:

$X4_{t-2}$
$X4_{t-1}$
$X4_{t}$
$X4_{t+1}$
$X4_{t+2}$

Where $X4_{t-2}$ represents the impact of the standard with a lag of two years, $X4_{t-1}$ represents the impact of the standard with a lag of one year, etc., and finally $X4_{t+2}$ represents the impact of the standard with a lead of two years.

If there is a general trend as well as an impact of the standard with lags and leads, this would lead to the 'typical' picture in Figure 5.

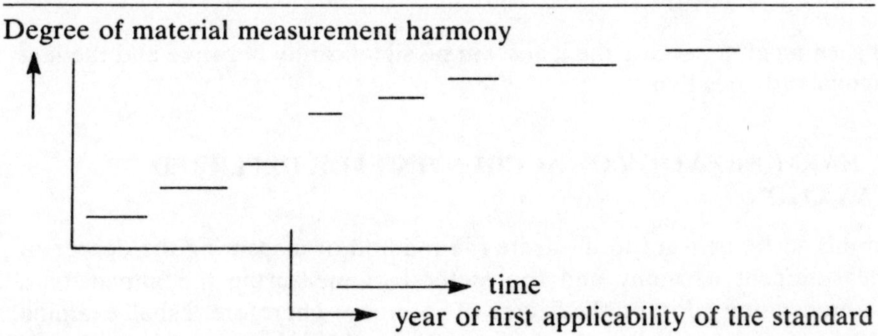

Figure 5

The corresponding independent variables of which the association with the dependent variable CINDEX would have to be tested are $X4_{t-2}$, $X4_{t-1}$, $X4_t$, $X4_{t+1}$, $X4_{t+2}$ and YR.

The question of what independent variables best explain the real-life data can be answered by applying multiple regression analysis with step-wise variable selection and examining the results critically in terms of R squared, significance level and Durbin-Watson statistics.

One must realize that the effect on material measurement harmony of a lead or lag in the introduction of a standard may also create the following typical picture if the degree of harmony is already high. Suppose all companies in a country apply method I and a directive is implemented requiring method II to be applied. If no lag or lead occurs the degree of harmony is 1, before as well as after the implementation of the directive. However, if some companies anticipate the implementation while others lag behind the implementation, the degree of material measurement harmony drops temporarily because in this period some of the companies apply method I while others apply method II. So an additional 'typical' picture arises (see Figure 6).

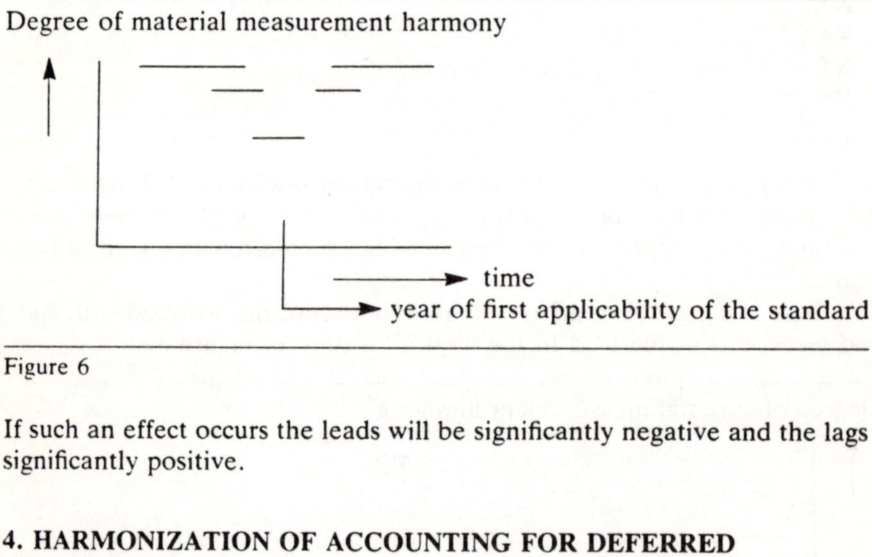

Figure 6

If such an effect occurs the leads will be significantly negative and the lags significantly positive.

4. HARMONIZATION OF ACCOUNTING FOR DEFERRED TAXATION

In this section I want to illustrate the method of measuring the degree of measurement harmony and the method of measuring the impact of a harmonization effort on the degree of harmony. Therefore, I shall examine the degree of material measurement harmony for accounting for deferred taxes in the years 1978–88 and the impact of the Fourth and Seventh EEC Directives thereon.

The necessary data are gathered from financial reports of companies in

Europe, taking twenty domestic companies listed on the national stock exchange of each of the nine member states that had implemented the Fourth EEC Directive before 1 January 1989 and examining their financial reports over the period 1978 (year in which the Fourth EEC Directive was adopted) to 1988. However, because of insufficient data and the limited number of domestic companies, other than pure holding companies, listed on the Luxembourg stock exchange, we could include only ten Greek and four Luxembourg companies. The survey is limited to listed companies. The reasons for this choice are:

- to avoid the problem of insufficient data. In some member states non-listed companies were not obliged to publish their financial reports before implementation of the Fourth and Seventh EEC Directive. Moreover, the financial reports of listed companies are easier to attain;
- the economic significance of the results. Listed companies are on the whole the larger companies having a more significant impact on the national and European economy; and
- the importance of the disclosure of information. Disclosure is especially important for listed companies because of the number of outside stakeholders.

A list of companies included in the survey is presented in Appendix I.

The limiting of the survey to listed companies, as well as the fact this is not a random sample of companies in the EC or even of EC companies to which the Fourth or Seventh EEC Directives apply, implies that the results cannot be considered a statistically valid estimation of the degree of harmony of financial reports of companies within the EC or a statistically valid test of the impact of the Fourth and Seventh EEC Directives. Instead, the survey should be considered as an illustration of the application possibilities of the methods of measuring harmonization and as an indication of the degree of material measurement harmony within the EC concerning some selected topics.

One of the problems encountered when collecting data was how to deal with differing financial years between companies. In order to measure the impact of the Fourth and Seventh EEC Directives it is necessary to assign each financial report to the appropriate year. Companies may have financial years deviating from the calendar year, or the implementation date of new standards may not be the start of a new financial year. We translated these various financial years into calendar years by taking the calendar year in which the standards implementing the Fourth EEC Directive became applicable as our benchmark in each country, and matching to it the financial year in which the standards first applied. For example, if the new standard is applicable to financial years starting on or after 1 January 19x1, the financial report of a company over the period 1 September 19x0 to 31 August 19x1 (i.e., this company's last report before the standards apply) will be called a report for calendar year 19x0. Each company's first financial year under the new standards will, in this country, be assigned to calendar year 19x1. This allows us to determine the impact of the new standards, and indirectly the impact of the Fourth EEC Directive, undisturbed by the fact that, on any given date up to a year after implementation, the new standards would not yet be applicable to some companies. In particular, the impact of the change in national provisions caused by the implementation of the Fourth and Seventh EEC Directives is examined. However, when the results indicate a significant impact of other standards such as standards set by accounting bodies or securities and exchange authorities, this impact is elaborated on in the notes.

Assessing the impact of a standard on material harmony provides some pitfalls. It is possible to determine whether a statistically significant correlation exists between the introduction of a standard and the degree of material harmony only. Such a correlation may suggest a causal connection, but this is not provable. The degree of material harmony could also have been influenced by a multitude of other factors, such as the verdict of a court of justice, the introduction of a standard in another country, the introduction of an international standard, an authoritative pronouncement by an academic, etc. In our survey we try to examine the impact of the Fourth, and where possible the Seventh, Directive on material measurement harmony between the financial reports surveyed. This is done by means of a statistical analysis of the correlation between the implementation of the Fourth and Seventh EEC Directives respectively and the changes in the degree of material measurement harmony, without considering any other factors. Where significant changes in the degree of material measurement harmony are measured which cannot be attributed to either of the directives but are clearly caused by some other factor this will be mentioned in the notes. This is, however, of secondary importance.

When accounting for deferred tax a choice must be made between the tax payable method and the deferred tax method. If the deferred tax method is applied a choice must be made between the comprehensive and the partial method and between valuation at nominal value or discounted value. Moreover, the deferred tax can be presented separately or can be included in the assets and liabilities to which they relate (net of tax method). This leads to seventeen different combinations. Some methods were not applied by the surveyed companies. On the other hand, some companies applied more than one combination. This leads to the following list of identified methods:

- A tax payable method;
- B at nominal value, comprehensive liability with separate deferred taxes;

- C at nominal value, comprehensive deferral method with separate deferred taxes;
- D at nominal value, partial liability with separate deferred taxes;
- E some deferred taxes are accounted for applying method B, and some using the net of tax method;
- F at discounted value, comprehensive liability, separate deferred taxes;
- G some deferred taxes are accounted for applying method B and some using method D;
- H the deferred taxes of some subsidiaries are not accounted for (tax payable method, A), the rest of deferred taxes are accounted for applying method C;
- I some of deferred taxes are accounted for applying the nominal, comprehensive liability method (B) and some are accounted for applying the discounted comprehensive liability method (F).

The Fourth EEC Directive requires companies applying the tax payable method (method A) to indicate in the notes on the accounts the full amounts of deferred taxation (method B), if this is material (art. 43, par. 11).

In this population we found the following forms of multiple reporting or additional data in the notes on the accounts as far as deferred taxation is concerned:

- Companies apply the tax payable method (A) but provide data in the notes on the accounts about the nature and amount of the various sources of deferred and accelerated taxes at current tax rates and based upon the current tax structure, calculated at nominal value (method B).
- Companies apply the comprehensive/deferral/nominal method (C) but state in the notes on the accounts what the impact on income and equity would have been if method B had been applied.
- Companies apply the partial/liability/nominal method (D) and provide data in the notes on the accounts about the nature and amount of the various timing differences not provided for because a liability is not expected to crystallize within the foreseeable future (D).

The results of our survey, with respect to accounting for deferred taxation, are presented and analysed below. The separate data for each member state are provided in Appendix II.

Individual accounts

We found the following application frequencies of the various methods of accounting for deferred taxes and multiple reporting or reconciliation data in the individual accounts (see Table 1). The methods not found are omitted. The last two columns contain the C index excluding and including reconciliation data respectively. The development of the C index, excluding as well as including reconciliation data, is illustrated in Figure 7.

Table 1 Accounting for deferred taxes in the individual accounts

Year	*Method*				*Reconcil.*		*No def. tax*	*C Index*	
	A	*B*	*D*	*I*	*A&B*	*B&D*		*Excl. recon.*	*Incl. recon.*
1978	29	22	20	0	2	13	83	0.333	0.476
1979	29	18	25	1	3	17	81	0.327	0.483
1980	29	17	25	1	1	18	82	0.329	0.463
1981	29	16	23	1	2	16	85	0.332	0.468
1982	29	15	22	1	2	15	87	0.336	0.464
1983	29	17	22	0	3	16	86	0.339	0.502
1984	30	16	23	0	20	17	84	0.344	0.742
1985	27	16	25	0	19	19	85	0.338	0.764
1986	27	19	21	0	22	16	87	0.331	0.817
1987	23	24	19	0	23	14	88	0.326	0.890
1988	22	25	19	0	22	13	88	0.327	0.869

A&B = Number of companies applying the tax payable method (A), but providing information in the notes on the accounts about the deferred taxes based upon method B

B&D = Number of companies applying the nominal, partial liability method (D) and providing information in the notes on the accounts about the deferred taxes not provided for based upon the nominal comprehensive method (B)

The degree of material measurement harmony, for the item deferred taxes in individual accounts, remains virtually the same over the period, if we take no account of the possibility of reconciling accounts based on different methods. But, if reconciliation data are taken into account, the C index rises sharply, especially in 1984 when many Belgian and French companies started to provide data in the notes on the accounts about deferred taxes measured according to method B. The developments in each of the individual member states can be seen in the data provided in Appendix II.

Impact of the directives

Only in Germany can a significant positive correlation be seen between the combined implementation of the Fourth and Seventh EEC Directives and the degree of harmony of accounting for deferred taxation in the primary accounts. A shift from method A to method B was found in 1987 with one company anticipating implementation by two years. This lead caused a temporary decrease in the degree of material measurement harmony. In Belgium and France all surveyed companies started to provide reconciliation data for method B in the notes on the accounts after the

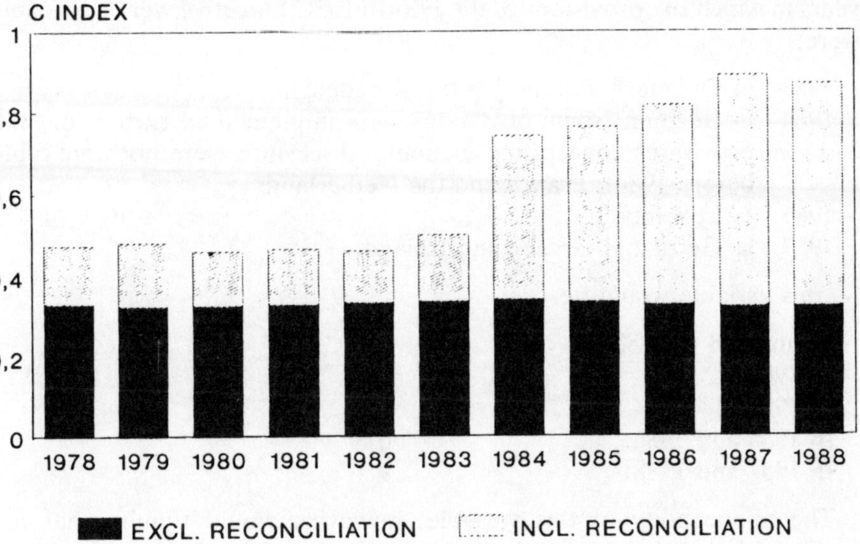

INDIVIDUAL ACCOUNTS

Figure 7 Deferred taxation in the EC: degree of harmony

implementation of the Fourth EEC Directive. Although this hardly affected the degree of national material measurement harmony, it did improve the degree of international material measurement harmony. The temporary decline in the degree of material measurement harmony, taking reconciliation data into account in Denmark around the date of implementation of the Fourth EEC Directive is not caused by a lead or lag on the Directive nor by the Directive itself.[2]

General trends

In Denmark a slight rising trend can be seen in the degree of material measurement harmony in the primary accounts. This applies whether or not reconciliation data are taken into account, and is due to the fact that a growing number of companies applied method B.

The first year in which the national law implementing the Fourth EEC Directive is applicable is different in the various member states. The same applies to the Seventh EEC Directive. This makes it difficult to measure the impact of the Directives on the total population of surveyed companies. We might try to overcome this problem by representing the degree of implementation of the Directive by a variable which is the total number of member states in which the provisions of the Directive had been implemented and were applicable in a particular year. The first calendar years in which the provisions of the Fourth EEC Directive were applicable were:

1983 in Denmark and the United Kingdom
1984 in Belgium (some provisions were implemented earlier, but the provisions concerning segmental disclosure were not applicable before 1984), France and the Netherlands
1985 in Luxembourg
1987 in Germany, Greece and Ireland.

So this variable would be:

From 1978 to 1982:	0
In 1983:	2
In 1984:	5
In 1985 and 1986:	6
In 1987 and 1988:	9

The applicability of this variable, however, would require that the number of companies in each member state be equal. In our population this is not the case, because the number of companies examined is different in each member state and because a varying number of surveyed companies in each member state had deferred taxes at all. This problem may be solved by weighting the countries by the number of companies in this country which have deferred taxes, divided by the total number of companies which have deferred taxes. The resulting data for this variable in our population are:

1978 to 1982:	0
1983:	0.382
1984:	0.797
1985:	0.794
1986:	0.806
1987 and 1988:	1

Applying the regression analysis described in section 6.3 identifies no significant correlation between the Fourth Directive and the degree of harmony of deferred taxation excluding reconciliation. However, when reconciliation is included in the degree of harmony, there is a significant correlation (R squared = 0.95, R squared adjusted = 0.944, and a correlation coefficient of 0.4, significant at the 0.0005 level) although the D-W statistic is poor (1.339) indicating some multicollinearity. There is no indication of a general trend in either of the two.

Consolidated accounts

The same data for the treatment of deferred taxes in consolidated accounts are provided in Table 2 and Figure 8.

Table 2 Accounting for deferred taxes in the consolidated accounts

Year	*Method*								*Reconciliation*			No def. tax	*C Index*	
	A	*B*	*C*	*D*	*E*	*G*	*H*	*I*	*A&B*	*B&C*	*B&D*		*Excl. recon.*	*Incl. recon.*
1978	27	32	9	37	1	1	0	1	2	0	30	22	0.268	0.456
1979	26	28	7	46	1	1	0	1	2	0	39	22	0.293	0.498
1980	25	27	8	46	1	1	0	1	1	0	40	22	0.291	0.486
1981	24	30	8	47	1	1	0	1	1	0	41	22	0.293	0.502
1982	25	29	9	47	1	1	1	1	1	0	41	20	0.283	0.478
1983	26	32	9	48	1	0	1	1	2	0	41	17	0.288	0.499
1984	26	33	9	48	0	0	2	1	2	0	41	15	0.287	0.501
1985	25	33	9	48	0	0	1	1	2	1	42	17	0.294	0.531
1986	20	42	9	48	0	0	1	1	2	0	43	17	0.305	0.577
1987	10	57	7	48	0	0	1	1	2	0	43	15	0.366	0.714
1988	10	62	4	49	0	0	1	1	2	0	43	13	0.390	0.749

A&B = Number of companies applying the tax payable method (A), but providing information in the notes on the accounts about the deferred taxes based upon method B.

B&C = Number of companies applying the nominal comprehensive deferral method (C) and providing information in the notes on the accounts concerning the impact application of the nominal comprehensive liability method would have had on equity and income.

B&D = Number of companies applying the nominal, partial liability method (D) and providing information in the notes on the accounts about the deferred taxes not provided for based upon the nominal comprehensive method (B).

The degree of material measurement harmony in the primary accounts (excluding reconciliation data and multiple reporting) increases, because more companies applied method B, and methods A and C were less used. The C index rises particularly in 1987, because the German companies switched from method A to method B. If we take account of reconciliation data and multiple reporting the degree of harmony also rises, especially in 1987, for the same reasons. Reconciliation data and multiple reporting have a smaller effect on the degree of material measurement harmony than was found in the individual accounts.

The data for individual states can be seen in Appendix II.

Impact of the directives

Around the time of the combined implementation of the Fourth and Seventh Directives in Germany, in 1987, the German companies switched from method A to method B in their consolidated accounts (with a lead

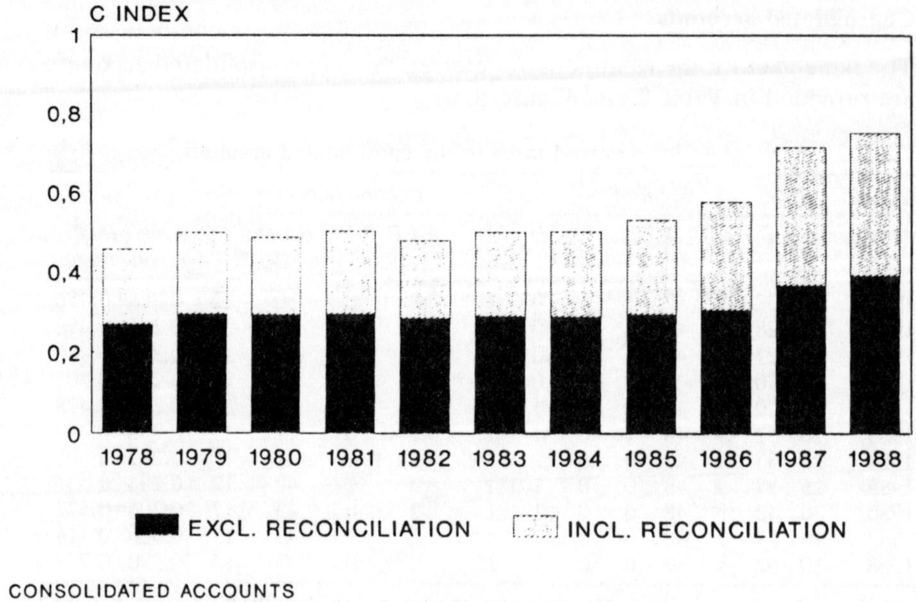

Figure 8 Deferred taxation in the EC: degree of harmony

of two years and a lag of one year). This lead and lag caused a temporary decline in the degree of material measurement harmony. Prior to 1989 the Seventh Directive was implemented *and* applicable in only one member state (France). Neither directive had a significant impact on the degree of material measurement harmony there.[3]

General trends

In Belgium a slight declining trend in the degree of material measurement harmony, when excluding reconciliation, was found, while in France a slight rising trend can be observed. Both are caused by a gradual shift from method A to method B in these countries.

If we evaluate the correlation between the implementation of the directives and the degree of harmony for the whole population the same way as described above for the individual accounts, we must apply the following weights:

1978 to 1982:	0
1983:	0.339
1984:	0.714
1985:	0.718
1986:	0.719
1987 and 1988:	1

But this does not indicate any significant correlation between the implementation of the Fourth Directive and the degree of harmony of deferred taxation in the consolidated accounts, neither when excluding reconciliation nor when including reconciliation.

5. CONCLUSION

Some results of the survey are that, as regards the individual accounts:

- the degree of harmony of the primary accounts, excluding reconciliation data in the notes on the accounts, is low and shows no significant movements during the examined period 1978 to 1988;
- the degree of harmony, taking reconciliation data in the notes on the accounts into account, increases sharply over the examined period;
- the impact of reconciliation data on the degree of harmony is very positive;
- the impact of the Fourth EEC Company Law Directive on harmony is very significantly positive.

As regards the consolidated accounts:

- the degree of harmony of the primary accounts, without taking reconciliation data in the notes on the accounts into account, is low but increases gradually over the examined period;
- the degree of harmony, taking account of reconciliation data in the notes on the accounts, increases importantly and is high at the end of the period;
- the impact of reconciliation data on the degree of harmony is very positive;
- the impact of the Fourth EEC Company Law Directive on harmony is not significant.

So a closer look at the degree of harmony of accounting for deferred taxation, taking account of reconciliation data and the difference between separate and consolidated accounts, reveals a more balanced and more positive picture of the degree of harmony of accounting for deferred taxation in the EC and the related harmonization efforts than expressed in the literature so far.

NOTES

The author is a member of the Department of Financial and Management Accounting, Erasmus University, Rotterdam, and temporarily seconded to the Commission of the European Communities by Moret Ernst & Young, Rotterdam.

The opinions expressed are those of the author. The author gratefully acknowledges the assistance of two anonymous reviewers.

1 *Official Journal of the European Communities*, L. 222, 14 August 1978: 11–31.
2 In Ireland and the United Kingdom, Statement of Standard Accounting Practice (SSAP) – 15 (applicable from 1979 onwards) initiated a change in accounting for deferred taxes by the companies. In SSAP–15 method D is prescribed with an obligation to disclose in the notes on the accounts the timing differences not provided for in the balance sheet (B&D). This caused the sharp increase in the degree of harmony in these countries in 1979 (and, because some companies in Ireland lagged upon the implementation, also in 1980).
3 In respect of the consolidated accounts of the surveyed Irish and UK companies the same developments can be observed as mentioned above when examining the individual accounts. SSAP–15 caused a shift in 1979 from application of method B to application of method D with additional information in the notes on the accounts about the deferred taxes not provided for.

APPENDIX I: LIST OF SURVEYED COMPANIES

Belgium

ACEC
Bekaert
Belgische Betonmaatschappij
Cimenteries CBR Cementbedrijven
CFE
Cockerill-Sambre (former Cockerill)
Gebroeders Delhaize en Cie 'De Leeuw'
GB-INNO BM
Glaverbel
Intercom
Mecaniver
Mettalurgie Hoboken Overpelt
Petrofina
Solvay
Tabacofina
Tiense Suikerraffinaderij
UCB
Unerg
Vieille-Montagne
Cie International Des Wagon-Lits et du Tourisme

Denmark

Aarhus Olie A/S
Bang & Olufsen A/S
Sophus Berendsen
Carlsberg A/S (former United Breweries Ltd)
A/S Dampskibsselskabet Torm A/S
Danfoss
S. Dyrop & Co A/S
The East Asiatic Company (Det Ostasiatiske Kompagni)

Fisker & Nielsen
Gyldendalske Boghandel Nordisk Forlag A/S
Icopal (Jens Villadsens Fabriker)
ISS
Jyske Bryggerier A/S
Kryolitselskabet Oresund
J. Lauritzen Rederierne
NKT A/S
Nordisk Fjerfabrik Holding A/S (former Nordisk Fjerfabrik A/S)
Novo Industri
SCS Holding
Thrige Titan

France

L'Air Liquide
Avions Marcel Dassault
BSN
Elf Aquitaine
Imetal
Lafarge Coppee (former Lafarge)
Legrand
Matra
Michelin
Moulinex
L'Oreal
Pechiney
PSA Peugeot-Citroen
Renault
Rhône-Poulenc
Sagem
Saint-Gobain
Schneider
Sommer Allibert
CIE Francaise de Petrol 'Total'

Federal Republic of Germany

Altana
BASF
Bayer
BMW
Daimler Benz
Hoechst
Holzmann
Karstadt
Kloeckner Werke
Linde
Lufthansa
Mannesmann
RWE

Schering
Siemens
Thyssen
Varta
VEBA
VEW
Volkswagen

Greece

Aluminium de Grèce
Elais
ETMA (Artificial Silk Company)
Lambropoulos Bros
Metka
Naoussa Spinning Mills
A. G. Petzetakis
Privileged Company of General Warehouses in Greece
Saint George's Mills
Titan Cement Company

Republic of Ireland

Arnotts
P. J. Carroll & Company (former Carroll Industries)
James Crean
CRH (former Cement-Roadstone Holdings)
Fitzwilton
Food Industries PLC (former Merchant's Warehousing Company PLC)
Grafton Group (former CPI Holdings)
R & H Hall
Heiton Holdings
Independent Newspapers
Irish Press PLC
Irish Ropes
R & W Jacob
The Jones Group
McInerney Properties
Readymix PLC
Ryan Hotels
Jefferson Smurfit Group
Unidare
Waterford Glass Group

Luxembourg

Arbed S.A.
Cegedel (Compagnie Grand-Ducale d'Electricité du Luxembourg)
Entreprises Quilmes SA
Metallurgique et Minière de Rodange-Athus SA

The Netherlands

Ahold NV
Akzo NV
Borsumij Wehry NV
Buehrmann Tetterode NV
Gist-Brocades NV
Heineken NV
Koninklijke Nederlandsche Hoogovens en Staalfabrieken NV
Internatio-Mueller NV
NV Koninklijke Bijenkorf Beheer KBB
Koninklijke Luchtvaartmaatschappij NV (KLM)
Koninklijke Nederlandsche Papierfabrieken NV (KNP)
Koninklijke Nedlloyd Groep
OCE van der Grinten NV
VOC (Van Ommeren Ceteco, former Phs. van Ommeren NV)
NV Philips' Gloeilampenfabrieken
Schuitema NV
Verenigde Machinefabrieken Stork NV
NV Verenigd Bezit VNU
Koninklijke Volker Stevin NV
Koninklijke Wessanen NV

United Kingdom

Allied-Lyons
Bass
BICC
Bowater
British Aerospace
British Petroleum
BTR
The Burmah Oil Company
Charter Consolidated
Courtaulds
Grand Metropolitan
Guest Keen & Nettlefolds
Hanson Trust
ICI
Lonrho
Marks & Spencer
RTZ (former Rio Tinto Zinc Corporation)
Rothmans International
Sears
Thorn EMI (former Thorn)

APPENDIX II: ACCOUNTING FOR DEFERRED TAXATION (SUMMARY OF RESULTS)

In this appendix the number of companies applying each of the accounting methods per member state are given. Additionally, the number of companies providing reconciliation information or multiple reports is stated, together with the C indices excluding, as well as including, reconciliation information and multiple reporting.

Explanation of characters

A	=	Tax payable method
B	=	Nominal, comprehensive, liability method with separate deferred taxes
C	=	Nominal, comprehensive, deferral method with separate deferred taxes.
D	=	Nominal, partial, liability method with separate deferred taxes.
E	=	Some deferred taxes are accounted for applying method B, some using the net of tax method
F	=	Discounted, comprehensive liability with separate deferred taxes
G	=	Some deferred taxes are accounted for applying method B, some using method D
H	=	The deferred taxes of some subsidiaries are not accounted for (tax payable method, A), the rest of deferred taxes are accounted for applying method C
I	=	Some deferred taxes are accounted for applying the nominal, comprehensive liability method (B), some are accounted for applying the discounted comprehensive liability method (F)
A&B	=	Number of companies applying the tax payable method (A), but providing information in the notes on the accounts on the deferred taxes based upon method B.
B&C	=	Number of companies applying the nominal comprehensive deferral method (C) and providing information in the notes on the accounts concerning the impact application of the nominal comprehensive liability method would have had on equity and income.
B&D	=	Number of companies applying the nominal, partial liability method (D) and providing information in the notes on the accounts about the deferred taxes not provided for based upon the nominal comprehensive method (B).

INDIVIDUAL ACCOUNTS

Belgium

Table 3 Accounting for deferred taxes in the individual accounts in Belgium

Year	Method	Reconc.	No def. tax	C index	
	A	A&B		Excl. recon.	Incl. recon.
1978	11	0	9	1	1
1979	11	0	9	1	1
1980	11	0	9	1	1
1981	11	0	9	1	1
1982	11	0	9	1	1
1983	11	1	9	1	1
1984	11	11	8	1	1
1985	11	11	8	1	1
1986	12	12	8	1	1
1987	11	11	9	1	1
1988	11	11	9	1	1

Denmark

Table 4 Accounting for deferred taxes in the individual accounts in Denmark

Year	Method			Reconcil.		No def. tax	C index	
	A	B	D	A&B	B&D		Excl. recon.	Incl. recon.
1978	4	5	8	2	4	3	0.324	0.603
1979	4	6	7	3	4	3	0.309	0.706
1980	4	6	6	1	4	4	0.3	0.583
1981	4	6	7	2	3	3	0.309	0.574
1982	4	6	6	2	2	4	0.3	0.533
1983	4	7	6	2	3	3	0.309	0.61
1984	4	7	7	2	4	2	0.314	0.641
1985	4	6	8	3	5	2	0.32	0.732
1986	3	9	6	3	4	2	0.353	0.843
1987	3	10	5	3	3	2	0.379	0.83
1988	3	10	6	3	4	1	0.368	0.848

France

Table 5 Accounting for deferred taxes in the individuals accounts in France

Year	*Method*		*Reconc.*	*No def. tax*	*C Index*	
	A	*B*	*A&B*		*Excl. recon.*	*Incl. recon.*
1978	7	0	0	13	1	1
1979	7	1	0	12	0.75	0.75
1980	7	1	0	12	0.75	0.75
1981	7	1	0	12	0.75	0.75
1982	7	1	0	12	0.75	0.75
1983	7	1	0	12	0.75	0.75
1984	8	0	7	12	1	1
1985	6	0	5	14	1	1
1986	7	0	7	13	1	1
1987	9	0	9	11	1	1
1988	8	1	8	11	0.778	1

Germany

Table 6 Accounting for deferred taxes in the individual accounts in Germany

Year	*Method*		*No def. tax*	*C index*	
	A	*B*		*Excl. reconc.*	*Incl. reconc*
1978	7	0	13	1	1
1979	7	0	13	1	1
1980	7	0	13	1	1
1981	7	0	13	1	1
1982	7	0	13	1	1
1983	7	0	13	1	1
1984	7	0	13	1	1
1985	6	1	13	0.714	0.714
1986	5	2	13	0.524	0.524
1987	0	7	13	1	1
1988	0	6	14	1	1

Ireland

Table 7 Accounting for deferred taxes in the individual accounts in Ireland

Year	*Method*		*Reconc.*	*No def. tax*	*C index*	
	B	*D*	*B&D*		*Excl. recon.*	*Incl. recon.*
1978	4	5	4	11	0.444	0.889
1979	1	8	6	11	0.778	0.944
1980	0	9	7	11	1	1
1981	0	8	7	12	1	1
1982	0	8	7	12	1	1
1983	0	8	7	12	1	1
1984	0	7	6	13	1	1
1985	0	7	6	13	1	1
1986	0	6	5	14	1	1
1987	0	6	5	14	1	1
1988	0	5	3	15	1	1

The Netherlands

Table 8 Accounting for deferred taxes in the individual accounts in The Netherlands

Year	Method		No def. tax	C index	
	B	I		Excl. recon.	Incl. recon.
1978	10	0	10	1	1
1979	9	1	10	0.8	0.8
1980	9	1	10	0.8	0.8
1981	8	1	11	0.778	0.778
1982	7	1	12	0.75	0.75
1983	8	0	12	1	1
1984	8	0	12	1	1
1985	8	0	12	1	1
1986	7	0	13	1	1
1987	6	0	14	1	1
1988	7	0	13	1	1

The United Kingdom

Table 9 Accounting for deferred taxes in the individual accounts in the United Kingdom

Year	Method		Reconc.	No def. tax	C Index	
	B	D	B&D		Excl. recon.	Incl. recon.
1978	3	7	5	10	0.533	0.867
1979	1	10	7	9	0.818	0.945
1980	1	10	7	9	0.818	0.945
1981	1	8	6	11	0.778	0.944
1982	1	8	6	11	0.778	0.944
1983	1	8	6	11	0.778	0.944
1984	1	9	7	10	0.8	0.956
1985	1	10	8	9	0.818	0.964
1986	1	9	7	10	0.8	0.956
1987	1	8	6	11	0.778	0.944
1988	1	7	6	12	0.75	0.964

CONSOLIDATED ACCOUNTS

Belgium

Table 10 Accounting for deferred taxes in the consolidated accounts in Belgium

Year	*Method*				*Reconc.*	*No def. tax*	*C index*	
	A	*B*	*D*	*H*	*B&D*		*Excl. recon.*	*Incl. recon.*
1978	4	2	0	0	0	7	0.467	0.467
1979	4	2	0	0	0	7	0.467	0.467
1980	4	2	0	0	0	7	0.467	0.467
1981	4	3	0	0	0	7	0.429	0.429
1982	4	2	0	1	0	6	0.333	0.333
1983	5	3	0	1	0	6	0.361	0.361
1984	5	3	0	1	0	5	0.361	0.361
1985	5	4	0	1	0	4	0.356	0.356
1986	6	4	1	1	1	4	0.318	0.379
1987	5	5	1	1	1	5	0.303	0.379
1988	6	6	1	1	1	3	0.33	0.396

Denmark

Table 11 Accounting for deferred taxes in the consolidated accounts in Denmark

Year	*Method*			*Reconcil.*		*No def. tax*	*C index*	
	A	*B*	*D*	*A&B*	*B&D*		*Excl. recon.*	*Incl. recon.*
1978	5	4	9	2	4	1	0.34	0.549
1979	5	5	9	2	4	1	0.327	0.55
1980	5	5	8	1	4	1	0.314	0.503
1981	5	6	8	1	4	1	0.31	0.509
1982	5	6	8	1	4	1	0.31	0.509
1983	5	7	8	2	4	0	0.311	0.574
1984	5	7	8	2	4	0	0.311	0.574
1985	5	5	9	2	6	1	0.327	0.632
1986	4	8	7	2	5	1	0.322	0.708
1987	4	9	6	2	4	1	0.333	0.708
1988	4	9	6	2	4	1	0.333	0.696

France

Table 12 Accounting for deferred taxes in the consolidated accounts in France

Year	Method					Reconc.	No def. tax	C index	
	A	B	C	D	H	B&C		Excl. recon.	Incl. recon.
1978	4	3	7	0	0	0	4	0.33	0.33
1979	3	4	7	0	0	0	4	0.33	0.33
1980	2	4	8	0	0	0	4	0.385	0.385
1981	1	5	8	0	0	0	4	0.418	0.418
1982	2	5	9	0	0	0	3	0.392	0.392
1983	2	6	9	0	0	0	2	0.382	0.382
1984	2	6	9	0	1	0	1	0.34	0.34
1985	2	6	9	0	0	1	2	0.382	0.426
1986	0	9	9	0	0	0	2	0.471	0.471
1987	0	12	7	1	0	0	0	0.458	0.458
1988	0	15	4	1	0	0	0	0.584	0.584

Germany

Table 13 Accounting for deferred taxes in the consolidated accounts in Germany

Year	Method		No def. tax	C index	
	A	B		Excl. recon.	Incl. recon.
1978	14	0	6	1	1
1979	14	0	6	1	1
1980	14	0	6	1	1
1981	14	0	6	1	1
1982	14	0	6	1	1
1983	14	0	6	1	1
1984	14	0	6	1	1
1985	13	1	6	0.857	0.857
1986	10	4	6	0.56	0.56
1987	1	13	6	0.857	0.857
1988	0	14	6	1	1

Ireland

Table 14 Accounting for deferred taxes in the consolidated accounts in Ireland

Year	Method		Reconc.	No def. tax	C. index	
	B	D	B&D		Excl. recon.	Incl. recon.
1978	4	14	14	1	0.634	1
1979	1	18	17	1	0.895	0.944
1980	0	19	18	1	1	1
1981	0	20	19	0	1	1
1982	0	20	19	0	1	1
1983	0	20	19	0	1	1
1984	0	20	19	0	1	1
1985	0	19	18	1	1	1
1986	0	20	19	0	1	1
1987	0	20	19	0	1	1
1988	0	20	19	0	1	1

The Netherlands

Table 15 Accounting for deferred taxes in the consolidated accounts in the Netherlands

Year	Method			No def. tax	C index	
	B	E	I		Excl. recon.	Incl. recon.
1978	16	1	1	2	0.784	0.784
1979	16	1	1	2	0.784	0.784
1980	16	1	1	2	0.784	0.784
1981	16	1	1	2	0.784	0.784
1982	16	1	1	2	0.784	0.784
1983	16	1	1	2	0.784	0.784
1984	17	0	1	2	0.889	0.889
1985	17	0	1	2	0.889	0.889
1986	17	0	1	2	0.889	0.889
1987	18	0	1	1	0.895	0.895
1988	18	0	1	1	0.882.	0.882

The United Kingdom

Table 16 Accounting for deferred taxes in the consolidated accounts in the United Kingdom

Year	*Method*				*Reconc.*	*No def. tax*	*C Index*	
	B	*C*	*D*	*G*	*B&D*		*Excl. recon.*	*Incl. recon.*
1978	3	2	14	1	12	0	0.5	0.689
1979	0	0	19	1	18	0	0.9	0.9
1980	0	0	19	1	18	0	0.9	0.9
1981	0	0	19	1	18	0	0.9	0.9
1982	0	0	19	1	18	0	0.9	0.9
1983	0	0	20	0	18	0	1	1
1984	0	0	20	0	18	0	1	1
1985	0	0	20	0	18	0	1	1
1986	0	0	20	0	18	0	1	1
1987	0	0	20	0	19	0	1	1
1988	0	0	20	0	18	0	1	1

REFERENCES

Accounting Standards Committee (1978) 'Statement of Standard Accounting Practice 15: Accounting for Deferred Taxation', *Accountancy*, November: 63–6, 68.

Doupnik, S. and Taylor, M. E. (1985) 'An Empirical Investigation of the Observance of IASC Standards in Western Europe', *Management International Review*, 25, 1: 27–33.

Evans, T. G. and Taylor, M. E. (1982) ' "Bottom Line Compliance" with the IASC: A Comparative Analysis', *The International Journal of Accounting (Education and Research)*, Fall: 115–28.

Kirkpatrick, J. L. (1986) 'The Role of the International Accounting Standards Committee' in *Harmonization of Accounting Standards: Achievements and Prospects*. Paris: Organization for Economic Co-operation and Development, pp. 87–92.

Mood, A. M., Graybill, F. A. and Boes, D. C. (1974) *Introduction to the Theory of Statistics*. Tokyo.

Nair, R. D. and Frank, W. G. (1981) 'The Harmonization of International Accounting Standards, 1973–1979', *The International Journal of Accounting (Education and Research)*, Fall: 61–77.

Nobes, C. W. (1987a) *Compliance by UK and US Corporations with IASC Standards*. Paper presented at the Tenth Annual Congress of the European Accounting Association in London, March; an amended version of this paper was published in the *British Accounting Review* (1990), 2: 41–9.

Nobes, C. W. (1987b) 'An Empirical Investigation of the Observance of IASC Standards in Western Europe: A Comment', *Management International Review*, 27, 4: 78–9.

Nobes, C. W. (1989) *Interpreting European Financial Statements: Towards 1992*. London/Edinburgh: Butterworth.

Tay, J. S. W. and Parker, R. H. (1990) 'Measuring International Harmonization and Standardization', *ABACUS*, 26, 1: 71–88.

Van der Tas, L. G. (1988) 'Measuring Harmonisation of Financial Reporting Practice', *Accounting & Business Research*, 18, 70: 157–69.

Van der Tas, L. G. (1992) *Harmonisation of Financial Reporting: With a Special Focus on the European Community*. Maastricht: Datawyse.

[6]

Accounting and Business Research, Vol. 23, No. 89, pp. 49-58, 1992

EC Accounting Harmonisation: An Empirical Study of Measurement Practices in France, Germany and the UK

Emmanuel N. Emenyonu and Sidney J. Gray*

Abstract—This research attempts to assess the extent to which accounting measurement practices in France, Germany and the UK are currently harmonised in the context of the major effort that has been made to promote EC accounting harmonisation. The statistical tests show that there are significant differences between France, Germany and the UK in respect of all the practices evaluated. Furthermore, the I-indices used to measure the overall level of international accounting harmony across the three countries indicate a wide and relatively low range of values.

Introduction

The topic of international accounting harmonisation has continued to generate interest among accounting practitioners, academics, investors and other users of corporate financial reports. A variety of organisations, including the International Accounting Standards Committee (IASC), the United Nations Centre on Transnational Corporations (UN), the Organisation for Economic Co-operation and Development (OECD), and the European Community (EC) have committed substantial resources in order to promote international understanding on accounting issues and to pursue the goal of international accounting harmonisation. However, in spite of all these endeavours, little has been done to devise a way of quantitatively determining the extent to which such efforts have been successful.

This study has two main purposes, which are related specifically to the problem of accounting harmonisation in the EC. First, an attempt is made to judge whether or not the asset and profit measurement practices of large companies in three major EC countries (France, Germany and the UK) are significantly different as at the end of 1989 in the context of the EC harmonisation effort, most notably in the form of the EC Fourth Directive (1978) which establishes the measurement methods to be followed in company accounts. Secondly, an effort is made to quantify the overall extent of international accounting uniformity or harmony across the three countries concerned. This study does not, however, attempt to measure the extent of international uniformity before the commencement of the EC harmonisation programme and the extent to which the situation has improved, deteriorated or remained the same since that time. The analysis is thus limited to an evaluation of the state of EC differences at a particular point.

In a bid to accomplish the aims of this paper, data was collected from the annual reports of 26 large industrial companies from each country. Six key asset and profit measurement practices were selected: stock valuation, depreciation, goodwill, research and development, valuation bases for fixed assets and the treatment of extraordinary/exceptional items. These practices were subjected to statistical tests to determine whether the pattern of their treatment in the three countries, within the limits of this study, could be said to be significantly different or not. Based on these variables, an international index was also computed to measure the overall level of harmony in respect of each of the measurement practices across the EC countries concerned.

Prior research and review of literature

In any endeavour to assess harmonisation, it is important to clarify the concepts involved. According to Choi and Mueller (1984, p. 470), harmonisation means that: '. . . different standards might prevail in individual countries, so long as they are "in harmony" with each other—meaning they should not logicallly conflict'. On the other hand,

*The authors are from the Centre for International Finance and Accounting, University of Glasgow.

standardisation 'means that a single standard or rule is applied to all situations'. Tay and Parker (1990, p. 71) see harmonisation as a process which entails 'a movement away from total diversity of practice' and standardisation also as a process but one which involves 'a movement towards uniformity'. While the objective of harmonisation is to move accounts away from total diversity, standardisation attempts to move them towards uniformity. In reality it might be very difficult to point out precisely at which point on the continuum an accounting regulatory process changes from harmonisation to standardisation. It is not impossible for even the EC harmonisation programme, in time, to move the accounting practices of companies in member nations from total diversity towards uniformity. As a result, the terms will be treated in conjunction with each other for the purposes of this paper.

Earlier researchers have written extensively on such issues as: the benefits and costs of harmonisation, obstacles and problems hindering harmonisation, scope for harmonisation, and factors that are encouraging the harmonisation drive (see, for example, Carey, 1970; Chevalier, 1977; Choi and Mueller, 1984; Fantl, 1971; Gray, 1984; McComb, 1979; Moulin, 1988; Nair and Frank, 1981; Turley, 1983; Turner, 1983). Therefore, this review of prior research will concentrate on those studies which are directly related to the measurement of international harmonisation.

Nair and Frank (1981, p. 76) set out to ascertain the impact of the harmonisation endeavours of the IASC. Consequently, they surveyed the effect of IAS 1 to 10 on the accounting practices of some 37 countries, using the Price Waterhouse surveys of 1973, 1975 and 1979. They found that the period of the IASC's existence had coincided with an increase in the harmonisation of accounting standards between the countries surveyed. These findings may be questioned, however, in that the Price Waterhouse surveys used by Nair and Frank are limited in terms of reliability, not least by their focus on regulations rather than actual practice (Nobes, 1981).

Evans and Taylor (1982, p. 118, 119), with aims similar to those of Nair and Frank (1981), studied the effect of IAS 2, 3, 4, 6 and 7 on financial reporting practices in France, Japan, UK, USA and West Germany. This study relied on the financial reports of selected companies in each of the countries from 1975–88 for its data. Based on their findings they concluded that the IASC had had very little effect on the accounting practices of the countries studied.

Doupnik and Taylor (1985) set out to assess the extent to which 16 western European countries conformed to a 'basic core of accounting practice', using IAS 1–8. Data collected through a survey questionnaire and the Price Waterhouse 1979 survey were analysed. The findings supported the hypothesis that many differences still existed in Western European accounting practices though some increased compliance with IASC standards was found. This latter finding was, however, disputed by Nobes (1987) who also concluded from a recent study of accounting practices of US multinationals that compliance with IASC standards was negligible (Nobes, 1990).

The Fédération des Experts Comptables Européens (FEE) has also produced some noteworthy surveys. The 1989 survey (FEE, 1989), covering 1987 accounts, set out to ascertain whether, after the implementation of the EC Fourth Directive on Annual Accounts, there was harmonisation of accounting practices within the member countries. Consequently, data was gathered from survey questionnaires and the annual reports of about 191 companies from 9 EC nations, namely: Belgium, Denmark, France, Germany, Greece, Ireland, Luxembourg, Netherlands and the United Kingdom. The survey concluded that, for those areas covered comprehensively by the Fourth Directive, a high level of harmonisation can be observed. On the other hand, an apparent lack of harmonisation can be seen in those areas covered only partially by the Directive. An update and extension of this survey based on 1989 accounts has also recently been published (FEE, 1991) which covers 441 companies from 15 European countries. A major finding of the survey is that other factors besides the EC Fourth Directive are having a significant influence on the evolution of accounting practice at the national level. What both of these surveys do not do, however, is attempt to quantify, in statistical terms, the existence of significant differences in practice and the current status of harmonisation.

Van der Tas (1988), in an exploratory article, set out to quantify harmony, to determine when and to what extent harmonisation has taken place and then to measure the impact of the organisations involved in international harmonisation. In order to accomplish the set goals, three indices of concentration measurement were developed and adapted. The basic tool was the Herfindahl index, or H-index, one of many measures used to assess industrial concentration or monopoly. Variants of the H-index were developed. The C-index was devised to handle national and the I-index to handle international harmonisation measurement. The use of a concentration index approach was justified on the grounds that harmonisation, i.e. moves towards standardisation or uniformity, may be likened to moves towards monopoly albeit in a different context.

Using these indices, van der Tas measured levels of harmonisation on the subject of Deferred Tax in the UK; accounting for the Investment Tax Credit in the Netherlands and the US; the Investment Tax Credit Equalisation Account in the Netherlands;

and the Valuation of Land and Buildings in the Netherlands. Finally, he attempted to compute a harmonisation index for the Investment Tax Credit in the US and the Netherlands. From these indices, which were computed over periods ranging from 1965 to 1985, it was possible at a glance to recognise periods of high and low harmonisation. However, this was an exploratory article and much work is still needed before the work of van der Tas can be fully operationalised. One important limitation of the indices he set out to calculate was how to measure the significance of changes in the indices involved.

Tay and Parker (1990), after reviewing van der Tas (1988) and other notable papers on the measurement of international harmonisation, identified the following as major problems: data sources, operationalisation of concepts, statistical methods employed, and distinguishing changes in accounting practice due to compliance with standards from changes due to other reasons. They went on to suggest an alternative approach to harmonisation measurement—a study focused on the actual practices of companies as disclosed in their annual reports rather than as stated by regulatory requirements. Evidence of harmony could be derived by subjecting data extracted from companies' annual reports to tests of statistical significance using, for instance, the chi-square test and by indices such as the I-index proposed by van der Tas.

This research attempts to implement some of the Tay and Parker suggestions, albeit in the limited context of EC harmonisation with particular reference to France, Germany and the UK. Objective statistical analysis (the chi-square test and the I-index) is used to form an opinion on the significance of differences and extent of harmony as at the end of 1989 in respect of the *de facto* measurement practices of companies from the three countries covered by this study.

However, perhaps most importantly, the purpose of this paper is not just to enable an opinion to be formed on the extent to which there are differences, or a lack of harmony, in financial reporting in the context of efforts to promote EC accounting harmonisation. A further significant aim is to contribute to the development and application of quantitative measures of international harmonisation.

Research methodology and hypotheses

The objectives of this research are twofold:

1. Assess, by using objective statistical tests, whether the pattern of usage of asset and profit measurement practices by large companies in France, Germany and the UK are significantly different;
2. Derive an index showing the extent of international harmonisation, using data on asset and profit measurement practices, across the three countries.

The variables selected for testing have been chosen because they can in solo or in concert significantly affect measures of assets and profits, depending on the choice of treatment adopted by a company. In addition, information relating to the particular method adopted for treating each of the variables is commonly available from the 'accounting policies' section of most companies' annual reports, or can be deduced from the notes to their accounts.

The relevant hypotheses are stated below in the null form for the purposes of statistical testing:

Ho_1: There is no significant difference in the stock valuation methods used by large French, German and UK companies.

Ho_2: There is no significant difference in the depreciation methods used by large French, German and UK companies.

Ho_3: There is no significant difference in the methods of treating goodwill used by large French, German and UK companies.

Ho_4: There is no significant difference in the methods of treating research and development expenditure used by large French, German and UK companies.

Ho_5: There is no significant difference in the valuation bases for fixed assets used by large French, German and UK companies.

Ho_6: There is no significant difference in the method of treating extraordinary/exceptional items used by large French, German and UK companies.

As already mentioned, the data for the study were collected from the 1989 annual reports of 26 large industrial companies[1] (with a turnover in excess of 1 billion), from each of France, Germany and the UK. For the 1989 financial year, 69 French, 77 German and 120 UK companies attained a turnover of 1 billion or more. The sample size for the study (26 from each country) thus represents about 38% of French companies in the class of interest, 34% for Germany and 22% for the UK. The samples were selected randomly, so as to guard against any biases. However, the fact that some industries were not represented in all of the country samples is recognised as a limitation. In this regard, it was not feasible to match the companies in each sample by industry. On the other hand, the samples were not biased by any particular industry groupings. The study was restricted to large companies because the need to promote

[1]The list of companies surveyed is available from the authors on request.

international investment is often cited as a justification for international accounting harmonisation. Hence, this study focuses on the class of companies most likely to attract the attention of international investors. The number of companies studied was limited by time and resource constraints.

Tools of analysis

Two statistical tools of analysis are employed. The Chi-square (χ^2) test is used to assess whether the pattern of usage of measurement practices by companies in France, Germany and the UK is significantly different. On the other hand, the I-index (a variant of Herfindahl's concentration measure) is used to compute the degree of international harmony that exists across the three countries. A brief discussion of each of the statistical tools now follows.

1. The Chi-square (χ^2) test

The hypotheses are treated using the Chi-square (χ^2) test for independent samples (see Siegel and Castellan, 1988, p. 191). The tests are conducted at the 5% level of significance.

2. The van der Tas I-index

The I-index employed by van der Tas (1988) is itself a variant of the Herfindahl index. While recognising that the Herfindahl index is just one of many possible concentration measures, Tay and Parker (1990, p. 83) argue that the use of a concentration index 'seems to be a useful way to evaluate the level of harmony, and track movements in harmonisation over time'.

The general formula for the I-index (van der Tas, 1988, p. 168), which includes a correction factor in the case of two or more countries, is:

$$I = \left(\sum_{i=1}^{n} (f^1 i \times f^2 i \times \cdots \times f^m i) \right)^{1/(m-1)}$$

where:

fi = relative frequency of method i in country m
m = number of countries
n = number of alternative accounting methods

By way of explanation, the I-index is computed by multiplying the relative frequency of use of a particular accounting method across countries and subsequently adding up the results for all alternative methods. Consequently, the index rises when more companies across countries use the same methods from the available accounting options. An example of a 3-country/2-method case is as follows:

Country	1	2	3
Method 1	0.7	0.5	0.6
Method 2	0.3	0.5	0.4

$I = (0.7 \times 0.5 \times 0.6 + 0.3 \times 0.5 \times 0.4)^{1/(3-1)}$
$= 0.27^{1/2} = 0.52.$

However, as indicated by Tay and Parker (1990), there may be problems in operationalising this approach in terms of identifying the range of accounting methods involved and the companies which are affected by a particular accounting method. Further, a test has yet to be devised to evaluate the significance of variations in index values. Users of the index are also expected to determine subjectively the desired value of the index for an acceptable degree of harmony to be said to exist.

Presentation of data and analysis of test results

In this section, the test results and main findings of the research are presented. This is accompanied by a discussion of the measurement provisions of the EC Fourth Directive and national requirements in each of the three countries with respect to the six practices studied. The EC Fourth Directive was implemented in France in 1983, Germany in 1985 and the UK in 1981. It should also be noted that the measurement provisions of the EC Fourth Directive were incorporated in the EC Seventh Directive (1983) relating to consolidated accounts which was implemented in France in 1986, Germany in 1985 and the UK in 1989. As far as possible, the discussion in this section is restricted to the six specified practices in the context of the three countries under study.

Stock Valuation Methods

Ho_1: There is no significant difference in the stock valuation methods used by large French, German and UK companies.

Article 39 of the EC Fourth Directive provides that current assets should be valued at purchase price or production cost or market value which ever is lower. Article 40 is flexible, though, as regards the bases for determining the cost of stocks: the 'first in, first out' (FIFO) method, weighted average costs, the 'last in, first out' (LIFO) method, or some similar method, are all permitted. However, France does not permit the use of the LIFO method, and it is rare in the UK where it is prohibited for tax purposes and not generally acceptable in the accounting standard (SSAP 9). Germany, on the other hand, allows it where it corresponds to actual or physical usage.

For the purposes of this study, three categories of methods were identified: cost, market value or lower of cost and market value. This categorisation was based on the stated accounting policies of the reporting firms. A test based on cost determination bases was not attempted since companies often use a combination of methods that would be too complex if not impossible to subject to testable categories. Worse still, many did not disclose the

Table 1
Stock Valuation Methods

Methods	*France*	*Germany*	*UK*	*Total*
Cost	16 (61%)	4 (15%)	0 (0%)	20 (26%)
Market value (MV)	0 (0%)	0 (0%)	2 (8%)	2 (2%)
Lower of cost/MV	10 (39%)	22 (85%)	24 (92%)	56 (72%)
Total companies	26	26	26	78
$\chi^2 = 27.97$		I-Index = 0.5481		

specific method used, i.e. LIFO, FIFO, weighted average etc. Market value is derived using either net realisable value or replacement cost.

From Table 1, it can be seen that a significant overall majority of companies (74%) use a lower of cost and market value approach. For purposes of the chi-square test, the market value and lower of cost and market value categories were combined to avoid the problem of small expected frequencies (Siegel and Castellan, 1988, p. 199).

The computed chi-square value of 27.97 shown in Table 1 is significant at the 5% level and, therefore, we reject the null hypothesis and conclude that the stock valuation methods used by large French, German and UK companies are significantly different. However, further statistical analysis using chi-square tests applied to pairs of countries (see Appendix A), indicates that there is no significant difference between methods adopted by German and UK companies. Hence, the overall significant result was due to variations in French practice relative to the other two countries. In this regard, however, it should be noted that the reported use of the cost method by French companies may be misleading, as the use of the 'lower of cost and market value' method generally leads to valuation at cost in any particular case.

The I-index of 0.5481 shown in Table 1 means that there is about a 54.81 percent level of harmony on the issue of stock valuation methods as described by large French, German and UK companies. As suggested earlier, there is no benchmark yet available to test whether this degree of harmony is acceptable or not.

Depreciation Methods

> *Ho_2: There is no significant difference in the depreciation methods used by large French, German and UK companies.*

According to Article 31 (i) of the Fourth Directive, 'account must be taken of all depreciation, whether the result of the financial year is a loss or a profit'. However, the directive is flexible in that it does not prescribe any particular method of reflecting depreciation in the books of accounts of companies in the member countries. To date, the straight line and declining balance methods remain the most widely used.

Owing to the German practice of starting with the declining balance method and then switching over to the straight line method when the figure derived from straight line exceeds that from declining balance, a third category combining both methods was created for analysis purposes as can be seen from Table 2. Clearly, there is a fairly even split overall between companies using straight line depreciation and those using a mix of straight line and reducing balance depreciation methods.

For the purposes of the chi-square test, the three companies in the declining balance category were excluded to avoid the problem of small expected frequencies. The computed chi-square value of 48.75 shown in Table 2 is significant at the 5%

Table 2
Depreciation Methods

Methods	*France*	*Germany*	*UK*	*Total*
A. Straight line (S)	15 (58%)	0 (0%)	25 (96%)	40 (51%)
B. Declining Bal (D)	1 (4%)	1 (4%)	1 (4%)	3 (4%)
C. (D) & (S)	10 (38%)	25 (96%)	0 (0%)	35 (45%)
Total companies	26	26	26	78
$\chi^2 = 48.75$		I-Index = 0.0076		

level, and thus we reject the null hypothesis and conclude that the depreciation methods used by large French, German and UK companies are significantly different.

The I-index of 0.0076 shown in Table 2 means that there is about a 1 percent degree of harmony on the issue of the depreciation methods used by large companies in France, Germany and the UK. The low degree of harmony in this respect can be explained by the influence of tax accounting on French and German financial reporting. While about 96% of the UK companies adopted the straight line method, about the same percentage of German companies preferred the declining balance method, switching over to the straight line method only when it offered tax advantages over the declining balance method. Though a sizeable percentage of French companies (58%) adopted the straight line method, the large degree of difference between German and UK practices appears to have neutralised the moderating effect of the French companies' depreciation policies.

Treatment of Goodwill

Ho_3: There is no significant difference in the methods of treating goodwill used by large French, German and UK companies.

Article 9 of the Fourth Directive is flexible in that it permits, but does not require, purchased goodwill to be carried in the balance sheet as an intangible asset. If capitalised, goodwill should normally be written off within a maximum period of five years (Article 37 (2)). Article 37 provides a derogation in that member states may permit companies to write off goodwill systematically over a period exceeding five years provided that this period does not exceed the useful economic life of the asset. All three countries have taken advantage of the Article 37 derogation by allowing amortisation in excess of 5 years depending on the expected useful economic life of the asset.

In Germany and the UK (see Table 3) the majority of companies have not capitalised goodwill, preferring to write it off against reserves and thus avoiding the amortisation provisions of the Fourth Directive. It can be seen that the chi-square value relating to the treatment of goodwill is 41.69. This is significant at the 5% level, and thus we reject the null hypothesis and conclude that the methods of treating goodwill adopted by large French, German and UK companies are significantly differently. However, when the analysis was done on a two-country basis, the difference between German and UK companies was found to be insignificant (see Appendix A). This suggests that the overall significant result arises because of the significant French result relative to both Germany and the UK.

The I-index of 0.2636 means that there is about a 26.36% level of harmony on the practice of treating goodwill adopted by large companies from the three countries. This relatively low degree of harmony can be explained by the relatively high use of the amortisation method prevalent among French companies (about 92%), in comparison with the low German (about 25%) and UK (about 4%) uses.

Research and Development Costs

Ho_4: There is no significant difference in the methods of treating research and development expenditure used by large French, German and UK companies.

As in the case of goodwill, the Fourth Directive is flexible in that it permits member states to authorise the treatment of research and development (R&D) costs as intangible assets (Article 37 (i)). Member states may also permit R&D costs to be amortised over a period in excess of five years. However, the reasons for exceeding five years must be disclosed in the notes on the accounts. In the individual countries, both France and Germany allow the capitalisation and amortisation of R&D costs. For the UK, Statement of Standard Accounting Practice No. 13 does not permit the capitalisation of research costs, but development expenses can be capitalised and amortised subject to meeting certain criteria. From Table 4 it can be seen that the overall majority of companies (63%) prefer the immediate write off method. In this case it was not possible to compute a chi-square statistic owing to the small expected frequencies and lack of policy disclosure. The I-index was also not computed due to the very high rate of German non-disclosure on this issue.

Table 3
Treatment of Goodwill

Methods	*France*	*Germany*	*UK*	*Total*
A. Immediate write off	2 (8%)	18 (75%)	23 (96%)	43 (60%)
B. Amortised over a period	22 (92%)	6 (25%)	1 (4%)	29 (40%)
Total companies	24	24	24	72
$\chi^2 = 41.69$		I-Index = 0.2636		

Table 4
Treatment of R & D Costs

Methods	*France*	*Germany*	*UK*	*Total*
A. Immediate write off	22 (85%)	2 (7%)	25 (96%)	49 (63%)
B. Deferred	1 (4%)	0 (0%)	1 (4%)	2 (2%)
C. Not disclosed	3 (11%)	24 (93%)	0 (0%)	27 (35%)
Total companies	26	26	26	78

While there is a very high degree of similarity between British (96.15% for immediate write off) and French (84.62% for immediate write off) practice, in Germany, the only two companies that disclosed their policies also used the immediate write off method and it would seem that this is the normal method used in practice. Hence, it can be said that the trend is in favour of immediate write off of research and development costs.

Valuation Bases for Fixed Assets

Ho_5: There is no significant difference in the valuation bases for fixed assets used by large French, German and UK companies.

Section 7 of the Fourth Directive sets out the rules for asset valuation. The basic valuation principle is historical cost. However, under Article 33, member states are permitted to authorise the use of replacement value, methods of valuation which take account of inflation, and revaluation on a periodic basis. However, in Germany, methods reflecting changing price levels are not permitted. Consequently, the use of the historical cost convention is mandatory. In France, the government and stock exchange bodies, having appreciated the effects of inflation on historical cost accounting, required index-based revaluation and hence some modification of the strict historical cost convention. However, the UK is the most liberal of the three countries. UK regulations permit periodic revaluations by companies on an *ad hoc* basis. The use of current cost accounting is also permitted in either primary or supplementary financial statements.

In order to test for the significance of the use of different valuation bases for fixed assets, three categories were identified: historical cost, modified historical cost (i.e. periodic revaluations) and current cost conventions. For the purposes of the chi-square test, however, the modified historical cost and current cost categories were combined to avoid the problem of small expected frequencies. From Table 5 it can be seen that, while historical cost is followed by the overall majority of companies (77%), there are a significant number of companies, mostly from the UK, using modified historical cost or current cost approaches in their primary financial statements.

The computed chi-square value of 25.77 shown in Table 5 is significant at the 5% level. Thus we reject the null hypothesis and conclude that the valuation bases used by large French, German and UK companies are significantly different. However, further statistical analysis shows that, when compared against each other, the difference between French and German companies was found not to be significant (see Appendix A). On the other hand, compared to France and Germany, the practice of UK companies was found to be significantly different.

From Table 5, it can be seen that the I-index is 0.6079, that is, there is about a 60.79% degree of harmony existing on the issue of the valuation bases adopted by large French, German and UK companies.

Treatment of Extraordinary and Exceptional Items

Ho_6: There is no significant difference in the method of treating extraordinary/exceptional items used by large French, German and UK companies.

Table 5
Valuation Bases for Fixed Assets

Methods	*France*	*Germany*	*UK*	*Total*
Historical cost	23 (88%)	26 (100%)	11 (42%)	60 (77%)
Modified historical	3 (12%)	0 (0%)	15 (58%)	18 (23%)
Total companies	26	26	26	78

$\chi^2 = 25.77$ I-index = 0.6079

Table 6
Treatment of Extraordinary and Exceptional Items

Methods	*France*	*Germany*	*UK*	*Total*
A. Treated in current year's income statement	23 (88%)	12 (46%)	22 (85%)	57 (73%)
B. Taken to reserves or retained earnings	3 (12%)	14 (54%)	4 (15%)	21 (27%)
Total companies	26	26	26	78
$\chi^2 = 14.47$		I-index = 0.5959		

The Fourth Directive defines extraordinary items as 'Income and charges that arise otherwise than in the course of the company's ordinary activities' (Article 29). However, no further guidance is given as to treatment other than to require separate disclosure of the gains and losses involved in the profit and loss account.

In the UK, the term 'exceptional items' refers to charges and incomes which are not regarded as being outside ordinary activities but are abnormal due to size or incidence, while in France both terms are translated as 'exceptionnel'. No matter how defined, it is hardly controversial to say that the treatment of extraordinary and exceptional items may significantly affect the profit result depending on whether or not such items are taken to reserves as opposed to treating them as part of the current year's profit or loss.

From Table 6, it can be seen that, while the majority of companies (73%) treat extraordinary/exceptional items as part of the current year's profit, a significant minority (27%) take such items to reserves. The chi-square test value is 14.47. This is significant at the 5% level. Thus, we reject the null hypothesis and conclude that the methods adopted by large French, German and UK companies for treating extraordinary and exceptional items are significantly different. Further analysis shows the difference between French companies compared to UK companies to be insignificant (see Appendix A). Hence, the overall significant result is likely to be due to the differences between Germany compared to France and Germany compared to the UK.

Table 7
Summary of I-index Values

Measurement Practices	*Index Values*	%
Depreciation	0.0076	0.8
Goodwill	0.2636	26.4
Stock valuation	0.5481	54.8
Extraordinary/exceptional items	0.5959	59.6
Valuation bases for fixed assets	0.6079	60.8

Table 6 shows an I-index of 0.5959. This suggests that there is about a 59.59% degree of harmony in the methods used by large French, German and UK companies for treating extraordinary and exceptional items. French and UK practice on this issue exhibits a high level of similarity. Over 84% of the selected companies in both countries include extraordinary and exceptional items in the current year's income statement as opposed to just over 46% by German companies.

Conclusion

Taken overall, the chi-square tests have yielded results that are not very encouraging to those concerned to eliminate or reduce differences in measurement practices between the EC countries. In all cases, apart from research and development where it was not possible to conduct the test, there were statistically significant differences in the measurement practices of large French, German and UK companies. As regards the overall extent of international harmony, the I-index yielded values as shown in Table 7 ranging from a high of 0.6079 for valuation bases for fixed assets to a low of 0.0076 for depreciation methods. This is a wide, and relatively low, range of values given the efforts of the EC and other international organisations such as the IASC to promote measurement practices that are harmonised internationally. Clearly, there are significant differences in the measurement treatment of a number of key items in major EC countries such as France, Germany and the UK. These differences tend to confirm the view that the measurement provisions of the EC Fourth Directive are inherently flexible. Thus, much is still to be achieved in terms of harmonising asset and profit measurement practices in the EC.

However, when the tests are restricted to two countries at a time, the results are a little more encouraging. As can be seen from Appendix A, the chi-square test results show that the difference between French compared to German companies was not significant for one item. The same holds true for French compared to UK companies. In the case of German compared to UK companies, two items were not significant.

At the same time, the lowest I-index value was 0.04 for depreciation methods in the case of Germany versus UK, while the highest value was 0.88 for France versus Germany on valuation methods. Also, the highest values for each pair of countries (0.88 France versus Germany; 0.85 Germany versus UK and 0.77 France versus UK), exceeds the highest value from the combined analysis of 0.6079.

In addition to the problem of accounting differences and a relative lack of harmony, there is the related problem of instances of inadequate disclosure and explanation of the measurement methods used, with particular reference to stock valuation and research and development.

Measuring the extent of harmony of accounting practices of companies internationally is still very much at an exploratory stage. Consequently, there is substantial scope for further research which could cover a larger sample of companies and include additional valuation and profit measurement practices such as deferred taxation, pensions, long-term contracts, treatment of long-term debt, and so on. Group accounting and consolidation practices could also be included. The measurement practices involved could also be studied in greater detail in terms of their quantitative and aggregate impact, subject to sufficient disclosures being made by the companies concerned. Furthermore, a study that embraces both measurement and disclosure practices promises to be even more revealing.

In terms of geographic scope, it would also be interesting to conduct a study embracing, say, all of the EC and OECD countries or, further still, all the developed market economies of the world. Such regional and global studies could help in the development of indices of international harmony which could assist organisations involved in accounting harmonisation to evaluate levels of harmony existing at various points in time. Harmonisation trend studies would also be useful as inter-temporal comparisons would help to sharpen our understanding of fluctuations in the levels of harmony over time. The above areas are just a few suggestions concerning harmonisation issues in need of further research.

References

Carey, J. L. (1970), 'How Can Barriers Against International Accounting Be Eliminated?', *International Journal of Accounting*, Fall, pp. 53–58.

Chevalier, G. (1977), 'Should Accounting Practices Be Universal?', *CA Magazine*, July, pp. 47–50.

Choi, F. D. S. and Mueller, G. G. (1984), *International Accounting*, Prentice Hall International.

Doupnik, S. and Taylor, M. E. (1985), 'An Empirical Investigation of the Observance of IASC Standards in Western Europe', *Management International Review*, Spring, pp. 27–33.

Evans, T. G. and Taylor, M. E. (1982), 'Bottom-line Compliance with the IASC: A Comparative Analysis', *International Journal of Accounting*, Fall, pp. 115–128.

Fantl, I. L. (1971), 'Case against International Uniformity', *Management Accounting*, May, pp. 13–16.

Fédération des Experts Comptables Européens (1989), *European Survey of Published Financial Statements in the Context of the Fourth EC Directive 1989*, Brussels.

Fédération des Experts Comptables Européens (1991), *European Survey of Published Accounts 1991*, Routledge.

Gray, S. J., Campbell L. G. and Shaw, J. C. (1984), *International Financial Reporting*, Macmillan.

McComb, D. (1982), 'International Accounting Standards and the EEC Harmonization Program: A Conflict of Disparate Objectives', *International Journal of Accounting*, Spring, Spring, pp. 35–48.

Moulin, D. J. (1988), 'Practical Means of Promoting Common Accounting and Auditing Standards', *Proceedings of the 13th Annual Conference of the International Organisation of Securities Commissions*, pp. 1–21.

Nair, R. D. and Frank, W. G. (1981), 'The Harmonization of International Accounting Standards, 1973–1979', *International Journal of Accounting*, Fall, pp. 61–77.

Nobes, C. W. (1987), 'An Empirical Investigation of the Observance of IASC Standards in Western Europe: A Comment', *Management International Review*, Winter, pp. 78–79.

Nobes, C. W. (1990), 'Compliance by US Corporations with IASC Standards', *British Accounting Review*, March, pp. 41–49.

Nobes, C. W. and Parker, R. H. (1991), *Comparative International Accounting*, Prentice Hall.

Siegel, S. and Castellan, N. J. (1988), *Non-Parametric Statistics for the Behavioral Sciences*, McGraw Hill.

Tay, J. S. W. and Parker, R. H. (1990), 'Measuring International Harmonization and Standardization', *Abacus*, Vol. 26, No. 1, 1990, pp. 71–87.

Turley, W. S. (1983), 'International Harmonization of Accounting: The Contribution of the EEC Fourth Directive on Company Law', *International Journal of Accounting*, Spring, pp. 13–28.

Turner, J. N. (1983), 'International Harmonisation: A Professional Goal', *Journal of Accountancy*, January, pp. 58–59.

Van der Tas, L. G. (1988), 'Measuring Harmonisation of Financial Reporting Practice', *Accounting and Business Research*, Spring, pp. 157–169.

Appendix A

Results of further country analysis

	France / Germany	France / UK	Germany / UK
Chi-square (χ^2) values:			
Stock valuation methods	11.70*	23.11*	4.33
Depreciation methods	21.09*	10.83*	48.15*
Goodwill	21.94*	36.81*	4.18

Valuation bases for fixed assets	3.18	12.24*	21.08*
Extraordinary/exceptional items	10.58*	0.17	8.50*

Critical value of χ^2 at the 5% level = 5.02.
*denotes significant results

I-index values:	(%)	(%)	(%)
Stock valuation methods	0.42 (42)	0.39 (39)	0.85 (85)
Depreciation methods	0.38 (38)	0.57 (57)	0.04 (4)
Goodwill	0.29 (29)	0.11 (11)	0.73 (73)
Valuation bases for fixed assets	0.88 (88)	0.44 (44)	0.42 (42)
Extraordinary/exceptional items	0.47 (47)	0.77 (77)	0.47 (47)

Part II
The International Accounting Standards Committee

[7]

The Harmonization of International Accounting Standards, 1973-1979

R. D. NAIR and WERNER G. FRANK*

In the decade of the 1970s, serious attempts were made to harmonize international accounting practices. This effort was deemed important because the growth of international trade and of multinational corporations necessitated the comparison of accounting data across national boundaries. Differences which existed in accounting practices constituted a barrier to international communication of valid financial data.

An assessment of these efforts at harmonization now needs to be made. Sufficient time has elapsed, a large number of accounting issues have been addressed in this effort, and enough empirical data are now available for such an assessment to be neither premature nor impractical. This assessment is particularly necessary because the barriers to harmonization are considerable. Economic, social, and political environments of nations differ, and these influences may lead to corresponding differences in accounting practices. Frank, and Nair and Frank found that underlying environmental variables were closely associated with groupings of countries based on their accounting practices.[1] Nair and Frank state the implications of such a finding are

* R. D. Nair and Werner G. Frank are respectively assistant professor and professor of accounting at the University of Wisconsin-Madison.

The authors express their appreciation to Thomas J. Linsmeier for his comments on an earlier draft of this paper.

[1] Werner G. Frank, "An Empirical Analysis of International Accounting Practices," *Journal of Accounting Research* (Autumn 1979): 593-605; and R. D. Nair and Werner G. Frank, "The Impact of Disclosure and Measurement Practices on International Accounting Classifications," *Accounting Review* (July 1980): 426-50.

that "reaching the goal of harmonization may be difficult because, given the . . . association, countries may be reluctant to make a change in accounting practices so long as the underlying environmental variables are significantly different."[2] It is of interest to see whether attempts at harmonization have succeeded despite such hurdles. In spite of these obstacles, the growing interdependence of countries and the growing commonality of worldwide economic conditions might have provided an added impetus to the trend toward harmonization.

The authors find in this study that the attempts at harmonization of accounting practices have met considerable success. The study isolates those practices on which progress has been made; relates those practices to the pronouncements of the major international standards-setting organization, the International Accounting Standards Committee (IASC); and examines which countries have made changes regarding those accounting practices. The authors also find that practices adopted in the United States seem to have had a considerable influence on the direction taken in the international accounting standard-setting process.

The first section of this study describes the institutional efforts directed toward harmonization. The second section describes the data sources used in this study, the accounting practices which were studied, and the countries which were examined. The third section details the methods of analysis which were used and the results of those analyses. The next section presents the analysis of national involvement in harmonization, and the final section presents the conclusions of this study.

EFFORTS AT HARMONIZATION

Several institutions have addressed the problem of differences in accounting standards between nations and the need to eliminate all unnecessary differences and to understand better those differences which are justified. A discussion of such efforts can be found in Cummings and Chetkovich[3] and Berton.[4] The most important of these institutions is undoubtedly the IASC, established in 1973 by the accounting bodies of nine countries: Australia, Canada, France, Germany, Japan, Mexico, the Netherlands, the United Kingdom and Ire-

[2] Nair and Frank, "Disclosure and Measurement Practices."

[3] Joseph P. Cummings and Michael N. Chetkovich, "World Accounting Enters a New Era," *Journal of Accountancy* (April 1978): 52-61.

[4] Lee Berton, "Arthur Young Professors' Roundtable: The International World of Accounting," *Journal of Accountancy* (August 1980): 74-79.

land (jointly), and the United States. At present, IASC's board consists of a representative from each of the founding countries and two representatives selected for members admitted after 1973. Members of the IASC have as their goal to ensure (1) that conformity exists between accounting standards in their own countries and those of the IASC, (2) that independent auditors examine financial statements for compliance with these standards, and (3) that noncompliance is either disclosed in the statements, or is referred to in the audit report. A discussion of the working procedures of IASC can be found in a publication from Deloitte Haskins & Sells.[5]

The authors have restricted their study to the first ten Statements of International Accounting Standards. These ten standards, listed in exhibit 1, were issued during the period for which the authors have survey data on the prevalent accounting practices in a wide range of countries, 1975 to 1978.[6]

Exhibit 1. IASC Statements of International Accounting Standards Issued Prior to January 1, 1979

(Date of issuance in parentheses)

No. 1 — Disclosure of Accounting Policies (January 1975)
No. 2 — Valuation and Presentation of Inventories in the Context of the Historical Cost System (October 1975)
No. 3 — Consolidated Financial Statements (June 1976)
No. 4 — Depreciation Accounting (October 1976)
No. 5 — Information to Be Disclosed in Financial Statements (October 1976)
No. 6 — Accounting Responses to Changing Prices (June 1977)
No. 7 — Statement of Changes in Financial Position (October 1977)
No. 8 — Unusual and Prior Period Items and Changes in Accounting Policies (February 1978)
No. 9 — Accounting for Research and Development Activities (July 1978)
No. 10 — Contingencies and Events Occurring after the Balance Sheet Date (October 1978)

[5] Deloitte Haskins & Sells, *International Accounting Standards Committee, Summary of Activities, January 1975-January 1980* (Deloitte Haskins & Sells, 1980).

[6] The most recent survey the authors use describes the accounting practices in use as of January 1, 1979. Although IASC Statements 7 to 10 became effective for financial statements covering periods beginning on or after January 1, 1979, they were issued from two to fourteen months prior to this date. The authors feel that if the IASC does, in fact, influence accounting practices, it is reasonable to assume that firms would begin to move toward recommended practices as soon as the IASC statements are issued.

An examination of these standards shows that many of them are quite similar to the authoritative pronouncements on those topics in the United States, although differences of varying degrees do exist. For example, with respect to valuation of inventories in the context of historical cost, IASC *Statement No. 2,* "Valuation and Presentation of Inventories," states that valuation should be at the lower of historical cost and net realizable value. The first-in, first-out or weighted-average methods are preferred, although the last-in, first-out or base-stock methods are also permitted. The treatment of unusual and prior period items by IASC is similar to the treatment outlined by the Accounting Principles Board (APB) in *Opinion No. 9,* "Reporting the Results of Operations," rather than the more stringent requirements of *Opinion No. 30,* "Reporting the Results of Operations," and *Statement of Financial Accounting Standards No. 16,* "Prior Period Adjustments," of the Financial Accounting Standards Board (FASB).

On the other hand, IASC required in June 1977, in *Statement No. 6,* "Accounting Responses to Changing Prices," that if no procedures had been adopted to show the impact of changing prices, whether of general or specific prices or both, that fact should be disclosed. In *Statement No. 9,* "Accounting for Research and Development Activities," IASC also permits deferral, and subsequent amortization, of research and development costs if certain criteria are satisfied, contrary to FASB *Statement of Financial Accounting Standards No. 2,* "Accounting for Research and Development Costs."

In sum, of the ten pronouncements, only the two dealing with changing prices and research and development can be regarded as being substantially in conflict with the U.S. posture on those topics at the time the standards were issued by the IASC. This is not surprising considering that five countries — Canada, Germany, Japan, Mexico, and the Netherlands — of the original nine members of IASC from 1973 were identified by Frank to be members of the "U.S. model."[7] In other words, these other countries followed accounting practices very similar to those in the United States. The authors would, therefore, expect the U.S. influences to prevail on IASC.

DATA SOURCES

The data for the analyses were drawn from three Price Waterhouse surveys of accounting principles and reporting practices in different countries, the first of which was published in 1973, the second in 1975,

[7] Frank, "International Accounting Practices."

and the third in 1980.[8] These surveys constitute an important data source for a longitudinal study of change such as this one, especially since the time span of the three surveys corresponds with the existence of IASC.

The Price Waterhouse survey data were compiled from information provided by their various offices around the world. Uniform procedures were used worldwide in collecting and compiling the data. Strenuous efforts were made to ensure accuracy of the data. The firm also made a conscious effort not to bias the responses in favor of the accounting practices of its own clients or its own views on the desirability of a given practice. However, in countries where a lack of publicly available information prevents an assessment of the degree of conformity of a given practice, the response represents the best judgment of the Price Waterhouse people in those countries. Similarly, judgment was used when a diversity of practice existed in a country. Moreover, the format of the survey responses makes it impossible to detect local variations in practice which may be of importance.

All responses were based on requirements applied to financial statements prepared for the shareholders of profit-oriented firms which issue their statements to the general public. The responses were also based on any other document which a firm is required by law to produce as part of its annual report to shareholders. It should be noted that the firms whose practices are surveyed may not themselves be comparable across countries. For example, many of the firms in one country may be involved in extracting natural resources, agriculture, or in the retailing industry while in another, manufacturing firms may constitute the major sector. However, the firms from a given country whose practices are surveyed are likely to be comparable over time. These shortcomings of the data should be kept in mind when evaluating the results. These limitations could not be corrected by the authors, who nevertheless feel that the value of the data, especially for a longitudinal study such as this, far outweighs their defects.

Although the procedures for collecting the data have been consistent over time, the number of countries in the survey, the type and number of questions asked, and the nature of the possible responses have changed. The methods for correcting for these changes are discussed next.

---

[8] Price Waterhouse International, *Accounting Principles and Reporting Practices* (Canada: Price Waterhouse, 1973); idem., *Accounting Principles and Reporting Practices* (Canada: Price Waterhouse, 1975); and idem., *International Survey of Accounting Principles and Reporting Practices* (Scarborough, Ontario: Butterworths, 1979).

The 1979 survey included sixty-four countries whereas the 1975 and 1973 surveys included forty-six and thirty-eight countries, respectively. The current study concentrated on the thirty-seven countries which were common to all three surveys because these were the countries for which comparisons at the three points in time could be made. These countries are listed in exhibit 2.

Exhibit 2. Countries Common to 1973, 1975, and 1979 Price Waterhouse Surveys

Argentina	Ireland	Philippines
Australia	Italy	Singapore
Bahamas	Jamaica	South Africa
Belgium	Japan	Spain
Bolivia	Kenya	Sweden
Brazil	Mexico	Switzerland
Canada	Netherlands	Trinidad and Tobago
Chile	New Zealand	United Kingdom
Colombia	Pakistan	United States
Fiji	Panama	Uruguay
France	Paraguay	Venezuela
Germany	Peru	Zimbabwe
India		

The number of accounting practices surveyed also changed; there were 233 practices in the 1973 survey, 264 in 1975, and 267 in 1979. In addition, not all the practices surveyed in a given year were included in subsequent surveys. Finally, the form in which some questions were asked also changed from one survey to the next. To ensure a consistent and comparable data set, the authors identified 131 practices which had been included in all three surveys.[9] In terms of general categories, these 131 practices could be classified as follows:

Broad concepts	7 practices or concepts
Accounting policies	2
Fixed assets and depreciation	25
Inventories	16
Investments	6
Receivables and liabilities	11
Long-term liabilities	3
Shareholders' equity	14
Other balance-sheet items	6
Income statement	18
Consolidations	16
Foreign currency	6
Directors' activities	1
	131 practices or concepts

[9] A complete list of these practices is available from the authors.

This selection procedure had the effect of ignoring changes with respect to certain accounting practices which were surveyed in 1979 but not in 1973 or 1975. Such issues were not as noteworthy during the early part of the decade but received greater attention in the latter part. Examples of such issues are accounting for price changes, and for segments of a business. A bias is therefore created in the sense that the study does not deal with a random sample of practices on which the authors were able to collect data in these thirty-seven countries in the three different years. Instead, these practices were the survivors in the sense that they were considered important in all three years. Because of this, practices on which harmonization took place toward the end of the period may have been excluded; alternatively, a disproportionately large number of those practices on which harmonization had already taken place may have been included. However, the fact that these practices were included in all three surveys indicates that they are not trivial issues.

The format of the responses also changed over time. The categories into which a country's position on a practice was classified were different in each of the three surveys. These categories are listed here.

In 1973	*In 1975*	*In 1979*
1. Required	1. Required	1. Required
2. Majority	2. Majority	2. Majority
3. About half	3. About half	3. Predominant practice
4. Minority	4. Minority	4. Minority practice
5. No application	5. Not found in practice	5. Rarely or not found
6. Not permitted	6. Not permitted	6. Not accepted
	7. No application	7. Not permitted
		8. No application

Before the analyses could proceed, these categories had to be made consistent over time. This was accomplished by collapsing certain categories in each survey to yield the following five broader categories:

1. Required (including Insisted upon from 1979);
2. Predominant practice (including Majority and About half from both 1973 and 1975);
3. Minority practice;
4. No application (including Not found in practice from 1975 and Rarely or not found from 1979); and
5. Not permitted (including Not accepted from 1979).

The analyses, presented in the next section, deal with these five new categories.

ANALYSIS AND RESULTS

To harmonize accounting standards is to bring them into agreement. Thus, with respect to the data base of this study, the authors accepted that harmonization on a given practice has taken place if all countries are in the same category with respect to that practice. Complete harmonization would require that all countries were in one or the other *extreme* category, Required or Not permitted. Even if all countries fell into one of the two intermediate categories, Predominant or Minority practice, this would indicate that true uniformity has not yet been achieved since some diversity of practice does exist within the individual countries. Clustering of all countries in the remaining category, No application, would indicate that the practice is not important with respect to these thirty-seven countries. Thus, for the purposes of this study, the authors concentrated on the extent to which the thirty-seven countries were to be found in either the Required or Not permitted categories.

An analysis was therefore conducted on each of the 131 accounting practices to determine how the thirty-seven countries were classified in each of the three years that the survey was conducted. For example, for the practice Depreciation methods are disclosed, the following distribution appeared:

Category/ Years	*Required*	*Predominant practice*	*Minority practice*	*No application*	*Not permitted*	*Total*
1973	9	7	15	6	0	37
1975	16	8	9	3	1	37
1979	28	2	5	2	0	37

This indicates that whereas only nine of the thirty-seven countries required disclosure of depreciation methods in 1973, twenty-eight of the same thirty-seven required such disclosure in 1979.

There was no accounting practice among the 131 for which all thirty-seven countries were in either the Required or Not permitted categories, that is, there was no practice on which complete harmonization had been achieved. Accordingly, a less stringent operational definition of harmonization was adopted. The authors looked for those practices on which more than half of the thirty-seven countries (nineteen or more countries) were to be found in either the Required or Not permitted categories by 1979. We identified 49 such practices, or approximately 37 percent, from the original 131. For 39 of these practices, the majority of countries were in the Required category while for the other 10, the majority were in the Not permitted category.

Even though more than half the countries were in agreement on these forty-nine practices, this harmony cannot be ascribed to the activities of the IASC without further analysis. For example, the countries may have been in agreement long before IASC came into existence. Therefore, the next step of the analysis was an attempt to determine the number of accounting practices of these forty-nine for which significant changes in distribution had taken place during the period 1973 to 1979.

To determine whether the shifts during the period were statistically significant, Friedman's Analysis of Variance[10] was utilized. The Friedman test can be used to examine the rankings on a criterion for the same group of cases (that is, countries) under two or more different conditions (such as might exist at different points in time). This technique was appropriate for the purposes here since the three surveys were not independent but instead constituted repeated measures on the same sample of thirty-seven countries. For this statistical test to be used, the data had to be recast in a different form. For example, assume the extent of usage on a given practice in two countries for the three years were as follows:

Country/ Year	*1973*	*1975*	*1979*
Country A	Minority practice (coded as 3)	No application (coded as 4)	Not permitted (coded as 5)
Country B	Predominant practice (coded as 2)	Predominant practice (coded as 2)	Required practice (coded as 1)

Then this data for each country (row) could be transformed into ranks as follows:

Country/ Year	*1973*	*1975*	*1979*
Country A	1	2	3
Country B	2.5	2.5	1

These rankings can then be analyzed by Friedman's Analysis of Variance to determine whether the overall change in ranks during the time period is statistically significant. The null hypothesis in such a test is that there is no difference in ranks over time. The test statistic follows a Chi-square distribution, and for the purposes of this study, a significance level of 5 percent was selected.

[10] Sidney Siegel, *Nonparametric Statistics for the Behavioral Sciences* (New York: McGraw-Hill Book Company, 1956).

The results indicate that of these forty-nine practices (those for which the presence of harmony of practice between countries had been detected), twenty-nine had significant changes in ranks between the three surveys.[11] Investigating further, it was found that for twenty-five of these twenty-nine practices, the significant shift occurred between the 1975 and 1979 surveys. (IASC Statement No. 1 was issued in January 1975, and thus it is not surprising that most of the significant changes should be observed after that date.) The twenty-nine practices are listed in exhibit 3. All of these practices except numbers 7, 21, 25, and 29 had significant shifts between 1975 and 1979. For nine of the practices, the majority of countries were in the Not permitted category rather than the Required category. These nine were numbers 13, 15, 16, 17, 21, 22, 23, 26, and 27.

In comparing the general topic areas covered by these twenty-nine practices with those covered by the IASC in their first ten pronounce-

Exhibit 3. Accounting Concepts and Practices Which Had Significant Movement to Harmonization — Sample of Thirty-seven Countries, 1973-1979

Accounting concept or practice (Description below title)	*Applicable IASC standard*	*Direction of movement*
1. Going Concern Concept Financial statements are drawn up on the premise that the business will continue in operation indefinitely.	Standard No. 1	Required
2. Consistency Concept Accounting principles and methods are applied on the same basis from period to period.	Standard No. 1	Required
3. Accrual Concept Revenues and costs are recorded in the financial statements of the period in which they are earned or incurred, and not as money is received or paid.	Standard No. 1	Required
4. Realization Concept Revenue is recognized when its realization is reasonably assured.	—	Required
5. Matching Concept Cost of sales and expenses are appropriately matched against sales and revenue.	—	Required

[11] Of these 131 practices, 39 had significant shifts in the period 1973 to 1979, but for 10 of these, the number of countries involved was less than nineteen; that is, the shift involved changes between the intermediate categories of Predominant practice, Minority practice, or No application.

Exhibit 3 (cont.)

Accounting concept or practice (Description below title)	*Applicable IASC standard*	*Direction of movement*
6. Historical Cost Convention Departures from the historical cost convention are disclosed.	—	Required
7. Accounting Policies When accounting principles or methods have not been applied on the same basis from period to period in the determination of results of operations or financial position, the effect of the change is disclosed.	Standard No. 1	Required
8. Fixed Assets When fixed assets are stated, in historical cost statements, at an amount in excess of cost, the basis of revaluation is disclosed.	—	Required
9. Fixed Assets When fixed assets are stated, in historical cost statements, at an amount in excess of cost, depreciation based on the revaluation is charged to income.	—	Required
10. Depreciation Depreciation methods are disclosed.	Standard No. 4	Required
11. Inventories The basis on which inventories are stated is disclosed.	Standard No. 2	Required
12. Inventories A breakdown of inventory by types, such as finished goods, work-in-progress, and materials is disclosed.	Standard No. 2	Required
13. Inventories Market value ("market") of inventories is interpreted to mean net realizable value defined as estimated selling price less reasonably predictable costs of completion and disposal and normal profit margin.	Standard No. 2*	Not Permitted
14. Inventories Inventories are stated at cost or market, whichever is lower.	Standard No. 2*	Not Permitted
15. Inventories Inventories are stated at cost although this may exceed market.	Standard No. 2*	Not Permitted
16. Inventories In historical cost statements, inventories are stated at market although this may exceed cost.	Standard No. 2*	Not Permitted

Exhibit 3 (cont.)

Accounting concept or practice (Description below title)	Applicable IASC standard	Direction of movement
17. Inventories Own manufactured goods are stated at estimated net realizable value when sale is assured.	Standard No. 2*	Not Permitted
18. Inventories The method of determining the cost of inventories (LIFO, FIFO, average, etc.) is disclosed.	Standard No. 2	Required
19. Investments When the carrying amount of an investment is permanently impaired, a provision is made for impairment.	Standard No. 3	Required
20. Receivables Receivables from affiliated companies are disclosed.	Standard No. 5	Required
21. Shareholders' Equity When there is no cash option, dividends satisfied by the issue of par value shares are recorded by the issues at the greater of market and par value of the share.	—	Not Permitted
22. Shareholders' Equity General reserves are set up by charges to income.	—	Not Permitted
23. Shareholders' Equity Reserves are used by absorb charges which would otherwise be charges against income of current or future years.	—	Not Permitted
24. Subsequent Events Events or transactions occurring between the date of the balance sheet and the date of the auditors' report which may have a material effect on the financial position or results of operations being reported upon are disclosed or reflected in those financial statements.	Standard No. 10	Required
25. Income Taxes Provision for income taxes on the current period's profits is shown separately before determining net income.	Standard No. 5	Required
26. Income Taxes Accounting practices adhere strictly to tax requirements.	Standard No. 12*	Not Permitted

Exhibit 3 (cont.)

Accounting concept or practice (Description below title)	*Applicable IASC standard*	*Direction of movement*
27. Consolidations Parent-company financial statements only are prepared for shareholders of a parent company.	Standard No. 3*	Not Permitted
28. Business Combinations In a business combination accounted for as a purchase, retained earnings of the acquired company prior to the combination are excluded from the retained earnings of the combined organization.	—	Required
29. Foreign Currency The basis for translating foreign currencies is disclosed.	Standard No. 1	Required

* With respect to practices 13, 14, 15, 16, 17, 26, and 27, the IASC standard listed prohibits the practice in question.

ments, it is of interest to note that all pronouncements except those dealing with changing prices, the statement of changes in financial position, and research and development of activities are reflected in the list. Exhibit 3 also relates these international accounting practices to the applicable IASC standard. It was found that twenty out of the twenty-nine practices could be related to seven IASC standards. In every case, the direction of change was consistent with the position espoused by IASC. With respect to reporting on changing prices and accounting for research and development, it should be recalled that the position of IASC was in conflict with the U.S. position. This suggests a possible association between the U.S. position on an issue and subsequent harmonization. This link will be explored later in the paper. Thus, there is some evidence from Price Waterhouse, a source independent of IASC, that these standards have been reflected in an associated harmonization of international accounting practices in those topic areas.

NATIONAL INVOLVEMENT IN HARMONIZATION

In the final step of this analysis, the authors investigated which countries were involved in the observed recent movement toward harmonization. For each of the twenty-five accounting practices for which a significant movement toward harmonization occurred between 1975 and 1979, those countries which had been involved were identified and were then grouped using the characterization developed by Frank based on the similarity of accounting practices in use in 1973.[12] He characterized the thirty-seven countries in this study (plus Ethiopia) as belonging to one of the following models: the British Commonwealth (twelve countries), Latin America (nine countries), Central Europe (eight countries), and the United States (eight countries).

For example, with respect to the Going concern concept (number 1 as listed in exhibit 3), it was found that twenty countries moved in the direction of increased harmonization (requiring the practices), fourteen made no change, and three moved in the opposite direction (toward prohibiting it).[13] Of the twenty countries that moved toward harmonization, nine were from the British Commonwealth group, six were from the Latin American group, four were from the Central European group, and only one was from the U.S. group. This same pattern (countries identified with the U.S. group being much less active than those in the other groups) was typical of all twenty-five practices. The authors found that a majority of the British Commonwealth countries changed in the direction of increased harmonization for seventeen of twenty-five practices. Similarly, a majority of the Latin American and of Central European countries moved toward increased harmonization for twenty and fifteen of the twenty-five practices, respectively. On the other hand, a majority of the U.S. group participated in such a change for only three of the twenty-five practices. This suggests two possible explanations: the U.S. group countries were not interested in change, or the other countries were moving toward the position the U.S. group countries had already taken.

To distinguish between these alternative explanations, the position of the United States in 1975 on the twenty-five practices was examined. This analysis showed that of the seventeen practices the rest of the world required in 1979, the United States had already mandated fourteen of them, two had no application, and one was followed by a majority of firms in 1975. Similarly, of the eight practices that the rest of the world had moved toward prohibition in 1979, the United

[12] Frank, "International Accounting Practices."

[13] Consistent with the definition of harmonization used in the first part of this study, *movement toward harmonization* is defined as movement in the direction taken by a majority of countries toward requiring (or prohibiting) a given accounting practice. For example, if a country moved from category 3, Minority practice, in 1975 to category 2, Predominant practice, in 1979, this was interpreted as a move in the direction of harmonization if a majority of countries required the use of this practice in 1979.

States had already prohibited seven, and one was followed by only a minority of firms in 1975.

This would tend to indicate that the United States enjoys a position of leadership in international accounting and that other countries tend to adopt the positions espoused by it. It confirms the observation made earlier on the pronouncements of the IASC and their relationships to U.S. pronouncements on the same topic. The inference of leadership by the United States is strengthened by the fact that harmonization was not detected on those issues on which the IASC's stand contradicted the U.S. position.

It is interesting to speculate on possible explanations underlying the apparent leadership role of the United States. Some insights into the nature of the standard-setting process are provided by examining the possible role of powerful groups in influencing decisions on accounting standards. This issue has drawn considerable attention in the United States where the actions of the APB and the FASB have been closely scrutinized. Horngren remarked that "... the setting of accounting standards is as much a product of political action as well as of flawless logic or empirical findings."[14] Solomons notes that "today, to judge from current discussions of the standard-setting process, accounting can no longer be thought of as nonpolitical."[15] The Staff Study of the Subcommittee on Reports, Accounting, and Management of the United States Senate is replete with charges of corporate dominance of the standard-setting process.[16] Empirical investigations of the influence exerted on policy makers and of the rationale for such behavior on the part of lobbyists can be found in Rockness and Nikolai[17] and Watts and Zimmerman.[18]

In the international arena, there is no reason to suspect that the setting of accounting standards is any more a product of "flawless logic or empirical findings" than it is domestically in the United States. The pressure may be exerted more on the behalf of national accounting

---

[14] Charles T. Horngren, "The Marketing of Accounting Standards," *Journal of Accountancy* (October 1973): 61-66.

[15] David Solomons, "The Politicization of Accounting," *Journal of Accountancy* (December 1978): 65-72.

[16] U.S. Congress, Senate, Subcommittee on Reports, Accounting and Management of the Committee on Government Operations, *The Accounting Establishment: A Staff Study* (Metcalf Staff Report) (Washington, D.C.: Government Printing Office, 1976).

[17] Howard O. Rockness and Loren A. Nikolai, "An Assessment of APB Voting Patterns," *Journal of Accounting Research* (Spring 1977): 154-67.

[18] Ross L. Watts and Jerold L. Zimmerman, "Towards a Positive Theory of the Determination of Accounting Standards," *Accounting Review* (January 1978): 112-34.

groups than from specific corporate or industry interests. These national accounting groups would be concerned with ensuring that the international accounting standard on a given issue varied as little as possible from the domestic standard on that issue. A national accounting group would lobby in this fashion in order to minimize the costs associated with changing to a new standard, or to avoid the stigma of noncompliance if it chooses instead to ignore the new international standard. One would expect the lobbying effort to be the greatest on the part of the accounting professions in those countries such as the United States which have devoted a great deal of effort and resources to developing an extensive and well-codified set of standards. These countries would have the most to lose if an international accounting standard was at variance with the domestically accepted accounting principle.

If the United States plays a leading role in IASC deliberations, then this suggests that rapid movement is not likely to occur in those standards which are the subject of heated controversy in the United States. Thus, in spite of the progress in accounting for the effect of changing prices in Europe, this topic has only just reached exposure draft form (Exposure Draft No. 17) with the IASC. This slow pace is also seen in the area of translating foreign currency. In the United States, the controversy surrounding FASB *Statement of Financial Accounting Standards No. 8,* "Accounting for the Translation of Foreign Currency Transactions and Foreign Financial Statements," caused that organization to issue a new exposure draft proposing changes from the existing requirements. Given the disagreement in the United States, it should not be surprising to find that no standard yet exists for this subject even though an exposure draft (No. 11) was issued in December 1977. Currently, efforts are being made to achieve a consensus on this subject by the professional accounting associations in the United States, Canada, and the United Kingdom.

Another implication of viewing the setting of standards as a political process is that governments, as well as the professional accounting organizations, would be expected to become involved. The European Economic Community (EEC), the United Nations, and the Organization for Economic Cooperation and Development are now taking an active role in developing international accounting standards. Directives issued by the EEC Council of Ministers are to be enacted into law by member countries, thus providing legal sanctions for the directives.

SUMMARY AND CONCLUSIONS

The authors examined 131 accounting practices common to the 1973, 1975, and 1979 surveys of international accounting practices made by Price Waterhouse. Although in 1973 a majority of the thirty-seven countries in the sample were in agreement on mandating adherence to only eight of 131 practices, by 1979 agreement had increased to forty-nine practices. In further analysis of these forty-nine practices, it was found that a significant change in position had taken place for twenty-nine practices during the period 1973-1979, and for twenty-five practices during the period 1975-1979. Further, the topics on which IASC had issued pronouncements during the period 1973 to 1979 were related to the accounting practices on which the authors had detected harmonization. Harmonization was not detected on those issues on which the stand of IASC was in conflict with the stand of the United States. With respect to where harmonization had occurred, it was found that the United States and countries with similar accounting practices were not very active in making such changes. Most of the movement was due to changes made by countries from the British Commonwealth, Central Europe, and Latin America. Pursuing the possible reason for such behavior, the authors noted that the practices which the rest of the world had moved toward requiring (or prohibiting) by 1979 had been already required (or prohibited) in the United States in 1975.

In conclusion, it should be observed that the inference of causation is no easy task and that there are more dangers than rewards in such an endeavor. Nonetheless, the authors can state that the period of the IASC's existence has coincided with a growing harmonization of accounting standards. This association between the two is strengthened by the fact that many of the topics on which the IASC has issued pronouncements are those on which the authors observe harmonization. Another conclusion to be drawn from this study is that the accounting practices in the United States seem to serve as a model for this harmonization process.

[8]

"Bottom Line Compliance" with the IASC: A Comparative Analysis

THOMAS G. EVANS and MARTIN E. TAYLOR*

BACKGROUND

Introduction

The problem of diversity in national accounting principles has a long history. When nations emerged as distinct political units because of divergent environmental factors such as culture, language, and political and economic systems, the conditions encouraged each nation to establish accounting standards which tended to mirror the nation's diverse factors.[1] This is not surprising, since nations also prefer their own currency, customs, and laws. A comparison of the accounting standards in the major nations today reveals that differences continue to exist.

Although understandable, this current situation of national diversity in accounting principles is not necessarily optimal for the worldwide allocation of economic resources. Distinct national economies do exist, but now there is also a world economy in which trade, investment, and capital flow freely from country to country. National differences in accounting principles, however, impede this flow since resource allocation decisions are thought to be based on accounting information that is heterogeneous in nature.

A recent study by Scott found that one of the most important categories of accounting problems was that of international accounting

* Thomas G. Evans and Martin E. Taylor are associate professors of accounting at the University of South Carolina.

[1] Financial Accounting Standards Board, "Objectives of Financial Reporting by Business Enterprises," *Statement of Financial Accounting Concepts No. 1* (Stamford, Conn.: FASB, 1978).

standards.[2] Within this category, the most important perceived problem was that the lack of international accounting standards greatly diminished the usefulness of financial statements to users in countries other than that on whose accounting standards the statements are based.

This problem was recognized as early as the late 1950s by Kraayenhof who made a personal plea for an effort to reduce the diversity.[3] As it became increasingly apparent that national diversity existed and was not economically desirable, attention was focused on ways to remedy this situation. Two general views emerged.

One school of thought emphasized the justification for such differences.[4] An extension of this view held that the natural evolution of accounting principles within each nation would narrow alternatives and this would, internationally, also reduce the degree of diversity found from country to country. Other natural forces, such as the international competition for capital, would also work to reduce diversity. Evidence of this latter phenomena was found.[5] Today, as illustrated by the consultation of the Financial Accounting Standards Board (FASB) with other countries while considering changes in Statement of Financial Accounting Standard (SFAS) No. 8, informal efforts are still being made to reduce diversity.

The other (more dominant) view posits that formal action should be taken to reduce the diversity. Consistent with this view, a number (approximately ten) of accounting standard-setting bodies which claim internationl jurisdiction for their pronouncements have emerged in the last decade. The four main organizations are the International Accounting Standards Committee (IASC), the European Economic Community, the United Nations, and the International Federation of Accountants. Each has been active in issuing accounting and financial reporting rules which, if followed, would reduce the diversity and result in greater harmony in accounting principles from country to country. These current attempts at international harmonization, however, have created a number of related problems, especially with regard to the composition and authority of these standard-setting bodies.

[2] G. Scott and P. Troberg, *Eighty-eight International Accounting Problems in Rank Order of Importance — A DELPHI Evaluation* (Sarasota, Fla.: American Accounting Association, 1980).

[3] Jacob Kraayenhof, "International Challenges for Accounting," *Journal of Accountancy* (January 1960).

[4] Irving L. Fantl, "Case against International Uniformity," *Management Accounting* (May 1971).

[5] Frederick Choi, "Multinational Financing and Accounting Harmony," *Management Accounting* (March 1974).

The failure of these agencies to coordinate their efforts has created problems of overlapping jurisdictions. Their productivity has created a bewildering array of new international accounting rules. For example, at last count, IASC has issued sixteen standards, has seven exposure drafts outstanding, and has authorized seven research projects. The question of the authority of these agencies is paramount, since almost all nations have retained their sovereignty to issue accounting standards.

THE IASC

Given these developments, it is now appropriate to evaluate this approach to achieving greater harmonization of international financial accounting standards by standard-setting bodies. The evaluation should focus on the IASC, the premier international body and the most productive issuer of international accounting standards. It is also the only body issuing statements with a global rather than a regional orientation. So far, it has raised most of the important questions regarding international accounting standards.[6]

The IASC was formed in 1973 by leading accounting professional bodies in nine nations: Australia, Canada, France, Germany, Japan, Mexico, the Netherlands, the United Kingdom and Ireland, and the United States. It is important to note that nations are not members of the IASC; instead, professional accounting bodies within nations are members (for example, the American Institute of Certified Public Accountants, not the FASB, is the representative of the United States). The objective of the IASC is simply to issue international accounting standards to be followed in the presentation of audited financial statements. Currently, sixty-one national accounting bodies are members of the IASC. Each member is pledged to use its "best endeavors" to ensure that (1) accounting standards in its respective country conform to those of the IASC, (2) the independent auditors satisfy themselves that the financial statements comply with these standards or that the fact of noncompliance is disclosed in the financial statements, and (3) in the event of nondisclosure, reference to noncompliance is made in the audit report.[7]

The IASC follows a due process procedure similar to that of the FASB. Such procedures followed in developing international accounting standards are these:

[6] Thomas G. Evans, "Can American Accountants Serve Two Masters: FASB and IASC?" *CPA Journal* (January 1976).

[7] International Accounting Standards Committee, *Preface to the Statements of International Accounting Standards* (London: IASC, 1974).

- The Board selects an *agenda* of subjects to be studied.
- A Steering Committee, comprised of three members drawn from different countries, is appointed to develop an exposure draft on each subject.
- The exposure draft is submitted to the Board for approval.
- When approved by a *two-thirds vote of the Board,* the exposure draft is sent to professional accounting bodies and others for *comment.* The comment period, generally, is a minimum of four months.
- The Steering Committee reviews the comments and *drafts a final Standard.*
- A final Standard, when approved by at least three-quarters of the Board, is issued.[8]

In addition, the IASC should be the focus of any evaluation of the impact of international harmonization of financial accounting standards because it has the longest history of any other organization and because it is widely recognized as the main body for achieving success in international harmonization: "The work of the IASC is without doubt the most promising development so far [in international harmonization]. . . ."[9] ". . . the IASC has been the most successful of any of the *large-scale* international efforts toward harmonizing accounting standards."[10] Concerning the IASC, it is particularly interesting that at least nine nations (Bahamas, Fiji, France, Malaysia, Nigeria, Pakistan, Singapore, Trinidad, and Zimbabwe Rhodesia) are reported to have accorded IASC standards the same status as domestic accounting standards.[11]

Research Issues

The preceding events raise the following questions concerning the ISAC's performance to date:

1. Have IASC standards been accepted and followed by firms in member nations? This question of acceptance is critical to the whole issue of international harmonization by direct action through a formal agency, such as the IASC. The IASC has attempted to bridge this gap through its pledge of "best endeavors" by members. Has this approach worked? Are IASC standards really being followed in those countries? If not, then IASC standards will not achieve international harmonization.

[8] Deloitte, Haskins & Sells, *International Accounting Standards Committee* (D, H & S, 1981).

[9] Frederick Choi and Gerhard Mueller, *An Introduction to Multinational Accounting* (Englewood Cliffs, N.J.: Prentice-Hall, 1978).

[10] J. Arpan and Lee Radebaugh, *International Accounting and Multinational Enterprises* (Boston: Warren, Gorham, and Lamont, 1981).

[11] R. Fitzgerald, A. Stickler, and T. Watts, eds., *International Survey of Accounting Principles and Reporting Practices* (Scarborough, Ontario, Canada: Price Waterhouse International, 1979).

2. What impact has the IASC had on the generally accepted accounting principles (GAAP) of developing countries? A special case for increased international harmonization can be made by asserting that the IASC directly benefits developing nations who lack a strong accounting profession and accounting infrastructure. If these nations can simply adopt IASC standards as their own GAAP, they will save themselves the effort and will also result in greater harmonization. The question then becomes whether the IASC has become the standard setter for those nations and how is it perceived in those nations. If the IASC is of benefit to those nations, how has this contributed to international harmonization?
3. How does the accounting profession (public accounting and industry) in developed nations, such as the United States, view the IASC and its standards? What are the perceptions of multinational firms which should be in compliance with IASC standards? This is a critical factor in the question of international harmonization and the IASC: lacking the formal authority to set accounting standards in member nations, has it been accorded the status it needs to obtain acceptance for its pronouncements?

RESEARCH METHODOLOGY

This paper reports on the first phase of an investigation into these problems. To determine the impact of IASC standards on the financial reporting in member nations, financial reports were analyzed. The IASC has issued sixteen standards to date; five of the earlier ones were selected and used to check compliance in a sample of five IASC member nations. The standards and their effective dates are as follows:

IASC standard		*Effective date*
No. 2	"Valuation and Presentation of Inventories"	12/31/76
No. 3	"Consolidated Financial Statements"	12/31/77
No. 4	"Depreciation Accounting"	12/31/77
No. 6	"Accounting Responses to Changing Prices"	12/31/78
No. 7	"Statement of Changes in Financial Position"	12/31/79

Major Provisions of IASC Standards

The major provisions for each of the five standards selected are presented here.

IAS No. 2 — "Valuation and Presentation of Inventories." In the context of the historical cost system, (1) inventories should be valued at the lower of historical cost and net realizable value; (2) inventories should be segregated in balance sheets or in notes to the financial statements to show the amounts held in different categories (such as materials, work-in-process, and finished goods), and the accounting policies adopted for valuation, including the cost method used, should be disclosed.

IAS No. 3 — "Consolidated Financial Statements." Minority interest in the equity of consolidated companies, and in the profits and losses of such companies, should be shown separately in the consolidated statements and should not be included in the shareholders' equity or consolidated net income. IAS No. 3 prescribes the equity method of accounting for investments included in consolidated statements when the investor may exercise significant influence over the investee (that is, holds 20 percent or more of the voting stock), or the investee is a subsidiary not consolidated because its activities are so dissimilar from those of the parent as to make consolidated statements meaningless.

IAS No. 4 — "Depreciation Accounting." A depreciable asset should be depreciated on a systematic basis, and its cost should be allocated to each accounting period during its useful life. Disclosures for each major class of depreciable assets should include the following: the depreciation method, useful lives or depreciation rates, depreciation expense for the period, and gross depreciable assets and accumulated depreciation.

IAS No. 6 — "Accounting Responses to Changing Prices." Information that describes the procedures adopted to reflect the impact on the financial statements of specific price changes or changes in the general level of prices, or both, should be disclosed in the financial statements. If no procedures have been adopted, that fact should be disclosed.

IAS No. 7 — "Statement of Changes in Financial Position." This requires that a statement of changes in financial position be presented as a basic financial statement.

These earlier standards were selected since countries should have had ample time to adopt them. The countries selected to determine whether they are implementing IASC standards are France, Japan, the United Kingdom, the United States, and West Germany. All of these nations are founding members of the IASC. In addition, France is the only developed country that has reportedly accorded IASC standards the same status as domestic standards.

Methodology

To determine the impact of IASC standards on financial reporting in these nations, the published financial statements of a sample of large corporations in each country were examined to determine whether the major provisions of the five IASC pronouncements just listed are being followed. (See Appendix for a list of the firms included in the analysis.) The analysis concentrated on the consolidated financial statements. All of the Japanese and part of the French and West German statements were English-language versions.

In general, nine or ten financial statements were examined for each country and each IASC standard with a few minor exceptions. The only major exception was the case for Japan for 1975 when only four financial statements were available. For this reason, the case for Japan for 1975 was not considered in the analysis. Published financial statements were examined for each firm for the period 1975-1980. Since the earliest IASC standard was effective 31 December 1976, the current authors were able to discern whether a firm was following a certain financial accounting principle before its adoption by the IASC in a standard. The examination of the published financial statements for these nations in regard to the five IASC standards provided insight into whether these standards have had an impact on financial reporting in those nations and especially when that impact took place. In some cases, for example in the United Kingdom and the United States, it was expected that firms had followed certain reporting principles before their adoption by the IASC, and so the IASC has had no impact. However, in other nations, it was expected that the IASC has had an impact on financial reporting.

ANALYSIS OF FINDINGS

IASC No. 2, "Valuation and Presentation of Inventories"

The results of the analysis of compliance with IASC No. 2 is presented in exhibit 1. Part A concentrates on the valuation of inventories, indicating that prior to the issuance of IASC No. 2, the largest percentage of the U.K. firms in the sample were in compliance with this standard, and that the degree of compliance in the U.K. firms rose after the effective year (1976) to 100 percent and then stabilized. This can be explained by the fact that during this period, U.K. accounting standards were changed to conform to IASC No. 2. In each of the other cases, except for West Germany, the results were disappointing in that none followed the U.K. experience. Surprisingly, the case for the United States is "spotty," mainly due to the unacceptability of LIFO inventory valuation which is very popular in the United States. By the end of the period covered by the analysis, a majority of firms in the sample

Exhibit 1. Compliance with International Accounting Standard No. 2, "Valuation and Presentation of Inventories" (effective for fiscal year ending 12/31/1976)

Part A: Inventories should be valued at the lower of historical cost and net realizable value

Year	*% compliance by country*				
	France	Japan	U.K.	U.S.	W. Germany
1975	50	NA	78	44	38
1976*	22	33	80	50	67
1977	30	33	100	56	60
1978	40	33	100	50	60
1979	40	33	100	50	60
1980	30	33	100	40	60

Part B: Segregation of inventories by major categories

Year	*% compliance by country*				
	France	Japan	U.K.	U.S.	W. Germany
1975	50	NA	33	56	25
1976*	56	100	60	60	22
1977	50	100	100	56	20
1978	50	100	100	50	20
1979	50	100	100	60	20
1980	50	100	100	70	20

* Year of effect.

from West Germany and the United Kingdom were in compliance with IASC No. 2's inventory valuation procedure.

Part B concentrated on the presentation of details concerning inventory on the balance sheet. It is clear that the IASC standard had an impact in the United Kingdom, based on the sample of firms. Only in the United Kingdom is the compliance pattern demonstrated clearly, with a one-year lag period. An increase in the percentage of firms in compliance with this aspect of IASC No. 2 is evident in the United States, but otherwise the results are disappointing from a compliance viewpoint. It should be noted here that when the financial statements examined referred to national legal requirements in regard to accounting methods, where the statements themselves did not give a clear evidence of compliance with the IASC standard, none was assumed.

IASC No. 3, "Consolidated Financial Statements"

The first part of exhibit 2 focuses on the disclosure of the minority interest in the sample firms. As the analysis shows, the IASC standard had no impact on U.K. firms in the sample, since they were fully in compliance before and after the effective date. Little impact was evident for Japan, West Germany, or France, and the record for the American firms is spotty. The wide difference in the degree of compliance with this IASC standard in 1976 regarding the disclosure of minority interest is interesting.

The use of the equity method of accounting for subsidiaries is presented in Part B of exhibit 2. As is obvious from the table based on the sample firms, the IASC standard has had no impact on the French, Japanese, and American statements. Only in the cases of the U.K. and West German firms was marginal impact noted. In West Germany, the prevalent practice is the cost method.

IASC No. 4, "Depreciation Accounting"

Two aspects of depreciation accounting are shown in exhibit 3. The first concentrates on the use of a systematic depreciation method. The

Exhibit 2. Compliance with International Accounting Standard No. 3, "Consolidated Financial Statements" (effective for fiscal year ending 12/31/1977)

Part A: Disclosure of minority interest

Year	*% compliance by country*				
	France	Japan	U.K.	U.S.	W. Germany
1975	80	NA	100	44	75
1976	78	22	100	50	78
1977*	80	22	100	56	80
1978	80	22	100	38	80
1979	80	22	100	50	80
1980	80	33	100	50	80

Part B: Use of equity method for firms in which between 20 percent and 50 percent of stock is owned

Year	*% compliance by country*				
	France	Japan	U.K.	U.S.	W. Germany
1975	90	NA	44	67	0
1976	89	33	50	70	0
1977*	90	33	50	89	10
1978	90	33	56	75	10
1979	90	33	60	80	10
1980	90	33	60	80	10

* Year of effect.

Exhibit 3. Compliance with International Accounting Standard No. 4, "Depreciation Accounting" (effective for fiscal year ending 12/31/1977)

Part A: Depreciable assets are depreciated using a systematic method

Year	*% compliance by country*				
	France	Japan	U.K.	U.S.	W. Germany
1975	70	NA	100	100	62
1976	67	67	100	100	67
1977*	70	67	100	100	70
1978	70	56	100	100	70
1979	60	56	100	100	70
1980	60	67	100	100	70

Part B: Disclosure of depreciation details

Year	*% compliance by country*				
	France	Japan	U.K.	U.S.	W. Germany
1975	10	NA	67	0	0
1976	0	11	60	10	11
1977*	10	11	50	11	0
1978	10	11	89	12	0
1979	10	11	100	30	0
1980	10	11	100	30	0

* Year of effect.

IASC standard has had no impact on any sample firms in the study. In general, a majority of firms in each of these cases were in compliance with this standard when it was issued.

A different situation existed, however, with regard to the disclosure of depreciation details, as shown in Part B of exhibit 3. When this standard became effective in 1977, the U.K. firms were the only ones near a majority in compliance with it. The overall low levels of compliance with this basic principle of disclosure is surprisingly evident for the period 1975-76. Dramatic improvement is evident only in the case of the U.K. firms, and it is also evident that the standard had no impact on France, Japan, and West Germany. An explanation for the low level of compliance of U.S. firms was a common deficiency concerning the disclosure of the useful lives or depreciation rates.

IASC No. 6, "Inflation Accounting Disclosures"

The results of the analysis of the disclosure of the impact of changing prices on the firms is presented in exhibit 4. As shown, the IASC

Exhibit 4. Compliance with International Accounting Standard No. 6, "Disclosure of Procedures to Reflect the Impact of Price Changes or Disclosure of the Fact That No Such Procedures Have Been Adopted"
(effective for fiscal year ending 12/31/1978)

Year	*% compliance by country*				
	France	Japan	U.K.	U.S.	W. Germany
1975	0	NA	11	11	0
1976	0	0	10	80	0
1977	0	0	44	100	0
1978*	0	11	44	100	0
1979	0	0	60	100	0
1980	0	0	100	100	0

*Year of effect.

standard had no impact in the case of France, West Germany, and the United States. Only in the case of the U.K. firms from 1978 through 1980 and for the Japanese firms in 1978 was there any evidence of an impact. U.S. compliance was affected by the Security and Exchange Commission's Accounting Series Release 190 passed in 1976 and FASB No. 33, effective in 1979. In the United Kingdom, Statement of Accounting Practice 16 on current-cost accounting was issued, effective for 1980. It is significant to note that only in the case of the latter two countries were any disclosures of the impact of inflation presented in the firm's annual reports by 1980.

IASC No. 7, "Statement of Changes in Financial Position"

Exhibit 5 shows the degree of compliance in the sample firms for the IASC standard requiring that a statement of changes in financial position be included as a basic financial statement. As shown by the analysis, this standard had no impact in any of the nations represented by firms in the sample: in no case did the percentage of compliance change. By 1980, a majority of U.K. and U.S. firms presented this statement; otherwise, it was not a majority practice.

SUMMARY AND CONCLUSIONS

Mueller has noted that the IASC attempts to review procedures currently in use in countries around the world and then harmonize them by recommending a limited set of alternatives.[12] The IASC has no

[12] Gerhard Mueller and L. Daley, "Accounting in the Arena of World Politics," *Journal of Accountancy* (February 1982).

"real authority" to implement its recommendations and must rely on the best efforts of its individual members which most often are not the accounting standard-setting bodies of those countries. The current study tends to indicate that the IASC has had very little impact on the accounting practices of the countries surveyed. Except for a few instances, a country following a particular method prior to the promulgation of an IASC standard continued to follow the same practice after the standard's issuance.

Exhibit 5. Compliance with International Accounting Standard No. 7, "Statement of Changes in Financial Position" (effective for fiscal year ending 12/31/1979)

Requires that a statement of changes in financial position be presented as a basic financial statement

Year	*% compliance by country*				
	France	Japan	U.K.	U.S.	W. Germany
1975	40	NA	89	100	11
1976	44	33	100	100	11
1977	40	33	100	100	10
1978	50	33	100	100	10
1979*	50	33	100	100	10
1980	50	33	100	100	10

*Year of effect.

APPENDIX. FIRMS INCLUDED IN SAMPLE

Country	*Firm*	*Principal lines of business*
France	Enterprise Minère et Chimique	Mining, chemicals
	Général Sucriere	Sugar
	Imetal	Mining, metallurgical products
	La Farge Copper	Cement, concrete, sanitary ware
	L'Oreal	Hair care, perfume, pharmaceuticals
	Sacilor	Steel
	Schneider	Heavy industry contractors, nuclear power plants, shipbuilding
	Thomson-CSF	Electronic equipment and components
	Union Laitiere Normande	Dairy products
Japan	Chizoda	Chemical engineering and construction
	Fuji Photo Film Co. Ltd.	Photographic film, cameras, magnetic tape
	Furakawa Electric	Electrical cable and wire
	Idemitsu Kosan Co. Ltd.	Oil products, chemicals, shipping
	Kubota	Agricultural machinery, pipe, building materials, industrial machinery
	Nippon Electric Co. Ltd.	Electronic products, data processing
	Sumitomo Metals	Steel, engineering
	Sumitomo Metal Mining	Metal mining and production
	Toyota Motor Co. Ltd.	Automobiles
United Kingdom	Allied Breweries	Alcoholic and nonalcoholic beverages, food
	Arthur Guiness Son & Co. Ltd.	Brewing, plastics, confections
	Cadbury Schweppes Ltd.	Confectionary, beverages
	Delta	Electrical equipment, metals, plumbing products
	General Electric Co. Ltd.	Manufacture of electrical and electronic products
	Grand Metropolitan Ltd.	Food, beverages, leisure
	ICL Ltd.	Computer systems
	RMC Group	Concrete
	Rolls-Royce Ltd.	Engineering, manufacturing
	The Welcome Foundation Ltd.	Pharmaceuticals, chemicals

Country	*Firm*	*Principal lines of business*
United States	Amax	Mining, energy
	Avon	Cosmetics, jewelry
	Control Data Corp.	Computers, data processing equipment
	CPC International	Foods
	Exxon	Oil, energy
	General Tire	Tires, rubber
	Honeywell	Computers, control systems, electronics
	J. P. Stevens	Textiles
	Lockheed	Aircraft, aerospace, electronics
	W. R. Grace	Chemicals, energy, consumer products
West Germany	Babcock	Power generating equipment and engineering
	Bazer	Chemicals, rubber, pharmaceuticals
	Continental	Tires
	FAG	Bearings, machine parts
	Magirns-Dentz A.G.	Trucks, buses
	Metallgesellschaft	Metals, manufacturing, engineering, chemicals
	Sachs	Manufacturing, motors
	Schering A.G.	Pharmaceuticals, chemicals
	Thyssen	Steel, manufacturing
	Volkswagenwerk	Automobiles

[9]

A Philosophical Perspective on the Development of International Accounting Standards

WILLIAM J. VIOLET*

Broadly speaking, accounting may be considered as either an art or an applied social science. The author submits that if international accounting standards (IAS) are to be established successfully, the establishment process must be accomplished within the perspective of accounting as a rational system, that is, a system based on a framework of universally accepted postulates. This discussion begins with a brief investigation of the consequences of viewing accounting as an art to illustrate several philosophical and cultural limitations.

Anyone who has attempted to discover the best finish for a piece of fine woodwork would certainly rely on an informal consensus of the generally recognized best practitioners. Where disagreements occur, no satisfactory way of resolving them exists; there are no canons of inquiry, no agreed-upon external standards. Furthermore, the knowledge which is the conceptual substance of the craft is lore — a historical accumulation which neither contains internal standards nor accepts external principles to separate the uselessness from the useful, the good from the bad. For all their theoretical deficiencies, however, the crafts provide beautifully finished furniture.

American accounting has been generally conceived of as an art or craft and has, as a result, the strengths and weaknesses of that conception. Rueschhoff refers to its development as "situationistic":

> The accounting objective also has been fulfilled through situationism. In fact a situationistic approach is common throughout the world (this is the pragmatic development of principles of conventions by individual countries). It

* William J. Violet is Assistant Professor of Accounting, Moorhead State University, Moorhead, Minnesota.

involves a loose type of structure that develops principles according to the situation. However, over time certain principles become generally accepted. This is the avenue that is prevalent in the United States.[1]

Although pragmatically derived accounting principles are quite satisfactory for what they are currently expected to accomplish, this trial-and-error method of developing principles has two severe flaws. First, the amassed results are often incoherent. R. J. Chambers has commented on the development and evolution of "generally accepted accounting principles."

> In all scientific, or otherwise disciplined pursuits, we proceed by what is loosely called "trial and error." If anything "tried" turns out to be in "error," because it does not procure what it is expected to procure, it is regarded as "on trial" until something else is found that is "less in error." The object of all research and development is to replace what is less effectual by something more effectual in bringing about what is desired or intended. The process has been described as a process of finding successively better approximations to an ideal — whether an ideal tool, an ideal programme or an ideal theory. It entails the search for flaws in a device or practice, the search for means of reducing those flaws and the rejection of devices or practices (or parts of them) which are "more-flawed" in favor of others that are "less-flawed."
>
> This has not been the method characteristic of accounting. The accounting method has been rather a method of trial and error-accretion. By no other method could there have been developed such a diverse and numerous set of rules or practices as those now available and permissable.[2]

The second flaw is that the trial-and-error results are tied to a specific culture and are, therefore, incapable of evolving into IAS.

American accountants have begun to realize the perceptual effects and behavioral limitations generated by generally accepted accounting principles (GAAP). As the American system transcends national borders into the complex international environment, the utility of GAAP greatly decreases. IAS are a necessity for multinational reporting of international transactions.

As cultures vary, so do accounting theories and applications. Because of this conceptual diversity, the establishment of IAS has met with limited success. Principles pragmatically developed in response to the needs of national users suffice for most domestic accounting applications. Because of the inherent limitations of accounting principles based on experience-oriented domestic systems, a domestic accounting system is useful beyond its national borders only to the extent that another country has a similar accounting system. Multinationals, like individual

---

[1] Norlin Rueschhoff, *International Accounting and Financial Reporting* (New York: Praeger, 1976), p. 147.

[2] R. J. Chambers, "Usefulness — The Vanishing Premise in Accounting Standards Setting," *ABACUS* (December 1979): 71-73.

nations, are continually confronted with a dilemma of diverse accounting systems, and the utility of reported financial data for various creditors, owners, and users decreases. IAS have attempted to rectify this situation; however, they are being established without a postulate framework as a reference point. A pragmatically developed international accounting system is even more questionable than a pragmatically developed domestic accounting system. If IAS are the forerunners of international accounting uniformity and theory, they must be developed from a postulate structure based on logic and scientific methodology. The question is whether IAS are intended to reflect universal truths or postulates of accounting. If IAS are to be truly world oriented, they must have the quality of universality. Postulates should be developed for establishing international principles and accounting standards. To be relevant to the world community and adaptable to international processes, IAS must be based on a sound conceptual, postulate basis. No individual domestic accounting system, developed on experience or pragmatism, could lead to the development of IAS. Pragmatically developed IAS will not be able to cope with infinite cultural diversity. It would be more effective for international accounting theories to conform conceptual differences before trying to resolve practice variances. An international system of accounting able to contend with the complexities facing nations and multinationals requires the establishment of universal postulates from which truly international "generally accepted accounting principles" and standards may be promulgated.

A pragmatic solution can neither resolve current variances nor cope with the dynamic international environment of the future; it can only extend the conventions or principles employed by a particular member nation such as the "generally accepted accounting conventions" employed in the United States into the international accounting environment. Such conceptual incoherence and the problems created could be resolved by considering accounting as a rational system which should have evolved from a postulate base.

In response to theoretical criticism demanding a closer alliance between accounting as a defined rational system and scientifically oriented research, accounting theory evolved from deductive relationalization, based on empirical research directed at supporting underlying premises and theories.

That accounting is not a science like physics does not deter it from functioning as an applied social science. Social sciences are not so much concerned with discovering absolute truths as with frequencies of occurrence and interrelationships between phenomena. Therefore, social scientists direct their efforts toward examining causal patterns (cause and effect) and functional analysis.

Functional analysis illustrates how components work together to support the structural whole and maintain systemic relationships and continuity. Functional explanation, unlike causal explanation, requires no time sequence; it is synchronic explanation.[3]

Both of these conceptual models are employed to explain phenomena. Phenomena are the focal points for observation and developing postulates for deriving principles. If accounting is an applied social science, it is subject to scientific criticism from a philosophical standpoint.

Accounting theory has developed pragmatically.[4] As a rational system parallel to the sciences, however, accounting, to be a meaningful discipline, must abide by a universal rationale found in all sciences. As a rational deductive system concerned with social phenomena, accounting is subject to certain scientific constraints affecting all sciences. Several parameters affecting any rational system can be demonstrated, but limits of space restrict consideration to one illustrative parameter only, the concept of measurement.

Paul Durbin introduces the importance of measurement as a concept:

Measurement is a foundation stone of the edifice of modern science, along with the experimentation so often necessary for exact measurement. It was exact measurement that made the difference between Galileo and the Aristotelians of his day; his "new sciences" were distinctive precisely insofar as they gave preeminence [*sic*] to mathematical-measurable effects.[5]

As M. R. Cohen and Ernest Nagel demonstrate, however, the concept of measurement is not a simple one:

Comparisons based upon counting . . . depend on our ability to distinguish clearly between different groups or different characters. Frequently, however, characters cannot be sharply distinguished because they form a continuous series with one another. Thus we may wish to distinguish different knives on the basis of their "sharpness." . . . What principles must we observe in using numbers to denote such differences in qualities?

It is often believed that because we can assign numbers to different degrees of a quality, the different degrees always bear to each other the same ratio as do the numbers we have assigned to them. . . .

We must note that numbers may have at least three distinct uses: (1) as tags, or identification marks; (2) as signs to indicate the position of the degree of

[3] Merwyn Garbarino, *Sociocultural Theory in Anthropology* (New York: Holt, Rinehart and Winston, 1977), p. 7.

[4] For a discussion on pragmatic development, see Maurice Moonitz, "Why Do We Need 'Postulates' and 'Principles?' " *Journal of Accountancy* (December 1963).

[5] Paul Durbin, *Philosophy of Science: An Introduction* (New York: McGraw-Hill, 1968), p. 126.

a quality in a series of degrees; and (3) as signs indicating the quantitative relations between qualities. . . .

We must make sure that we do not allow different numbers to be assigned to the same object. Thus suppose the weight of object A is regarded as the unit or 1, and that we can assign weights to other objects by this process so that A_2 will have weight 2, A_4 weight 4, and A_6 weight 6. Can we be sure that A_2 and A_4 placed together in one pan will just balance A_6 placed in the other? It is very important to note that we cannot be certain of this until we perform the experiment. The proposition that $2 + 4 = 6$ can be demonstrated in pure arithmetic without experiment. But until we perform the proper experiments we cannot be certain that the physical operation of addition of weights does conform to the familiar properties of pure arithmetical addition.[6]

The subject of accounting has always been concerned with the concept of measurement against some rationally developed standard. Several noted accounting authors have questioned the qualities of measurement as applied in their field. For example, Chambers questions the extensive or additive properties presented in a balance sheet. Is it conceptually correct to add current assets to fixed assets for presenting the economic resources available to an entity? Chambers discusses at length the fallacy of adding various elements of a balance sheet.

All allusions to financial position, and the general practice of drawing up balance sheets, entail that what is represented is aggregative. The aggregate amounts of assets, liabilities and owners' equity are determined; and there are subaggregates in each case. In the context of a double-entry system, balance sheet aggregations may be thought simply to be a check on the mechanical completeness of the record. But aggregation has a more substantial justification.

The very use of class names, "assets," "liabilities" and "owners' equity," implies that the amounts by which the items in each class are represented are homogeneous amounts, properly aggregable (or subtractable). APBS4 describes owners' equity as the excess of assets over liabilities (par. 132), and net income as "the net increase in owners' equity . . . from profit-directed activities" (par. 134). If the amounts of the three classes (and of net income) were not homogeneous, the differences would not be valid differences. All the documents, whether explicit about the matter or not, contemplate that users of financial statements are concerned with aggregates, and in particular, with the financial positions of whole enterprises. . . .

An aggregative position cannot be represented by improper aggregations. Yet APBS4 and all practice under generally accepted accounting principles tolerate improper aggregation. . . .

Other fictions, of course, contribute to the fictional character of aggregates under generally accepted accounting principles. Allocations give rise to fictions: a lower of cost and market valuation is a fiction: a valuation based

[6] M. R. Cohen and Ernest Nagel, *An Introduction to Logic and Scientific Method* (New York: Harcourt, Brace and World, 1934), pp. 293-97.

on straight-line depreciation or any other calculation by formula is a fiction. The burden of demonstrating that they are serviceable fictions, for balance sheet purposes, rests on their supporters.[7]

James A. Schweikart discusses particular factors affecting the concept of measurement in the international setting:

Foreign subsidiaries operate in different legal, social, political and economic environments. Not only does this situation affect the accounting principles which are applied, but also the meaning of values attached to assets and expenses is affected. For example, in West Germany a building may cost $575,000. The same building may cost $300,000 in South Korea. What value should be attached to these two assets? . . .

Another facet of the foreign operating environment is the risk of assets abroad. Do the assets located abroad really have any values? . . .

Therefore, incomes with the esoteric meanings and assets with their unknown true values are included in U.S. consolidated statements as if they are U.S. assets and U.S. incomes.[8]

Even within our own system, the concept of measurement employing the dollar as a measuring unit is troubling, as Herbert Taggart points out:

Accountants are as aware as anyone that it is absurdity to deduct peaches from apples and expect to get an intelligible answer. It is most uncomfortable for the accountant to be told that he is performing equally futile arithmetic when he adds or subtracts dollars spent at different times and representing differing purchasing power. It is no wonder that accountants have by tradition stubbornly ignored changes in the magnitude of their measuring unit. To give in on this point cuts the very foundations of their beliefs from under them. . . .

Continued failure to give expressions to the profound and prolonged change in the price level has led to much misinterpretation of financial statements, and especially of the statement of income.[9]

In addition to the constraint of measurement, a myriad of other constraints governing science and accounting exists. Accounting as a rational system must obey the "laws" of logic for presenting valid and relevant data. Science has accepted, as a matter of practicality and necessity, "certain a priori" truths which it does not attempt to test, although metaphysically such theories or assumptions will continue as matters of conjecture and controversy. Such truths have evolved into postulates. Postulates are necessary to provide relevant data. Postulates demand logical reasoning and form a base for empirical testing. They

[7] Chambers, "Usefulness — The Vanishing Premise," pp. 77-79.

[8] James A. Schweikart, "We Must End Consolidation of Foreign Subsidiaries," *Management Accounting* (August 1981): 17.

[9] Herbert Taggart, "Sacred Cows in Accounting," *Accounting Review* (July 1953): 315-16.

permit and necessitate a conceptual conformity between all the sciences and allow for the development of new sciences or rationally applied systems, such as accounting. Logic entails a set of postulates to formulate accounting principles. Maurice Moonitz, a pioneer in the research for a set of accounting postulates, stated several years ago:

For many years now, the expressed policy of the American Institute of CPAs in the field of accounting has been to determine appropriate practice and to narrow the areas of difference and inconsistency in practice. . . .

In essence this new approach contemplated the formulation of a "fairly broad set of co-ordinated accounting principles" on the basis of a previously established set of postulates. The postulates and principles taken together would then serve as a "framework of reference" for solving specific issues and detailed problems. . . . Clearly, then, the special committee expected . . . to seek the help of logic in determining the "rules of accounting."

In this respect accounting is merely repeating the history of many other fields. Up to a certain point, experience is the touchstone that solves problems and does it in a satisfactory manner, but beyond that point, more is needed.[10]

What this "more" is becomes clearer from Moonitz's comments on Accounting Research Study No. 1:

. . . research study (Accounting Research Study No. 1) took the form of a search for "self-evident propositions," for assertions about the environment in which accounting functions. . . .

As was to be expected, certain issues kept recurring in all sorts of situations, for example, income determination, financial position, control over goods and services, etc. These leads were pursued into the business, economic, and political setting in which accounting operates. A vast amount of evidence had to be reviewed and sifted to obtain the relatively few usable propositions that were reported in the published study.

To be fruitful, the postulates of accounting must of necessity relate to [be inferred from] a world that does exist and not to one that is a fiction. It may not ever be possible to demonstrate the "truth" of a postulate because no one person or group can possess all the necessary knowledge, (this is a philosophical deduction; complete understanding of any element, cause, or event would be absurd) but the proposition set forth as a postulate must be plausible and must rest upon a large amount of positive factual knowledge of the environment in which accounting functions.

Once the basic inferences are drawn they become obvious [self-evident?] to everyone and serve as a starting point from that time on. In this light, accounting postulates may be viewed as the inferences drawn from the mass of data concerning the environment in which accounting functions.[11]

Even if accounting is not a science, it is, after all, a rational system aligned with science. To exist as a rational system reporting on social phenomena through discovery, observation, explanation, confirmation,

[10] Moonitz, "Why Do We Need 'Postulates,' " p. 42.
[11] Ibid., pp. 44-45.

and prediction, accounting will eventually need to establish a set of postulates for operating in a complex, dynamic environment.

Repeatedly, scientists are required to apply theory to reality. Often theoretical application must be modified to adapt simplistic theory modeling to the infinite complexities of a dynamic environment. To ensure continual development of science in its quest for truth, the theoretical framework of science must not be rigid but must have an underlying structure combining short-run stability with long-run flexibility. To ensure adaptability from the conceptual plane to reality, science must operate from a set of postulates. The postulates form the foundation of science and provide the framework for continual modification.

To facilitate the domestic beneficiaries (practitioners), accounting theory currently employs a pragmatic or practical orientation for establishing so-called "generally accepted accounting principles." Continued use of such a practice will, however, limit the capacity of accounting theory to resolve the more complex issues it will eventually face.

At the domestic level, pragmatic application can be satisfactorily utilized. The proximity of the theoretician, practitioner, and a domestic environment enhances the pragmatic (or trial and error, through experience) development of accounting principles. Such pragmatically developed "generally accepted accounting principles" are domestic conventions. Moonitz clarifies the term "conventional" as it relates to accounting.

> Accounting is often described as "conventional" in nature, and its principles as "conventions." These two terms, conventions and conventional, are ambiguous; the statement that accounting is conventional may be true or false depending on which meaning is intended. It is true if it refers to such things as the use of Arabic numerals, the use of the dollar sign, or the sequence in which assets, liabilities, revenues, and expenses are listed in financial statements because other symbols and forms could be used to convey precisely the same message. It is not true if the statement means that any proposition which accountants accept is a valid one. . . .
>
> Suppose, however, that the assertion about accounting principles as "conventions" is intended to convey the idea that they are generalizations, inferences drawn from a large body of data, and that they are not intended to be literal descriptions of reality. "Conventions" and "conventional" are clearly valid descriptions, then, but not because accounting is unique. Instead, accounting is like every other field of human endeavor in this one respect: its basic propositions are generalizations or abstractions and not minute descriptions of every aspect of "reality."[12]

Principles originally developed from experience may resemble principles formulated from a set of postulates; however, since no framework

[12] Ibid., pp. 45-46.

exists for postulate-to-principle sequential development and modification, environmental influences will greatly affect the evolution of the originating principles. Domestic pressures create an environment contraproductive to future postulate creation. Further, the pragmatic development conventionalizes domestic "generally accepted accounting principles." The pragmatic principles become "conventions" of a particular sociopolitical entity. The "generally accepted accounting principles" are not principles but conventions of a particular society.

Our generally accepted accounting principles, the product of the highly technological environment of the United States, are not generally accepted by the great majority of other countries, and diverse accounting principles in various developmental stages occur throughout the world.

Cultural diversity inhibits the establishment and enforcement of IAS. Current approaches for harmonization of accounting practices have advocated understanding accounting differences. A more acceptable or meaningful approach would be to strive for harmonization based on a knowledge of cultural differences. We cannot expect accounting as a reflection of a particular society to have exactly the same objectives from one culture to another.

Further, a postulate framework for accounting, specifically, international accounting, must be developed to facilitate the development of international accounting standards. Such a structure would provide the necessary flexibility for developing and employing IAS in diverse cultural settings. This framework would also establish and clarify accounting concepts throughout the accounting environment. The profession needs this added clarity. A postulate structure will clarify theoretical positions, and such a step is a necessary precondition to harmonizing international theories and variances.

A framework of universal postulates will also promote and enhance an understanding of cultural determinants and variables. A knowledge of cultural relativity will assist the International Accounting Standards Committee in defining the cultural requirements which must be met before IAS can be universally accepted, established, and enforceable.

SELECTED BIBLIOGRAPHY

Articles

Ahmed Belkaoui. "The Interprofessional Linguistic Communication of Accounting Concepts: An Experiment in Sociolinguistics." *Journal of Accounting Research* (Autumn 1980): 362-74.

Sir Henry Benson. "International Accounting — The Challenges of the Future." *Journal of Accountancy* (November 1977): 93-96.

Lee Berton. "Arthur Young Professors' Roundtable: The International World of Accounting." *Journal of Accountancy* (August 1980): 74-79.

Jan G. Brown. "The Development of International Accounting Standards." *Woman CPA* (October 1977): 9-11.

R. Lee Brummet. "Internationalism and the Future of Accounting Education." *International Journal of Accounting* (Fall 1975): 161-66.

R. J. Chambers. "Usefulness — The Vanishing Premise in Accounting Standards Setting." *ABACUS* (December 1979): 71-92.

Frederick Choi. "Primary-Secondary Reporting: A Cross-Cultural Analysis." *International Journal of Accounting* (Fall 1980): 83-104.

Alvin Clay. "Undergraduate International Accounting Education." *International Journal of Accounting* (Fall 1975): 187-92.

Percy Cohen. "Economic Analysis and Economic Man." *Themes in Economic Anthropology*. New York: Travistock Publications, 1967, pp. 91-117.

Joseph Cummings. "The International Accounting Standards Committee: Current and Future Developments." *International Journal of Accounting* (Fall 1975): 31-38.

———."Progress in the Establishment and Enforcement of International Accounting Standards." *Accounting Forum* (May 1976): 1-6.

Irving Fantl. "Frustrations Facing Accounting Uniformity." *Accounting Forum* (May 1976): 27-31.

E. Flamholtz and E. Cook. "Cognitive Meaning and Its Role in Accounting Change: A Field Study." *Accounting Organizations and Society* (October 1978): 115-40.

Henry Hatfield. "An Historical Defense of Bookkeeping." *Journal of Accountancy* (April 1924): 241-53.

Donald Hayes. "The International Accounting Standards Committee — Recent Developments and Current Problems." *International Journal of Accounting* (Fall 1980): 1-10.

John Hepworth. "International Accounting Standards." *Chartered Accountant in Australia* (August 1977): 17-19.

William S. Kanaga. "International Accounting: The Challenge and the Changes." *Journal of Accountancy* (November 1980): 55-60.

Alexander Keyserlingk. "International Public Accounting: An Underdeveloped Profession." *International Journal of Accounting* (Fall 1975): 15-22.

Robert Libby. "Bankers' and Auditors' Perceptions of the Message Communicated by the Audit Report." *Journal of Accounting Research* (Spring 1979): 99-122.

J. N. Miles. "The Development of International Accounting Standards." *Chartered Accountant in Australia* (August 1978): 26-32.

Steven Mintz. "Internationalization of the Accounting Curriculum." *International Journal of Accounting* (Fall 1980): 137-52.

Maurice Moonitz. "Why Do We Need 'Postulates' and 'Principles'?" *Journal of Accountancy* (December 1963): 42-46.

Gerhard Mueller. "The Dual System for Transnational Financial Reporting." *Accounting Forum* (May 1976): 17-25.

———. "International Accounting Standards." *Accountant* (October 1977): 446-49.

Walter O'Conner. "The Multinational Corporation and the Developing Country." *Accounting Forum* (May 1976): 33-40.
Bruce L. Oliver. "Semantic Differential: A Device for Measuring the Interprofessional Communication of Selected Accounting Concepts." *Journal of Accounting Research* (Autumn 1974): 229-316.
James Schweikart. "We Must End Consolidation of Foreign Subsidiaries." *Management Accounting* (August 1981): 15-18.
Michael Silverstein. "Shifters, Linguistic Categories and Cultural Description." *Meaning in Anthropology*. Albuquerque: University of New Mexico, 1976, pp. 11-56.
Robert Sterling. "Accounting Research, Eduation and Practice." *Journal of Accountancy* (September 1973): 44-52.
Washington Sy Cyp. "Establishing and Applying Standards in Diverse Economic and Social Environments." *International World of Accounting Challenges and Opportunities*, ed. by John Burton. New York: Arthur Young, 1981, pp. 85-96.
Herbert Taggart. "Sacred Cows in Accounting." *Accounting Review* (July 1953): 313-19.
Arthur Young and Co. "Keeping Up-to-Date with International Accounting Developments." *Arthur Young Client Memorandum* (March 21, 1980): 1-19.
Stephen A. Zeff. "Chronology of Significant Developments in the Establishing of Accounting Principles in the United States, 1926-1972." *Journal of Accounting Research* (Spring 1972): 217-27.

Books

Accountants International Study Group. *International Financial Reporting Study No. 11*. Toronto: AISG, 1975.
American Accounting Association. *A Statement of Basic Accounting Theory*. Evanston, Ill.: AAA, 1966.
American Institute of Certified Public Accountants. *Professional Standards*, vol. 3. New York: Commerce Clearing House, 1981.
Association of Social Anthropologists of the Commonwealth. *Themes in Economic Anthropology*. London: Travistock Publications, 1967.
Anthropological Society of Washington. *Anthropology and Human Behavior*. Washington, D.C.: ASW, 1962.
Keith Basso and Henry Selby. *Meaning in Anthropology*. Albuquerque: University of New Mexico, 1976.
Ruth Benedict. *Patterns of Culture*. Preface by Margaret Mead. Boston: Houghton Mifflin Company, 1934.
Franz Boas. *Social Evolution*. Cleveland: Meridan Publishing, 1963.
James A. Boon. *From Symbolism to Structuralism*. New York: Harper and Row, 1972.
Michael Chatfield. *Contemporary Studies in the Evolution of Accounting Thought*. Belmont, Calif.: Dickenson Publishing, 1968.
Irvin Child and John Whiting. *Child Training and Personality: A Cross-Cultural Study*. New Haven: Yale University Press, 1953.
M. R. Cohen and Ernest Nagel. *An Introduction to Logic and Scientific Method*. New York: Harcourt, Brace and World, 1934.

Paul R. Durbin. *Philosophy of Science an Introduction*. New York: McGraw-Hill, 1968.

Raymond Firth, ed. *Themes in Economic Anthropology*. New York: Travistock Publications, 1967.

Merwyn S. Garbarino. *Sociocultural Theory in Anthropology*. Edited by George and Louise Spindler. New York: Holt, Rinehart and Winston, 1977.

Clifford Geerty. *The Interpretation of Cultures*. New York: Basic Books, 1973.

Ernest Hilgard, Richard Atkinson, and Rita Atkinson. *Introduction to Psychology*. 6th ed. New York: Harcourt, Brace, Jovanovich, 1975.

E. Adamson Hoebel. *Anthropology: The Study of Man*. 4th ed. New York: McGraw-Hill, 1972.

Conrad P. Kiltak. *Anthropology, the Exploration of Human Diversity*. New York: Random House, 1974.

Elsa P. Kimball. *Sociology and Education: An Analysis of the Theories of Spencer and Ward*. New York: AMS Press, 1968.

Adam Kuper, ed. *The Social Anthropology of Radcliffe-Brown*. London: Routledge and Kegan Paul, 1977.

Claude Levi-Strauss. *Structural Anthropology*. New York: Basic Books, 1963.

Bronislaw Malinowski. *A Scientific Theory of Culture and Other Essays*. Preface by Huntington Cairns. Chapel Hill, N.C.: University of North Carolina, 1944.

John S. Mill. *Auguste Comte and Positivism*. Ann Arbor: University of Michigan, Toronto Ambassador Books, 1961; Ann Arbor Paperbacks, 1961.

Gerhard Mueller. *Accounting Practices in the Netherlands*. Seattle: University of Washington, 1962.

———. *Accounting Practices in West Germany*. Seattle: University of Washington, 1964.

———. *International Accounting*. New York: Macmillan, 1967.

Gianfranco Poggi. *Images of Society*. Stanford: Stanford University, 1972.

Price Waterhouse and Co. *Guide for the Reader of Foreign Financial Statements*. Edited by George Watt. 2nd ed. New York: Price Waterhouse and Co., 1975.

Norlin Rueschhoff. *International Accounting and Financial Reporting*. New York: Praeger, 1976.

Edward Sapir. *Culture, Language and Personality*. Berkeley: University of California, 1958.

———. *Language*. New York: Harcourt, 1921.

George Scott. *Accounting and Developing Nations*. Seattle: International Accounting Studies Institute and University of Washington, 1970.

Herbert Shenton, Edward Sapir, and Otto Jespersen. *International Communication*. London: Kegan Paul, Trench, Trubner and Co., 1931.

W. Stark. *Montesqieu Pioneer of the Sociology of Knowledge*. Toronto: University of Toronto, 1961.

Edward Tylor. *Researches into the Early History of Mankind and the Development of Civilization*. Edited by Paul Bohannan. Chicago and London: University of Chicago Press, University of Toronto, 1964.

Anita Tyra. *Companies, Laws, and Financial Reporting: West Germany, France, and the United Kingdom*. Seattle: University of Washington, 1971.

Leslie A. White. *The Science of Culture*. New York: Farrar, Straus and Company, 1949.
B. L. Whorf. *Language, Thought and Reality*. Cambridge: MIT Press, 1956.
Arthur Young. *The International World of Accounting Challenges and Opportunities*. Edited by John Burton. New York: Arthur Young, 1981.
V. K. Zimmerman, ed. *The Multinational Corporation: Accounting and Social Implications*. Urbana, Ill.: University of Illinois, 1977.

[10]

The International Accounting Standards Committee: A Performance Evaluation

S. M. McKINNON and PAUL JANELL*

The International Accounting Standards Committee (IASC) was established in 1973 by the professional accounting institutes of nine major countries in response to increasing calls for harmonization of worldwide accounting regulations. Since its inception, the IASC has expanded to include accountancy bodies in sixty-five countries. It has been acclaimed as the most successful and influential international body in achieving some degree of harmonization of standards. A review of the IASC, its objectives, and its achievements in order to evaluate the overall performance of the IASC in its first twelve years is appropriate.

This study analyzes the role of the IASC. After briefly commenting on the general desirability of harmonization, the study identifies the IASC objectives and analyzes three contemporary accounting issues in light of these objectives. The final step is an analysis of the role the IASC should play in consideration of its successes and failures.

IS HARMONIZATION DESIRABLE?

Much of the impetus for harmonization has focused on the need for comparative information in a world of expanding capital markets. Growing competition for both domestic and international financing has produced a seller's market for money, where the sellers have the power to demand additional information concerning potential investments. Differing standards present an obstacle to optimal economic resource allocation, and the necessity to

* S. M. McKinnon and Paul Janell are Associate Professor and Professor, College of Business Administration, Northeastern University.

accommodate differing accounting standards places a dual burden on the multinational executive concerned with financial reporting.

Since Jacob Kraayenhof's seminal paper on international harmonization,[1] few have questioned the desirability of harmonized standards. Most opponents have focused on the practical difficulties of achieving agreements among different countries, given the differences in background, tradition, needs of economic environments, and the inevitable challenge of uniformity to state sovereignty.

HOW EFFECTIVE HAS THE IASC BEEN?

The fact that harmonization itself can be assumed to be a worthwhile goal is not sufficient justification to conclude that the efforts of the IASC have been the best way to fulfill that goal. Critics of harmonization may be quite right when they state that complete international standardization is impossible. Since that objective is the essential premise of the IASC's existence, the IASC objectives should be analyzed in relation to what it has actually accomplished in its brief years of operation.

IASC Objectives

The board of the IASC is charged with directing its major operations. The board has two representatives from the original founding members, plus two representatives from two additional member accounting organizations. The board issues exposure drafts (EDs) of proposed standards generally followed by the standards themselves. To take effect, a standard must be approved by a minimum of three-fourths of the committee membership. As of May 1985, IASC had issued over twenty Statements of International Accounting Standards, and numerous exposure drafts were outstanding.

The objectives of the IASC, as expressed in the agreement under which it was established, are ". . . to formulate and publish in the public interest, basic standards to be observed in the presentation of audited accounts and financial statements and to promote their worldwide acceptance and observance."[2] Several key points are expressed in this statement. The statement identifies two major goals: (1) to formulate standards, and (2) to promote their accep-

[1] Jacob Kraayenhof, "International Challenges for Accounting," *Journal of Accountancy* (January 1959), 34-38.

[2] George C. Watt, Richard M. Hammer, and Marianne Burge, *Accounting for the Multinational Corporation* (Financial Executives Research Foundation, 1977), 166-67.

tance and observance. Within the first of these goals is the qualification to formulate basic rather than detailed standards. Paragraph 10 of the *Preface to Statement of International Accounting Standards,* published by the IASC in 1975, states:

> . . . it is the intention of the IASC . . . to concentrate on basic standards. It will therefore endeavor to confine the International Accounting Standards to essentials and not to make them so complex that they cannot be applied effectively on a worldwide basis. . . .[3]

The second goal was further elaborated in an agreement by member accounting institutes to use their best endeavors to:

1. Ensure that published accounts comply with these standards or that there is disclosure of differences;
2. Persuade governments, securities markets, and the business community that published accounts should comply with these standards; and
3. Ensure that auditors report differences from these standards.[4]

Are these goals being met? In the next section, the authors examine three topics considered by the IASC: depreciation, the equity method, and foreign currency translation. Each is different in the points raised as to the effectiveness of the IASC, but none is a special case. These three subjects provide reasonable examples of the degree of acceptance of IASC standards throughout the world.

Depreciation

The standard on depreciation (IAS No. 4) was chosen because it was relatively noncontroversial and was one of the earliest standards issued, becoming effective January 1, 1977. IAS No. 4 is a prime example of the approach initially taken by the IASC to address those issues that would most likely be accepted first. Greater acceptance would be found for standards on which a consensus could be achieved among the members of the voting committee. Other countries would find adoption fairly easy, and the IASC would gain more influence and credibility as a standard-setting body.

This standard seems ideal for meeting the goal of setting basic general principles, yet the IASC initially fell into the trap of being too specific and narrow in its prescribed choices. The exposure draft chose the straight-line method as preferable and called for disclosure of any differences in income attributable to using a

[3] International Accounting Standards Committee, *Preface to Statements of International Accounting Standards* (1974), par. 10.

[4] Watt, Hammer, and Burge, *Multinational Corporation.*

different method. This went beyond the requirements of any national professional body and was quickly eliminated.[5]

The final statement is general in its requirements, calling for depreciation of assets charged to income in a systematic fashion over the life of the asset. Depreciable cost is historical cost less estimated salvage. Disclosures of method, depreciation expense, and both the gross amount of the assets and the accumulated depreciation are mandated.

In analyzing the effect of IAS No. 4 on worldwide practice, two questions are important. First, does practice conform to the standards of the IASC? Second, has practice *changed* to reflect the new standard, or does practice conform for other reasons, such as existing local legislation? To help answer these questions, we referred to a study by Price Waterhouse International.[6] Sixty-four countries were surveyed, including thirty-three that are members of IASC. Practice in the surveyed countries on 267 reporting practices was classified into categories of acceptance, ranging from "Required" to "Not Permitted."[7]

These data cannot be used to measure conformity exactly, for many reasons. First, at least ten IASC member countries were not included in the study. Generalizations of practice in these countries cannot be drawn, for they include such diverse nations as Yugoslavia, Israel, Bangladesh, and Finland. Second, the survey covered practice as of January 1979, only two years after IASC No. 4, possibly not allowing enough time for the countries which may have been in the process of changing standards. Third, categories, such as "Required" and "Insisted Upon," always lead to arbitrary classifications by respondents who perceive the definitions of the groups in different ways. Despite these flaws, the study is valuable for providing a general overview of acceptance; it represents the most comprehensive collection of worldwide accounting practices available.

In all but five of the countries surveyed, depreciation charges to income are the predominant practice and the minority practice in those five. Of the IASC members surveyed, all except Jamaica

[5] International Accounting Standards Committee, "Accounting for Business Combinations," *Exposure Draft* (1976).

[6] R. D. Fitzgerald, A. D. Stickler, and T. R. Watts, eds., *International Survey of Accounting Principles and Reporting Practices* (London: Price Waterhouse International and Butterworths, 1979).

[7] In order of their level of acceptance, these categories are "Required," "Insisted Upon," "Predominant Practice," "Minority Practice," "Rarely or Not Found," "Not Accepted," and "Not Permitted."

and Portugal either require depreciation or insist upon it for an unqualified auditor's report; in these two countries, it is standard practice even though not mandatory. Quite obviously, the IASC tread on no toes by advocating depreciation charges. A slightly more stringent requirement of IASC No. 4 is the need to reflect salvage value in the estimated charges. Of the countries surveyed, only 37 percent require or insist on the consideration of salvage, even though another 16 percent indicate this as the predominant practice. (Actual figures are presented in exhibit 1.) The situation is slightly better for IASC member countries: 58 percent require or insist upon consideration of salvage, and an additional 12 percent say it is the majority practice.

These data may appear to give credence to the belief that IASC standards are being adopted in the member countries, but this assumption fails after an analysis of the source of the standards in the countries reporting high compliance. Exhibit 2 presents the analysis of countries by category and by membership in IASC. The most striking point of the IASC members reporting at least predominant practice is the number of recent former British colonies on the list. When they are removed, the only remaining nations are Japan, France, Korea, Mexico, the Netherlands, and the United States. The British established sophisticated accounting procedures throughout the empire years before the IASC was formed; eight of the former colonies cite IAS No. 4 as their authoritative source rather than credit the British systems installed years ago. Of the remaining nations, Japan, the Netherlands, and

Exhibit 1. Countries Reflecting Salvage Value in Determining Depreciation Charge

	Total survey		IASC members	
	Number	Percent	Number	Percent
Required	18	28	17	52
Insisted upon	6	9	2	6
Predominant practice	10	16	4	12
Minority practice	22	34	8	24
Rarely or not found	8	13	2	6
Total	64	100	33	100

Source: Table 58, Price Waterhouse Survey.

Exhibit 2. Consideration of Salvage — By Country

ISAC members

Required
Australia
Fiji
France
Hong Kong
Ireland
Korea
Malaysia
Mexico
Netherlands
New Zealand
Nigeria
Pakistan
Singapore
Trinidad and Tobago
United Kingdom
United States
Zimbabwe/Rhodesia

Insisted upon
Canada
Jamaica

Predominant practice
India
Japan
South Africa
Zambia

Minority practice
Belgium
Denmark
Germany
Norway
Philippines
Portugal
Spain
Sweden

Rarely or none
Brazil
Greece

Other countries

Required
Bahamas

Insisted upon
Bermuda
Botswana
Dominican Republic
Venezuela

Predominant practice
Argentina
El Salvador
Jersey
Kenya
Nicaragua
Taiwan

Minority practice
Bolivia
Chile
Colombia
Costa Rica
Ecuador
Guatemala
Honduras
Iran
Italy
Malawi
Panama
Paraguay
Switzerland
Uruguay

Rarely or none
Austria
Ivory Coast
Morocco
Peru
Senegal
Zaire

Source: Table 58, Price Waterhouse Survey.

the United States take pride in their accounting independence; Korea and Mexico were influenced directly through trade ties with the United States; France, which credits the IASC standard, is actually strictly governed by its uniform Plan Comptable. Among those countries where consideration of salvage is a minority practice or not seen at all are eight European countries; four are members of the European Economic Community (EEC). While IAS No. 4 was not enough to convince them to change their ways, these four, with Spain and Portugal, upon their entrance into the EEC in the 1980s, will need to consider salvage value when the EEC's Fourth Directive is incorporated into the national law. As for Brazil, with hyperinflation, one understands the reluctance to estimate future salvage value in terms of present dollars.

What does this exercise indicate of the depreciation standard? Simply based on this analysis, several points can be made:

1. The IASC succeeded in identifying and codifying standard practice in much of the world.
2. The IASC did not succeed in influencing practice in either its member countries or nonmember countries listed in the survey.
3. In this case, practice correlates somewhat to the IAS standard in terms of considering salvage value, but practice is based on previous standards.

The Equity Method

The equity method of accounting for minority-owned intercorporate investments is a much more controversial subject than the need to depreciate fixed assets. In the United Kingdom and United States, the equity method is required for investments where significant influence exists, generally defined as from the 20 to 50 percent ownership levels. Because the investor is considered to have such influence that dividend policy could be affected, dividends are considered as a return of capital, reducing the investment instead of increasing income. Profit or loss from the investment is counted as the ownership percentage of the associated company's profit or loss.

Practice in the United Kingdom and the United States is almost identical to the requirements of IAS No. 3, the statement on consolidations issued in 1976. This is not surprising, for the equity method is singularly suited to a reporting environment which emphasizes the investor. It attempts to measure the value of the investment, rather than only the immediate proceeds of the investment. This is also the controversial point as to its use. The equity method raises issues of the realization of profits and losses. Particularly in those countries where tax reporting is based on financial reporting, claiming profits and losses which have not been realized in a more concrete sense is not considered acceptable.

The equity method is a controversial topic, unlike depreciation. Its use has increased dramatically in the last ten years as more countries have accepted or legislated stricter requirements for financial relationships between companies. This is an area where the IASC has had a great opportunity to influence evolving practice. The Price Waterhouse (PW) study shows results similar to the depreciation issue. A brief review of the percent of countries using the equity method is presented in exhibit 3. The same country-by-country analysis could be done as with the salvage issue.

Much more interesting analysis of this issue can be made by considering individual countries which have adopted the equity method within the past five years (or are in the process of adopting it).

The PW study lists Japan as an IASC member with minimal acceptance of the equity method. This is changing rapidly; in the years since the PW study was undertaken, the classification has probably reached "predominant practice." This is not in response to IAS No. 3 but to new securities legislation. The growth of the stock market in Japan has led to new and more detailed securities laws, one of which required consolidated statements after April 1, 1977. The same regulation called for the equity method for 20 to 50 percent investments but allowed an interim period during which companies can change from the cost method. The Japanese have stated that their primary impetus for changing standards is to conform to foreign securities markets' requirements.[8]

Germany is an entirely different case and a classic example of the influence of taxes on financial reporting. In Germany, use of the equity method is not allowed. However, Germany is included here as an example because, within the next five years, the equity

Exhibit 3. Countries Using the Equity Method for Significant Investments

	Total survey		IASC members	
	Number	Percent	Number	Percent
Required	19	30	14	14
Insisted upon	1	2	0	0
Predominant practice	4	6	2	6
Minority practice	12	19	7	22
Rarely or not found	21	32	5	15
Not permitted	7	11	5	15
Total	64	100	33	100

Source: Table 103, Price Waterhouse Survey.

[8] Organization for Economic Cooperation and Development, *International Investment and Multinational Enterprises: Accounting Practices in OECD Member Countries* (1980), 194.

method will be required procedure. This dramatic reversal will result from the implementation of the Seventh Company Law Directive of the EEC. The Seventh Directive requires use of the equity method when significant influence exists; therefore, Germany will need to change to a method of which many Germans have severe reservations.

Another EEC country changing its methods is Denmark, which traditionally had conformity between tax and financial reporting, but which has separated the two completely in the last decade. The PW study lists the equity method as rare in Denmark, but this is now inaccurate. Although the equity method is not yet required, its use is increasing, and in an interesting way. To cope with the problem of recognizing income, the Danes have modified the equity method, transferring the ownership percentage of profit and loss to a reserve account in owners' equity instead of the income statement. This does not conform to IAS No. 3 and will change when the Seventh Directive is implemented.

The last interesting example is Italy. The PW study lists Italy as a country where use of the equity method is rare. This is true, but it has existed, although it is not allowed for tax purposes. Many companies have voluntarily been presenting consolidated statements and using the equity method experimentally. No longer will this be voluntary. A move is under way by the new national stock exchange commission to require large listed companies to consolidate accounts. Most companies will probably follow rules advocated by the new accounting organization, ASSIREVI. These rules are quite openly based on U.K. and U.S. principles and include use of the equity method. The reason for this is the influence of the "Big 8" accounting firms in Italy, which began by auditing U.K. and U.S. subsidiaries, but whose work has expanded to include a large percentage of Italian firms.

In comparing the IASC and the equity method, we should make several points:

1. The IASC has succeeded in identifying and codifying practice which is predominant in investor-oriented countries and, since that is the growing trend, it has succeeded in advocating increasingly popular practice.
2. In countries where the equity method has recently been adopted, there are equally compelling reasons other than adherence to IASC No. 3. These reasons concern securities legislation, compliance with legal requirements imposed through community organizations

such as the EEC, cooperation with trading partners, and the influence of the United Kingdom and United States.
3. The IASC has not greatly influenced either member or non-member nations to adopt the equity method.

Foreign Currency Translation

The last area is the turbulent topic of foreign currency translation. A chronology of statements on foreign currency translation by the three major parties involved in the controversy is interesting. Without attempting to explain the major methods involved, the chronology of important events follows. Statement No. 8 by the Financial Accounting Standards Board (FASB) in 1975 called for the use of the temporal method and immediate recognition of gains and losses on translation. This was bitterly opposed by companies which found their earnings shifting dramatically due to currency swings.

In 1978, the IASC issued ED 11, which was basically all things to all people. It allowed a choice between the temporal method and the closing rate method and allowed various alternatives as to recognition of translation gains and losses through both the income statement and direct movements to owners' equity. These choices were allowed even though the known preferred alternative of the majority of IASC members was the closing rate method. Why was the IASC hesitant to take a stand? Unlike depreciation, and even unlike the equity method, foreign currency translation is so emotionally charged that it actually renders the IASC somewhat powerless. The two major powers, the United Kingdom and the United States, were almost diametrically opposed in philosophy at that time, and any stand by the IASC would have been certain to contravene accepted practice in one of the two countries.

At approximately the same time, the Accounting Standards Committee (ASC) of the United Kingdom released ED 21 on the topic of accounting for foreign statement translation. Discussion leading to ED 21 was almost unanimously in favor of the closing rate method, yet the ED allowed the choice of either the temporal method or the closing rate method. Many British experts felt at the time that it would be difficult to adopt a method contrary to the U.S. method when the IASC was flexible enough to allow both.

The controversy continued, fueled by the decision of the FASB to re-evaluate foreign currency translation. A task force was established, and the IASC was represented at each meeting. Subsequently, the FASB issued Statement No. 52, requiring the current rate (closing rate) method in all but exceptional cases. The advocacy of the current rate method could be seen as a victory for the IASC in some ways. The extent of its influence is difficult to judge, however, for the major influence was obviously the American business community. The FASB has shown little inclination to do more than consider international standards briefly in setting U.S. standards.[9] No doubt the FASB was influenced somewhat because the major trading partners of the United States were strong proponents of the current rate method.

An analysis of the IASC role in the foreign currency issue is difficult because of the other factors involved. It is easy to state that the IASC exhibited weakness in its failure to issue a standard advocating the current rate method. Whether or not the IASC was influential behind the scenes is unknown. The FASB task force meetings and open hearings held on the subject indicate only cursory attention to international standards.

Impediments to IASC Effectiveness

Earlier in this paper, the authors presented the aims of the member institutes' individual efforts to achieve the acceptance of IASC standards. The extent to which compliance has been achieved was categorized by the IASC into three areas in a discussion paper titled "Acceptance and Observance of International Accounting Standards."

1. Those countries where IASC standards are awarded the same status as domestic standards. (Mandatory compliance)
2. Those countries where accountancy bodies have declared support for IASC standards and advise disclosure of any areas where local standards differ from international standards. (Preferable compliance)
3. Those countries where no formal status of standards has been determined. (None or accidental compliance)

Few countries fit the first category, although the Bahamas, Figi, Malaysia, Nigeria, Pakistan, Singapore, Trinidad and Tobago, and Zimbabwe come very close. A number of countries, particularly those with long established standard-setting mechanisms, fit the second category. These include the United Kingdom, Canada, and, to a lesser extent, the United States. Many more countries comprise the latter category.

[9] In early 1982, a vote was taken among the FASB and its constituency as to the most important problems requiring the board's consideration. The need for international standards ranked near the bottom on a list of over thirty subjects.

Lack of enforcement. A primary impediment to the IASC's effectiveness is its lack of enforcement powers. The IASC depends on voluntary compliance and the influence of the accounting institutes in each country to achieve incorporation of its recommendations into local standards. Despite the goals of these institutes, there is little evidence that much has been achieved.

In 1980, the Organization for Economic Cooperation and Development (OECD) published a survey of accounting practices in member countries.[10] The OECD lists among its members seventeen IASC members, comprising most of the "developed" world, and eight of the founding countries of the IASC. The survey included a question concerning the degree of flexibility existing in each country for accommodating recommendations on standards from international bodies. Of the eight IASC founders, only respondents from the United Kingdom and Ireland stated that IASC standards would be followed. Much more common were responses such as that of Germany: "International recommendations can be taken into account as far as they are compatible with existing legal provisions." Of the twenty OECD nations surveyed, fifteen expressed the view that international standards were often considered when local decisions were made, but that they were overridden by national concerns, particularly where accounting standards are actually enacted into law. Austria and Switzerland, nonmembers of IASC, claim no efforts to consider IASC standards, and France states that its national law goes beyond (and therefore includes) IASC standards, a debatable statement.

The IASC depends on others for its enforcement. Often these other parties are ineffectual in achieving compliance. Even in the United Kingdom, where the ASC has announced its intention to harmonize U.K. standards as far as possible with the IASC's statements, differences remain. A comparison of U.K. accounting practices with international standards produces a list of divergent requirements in at least seven of the first thirteen subjects addressed by the IASC.[11] In the United States, representation on the IASC is through the American Institute of Certified Public Accountants (AICPA) instead of the FASB. No longer does the AICPA have direct power over standard setting; therefore, it must attempt to influence adherence with international standards indirectly through opinions addressed to the FASB and the AICPA membership.

---

[10] Organization for Economic Cooperation and Development, *International Investment*, 194.

[11] Arthur Young International, "The United Kingdom," *World Business Reports* (AYI, 1981), 24, exhibit 9.

Other international bodies. An additional problem with setting international standards concerns the number of organizations which have decided to consider the subject. These groups represent diverse constituencies and include international organizations, such as the OECD and the United Nations (UN), and regional standard-setting groups such as the EEC.

The OECD and UN can be loosely typified as representing the "developed" and "developing" world, respectively. Each has recently compiled a code of behavior for multinational firms, including rules for reporting. Each must also rely on voluntary compliance. Their primary difference is their emphasis; standards applicable to industrialized nations are not necessarily appropriate for nations in the early stages of development.

In contrast, the EEC is not forced to rely on voluntary compliance. All member countries must pass national laws to include requirements complying with EEC company law directives, several of which include detailed accounting rules. Although regional in nature rather than worldwide, the EEC efforts are the most significant in terms of world harmonization because of the consensus required in choosing standards, the vast differences in the countries involved, and the agreement to make regional standards national law.

The combination of UN, OECD, IASC, and EEC efforts is often confusing and appears unnecessasry to many people. The IASC is hindered in not being the only recognized world authority, for how can there be more than one international standard?

IS THERE A BETTER ROLE FOR THE IASC?

To answer this question, it is necessary to examine the present objectives of the IASC in comparison to the areas where they have been most and least effective. The two objectives were stated earlier as (1) to formulate basic standards and (2) to promote worldwide compliance with these standards.

In this paper, the case has been made that the IASC has had great difficulty in meeting the second objective. It has not been successful in either changing existing rules or in achieving compliance with new standards. It has been hindered by a lack of authority, a tendency to emphasize details, and questionable support from member nations intent on protecting local interests.

There are some areas, however, where the IASC has been influential. An examination of these areas provides a starting point to define a new role for the IASC more in keeping with the present stage of the international harmonization process, and which would be more realistic. The IASC has been effective in three major ways:

1. It has succeeded in identifying and codifying the most generally accepted principles in use in the developed nations of the world.
2. Its standards have provided a neutral source for countries in the process of standard setting.
3. The most effective way of influencing world harmonization has been through the IASC's ability to have its standards considered by other, more powerful groups.

The first point correlates closely to the first objective of the IASC: to formulate basic standards. To date, the standards have represented practice in the industrialized world with an emphasis on investor-oriented societies. The IASC should continue to codify the best of present practice in statement form but should expand this role to one which includes research as to how different standards are suitable to different reporting environments. Little work has been done in this area; the IASC could serve as a non-affiliated clearinghouse for efforts to determine the best principles applicable to countries in different stages of development. This research should include the suitability of basic principles such as revenue recognition and matching to different political and industrial environments.

The second way in which IASC standards have proven to be effective has been as a reference for nations and companies needing neutral sources. Earlier, it was stated that many former British colonies refer to IASC standards rather than to U.K. standards as their source of practice. This is not a trivial role for the IASC to endorse for itself. Not all countries are as willing as Italy to adopt American or British standards openly as their own, yet many need an outside source to help legitimize choices of principles. IASC standards should serve as basic models which local standard-setting bodies can use as benchmarks to evaluate existing practice. They should provide guidance in areas where local standards have not yet been formulated. A further need would be served by giving multinational corporations a reference point to deal with numerous divergent reporting requirements.

The IASC has been most effective when it has been able to obtain endorsements for its opinions by parties having greater enforcement powers. Although IASC standards are not recognized as law in many countries, they are endorsed by the International

Federation of Stock Exchanges, which has the power to require adherence to IASC rules by companies listed on the major exchanges of the world.[12] The IASC lobbies to have its standards considered by the FASB and ASC, and its power to influence EEC law directives is considerable. This suggests that working toward the adoption of IASC standards should be secondary to working toward the incorporation of IASC principles into national standards. The IASC should assume the role of consultant to those groups which *do* have powers of enforcement.

SUMMARY

This paper has examined the role of the IASC. Given the assumption that the harmonization of standards is a worthwhile goal, the IASC was evaluated in terms of its ability to date to achieve its stated objectives. This analysis leads to conclusions that the IASC has not succeeded in changing existing standards or setting new standards. It has succeeded in codifying generally accepted practice, in serving as a neutral source for standards, and in influencing groups with enforcement powers. These successes indicate that the IASC objectives should be changed to the following:

1. To serve as a research clearinghouse to study the effects of different principles in different reporting environments.
2. To provide a neutral model of possible standards for countries in the process of standard setting and for multinational firms dealing with divergent regulations.
3. To provide temporary standards to fill the void existing before local standards can be set.
4. To serve as a consulting body for organizations in the standard-setting process.
5. To channel efforts to influence harmonization to incorporation of IASC principles into local legislation rather than to adoption of IASC standards themselves.

The national differences preventing immediate worldwide harmonization of standards may disappear more quickly than many people think. The primary impetus will probably come from companies themselves. As more firms seek to raise funds in world securities markets, they will be forced to change standards to meet filing requirements. Such de facto harmonization may thus succeed in eliminating present barriers preventing worldwide cooperation.

[12] Fitzgerald, Stickler, and Watts, *International Survey*.

By providing a more research- and consulting-oriented role, the IASC will have a greater opportunity to influence the eventual content of international accounting standards.

ADDITIONAL REFERENCES

Fantl, Irving L. "Case Against International Uniformity." *Management Accounting* (May 1971):13-16.

International Accounting Standards Committee. "Accounting for Business Combinations." *Statement of International Accounting Standards No. 3* (1977).

———. "Accounting for Depreciation." *Statement of International Accounting Standards No. 4* (1977).

———. "Foreign Currency Translation." *Exposure Draft* (1978).

[11]

*S. Doupnik / M. E. Taylor**

An Empirical Investigation of the Observance of IASC Standards in Western Europe

Introduction

The problem of diversity in national accounting practices has been widely discussed over the years. A world economy exists today in which trade and investment show no regard for national borders. Differences in accounting practices among countries impede the flow of capital across borders necessary for the optimal allocation of scarce resources worldwide.

Much effort has been devoted over the last decade to harmonize corporate financial reporting on an international level. One of the most important factors in the harmonization process has been the establishment of the International Accounting Standards Committee (IASC). As of October 1983, the IASC had issued 21 standards of accounting and had a number of proposed standards out for exposure.

The IASC has been criticized for considering "only noncontroversial subjects and for taking a 'lowest common denominator' approach to standard setting" (Fitzgerald, 1981, p. 26). Although IASC standards to date perhaps have not addressed the most controversial topics in accounting, as a whole they do reflect a basic core of accounting practice necessary for providing useful information. Given their "lowest common denominator" nature, if the basic accounting and disclosure practices recommended in IASC standards are not followed, there is little chance that valid comparisons of financial results can be made between business enterprises in different countries.

The nations of Western Europe comprise one of the most economically developed regions in the world. Trade and investment across national borders is perhaps more prevalent here than anywhere else. Despite their geographic proximity, and the apparent benefits to be derived from comparable corporate financial statements, European countries possess disparate sociopolitical, legal, and economic characteristics that tend to hamper harmonization within the region (McComb, 1982, p. 38). The objectives of this study are to ascertain the extent to which the countries of Western Europe are conforming to a basic core of accounting practice (as evidenced by the level of compliance with the first eight IASC standards) and examine the change in the level of conformity over time. This is accomplished by measuring and comparing the level of compliance with a number of IASC standards at two dates – January 1, 1979 and January 1, 1983.

* *Timothy S. Doupnik, Assistant Professor, Martin E. Taylor, Doctoral Student, College of Business Administration, University of South Carolina, Columbia, SC., U.S.A.* *Manuscript received January 1984.*

Methodology

In 1979, Price Waterhouse (PW) published an "International Survey of Accounting Principles and Reporting Practices" containing information on how 267 accounting propositions were presented in the financial statements of business firms in 64 countries as of January 1, 1979. The survey included propositions representing measurement procedures and disclosure requirements recommended in the first eight IASC standards. That portion of the PW survey related to these standards was updated to January 1, 1983 by mailing a questionnaire containing 53 accounting propositions to PW offices worldwide. Participants were asked to indicate for each measurement procedure or disclosure practice described which of the following assessments was true at January 1, 1983:

Required – application of the principle of practice is required by a pronouncement of a professional accountancy body or by law.

Majority practice – the principle or practice is the one which is most frequently followed.

Minority practice – the principle or practice is followed less frequently than an alternative.

Rarely or not found – the principle or practice is not followed in financial statements, or is found in isolated examples only.

Not permitted – the opposite of Required; application of the principle or practice is prohibited by a pronouncement of a professional body or by law.

Not applicable – the proposition addresses a situation which does not occur in your country.

Fifty (50) countries had responded to the survey by December 1, 1983, sixteen (16) of which are located in Western Europe.

Weighted-average scores have been calculated for each country using the following weighting scheme:

Required	= 4.00
Majority practice	= 3.00
Minority practice	= 2.00
Rarely or not found	= 1.00
Not permitted	= 0.00

Thus, weighted-average scores can range from a low of 0.00 if all propositions were "not permitted," to a high of 4.00 if all propositions were "required." The larger the score, the greater the level of compliance with IASC standards. Weighted-average scores have been calculated from the results of the current survey as well as from the 1979 PW survey. In addition to the six responses possible in the 1983 survey, the PW survey had "insisted upon" and "not accepted" as possible responses. A weight of 4.00 has been attached to the first and a weight of 0.00 to the second in calculating scores.

Analysis of Weighted-Average Scores

In this section, mean weighted-average scores for five geographic areas are first examined to determine the relative quality of financial reporting in Europe vis-à-vis other regions. Scores for individual countries of Western Europe are then analyzed. As a part of this analysis, European countries are dichotomized into "EC" and "non-EC" groups to compare the relative quality of financial reporting between them. In addition, propositions are dichotomized into "disclosure" and "measurement" groups to compare the relative level at which they are being applied by European countries.

Analysis of Geographic Areas

The 50 countries responding to the current survey have been grouped into five broadly-defined geographic areas. Table 1 shows the number of countries in each geographic area (N), and mean weighted-average scores for 1979 and 1983. The Kruskal-Wallis one-way analysis of variance of ranks (Siegel, 1956, pp. 184–193) has been used to test the hypothesis that there is no difference in mean scores among the various geographic areas. The null has been rejected at the 0.01 level for 1979 and the 0.02 level for 1983. This indicates that statistically significant differences in mean weighted-average scores exist.

Table 1: Mean Weighted-Average Scores by Geographic Area

Area	N	1979	1983
Africa	(7)	3.23	3.19
Asia & Australia	(8)	3.59	3.65
Europe	(16)	2.97	3.11
Latin America	(15)	3.07	3.18
North America	(4)	3.84	3.82

That table shows that Europe has the lowest mean scores in both 1979 and 1983. This is somewhat surprising given the fact that Europe as a region is relatively highly developed, both economically and in terms of the overall accounting environment. One explanation for this apparent contradiction could be the fact that individual European countries long ago developed their own accounting standard-setting processes and feel less obliged to conform to standards set by an international body. Accounting standard-setting processes in other regions are relatively less advanced compared with Europe, and therefore may be more influenced by IASC pronouncements.

Considering the changes in mean scores from 1979 to 1983, Europe registers the greatest percentage increase (+4.7 percent), followed by Latin America (+3.6 percent), while North America and Africa have actually decreased in their overall level of compliance. This shows that although Europe started at the lowest level, it has made the greatest advances over the period 1979 to 1983.

Analysis of Country Scores

Weighted-average scores for individual European countries are given in Table 2. Scores are presented for 1979 and 1983, along with an indication of whether the score for each country has increased (+), decreased (–), or remained the same (0) during the period 1979 to 1983.

Table 2: Weighted-Average Scores by Country

Country	1979	1983	Δ
Austria	2.27	2.19	–
Belgium	3.27	3.43	+
Denmark	3.09	3.40	+
France	4.00	3.81	–
Germany	3.04	3.04	0
Greece	2.17	2.19	+
Ireland	3.89	3.92	+
Italy	2.94	3.08	+
Jersey	2.38	3.53	+
Netherlands	3.66	3.75	+
Norway	3.17	3.32	+
Portugal	2.59	2.60	+
Spain	1.90	2.26	+
Sweden	3.26	3.32	+
Switzerland	1.98	1.98	0
United Kingdom	3.83	3.91	+
mean	2.97	3.11	

Examination of the changes from 1979 to 1983 shows that weighted-average scores have increased for 12 countries, remained the same for 2 countries, and actually decreased for 2 countries. This indicates that the level of compliance has improved in 75 percent of the European countries included in this study and has either remained the same or declined in 25 percent of those countries.

Analysis of the relative magnitude of individual country scores shows that France had a score of 4.00 in 1979, indicating full compliance with the 53 propositions included in the study. There are no countries exhibiting full compliance in 1983. The second highest-score country in 1979 is Ireland (3.89), followed by the United Kingdom (3.83) and the Netherlands (3.66). The country with the lowest score in 1979 is Spain (1.90). Other countries with relatively low scores in 1979 are Switzerland (1.98), Greece (2.17), and Austria (2.27).

The countries with the highest scores in 1979 also have the highest scores in 1983. Ireland has the highest score in 1983 (3.92), followed by the United Kingdom (3.91), France (3.81), and the Netherlands (3.75). Those four countries with lowest scores in 1979 also exhibit the lowest scores in 1983. Switzerland has the lowest score in 1983 (1.98), preceded by Austria and Greece (2.19), and then Spain (2.26).

Countries showing the greatest increase im weighted-average scores over the period 1979 to 1983 are Jersey (+48 percent), Spain (+19 percent), and Denmark (+10 percent). Except for Spain, countries exhibiting relatively low compliance in 1979 have not improved much over the period 1979 to 1983. Greece improves negligibly, Switzerland remains the same, and Austria in fact declines in overall compliance.

Notice that the four highest-score countries in both 1979 and 1983 are members of the EEC, whereas three of the four lowest-score countries in both 1979 and 1983 are nonmembers. One might hypothesize that the level of compliance is greater for members of the EEC than for nonmembers. To examine this hypothesis, countries have been dichotomized into two groups and mean weighted-average scores computed for each. Of the ten members of the EC, only Luxembourg is not included in the study.

Table 3: Mean Weighted-Average Scores

EC	N	1979	1983
Member	(9)	3.32	3.39
Nonmember	(7)	2.51	2.74

Comparison of the mean scores presented in Table 3 shows that the EC countries as a group have dramatically higher scores than non-EC European countries. Scores for the former group are 32 percent higher in 1979 and 24 percent higher in 1983 than scores in the latter group. The Mann-Whitney U test (Siegel, pp. 116–126) has been used to test the null hypothesis that these two groups of scores come from the same population. The null has been rejected at the 0.01 level for both 1979 and 1983, indicating that statistically significant differences in group scores exist. Thus, it can be concluded that compliance with the 53 propositions included in this study is greater for those countries in Europe which are members of the EC than for those countries which are not.

Propositions incorporated in the 1983 survey reflect either a disclosure of relevant information or the choice among alternative accounting measurement procedures. Propositions have been dichotomized into "disclosure" and "measurement" groups and weighted-average scores calculated on a country basis to examine whether the level of compliance differs depending upon the type of proposition involved. Table 4 shows scores for each country for the 36 disclosure requirements and 17 measurement procedures included in the study.

Comparison of mean scores in that table shows that compliance with those propositions representing disclosure requirements is greater in both 1979 and 1983 than compliance

Table 4: Weighted-Average Scores

Country	Disclosure (36)			Measurement (17)		
	1979	1983	Δ	1979	1983	Δ
Austria	2.29	2.26	–	2.33	2.08	–
Belgium	3.51	3.51	0	2.77	2.83	+
Denmark	3.25	3.50	+	2.76	3.18	+
France	4.00	3.83	–	4.00	3.76	–
Germany	3.49	3.49	0	3.18	3.18	0
Greece	2.06	2.91	+	2.46	2.46	0
Ireland	3.83	3.92	+	4.00	4.00	0
Italy	2.94	3.31	+	2.92	2.94	+
Jersey	2.64	3.58	+	2.24	3.53	+
Netherlands	3.81	3.81	0	3.35	3.65	+
Norway	3.33	3.47	+	2.82	2.88	+
Portugal	2.56	2.69	+	2.69	2.41	+
Spain	1.64	2.19	+	2.47	2.64	+
Sweden	3.44	3.36	–	3.12	3.24	+
Switzerland	2.03	2.03	0	1.91	1.91	0
United Kingdom	3.92	3.86	–	4.00	4.00	0
mean	3.05	3.23		2.94	3.02	

with those propositions reflecting a choice among measurement procedures. Moreover, the difference in mean scores between the two types of proposition has increased from 1979 to 1983. Examination of relative magnitudes shows that only France exhibits full compliance with the 36 disclosure propositions in 1979 and no country shows full compliance in 1983. Three countries were in full compliance with the 17 measurement propositions in 1979 (France, Ireland, and the United Kingdom), but only Ireland and the United Kingdom have scores of 4.00 in 1983. The lowest score found in Table 4 is the disclosure score for Spain in 1979 (1.64). The only other scores less than 2.00 are the measurement scores for Switzerland in both 1979 and 1983 (1.91).

The changes in scores from 1979 to 1983 show that eight countries (50 percent) have increased their level of compliance with disclosure propositions and eight have increased their compliance with measurement propositions. Only Austria and France have declines in scores for both types of propositions. The direction of the change in scores for some countries is different between the two types of propositions. Sweden has a decline in disclosure score, but an increase in measurement score. Portugal, on the other hand, has an increase in disclosure score, but a decrease in measurement score.

Calculation of weighted-average scores for individual propositions across countries reveals that two of the three highest-score propositions among the European countries in both 1979 and 1983 are disclosure propositions, and two of the three lowest-score propositions in both 1979 and 1983 are measurement propositions. The three propositions sharing the highest score (3.69) in 1979 are: disclosure of fixed assets by category, disclosure of depreciation charges, and taking gains on sales of fixed assets to income. The first and third of these share the highest score in 1983 (3.88). The relatively high level of compliance with these propositions seems to indicate that accounting for fixed assets in general is afforded a high level of importance in European countries.

The lowest score in 1979 (1.56) is shared by two propositions related to the use of the equity method: application of the equity method in less than 50% investments when the investor exercises significant influence, and making adjustments similar to elimination entries on consolidation when the equity method is applied. The third lowest score (1.60) is found for the proposition requiring the disclosure of contingent assets. These propositions also have the three lowest scores in 1983. The proposition related to making adjustments when the equity method is used registers the lowest score in 1983 (1.50). Notice that compliance with this particular proposition has declined over the period 1979 to 1983.

Summary and Conclusions

The objectives of this study were to examine the extent to which the countries of Western Europe are conforming to a basic core of accounting practice (as evidenced by compliance with IASC standards) and examine the change in the level of conformity over the period 1979 to 1983.

Analysis reveals that Europe registers the lowest level of compliance with IASC standards among five broadly-defined geographic areas. There appears to be some resistance to conforming to a "lowest common denominator" level of accounting practice on the part of the countries of Western Europe. Although Europe had the lowest level of compliance in both 1979 and 1983, it showed the greatest percentage increase in mean score over the period 1979 to 1983. This may indicate that resistance to conformity is lessening.

Analysis of individual country scores indicates that there is a wide range in the level of application of the basic core of accounting procedures prescribed by the IASC among the countries of Europe. In general, the English-speaking countries, France, and the Netherlands are in greatest conformity, and the German-speaking and Southern European countries are in least conformity. Comparisons of financial statements between some pairs of countries in Europe appear to be valid, while comparisons between other country-pairs probably should not be attempted.

Members of the EC have been found to exhibit a higher level of compliance with IASC standards than nonmember European countries, but the difference has shrunk over the period 1979 to 1983. The efforts of the EC to harmonize accounting practices within the community possibly have helped to improve the overall quality of financial reporting in those countries.

European countries were more inclined to conform to propositions related to disclosure requirements than those related to measurement practices. Moreover, the difference in the level of conformity has increased from 1979 to 1983.

A partial examination of individual propositions indicates that European countries are most inclined to follow those international standards of accounting related to fixed assets. Certain aspects of applying the equity method of accounting for stock investments, on the other hand, have not met with much support in the European countries.

Overall, the general conclusions are that Europe as a whole lags behind the rest of the world in achieving a "lowest common denominator" level of accounting practice, and that much diversity continues to exist among the countries of Western Europe regarding conformity to a basic core of accounting practice.

References

Fitzgerald, Richard D. (1981): "International Harmonization of Accounting and Reporting," International Journal of Accounting, Fall, pp. 21–32.

International Accounting Standards Committee: International Accounting Standards Nos. 1 through 8. London: IASC.

McComb, Desmond (1982): "International Accounting Standards and the EEC Harmonization Program: A Conflict of Disparate Objectives," International Journal of Accounting, Spring, pp.35–48.

Price Waterhouse International (1979): International Survey of Accounting Principles and Reporting Practices. Price Waterhouse.

Siegel, Sidney (1956): Nonparametric Statistics. New York: McGraw Hill.

[12]

COMMENTS

C. W. Nobes*

An Empirical Investigation of the Observance of IASC Standards in Western Europe: A Comment

Doupnik and Taylor (1985) purport to examine compliance with IASC standards over time and across regions. For data on practices in 1979 they rely on a Price Waterhouse survey; for 1983 they conducted their own questionnaire to Price Waterhouse offices, receiving 50 country responses. Their conclusions are not credible in some respects, particularly because they do not recognise the limitations of the data.

It has been pointed out that Price Waterhouse data are unreliable and unsuitable for classification purposes (Nobes, 1981). It is also unsuitable for the purposes of Doupnik and Taylor, who perpetuate the problems in their own questionnaire. For example, the response category "Required – application ... is required by a pronouncement of a professional accountancy body or by law" is highly misleading. To take one instance, the 1979 data shows that only

> France had a score of 4.00 in 1979, indicating full compliance with the 53 propositions ... There are no countries exhibiting full compliance in 1983.

This apparent full compliance rests on the 1979 Survey giving scores of "required" for France on the basis that IASC standards had been issued in France. However, French law, French standards and French companies did not fully comply with IASC standards in 1979. As just one example of this, data from the Commission des Opérations de Bourse (1980) show that only about half of even the listed French companies prepared consolidated accounts (as required by IAS 3) in 1979. The "full compliance" of France in 1979 is total fiction, but this is merely the most obvious case. The apparent fall in compliance from 1979 to 1983 results from a change in response not a change in reality.

A less important case, but one that further illustrates the problem, is that, for 1983, Jersey gets a score of 3.53 which is only possible if over half the propositions are "required". In fact, there is no relevant law in Jersey, and UK standards are merely voluntarily followed (presumably about half of the propositions coincide with those UK rules used in Price Waterhouse's Jersey office).

The clear-cut errors for France and Jersey suggest that there are also many subtler problems with the scores for other countries. The most obvious cause of error is that a "pronouncement of a professional accountancy body" can range from one that is legally enforced (e.g. Canada), to one that is usually obeyed and is binding on auditors (e.g.

* *Professor Christopher W. Nobes, Department of Economics, Faculty of Letters and Social Sciences, University of Reading, Whiteknights, Reading, England. Manuscript received April 1987.*

UK), to one that is persuasive (e.g. the Netherlands), to one that is unimportant (e.g. domestic pronouncement of the accountancy body in West Germany), to one that is largely unknown to companies or auditors (e.g. an IASC standard in Frace, although referred to by the Price Waterhouse survey).

This suggests that, at least in some cases, Doupnik and Taylor's detailed discussions of increases and decreases in country scores bear little relationship to reality. In passing, it should be noted that the score for the UK is shown to rise in Table 2, whereas its components fall in Table 4. This is numerically impossible.

On another point, the authors' suggestion that the harmonization efforts of the European Communities "possibly have helped to improve the overall quality of financial reporting" seems unlikely to be an important factor. This is because only two countries out of the ten had brought the earliest accounting Directive into force (only Denmark and the UK had implemented the Fourth Directive by 1. 1. 83, although there may have been some effect of partial anticipations, e.g. in Belgium).

In summary, the data are too weak to support the detailed numerical analysis, descriptions and conclusions of Doupnik and Taylor. Even if this were not the case, the paper's frequent reference to "compliance with IAS standards" would be quite misleading since no evidence is offered to suggest causality.

References

Commission des Opérations de Bourse (1980): *Annual Report.*

Doupnik, S. and M. E. Taylor (1985): "An Empirical Investigation of the Observance of IASC Standards in Western Europe", *Management International Review,* Vol. 25, 1, pp. 27–33.

Nobes, C. W. (1981): "An Empirical Analysis of International Accounting Principles: A Comment", *Journal of Accounting Research,* Vol. 19, 1, pp. 268–270.

[13]

Int J Acctg (1989) 24:320–341

The International Journal of Accounting

The Internationalization of Accounting Standards: Past Problems and Current Prospects

Juan M. Rivera

Associate Professor of Accounting, University of Notre Dame, Notre Dame, IN 46556, USA

Key words: Harmonization; Internationalization; International accounting standards; International Accounting Standards Committee; Regional accounting standards

Abstract: *The search for international accounting standards continues. Several groups are contributing to the process. The most prominent is the International Accounting Standards Committee which has issued nearly 30 international accounting principles. Despite these results, concerns as to the validity and worth of the harmonization process remain. A lack of a structured theoretical accounting framework underlying the specific standards, a multiplicity of permitted reporting and reporting alternatives introduced in the issued standards, a tendency to address only those issues developed or related to advanced economic eivironments, and a lack of enforceability have all been mentioned. Problems of acceptance and enforcement of these international standards remain. To be accepted, the international accounting standards must recognise the existence of domestic requirements and needs of individual nations to assure that international standards are representative and responsive to all the countries and not simply to the larger members of the standard setting group.*

The topic of international accounting standards is thought to have received the most attention in recent international accounting literature, with approximately half of the papers written addressing this issue.[1] Moreover, interest in the subject is not circumscribed to only a few institutions. Most (Ref.2, p.10) identified a variety of organizations involved in the international accounting standard-setting process. They include intergovernmental groups such as the United Nations (UN), the European Economic Community (EEC), and the Organization for Economic Co-operation and Development (OECD); professional accounting bodies, such as the International Accounting Standards Committee (IASC), and the Union of

Accepted for publication: December, 1989

European Accountants (UEC); and regional accounting associations, such as the Arab Society of Certified Accountants (ASCA) and the Confederation of Asian and Pacific Accountants (CAPA).[3] Among these groups, the most prominent and prolific in setting standards has been the IASC, which has issued 29 international accounting principles and a comprehensive accounting framework for financial statements since its formation in 1973.[5]

Attempts to harmonize accounting standards at the international level began in 1966 when accountants from the United States, Canada, and the United Kingdom formed the Accountants International Study Group (AISG). Subsequently, a group of nine countries, including the member countries of the AISG, constituted the IASC, the multinational accounting organization that now includes 98 professional accounting associations from 74 countries. Also important in this process of international accounting standardization has been the International Federation of Accountants (IFAC), an organization that developed parallel to the IASC and currently has the same membership. Distinct from its twin institution, the IFAC has focused exclusively on the issuance of international guidelines which deal with auditing, ethics, and accounting educational requirements.

Notwithstanding the amount of interest in this area of international accounting standardization, doubts about the validity and worth of this harmonization process remain. Even though the number of accounting standards issued by the IASC is substantial (29 official pronouncements), their recognition and general acceptance is still an unrealized goal (see, for instance, Ref.7). The IASC's attempts at accounting harmonization have been unsuccessful because of the following observable conditions:

(1) lack of a structured theoretical accounting framework underlying the issuance of specific standards,[8]

(2) a multiplicity of permitted reporting and recording options introduced in the current standards,

(3) a tendency to address only those issues developed in or related to advanced economic environments where sophisticated markets and information prevail, and

(4) lack of enforceability of those international standards at the local and international levels.

Because of all these conditions, the persistent variety of inherent accounting practices in different geographical settings remains.[10] These conditions have divided academicians and practitioners alike between those who support harmonization at the international level and those who consider it a futile exercise.

Support for Standardization

There is a general consensus that a world-wide standardization of accounting principles could benefit users of financial information which originates in different geographical locations (see, for instance, Ref.12). Mason[13] identified 10 types of beneficiaries from international standardization. Increasing the comparability of financial reports of companies from different countries is another reason to support standardization.[2,14] In general, the interests of the investor as a user of financial information must be met.[15] The recent expansion of international capital markets and the availability of instantaneous global communications have placed on accounting the onus to provide useful and comparable information across international borders.

The demand for the international standardization of accounting principles stemmed from a need for information by the capital markets in developed countries and in accounting problems arising from a corporation's foreign operations.[16] Even with the proliferation of accounting statements by the IASC, many still perceive the absence of international accounting standards to be a fundamental problem. Studies by Scott[17] and Scott and Troberg[18] found that a group of accounting experts from different countries placed the lack of international accounting standards as sixth in a list of 88 problems in international accounting.

Standardization of accounting principles internationally is more of a harmonizing than a uniformity process. Nobes and Parker[19] considered harmonization as a process of making diverse accounting principles from different countries more compatible. The issue is also related to principles of accounting for private enterprises, exclusive of those for governmental entities in a centrally planned economy.

Arguments Against Harmonization

Even though the general trend in the literature supports harmonization some significant arguments have been advanced against that process. Both practical and theoretical considerations are mentioned as reasons for discouraging the standardization of accounting principles internationally (see, for instance, Ref.20, pp.100–108). The main argument is that socioeconomic and cultural differences between countries that cause the objectives of those countries' accounting systems actually or potentially to be different (Ref.21, pp.23–28; Ref.22), will always exist.[23] Thus the harmonization of accounting standards in different countries would tend to fail.

Choi and Mueller[21] identified numerous environmental variables that affect accounting development. For example, the degree of sophistication of a country's capital market affects business information requirements. Few of the less-developed countries have a structured capital market. The specific ownership structure of business enterprises constitutes another variable. In some countries, ownership is widely spread among investors who are normally absent form managing the business. In other countries, ownership and management fall to the same individuals. The need for disclosure and the emphasis on agency theory, so common in the more developed countries, are not a concern in many developing nations.

At the national level, unresolved questions remain on the objectives of accounting, and on the standards themselves, if any have been issued. A strong argument against the standardization of international accounting principles proposes that the conditions in developing countries differ from those in the developed nations. Because the process of standard setting has been predominantly controlled by the developed countries, the less-developed nations complain of not having enough participation in the process.[24]

The question remaining is whether a need for international accounting standards really exists, especially because lack of compliance with the international accounting rules has not impeded the development of international financial markets and foreign operations. Even before the IASC was formed, Most[27] found that when comparing financial statements of U.S. and European companies, a skilled analyst could find the information useful. Using financial statements of five leading chemical companies from five different countries to prepare a ratio analysis, he observed that European financial reports were comparable to those published in the United States. In the same vein, Choi and Bavishi[28] examined 1000 financial statements from public corporations with headquarters in 24 countries. A major finding of their comparison of the set of foreign companies with those based in the United States was that the fundamental differences in accounting standards among the countries sampled were not as extensive as expected. Also, using a sample of 26 foreign companies registered with the Securities and Exchange Commission (SEC), Meek[29] detected that responses in U.S. share prices were similar when the earnings announcements occurred, whether those earnings were measured with foreign or U.S. generally accepted accounting principles (GAAP).

Harmonization of International Accounting Principles by Intergovernmental Organizations

Both the UN and the OECD have studied the activities of transnational corporations (TNCs). The UN has shown concern with the divergent accounting and reporting practices TNCs follow and with the lack of comparability in the information they disclose. The Group of Experts on International Standards of Accounting and Reporting, an *ad hoc* unit appointed by the UN Centre on Transnational Corporations, seeks the harmonization of accounting practices and disclosures to meet user needs, particularly the needs of users in the developing countries. The Group of Experts has issued a few objectives upon which accounting standards could be built (Ref.11, pp.4–5). However, most of the work of the Centre on Transnational Corporations on the subject of accounting standards has consisted of a description of the development of accounting practices and standards in different countries.[11,30,31] Even though the intention of the UN and its Group of Accounting Experts is to formulate lists of minimum requirements of corporate financial information and disclosure, they have opted to reserve that task for private professional groups.

An important intergovernmental body involved in the establishment of international accounting standards is the European Economic Commission. This regional group attempts to harmonize accounting practices in the 12 member countries of the EEC through its Fourth and Seventh Directives. On a supra-national level, this is the only organization at present capable of enforcing its accounting norms. According to the EEC parliamentary agreements, its member nations must enact the appropriate laws to implement the accounting methods and standards contained in the Commission's Directives.[32] With the upcoming elimination of trade barriers among the 12 members of the EEC in 1992, a surge in the harmonization of accounting policies and practices in that region is expected to develop. Whether those EEC directives would be compatible with the IASC pronouncements or with accounting standards in non-EEC countries is still uncertain.

The Record of the IASC: Many Pronouncements and Few Endorsements

The IASC has been successful in publishing 28 pronouncements and in attracting new member countries since its inception in 1973. Unfortunately, the IASC's standards are not enforceable and have not yet received "generally accepted" status world-wide.

The model under which the IASC operates is strongly influenced by the accounting practice of developed countries, particularly the United States. Hall[34] observed that the IASC was created under the tutelage of a few dominant countries, especially the United States, the United Kingdom and, to a lesser extent, West Germany and The Netherlands. There was the patronizing assumption that the standards from these developed countries could be adapted to other countries, particularly those in the Third World. Attempts to transplant elaborate principles to environments where different conditions prevail make the accounting standards process questionable and often inefficient. Thus, recent subjects addressed by the IASC's principles, such as those dealing with pension accounting and leases, are superfluous for countries where capital-lease transactions are not practiced.[35] Even the IASC has been self-critical when stating that in the past, it "tended to follow the developments in standard-setting that have taken place in countries where the regulatory environment and the accounting profession are well developed" (Ref.26, p.16)

Evidence of a strong dependent relationship between the IASC's standards and the accounting principles (GAAP) issued in the United States is provided by the comparative analysis presented in the Appendix. It should be noted that only two of the 28 international standards advanced by the IASC – IAS 20: Accounting for Government Grants, and IAS 29: Financial Accounting in Hyperinflationary Economies – had not been preceded by a U.S. accounting pronouncement which dealt with the same subject matter and arrived in general at the same acceptable methods and procedures. The fact that the AICPA has found very few and only minor differences between the IASC's standards and U.S. GAAP[25] corroborates the perceived relationship between those two sets of accounting principles.[36]

Additionally, the harmonization of international accounting standards that the IASC has tried to achieve has been limited because flexibility is ingrained in its outstanding pronouncements. In a search for the intrinsic uniformity of international accounting standards, Rueschhoff[37] found that flexibility is permitted in the international standards, just as flexibility is present in the U.S. GAAP in a number of cases. Most[2] found that in eight of the 24 international standards issued up to 1984, i.e., in one-third of the standards, alternative solutions were permitted. Similarly, Choi and Bavishi[28] found that eight of the initial 16 standards issued by the IASC permit alternative accounting treatments, and hence allow flexibility.

The IASC has recognized the impediments to improved harmonization caused by the free choices of accounting treatment permitted for similar transaction or events in its current international standards. The flexibility introduced in those standards was probably an attempt to accommodate the variety of treatments that existed in reporting standards already adopted by developed countries.[38] In an effort to ameliorate the problem of the observance of international accounting standards in the future and thus aim for wider comparability of financial statements, the IASC has proposed amendments to 13 of its existing standards.[6] The changes would eliminate choices of treatments and/or prescribe preferred solutions whenever options cannot be dismissed. Reporting companies which opt for an allowed alternative would need to disclose information reconciling the effect of the alternative selected against the one considered as preferred.

The Problem of Enforcement of IASC Standards

The degree to which IASC standards are observed world-wide is generally discouraging. In a few countries, such as Cyprus, Malawi, Malaysia, and Zimbabwe, where the accounting profession is relatively young, the international accounting standards (IAS) generally have been incorporated into the official local accounting principles (Ref.26, pp.9–12). For other countries, such as Fiji, India, Kenya, and Singapore, the principles issued by the IASC serve as a basis for the formulation of local accounting rules (Ref.26, pp.12–14). Still only in exceptional cases do particular firms make reference to compliance with IAS in the financial statements. Likewise, reference to IAS in the auditors' reports of published financial statements of these countries is missing. It is evident that professional accountants must abide by existing accounting standards at the local level, and that the power or persuasion to incorporate the use of and reference to IAS has not materialized into disclosure of their observance.

Because of the large number of options permitted in the published IAS, the actual level of agreement with IAS is conceivably substantially higher than the level of disclosure of that compliance. In an effort to test the use and application of its international standards, in 1987 the IASC conducted a survey among its member bodies from 70 countries (see Ref.26). Results of this survey showed that in most of the responding countries, the national requirements or accounting practice conformed with 23 of the 25 IAS then outstanding (Ref.26, p.3). The two exceptions corresponded to IAS 14 and IAS 15, which deal with segmental information and with information to reflect the effect of changing prices, respectively.

A close scrutiny of the IASC's survey results provides additional evidence that its standards have accommodated accounting principles in effect in a few of the developed countries. The responses received from the United Kingdom, Canada, the United States, France, Belgium, and Japan indicated the highest level of conformity between the standards developed there and those promulgated by the IASC[39] (Ref.26, pp.21–69). This would imply that, at least on issues such as those covered by IAS, a good level of accounting harmonization has been achieved in those countries. Therefore, the development of standards to mirror those where agreement already exists would be a redundant task. Nonetheless, the apparent high level of conformity may be the result more of the flexibility allowed by the IASC's standards than of the actual correspondence of accounting rules and practices among those countries surveyed.

Whatever power of enforcement the IASC could have possessed, it has diminished substantially through time. When the IASC was founded, its members agreed to use their best endeavors and persuasive influence to ensure compliance with the standards. Each professional accounting association within the IASC was to ensure that the external auditors would satisfy themselves of the standards' observance and would disclose cases of noncompliance. Appropriate action was to be taken against any auditor who did not follow these recommendations. Later, revised wording of the agreement among members acknowledged that the IASC's pronouncements would not override the standards followed by individual countries. In the most recent version of the agreement, dated October 1982, the members' obligation is to use "their best endeavors to ensure that financial statements comply with the IAS in all material respects and disclose the fact of such compliance" and "to ensure that auditors satisfy themselves that the financial statements comply with those standards in all material respects" (Ref.25, Appendix). However, the earlier requirement that auditors should disclose the extent of noncompliance and refer to it in the audit report is no longer present. Actual observance of the IASC's standards is very difficult to document in practice because very few companies make reference to them in their financial reports. For instance, although the International Stock Exchange of the United Kingdom and the Republic of Ireland permits foreign companies to file financial statements that comply with IAS rather than with the British ones, disclosure of that fact is still very rate (Ref.25, p.77). The exception to the norm is Canada, where efforts undertaken by the organized accounting profession have led to a widespread practice of listed companies disclosing their observance of IAS.[40]

To assess the extent of references to IAS in published financial statements, a search for these disclosures was performed, using financial reports compiled by the National Automated Accounting Research System (NAARS). The sample included approximately 22 600 documents filed during the years 1983–1988. The sample comprised entities that were listed companies traded in the major U.S. stock exchanges or in the over-the-counter market. The results of this analysis, as reported in Table 1, reveal that disclosures of compliance with IAS are extremely limited. Although this type of disclosure is increasing, on average only 14

Table 1. References to IAS in Published Financial Reports

Name of company or institution	Country	1983 F	1983 M	1984 F	1984 M	1985 F	1985 M	1986 F	1986 M	1987 F	1987 M	1988 F	1988 M	Total cases F	Total cases M
1. Alcan Aluminum, Ltd.	Canada		x		x		x		x		x		x		6
2. AICPA	U.S.A.	x		x		x		x						4	
3. Bell Canada (BCE)	Canada	x		x		x		x		x		x		6	
4. Bow Valley Industries, Ltd.	Canada	x					x		x		x		x	1	4
5. CPC Intl. Corp.	U.S.A.										x		x		2
6. Campeau Corporation	Canada							x		x				2	
7. Dominion Textile Inc.	Canada							x	x	x	x	x	x	3	3
8. Echo Bay Mines, Ltd.	Canada			x		x		x		x				4	
9. Elscint, Ltd.	Israel					x								1	
10. Exxon Corporation	U.S.A.						x	x		x		x		3	1
11. FMC Corporation	U.S.A.								x		x		x		3
12. Gandalf Technologies	Canada											x		1	
13. General Electric Co.	U.S.A.				x		x		x		x		x		5
14. Hudson Bay Mines, Ltd.	Canada				x						x				2
15. Imperial Oil, Ltd.	Canada	x		x		x		x		x				5	
16. Interhome Energy, Inc.	Canada											x		1	
17. IFAC[a]	U.S.A.			x						x		x		3	
18. Interprovincial Pipe Line, Ltd.	Canada	x		x		x		x		x				5	
19. McIntyre Mines, Ltd.	Canada	x		x										2	
20. Montedison, SPA[a]	Italy									x				1	
21. Northern Telecom, Ltd.	Canada	x		x		x		x		x		x		6	
22. Page Petroleum, Ltd.	Canada	x		x		x		x						4	
23. Texaco Canada, Inc.	Canada			x		x								2	
24. Transcanada Pipeline, Ltd.	Canada	x	x	x	x		x	x	x	x	x		x	4	6
25. Union Gas, Ltd.	Canada									x	x			1	1
26. Velcro Industries, Ltd.	Neth. Antilles							x		x				2	
Cases per type/year		9	2	11	4	9	5	12	6	13	9	7	7	61	33
Total companies/year		10		14		14		16		19		13			

[a]Case reported included a reference to IAS compliance in the auditor's report.

F = Footnote in financial statements.

M = Included in the text of the management report.

Source: Annual files from the National Automated Accounting Research System (NAARS) for the years 1983-1988, comprising ca. 22 600 financial reports.

financial statements have alluded to IAS every year.[41] In general, the references reported in footnotes have outnumbered those included in the management report by a margin of two to one. As for the country of origin of the disclosing companies, 17 of those 26 reporting firms were incorporated in Canada. Only four U.S. companies referred to IAS during the 6-year period examined. With the exception of one Italian company, no mention to IAS was found in the auditor's report of the corporate financial statements reviewed.

Criticism of the IASC's Standard-Setting Process

A basic criticism of the IASC is that it has not paid sufficient attention to the objectives of financial accounting and reporting in an international context. The IASC's focus has been more on legitimizing certain practices already tried in influential, developed economies. Initially, the IASC (Ref.42, para.6–10) recognized the following three fundamental assumptions in accounting: (1) going concern; (2) consistency; and (3) accrual process, together with the following three governing "considerations" in the preparation of financial information: (1) prudence; (2) substance over form; and (3) materiality.[43] However, the viability of assumptions such as these has not been tested under different economic environments. Assessment of the applicability of standards on materiality, prudence, cost–benefit, and relevance under varying conditions of inflation, unemployment, exchange controls, absence or inefficiencies of capital markets, and similar factors has not yet occurred.

The internationalization of accounting principles has suffered from a lack of synchronization between the issuance of standards at the national level in difference countries and the formulation of standards by the IASC. Based on the type of subjects covered, it seems that the IASC follows those undertaken by the Financial Accounting Standards Board (FASB), as can be inferred from the analysis of corresponding standards presented in the Appendix. In itself, the IASC's process for formulation of accounting principles is very similar to that followed by the FASB, its U.S. counterpart. Thus, for each standard, an exposure draft invites comments from interested parties. Further, an international standard in its definite form requires the approval of at least two-thirds of the members of the steering committee before its final release to the membership for implementation.[44]

The first standards from the IASC were basic and simple, and largely noncontroversial. Later they became more complex, with attempts to deal with problematic subjects in vogue in the leading accounting countries. Some researchers stated that the IASC is generally reluctant to issue a standard that conflicts with U.S. or U.K. principles (Ref.45, p.31). This implies that the task of standard setting cannot remain politically neutral. Both the IASC and the U.S. FASB have been categorized as political bodies whose standards are those appropriate for industrial countries with a large private sector and a well-developed capital market.[46,47] Most of the IAS issued probably have been made deliberately flexible so as not to upset any of the leading accounting countries. This produces more confusion in a profession already overburdened with an overload of standards and multiple accommodating options that hinder comparison and harmonization.

Shortcomings of Past Research

Smith and Shalchi[48] have signalled a lack of rigorous methodology and analysis in international accounting research. Many of the international accounting papers are descriptive and show an excessive concern with one aspect of the problem, namely, the harmonization of accounting principles. The research undertaken in this area is generally not supported by theory or paradigms but depends rather on subjective opinions. The studies have been of the fact-finding, data-collection type, and the results have not been sufficient to conclude with confidence whether recommendations or statements made by the researchers constitute the "best" alternative. It is still not possible to determine whether current harmonization attempts such as those of the IASC, lead to better investment decisions or whether a uniform accounting system, such as that of France, facilitates national economic planning and true harmonization.

Much of the literature on international accounting has concentrated on describing the methods used in a particular country or comparing them with those used elsewhere. Another popular topic, the classification of countries into groups according to their accounting practices or economic features, provides logical comparisons but has not produced normative research (Refs.22;49;50, pp.15–19). Even the more scientific approaches of discriminant and factor analyses for classification of countries have been criticized for using a secondary, inefficient empirical base.[51] In any event, the classification of accounting practices using sophisticated techniques has accentuated the reasons for international differences in accounting and has challenged the rationale for harmonization.[52]

Toward a Research Agenda for the Future

No apparent agreement exists on the objectives of the international standards-setting process, and serious research on this subject has good potential. Worldwide, at least 20 national standard-setting organizations or boards exist, with very little interaction and synchronization among them.[53] The area of standards harmonization demands better answers on its validity and future direction. A cost–benefit assessment of the international standards process could produce interesting research results. Also, although some research of the descriptive–comparative type[54] has been conducted, the subset of international auditing standards and practices holds promising research potential.

The level of financial reporting reached in a particular environment depends on two main forces, namely, the needs of the users and the interest of corporations in supplying the information that is demanded. At the international level, the information needs of users in different environments is yet to be defined, thus opening an area for potentially interesting research. The information needs of users as distinct from shareholders and lenders, and the impact of these needs on the nature of accounting standards constitute another area for research.

The process of harmonization could operate at lower levels of aggregation, apart from the attempts at global standardization that have been proven far from successful. As a practical solution, the classification of countries could be used to create standard-setting organizations for those regions of the world identified as homogeneous. This process could function with direct participation of the countries involved. At some point, some basic, but, it is hoped, useful, standards could be formulated at higher levels of national aggregates. Gray et al.[1] advanced this idea of segmenting the area where international standards of accounting should be applied. They discussed the use of standards by only multinational corporations as a desirable alternative to the IASC's approach.[55] To date, the IASC's standards have been destined for application to all companies without distinguishing those that are uninational from those multinational firms – an essential distinction. Research endeavors which deal with these alternatives could produce interesting findings.

In the area of international accounting, new approaches should be introduced, borrowing from other disciplines such as statistics or behavioral sciences, as has already happened in other fields of accounting research. Attention should be turned also to issues of management accounting, particularly because in many countries the same individuals own and manage businesses. In Third World countries disclosure of accounting information for outsiders, on which the traditional accounting model has been based, is not common because there are essentially no capital markets.[56]

For empirical research, opportunities are plentiful in international accounting. So far, for instance, no research has asked U.S. investors who have passive investments in foreign companies what type of information would be useful for their decisions. The same kind of questions can be asked of foreign investors in U.S. companies. Determining a risk–return paradigm for such decision-makers is a subject worth investigation. Comparing their decision models with a standard used by a U.S. domestic investor could give support for more or less financial reporting uniformity on a world-wide or regional basis.

If a need for harmonization in international accounting practices were perceived, and assuming that harmonization efforts by the different organizations are not successful, other options could be identified through direct investigation. If the need for re-expression or adjustments of financial data to fit the particular needs of some decision-makers is essential, empirical analysis would help to determine whether it is worth producing. Perhaps the services of financial analysts or public accounting firms, either foreign- or U.S.-based, are already filling the gap.

If the harmonization of international accounting practices and standards is proven to be theoretically unsustainable, consideration of the need for and availability of other types of business information is in order. The traditional accounting information model should then be set aside and instead other indices should be built on market, management, or risk considerations more susceptible to measurement and international comparisons.

The areas for research mentioned here must be addressed through rigorous research techniques, if for no other reason than to provide evidence to critics of international accounting that this area has achieved the mature status it deserves.

Summary

More than a decade of efforts by an array of organizations in the development of international accounting standards has not produced the world-wide harmonization of accounting and reporting practices that was intended. As proven many times, the financial reporting process must attend to domestic requirements of information, which derive from the specific economic, legal, and cultural circumstances encountered in each geographical location. Often the standard-setting apparatus within specific countries lacks sufficient consensus and support from the professional groups involved in standards implementation. This is understandably so because the process is commonly characterized as a political one, with the interested parties vying for a particular course of action concomitant with their interest. Normally, the local accounting professional associations are in charge of issuing accounting principles "generally acceptable" among their membership.

The most prominent of the accounting standard-setting bodies at the international level, the IASC, follows the structural pattern of the local accounting organizations. Composed of the professional accounting associations from 74 countries, it suffers from the same defects that have plagued the determination of accounting principles at the local level. In its attempts to be politically acceptable, the IASC has followed the practice of endorsing accounting principles applied in the leading accounting countries, mainly the United States. Flexibility has also been permitted in the accounting pronouncements to accommodate divergent practices in different nations or not to upset accounting as practiced in the leading influential economies. This approach produces a result that can hardly claim to advance "harmonization". Recent attempts by the IASC[6] to reduce the free choices allowed in the current international standards could provoke further reluctance of companies to comply. The distinction of preferred and allowed methods introduced in the proposed amendments[6] would burden those companies that choose the allowed options. In these cases, the reporting company would have to reconcile its financial reported data not only against the national accounting requirements, but also against those prescribed in the "preferred" method.

It is time to question through serious research the value of the harmonization of international accounting standards. Measuring the real benefits and costs of harmonization could provide clues to support or challenge the existence of institutions such as the IASC. Even though these organizations have issued general standards, they have failed to ensure observance and disclosures even among their member countries. Part of the reason might be that the peculiar economic and cultural characteristics of each country defy any attempt for a global harmonization of accounting principles. Essentially, it is not theoretically acceptable to envision a set of accounting standards without previously defining a fundamental core of accounting theory with basic postulates. The IASC has only recently amended this mistake through the issuance of a theoretical accounting framework.[9] Whether this is the basic accounting theory acceptable on a world-wide basis remains questionable. Assuming that these basic postulates are proven operational in different geographical settings, the review and implementation of international accounting standards might have better chances of success.

Finally, perhaps a more realistic option is to seek regional harmonization. This could develop from the classification of countries into homogeneous economic or cultural regions where common accounting standards have a better chance of being observed. Perhaps institutions such as the IASC should be only guiding mechanisms or clearing houses of the accounting principles, measurement, and disclosures as applied in different parts of the world.

Appendix. Accounting Standards Issued by IASC

IAS	Subject area and content	Issue date	U.S. GAAP	Subject area and content	Issue date
1	Disclosure of Accounting Policies. Three fundamental assumptions and three criteria given for selection and application of accounting policies. Disclosure of all policies required.	January 1975	APB Opinion 22	Disclosure of Accounting Policies. Requires disclosure of accounting policies selected among permitted alternatives.	April 1972
2	Valuation and Presentation of Inventories in the Context of the Historical Cost System. Inventories to be valued at lower of cost or net realizable value. Several methods permitted to report cost, including LIFO base stock and standard costing.	October 1975	ARB 43 (Chapter 4)	Inventory Pricing. Inventory Valuation at cost or lower-of-cost-of-market. Cost methods are FIFO, Average or FIFO.	June 1953
3	Consolidated Financial Statements. Defines relationship between investor and investee and degree of control for application of consolidation or equity methods. Cost method applied when no significant influence exercised by investor.	June 1976	ARB 51, and APB Opinion 18	Consolidation of Foreign Operations; and The Equity Method of Accounting for Investments in Common Stock. Provide criteria to apply consolidation, cost or equity methods to report investments in other entities.	August 1959 and March 1971 respectively
4	Depreciation Accounting. Discusses concept of depreciation and type of assets subject to depreciation accounting. Disclosures required include methods of depreciation, and useful lives of assets or depreciation rates used.	October 1976	ARB 43 (Chapter 9c) and APB Opinion 12	Depreciation Concepts, Methods and Disclosures.	June 1953 and December 1967 respectively
5	Information to be Disclosed in Financial Staements. Identifies the balance sheet, income statement, notes and other statements and explanatory material as part of the financial statements. Lists specific items and groups of accounts for presentation in the statements.	October 1976	ARB 43 (Chapters 2 to 9)	Discusses the main elements comprising a set of comparative financial statements and the applicable methods to recognize, report and classify them.	June 1953

IAS	Subject area and content	Issue date	U.S. GAAP	Subject area and content	Issue date
7	Statement of Changes in Financial Position. Considers the statement of changes in financial position as integral part of financial statements. Funds provided from or used in the operation should be disclosed separately. Funds broadly defined to be cash, cash and cash equivalents, or working capital.	October 1977	APB Opinion 19	Reporting Changes in Financial Position. Concept of Funds to mean working capital or cash. Funds from or used for operations to be disclosed separately from other sources and uses.	March 1971
8	Unusual and Prior Period Items and Changes in Accounting Principles. Gains/losses from unusual transactions or events should be separately disclosed within the income statement. Prior period adjustments reported either in retained earnings or in current income. Effect of changes in accounting estimates can be accounted in the current or in both current and future periods.	February 1978	APB Opinion 9 and SFAS 16	Treatment of Extraordinary Items and Prior Period Adjustments. Accounting treatment and disclosures for prior period adjustments, changes in accounting principles, and effects of changes in accounting estimates.	March 1971 and June 1977 respectively
9	Accounting for Research and Development Activities. Lists typical items included in research and development costs. These costs are charged as expenses in the period when they are incurred. Development costs may be deferred to future periods if certain criteria for ensuring future benefits are satisfied.	July 1978	SFAS 2	Accounting For Research and Development Costs. Defines activities that constitute research and development and the cost elements associated with them. All research and development costs should be charged to expenses when incurred.	October 1974
10	Contingencies and Events Occurring After the Balance Sheet Date. Dictates accrual of contingency losses if contingent future event is probable, and if a reasonable estimate of the loss can be made. Contingency gains are not to be accrued. After balance sheet events require adjustment of the balance sheet if related to conditions	October 1978	SFAS 5	Accounting for Contingencies. Establishes criteria to help define if a loss contingency exists and if actual and/or disclosure in the financial statements should proceed.	July 1975

IAS	Subject area and content	Issue date	U.S. GAAP	Subject area and content	Issue date
11	Accounting for Construction Contracts. Permits the recognition of income through a percentage of completion or a completed contract method, establishing the conditions under which one or the other method applies.	March 1979	ARB 45	Long-Term Construction-Type Contracts. Income from construction contracts recognized under a percentage of completion or a completed contract approach, depending on the conditions of the contractual operation.	October 1955
12	Accounting for Taxes on Income. Prescribes tax expense which should be recorded according to tax effect accounting, using the deferral or the liability method. Effect of timing differences to be included in deferred assets or liabilities, unless no reversal is foreseeable in at least 3 years ahead.	July 1979	APB Opinion 11	Accounting for Income Taxes. Income tax expense calculated on reportable pre-tax accounting income. Resulting timing differences are included in deferred taxes receivable or payable. Includes accounting for loss carry-back and carry-forward.	December 1967
13	Presentation of Current Assets and Current Liabilities. Decision to present the classification of current/non-current assets and liabilities in the financial statements is left to the enterprise. Typical items to include among the current assets/liabilities group are listed.	November 1979	ARB 43 (Chapter 3)	Current Assets and Current Liabilities. Criteria to define the current/non-current attributes of an asset or liability. Corresponding disclosures.	June 1953
14	Reporting Financial Information by Segment. Disclosure of material line-of-business and geographical segments for firms whose securities are publicly traded. For each reportable industry or geographical segment, sales, profit, assets and inter-company pricing should be disclosed. Materiality of a segment to trigger its disclosure is set at 10% of consolidated total sales, profits, or assets.	August 1981	SFAS 14	Financial Reporting for Segments of a Business Enterprise. Requires disaggregated information by line-of-business or geographical units for segments of a firm representing 10% or more of the company's consolidated sales, profits, or assets. The existence of major customers, representing 10% or more of total sales, should also be reported.	December 1976

IAS	Subject area and content	Issue date	U.S. GAAP	Subject area and content	Issue date
15	Information Reflecting the Effects of Changing Prices. Superseded IAS 6. Applies to businesses whose levels of revenues, assets, profits or employment are significant in their environment. Information adjusted for price changes can be prepared though price indices or current cost methods. Disclosures are in the form of supplementary data, unless the firm routinely presents that information in the primary financial statements.	November 1981	SFAS 33[a]	Financial Reporting and Changing Prices. Applies to public enterprises of a given material size as defined in the standard. Supplementary information to reflect effect of changing prices on selected items, plus the current cost of inventories, property plant and equipment.	September 1979
16	Accounting for Property, Plant and Equipment. Carrying value of an asset in property, plant and equipment is historical cost or revaluation amount. General guidelines for acquisition of assets through asset exchanges are established. Revaluation of assets is permitted, provided the difference between revalued amount and cost is directly reported in shareholders' equity.	March 1982	FASB Concept 6	Elements of Financial Statements. Replaced FASB concepts statement No. 3, thus extending the theoretical concepts supporting valuation and reporting of the items in the financial statements.	December 1985
17	Accounting for Leases. Provides general guidelines for the accounting and disclosure of operating and finance leases for both the lessee and the lessor. Finance leases are classified into sale-type or strict financing ones. Sale and lease-back option is also covered.	September 1982	SFAS 13	Accounting for Leases. Leases classified into operating and capital types, according to criteria that focus on the substance of the transaction. Capital leases can be sales- and financing-types. Disclosures for the lessee and the lessor are discussed. Accounting treatment for sale–leasebacks is included.	November 1976

[a] SFAS 82 eliminated reporting of price-level adjusted data when current cost information was supplied. Further, the FASB made only voluntary the reporting of SFAS 33 disclosures.

IAS	Subject area and content	Issue date	U.S. GAAP	Subject area and content	Issue date
18	Revenue Recognition. Establishes criteria to recognize revenue from sales or service transactions. Recognition of service revenue is permitted under the completed contract or percentage of completion methods.	December 1982	ARB 43 (Chapter 1A and 8)	Recognition of revenue and gains as part of realization and matching concepts.	June 1953
19	Accounting for Retirement Benefits in the Financial Statement of Employers. Definitions of current and past service costs, vested benefits, funding, actuarial methods, accrued and projected benefits, etc., are introduced. Gives guidelines for the accounting and reporting of a defined benefit plan in the financial statements of the employer.	January 1983	SFAS 36	Disclosure of Pension Information. Requires revised disclosures of defined benefit pension plans in the financial statements of the employer. The disclosures include the present value of the accumulated plan benefits, and the funded assets for the pension plan obligations.	May 1980
20	Accounting for Government Grants and Disclosure of Government Assistance. Government grants are to be included in the income statement. Recognition is during the period(s) when the corresponding costs intended to be compensated with the grant are incurred.	April 1983		No corresponding standard is available.	
21	Accounting for the Effects of Changes in Foreign Exchange Rates. Provides guidelines to account and report transactions involving foreign operations. Exchange differences from intercompany monetary items are to be reflected in shareholders' interests. Exchange rate differences from long-term monetary items can be deferred, or recognized in current income.	July 1983	SFAS 52	Foreign Currency Translation. Superseded SFAS No. 8. Introduces the concept of "Functional Currency" to translate foreign operations to a reporting currency, using current exchange rates. Translation adjustments are accrued in a separate component of consolidated shareholders' equity. Special treatment is applied to translating foreign operations from a subsidiary operating in highly inflationary environments.	December 1981

IAS	Subject area and content	Issue date	U.S. GAAP	Subject area and content	Issue date
22	Accounting for Business Combinations. The general treatment for a business combination is to account it under the purchase method. If combination is deemed a uniting of interests, the pooling of interests method may be applied. Differences between the cost of acquisition and fair values of the assets acquired can be recognized in income or adjusted to shareholders' equity. Positive goodwill arising in the acquisition should be recognized as a deferred asset.	November 1983	APB Opinion 16	Business Combinations. Considers the purchase method and the pooling of interest method as acceptable approaches to account for business combinations. The combination must meet specified criteria to be treated as a pooling of interest case. For acquisitions considered purchases, if cost of acquisition exceeds the fair value of net assets bought an amortizable goodwill is recorded.	August 1970
23	Capitalization of Borrowing Costs. Borrowing costs should be capitalized as part of the cost of an asset up to the point in time when the asset is ready for its intended use or sale.	March 1984	SFAS 34	Capitalization of Interest Cost. Standards for capitalizing the interest cost as part of the acquisition cost of an asset. Interest is for the period required to complete the asset. Interest cannot be capitalized for inventories that are routinely manufactured.	October 1979
24	Related Party Disclosures. After identifying who constitutes related parties, full disclosure is called for transactions involving the reporting enterprise and the related party.	July 1984	SFAS 5	Related Party Disclosures. Establishes the required content for disclosures of material related party transactions. Excludes compensation arrangements, expense allowance and similar items from the obligation to disclose.	March 1982
25	Accounting for Investments. Valuation and disclosure rules are stated for both short-term and long-term investments in securities. Accounting is for investments in securities different from those reportable under consolidation or equity methods. Long-term investments in tangible assets are also covered.	April 1986	SFAS 12	Accounting for Certain Marketable Securities. Provides standards for accounting and reporting investments in marketable equity securities, including the resulting gain or loss from their valuation and disposal.	December 1975

IAS	Subject area and content	Issue date	U.S. GAAP	Subject area and content	Issue date
26	Accounting and Reporting by Retirement Benefit Plans. Addresses the disclosures needed in reports by defined retirement benefit plans. The report should disclose net assets available for benefits, present value of the promised retirement benefits, and the resulting excess or deficit between those two items.	January 1987	SFAS 35	Accounting and Reporting by Defined Benefit Pension Plans. Establishes guidelines for supplying information relevant to the status of the plan. Disclosures must include net assets available in the plan, present value of accumulated benefits, and changes affecting the actuarial computations of the accumulated plan benefits.	March 1980
27	Consolidated Financial Statements and Accounting for Investments in Subsidiaries. Relates to the preparation and reporting of consolidated financial statements for parent and subsidiaries. Control needed to proceed with consolidation is presumed if the investor owns more than 50% of the voting shares of the investee.	April 1989	SFAS 94	Consolidation of All Majority-Owned Subsidiaries Requires consolidation of all majority-owned subsidiaries on substantially all cases, except where control is likely to be temporary or when special circumstances preclude control by the majority owner.	
28	Accounting for Investments in Associates. Modifies IAS 3 in relation to investments in associated companies under the equity method. It is assumed than an investor holding 20% or more of the voting stock of the investee has "significant influence" over the investee's policies and decisions to require reporting under the equity method.	April 1989	APB Opinion 18	The Equity Method of Accounting for Investments in Common Stock. Provides guidelines in using the equity method for investments where the investor, not having majority control, exercises significant influence on the investee. Significant influence is presumed if investor holds 20% or more of the investee's voting stock.	March 1979
29	Financial Reporting in Hyperinflationary Economies. Requires enterprises reporting in the currency of a hyperinflationary economy to restate the primary financial statement to account for changes in the domestic price levels. Gains or losses resulting from the adjusted net monetary position should be included in net income.	April 1989		No corresponding standard is available (for a related item, see IAS 15 and the corresponding footnote to SFAS 33).	

Acknowledgements: Financial support for this study from Peat, Marwick and Main is acknowledged and appreciated.

References

1. S.J. Gray, J.C. Shaw and L.B. McSweeney. "Accounting Standards and Multinational Corporations," in F.D.S. Choi and G.G. Mueller (eds.), *Frontiers in International Accounting. An Anthology* (Ann Arbor, MI: UMI Research Press, 1985), 136–156.
2. K.S. Most. *International Conflict of Accounting Standards, A research Report* (Vancouver: The Canadian Certified General Accountants' Research Foundation, 1984).
3. A similar list and discussion of the actors involved in this process was presented by Belkhaoui (Ref.4, pp. 57–84).
4. A. Belkhaoui. *International Accounting. Issues and Solutions* (Westport, CT: Quorum Books, 1985). 57–84.
5. The Appendix presents a list of the accounting standards issued by the IASC, with a brief description of their content and a cross-correspondence to U.S. accounting principles which address similar subject matters. In addition to the standards issued, there are currently three IASC Exposure Drafts (E) outstanding, namely, E32: Comparability of Financial Statements;[6] E33: Accounting for Taxes on Income; and E34: Disclosures in the Financial Statements of Banks and similar Financial Institutions.
6. IASC. E32 Exposure Draft. *Comparability of Financial Statements* (New York: AICPA, Product G00392, 1989).
7. D.T. Hayes. "The International Accounting Standards Committee: Recent Development and Current Problems," *International Journal of Accounting* (Fall 1980), 1–10.
8. The recent accounting framework prepared by the IASC[9] is expected to provide the basis needed to develop international accounting standards in the future.
9. IASC. *Framework for the Preparation and Presentation of Financial Statements* (London: IASC, 1989)
10. A survey conducted by the UN (Ref.11, pp. 21–64) on 42 of its affiliated members exemplified the diversity of accounting principles followed by the countries surveyed.
11. UN. *International Accounting and Reporting Issues: 1984 Review* (New York: United Nations, 1985).
12. CCA (The Canadian Chartered Accountant). "The Need for International Standards in Accounting," in K.B. Berg, G.G. Mueller and L.M. Walker (eds.). *Readings in International Accounting* (Boston: Houghton Mifflin, 1969), 189–191.
13. A.K. Mason. *International Financial Reporting Standards: Problems and Prospects* (Lancaster, U.K. University of Lancaster, 1977).
14. J.C. Burton (ed.). *The International World of Accounting, Challenges and Opportunities, 1980 Proceedings of the Arthur Young Professors' Roundtable* (Reston, VA: Arthur Young, 1981).
15. S.J. Gray. "The Impact of International Accounting Differences from a Security-Analysis Perspective: Some European Evidence," *Journal of Accounting Research* (Spring 1980), 64–76.
16. B.R. Doyle and S.D. Spencer. "International Accounting Standards. Why They Merit Support?" *Management Accounting* (October 1986), 28–29.
17. G.M. Scott. "Topical Priorities in Multinational Accounting," in F.D.S. Choi (ed.), *Multinational Accounting. A Research Framework for the Eighties* (Ann Arbor, MI: UMI Research Press, 1981), 5–19.
18. G.M. Scott and P. Troberg. *Eighty-eight International Accounting Problems in Rank Order of Importance – A DELPHI Evaluation* (Sarasota, FL: American Accounting Association, 1980).
19. C.W. Nobes and R.H. Parker. *Comparative International Accounting* (Oxford: Philip Allan, 1981).
20. J.M. Samuels and A.G. Piper. *International Accounting: A Survey* (New York: St. Martin Press, 1985).
21. F.D.S. Choi and G.G. Mueller. *An Introduction to Multinational Accounting* (Englewood Cliffs, NJ: Prentice-Hall, 1978).
22. W.G. Frank. "An Empirical Analysis of International Accounting Principles," *Journal of Accounting Research* (Autumn 1979), 593–605.
23. The variety of social, economic, and legal circumstances as causal factors for differences in financial statements across countries has been acknowledged by the IASC (Ref.9, Preface).

24. Although the operating structure of the IASC calls for a policy preferably to include a minimum of three developing countries in its 13-member Board (see IASC Objectives and Procedures in Ref.25, p.11 053) only one developing country (Jordan) is currently included. In addition, only the U.S. standard-setting type of institution (The Financial Accounting Standards Board) is a representative in the IASC's 10-member Consultative Group (Ref.26, Appendix 2).
25. AICPA (American Institute of Certified Public Accountants). International Accounting and Auditing Standards (New York: AICPA, 1988).
26. IASC.; *Survey of the Use and Application of International Accounting Standards* (London: IASC, 1988).
27. K.S. Most. "How Bad are European Accounts?" in K.B. Berg, G.G. Mueller and L.M. Walker (eds.) *Readings in International Accounting* (Boston: Houghton Mifflin, 1969) 208–222.
28. F.D.S. Choi and V.B. Bavishi. "Financial Accounting Standards: A Multinational Synthesis and Policy Framework," *International Journal of Accounting* (Fall 1982), 159–183.
29. G.K. Meek. "U.S. Securities Market Responses to Alternate Earnings Disclosures of Non-U.S. Multinational Corporations," *The Accounting Review* (April 1983), 394–402.
30. UN (United Nations Centre on Transnational Corporations). Towards International Standardization of Corporate Accounting and Reporting (New York: United Nations, 1982).
31. UN. *International Accounting and Reporting Issues: 1985 Review* (New York: United Nations, (1985).
32. Rueschhoff[33] analyzed similarities and differences between the IASC's and the EEC's pronouncements as well as between the IFAC's and the UEC's statements and guidelines.
33. N.G. Rueschhoff. "European Accounting and Auditing Standards: A Comparative Study with International Standards and Guidelines," in V.K. Zimmerman (ed.), *The Recent Accounting and Economic developments in Western Europe* (Champaign, IL: University of Illinois, Center for International Education and Research in Accounting, 1985), 91–114.
34. W. Hall, "Establishing Standards for International Financial Reporting," in J.J. Davis (ed.), *1977 Accounting Research Convocation on the Subject of Patterns of Change* (Tuscaloosa: University of Alabama Press, 1977), 95–106.
35. As another example, in many countries – particularly those in Latin America – the severance payment to an employee upon dismissal or retirement is a totally different construct from pension benefits as thought of in the United States.
36. The trend is apparently continuing, because two of the three IASC's exposure drafts outstanding and one under study – on financial instruments – have also been in the agenda of the FASB.
37. N.G. Rueschhoff. "The Intrinsic Uniformity of International Accounting Standards," in K.S. Most (ed.), *Advances in International Accounting*, Vol. 1 (Greenwich, CT: JAI Press, 1987), 23–38.
38. As an example, IAS 9 on Accounting for Research and Development allows development costs to be either expensed (as required in U.S. GAAP) or deferred if certain conditions are met (as dictated in the U.K. standards).
39. For the countries listed, conformity in all material respects was reported for 17 or more of the 25 standards issued. On the other hand, the West German and Swiss accounting requirement did not conform to those advanced by the IASC in 18 and 15, respectively, of the 25 standards checked.
40. The recent IASC (Ref.27) survey states that in 1987, from a sample of 129 companies listed in the Toronto Stock Exchange, 102 disclosed such compliance.
41. In most cases, referral to IAS consisted in stating that the financial statements have been prepared according to the generally accepted accounting principles of the particular country, and that such principles were in conformity, in all material respects, with IAS.
42. IASC (International Accounting Standards Committee). International Accounting Standard. IAS 1. Disclosure of Accounting Policies (London: IASC, 1975).
43. The assumption of consistency is absent in the new framework developed by the IASC. The "considerations" have been broadened and renamed "qualitative characteristics of accounting information" (see Ref.9).
44. Details of this process are described in the IASC's Objectives and Procedures (Ref.24, pp. 11 051–11 057)
45. H. Benson, "Establishing Standards Through a Voluntary Professional Process Across National Boundaries," in J.C. Burton (ed.). *The International World of Accounting, Challenges and Opportunities, 1980 Proceedings of the Arthur Young Professors' Roundtable* (Reston, VA: Arthur Young, 1981), 27–48.
46. J.M. Samuels and J.C. Oliga. "Accounting Standards in Developing Countries," *International Journal of Accounting* (Fall 1982), 69–88.
47. R.G. May and G. Sundem. "Research for Accounting Policy: An Overview," *Accounting Review* (October 1976), 747–763.

48. C.H. Smith and H. Shalchi. "Multinational Accounting: Some Methodological Considerations," in F.D.S. Choi (ed.), *Multinational Accounting: A Research Framework for the Eighties* (Ann Arbor, MI: UMI Research Press, 1981), 21–37.
49. R.C. Da Costa, J.C. Burgeois and W.M. Lawson. "A Classification of International Financial Accounting Practices." *International Journal of Accounting* (Spring 1978), 73–85.
50. G.G. Mueller, H. Gernon and G. Meek. *Accounting: An International Perspective* (Homewood, IL: Irwin, 1987).
51. C.W. Nobes. "An Empirical Analysis of International Accounting Principles: A Comment," *Journal of Accounting Research* (Spring 1981), 268–270.
52. C.W. Nobes. *International Classification of Financial Reporting* (London: Croom Helm, 1984).
53. L.A. Daley and G.G. Mueller. "Accounting in the Arena of World Politics: Crosscurrents of International Standard-setting Activities," in F.D.S. Choi and G.G. Mueller (eds.), *Frontiers of International Accounting, An Anthology* (Ann Arbor, MI: UMI Research Press, 1985), 157–170.
54. B.E. Needles, Jr. *Comparative International Auditing Standards* (Sarasota, FL: American Accounting Association, 1985).
55. The proposal that harmonization should apply only to companies with international dimension has also been suggested by Nobes (Ref.52, p. 96).
56. Although academicians and practitioners have discussed topics of managerial accounting, these have been approached from the standpoint of the multinational corporation's interest only.[57]
57. V.K. Zimmerman (ed.). *Managerial Accounting: An Analysis of Current International Applications* (Champaign, IL: University of Illinois Center for International Education and Research in Accounting, 1984).

Correspondence and offprint requests to: Juan M. Rivera, Associate Professor of Accounting, University of Notre Dame, Notre Dame, Indiana 46556, USA.

[14]

Survival Strategies of a Global Organization: The Case of the International Accounting Standards Committee

R. S. Olusegun Wallace

R. S. Olusegun Wallace is Lecturer in Accountancy at the University of Exeter, and IASC's International Accounting Research Fellow.

This paper is based on the premise that the IASC is a legitimate organization because it continues to be acceptable to its constituencies, in spite of the challenges posed to its credibility by the inevitable crises that surround the pursuit of its goals. In fact, legitimacy implies acceptability in the face of uncertainty; and that, in turn, as Johnson and Solomons[1] argue, implies organizational durability. Whether they focus on the IASC's explicit objectives or its standards, current explanations treat the IASC too superficially and posit a relationship between it and its social environment that seems inflexible. Given the IASC's survival, this paper abandons the assumption that the worst will happen and that unintended consequences will invariably be negative. It separates out the IASC from its standards or actual activity so as to explain why and how it continues to survive.

The paper is in three parts. The first part introduces the topic in the context of a contingency theory which provides the stimulus for the study of the survival strategies of the IASC. The second part presents the survival strategies concerned with the management of technical core resources and the procedural process. The third part explains how the IASC manages its external environment.

INTRODUCTION

Researchers studying the IASC have emphasized its standards and treated these standards as choices made by a single actor, and have likened them to those of an individual human being. The authors state propositions about the explicit goals of the IASC which are then presumed to be the only principles for evolving accounting standards. An alternative approach is to focus upon the IASC itself rather than upon its standards, in order to utilize its peculiar characteristics to examine the rationality of its goals, options and consequences. This will enable a researcher to consider either (a) the propensities or institutional traits of the IASC, (b) the values shared by its membership or (c) the special principles of action such as a change in its goals or a narrowing of its alternatives or consequences. This focus could concentrate on the IASC's strategic objectives including its own perpetuation rather than its explicit goals. Yet another approach is the political; the recognition of the existence of several actors within the IASC's central mechanism. The last two approaches could help to explain how the IASC has adapted to, created or shaped its own environment. As Solomons[2] has pointed out:

The author acknowledges the helpful comments on earlier drafts of this paper from Professor R. H. Parker and Dr. Terry E. Cooke of the University of Exeter, Professor C. W. Nobes of the University of Reading, Professor Helen Gernon of the University of Oregon and David Cairns, Secretary-General of the IASC. The author served as Technical Adviser to the Nigerian members on the IASC's Board from 1983 to 1988. The personal views expressed in this paper are neither those of the Nigerian delegation nor of the IASC.

[1]Steven B. Johnson and David Solomons, "Institutional Legitimacy and the FASB," *Journal of Accounting and Public Policy* (Vol. 3, No. 3, Fall 1984), p. 167.

[2]David Solomons, *Making Accounting Policy: The Quest for Credility in Financial Reporting* (New York, Oxford University Press, 1986), pp. 59-60.

International accounting standards [IASs] are not exclusively the concern of any one organization, for governments have not been willing to leave this matter entirely to private initiative. The IASC is unquestionably the voice of the private sector in this field, but it does not have the field to itself. The OECD, made up of highly developed countries, has prepared a Code of Conduct for Multinational Enterprises, which includes, among other things, prescriptions for financial disclosure by multinationals. At the urging of the developing nations, the United Nations has formed an Intergovernmental Group on International Accounting Standards and Reporting.

This quotation emphasizes the market for the supply of global accounting standards in which the IASC is a dominant (not the sole) supplier. To understand such a dominant role, one needs to consider the factors which affect the structure and effectiveness of the IASC. Such an understanding can be informed by a contingency theory of the existence (and survival) of the IASC.

Contingency Theory

Previous studies of the IASC have conceptualized the contingency approach very restrictively. Choi and Mueller[3] use varying cross-national differences in environmental characteristics of countries to argue that the IASC cannot be a sustainable entity.[4] Aitken and Islam[5] disagree with this contention. They argue that the transactions and events which accountants seek to measure, value and report are similar across countries and that the IASC's task is to harmonize the different measurement, valuation and reporting practices.

Similarity of business transactions and events occurring in different countries and different environmental factors are two of the many variables capable of informing an understanding of the IASC's activities and survival. An enlarged perspective on contingency theory, with the inclusion of contextual, environmental and socio-cultural variables can provide a comprehensive understanding of the determinants of the organizational patterns and effectiveness of IASC. An integrative model [Figure 1] provides a means of conceptualizing these variables by visualizing three successive environments: the IASC's internal environment (the core); its tasks and constituencies (the inner boundary) and the varying international environment (the outer boundary). This model stresses the "patterns of relationships" rather than causal linkages. It is from these patterns that one can perceive the intentions of the IASC and its membership.

The internal environment is shown in the center with the Secretary-General and Chairman to the Board determining, in consultation with the Organization and Planning Committee [OPC], the patterns and survival strategies of the IASC. Also determining the scope of operations of the IASC is the size of its staff and budget. Shown on either side to represent what keeps the IASC in existence are business transactions and events, and accounting policy options. Accounting standards are developed, after due process, to resolve measurement, valuation and reporting problems arising from business transactions and events. The standards are the result of choices from among many accounting and disclosure options. Guiding all these operations is the primary goal of the IASC [harmonization] and the know-how of the Board's members.

Surrounding all these activities are the various groups of coalition. The members of International Federation of Accountants [IFAC] who are also members of the IASC are shown at the top. The national accounting standards setting bodies which determine the international recognition of the IASC are shown below. The various external constitu-

[3]F. D. S. Choi and G. G. Mueller, *International Accounting* (Englewood Cliffs, New Jersey: Prentice-Hall Inc., 1984).

[4]Other scholars have doubted the continued survival of the IASC. These include D. De Bruyne, "Global Standards: A Tower of Babel?", *Financial Executive* (February 1980) and C. W. Nobes, "Is the IASC Worthwhile?", *International Accounting Bulletin* (February 1986), p. 14.

[5]M. J. Aitken and M. A. Islam, "Dispelling Arguments Against International Accounting Standards," *The International Journal of Accounting Education and Research* (Vol. 19, No. 2, Spring 1984), pp. 35-46.

FIGURE 1

Environmental Factors Influencing IASC's Patterns and Survival

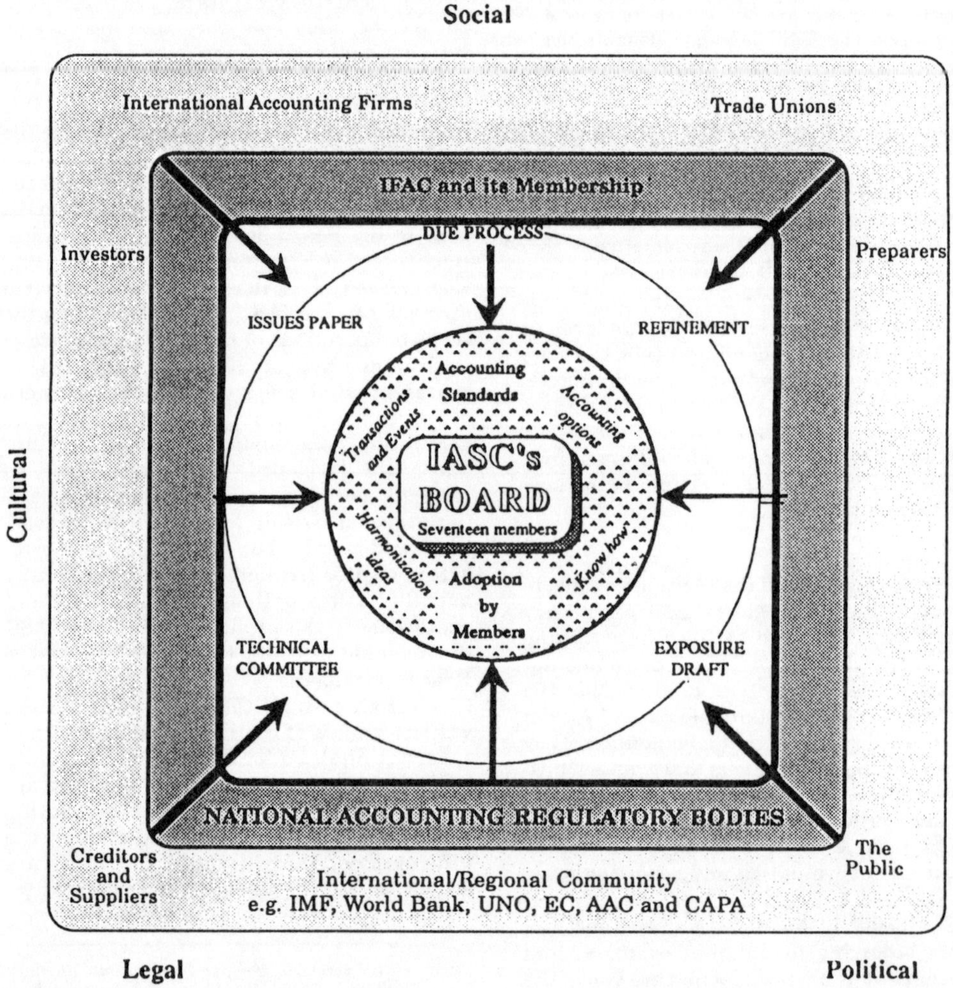

encies including investors, preparers, creditors/suppliers and other external parties are shown to form a ring around the entire core, in effect influencing or being influenced by every part of it. Finally, all these groups of interested parties are influenced by different (national) and sometimes common (international) social, cultural, legal, political and economic factors.

This contingency model equates social behavior with political and rational behavior. It posits the existence of a core structure within the IASC composed of some member-bodies (nominated to its Board) with regular, routine and easy access to the IASC's core activities. Member-bodies excluded from the core are denied the ready access and some strive to join the core to gain such privileges. The core is dominated by developed countries while the excluded group is populated by developing countries. However, the core is a conglomeration of independent bodies that promote and defend their own interests.

But many member-bodies share a sufficient level of individual needs (e.g., harmonization of accounting practices) and grievances (e.g., increasing power of transnational enterprises [TNEs]) to produce a common purpose. Their support of the IASC can be seen as a product of environmental forces, internal and external to the IASC. Internal forces include leadership qualities, level of available resources, and the small size and level of professional competence of the IASC's establishment. External forces include the level of the IASC's recognition, extent of external sympathizers [third party constituencies] and the professional capability, capacity and influence of each non-core member-body. The interplay of these various factors can be said to determine the development and behavior of the IASC.

SURVIVAL STRATEGIES: MANAGING CORE ACTIVITIES

It may be argued that the survival of IASC is a non-issue because the IASC has been functioning since 1973. Institutional survival is an elusive concept which needs to be bounded for a meaningful discourse. Survival, in the context of this paper, connotes the methods by which the IASC sustains itself, adapts to change and the demands of its internal and external environment. The requirements for IASC's survival are examined along the following lines: (a) the resources at its disposal; (b) the diversification of its tasks; (c) the goals it pursues and how such goals are sustained and renewed; (d) the legitimacy of its tasks and procedures and (e) the management of its external environment. Each of these requirements is discussed below and summarized in Figure 2, as the management of (a) technical core resources, (b) procedural process and (c) external environment.

Gradualism and discretion are the hallmarks of the IASC's survival in a potentially hostile environment. Abrupt pursuit of harmonization would attract resistance and place the IASC in jeopardy. But if it acts gradually and quietly, positive steps can be taken, while letting its constituencies build up their support, to help the process of harmonization along. This evolutionary process can be perceived in the way the IASC seeks the support of its member-bodies. It started off in 1973 by emphasizing and strengthening the independence of individual member-bodies. In the 1980s, it sought to strike a sensitive balance between its collective actions and the desires of individual members. This balancing act is now giving way to the need to strengthen the organs of collective responsibility; to let the IASC emerge as a rational actor, different from its individual members.

Technical Core Resources

The core activities of the IASC can be categorized for analytic convenience into two: the management of technical core resources like the organization of the IASC's office, staffing; and the management of the procedural process. The IASC operates on a meager budget[6] compared to any national regulatory body in the developed world. It has no more than three professionally qualified accountants (including the Secretary-General) on its staff at any time. Ninety percent of the IASC's annual budget is financed, on an equal basis, by its Board members and the rest by IFAC on behalf of its entire membership. No funding comes from its constituencies. As McCarthy and Zald[7] state, "the growth or main-

[6]Its annual revenue and capital expenditure has risen from £100,000 in 1973 to £400,000 in the 1989 budget. Its earnings from sales of standards and other publications are insignificant.

[7]J. D. McCarthy and M. N. Zald, *The Trend of Social Movements in America: Professionalization and Resource Mobilization* (Morristown, NJ: General Learning Corporation, 1973), p. 18, emphasis added.

tenance of organizations whose formal goals are aimed at helping one population but who *depend* on a different population for funding is ultimately more *dependent* on the latter than the former." This suggests that the IASC is more likely to conform to the wishes of the funding population [its Board members] than the wishes of the beneficiary population [TNEs, stock exchanges, national accounting regulatory bodies of the Third World]. Thus it can be argued that the IASC cannot be said to represent the views of the constituencies it is supposed to serve.

An underlying assumption of the small budget and administrative machinery is that the IASC can draw on the knowledge, perspectives, experience and resources of its many member-bodies especially those of its Board members. The raw materials for forging solutions to global accounting problems are neither concentrated in a single country nor a global accounting profession, but rather are widely dispersed among the various countries' accounting professions and other global non-accounting professional bodies. For any given accounting problem there is a variety of classes of expertise. Every affected party is an expert on some aspect of the problem and its solution. But members do not and cannot contribute equally to the resolution of IASC's problems. For example, the extent of participation in IASC's technical committees, and "procedural due process" depends on the extent of standard-setting experience of a member country.[8] There are three different ways of classifying countries on the basis of capability to set standards:[9]

[8]A member country is one in which a member body of the IASC is located.

[9]Examples of countries suggested are taken from the IASC's *Survey of the Use and Application of International Accounting Standards, 1988* (London: IASC).

FIGURE 2

IASC'S Survival Strategies

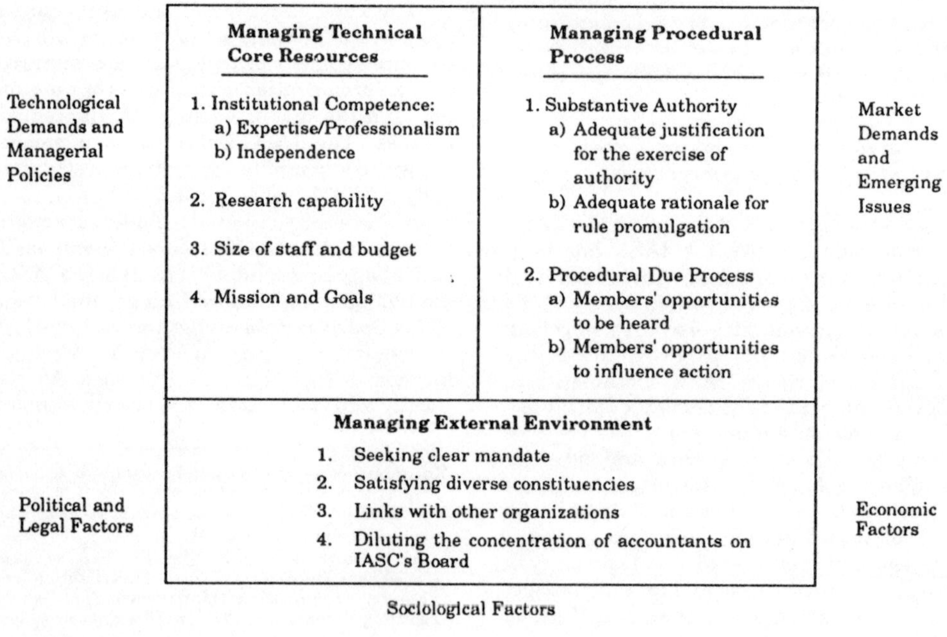

1. those that originate standards with little or no references to other countries. These are countries with developed standard-setting procedures [i.e., the standard setters]; for example, Australia, Canada, the UK, the Netherlands, and the US. The first three countries, however, make reference to the US and to each other.
2. those that take standards prepared in other countries or by other agencies outside their own countries, without ensuring that such standards are suitable for their environment because they lack the capability and capacity, that is, they do not possess the technical expertise, cannot afford the costs, are afraid of being exposed to *ex ante* complaints or do not want to be held responsible for the scandals which may arise from such disclosure rules *ex post*. Examples are Cyprus, Malawi, Pakistan, Trinidad, and Zimbabwe.
3. those that blend standards from outside sources into their internally generated standards; for example, Egypt, France, Fiji, Germany, India, Japan, Kenya, Nigeria and Singapore.

Many countries in category 1 have accounting professional bodies or regulators that are keenly interested in exporting their internally generated accounting standards to other countries. Although every country is free to "set" its own standards, only a few can originate their standards from scratch. This requires knowledge of available options, exposure to situations requiring accounting regulation (such as an active stock exchange) and adequate resources. While it might be argued that there is usually no need to travel through a well-trodden path in search of a similar solution to a similar problem, it is important to realize that such a journey may be worthwhile if the solution is to be relevant to its environment.

Essentially, if a country has greater resource endowments and capabilities, relatively superior experience in accounting practice and standard-setting process, a litigious citizenry (as in the U.S.), a knowledgeable and free financial press and many companies with foreign subsidiaries and branches, it is more likely that such a country would have more to offer to (than receive from) any institution concerned with international harmonization of financial disclosure practices. This may explain why some members are more capable than others of serving the IASC and why the IASC seeks to utilize the capabilities of these members. Table 1 provides information on the level of participation of member countries in the IASC's technical committees since its establishment.[10]

There are two methods for assessing the extent of the IASC's utilization of individual member's capabilities. The first is to measure the difference between the scope and contents of IASs and the average scope and contents of member countries' standards to reflect how effectively the IASC has benefitted from its members' capabilities in arriving at its output.[11] The second is to measure whether the IASC's output exceeds that of its best member country.[12] Both methods would focus on the synergistic effects of the interaction of the members of IASC. Synergy would exist if the

---

[10]There have been 46 technical steering committees between June 1973 and October 1989. These are made up of (a) nine ongoing (active) committees, three of which have issued Exposure Drafts 32, 33 and 34; (b) completed committees resulting in 29 IASs [two of which have been withdrawn—IASs 3 and 6]; (c) one on the completed conceptual framework; (d) one led to the issue of a discussion paper on accounting for banks; (e) three committees reviewed IASs 1, 3 and 6 and (f) three committees on assets, liabilities and objectives of financial statements dissolved when the committee on the conceptual framework was constituted.

[11]This method assumes that all members have developed the standards under investigation before the IASC issued its own which is not always the case. For three examples of IAS topics not covered by any extant accounting standards in the U.S. see C. W. Nobes "A Note on the Compliance by U.S. Corporations with IASC Standards," *British Accounting Review* (Vol. 22, No. 1, March 1990), pp. 41-49.

[12]This is based on the belief that two or more heads are better than one. However, compared to the U.S., which can, intuitively, be described as the "best" member of the IASC in the context of the number and quality of extant accounting standards developed by each member country, the IASC's standards are poorer "cousins."

TABLE 1

Participation in All 46 IASC's Technical Steering Committees 1973–1989+

Countries	Number of Committees		
Board Members	**Active**	**Concluded**	**Total**
Australia (1973)	2	8	10
Canada (1973)	3	10	13
Denmark (1988)	1	2	3
France (1973)	3	9	12
Germany (1973)	1	10	11
Italy (1983)	2	2	4
Japan (1973)	3	8	11
Jordan (1988)	1	–	1
Korea (1988)	–	–	–
Netherlands (1973)	4	9	13
South Africa (1978)	2	4	6
United Kingdom (1973)	5	10	15
USA (1973)	5	10	15
ICCFAA (1986)	1	1	2
Former Board Members			
Mexico (1973-87)	1	8	9
Nigeria (1978-87)	–	3	3
Taiwan (1984-87)	–	1	1
Non-Board Members			
Austria	–	1	1
Belgium	–	1	1
Brazil	1	2	3
Egypt	–	1	1
Greece	1	–	1
Hong Kong*	–	1	1
India	1	1	2
Indonesia	–	1	1
Israel	1	2	3
Lebanon	–	1	1
Malaysia	–	1	1
New Zealand	2	2	4
Norway	–	2	2
Pakistan	–	2	2
Philippines	1	1	2
Singapore*	–	1	1
Spain	–	1	1
Sri Lanka	–	1	1
Sweden	1	2	3
Venezuela*	–	1	1
Yugoslavia	–	1	1
Zimbabwe	–	1	1
Former Non-Board Member			
Argentina**	–	1	1

Non-Board members which have never participated in a Steering Committe

Bahamas	Ghana	Paraguay
Bahrain	Iceland	Portugal
Bangladesh	Iraq	Swaziland
Barbados	Jamaica	Switzerland*
Bolivia	Kenya	Syria
Botswana	Kuwait	Tanzania
Chile	Lesotho	Thailand
Colombia	Liberia	Trinidad & Tobago
Cyprus	Libya	Tunisia
Dominican Rep	Luxembourg	Turkey
Ecuador	Malawi	Uruguay
Fiji	Malta	Zambia
Finland*	Morocco	
	Panama*	

Participation by Board Members in Active Technical Steering Committees

Australia (2)	Fin. Instruments
	Joint Ventures
Canada (3)	Joint Ventures++
	Fin Instruments
	Improvements
Denmark (1)	Cash Flows
France (3)	Comparability of F.S.
	Review of IAS 12++
	Fin Instruments
Germany (1)	Banks' F.S.
Italy (2)	Fin. Instruments
	Intangibles
Japan (3)	Banks' F.S.
	Comparability of F. S.
	Fin Instruments
Jordan (1)	Improvements
Netherlands (4)	Review of IAS 15++
	Comparability of F.S.
	Fin. Instruments
	Improvements
South Africa (2)	Comparability of F.S.
	Cash Flows++
UK (5)	Banks' F.S.++
	Review of IAS 15
	Fin. Instruments
	Intangibles++
	Improvements
USA (5)	Banks' F.S.
	Comparability of F.S.++
	Fin. Instruments++
	Joint Ventures
	Improvements++
ICCFAA (1)'	Review of IAS 15

NOTES:

+ The author is grateful to David Cairns, Current Secretary-General of the IASC, for supplying this information, on request. This information is current to the end of October 1989 and excludes membership of the Task Force on the needs of developing countries.

++ Chairman of Technical Steering Committee.

* These non-Board members have, in the past, declined an invitation by the IASC to participate in a particular proposed technical Steering Committee.

** This non-Board member has served on an IASC technical Steering Committee but is no longer a member of IASC and IFAC.

( ) Date since joining the Board of IASC or period on the Board.

IASC's capabilities surpass those of its members. This is likely to arise when members effectively exchange, constructively criticize and build upon each other's ideas.

Degree of Professionalization

The Board of the IASC is a professional polity in the sense of achieving coordination essentially by calling upon the professional skills and experience of members acquired through education, training and exposure in their respective countries.[13] Most of the representatives of its members enter with professional qualifications and experience in accounting and/or auditing. Many have had experience as members of national accounting regulatory boards. Many have served as Presidents or Council members of their country's accountancy profession or as heads of the nominating organization. The high professional profile of each person nominated to the Board of the IASC by each member-body springs from the need of each Board member-body to ensure that its candidate goes to represent and secure for it the best terms (output) from the IASC. The concentration of expertise on the Board probably accounts for the high quality of the IASs and the emphasis of those standards on transactions and events that are not peculiar to a particular industry or region; thus ignoring issues of particular relevance to developing countries.

Diversification Strategy

The IASC seems to prefer topics of a general nature to industry-specific and region-specific topics. This is probably because the IASC is a mirror of what prevails in many member countries, where industry regulation is less preferred to regulation of transactions and events of a general nature. To embark upon industry-specific regulation is to limit the scope of the IASC's market.[14] Such a regulation will create a bilateral monopoly, where there will be one user group of the IASC's standards—the relevant industry. Also if the IASC regulates all aspects of corporate reporting for such an industry, the industry has only one place where it can buy such regulation. But by adopting the general transactions/events regulation strategy the IASC seeks not only to expand its market, but also to produce parcels of standards which can be distributed across many separated markets and countries. In short, general transactions/events regulation is an improved product. It increases the scope of the IASC's activities immensely, increases the number of affected interest groups and reduces the IASC's dependence on any one industry or group of countries. This diversification strategy provides one explanation of the IASC's global influence.

Under industry- or sector-specific regulation, the IASC would serve fewer groups—the specific industry/sector and its customer class.[15] Since the marginal benefits to the customer class are probably very small, that group will most probably not bother to seek regulation.[16] Therefore, the standards would exist to serve only one industry or one sector. Under general transactions/events regulation, the market for IASs is expanded in two ways. First, the IASC provides service to more than one industry/sector. Second, the standards are likely to be perceived as having a larger impact on many users because they deal with topics from which many different issues and interpretations tend to emerge. Rutherford's[17] specification of the wide variety of the different ways the IASC's standard is used confirms the preceding argument:

---

[13]For more on the concept of professional bureaucracy, see H. Mintzberg, *The Structuring of Organizations* (Englewood Cliffs: Prentice-Hall, 1979).

[14]It can be argued that the evolutionary (rather than revolutionary) profile of the IASC compels the pursuit of transactions/events of general nature and that industry regulation may follow after key underlying issues have been dealt with as in the U.S. and the U.K.

[15]The customer class includes national accounting regulators for the specific industry/sector, preparers, users and auditors of corporate annual reports in the specific industry/sector not all of which actively seek regulation.

[16]IASC's detour into regulation of financial reporting in the banking industry may be due to the fact that it perceives the marginal benefits to its constituencies to be high.

[17]Brian Rutherford, "A Pat on the Back but Time for a Change," *Accountancy* (July 1987), p. 18.

[IASC standards] are used as a vehicle for harmonization within the developed Anglo-American oriented world; as a means by which sophisticated enterprises in one country can communicate with sophisticated investors in other countries; as a source of standards for indigenous enterprises in Third World countries; as a means of regulating the activities of multinationals within the Third World; as a uniform body of standards to be used by companies quoted on several national stock exchanges.

There are innumerable difficulties in balancing these tasks. As McDougall[18] has suggested:

What is, perhaps, not so obvious is that there are, and must be differences between "what is good for General Motors" [a transnational enterprise] on the one hand and what is good for any nation-state (not excluding the USA) as regards the relations within its own territory between that nation-state and General Motors, between that nation-state and its own companies, and between those national companies and the local subsidiary of General Motors. Problems such as those relating to group accounts, associated and subsidiary companies, transfer pricing, translation of foreign currencies, inflation accounting and costing policies in the extractive industries are among the many where highly skilled accountants can produce very different proposed solutions, all backed by strong arguments that are likely to appeal to those whose interests it is their duty to serve.

It follows that the profession must not allow itself to be dominated—nationally and internationally—by thinking dictated by consideration only of what is good for, say, transnational companies. There must be an opportunity for the interest of all types of businesses to be represented both on the national and international level.

The preceding discussion suggests a multiplicity of underlying rationales. The internationality of an accounting problem, transboundary transactions (including related-party transactions and debt swaps), the perceived seriousness of an accounting problem in the light of the inadequacy of most or even all national solutions (e.g., financial instruments and off balance sheet transactions), the greater efficiency of collective solutions and the objective of eliminating distortions of the global market for capital—all may help to explain the identification and development of candidates for harmonization and/or the substantive solutions adopted. The interests of Third World countries require, in some cases, particular attention like IAS 29 on financial reporting for hyper-inflationary economies. It is, of course, not easy to identify a single rationale even for an accounting standard.

A genuinely global system of standard-setting contains serious internal strains. If it is to be a system, there must be a measure of coherence between the purposes being pursued by its different member-bodies. If it is to be global, there must be a measure of independence accorded the different members, so that standard-setting in each member-country may respond appropriately to the particular constellations of interests confronting corporate reporting. The IASC's system has evolved a set of arrangements and procedures which may alleviate these internal strains in its quest for harmonization. Before these are discussed, it is necessary to determine what the IASC means by harmonization.

The Mission and Goals of the IASC

The implicit primary goal of the IASC is harmonization but its official goal (or mission) is "to formulate and publish, in the public interest, accounting standards to be used in the presentation of financial statements." Harmonization can, however, be attained by means other than the development of IASs.

Types of Harmonization

The definition of harmonization provided by Nobes[19] as "a process of increasing the compatibility of accounting practices by setting bounds to their degree of variation," suggests that there are other ways of achiev-

[18]E. H. V. McDougall, "Regional Accountancy Bodies," in *The Internationalization of the Accountancy Profession*, J. W. Brennan (ed.) (Toronto: The Canadian Institute of Chartered Accountants, 1979), p. 18. For a similar argument with an explicit diagrammatic illustration see C. Nobes, "Harmonization of Financial Reporting," in C. W. Nobes and R. H. Parker (eds.), *Comparative International Accounting* (Oxford: Philip Allan, 1985), pp. 341-2.

[19]C. Nobes, "Harmonization...," op. cit., p. 331.

ing harmonization. For example. each national stock exchange can issue certificates to its domestic registrants whose financial statements have met its standardized review protocols. If such certification is recognized by other national stock exchanges, harmonization is enhanced by the elimination or reduction of repetitive review procedures. Another process of harmonization may be to allow countries to set accounting and disclosure standards in the first instance, subject to centralized review under general criteria, as in the European Communities [EC] model. Yet another is the institutional mechanism operated by the defunct Accountants International Study Group [1966-1977]. This Group founded by Canada, the UK and the US undertook research into the differences in the accounting practices of the three countries and made recommendations on how to harmonize the different practices.

In the context of the approach adopted by the IASC, harmonization is not a matter of either-or propositions but a matter of degree. In an objective appreciation of its inability to force its standards on member-countries, the IASC acknowledges, in its Constitution, that its standards are not intended to supersede local standards. It expects, however, that its member-bodies will use their best endeavors in their respective countries to procure the acceptance of its standards. The problem with this expectation is that member-bodies are not, in many cases, the bodies responsible for regulating accounting principles and practices in their countries. The degree of harmonization which the IASC can pursue and attain depends, therefore, upon the ability of each member-body to use its "best endeavors" to ensure that IASs are adopted within its own country. A full knowledge of the different degrees, will help our understanding of the one which represents the IASC's goals.

Total harmonization would occur when all countries[20] adopt and enforce the same accounting and disclosure standards. This would strengthen the concept of collective responsibility. While there are overwhelming disincentives to total harmonization [variation in preferences, differences in geographical, economic, political, social and cultural conditions; resentment of centralized directions and opposition from reporting TNEs], there are other degrees of harmonization which can mediate the competing claims of total harmonization and national autonomy. These are minimum, partial, optional and alternative harmonization.

Minimum harmonization would occur when member countries adopt standards which are at least as stringent[21] as those recommended by the IASC. But it would not allow member countries to adopt less stringent standards. The minimum "floor" limits member countries' use of weaker accounting standards as incentives for attracting companies to locate in their territories, but allows countries to give effect to more stringent standards. This approach can, however, increase the reporting costs of companies seeking to enter these countries from a country with minimum standards; thus increasing the height of barriers to entry.

Partial harmonization would allow a country to impose stricter or laxer standards on domestic enterprises[22] but forbids imposition of stricter standards on foreign companies. This is what the IASC's current comparability exercise is seeking to achieve: a situation

---

[20]A country represents a national accounting regulatory body. It may be a professional accounting body that is a member of the IASC, a government agency, a body made up of a mixture of accounting profession, government agency and other interested users and preparers of accounts. It may also stand for generally accepted accounting practices in a country with no identifiable regulatory agency.

[21]Stringency, in the context of accounting standards, refers to a demand for more rather than less disclosure and to a decision to prescribe or proscribe specific measurement and/or disclosure (i.e., presentation) methods rather than to permit all available options.

[22]This raises the problem of which entities should come within global harmonization rules—should it be TNEs, local companies with no multinational interests, public or private limited companies, government-owned enterprises, joint ventures between two or more enterprises/governments from different countries? The IASC believes that its standards apply to all. The earlier quotation from Brian Rutherford ("A Pat on the Back..." op. cit.), a former Assistant Secretary of the IASC, attests to this belief.

where corporate reports presented on the basis of its own standards will be acceptable to securities regulating organizations in other countries. This may give foreign companies unfair advantage or disadvantage over domestic companies.

Optional harmonization would allow a country to adopt standards different from the global standards but requires the country to allow domestic or foreign companies operating in that country to elect which of the standards to comply with. This is similar to partial harmonization but there are two important differences. First, a country must specifically "opt out" of the global standards. Second, when Country X adopts less stringent standards, foreign companies located in Country X need only comply with its standards rather than the global standards, undercutting the competitive advantage that domestic companies would otherwise enjoy.

Alternative harmonization is the current option of the IASC which allows two or more alternative accounting and/or disclosure methods from which a member country may elect. The IASC may identify a clear preference for one set of methods as in its current proposal to limit allowable options. In such cases, selection of alternatives will ordinarily be allowed only under narrowly defined criteria and this may be subject to later reviews.

The preceding discussion on the resources and mission of the IASC does not explain the potential weaknesses of the IASC's standard-setting process, its vulnerability to political manipulation, its lack of constitutional and legalistic legitimacy and its potential conflict with the culture of many countries. How can (or does) the IASC protect itself against political interference (or manipulation) and ward off attacks on its regulatory process on constitutional and other grounds? This is a question of institutional legitimacy.

Institutional Legitimacy

Three conditions for assessing legitimacy (acceptability or defensibility) of a regulatory machinery were presented by Johnson and Solomons.[23] The three conditions for the defense of institutional legitimacy they suggested as collectively sufficient to ward off attacks on the standard-setting process are:

1. The organization must possess a level of authority sufficient to carry out its intended regulatory function given the environment in which it must operate. Possession of "sufficient authority" comes about as a result of proper delegation and institutional competency.[24]
2. The decision-making process of the organization must be impartial and objective and each exercise of authority must bear a direct and substantial relationship to the organizational remit. This condition, referred to as "substantive due process" requires that the organization acts as a fiduciary in arbitrating disputes that may arise between the various interested parties, not as agent of any one party or group.[25]
3. The organization must provide an adequate and an impartial opportunity for interested parties to provide input into the standard-setting process. This "procedural due process" requires that interested parties are kept informed of matters considered by the organization and be given an adequate opportunity to have their views and evidence heard.[26]

In short, institutional legitimacy [IL] is a function of sufficient authority [SA], substantive due process [SDP] and procedural due process [PDP]. An organization's survival is potentially threatened if it lacks any of the characteristics of the elements of IL.

Sufficient Authority

SA can be attained when there is a clear mandate and institutional competence. It has been argued that the IASC possesses institutional competence. However, the IASC has no clear mandate, that is, it lacks *de jure* IL. No

---

[23]Johnson and Solomons, op. cit., pp. 172-79.

[24]Ibid., p. 172.

[25]Ibid., p. 173.

[26]Ibid., p. 174.

country has delegated to it the power to prepare its accounting standards. Neither the United Nations which has a broad though vague remit for global order, the OECD concerned with economic cooperation and development among industrialized nations nor the EC has asked it to regulate accounting at the global level on its behalf. Although the IASC does not act directly as agent for any group, the present situation whereby some countries have a permanent seat[27] on its Board creates an apparent over-representation of the interests of developed countries. While it might be argued that the exposure draft procedure and the consultative committee process offer some opportunities for many member countries and non-accounting groups to participate in its substantive due process, it is not apparent that the views and evidence of the majority [the developing countries] are being heard and considered.

Substantive Due Process

SDP legitimacy exists if the IASC can justify its authority and provide adequate rationale for its standards. It has been suggested that there are multiple rationales for its standards. The lack of adequate justification tends to invite political interference. Solomons[28] has suggested three kinds of defenses against political interference to national accounting regulation: educational, conceptual and structural. One would agree with Solomons that much of the political heat generated by so many accounting arguments could be avoided if the limited significance of many accounting numbers were better understood. Much of the argument arises from the need to enhance the "bottom line" in corporate reports. Educational defense involves the use of persuasive devices to remove the "bottom line" mentality. On conceptual defense, Solomons emphasized that an explicit theoretical foundation, that is, the provision of a conceptual framework [and the IASC has recently issued its own framework] is an indispensable defense against political interference, but as Peasnell[29] argued, this is not the case with the Accounting Standards Committee in the U.K. whose regulatory process is characterized by bargaining. The conceptual framework might be more of a hindrance than a help, since flexibility is the more important in a predominantly bargaining environment; but flexibility seems to be what a conceptual framework is intended to eliminate.

Structural defense is the installation of institutional machineries to ensure that constituencies perceive the legitimacy of the standard-setting process. Solomons does not give a clear statement of how to determine the acceptability of a regulatory process. The two illustrations provided in his paper are only inferential. One is the validity of the process which, in the U.K. context, requires that an accounting standard developed by the Accounting Standards Committee [ASC] needs the approval of each member-body of the Consultative Committee of Accounting Bodies [CCAB] to be operative. The other concerns the independence of the Board members of

---

[27]As will become clear in the discussion of the link between the IASC and IFAC, no member now has a permanent seat. In practice, however, some probably will have, because of their expertise and long-standing experience in the standard-setting process. Since membership of the IASC implies neither activity nor much in the way of financial support, the members with little or no expertise and finance to contribute could not have been expected to have a serious voice in the policy formulation of the IASC.

[28]D. Solomons, "The Political Implications of Accounting and Accounting Standard Setting," *Accounting and Business Research* (Vol. 13, No. 50, Spring 1983), p. 115.

[29]K. V. Peasnell, "The Function of a Conceptual Framework for Corporate Financial Reporting," *Accounting and Business Research* (Vol. 12, No. 48, Autumn 1982), pp. 243-56. Recently, more interests have been shown by some members of the Accounting Standards Committee in the U.K. David Solomons addressed to the Accounting Standards Committee a report, *Guidelines for Financial Reporting* (1989), prepared for the Research Board of the Institute of Chartered Accountants in England and Wales. The Institute of Chartered Accountants, Scotland also produced a document on *Making Corporate Reports Valuable* (1988). More importantly, the Accounting Standards Committee in the U.K. announced that it proposes to use the IASC's *Framework for the Preparation and Presentation of Financial Statements* (1989) as a benchmark against which its future proposals will be measured.

the ASC who as part-time members are not likely to be perceived as neutral by the very fact of their affiliation to bodies which may be interested in the output of the ASC. These two points apply to the IASC as well. In the first place, there is the expectation that member-bodies of the IASC would use their best endeavors to ensure that the standards issued by the IASC would become acceptable in member countries. A recent survey by the IASC[30] provides overwhelming evidence that only in a few developing countries have such endeavors resulted in a total incorporation of the provisions of IASs into national accounting rules, though many other countries have used the IASs as a basis for their own national standards. If member- bodies have little or no clout in the standard-setting process of their countries, they are not likely to succeed in ensuring the conformity of their national standards with IASs. In respect of the independence of Board members, many of them have affinity with the big international auditing firms or TNEs—two major groups likely to be affected by the output of the IASC. In this case, there is the potential for the IASC to be captured by those it seeks to regulate.

Procedural Due Process

A legitimate PDP must provide interested parties with sufficient opportunities to be heard and to influence outcome. The presumed endeavor of the IASC, its Board and its entire membership is to arrive at a consensus based on the preferences of the various participants. That is why information about the topic and contents of a future standard is widely circulated among members of the Board, other member-bodies and an international consultative group of interested institutions. In the process a topic takes, on the average, two to three years to become a standard. It is also possible for the Board, at any time during this period, to stop the progress of an evolving standard and to decide to issue a discussion paper on the topic instead.

In resolving differences on any topic, attention is paid to criteria which would ensure the acceptability of a standard. The unwritten but operational procedure is to ensure that the document which finally evolves is satisfactorily received by all target groups—this involves an *ex ante* estimation of the preferences elicited from its membership, various national accounting standard setting bodies and the other target groups such as TNEs and national stock exchanges. To achieve this, there are three possible options which provide alternative ways of understanding the actions or reactions of member-countries to IASs.

The first is the flexibility option. This seeks to capture all present and potential regulators of corporate reporting practices across the world. It aims at the maximization of the number of feasible or acceptable methods (or techniques) for each and every issue covered by a standard. It is because this option recognizes rather than harmonizes differences in accounting practices that the IASC is seeking to reduce the number of options in its current IASs.

The second is the maximum likelihood option. In contrast to the flexibility option, this seeks to identify those methods and techniques with which all countries from which Board members are drawn agree, in the belief that the Board membership is truly representative of the member countries. This belief assumes "vicarious representation" which is the satisfaction or dissatisfaction felt by one member as the direct consequence of the representation of another. Concern about the welfare of others can motivate individuals just as self-interest does. This option suggests as a decision criterion the probability that a choice from among competing methods of recognizing, measuring or disclosing a transaction or event will be optimal when there is uncertainty with regard to preferences associated with the different alternatives by member countries. The task of the IASC will then be to focus on the methods which are acceptable to all its members—a sort of convergent standard or what is described as the lowest common denominator

[30] IASC's Survey...op. cit.

approach.[31] This means that the IASC seeks a middle path between more detailed and less detailed standards. It draws heavily on the work of other national standard setting bodies (especially the U.S., the U.K., Canada, Australia and the Netherlands). It does not carry out much, if any, original work, and it is therefore, not surprising that its standards represent some sort of compromise. This reduces IASs to the level of "second-rate" standards in countries with greater "topic" coverage but it has also enabled the IAS to become a sort of minimum benchmark which some other countries seek to attain. This probably suggests that most member-bodies see the attainment of minimum harmonization as the goal of the IASC.

The third option, which derives from the previous one (though different from it), is the versatility option by which the IASC would prefer to see itself as an organization independent of and distinguishable from its member-bodies. The aim of the IASC would be to ensure that its standards would attain an acceptable level of adoption across the world. The strategy for generating this acceptability would be:

1. to ensure that any group most likely to determine its continued survival as an organization is not "offended" [the 'vital countries hypothesis' of Mason[32]]; or
2. to seek to develop standards which will be acceptable to the majority rather than all the membership.

This strategy is based on the assumption that the IASC is a risk-averse satisficer[33] that aims to minimize the likelihood of not attaining its chosen objectives, one of which is the adoption of its standards by all possible target groups. In this endeavor, the IASC makes it a point of duty to go round all member countries to persuade national accounting regulatory bodies to adopt or recognize its standards. The versatility option is more useful than the others in explaining (i) the strategies of the IASC for survival in an international arena where there are heterogeneous preferences about the IASC's agenda of regulatory items, information needs and the targets which should be regulated and (ii) the adoption of IASs by developing countries instead of the development of accounting and disclosure standards suited to their needs.

Without SA, the drive toward harmonization, to which the IASC has contributed so much, may ultimately be futile. Without SDP legitimacy based on the superiority of solutions to measurement and disclosure problems, the effects of continuing harmonization of corporate disclosure may be the increasing repression of the IASC. These deficiencies of the IASC are presently being overcome by a deliberate management of its external environment, to convert potentially hostile external parties to friendly and supportive allies.

MANAGING THE EXTERNAL ENVIRONMENT

The UN Link

The United Nations' interest in the standardization of the contents of corporate reports started in the early 1970s, when it created the United Nations Commission for Transnational Corporations [UNCTNC] which discovered in its attempt to assess the impact of TNEs on international business and developing countries that there was a lack of usable financial and non-financial information

---

[31]This term was used to describe the IASC's approach by R. D. Fitzgerald in "International Harmonization of Accounting and Reporting," *The International Journal of Accounting Education and Research* (Vol. 17, No. 1, Fall 1981), pp. 22-32. Fitzgerald's meaning of the term must be distinguished from its meaning here. In the context used here, it refers to a set of standards or practices applicable in all countries—a sort of convergent standard. In the context of Fitzgerald's meaning, an IAS is a set of composite standards from different countries. What prevailed when Fitzgerald wrote was an IAS that allowed each country to more or less have its own way.

[32]A. K. Mason, *The Development of International Financial Reporting Standards,* ICRA Occasional Paper No. 17 (International Centre for Research in Accounting, University of Lancaster, U.K., 1978), p. 40.

[33]See Herbert Simon, "A Behavioural Model of Rational Choice," *Quarterly Journal of Economics,*(Vol. 69, No. 1, 1955)), pp. 99-114.

on TNEs. The different styles of corporate reporting made it difficult to compare TNEs. This led to the creation of a 14-man Group of Experts on International Standards of Accounting and Reporting [GEISAR] in 1974. The experts were chosen from different regional groupings on the basis of professional and academic experience with accounting practices in their regions. The group reported in 1977 and recommended, among other things, the compilation of a list of minimal disclosure items which should be found in TNE's corporate annual report and accounts. The desire to elaborate on the broad and vague recommendations of GEISAR led to the creation in 1979 of an "Ad Hoc Intergovernmental Working Group of Experts on International Standardization of Accounting and Reporting" [Group of Experts]. This 34-member group of experts is made up of government representatives many of whom do not possess the technological competence of the members of GEISAR. Their discussion became more politicized and polarized and fundamental issues in accounting were viewed more from the perspective of economic and regional consequences than from professional validity. This made it impossible for the group of experts to pursue the task of compiling a list of minimum disclosure items with a singular focus. But their deliberations revealed deficiencies in current "general purpose" corporate reporting and led to the conclusion that each country should not discriminate between foreign and domestic companies in its corporate disclosure regulation [one step toward partial or optional harmonization]. The effort of the group of experts towards the development of global accounting standards waned because (i) the UN has no technical competence in the development of accounting standards, (ii) members of the group of experts from the developed world saw this as a duplication (if not dissipation) of the effort of the IASC, (iii) the IASC was granted an observer status at the group's meeting, thus recognizing it as the global standard-setting body and (iv) the group's discussions and deliberations tend to be overwhelmed by political rather than technical considerations. The group decided in 1984 that it should not become involved in standard-setting but should serve instead as a forum for discussion of member needs. The group now sees its role as that of compiling, comparing and reporting regulatory practices in different countries. This shift in emphasis is probably a reflection of the growing influence of the IASC, the difficulty of obtaining a mandate from the Security Council to take on the role, and the concerted efforts of developed countries to discourage the group from pursuing that course.[34] The IASC in concert with others has succeeded in out-maneuvering the UN's attempt to set corporate reporting standards for the TNEs.

Link with Regional Bodies

The major strategy of the IASC's relationship with regional groups is to keep its secretariat and Board membership informed of regional activities, to attend major regional conferences with potential impact on accounting harmonization and present papers on the IASC and its activities at such conferences. In addition, the Board members of IASC in Europe have continued to play a significant role in weakening the potential threat[35] to the survival of IASC because of the effect of the apparent incongruence between the objectives of the EC intent on harmonizing accounting regulation by the use of alternative harmonization and those of the IASC on those countries which are members of the two institutions.

Link with IFAC

Although IFAC was founded in 1977, four years after the IASC, an agreement of the nature of an absorption [described as "mu-

[34]This is probably because the developed countries, particularly the U.S., were concerned that their influence would not be as extensive at the UN compared with the IASC.

[35]For a full discussion of such a threat see, D. McComb "International Accounting Standards and the EEC Harmonization Program: A Conflict of Disparate Objectives," *The International Journal of Accounting Education and Research* (Vol. 17, No. 2, Spring 1982), pp. 35-48.

tual commitments"] was entered into between IFAC and the IASC. This "mutual commitment" came into effect in January 1983. It allows the rationalization of the membership of the two bodies. This meant that professional bodies no longer need to be members of both bodies but only need to be fee-paying members of IFAC to enjoy the benefits of the IASC's membership. The agreement allowed the IASC to retain full autonomy in setting corporate reporting standards and IFAC to endorse automatically all such standards. For the loss of direct subscription from its membership the IASC was to be (and is) given 10 percent of its annual budget by IFAC which also agreed to defray the costs incurred by non-Board member-bodies for participating in steering committees. In return for these contributions, IFAC appoints 13 member-bodies to the 17-member Board of the IASC from July 1986 and has an observer status at the Board meeting of the IASC. The remaining four members of the IASC's Board are co-opted from non-accounting user and interest groups that are not members of IFAC.[36]

The mutual commitment between IFAC and the IASC probably ensures the capture of the IASC by the accounting profession which founded it but prevents it from adopting the current practice of broadening the membership of accounting standard-setting bodies across the world. National accounting regulatory bodies are no longer the exclusive monopoly of the accounting profession.[37] Many now have non-accountants on their boards and are controlled by bodies which seek to protect the interests of the predominant users of corporate annual reports. In the interest of international harmonization of corporate reporting and the legitimacy of the IASC, it is appropriate that both IFAC and the IASC reconsider the propriety of their mutual commitments. Membership of the IASC should belong to standard-setting organizations [not accounting professional bodies] from each country. This is because the "best endeavor pledge" of professional accounting bodies that are not responsible for standard setting in their countries is ineffectual. The IASC should be made up of such organizations as the Council for Annual Reporting in the Netherlands, the Financial Accounting Standards Board in the U.S. and the Australian Accounting Standards Review Board. There is also a need for IFAC to (a) relinquish its hold on the IASC and (b) sponsor the formation of a Global Financial Reporting Foundation to superintend over the affairs of the IASC (that is, to take over the functions now performed by IFAC) and to seek to resource it adequately. The Foundation may comprise IOSCO, IFAC, ICCFAA, the International Financial Executive Institutes, the UNCTNC and the World Bank among others.

Link with Board Member Countries

The most important and pervasive aspect of the IASC's influence is its practice of rotating the venue of its Board meeting from one Board member country to another. Another is the special alliance which the IASC cultivates with its Board members. This relationship is embedded in the understanding which has evolved over time that the IASC's staff are to deal with such professional bodies through their representatives on its Board and vice versa. This special relationship has two disadvantages. First, there is the danger of the IASC being captured by its professional member-bodies for their domestic purposes. Second, such relationships limit the IASC's access to other agencies that might be more suitable for negotiating certain aspects of its agenda. A good example is the time it took the IASC to evolve a working relationship with the FASB in the U.S. and the little or no relationship between the IASC and other regulatory bodies in countries where the member-bodies do not control accounting regulation.

---

[36]Only one of these seats has been filled by the International Coordinating Committee of Financial Analysts' Associations [ICCFAA]. It has recently been suggested that one of the seats be offered to the International Organization of Securities Commissions.

[37]In countries like France, Germany, Japan, etc., accounting regulatory bodies never were in the hands of the accounting profession.

Link with Non-Board Member-Countries

The link with non-Board member-countries includes (a) the use of IASs by member-countries; rather than duplicate the IASC's effort, some members rely on the IASC's standards for input into their standard setting process or adopt them with or without amendments as their own standards; (b) the request for nominations to the technical committees on issues in which the IASC believes a member-country can contribute. The most critical issue concerning the adoption of IASs is their relevance to developing countries.[38] For example, a comparative study of the perceptions of users and accountants in Nigeria on the one hand and those of the Board members of the IASC on the other revealed that the IASC does not perceive the same set of measurement and disclosure items as important as do users and accountants in Nigeria.[39] Another critical link is the desire to develop standard setting procedures in member-countries with no experience in this area. The Chairman and Secretary-General of the IASC make regular visits to member-countries to discuss their problems and to advise them on how to use IASs or on how to embark on the development of corporate disclosure standards.

Link with User Groups

Initially the IASC was less interested in the views of dominant users of its standards, relying principally on the pledge of its members to use their best endeavors to ensure that IASs are adopted in their respective countries. This may be the most appropriate strategy to start with but it did not seem to work, and the legitimacy of the IASC, as a body composed of professional accountants, to set corporate financial reporting standards at the global level was regularly questioned. At a low level, prior to 1982, and more so thereafter, the IASC opened up a "continuing dialogue" with regulatory bodies and international organizations [such as the potential users of corporate reports prepared on the basis of its standards] as an essential part of its program. It is the increasing intensity of this "continuing dialogue" with the international user community that is a distinguishing feature of the IASC's management of its environment. Although only a few members of the user community recognize what the IASC is, the IASC makes sure that that part of the user community most active in influencing corporate reporting activities of TNEs and government-owned enterprises operating in and from different countries know what it is doing and what it can do for them. These awareness activities are pursued in two ways.

The first is the introduction, in October 1981, of user consultation into the standard-setting process. A consultative group comprising international bodies representing valuers, bankers, financial executives, lawyers, chambers of commerce, trade unions, securities commissions, the World Bank, the International Finance Corporation, and the FASB in the U.S. was formed. The European Commission has recently been invited to join this group. The goal is for the group to include representatives of preparers and users of financial statements and standard-setting bodies. The group meets regularly with the IASC Board to discuss matters of principles and policy arising from the IASC's work and the practical and conceptual issues that affect the acceptability of IASs. The OECD and UNCTNC attend as observers.

The second approach is to co-opt some representatives of international preparers and users to its Board. One such co-option was the admission of the International Coordi-

---

[38] For arguments on the irrelevance of the IASC's standards to developing countries see, R. J. Briston, "The Evolution of Accounting in Developing Countries," *The International Journal of Accounting Education and Research* (Vol. 14, No. 1, Fall 1978), pp. 105-20 and J. M. Samuels and J. C. Oliga, "Accounting Standards in Developing Countries," *The International Journal of Accounting Education and Research* (Vol. 18, No. 1, Fall 1982), pp. 69-88.

[39] R. S. O. Wallace, "Intranational and International Consensus on the Importance of Disclosure Items in Financial Reports: A Nigerian Case Study," *British Accounting Review* (Vol. 20, No. 2, December 1988), pp. 223-65.

nating Committee of Financial Analysts Association to the Board in June 1985. Another is the moral suasion of national member-bodies to ensure that their nominations to the Board include both preparers and auditors.

Link with Stock Exchanges and Securities Organizations

Apart from the best endeavors of its members, the IASC has sought to make the adoption of its standards visible by advocating the desirability of TNEs to disclose conformity with or identify deviations from IASs. The most important ally in the propagation of IASs is Canada. In that country, the President and Chief Executive of the Toronto Stock Exchange invites, on an annual basis, enterprises listed on the Exchange to disclose the fact of conformity with IASs. Similarly, the Chairman of the Canadian Accounting Standards Committee urges all major accounting firms to encourage their audit clients to comply with IASs and disclose the fact of such compliance in their financial statements. These efforts have resulted in increased disclosure in the annual reports of Canadian listed enterprises. The IASC reported that in 1980, 49 out of a sample of 140 of the large Canadian enterprises listed on the Toronto Stock Exchange made a compliance disclosure. By 1987, 102 out of a sample of 129 such enterprises disclosed compliance with IASs.[40] This overwhelming support is limited to Canada but the IASC will probably not relent in its efforts to increase the support of other national Stock Exchanges.

In February 1985, the US SEC published a consultative document calling for comments on two approaches for the harmonization of disclosure practices in prospectuses and facilitation of transnational securities offerings by enterprises in Canada, the UK and the US.[41] The document suggested two harmonization approaches: (a) *reciprocal*—by which the offering document used by an issuer in its own country would be accepted for offerings in each of the other countries and (b) *common prospectus*—to which all three countries would agree on disclosure standards for an offering document which would be used in more than one country. Although there were 70 responses[42] (50 of which favored the reciprocal approach and 21 [including the IASC's] the common prospectus approach), the US SEC has not decided on how to proceed. This is probably due to the desire to extend the arrangement to other countries, especially Japan. This desire has led to the transformation of the Interamerican Conference of Securities Agencies and Similar Organizations from a regional group to a global body now named the International Organization of Securities Commissions and Similar Organizations [IOSCO]. This new organization has 49 regular members from 45 countries and one affiliate member [the International Finance Corporation]. IOSCO's objectives include (a) to establish standards and an effective surveillance of international securities transactions and (b) to provide mutual assistance to ensure the integrity of the markets by a rigorous application of the standards and by effective enforcement against offenses. IOSCO has set up six working parties to review and propose solutions to regulatory problems related to international securities transactions. One working party would work with the IASC with a view to identifying accounting standards which securities regulators might be ready to accept in the case of multinational offerings. It is more likely that a global grouping of national organizations with jurisdiction over corporate disclosure regulation in their respective countries would want to take over the control of a global body formulating corporate reporting standards.

In 1987, IOSCO accepted an invitation to join the IASC consultative group. IOSCO's membership has meant that it could influence the work of the IASC especially if it believes that IASs could form the basis of the

[40] IASC's Survey...op. cit., pp. 70-71.

[41] See Securities Act Release No. 6568 (February 28, 1985) or *Federal Register*, Vol. 50, No. 45, March 7, 1985.

[42] See Clarence Sampson, "Facilitation of Multinational Securities Offerings," in *Research in Accounting Regulation*, edited by Gary J. Previts, Volume 2 (Connecticut, JAI Press Inc., 1988), p. 216.

common standards of accounting in prospectuses which it desires to evolve. While IOSCO does not agree that the present portfolio of IASs is adequate for this purpose, it has agreed to take part in IASC's projects concerned with the (a) reduction of options in IASs and (b) improvement of extant IASs to a level which would be acceptable to IOSCO.

At its recent meeting in November 1988, IOSCO issued the following statement which confirms its desire to support the harmonization efforts of the IASC:

> The Technical Committee of IOSCO supports the initiatives by the IASC to revise and expand international accounting standards. A primary impediment to international offerings of securities is that different countries have different accounting standards. Mutually acceptable international accounting standards are a critical goal because they will reduce the unnecessary regulatory burdens resulting from current disparities between the various national accounting standards, while protecting investors through adequate disclosure in financial statements.[43]

Future Directions

Recently [November 1988], the Board of IASC considered and approved that the IASC should focus its attention, during the five years to 1993, on the demands for:

a. truly international standards of accounting and disclosure that can be used by international capital markets and the international business community;
b. the comparability of national and international standards; and
c. accounting standards that developing (and other) countries can use as the basis for national standards and assistance with the implementation of such standards.

If the IASC continues with the "co-option" policy of inviting non-accounting international bodies to join its Board as well as emphasizing its consultation strategies, it will soon become a multilateral professional organization with a potential for responding to emerging international business transactions and events based on its expertise and neutrality. Such a potential would arise from the fact that it would be in a position to draw from a global pool of diversified competences in the interest of international harmonization of accounting practices. This will probably increase its influence as a dominant actor in international regulation of business. As the world of "big" business becomes more and more integrated through the coordination of the world's major stock exchanges and the continuation of cross-national merger arrangements of businesses and auditing firms, the need for corporate reporting standards at the global level will become more pronounced and the legitimacy of a private-sector body affiliated to an international accounting organization [IFAC] will be intensely questioned. At present, enterprises seeking finance for growth from other countries and those seeking to be quoted on foreign stock exchanges have to bear the costs of preparing different sets of corporate reports to satisfy the regulatory bodies in the different countries in which they operate. Such increasing costs make it more compelling that these enterprises welcome any international efforts to narrow and rationalize the many corporate reporting differences into a set of identifiable rules. But that set of rules must not be too permissive. If the IASs cannot be prescriptive [i.e., identify a particular option as the only preferred option], they can at least be proscriptive [i.e., disallow one or more options by reducing the domain and range of options allowable in its standards]. The IASC has decided to adopt the latter.

The IASC has recently issued Exposure Draft No. 32 on "Comparability of Financial Statements." The aim of this draft is "to eliminate most of the choices of accounting treatment currently permitted under IASs," so that like transactions and events can be accounted for in the same way, wherever in the world they are being reported.

---

[43]See *IASC News*, The Newsletter of the IASC, Vol. 18, No. 1, January, 1989, pp. 2-3.

The IASC indicated that it will be guided by the undernoted preferability criteria in its attempt to proscribe accounting practices:

a. current worldwide practice and trends in national accounting standards, law and generally accepted accounting principles [especially if they all point to one or two specific options];

b. conformity with its Framework for the Preparation and Presentation of Financial Statements which is its own conceptual basis of accounting;

c. the views of regulators and their representative organizations, such as IOSCO; and

d. consistency within an IAS and with other IASs.

There are many reasons for this obvious change of direction in the IASC's operational strategy. The first is the increasing presence of many non-accounting organizations in the IASC's core deliberations—many of these organizations desire accounting standards documents to have internal consistency and integrity. Of particular relevance is the indication of many securities regulators [including the SEC in the U.S.] that they are willing to consider the possibility of allowing foreign TNEs quoted on their stock exchanges to file corporate annual reports and accounts prepared on the basis of IASs if the IASC will reduce many of the options in its current stock of IASs. The second reason is the increasing convergence of the different corporate reporting rules of the member countries of the EC. Their demands for the inclusion of country-specific accounting options in IASs is probably not as intense as it was before the 4th Directive of the EC was implemented by member countries. The third is the need to enhance the comparability of accounting statements prepared by enterprises located in different parts of the world.

There are, however, potential problems for the IASC. The Dearing Committee (set up to review the accounting standard-setting process in the UK) suggests that the attempt of the IASC to reduce the number of options in its standards may pose some difficulties for the U.K. Accounting Standards Committee, especially if the IASC comes down against some options favored in the U.K.[44] This is probably true of many countries with developed accounting standard-setting procedure. Another problem is the possibility that some Third World countries currently conforming with the IASs may discontinue the practice because the options they prefer are no longer permitted and the permitted options are evolved on the assumptions that there is an efficient stock market and that the accounting competence of all countries is comparable to that in the developed world. For example, it is proposed to eliminate the completed contract method as an option for the recognition of revenue and net income on construction contracts. Many construction contracts in developing countries are undertaken by joint ventures between Third World investors and/or governments and TNEs/governments of developed countries. If profits are only allowed to accrue without recognition of the uncompleted portion of a contract, an abandoned contract would create a burden on local investors especially if foreign partners have remitted their share of recognized profits and have left the resolution of post-completion problems to local partners. In some cases, the post-completion costs may overwhelm the profits which had accrued to local partners.

The point was made earlier that Third World countries require more assistance if they are expected to move along with the international community. In pursuit of this goal, the IASC can play the role of a catalyst by introducing programs which will help to train people of the Third World in setting their own standards. The IASC can also develop a system of providing experts on secondment to accounting standard-setting bodies of the Third World. This would require more funds than is available to the IASC at present. But

[44]Accounting Standards Committee (UK),, *The Making of Accounting Standards*, Report of the Review Committee under the Chairmanship of Sir Ron Dearing CB (London: The Institute of Chartered Accountants in England and Wales, 1988), p. 5.

given the will, and its international prestige, the IASC can collaborate with international development organizations to raise such funds. The IASC can also undertake research studies of the state of accounting in specific countries and sectors and on specific accounting problems. This will provide immense assistance to the international community and will also identify many issues worthy of inclusion in the agenda of the IASC.

There are still important accounting topics and corporate disclosure issues which require further harmonization and collective solutions at the global level. One such issue is accounting for financial instruments. Many new financial instruments (including the swapping of Third World debts) which are being created across national borders by financial institutions do not come under any extant national corporate disclosure regulation and are hardly reported in corporate reports of the affected parties. An attempt is presently being made to evolve a global solution. The IASC and the Canadian Institute of Chartered Accountants have formed a joint working party to study the problems and to develop an exposure draft in this area for adoption by the two bodies. There are other disclosure problems—like the treatment of taxation in corporate reports, cash flow statements, interim financial reporting and the computation and reporting of earnings per share—where divergent national measures justify the intervention of the IASC in the interest of international harmonization of corporate financial reporting. There is also the need to enhance the level of participation of the Third World. The present situation whereby these countries adopt the standards developed by the IASC and some standard setting bodies from the developed world regardless of the relevance of these standards to their environments will not do.

CONCLUSION

The IASC is probably here to stay. Its inadequacies and survival strategies have been examined. Despite its lack of *de jure* institutional legitimacy, the IASC has managed to generate a global constituency of broad public support. Its survival is being sustained by (a) the increasing internationalization of business and finance which make global harmonization of accounting and disclosure practices desirable, (b) the composite nature of its standards and its preoccupation with topics of a general nature, (c) its evolutionary strategy and (d) the absence of a rival organization with keen and prolonged interest in the development and marketing of global accounting standards.

If the IASC did not exist, there would be a need for an organization to harmonize differing national accounting and disclosure standards. The appearance of IOSCO in 1985 with a desire to harmonize differing national rules for securities offerings increases the need for an international organization to harmonize differing national and international corporate disclosure rules and poses a threat to IASC's survival. But IOSCO seems to have left this task to the IASC. So the critical question is not whether one needs an IASC but whether we have the appropriate IASC. One suggestion concerns the potential benefit to the Board of the IASC of a restructuring of its membership and the injection of non-accounting international bodies interested in corporate reporting as regulators, users, preparers and advisers. Another suggestion is the improvement in the manpower and funding of the IASC. International harmonization of corporate disclosure practices seeks to serve more than the accounting profession. Such pursuits should be endowed with much more financial and technical staff than is presently available. Yet another suggestion concerns the probable improvement in the acceptance and relevance of IASs if the IASC seeks to evolve a tiered standardization process which can differentiate between big and small TNEs found in developed countries, and smaller TNEs emerging from developing and newly industrialized countries on the one hand, and big and small domestic enterprises on the other. It seems inappropriate to apply a single IAS uniformly to all reporting enterprises of different sizes, especially when it is obvious that the benefits of that application far outweigh the costs for only a few of them. An IAS that is worthwhile in terms of benefit/cost analysis for a TNE may be less worthwhile for a domestic enterprise in a developing country.

As enterprises, investors and lenders continue to ignore national boundaries and cultures they would continue to support those efforts which seek to encourage the increasing internationalization of business and finance. It is on such a support that the survival and future prospects of the IASC depend. The comparability project is probably a turning point in the history of the IASC. It is more likely that the IASC will spend less time on the development of new standards but more on the review of existing standards and the removal of options which are mutually unacceptable in the international arena. The IASC may increase its interest in the promotion and liaison work in order to increase further the use of IASs. Following from its ongoing project on the search for the needs of financial reporting in developing and newly industrialized countries, the IASC could begin to provide help to developing countries in the creation of a standard-setting process and the interpretation of IASs.

European Accounting Review 1993, **3**, 531–554

Lobbying behaviour and the development of international accounting standards

The case of the IASC's joint venture project

Sara York Kenny and Robert K. Larson
University of Utah and Pennsylvania State University – Harrisburg

ABSTRACT

This paper studies the role of lobbying in an international (i.e., harmonization) accounting standards setting and examines the IASC's process of promulgating International Accounting Standard (IAS) 31, 'Financial Reporting of Interests in Joint Ventures'. Our study begins with an examination of the Exposure Draft (ED 35, 'Financial Reporting of Interests in Joint Ventures') preceding IAS 31 and analyses the lobbying efforts observed during the promulgation process. Consistent with prior literature, the paper analyses lobbyists and their lobbying positions. During the time frame of the study (1989 and 1990), the IASC changed its due process, which affords us the opportunity also to analyse the IASC's strategic approach to public input. Accordingly, this study incorporates aspects of institutional theory as it relates to strategic choice by organizations.

The comment letters received by the IASC regarding ED 35 were analysed using a form of content analysis. The analyses generally support the hypothesized relationships; namely, lobbying firms tend to be very large, and they lobby against any change in the *status quo*; professional and trade organizations lobby on behalf of their constituents and tend to support the majority positions held by those constituents; and the regulatory body (IASC) seeks acceptance from its constituency by adapting its position to that which is more palatable to the lobbyists. The interaction between respondents and the IASC is consistent with an institutional theory explanation of organizational change and adaptation to environment pressures.

Few individual firms lobbied the IASC. Rather, the bulk of the respondents to ED 35 were professional associations and organizations. The result contrasts markedly with both our expectations and prior research involving lobbying of the FASB. The dearth of corporate respondents to ED 35 implies that multinational corporations do not yet see the IASC as a serious regulatory organization. Further, few legal, governmental or regulatory organizations required compliance with IASs during 1989 and 1990, when IAS 31 was being deliberated,

Address for correspondence
Sara York Kenny, David Eccles School of Business, University of Utah, Salt Lake City, UT 84112, USA.

but many organizations and countries were considering such regulation (Guy, 1992; Denman, 1991). As of early 1993, both the London and Hong Kong Stock Exchanges began allowing foreign issuers to provide only reconciliations from home country GAAP to IASs (Cairns, 1992). Additionally, the International Organization of Securities Commissions (IOSCO) has been increasingly supportive of the IASC's harmonization efforts (Chandler, 1992; Wyatt, 1992; Wallace 1990). Coupled with the IASC's efforts to achieve institutional legitimacy (Wallace, 1990), the lack of corporate respondents might be rather disturbing except for one factor: the Exposure Draft (ED) analysed in this study represents one of the first standards promulgated under the IASC's new due process, and it may be that multinational corporations (MNCs) simply have not yet focused on the IASC. If this is the case, a steady increase in both the number and the intensity of respondents to future IASC exposure drafts would be expected.

This study raises several questions for future study. As the IASC embarks on its future goals towards internationalization and harmonization of accounting standards, these questions of legitimization, acceptance, flexibility and economic consequences will grow in importance.

A substantial amount of academic literature addresses the role of lobbying in the accounting standards-setting process. These studies primarily focus on lobbyists and lobbying positions directed towards the Financial Accounting Standards Board (FASB) or the Governmental Accounting Standards Board (GASB) in the United States (Watts and Zimmerman, 1978; Kelly, 1983; Deakin, 1989; Roberts and Kurtenbach, 1990; Tandy and Wilburn, 1992). Of increasing importance, however, is the development and harmonization of international accounting standards, i.e., financial reporting standards and practices which apply in a wide range of countries and economies. Although there is some descriptive and theoretical research comparing lobbying behaviour in the US to that in the UK (Benston, 1980; Sutton, 1984), little research addresses the question of lobbying efforts directed towards the International Accounting Standards Committee (IASC), the major international accounting standards-setting organization (Coopers & Lybrand, 1991; Wallace, 1990; Grinyer and Russell, 1992).[1]

Since its inception in 1973 until 1989, the IASC invited commentary from selected interested parties regarding proposed international accounting issues, but carried out its deliberations in relative private, with little, if any, unsolicited public input. Written commentary submitted to the IASC was not released to the public. In 1989, the IASC changed the policy and began soliciting a wider range of public input. Comment letters received by the IASC began being released, upon request, to the general public. In other words, the IASC changed from a relatively introverted strategy of standards setting to a more public strategy, which is similar to that followed by the FASB.

This paper provides the first study dealing with the role of lobbying in an international (i.e., harmonization) accounting standards setting and examines the IASC's process of promulgating International Accounting

Standard (IAS) 31, 'Financial Reporting of Interests in Joint Ventures'. Our study begins with an examination of the Exposure Draft (ED 35, 'Financial Reporting of Interests in Joint Ventures') preceding IAS 31 and analyses the lobbying efforts observed during the promulgation process. Consistent with prior literature, our paper analyses lobbyists and their lobbying positions. The observed change in the due process affords us the opportunity also to analyse the IASC's strategic approach to public input. Accordingly, this study incorporates aspects of institutional theory as it relates to strategic choice by organizations.

The comment letters received by the IASC regarding ED 35 were analysed using a form of content analysis. The analyses generally support the hypothesized relationships; namely, lobbying firms tend to be very large, and they lobby against any change in the *status quo*; professional and trade organizations lobby on behalf of their constituents and tend to support the majority positions held by those constituents; and the regulatory body (IASC) seeks acceptance from its constituency by adapting its position to that which is more palatable to the lobbyists.

Few individual firms lobbied the IASC. Rather, the bulk of the respondents to ED 35 were professional associations and organizations. The result contrasts markedly with both our expectations and prior research involving lobbying of the FASB. The dearth of corporate respondents to ED 35 implies that multinational corporations do not yet see the IASC as a serious regulatory organization. In light of the IASC's efforts to achieve institutional legitimacy (Wallace, 1990), the lack of corporate respondents might be rather disturbing except for one factor: the Exposure Draft (ED) analysed in this study represents one of the first standards promulgated under the IASC's new due process, and it may be that multinational corporations (MNCs) simply have not yet 'tuned in' to the IASC. If this is the case, a steady increase in both the number and the intensity of respondents to future IASC exposure drafts would be expected.

While few legal, governmental or regulatory organizations required compliance with IASs during 1989 and 1990, when IAS 31 was being deliberated, many organizations and countries were considering such regulation (Guy, 1992; Denman, 1991). As of early 1993, both the London and Hong Kong Stock Exchanges began allowing foreign issuers to provide only reconciliations from home country GAAP to IASs (Cairns, 1992). Additionally, the International Organization of Securities Commissions (IOSCO) has been increasingly supportive of the IASC's harmonization efforts (Chandler, 1992; Wyatt, 1992; Wallace, 1990). Support from IOSCO is considered to be very important to the IASC because IOSCO represents securities commissions throughout the world, and harmonization is considered to be most possible through efforts of the international capital and securities markets (Guy, 1992; Radebaugh and Gray, 1993; Wyatt, 1992). The relationship between accounting and capital flows is well documented

(Radebaugh and Gray, 1993). Therefore, as Fogarty (1992: 348) suggests, studying the organizations which determine acceptable accounting techniques should be 'a special priority'.

The remainder of the paper is organized as follows. Background information about the IASC's due process and the evolution of ED 35 into IAS 31 are presented in the first section. Prior economic consequences literature is reviewed and applied to the IASC case in the second section. Institutional theory is discussed and applicable hypothesized relationships are introduced in the third section. The fourth section contains research design and data collection discussions. The results are analysed in the next section and the final section presents the conclusions and implications of the study.

BACKGROUND

From its formation in 1973 until 1989, the IASC promulgated IASs with input from a select group of interested parties. Besides the IASC Board members the IASC invited commentary from IASC members, professional associations, government agencies, public accounting firms and corporations. Eventually part of this process was formalized into an official IASC Consultative Group. Table 1 lists the board members and Table 2 lists the members of the consultative group during the focus of this study's time frame. Most of the IASC's deliberations were conducted essentially

Table 1 Members of IASC Board (1989)

Representatives of the accountancy profession from:
Australia*
Canada*
Denmark
France
Germany
Italy
Japan
Jordan
Korea
Netherlands
South Africa
United Kingdom
United States*
and representations of up to four other organizations with an interest in financial reporting (then only one):
International Co-ordinating Committee of Financial Analysts' Associations

* Participated on Joint Venture Technical Steering Committee.

Source: ISAC (1989)

Table 2 Members of IASC Consultative Group (1989)

Federation Internationale des Bourses de Valeurs (FIBV)
Financial Accounting Standards Board (FASB)
International Association of Financial Executives Institutes (IAFEI)
International Banking Associations
International Bar Association (IBA)
International Chamber of Commerce (ICC)
International Confederation of Free Trade Unions (ICFTU) and World Confederation of Labour
International Finance Corporation (IFC)
International Organization of Securities Commissions (IOSCO)
The World Bank
Organization for Economic Co-operation and Development (OECD)*
United Nations Centre on Transnational Corporations (UNCTC)*

* Denotes observer status.

Source: IASC (1989)

in private, and comment letters were not released to the public.

Beginning with ED 32, issued in 1989, the IASC began a new due process which more closely mirrors that of the FASB, including public input and a form of public hearings. ED 32, 'Comparability of Financial Statements', generated over 125 comment letters, including forty-seven from various multinational enterprises; most of the comment letters concerning ED 32 were released to the public. However, ED 32 did not result in an IAS; rather, ED 32 was split into several separate exposure drafts. At the time of this study, the comment letters on the separate exposure drafts had not been released to the public. ED 33, 'Accounting for Income Taxes', was released in 1989 and generated considerable commentary as well. As of early 1993, the IASC has not resolved the issue of accounting for income taxes (IASC 1993). Thus, neither ED 32 or ED 33 followed smoothly the IASC's new due process and, thus, could not be used in this study.

Two EDs, 34 and 35, followed the IASC's new due process from inception to promulgation of an IAS. ED 34, 'Disclosures in the Financial Statements of Banks and Similar Financial Institutions', generated thirty-three comment letters which were released to the public and culminated in IAS 30. ED 35, 'Financial Reporting of Interests in Joint Ventures', generated fifty comment letters and culminated in IAS 31. Since the issue addressed in ED 34 applied only to financial institutions, we hypothesized that ED 34 might not generate much public input from industrial multinationals. ED 35, however, dealt with a salient issue of MNCs, accounting for joint ventures, and we expected considerable public input from multinationals. Accordingly, we chose to study the deliberation process of ED 35 (IAS 31) in this research project. We were interested in the entire deliberation process, so we analysed both lobbying behaviour (comment letters from constituents) and the IASC's reactions and behaviour.

The IASC issued ED 35, 'Financial Reporting of Interests in Joint Ventures', in December 1989. Comment letters were due to the IASC by May 1990. The IASC received fifty comment letters on ED 35 from fifty-two organizations, trade/professional associations and individuals from eighteen different countries.[2] The final standard, IAS 31, 'Financial Reporting of Interests in Joint Ventures', was issued in November 1990.

ED 35 defines the nature of joint operations and prescribes various accounting treatments for several types of joint venture operations. ED 35 defines joint ventures broadly, including not only jointly controlled entities, but also jointly controlled operations and jointly controlled assets. The general tone of the ED stresses the relative importance of the economic substance of relationships within the joint ventures over the legal form of those relationships. Also, the lack of unilateral control by any one venturer and consensus in all major decision making is key to the joint venture relationship in ED 35. Thus, venturers would include in their own financial statements their ownership/responsibility of jointly controlled assets, liabilities, revenues and expenses. Further, ED 35 suggests proportional consolidation for jointly controlled entities. Gains and losses on capital contributions are then to be limited to that portion attributable to the interests of the other venturers/partners. ED 35 also encourages substantial disclosures regarding the nature and scope of joint venture operations.

Although IAS 31 retains much of the flavour of the ED, the IASC did recant its insistence on proportional consolidation for jointly controlled entities by allowing the equity method as an acceptable accounting alternative. In addition, the IASC deleted some of the disclosure requirements in ED 35 and more carefully defined 'unilateral control' and consensus in decision making to encompass a wider range of joint venture arrangements.

LITERATURE REVIEW

Prior literature regarding lobbying activities directed towards accounting standards-setting organizations follows two basic paths: (1) as a subset of accounting choice research, lobbying has been studied from management's perspective, and (2) the relevant influence of various parties on standards setters has been analysed. Both of these paths of research follow an economic consequences model, assuming self-interest motivations on the part of the lobbyists. To date, the literature has not tied together these two lines of research in an international accounting lobbying context. Rather, the extant literature has tended to study behaviour of standards-setting organizations (primarily the FASB) as separate from that of the lobbyists. Our research introduces an institutional theory framework which affords us the opportunity to study the relationship of the standards-setting organization (in this case, the IASC) to its constituents from a strategy standpoint.[3]

Much of the prior literature views lobbying accounting standards setters as a subset of accounting choice research (Francis, 1987; Deakin, 1989; Kelly, 1985). In this context, the purpose of the research has been to identify economic incentives associated with management's choices, with respect to either accounting methods or lobbying activities (Francis, 1987). From this line of research, several hypotheses have evolved and have been well supported:

1. Lobbying firms tend to be very large because lobbying is costly, and only the very large firm can receive enough benefit to justify the cost. Additionally, the very large firms are the only ones which can hope to influence standards setters. Finally, lobbying is a means of mitigating political costs (such as tax or antitrust) borne by the very large firms.
2. Debt position (leverage) is a factor significantly influencing a firm's decision to lobby because of the impacts of accounting upon lending agreements (debt covenants) and perceived risk in the marketplace for debt financing.
3. In general, firms will lobby for accounting treatments which broaden their abilities to manage reported income.
4. If management's compensation is based upon reported income, management will prefer accounting methods which maximize its income.

The accounting choice research in lobbying behaviour assumes that lobbying will significantly influence the standards setters' activities, and that lobbyists will get what they want in the process. This line of research implicitly assumes that management feels financial reporting techniques have economic consequences and that changes in accounting standards can significantly impact on firm valuation. Further, as Tandy and Wilburn (1992) note, disagreement with a proposed standard seems to induce response.

In terms of the question addressed in this study, accounting for joint ventures, the economic consequences literature should lead us to hypothesize that large MNCs involved heavily or contemplating involvement in joint venture projects should be interested in the ED. Further, since the ED supported a method which differed from that which the MNC was presently using (as in the case of proportional consolidation), the economic consequences literature would predict voluminous and negative commentary on the part of MNCs.

Another area of lobbying research studied the relative influence of various lobbying organizations. Initially, the research studied the contention that public accounting firms have undue influence on standards-setting organizations (US Senate, 1976; Haring, 1979; Hussein and Ketz, 1980; Brown, 1981; Newman, 1981). Although the research has evolved into more general studies of the relative influence of various types of organizations on standards-setting bodies (Puro, 1985; Taylor, 1987; Tandy and Wilburn, 1992), the question of public accounting influence on the IASC has been noted (IASC, 1992). While the general consensus of this line of research is that public accounting firms do not exhibit undue influence on standards-setting organizations (at least, not on the FASB), at least two observations about the lobbying behaviour of public accounting firms have been supported in the literature:

1. Accounting firms will lobby to express their views.
2. Large multinational accounting firms are more likely to lobby than are small and medium-sized firms.

In summary, the prior literature seems to tell us who will lobby and why, and the prior literature implicitly assumes the standards-setting organization will be influenced by lobbying activities. However, the strategy of the standards-setting organization to deal with and/or encourage participation has not been addressed in the economic consequences literature. In the next section, we discuss this dimension as guided by institutional theory.

INSTITUTIONAL THEORETICAL FRAMEWORK

Institutional theory places organizations within a social setting and explicitly recognizes the influences and interactions of the external social environment on the internal activities of the organization (Selznick, 1957; Scott, 1987). A key element of institutional theory is that an organization strives to be legitimized by becoming or remaining acceptable within the social environment (Dowling and Pfeffer, 1975; Oliver, 1990; Meyer and Scott, 1983; Meyer and Rowen, 1977). In this context, organizations such as the IASC must remain acceptable to their constituencies to survive. Therefore, organizations will continuously monitor the needs and influences of their constituencies and will adjust accordingly to meet those needs.

In the case of the IASC, we observe an organization which solicits direct commentary about its products (accounting standards) from its constituents. An institutional theory framework would assume that the IASC plans to use the commentary in its deliberations. Lobbying in the form of commentary on exposure drafts should be an effective way for constituencies to make known their wishes and influence the outcome of the regulation, e.g. accounting standard. Consistent with the predictions of economic consequences theories in this instance, institutional theories would predict that constituents will respond to the IASC's requests for commentary.

Institutional theory predicts that an organization will be responsive to its environment and will change itself to adapt to (real and/or perceived) shifts in its environment (Scott, 1987). Institutional theorists emphasize that environmental forces make organizations adopt forms which best meet imposed needs, thereby encouraging continuous interaction between an organization and its environment (Thompson, 1976). Although changes in organizational form and strategy may be induced by a variety of factors and may be explained under a variety of rhetorics in the institutional theory literature, organizational change, while difficult, is virtually a foregone conclusion (Zucker, 1977, 1983, 1988; Fogarty, 1992; Scott, 1987).

The IASC's 1989 policy shift triggered our interest in the organization and the process by which it established international accounting standards. The policy shift seemed consistent with an institutional theory explanation of mimetic institutional influence (DiMaggio and Powell, 1983).[4] Mimetic institutional influence suggests that organizations will try to model themselves after other organizations which they perceive as successful or legitimized because to do so enhances their own legitimacy and reduces their exposure to environmental uncertainty. Since the FASB and the IASC were formed in the same year (1973), and the FASB has been more fully legitimized, the mimetic institutional influence explanation might predict that the rational strategy for the IASC to take was to imitate the FASB's format.[5]

International stock exchanges, professional accounting organizations and multinational corporations (MNCs) are the IASC's targeted constituency. Based upon this relationship, MNCs and organizations representing MNCs should be highly inclined to respond to IASC exposure drafts. Institutional theory would also predict that the IASC will try to accommodate the strongest wishes of its constituency when doing so enhances the organization's acceptability without seriously impairing its integrity. This 'give and take' process will usually result in at least some flexibility in the accounting standards in order to accommodate as many of its constituents as possible.[6]

As Fogarty (1992) points out, the notion of resource dependency also enriches the institutional theory perspective. Resource dependency concepts focus on the firm's competition for external sources of funding (Tolbert, 1985; Oliver, 1990). The successful competition for scarce resources enhances the organization's legitimization and increases its likelihood of survival (Dowling and Pfeffer,1975; DiMaggio, 1988; Oliver, 1990). In the case of the IASC, resources consist primarily of contributions and, to a lesser extent, rhetorical support. In this regard, the IASC may be in competition with the FASB and other standards-setting organizations for contributions. As we studied the IASC, we observed increasing levels of support from various international organizations, including the International Federation of Stock Exchanges (FIBV), the International Bar Association and the IOSCO.[7] Coupled with the IASC's deliberate attempts to invite a wider range of participants into the standards-setting process, we hypothesize an adaptation and resource-seeking strategy designed to further legitimize the IASC. The change in due process policy may simply be a survival strategy, as Wallace (1990) suggests, but even that explanation is generally consistent within an institutional theory framework.

Consistent with the accounting choice research and economic consequences theory, we agree that very large firms will respond to IASC's exposure drafts because (1) the cost of response is relatively high, (2) very large (multinational) firms are significantly affected by IASC standards and (3) only very large (multinational) firms can hope to have the clout to influence the behaviour of standards-setting organizations. The accounting choice/economic consequences theory hypothesizes that debt position, income manipulation and management compensation plans are factors in the decision to lobby. These three factors are only relevant if the proposed standards affect them. While ED 35 cannot be used to test the income manipulation and management compensation issues because it does not increase or decrease income, the debt position is relevant since proportional consolidation may result in a different balance sheet.

In summary, a large number of MNCs are expected to respond because the issue, joint venture accounting, affects most MNCs. Further, we expected MNCs to oppose any method which required a change from their current practice, such as would be the case with proportional consolidation. Finally, we expected responses from IASC member bodies, the large international accounting firms and other interest parties, especially those who oppose at least part of ED 35.

RESEARCH DESIGN

Table 3 lists the respondents to ED 35. Respondents were categorized by size, type of organization, country of origin, multinational operations and activity in joint ventures. This data was gathered from a variety of sources, including Disclosure, ABI Inform and NAARS.

The responses were analysed using content analysis and categorized based upon their general support of the standard and/or the IASC's joint venture project as well as their comments on various parts of ED 35. Consistent with Holsti (1969), responses were analysed both for commentary and tone of commentary. In general, however, respondents' letters were quite straightforward and often almost terse, so the concerns often present in content analysis may be somewhat lessened in this study.

The demographic data about the respondents was combined with the

Table 3 Respondents to IASC Exposure Draft 35 on Joint Ventures

Member bodies of the IASC:	
CIC	Accounting Standards Steering Committee of the Canadian Institute of Chartered Accountants
CGA	Certified General Accountants' Association of Canada
CYP	Institute of Certified Public Accountants of Cyprus
FRN	Compagnie Nationale des Commissaires aux Comptes and Orde des Experts Comptables et des Comptables Agrees (France)
GER	Institut der Wirtschaftsprufer (Federal Republic of Germany)
JPN	Japanese Institute of Certified Public Accountants
NZ	New Zealand Society of Accountants
NRW	Norwegian Institute of State Authorized Public Accountants, Norwegian Accounting Standards Board, and Oslo Stock Exchange
SNG	Institute of Certified Public Accountants of Singapore
SA	South African Institute of Chartered Accountants
SWD	Foreningen Auktoriserade Revisorer FAR (Sweden)
SWZ	Schweizereische Kammer der Bucher-Steuer-und Treuhendexperten (Switzerland)
AIC	American Institute of Certified Public Accountants
NAA	National Association of Accountants (now IMA)
ZMB	Institute of Chartered Accountants of Zimbabwe
Regional and other accounting bodies:	
FEE	Federation des Experts Comptables Européens
NJ	New Jersey Society of Certified Public Accountants
Standard-setting bodies:	
NTH	Raad Voor De Jaarverslaggeving – Council for Annual Reporting (The Netherlands)
UK	Accounting Standards Committee of the United Kingdom and Ireland
GSB	The staff of the Governmental Accounting Standards Board
Stock exchanges:	
JSE	Johannesburg Stock Exchange
Other organizations:	
SEC	Securities and Exchange Commission
FEI	Financial Executive Institute
SJP	Security Analysts Association of Japan
Corporations – industry and commerce:	
BHP	Broken Hill Proprietary (Australia)
RDS	Royal Dutch Shell (Netherlands & UK)
ABL	Abbott Laboratories
ELI	Eli Lilly and Company
ITT	ITT Corporation
MRC	Merck & Co., Inc.
SAL	Salomon Inc
SHL	Shell Oil Company
TEX	Texaco Inc

Table 3—*continued*

Representative organizations – industry and commerce:	
100	The Hundred Group (UK)
Banks and banking associations:	
CIT	Citicorp – Citibank N.A.
BAA	British Bankers' Association
Accounting firms:	
AA	Arthur Andersen & Co (International)
HI	Hodgson Impey (UK)
PW	Price Waterhouse (USA)
Individual, but member of accounting firm:	
CLC	M.P. Carscallen, Coopers & Lybrand (Canada)
Those who responded, but desired that their responses remain confidential:	
Bahamas Institute of Chartered Accountants	
Association for Investment Management and Research (USA)	
CIGNA Corporation	
E. I. Du Pont de Nemours & Company	
General Electric Company	
Texas Instruments	
AT&T	
Coopers & Lybrand (USA)	
Plus two other unknown respondents	

results of the content analysis in order to perform several tests analysing the existence of any patterns between responses and respondents.

Finally, the comments and suggestions of the respondents were compared to the requirements in the final standard to see what influence, if any, the respondents had on the IASC. This last step was designed to test the IASC's adaptability and desire to be acceptable to its constituency, as well as to be a weak test of the significance of influence of any one group on the IASC.

RESULTS

Characteristics of respondents

The bulk of the fifty comment letters to ED 35 came from professional organizations and standards-setting bodies. Four public accounting firms and one partner of a large international accounting firm also submitted responses. Of the fifty responses, only fifteen responses were from industrial or financial institutions, contrary to expectations. Of the fifty responses, however, only forty were made public.[8]

The fifteen corporations that did respond were, as predicted, extremely large MNCs. Thirteen of the fifteen businesses responding were US-based multinational corporations, representing several industries, including the oil and gas, financial services and pharmaceutical sectors. The two non-US firms were gigantic mining and oil and gas firms (Royal Dutch Shell and BHP). Each of the US responding corporations was consistently listed in the Fortune 500 in the past decade. The 1988, 1989 and 1990 annual reports for the MNC respondents were reviewed and, interestingly, only six of the thirteen US corporate respondents mentioned international joint venture activities in their annual reports.[9]

Further, NAARS search indicated that the corporate respondents were not particularly representative of those firms which engage heavily in joint ventures. One hundred and nine companies reported significant international joint venture activity in either their 1989 or 1990 annual reports. The companies represented several industries, including oil and gas, automotive, manufacturing and pharmaceutical industries. Several of the joint venture discussions in the annual reports were lengthy and discussed activities in virtually all sectors of the world. We wondered why these firms had not responded to the IASC's exposure draft regarding joint venture accounting. We thought at first that perhaps these firms simply did not lobby standards-setting organizations at all, but a quick review of FASB respondents found the contrary. More often than not these firms did officially comment on FASB exposure drafts.

So, while this study finds some evidence that only very large firms lobby, it does not fully support the economic consequences theory literature. The paucity of responses from seemingly affected firms casts doubt on the perceived economic consequences of the IASC's standards. An alternative explanation may be that many of these firms do not perceive themselves to be affected by IASC standards and, thus, are not part of its constituency. The ramifications of this alternative explanation are discussed more fully later in the paper.

Content analysis of comment letters

Respondents' comment letters were analysed to determine the major areas of comment or concern. The content analysis indicated that the respondents were concerned with three major issues: (1) general need for a joint venture standard, (2) proportionate consolidation and (3) disclosure requirements. On each of these points, respondents were fairly clear and consistent; that is, respondents either supported the issue or they did not, and there was very little evidence of indecision or 'degrees' of support. Accordingly, responses were coded nominally.

Table 4 Respondents' positions listed and grouped based upon overall support, proportionate consolidation and disclosure requirements

Respondent		*Overall support (S=support, N=neutral or no comment, O=oppose)*	*Proportionate consolidation (S=support, N=neutral or no comment, O=oppose)*	*Disclosure requirements (S=support, N=neutral or no comment, O=oppose)*
CLC	Can Coopers & L	O	O	N
HI	UK Hodgson Imp	O	O	N
CIT	US Citicorp	O	O	N
ITT	US ITT	O	O	N
RDS	Royal Dutch Sh	O	O	N
TEX	US Texaco	O	O	N
FEE	Fed Eurp Accts	O	O	N
GER	Germany	O	O	N
GSB	US GASB	O	O	N
NAA	US NAA (IMA)	O	O	N
NZ	New Zealand	O	O	N
SEC	US SEC	O	O	N
SAL	US Salomon	O	O	S
100	UK Hundred Grp	O	O	O
ELI	US Eli Lilly	O	O	O
SHL	Shell Oil	O	O	O
FEI	Finl Exec Inst	O	O	O
NTH	Netherlands	O	O	O
UK	UK ASC	O	O	O
AA	Arthur Andersn	S	O	N
BHP	Aust Broken Hl	S	O	N
NRW	Norway	S	O	N
SJP	Jp Security Anl	S	O	N
CYP	Cyprus	N	N	N
SNG	Singapore	N	N	N
ZMB	Zimbabwe	N	N	N
ABL	US Abbott Labs	S	S	O
BAA	UK Bankers	S	S	O
FRN	France	S	S	O
PW	Price Waterhse	S	S	S
SA	South Africa	S	S	S
MRC	US Merck	S	S	N
CGA	Can CGA	S	S	N
JSE	JohannesburgSE	S	S	N
NJ	US New Jersey	S	S	N
JPN	Japan	S	S	N
SWD	Sweden	S	S	N
SWZ	Switzerland	S	S	N
CIC	Can CICA	O	S	O

Analysis of respondents' positions

Tables 4 and 5 present the results of the content analysis.[10] In general, the comment letters expressed support for the process of internationalization and harmonization of accounting standards, even though many comments had specific disagreements with certain aspects of this particular proposed standard.

Table 5 Summary of respondents' positions on three main issues

	Overall support	*Proportionate consolidation*	*Disclosure requirements*
Support	16	13	3
Neutral/no comment	3	3	27
Oppose	21	24	10

The first column in Table 4 presents the 'overall support' category. 'Overall support' is based on respondents' general comments regarding ED 35 and/or their comments regarding the mission of the IASC in the area of joint venture accounting. Sixteen respondents expressed support for ED 35. While less than the majority of respondents, we interpret these responses as evidence to suggest that at least a portion of the IASC's constituency seems to be legitimizing the IASC by acceptance and support. Although twenty-one respondents expressed strong concerns about the appropriateness of ED 35, these respondents seemed to focus primarily on proportionate consolidation issues, as opposed to the overall intent of harmonization of joint venture accounting and the IASC.

The second column of Table 4 presents the issue of proportionate consolidation for jointly controlled entities. The area of proportional consolidation generated the most responses of all separable issues in ED 35. Two diametrically opposed groups formed. The larger group of twenty-four respondents opposed proportional consolidation and is dominated by most of the US, UK and German professional organizations and industrials which responded.

The other group of thirteen respondents supported proportional consolidation and represents a diverse group, including one US public accounting firm (Price Waterhouse), two US pharmaceutical corporations (Merck and Abbott Labs), the British Bankers Association and the professional accounting organizations for France, South Africa, Japan, Sweden and Switzerland. Interestingly, while both Canadian professional accountancy organizations are in this group and support proportionate consolidation, a representative of Coopers & Lybrand (Canada) opposed proportionate consolidation. However, since no Canadian corporations responded, it is not possible to assess which position is representative of Canadian industrials.

The link between the respondents in each opposing group is not well explained by either of the theoretical frameworks used in this study. The evidence appears to support most strongly the view that firms and organizations lobby to maintain the status quo. Inasmuch as the equity method is presently acceptable in the US, the UK and Germany, the domination of the group opposing proportionate consolidation by representatives from these countries appears consistent.

Next, comparisons were made of the first two columns in Table 4, based on general support and proportionate consolidation. Interestingly, respondents who oppose proportionate consolidation also seem to dismiss ED 35 in general. Even though the relationship is interesting, it tends to cloud the application of institutional and legitimacy theories to this scenario. From the tenor of the responses, it was not determined if the respondents generally support the IASC's efforts and simply oppose proportionate consolidation, or if they dismissed both. To try and understand this relationship, the respondents to ED 34 were briefly analysed. Seventeen of the ED 35 respondents also responded to ED 34, although none of the dual respondents were corporations. Thus, if response can be at all interpreted as either support, legitimization or acknowledgement of importance, then legitimization is being given to the IASC only by the professional accounting organizations. At this time corporations may not feel a need to respond to each ED from the IASC, either because the IASC is not important, the accounting issue is not important or because corporations are willing to allow professional organizations to handle it.

The third column in Table 4 lists whether respondents support the disclosure requirements. Only ten of the respondents to ED 35 opposed or suggested an alteration in the proposed disclosure requirements. While that number does not, on the surface, seem important, it is because twenty-seven of the respondents made no comment on the disclosure requirements.

Next, all three issues were examined together: general support, proportionate consolidation and support of disclosure requirements. The first group of thirteen respondents oppose both ED 35 in general and proportionate consolidation specifically. They are silent with respect to additional disclosures, which might mean that by dismissing the overall content of the ED, they have also effectively dismissed the disclosure requirements. While this cluster is dominated by US respondents, it is by no means representative of all US respondents, either corporations, regulatory bodies or professional organizations.

Other respondents, when grouped by their common position, were fairly diverse and did not appear to have a common link, at least as explained by the theoretical frameworks. The BHP, AA, NRW and SJP group of respondents, however, while tiny, is quite interesting. This group is made up of respondents who expressed general support for ED 35, opposed proportionate consolidation and were silent with respect to additional disclosures. This might be the type of response one would expect to see to support the legitimizing theories; that is, the constituencies support the institution in principle, but oppose some of its edicts. This is precisely the type of response a 'legitimate' organization would generate, much like that observed with respect to the FASB.

That this group is so tiny may be interpreted in the context of institutional theory. One might argue that, since the IASC has a new due process, the need for public legitimization by respondents is not understood by the IASC's constituents. Further, the 'constituency' may not yet realize that it is the constituency. This interpretation would imply that, once constituents understand this need, future EDs should generate more responses and interest by both professional organizations and corporations. Of course, any increase in the level and/or intensity of response might also indicate an increasing economic consequences perspective.

Analysis of positions by group membership

We further analysed the groups formed by the issues 'overall support', 'proportional consolidation' and 'disclosure', to see if certain types of organizations held similar views. The respondents were grouped by country (grouping US and UK together and comparing them to other countries), and industry (including categories for corporate, public accounting and professional organizations). These analyses are presented in Table 6.

Table 6 Analysis of responses by country of origin: difference of means tests

	N	*Overall support*	*Proportional consolidation*	*Disclosure requirements*
US/UK	21	–.4286	–.5238	–.2381
Other countries	19	.2105	.0000	-.1053
t-value		2.19**	1.82*	.76

* significant at .076 confidence level (two-tailed test).
** significant at .035 confidence level (two-tailed test).

Grouping by industry/organization was uniformly insignificant. No issue identified divided respondents based on their type of organization. Grouping by country, however, was significant in the 'overall support' and 'proportional consolidation' issues. With a mean response of –.43, the US/UK group is significantly different (and generally non-supportive of ED 35) from the other countries responding. This difference is significant at a .035 level 38 with degrees of freedom. In other words, in general, US or UK respondents were less likely to support ED 35 than respondents from other countries. Further, the US/UK group tended generally to oppose proportional consolidation, with a mean response of −.52; and was significantly different from respondents from other countries on this issue, with a confidence level of .076. We find this result odd in light of recent criticisms directed towards the IASC which claim that the IASC is dominated by US and UK influences. Though this criticism appears somewhat validated later by the IASC's response to objections from the US and UK.

The US/UK versus everyone else split led us to review the comment letters again. The data lend supports to the economic consequences view that respondents are unwilling to change from the status quo. In the case of ED 35, proportional consolidation represented a change from the status quo, which appeared to be unacceptable to US and UK respondents. Proportional consolidation, while having no differential impact on net income than the equity method, changes the picture of the balance sheet. The relationships on the balance sheet should be similar under both methods, but the increase in both assets and liabilities may be undesirable to companies used to using the equity method, especially those with debt covenant restrictions.

Analysis of the IASC's response

The final analysis compared the requirements of the ED with the IAS, given the nature and intensity of respondents' comments. Of major importance was that the IASC modified the ED to allow the equity method for accounting for jointly controlled entities. The IASC also modified the descriptions and requirements for disclosures in accordance with respondents' comments. This action is consistent with institutional theory. Seeking legitimization and survival, the IASC must remain acceptable to its constituency. If the IASC is to achieve its goal of harmonization, it must accomplish these objectives (Wallace, 1990). One strategy to accomplish these goals is to maintain a posture of flexibility and receptivity to public input (Wallace, 1990).[11] This does, however, also reinforce criticism of the IASC as being dominated by UK and US interests (Hove, 1990).

One important note is that the IASC, in order to pass a new IAS, must get three-fourths of the vote of the IASC board members (IASC, 1989). Thus the IAS must be acceptable to the vast majority of the Board. Of the letters from respondents from countries represented on the IASC Board, a majority opposed proportional consolidation (see Table 7). Therefore, assuming that Board members at least consider the desires of those in their own country as well as seek general legitimacy, some compromise

Table 7 Analysis of respondents from IASC board member countries

	All support	*Most support*	*Split*	*Most oppose*	*All oppose*
Position on proportionate consolidation	France South Africa	Canada	Japan	United Kingdom United States	Australia Germany Netherlands

was required in order to achieve the required number of votes to approve a joint venture IAS.

A final issue considered was the relationship of the funding of the IASC to its decision, i.e. the resource dependency issue. Historically, the primary sources of funding for the IASC were the International Federation of Accountants (IFAC) and the IASC board members themselves. More recently, funds have also been contributed by the six largest international accounting firms, as well as by other accounting firms and corporations, including BHP (Australia) and ITT (IASC, 1991). Of those known for both taking positions on ED 35 and contributing to the IASC, both corporations (BHP and ITT) were opposed to proportional consolidation, while the accounting firms were split on the issue. While contributions may be made in order to increase an organization's influence on the IASC, insufficient information is currently available in order to reach any real conclusion on this matter.

CONCLUSION

This study examined the IASC's process of promulgating IAS 31, 'Financial Reporting of Interests in Joint Ventures', the lobbying efforts observed during the process and the interaction between the IASC and its constituents. The interaction between respondents and the IASC is consistent with an institutional theory explanation of organizational change and adaptation to environment pressures. The results were also consistent with an economic consequences model in that only very large firms lobby and they lobby against virtually any change in the *status quo*. Further, the respondents did tend to cluster around a few salient issues. However, their behaviour and the small number of corporate respondents did not strongly support an economic consequences explanation.

Also interesting from both an economic consequences viewpoint and an institutional legitimacy standpoint is the fact that US companies heavily involved in international joint ventures did not respond to the IASC. Given the recent attention paid to harmonization of financial reporting standards in both the academic and popular press and the attention the issue is receiving from international stock exchanges, more responses from

MNCs were expected. However, further study of both the data and MNCs active in international joint venture activity led us to conclude that the IASC probably was not perceived as a salient regulatory body by most of those companies. In addition, we studied one of IASC's 'new due process' standards, which may not have attracted much attention from these corporations since the IASC's new standards-setting process was such a recent event.

The study, like most lobbying studies, is subject to several limitations. For example, the decision to lobby is inherently a respondent specific choice, and, thus, any study of lobbyists represents a choice-based sample. In this context, that bias is acceptable since we were primarily interested in those who did lobby as opposed to those who did not. However, future research in this area may choose to concentrate on those organizations involved in joint venture activities who did not lobby, especially given evidence to suggest that this population is large.

Another criticism of lobbying studies is that each study tends to treat lobbying as a single-issue, single-period decision, when it actually may be a multiple-issue, multiple-period decision. Inasmuch as ED 35 represents only one of the first two standards to have endured the entire process under the IASC's new rules, we have no way currently of assessing the impact (if any) of this criticism. As the IASC continues under its new due process, future research may involve longitudinal studies of the process of lobbying over time by particular firms and/or organizations. Another area for future research may focus on multiple entity lobbying, i.e., a study of firms who lobby a variety of accounting standards-setting bodies.

Additionally, we chose to study an ED which eventually became an IAS. From an institutional theory standpoint, a study of those EDs which did not become IASs may also be relevant. Our focus in this paper was the more complete due process, but future research may include studies of 'unsuccessful' EDs.

The conclusions of this study suggest a basis for future research examining MNC reaction to forthcoming IASC exposure drafts. The IASC is publicizing its activities more fully and has recently gained the support of IOSCO and the interest of the SEC. Harmonization continues to be a popular idea, both in the EC and the Pacific Rim. Even the AICPA (American Institute of Certified Public Accountants) and the IMA (Institute of Management Accountants) are now regularly announcing new IASC EDs in their publications. Accordingly, we expect to see an increase in both the number and intensity of responses to future IASC exposure drafts. The current study provides a base from which to launch those future studies.

This study also motivates future research dealing with the IASC's move towards more restrictive accounting standards (as evidenced by the many recently released EDs). As these EDs, most of which are components of

ED 32, move through the due process, the interaction between the IASC and its constituencies may be compared to the actions predicted by institutional theories and economic consequences theories.

While this study raises interesting questions for future study, it also contributes to the current literature in at least two important areas. First, this study represents some of the first empirical work examining lobbying accounting standards setting bodies in an international context. Second, this study addresses the applicability of two theoretical frameworks, each developed in a US context, to an international context.

NOTES

We gratefully acknowledge the helpful comments from our colleagues at the University of Utah, Jerry Searfoss of Deloitte and Touche, Anne Loft (the editor) and an anonymous reviewer. We thank the Center for International Business Education and Research at the University of Utah for its support of this project. Any remaining errors are our own.

The data used in this study were purchased from a variety of sources, all of which are available to the public. Included in the data sources are: the IASC, *NAARS, Disclosure* and *ABI Inform*.

1 Wallace (1990) discusses the issue of lobbying the IASC, but his focus is the IASC's reactions to lobbying as opposed to the motivations and/or behaviours of the lobbyists. While Grinyer and Russell (1992) discuss whether the IASC affects the UK standard setting process, their focus is lobbying efforts towards the UK's Accounting Standard Committee.
2 In one instance three Norwegian organizations jointly penned responses to ED 35, thus providing fifty letters in total from fifty-two organizations.
3 Fogarty (1992) suggests studying the FASB from an institutional theory standpoint.
4 For a discussion of mimetic institutional influence as applied to the FASB, see Fogarty (1992).
5 For a discussion of the legitimization of the FASB, see Johnson and Solomons (1984).
6 Though with the increased involvement of IOSCO in the activities of the IASC, the push for narrower standards may eventually outweigh the push for flexible standards.
7 For a more detailed discussion of this point, see FIBV (1991) and IOSCO (1991).
8 In the transition to the 'new due process', the IASC allowed respondents confidentiality if they so chose. Five corporate respondents elected that option.
9 Respondents mentioning joint venture activity in the Form 10-K include AT&T, General Electric, ITT, Merck, Shell and Texaco.
10 Cluster analysis was also performed with the data and provided similar results.
11 Again, it will be interesting to see if the IASC continues to allow flexible IASs in the future, given that IOSCO, a new major constituent, is strongly lobbying for narrower IASs.

REFERENCES

Benston, G. J. (1980) 'The Establishment and Enforcement of Accounting Standards: Methods, Benefits and Costs', *Accounting and Business Research*, Winter: 51–60.

Brown, P. R. (1981) 'A Descriptive Analysis of Select Input Bases of the Financial Accounting Standards Board', *Journal of Accounting Research*, 19: 232–46.

Cairns, D. (1989) 'IASC's Blueprint for the Future', *Accountancy*, 104 (1156): 80–2.

Cairns, D. (1992) 'FIBV/Toronto Stock Exchange Workshop: Should Listed Companies Conform with IAS?', *IASC Insight*, July: 7–8.

Campbell, A. (1990) *Lobbying Intensity and Corporate Management's Opinion: The Marketable Securities Case, 1975*, working paper, University of Colorado at Boulder.

Chandler, R. A. (1992) 'The International Harmonization of Accounting: In Search of Influence', *International Journal of Accounting*, 27: 222–33.

Choi, F. D. S. and Mueller, G. G. (1992) *International Accounting*, 2nd edition. Englewood Cliffs, NJ: Prentice-Hall.

Coopers & Lybrand (International) (1991) *1991 International Accounting Summaries: A Guide for Interpretation and Comparison*. New York: Wiley.

Deakin, E. B. (1989) 'Rational Economic Behavior and Lobbying on Accounting Issues: Evidence from the Oil and Gas Industry', *The Accounting Review*, January: 137–51.

Denman, J. H. (1991) *The Comparative Analysis of Financial Statements by Use of International Accounting Standards*, paper presented at the Third Asian-Pacific Conference on Accounting Issues, Honolulu, 18 October.

DiMaggio, P. (1988) 'Interest and Agency in International Theory,' in *Institutional Patterns and Organizations*, Zucler, L. (ed.) Cambridge, MA: Ballinger Press: 3–21.

DiMaggio, P. and Powell, W. (1983) 'The Iron Cage Revisited: Institutional Isomorphism and Collective Rationality in Organizational Fields', *American Sociological Review*, 48: 147–60.

Dowling. J. and Pfeffer, J. (1975) 'Organizational Legitimacy: Social Values and Organizational Behaviour' *Pacific Sociological Review* 18(1): 122–36.

Francis, J. R. (1987) 'Lobbying Against Proposed Accounting Standards: The Case of Employers Pension Accounting', *Journal of Accounting and Public Policy*, 6: 35–57.

Federation Internationale Des Bourses De Valeurs (FIBV) (1991) *Annual Report 1990*. Paris: FIBV.

Fogarty, T. J. (1992) 'Financial Accounting Standard Setting as an Institutionalized Action Field: Constraints, Opportunities and Dilemmas', *Journal of Accounting and Public Policy*, 11: 331–55.

Grinyer, J. R. and Russell, A. (1992) 'National Impediments to International Harmonization: Evidence of Lobbying in the UK', *Journal of International Accounting Auditing and Taxation*, 1(1): 13–31.

Guy, P. (1992) 'Regulatory Harmonization to Achieve Effective International Competition', in Edwards, F. R. and Patrick, H. T. (eds) *Regulating International Financial Markets: Issues and Policies*. Boston: Kluwer Academic.

Haring, J. R. (1979) 'Accounting Rules and "The Accounting Establishment"', *Journal of Business*, 52(4): 507–19.

Holsti, O. E. (1969) *Content Analysis for the Social Sciences and Humanities*. Addison-Wesley.

Hove, M. R. (1990) 'The Anglo-American Influence on International Accounting Standards: The Case of the Disclosure Standards of the International Accounting Standards Committee', in R. S. O. Wallace (ed.) *Research in Third World Accounting*, Vol. 1. London: JAI Press, pp. 55–66.

Hussein, M. E. and Ketz, J. E. (1980) 'Ruling Elites of the FASB: A Study of the Big Eight', *Journal of Accounting, Auditing and Finance*, 3(4): 354–67.

Hussein, M. E. and Ketz, J. E. (1991) 'Accounting Standards-Setting in the U.S.: An Analysis of Power and Social Exchange', *Journal of Accounting and Public Policy*, 10: 59–81.

International Accounting Standards Committee (1988) *Survey of the Use and Application of International Accounting Standards 1988*. London: IASC.

International Accounting Standards Committee (1989) *International Accounting Standards 1990*. London: IASC.

International Accounting Standards Committee (1990) 'Financial Reporting of Interests in Joint Ventures: From E35 to IAS 31', *IASC News*, 19: 7–11.

International Accounting Standards Committee (1991) 'IASC Funding: New Contributions From Business Community', *IASC Insight*, October: 2.

International Accounting Standards Committee (1992a) *International Accounting Standards 1993*. London: IASC.

International Accounting Standards Committee (1992b) 'Involving the Business Community', *IASC Insight*, March: 1.

International Organization of Securities Commissions (IOSCO) (1991) *Annual Report 1991*. Montreal: IOSCO.

Jensen, M. C. and Meckling, W. H. (1976) 'Theory of the Firm: Managerial Behavior, Agency Costs and Ownership Structure', *Journal of Financial Economics*, October: 305–60.

Johnson, S. B. and Solomons, D. (1984) 'Institutional Legitimacy and the FASB', *Journal of Accounting and Public Policy* 3(2): 165–83.

Kelly, L. (1982) 'Corporate Lobbying and Changes in Financing or Operating Activities in Reaction to FAS No. 8', *Journal of Accounting and Public Policy*, 1(2): 153–73.

Kelly, L. (1983) 'The Development of a Positive Theory of Corporate Management's Role in External Financial Reporting', *Journal of Accounting Literature*, 2: 111–50.

Kelly, L. (1985) 'Corporate Management Lobbying on FAS No. 8: Some Further Evidence', *Journal of Accounting Research*, 23: 619–33.

Meyer, J. W. and Rowan, B. (1977) 'Institutionalized Organizations: Formal Structure as Myth and Ceremony', in Meyer, J. W. and Scott, W. R. (eds) *Organizational Environments*. Beverly Hills, CA: Sage, pp. 45–67.

Meyer, J. W. and Scott, W. R. (1983) *Organizational Environments*. Beverly Hills, CA: Sage.

Newman, D. P. (1981) 'An Investigation of the Distribution of Power in the APB and FASB', *Journal of Accounting Research*, 19: 247–62.

Oliver, C. (1990) 'Determinants of Interorganizational Relationship: Integration and Future Developments', *Academy of Management Review*, 15(2): 241–65.

Puro, M. (1985) 'Do Large Accounting Firms Collude in the Standards-Setting Process?', *Journal of Accounting, Auditing, and Finance*, 8(3): 165–77.

Radebaugh, L. and Gray, S. (1993) *International Accounting and Multinational Enterprises*, 2nd edition. New York: Wiley.

Roberts, R. W. and Kurtenbach, J. M. (1990) 'An Analysis of Lobbying Activities before the Governmental Accounting Standards Board', working paper, University of Missouri-Columbia.

Scott, W. R. (1987) 'The Adolescence of Institutional Theory', *Administrative Science Quarterly*, 32: 493–511.

Selznick, P. (1957) *Leadership in Administration*. New York: Harper & Row.

Sutton, T. (1984) 'Lobbying of Accounting Standard-Setting Bodies in the U.K. and the U.S.A.: A Downsian Analysis', *Accounting, Organizations, and Society*, 9(1): 81–95.

Tandy, P. R. and Wilburn, N. L. (1992) 'Constituent Participation in Standard-Setting: The FASB's First 100 Statements', *Accounting Horizons*, 6: 47–58.

Taylor, S. L. (1987) 'International Accounting Standards: An Alternative Rationale', *Abacus*, (23)2: 157–71.

Thompson, J. D. (1976) *Organizations and Beyond: Selected Essays of James D. Thompson*, ed. W. A. Rushing and M. N. Zald. Lexington, Mass.: Lexington Books, D. C. Heath.

Tolbert, P. (1985) 'Institutional Environments and Resource Dependence: Sources of Administrative Structure in Higher Education', *Administrative Science Quarterly*, 30(1): 1–13.

US Senate (1976) 'Subcommittee on Reports, Accounting and Management of the Senate Committee on Government Operations, 94th Congress, 2nd Session', *The Accounting Establishment: A Staff Study (Metcalf Report)*. Washington, DC: Government Printing Office.

Wallace, R. S. O. (1990) 'Survival Strategies of a Global Organization: The Case of the International Accounting Standards Committee', *Accounting Horizons*, 4: 1–22.

Watts, R. L. and Zimmerman, J. L. (1978) 'Towards a Positive Theory of the Determination of Accounting Standards', *The Accounting Review*, 53: 112–34.

Watts, R. L. and Zimmerman, J. L. (1986) *Positive Accounting Theory*. Englewood Cliffs, NJ: Prentice-Hall.

Wyatt, A. R. (1991) 'International Accounting Standards and Organizations: Quo Vadis?' in Choi, F. D. S. (ed.) *Handbook of International Accounting*. New York: Wiley.

Wyatt, A. R. (1992) 'An Era of Harmonization', *Journal of International Financial Management & Accounting*, 4(1): 63–80.

Zucker, L. (1977) 'The Role of Institutions in Cultural Persistence', *American Sociological Review*, 42(5): 726–43.

Zucker, L. (1983) 'Organizations as Institutions', in Bacharach, S. (ed.) *Advances in Organizational Theory and Research*. New York: JAI Press, pp. 1–43.

Zucker, L. (1988) 'Where Do Institutional Patterns Come From?', in Zucker, L. (ed.) *Institutional Patterns and Organizations*. Cambridge, Mass.: Ballinger, pp. 23–49.

Part III
European Harmonization

[16]

EEC Accounting Harmonisation:
Implementation and Impact of the Fourth Directive
S.J. Gray and A.G. Coenenberg (editors)

1. THE AIMS OF EEC COMPANY LAW HARMONISATION: CORPORATE ACCOUNTING AND DISCLOSURE ISSUES

Robert Coleman
Commission of the European Communities

Before dealing with the objectives of company law harmonisation, and its goals as regards corporate accounting and disclosure in particular, it is useful to address a more general question: just what is the European Economic Community?

1. THE NATURE OF THE EEC

The answer to the question is important not simply so as to avoid any possible misunderstanding in the abstract interests of clarity and accuracy, but more concretely because the nature of the Community conditions its whole approach to corporate accounting and reporting, a matter to which I will return subsequently.

What is the creature then? One of the best answers is, I think, that it is **an adolescent federation:** an association of formerly independent, and ticklishy "sovereign", Nation States which have agreed amongst themselves to deal through a common legal and institutional framework with a number of mostly economic problems. The long term objective is to extend the range of common action to include all matters that are the concern of national governments in the modern State. Of course, this mature stage, what we might call **full** federation, is a long way off. And like many adolescents ours is rather spotty, not always well co-ordinated, and from time to time it relapses into childhood with a lot of screaming and shouting ("I want my money back!" "Cheat!" "Shan't!" "Won't!" etc.).

Be that as it may, the association has not been dissolved after more than 20 years of sometimes painful evolution. On the contrary, it has increased substantially in size. In addition, real progress has been made, if sometimes slowly, in many fields including the harmonization of company laws and more particularly the legal requirements of the Member States as to corporate accounting and reporting, our subject to-day.

2. THE OBJECTIVES OF THE COMMUNITY'S COMPANY LAW HARMONISATION MEASURES, WITH PARTICULAR REFERENCE TO THOSE ON ACCOUNTING AND REPORTING

The starting point is the EEC Treaty (the Treaty of Rome) itself, and in particular those of its provisions dealing with the freedom of establishment of firms (Article 52 to 58, and especially Article 54(3)(g)). In brief, in those articles, the Member States have agreed to harmonize their company laws **"to co-ordinate the safeguards"** contained therein **"for the protection of the interests of members and others...with a view to making such safeguards equivalent."** Why? What were they hoping to achieve?

The fundamental, strategic objectives were essentially two-fold. First, they wished to remove the obstacles consituted by differences in their national laws of the full exercise of certain basic liberties consecrated by the Treaty, namely the freedom of establishment of companies and firms and the free movement of capital. Second, and in many ways the other side of the coin, they sought to co-ordinate the safeguards contained in national company laws in order to ensure that **throughout the Community** certain **minimum standards** at least figure in all national legal systems.

To return to the **first objective, removal of barriers**, the Member States considered that differences in national legal requirements applicable to companies and firms complicate the lives of enterprises and investors seeking to operate across national frontiers and thereby, to a real extent, discourage their activities.

In the field of corporate accounting, examples are not hard to find or imagine. Though it is becoming (slowly) less true, to compare the accounts of companies incorporated in different Member States often requires a difficult operation of retreatment of the accounts concerned. This must frequently be done on the basis of assumptions that cannot be specified with certainty. From the early days of the company law programme, the European Federation of Association of Financial Analysts has consistently drawn attention to this problem and supported the Commission's harmonization proposals as a necessary and appropriate solution to the problems experienced daily by companies' shareholders, clients, suppliers, bankers (actual and, more important from the point of view of the development of the Community, potential).

From the perspective of enterprises themselves, seeking to adapt themselves to the new dimension of the Community market, divergent reporting and accounting requirements create obvious difficulties. Not only must different affiliates account and report on different bases, but the enterprise as a whole may find itself having to account in different ways in different contexts. Of course, enterprises can operate under these conditions, indeed they are obliged to. But the costs are real and cross-frontier activities are to a significant extent discouraged. Moreover, the problem risks becoming more acute as pressures for new forms of disclosure at national level produce national political responses and new national legislation.

Imagine, for example, what would probably have happened as regards **consolidation** requirements, if there had been no Community discussion of a seventh directive. Quite recently, another good example has arisen here in Belgium. The Belgian government has indicated an intention to legislate to give itself power to require the branches of foreign companies established in Belgium to account separately for the branch as if it were a separate company. Quite apart from the doubtful utility of such accounts, the multiplication of requirements clearly does not encourage foreign companies to take advantage of their rights under the Community Treaty and extend their activities to Belgium by opening a branch there. Indeed, we at the Commission take the view that the proposed Belgian requirements are not simply regrettable. They are also an infringement of the Community Treaty, since they might impose legal obligations on firms from other Member States that are not imposed on Belgian enterprises. We have approached the Belgian authorities officially to make known our views that their proposed requirements would be contrary to Articles 7 and 52 of the EEC Treaty and it will be interesting to see what develops.

For us, the issue is one of great importance since the **simplification** or **de-regulatory** effects of harmonisation from the point of view of enterprises would be seriously undermined if, even after the adoption of Community legislation on companies' annual accounts, Member States felt free to impose significant additional obligations on companies incorporated in other Member States which are not imposed on their own national firms. What is the point of co-ordinating the safeguards contained in national company laws as regards annual accounts, if additional requirements nevertheless will continue to be imposed on such companies seeking to operate through branches in another Member State?

This bring us neatly to **the second strategic objective,** the **co-ordination of safeguards.** The Treaty itself creates the right of establishment for companies and firms. They have a directly enforceable right to establish themselves, whether by opening up a branch or by incorporating or acquiring a subsidiary, in other Member States and to operate there under the same conditions as local firms. Hence, our challenge to the Belgian requirement on branch accounting. But if cross-frontier activities are to become more and more frequent, as indeed they have, the Member States have a clear interest in a programme that will ensure that all participants respect certain basic rules designed to protect interests likely to be affected. To put it rather dramatically, there are to be no "Delawares" in the EEC: no legal havens where systematic "laisser faire" could be used to secure economic advantage. If some Member States might seek to impose obligations on foreign enterprises that would discourage them from treating the common market as a single entity, others might on the other hand be tempted to attract enterprises to operate under their legal system rather than somebody else's. The advantages of such a policy for some Member States are rather obvious. It should be recalled that the interests of the Member States in this regard are not the same. Some have more to gain and less to lose than others.

That the problem is not an academic nightmare essentially divorced from reality has been clearly demonstrated by the experience of the United States. In the nineteenth century, a right of establishment had been recognized pursuant to the commerce and "full faith and credit" clauses of the US Constitution and as industrial and commercial development gathered momentum, certain States of the Union had indeed entered into a somewhat unholy competition to provide a company law most attractive to entrepreneurs. They competed by reducing the mandatory content of their laws. This competition, it is generally agreed, has been won by Delaware, with New Jersey a close finisher, though in truth, the competition continues to this day, which explains why large US corporations still tend to incorporate in those States rather than in Illinois or California, for example[2]. Moreover, it is interesting to note that despite the intervention of the federal government in the 'thirties to regulate the securities market and thereby indirectly the disclosure requirements for many larger companies, in recent years, an increasing number of commentators have called for action of a more direct kind to fill what they consider to be a legislative vacuum. Federal chartering of large corporations, and more realistically, some form of minimum standard setting for State laws have both been suggested as possible solutions. The latter idea has in the recent past won Congressional support. At present, political conditions are clearly not favourable to legislative initiatives of this kind, but with the swing of the political pendulum, it will be surprising if the idea does not surface again.

A single environment for the enterprise

The two objectives of which I have spoken, the removal of barriers and the co-ordination of safeguards, are different, related expressions of a more fundamental idea: the Community as a single environment for business. The enterprise, operating to take best advantage of the Community-wide market of over 260 million consumers, should in time be able to assume that the national company laws applying to its operations are not so disparate either that those operations are obstructed or that some companies are given unfair advantage by certain national jurisdictions.

3. THE STARTING POINT: DIVERGENT NATIONAL TRADITIONS, AND THE NEED FOR CONSENSUS

However, to speak only of our objectives and not of the realities of our point of departure is to tell only half the story.

[1]Leleux, Corporation law in the United States and the EEC, **Common Market Law Review**, 1967/68, p.133

[2]Smith, Delaware works hard to stay a corporate home sweet home. **Fortune**, 13 February 1978, p.132

The Community's starting point is ten divergent national systems with very deep roots and the reduction of these differences is achieved through a political system based on consensus. Although majority voting is possible in Council, and has indeed been used in the accounting field, it is the exception. Most issues are resolved through compromise and in some cases these compromises inevitably have a framework character permitting alternative solutions, provided that the minimum necessary comparability is achieved.

Sometimes it is suggested, rather critically, that there are an excessive number of options in the Fourth Directive: so many that the objective of ensuring the publication of comparable information will not be achieved. The honest answer to this criticism is that we will have to wait and see. But in my opinion the criticism is likely to prove exaggerated. Many of the options are purely formal: information may appear in the notes instead of the accounts or vice versa. Where options are more significant, in the valuation field, for example, conditions have been included to preserve the necessary minimum of comparability. If Member States decide to permit or require the use of current values instead of historic costs, Article 33 (4) requires information to be given in any event on an historic cost basis so that comparisons may be made. Similarly, when asset values have been adjusted for fiscal purposes, as they must be in some Member States, the amount of such adjustments must be disclosed (Articles 35 (1)(d) and 39(1)(e)). These limitations should preserve a sufficient degree of comparability, and we should not overlook that this kind of technique enabled us to overcome certain obstacles, deriving from deep-rooted economic and political factors in the Member States, which threatened to prevent the adoption of any Community directive in the field.

Furthermore, in saying that we would have to wait and see, I do not wish to imply a passive, unquestioning acceptance of the present state of affairs. The Fourth Directive was always conceived as a beginning rather than the end of Community's involvement in corporate accounting. The directive itself explicitly contemplates a re-examination of the question of current values by 1985. In addition, with the help of the Study Group of the Community's accounting professions, we shall be examining closely the ways in which the Member States implement the directive to establish whether in reality the so-called options have resulted in undesirably divergent national approaches. If so, we shall be making further proposals to deal with the problems.

Of course, this kind of approach has its risks. Alternative solutions without conditions ensuring sufficient comparability would mean that harmonisation was apparent rather than substantial. Further, achievements painfully realised may be overtaken by events. In this respect, we shall have to monitor carefully how Member States use the possibility to authorise departures from specific rules in the Fourth Directive by relying on the true and fair view principle. Abuse of this possiblity could as it were turn the flank of the Community's harmonisation problem.

These real problems and risks underline the importance of conferences and seminars such as this. The academic world has a particular contribution to make as regards the critical evaluation of the Community's programme. All we ask is that the evaluation should be constructively critical **and** show understanding of the real nature of the process under way. By all means tell us what remains to be done if our objectives are to be adequately realities, but at the same time give due weight to the real difficulties, historical and political, that the harmonisation process is confronting.

WINTER 1983

The Evolution of the Harmonising Provisions of the 1980 and 1981 Companies Acts*

C. W. Nobes

The 1980 and 1981 Companies Acts of the United Kingdom are substantial pieces of legislation. They dramatically affect financial reporting, in ways which may not be anticipated by a study of the Companies Acts 1948, 1967 and 1976 (which are added to, rather than repealed by, the above Acts). This is because the origins of the new legislation lie outside the Anglo-Saxon accounting tradition;[1] these Acts are part of a process of harmonisation of laws within the European Communities (EC).[2] In this case, particularly for the 1981 Act, the pattern which was originally chosen as a basis for harmonisation was German, as will be shown.

It is fairly well established that, if one organised the countries of the developed Western world into a small number of groups by their accounting practices, the United Kingdom and West Germany would be in different groups (Mueller, 1967; Nair and Frank, 1980; Nobes and Parker, 1981). The United Kingdom presents a good example of 'accounting as an independent discipline'; of pragmatic accounting; of accounting based on the judgement of 'fairness'. West German accounting, on the other hand, is held up as an example of detailed prescription (by company and tax laws) of formats, measurement rules and disclosure; of accounting which seeks correctness and legality. Thus, it is not surprising that the new UK legislation, being based on German law, introduces many changes, some of which are revolutionary.

This paper is concerned with those substantial parts of the 1980 and 1981 Acts which result from Directives[3] of the EC. Topic by topic, the origins of the new British legislation will be traced to earlier continental law. It should be stressed that the object of this paper is not directly to examine EC harmonisation or the changes to accounting in any other country.

Evolution of the 1980 Act

Those provisions of the 1980 Companies Act which are analysed here result from the second Directive. This section examines how they fit in with existing continental European practice, which is clearly the origin of the second Directive, both drafts of which were published before the UK acceded to the EC (see Figure 1).

1. *Company Names*

In most Member States of the EC it has long been possible to tell whether a company is public or private by looking at its name.[4] The split in Germany goes well back into the last century. In France, the 'private company' (*Sàrl*)[4] form dates from 1925, after the absorption into France of the former German territories of Alsace and Lorraine following the post-war Treaty of Versailles. At that point many *GmbH*[4] companies suddenly became French; the form was legalised and it spread rapidly. In the Netherlands, the *BV*[4] was invented in 1971 following the first draft of the second Directive.

The second Directive demands such separation. For the UK, the 1980 Companies Act achieved this by leaving private companies' names unchanged, and causing public companies (which are fewer and

*I gratefully acknowledge the useful comments of D. A. R. Forrester, R. H. Parker, I. C. Stewart and an anonymous referee on earlier drafts of this paper.

[1]The 'Anglo-Saxon accounting tradition' is used throughout this paper to refer to the broad consensus, of British origin, which exists on accounting matters throughout most of the English-speaking world. This is perhaps typified by 'fairness' and 'substance over form'.

[2]In 1983, these are ten: Belgium, Denmark, France, Greece, Luxembourg, Ireland, Italy, Netherlands, United Kingdom and West Germany. The word 'communities' refers to the European Economic Community (Common Market), the European Coal and Steel Community and Euratom.

[3]Directives are pieces of 'secondary legislation'. They are drafted by the EC Commission, approved by the Council of Ministers, and sent to the governments of Member States for enactment as national laws.

[4]The private company forms in West Germany, France and the Netherlands are *Gesellschaft mit beschränkter Haftung (GmbH)*, *Societé à responsibilité limitée (Sàrl)* and *Besloten Vennootschap (BV)*, respectively. These are not the exact equivalents of the UK private company. Instead, they have some elements of partnerships, particularly in the way in which capital is held.

Figure 1
EC Directives of Especial Relevance to Accounting

Directives on Company Law	*Dates of Drafts*	*Date Approved in Brussels*	*UK Law*
Second	1970, 1972	1976	1980
Fourth	1971, 1974	1978	1981
Seventh	1976, 1978	1983	

more easily visible) to change their names to include 'public limited company' or 'p.l.c.' (S2). The use of the expression, 'proprietary company,' which is found in several Commonwealth countries, was proposed for small private companies in the Green Paper (DOT, 1979) which preceded the 1981 Act. However, this proposal was not enacted.

The legal distinction remains that only a public company's shares may be offered to the public. Thus a listed company must be public. However, there is little point in stressing this distinction unless other differences also follow. Both the 1980 and the 1981 Acts do introduce further differences.

2. *Minimum Capital Requirements*

It has been normal in continental Europe for there to be minimum capital requirements for companies. (For examples, see footnote 5.) The second Directive imposes such a requirement for public companies. The UK has now inherited these continental provisions in that the 1980 Act introduced a minimum requirement of £50,000 issued share capital for UK public companies (S85). No such requirement has been introduced in the UK for private companies.

3. *Number of Members*

The minimum number of members of a public company is reduced from 7 to 2 (S2). This does not seem to be predictable from the continental European practice ruling before the second Directive (see footnote 6). However, there is now harmonisation on a minimum of 2 for all types of companies throughout the EC.

4. *Distributable Income*

Until 1980, the definition of legally distributable income was not to be found in British statute law, but in a miscellany of cases dating back to the last century; for example, *Lee v. Neuchatel Asphalte Co.* (1889) and *Verner v. General and Commercial Investment Trust Ltd.* (1894). These cases were sometimes difficult to apply, and appeared contradictory.

In Germany, there has been no similar problem. The strict and uniform application of detailed historic cost rules has been designed to lead to a conservative and reliable figure for distributable profit to protect creditors. The same figure is used for accounting profit and for taxable profit. Such a coincidence is attempted in the definition of distributable profit of a company in the second Directive and the UK's 1980 Companies Act (S39): 'its accumulated realised profits . . . less its accumulated realised losses'. However, since it is clear that UK law does not impose uniform rules for the measurement of accounting profit, the Act lays down that, irrespective of the accounting methods used by a company, the legally distributable profit must be based on strict historic cost rules. For example, if any fixed assets have been revalued and depreciation has been based on the revalued amounts, then an adjustment must be made to 'correct' the depreciation charge for the purposes of calculating distributable profits. However, such a calculation, or its result, need not be disclosed in the published accounts. Familiarity with the strict application of the principle of 'purchase price or production cost' in German accounting as determined by the 1965 *Aktiengesetz* (share law or public company law) would render these rules unsurprising. The Directive and the 1980 Act go further by adding more restrictions relating only to public companies.[7]

It is one of the ironies of the legal system of Britain and parts of the Commonwealth that the archaic British case law on distributable profits now applies in several countries (e.g. Australia and New Zealand) but not in the UK.

Evolution of the 1981 Act

In the case of the fourth Directive, the EC Commission entrusted the task of preparing the *avant projet* (the unpublished preliminary draft) to a working party chaired by a German, Professor Elmendorff. It is not surprising, then, that the first draft of the Directive, published in 1971, bears resemblances to the German *Aktiengesetz (AktG)* of 1965. The Directive applies to public and private

[5]Before the enactment of the second Directive, the West German minimum capital requirements were: DM 20,000 (*GmbH*), DM 100,000 (unlisted *AG*), and DM 500,000 (listed *AG*). The French figures were the same in francs. Other EC countries also had such requirements.

[6]The pre-Directive numbers, for private and public companies respectively, were: West Germany (2 and 5); France (2 and 7); Netherlands (2 and 2); Italy (1 and 2); UK (2 and 7).

[7]S40 states that a distribution must not be made by a public company if it would reduce net assets below the aggregate of capital and undistributable reserves. The latter are defined at length, and include share premium and capital redemption reserve fund. This requirement will only be more restrictive than S39 where there is an unrealised deficit on revaluation. A connected new requirement in the 1980 Act (S34) is that, where the net assets of a *public* company fall to half or less of the called-up share capital, an extraordinary general meeting shall be called.

companies (except for banking, insurance and shipping companies) of all Member States. It deals with statutory annual balance sheets, profit and loss accounts and notes, but not with supplementary statements like current cost accounts or funds flow statements.

One curious feature of the 1981 Act is that it contains no instructions[8] about consolidation, and that in various places (like the standard formats) adjustments have to be made for this. Given that statutory accounts for groups of companies in the UK are usually consolidated accounts, this omission might seem hard to understand. However, although the *AktG* required consolidation of domestic subsidiaries by German public companies, consolidation is rare in much of continental Europe (Parker, 1981a) and was rarer still in the days of the early drafts of the fourth Directive. This may explain its absence from the fourth Directive and thus from the 1981 Companies Act. The accession of the UK, Ireland and Denmark to the EC in 1973 was followed by the drafting of the seventh Directive (see Figure 1) which deals with consolidation. This is a substantially Anglo-Saxon document.

The evolution of the accounting provisions of the 1981 Act will be analysed under four headings. In each case, the concentration will be on locating the source of the provisions. In most cases, this will involve tracing provisions from the 1965 *AktG*, through the various drafts of the fourth Directive, to the 1981 Act.

It is not intended here to discuss whether the changes brought from German legislation into British legislation are 'good' or 'bad'. There has been much prior argument about, for example, whether the imposition of uniformity in accounting would be useful. This might now be regarded as a case for empirical investigation rather than further speculation.

1. *Formats*

Compared with traditional Anglo-Saxon accounting, perhaps the most obvious feature of the *AktG*, the fourth Directive, and the 1981 Companies Act is the prescription of uniform formats. In the UK, formats have not been compulsorily imposed by statute before, except for special companies, like those in life assurance or public utilities. Also, there have never even been format rules in accounting standards.[9] This revolutionary change is not only the most obvious of the changes imposed by the 1981 Act, but also one which will be very difficult to avoid. As will be shown later, although the letter of the law also introduces some fundamental changes of principle and detail in the areas of valuation and measurement, it will probably be possible for many companies to avoid important changes to their practices in these areas in the short run.

When tracing the history of formats back into the last century one does come across an optional format for balance sheets in the British Companies Act of 1856 and the consolidating Act of 1862, which remained in force until 1908 (Edey, 1979; Parker, 1981b). Nevertheless, the evolution of the 1981 Act must be traced through previous German law not previous British law.

Perhaps because of the importance of banks and creditors, and the lack of importance of individual shareholders, German accounting has concentrated on the protection of creditors and on cost and management accounting, not on financial statements for shareholders. It was for internal, management accounting purposes that uniform formats were first developed. It appears that the first comprehensive chart of accounts was published in Germany by J. F. Schaer in 1911 (Scherpf, 1955). Such charts were used by industry in the first World War. In 1927, Schmalenbach published *Der Kontenrahmen*, which was followed by the publication of model charts for different industries (Forrester, 1977). Under the National Socialists, the ascendant ideology of controlling the economy led naturally to the compulsory adoption of charts of accounts, particularly as the price mechanism was not operating due to controls on prices and money, and thus some alternative allocation mechanism was needed (Singer, 1943). The Germans also used a system of uniform cost accounting in France in the early 1940s.

As for uniform published financial statements, these were developed in Germany, France and other continental countries. The Germans introduced compulsory formats in the law of 1931 (Barth, 1953). The French first issued a national accounting plan *(plan comptable général)* in 1947 (revised 1957 and 1979). This included both a chart of accounts and formats for published accounts (Most, 1971).

The *AktG* of 1965 lays down formats in its sections 151 and 157 (Mueller and Galbraith, 1966). The *AktG* offered no choice between formats, nor any substantial flexibility within a format. As might have been expected, there was considerable difficulty in arriving at agreed formats for the first draft of the fourth Directive (EC Commission, 1971), even among the six Member States belonging to the EC in 1971 (Niehus, 1971). This shows itself in the inclusion in the Directive of two balance sheet formats and four profit and

[8]There are references to group accounts in the 1981 Act, but only to make clear that the Act applies to them.

[9]SSAP 10 (published by the UK accountancy bodies in 1975) gives formats for funds flow statements in an appendix, but clearly states that they are merely suggestions. SSAP 16 (CCA, 1980) also provides suggested formats, and SSAP 6 (1974) suggests a presentation for extraordinary items.

Figure 2
The Evolution of the Balance Sheet (Abbreviated Versions)

AktG (S151)	1971 Draft (Art. 8)	1981 Act (Format 2)
I Unpaid Capital	A Unpaid Capital	A Unpaid Capital
	B Formation Expenses	
II Fixed and Financial	C Fixed Assets	B Fixed Assets
A Fixed & Intangible	I Intangible	I Intangible
B Financial	II Tangible	II Tangible
	III Participations	III Investments
III Current Assets	D Current Assets	C Current Assets
A Inventories	I Stocks	I Stocks
B Other Current	II Debtors	II Debtors
	III Securities	III Investments
		IV Cash
IV Deferred Charges	E Prepayments	D Prepayments
V Accumulated Losses	F Loss	
	I For the Year	
	II Brought Forward	
– – –	– – –	– – –
I Share Capital	A Subscribed Capital	A Capital and Reserves
II Disclosed Reserves	B Reserves	I Called up Capital
III Provisions for Diminutions	C Value Adjustments	II Share Premium
		III Revaluation Reserve
		IV Other Reserves
		V Profit and Loss
IV Provisions for Liabilities	D Provisions for Charges	B Provisions for Liabilities and Charges
V Liabilities (4 years +)	E Creditors	C Creditors
VI Other Liabilities		
VII Deferred Income	F Accruals	D Accruals
VIII Retained Earnings	G Profit	
	I For the Year	
	II Brought Forward	

loss account formats. These remained largely unaltered in the second draft (EC Commission, 1974) and the final Directive (EC Commission, 1978).

Looking first at the balance sheet, *AktG* S151 was reproduced with slight amendment as Article 8 of the 1971 draft of the fourth Directive (see Figure 2). This is a two-sided (or horizontal) balance sheet, with assets on the left. The only significant change between the 1971 draft and those of 1974 and 1978 is in the classification of reserves. The *AktG* and the 1971 draft Directive show profits as the last item on the *credit* side of the balance sheet, and losses as the last item on the *debit* side. Such a treatment of profits fits better with a creditors' or entity view rather than a proprietors' view: 'it contains no implications that . . . the proprietors possess any particular lien' (Edwards, 1981, p. 17). This had been the presentation shown in the British 1856 Act, and was common in Britain before the Second World War. Edwards (1981, p. 17) notes that perhaps 'it reflects the mechanical approach to accounts construction then prevailing'.

However, in the final Directive, a more Anglo-Saxon approach to reserves is allowed. Format 2 of the 1981 Act (see Figure 2) follows the Directive, except for permitted deletions like formation expenses, which was a necessary heading for practice in some countries. Figure 2 illustrates the gradual and slight changes in the formats over the sixteen year period. It shows only the first two levels of headings. A third level (of sub-sub-headings) is omitted from Figure 2, but in each case does exist and is preceded by Arabic numbers.

However, it should not be supposed that UK balance sheets will in future look like the expanded version of this Format 2 of the 1981 Act. There are several reasons why this will probably not be the case. First, the Directive contains another format.[10]

[10]Article 9 of the 1971 and 1974 drafts, which became Article 10 in the 1978 version.

Figure 3
Balance Sheet Format 1 from the 1981 Companies Act

A. *Called up share capital not paid*
B. Fixed assets
 I Intangible assets
  1. Development costs
  2. Concessions, patents, licences, trade marks and similar rights and assets.
  3. Goodwill
  4. *Payments on account*
 II Tangible assets
  1. Land and buildings
  2. Plant and machinery
  3. Fixtures, fittings, tools and equipment
  4. *Payments on account and assets in course of construction*
 III Investments
  1. *Shares in group companies*
  2. *Loans to group companies*
  3. *Shares in related companies*
  4. *Loans to related companies*
  5. Other investments other than loans
  6. Other loans
  7. *Own shares*
C. Current assets
 I Stocks
  1. Raw materials and consumables
  2. Work in progress
  3. Finished goods and goods for resale
  4. *Payments on account*
 II Debtors
  1. Trade debtors
  2. *Amounts owed by group companies*
  3. *Amounts owed by related companies*
  4. Other debtors
  5. Called up share capital not paid
  6. Prepayments and accrued income
 III Investments
  1. *Shares in group companies*
  2. *Own shares*
  3. Other investments
 IV Cash at bank and in hand
D. *Prepayments and accrued income*
E. Creditors: amounts falling due within one year
  1. Debenture loans
  2. Bank loans and overdrafts
  3. Payments received on account
  4. Trade creditors
  5. Bills of exchange payable
  6. *Amounts owed to group companies*
  7. *Amounts owed to related companies*
  8. Other creditors including taxation and social security
  9. Accruals and deferred income
F. Net current assets (liabilities)
G. Total assets less current liabilities
H. Creditors: amounts falling due after more than one year
  1. Debenture loans
  2. Bank loans and overdrafts
  3. Payments received on account
  4. Trade creditors
  5. Bills of exchange payable
  6. *Amounts owed to group companies*
  7. *Amounts owed to related companies*
  8. Other creditors including taxation and social security
  9. Accruals and deferred income
I. Provisions for liabilities and charges
  1. Pensions and similar obligations
  2. Taxation, including deferred taxation
  3. Other provisions
J. *Accruals and deferred income*
K. Capital and reserves
 I Called up share capital
 II Share premium account
 III Revaluation reserve
 IV Other reserves
  1. Capital redemption reserve
  2. Reserve for own shares
  3. Reserves provided for by the articles of association
  4. Other reserves
 V Profit and loss account

This is shown in Figure 3, and is a vertical or statement form of the format in Figure 2. Member States are allowed to adopt one format or to permit companies to make the choice, as long as they are consistent. The 1981 Act does the latter, and presents the vertical form as 'Format 1', presumably on the grounds that it corresponds much more closely with previous UK practice for published accounts (at least those of large companies) (ICAEW, 1980). Format 1 contains broadly the same headings, sub-headings and sub-sub-headings as Format 2, except that current liabilities are shown separately and positioned so as to enable a calculation of net current assets and then assets net of current liabilities.

Secondly, there are several ways in which flexibility is allowed. The *AktG* in S151 permits (i) different classifications for particular trades, (ii) extra detail to be added, and (iii) empty headings to be omitted. The Directive contains these provisions, and also allows Arabic number headings to be combined where the amounts are separately immaterial or where this would lead to greater clarity.[11] The 1981 Act includes these provisions, and also notes that the letters and numerals preceding the headings need not be shown. This

[11]In this latter case, the information must be shown by note (Article 4).

accords with continental practice, but is not actually stated in the *AktG* or the Directive.

Thirdly, extra flexibility exists within the Directive's and hence the Act's formats, which was not present in the *AktG*. This takes the form of several alternative presentations of particular items,[12] in addition to the deletions mentioned above (e.g. formation expenses). This compromising of the original inflexible German format leads to uneasy results. For example, if the option is taken to show all accruals under J (a Germanic position) within Figure 3 (the British-style format), the size of 'net current assets' can be artificially increased by the amount of the short-term accruals.

All these provisions and the formats themselves are contained in Part I of Schedule 1 of the 1981 Act. Rather confusingly, this Schedule, which also contains accounting principles and disclosure rules, became Schedule 8 of the 1948 Companies Act. Taking all the most Anglo-Saxon options, and assuming that certain items will be immaterial or may be removed to notes, might mean that the italicised items in Figure 3 will not appear in many British balance sheets. Naturally, the letters and numerals will also be omitted. Also, given that one is concerned with a consolidated balance sheet, further items have been italicised; but a heading would need to be inserted for 'minority interests'. The lack of references to, or suitable headings for, consolidation in the 1981 Act has already been mentioned.

Another feature which may require explanation for Anglo-Saxon accountants is the omission of proposed dividends (as current liabilities in the balance sheet, and as appropriations 'below the line' in the profit and loss account). Again, the explanation lies in the predominant, 'legalistic' continental view of proposed dividends as amounts not established at the balance sheet date because they require the later approval of the shareholders. The 1981 Companies Act specifically (in Part I, Sch. 1) requires companies to adjust the profit and loss account for this. There is no instruction to adjust the balance sheet. Thus, proposed dividends may be shown separately under creditors or may be included under some other heading.

Turning now to the profit and loss account, there is one format only in the *AktG* (S157), but four in each of the versions of the Directive and in the 1981 Act. The format in the *AktG* contains 32 headings, whereas the nearest to it in the Directive and the 1981 Act[13] contains about 20 headings. These are statement formats, which combine together expenses and revenues by their financial accounting nature; for example, all salaries together and all depreciation together (see Figure 4). This Germanic format might also be said to be production-oriented; it compares input with output (not sales with cost of sales), which is perhaps more the view of a business economist than of an accountant. Thus, the turnover is adjusted for changes in stocks and for use in the construction of fixed assets. The effect is reminiscent of a value added statement, and might seem attractive to some users as a compromise between that and a traditional profit and loss account.

The alternative in the Directive which will probably be most popular in the UK is presented in the 1981 Act as Format 1 (see Figure 5). This is also a vertical statement format and is identical to Format 2 from line 7, but it is sales-oriented and it combines expenses by stage of production. This format involves the disclosure of cost of sales and gross profit, whereas Format 2 does not, because of lack of information about how much wages, depreciation, etc to include in cost of sales. Some UK companies thus prefer Format 2.

The remaining two formats in the Directive and the Act are two-sided versions of Format 1 and Format 2, with charges (i.e. *debits*) on the left and income (i.e. *credits*) on the right.

The provisions relating to flexibility are the same as for the balance sheet, and one might note that all the headings in Figure 4 are preceded by Arabic numbers. The Act requires the inclusion of items for dividends, movements on reserves and pre-tax profit. Other items, like 'minority's share of profit' may be added.

Overall, profit and loss accounts in the UK have become much more detailed, with the disclosure of more information about expenses. Such details have been normal in German accounts.

These provisions relating to formats apply for *all* companies to the statutory annual accounts as drawn up for shareholders and audited. Although the Directive allowed some exemptions here, there are no exemptions in the UK's 1981 Act from the requirements to send full audited accounts to shareholders. However, there are some exemptions from *publication* for smaller *private* companies, as will now be discussed.

2. *Publication*

A further innovation in British law is that the 1981 Act introduces reduced *publication* requirements by size of company. This only applies to private companies. All public companies and large private companies must send to the Registrar of Companies, who gives access to the public, the full accounts as drawn up and audited.

Differential publication requirements were a feature of British Acts until 1947.[14] For example, the

[12]For example, in Figure 3, unpaid capital (A) and prepayments (D) may be (and, in the UK, presumably will be) shown under debtors (C, II, 5 and 6).

[13]Article 20 in 1971 and 1974; Article 21 in 1978, and Format 2 of the 1981 Act.

[14]To a large extent the 1948 Act removed the differentiation between private and public companies. However, a special class of 'exempt private companies' survived until the 1967 Act.

Figure 4
Profit and Loss Account Format 2 (1981 Companies Act)

1. Turnover
2. Change in stocks of finished goods and work in progress
3. Own work capitalised
4. Other operating income
5. (a) Raw materials and consumables
   (b) Other external charges
6. Staff costs:
   (a) wages and salaries
   (b) social security costs
   (c) other pension costs
7. (a) Depreciation and other amounts written off tangible and intangible fixed assets
   (b) Exceptional amounts written off current assets
8. Other operating charges
9. Income from shares in group companies
10. Income from shares in related companies
11. Income from other fixed asset investments
12. Other interest receivable and similar income
13. Amounts written off investments
14. Interest payable and similar charges
15. Tax on profit or loss on ordinary activities
16. Profit or loss on ordinary activities after taxation
17. Extraordinary income
18. Extraordinary charges
19. Extraordinary profit or loss
20. Tax on extraordinary profit or loss
21. Other taxes not shown under the above items
22. Profit or loss for the financial year

1907 Act required disclosure of balance sheet information by public companies but not private companies; the 1928 Act required companies to circulate profit and loss accounts to shareholders but not to the Registrar (Edwards, 1981, part II). Nevertheless, the 1981 Act cannot sensibly be traced to these precedents, which are too distant and do not concern exemptions by *size* of company. However, publication requirements dependent upon size are commonplace in continental Europe. They are found in the *AktG* (S157), which exempts an unlisted company from showing the details making up gross profit in the profit and loss account, if the company's balance sheet total does not exceed DM 3m (or it is a family company not exceeding DM 10m). Also, such provisions are found in a later German law, the Publicity Law (*Publizitätsgesetz*) of 1969, which requires all legal entities to publish audited accounts, irrespective of their business form, if they are above two of three size criteria for two years (see Figure 6).

There are somewhat similar rules in the Netherlands, where *BV*s are exempted from the need to publish profit and loss accounts where they fall below the limits shown in Figure 6. Also, in France, listed companies with assets in excess of FF 10m have been obliged to publish annual and interim figures in the *Bulletin des annonces légales et obligatoires*.

The Directive allows various exemptions which may be traced to the above precedents.[15] The 1981

Figure 5
Profit and Loss Account Format 1
(1981 Companies Act)

1. Turnover
2. Cost of sales
3. Gross profit or loss
4. Distribution costs
5. Administrative expenses
6. Other operating income
7. Income from shares in group companies
8. Income from shares in related companies
9. Income from other fixed asset investments
10. Other interest receivable and similar income
11. Amounts written off investments
12. Interest payable and similar charges
13. Tax on profit or loss on ordinary activities
14. Profit or loss on ordinary activities after taxation
15. Extraordinary income
16. Extraordinary charges
17. Extraordinary profit or loss
18. Tax on extraordinary profit or loss
19. Other taxes not shown under the above items
20. Profit or loss for the financial year

[15]Articles 11, 12, 27, 44 and 47 of the 1978 Directive.

Figure 6
Publication Requirement Size Criteria

	Germany–1969 Publizitäts-gesetz*	Netherlands BVs	UK 1981 Act* Small	UK 1981 Act* Medium
Balance Sheet Total	DM.125m	Fl.8m	£0.7m	£2.8
Turnover	DM.250m		£1.4m	£5.75
No. of Employees	5000	100	50	250

*A company must fall below two out of the three limits.

Act does not take full advantage of these exemptions (SS5–11), but does allow small private companies (see Figure 6) not to publish profit and loss accounts and most notes, and to abridge the balance sheet by omitting the headings and amounts preceded by Arabic numbers. This is reminiscent of the rules for *BV*s in the Netherlands. Medium-sized private companies are allowed to combine the gross profit items in their *published* profit and loss accounts. This is reminiscent of S157 of the *AktG*.

3. *Accounting 'Principles'*

In the area of accounting 'principles' there are also major changes for British accounting in the 1981 Companies Act. There are three levels of 'principles' (the word used in the Act). The first, and 'vaguest', level consists of a strengthened re-affirmation of the requirement for accounts to present a true and fair view. The paramount nature of the principle is made much clearer in S1 of the 1981 Act, which revises S149 of the 1948 Act:

> Subsection (2) above [the true and fair view] overrides the requirements of Schedule 8 to this Act and all other requirements of the Companies Acts 1948 to 1981 . . . .
> (b) if, owing to special circumstances . . . , compliance with any . . . requirement . . . would prevent . . . complying with that subsection . . . , the directors . . . shall depart from that requirement . . .

This principle was not contained in German Law, nor in the first draft of the fourth Directive. However, presumably as a result of pressure from the governments of the UK, Ireland and the Netherlands, the principle was inserted in the 1974 draft and became predominant in the final Directive. This process is illustrated in Figure 7. It should be noted that the UK parliament did not define the 'special circumstances' in S1 of the 1981 Act, as the Directive would have allowed. It will become clear below that the British accountancy profession intends to claim exemption from some detailed provisions on this ground.

The second level of principles has again been substantially affected by Anglo-Saxon accounting. Four accounting conventions of a British accounting standard, SSAP 2 (ASC, 1971), are enshrined in Article 31 of the Directive and in Part II of Schedule 1 of the 1981 Act. The conventions are: going concern, consistency, prudence and accruals. The first and the last were missing from the first draft of the Directive. However, a fifth principle has been taken from German law, i.e. that assets and liabilities should be valued separately (for example, using the lower of cost and net realisable value) before being added together. More importantly, it is of course a fundamental change of philosophy to find fairly detailed accounting concepts imposed by statute in the UK. This change clearly results from the *AktG*, which enacted accounting principles, including three of the five in the 1981 Act.

The third level of principles is more detailed and involves the encroachment of statute into territory previously regarded as that of the profession. Here, the influence of the *AktG* on the new British legislation is again clear. In order to enable comparisons within and between industries, to perform sensible aggregations of companies' accounting figures, and to control the economy, it has seemed appropriate in several continental countries not just to establish uniform formats but to ensure that the items within them are uniformly valued and measured.

The following rules are found in the *AktG*, the Directive and the 1981 Companies Act (Schedule 1); the sources are noted in that order in brackets after each item:

(i) Fixed assets shall be carried at purchase price or construction cost (S153; Art32; para. 18).
(ii) Intangibles may only be shown as assets if acquired for valuable consideration (S153; Arts 9 and 10; para. 8, notes 2 and 3).
(iii) Fixed assets with limited useful lives must be depreciated (S154; Art35; para. 18).
(iv) The basic rule for valuing current assets is 'lower of cost or net realisable value' (S155; Art39; para. 23).
(v) Current asset valuation may use FIFO, LIFO, or similar method (S155; Art40; para. 27).

Figure 7
'True and Fair' in the Fourth Directive

1965 *Aktiengesetz* (S149):	1.	The annual financial statements shall conform to proper bookkeeping principles. They shall be clear and well set out and give as sure a view of the company's financial position and its operating results as is possible pursuant to the valuation provisions.
1971 Draft (Art2):	1.	The annual accounts shall comprise the balance sheet, the profit and loss account and the notes on the accounts. These documents shall constitute a composite whole.
	2.	The annual accounts shall conform to the principles of regular and proper accounting.
	3.	They shall be drawn up clearly and, in the context of the provisions regarding the valuation of assets and liabilities and the lay-out of accounts, shall reflect as accurately as possible the company's assets, liabilities, financial position and results.
1974 Draft (Art2):	1.	(as 1971 Draft).
	2.	The annual accounts shall give a true and fair view of the company's assets, liabilities, financial position and results.
	3.	They shall be drawn up clearly and in conformity with the provisions of this Directive.
1978 Final (Art2):	1.	(as 1971 Draft).
	2.	They shall be drawn up clearly and in accordance with the provisions of this Directive.
	3.	The annual accounts shall give a true and fair view of the company's assets, liabilities, financial position and profit or loss.
	4.	Where the application of the provisions of this Directive would not be sufficient to give a true and fair view within the meaning of paragraph 3, additional information must be given.
	5.	Where in exceptional cases the application of a provision of this Directive is incompatible with the obligation laid down in paragraph 3, that provision must be departed from in order to give a true and fair view within the meaning of paragraph 3. Any such departure must be disclosed in the notes on the accounts together with an explanation of the reasons for it and a statement of its effect on the assets, liabilities, financial position and profit or loss. The Member States may define the exceptional cases in question and lay down the relevant special rules.

Further rules, which are consistent with German practice, are:

(vi) Research costs, preliminary expenses and expenses on issue of securities must not be capitalised (para. 3).

(vii) Purchased goodwill (where capitalised) must be written off over its useful life (para. 21). This does not apply to goodwill on consolidation.

The above are merely examples of the detail to which the 1981 Act specifies valuation rules. The *content* of the rules is not out of character for British accounting, but their statutory nature is a fundamental change. However, there follow four examples of the way in which the character of traditional British accounting will probably overcome the new rules in particular cases:

(a) In order to avoid writing off purchased goodwill through the profit and loss account [see (iii) and (vii) above], British companies will probably write off existing goodwill against reserves before preparing their first balance sheet under the Act. In future, they may ensure that goodwill is never capitalised and thus needs no depreciation. Incidentally, although goodwill on consolidation is not covered by the 1981 Act, the requirements to be introduced as a result of the seventh Directive will be similar.

(b) The Act defines prudence as the inclusion only of 'profits realised' (Sch. 1, para. 12). This in itself seems more restrictive than the Directive, which refers to 'profits made' (Art31). However, after representations from the accountancy bodies, the Act included a note that 'realised' should be taken in the context of 'principles generally accepted' (Sch. 1, para. 90). Thus, for example, it will be acceptable to take a proportion of profit on long-term contracts as they proceed (SSAP 9, ASC, 1975).

(c) In direct contravention of (iii) above, it will still be possible for companies not to depreciate investment properties. Again an appeal to the overriding principle of 'true and fair' will be made, backed up by reference to SSAP 19, the standard which allows this (ASC, 1981). This standard was issued after the 1981 Act, and the ASC made specific reference to this.[16]

(d) In the UK before the 1981 Act, LIFO was normally unacceptable for both financial accounting and taxation purposes (ASC, 1975, App. I, para. 12). The enactment of the provision which specifically allows LIFO will not necessarily alter this. The accounting standard remains in force, and the Accounting Standards Committee might reasonably hold that the Act is 'minimum' legislation which by no means stops the profession from narrowing down from what is legally available to what gives a true and fair view. (Tweedie, 1983; Hoffman and Arden, 1983.)

Nevertheless, the imposition of valuation rules by statute is not just important as a philosophical change; it will be very significant in practice in some areas. For example, the following practices, some of which were certainly found in the UK particularly among smaller companies, are made illegal:

(a) capitalisation of certain costs, as in (vi) above;

(b) failure to depreciate goodwill (when capitalised) or most buildings (in the latter case, some companies have previously put up with audit qualifications as a price of this) (Sch. 1, paras 18 and 21);

(c) failure to use 'lower of cost and net realisable value' for stocks or (more frequently) current asset investments.

Another main area where the strictness of the *AktG* has been watered down concerns historical cost. Although the 1981 Act, like the 1980 Act, is written in the context of historical cost, there are provisions in the Directive (Art33) and the 1981 Act (Sch. 1, paras 29–34) which allow alternative rules to a strict Germanic interpretation of this. Departures from historical cost are allowed, ranging from *ad hoc* revaluations of fixed assets to full scale current cost accounting (CCA) as statutory accounts. Even the first draft of the Directive (before British entry to the EC) allowed for such departures, which would have been necessary to allow for the practice of many Dutch companies (Arts 30 and 31). However, the effect is clearly to destroy the attempt to establish uniform accounting measurement rules.

Nevertheless, there is a fundamental change from the previous UK position, in which a company could present statutory CCA accounts without historical cost information. As part of the price for adopting (or having previously adopted) an alternative to 'Germanic Accounting' for any item, many disclosures are required by Schedule 1 of the 1981 Act.[17] In effect, these would allow the reconstruction of historical cost accounts, which does represent a measure of harmonisation (as opposed to standardisation).

Disclosure

The fourth major area of accounting provisions in the 1981 Act is a series of disclosure requirements[18] which are additional to those of the Companies Act 1948 to 1980. Many of them may be traced to the *AktG*.

Conclusion

During the twentieth century, until the 1980 Companies Act, British legislation relating to financial reporting has been fairly sparse and has moved forward in an evolutionary way, often *following* 'best practice'. The advent of the 1980 and 1981 Companies Acts brings about several changes. Some of these changes are revolutionary because their inspiration comes from outside the Anglo-Saxon world; the most obvious single source being the German *Aktiengesetz* of 1965. For example, introduction of a distinct label and minimum capital requirements for public companies, of compulsory formats and detailed measurement rules for financial reports, and of reduced publication requirements for smaller companies may be better understood by tracing their ancestry. There are some cases where the British accounting tradition may manage to side-step the detailed requirements of the new legislation, but even here the changed letter of the law may have an important influence in the longer run.

[16]Paras. 9–13 of the supplementary statement to SSAP 19.

[17]The disclosures include: (i) the valuation basis used (para. 33), (ii) the comparable historical cost amount or the difference therefrom (para. 33), (iii) the comparable accumulated depreciation under historical cost or the difference (para. 33), (iv) the revaluation reserve relating to all departures (para. 34), (v) a note of valuation revisions due to adoption of alternative methods in the year (para. 42), (vi) the year of valuation (para. 43), (vii) for assets revalued in the year, the names or qualifications of the valuers (para. 43).

[18]These are to be found in part III of Schedule 1 of the 1981 Act, which replaced Schedule 8 of the 1948 Act. Article 32 of the Directive contains many of them. There is one repeal, in that S16 of the 1981 Act removes the requirement of S20 of the 1967 Act to disclose exports.

References

ASC, *Accounting for Investment Properties, SSAP 19*, Accountancy Bodies, London 1981.

ASC, *Stocks and Work in Progress, SSAP 9*, Accountancy Bodies, London 1975.

Barth, K., *Die Entwicklung des deutschen Bilanzrechts*, Band I Handelsrechtlich, Stuttgart 1953, pp. 291–3.

DOT, *Company Accounting and Disclosure*, Cmnd. 7654, HMSO, 1979.

EC Commission, 'Proposal for a Fourth Directive', *Bulletin of the European Communities*, November 1971.

EC Commission, *Industrial Policy and the European Community*, Brussels, November 1972, p. 5.

EC Commission, 'Amended Proposal for a Fourth Directive', *Bulletin of the European Communities*, Supplement 6, 1974.

EC Commission, 'Fourth Directive on Company Law, 78/660', *Official Journal*, 1978, L 222/11, or *Trade and Industry*, 11 August 1978.

Edey, H. C., 'Company Accounting in the Nineteenth and Twentieth Centuries' in T. A. Lee and R. H. Parker, *The Evolution of Corporate Financial Reporting*, Nelson, London 1979.

Edwards, J. R., *Company Legislation and Changing Patterns of Disclosure in British Company Accounts 1900–1940*, Institute of Chartered Accountants in England and Wales, London 1981.

Forrester, D. A. R., *Schmalenbach and After*, Strathclyde Convergencies, Glasgow 1977.

Hoffman, L. and M. H. Arden, 'Legal Opinion on True and Fair View', *Accountancy*, November 1983.

ICAEW, *Survey of Published Accounts*, Institute of Chartered Accountants in England and Wales, London 1980, p. 182.

Most, K. S., 'The French Accounting Experiment', *International Journal of Accounting*, Fall 1971.

Mueller, G. G., *International Accounting*, Macmillan, New York 1967, Part I.

Mueller, R. and E. G. Galbraith, *The German Stock Corporation Law*, Knapp, Frankfurt 1976.

Nair, R. D. and W. G. Frank, 'The Impact of Disclosure and Measurement Practices on International Accounting Classifications', *Accounting Review*, July 1980.

Neihus, R., 'Harmonized EEC Accounting—A German View of the Draft Directive for Uniform Accounting Rules', *International Journal of Accounting*, Spring 1972, p. 102.

Nobes, C. W. and R. H. Parker, *Comparative International Accounting*, Philip Allan, Oxford 1981, chs. 3, 5 and 7.

Parker, R. H. (a), 'Consolidation Accounting' in Nobes and Parker (1981).

Parker, R. H. (b), 'The Want of Uniformity in Accounts: A Nineteeth Century Debate', in D. M. Emanuel and I. C. Stewart, *Essays in Honour of Trevor R. Johnston*, University of Auckland 1981.

Scherpf, P., cited in Niehus [1972] as *Der Kontenrahmen*, Max Verlag, Munich 1955, p. 8.

Singer, H. W., *Standardized Accountancy in Germany*, Cambridge University Press 1943.

Tweedie, D., 'The ASC in Chains: Whither Self-Regulation Now?', *Accountancy*, March 1983; and 'True and Fair Rules', *Accountants' Magazine*, November 1983.

[18]

The Route of the Seventh Directive of the EEC on Consolidated Accounts — Slow, Steady, Studied, and Successful

RICHARD VANGERMEERSCH*

Although proposed in 1974, the Seventh Directive, which deals with consolidated accounts, was not adopted by the European Economic Community (EEC) until 1983. The process began with a memorandum on the topic of consolidated accounts by the Study Group of Expert Accountants (Groups D'Etudes des Experts Comptables de la C.E.E.). In 1976, the EEC's administrative staff published its first draft on this topic. In February 1977, the EEC Economic and Social Committee gave its official opinion. In October 1978, the European Parliament endorsed the report of its Legal Affairs Committee on the Seventh Directive. In January 1979, the EEC administrative staff presented its second draft, and finally, the EEC Council of Ministers passed the Seventh Directive on June 13, 1983.

The EEC's goal is to harmonize the company laws of its member states, and it has used the directive process to reach this goal.[1] This harmonization is necessary to meet a requirement of the Treaty of Rome, the founding document of the EEC, to abolish obstacles to freedom of movement of persons, services, and capital among member states.[2] The EEC has not only been concerned with harmonizing company laws to have equitable reporting re-

* Richard Vangermeersch is Professor of Accounting, the University of Rhode Island.

[1] Price Waterhouse, *Doing Business in the European Communities* (New York: Price Waterhouse Center for Transnational Taxation, 1983), 55.

[2] Sharon M. McKinnon, *Consolidated Accounts: The Seventh EEC Directive* (Netherlands: AMSA and Arthur Young International, 1983), 12.

quirements for companies but also is interested in the rights of shareholders, creditors, and employees.[3] The Seventh Directive on consolidated accounts was issued as an important part of this goal of harmonization.

The specifics of the accounting requirements of the 1983 promulgation have already been reviewed by many organizations, such as the larger international public accounting firms.[4] The purpose of this study is to elaborate on the history of the directive as it passed through the stages of (1) the 1974 memorandum of the Study Group of Expert Accountants, (2) the 1976 first draft of the EEC administrative staff, (3) the February 1977 opinion of the Economic and Social Committee, (4) the opinion of the European Parliament in October 1978, (5) the January 1979 second draft of the EEC administrative staff, and (6) the final promulgation by the EEC Council of Ministers on June 13, 1983. The goals of this study are to describe each of the stages, to highlight the key issues of each stage, and then to propose conclusions concerning the EEC process for the Seventh Directive.

THE MEMORANDUM OF THE STUDY GROUP OF EXPERT ACCOUNTANTS

The Study Group of Expert Accountants of the EEC is composed of members appointed by the national accounting professional bodies and has a national representative and a technical adviser for each EEC member state. The national representative may also add other technical advisers to the delegation.[5] The Study Group has its office in Brussels and is a part of the Union Europeane des Experts Comptables Economiques and Financiers (UEC),[6] which is similar to the EEC in that it has adopted a policy of low profile non-antagonistic, incremental progress toward change. The EEC places great weight on the Study Group's opinions if there are no political consequences. Political realities often overtake technical arguments.[7]

The Study Group prepared the memorandum "On the Rules to Advocate on the Subject of Consolidated Accounts" in 1974 in

[3] Ibid., 13.
[4] Ibid., 1–392 and Price Waterhouse, *Special Supplement on the EEC Seventh Directive: Consolidated Financial Statements EEC Bulletin* (Brussels: EEC Services Group, Price Waterhouse, 1983), 35 pp.
[5] Letter from a member of the EEC Services Group of Price Waterhouse in Brussels.
[6] A. M. El-Agraa, ed., *The Economics of the European Community* (New York: St. Martin's Press, 1980), 301.
[7] Ibid., 301–2.

response to a request from the EEC administrative staff.[8] The memorandum by the Study Group was the first stage of the EEC process;[9] the use of an independent party to write the preliminary report is not uncommon.[10] This EEC request was a part of the process of the proposal for the EEC's Fourth Directive, which dealt with the format of annual accounts, valuation methods to be adopted for preparation of annual accounts, content of annual reports, and provisions concerning publication of the accounts.[11] The Fourth Directive did not consider the preparation of consolidated accounts.[12]

The Study Group expressed its overriding philosophy:

> Numerous and complex aspects can arise in the preparation of consolidated accounts and the practices and methods in order to prepare such accounts are still evolving. . . . It is desirable that the directive to prepare consolidated accounts must, therefore, be as general as possible and not be in the form of fundamental rules. The questions of very complex applications should be left to the preference of competent national or international accounting organizations.[13]

The Study Group took the legal approach to consolidations by requiring consolidated accounts for a parent and companies in which the parent owns, directly or indirectly, more than 50 percent of the voting common shares.[14] A second level of control in which the parent has by contract the power to name a majority of the board of directors of a company or has an effective majority of the voting stock could exist.[15] This second level may be labeled the economic approach to consolidations. Such companies, the Study Group recommended, ought to be permitted to consolidate.[16] This "ought to be permitted" would have given considerable leeway to the national accounting and legislative bodies of the member states, since there would have been an option available

[8] Study Group of Expert Accountants of the European Economic Community, *Memorandum on the Rules to Advocate on the Subject of Consolidation of Accounts* (Brussels: Study Group, 1974), 1.
[9] Price Waterhouse, *Doing Business in the European Communities*, 23.
[10] Study Group of Expert Accountants of the European Economic Community, *Memorandum on the Rules*, 1.
[11] Price Waterhouse, *Doing Business in the European Communities*, 57–58.
[12] Interview with member of the staff of the EEC's Directorate — General III, Internal Marketing and Industrial Affairs, Directorate D, Approximation of laws, freedom of establishment and freedom to provide services, Number 2, Company law, industrial democracy and standards.
[13] Study Group, *Memorandum*, 1.
[14] Ibid.
[15] Ibid.
[16] Ibid., 2.

to them without a mandated requirement, as in the case of the more than 50 percent ownership. The Belgian and French delegations were in favor of an obligatory consolidation whenever the parent possessed more than 50 percent of the general voting stock.[17] Since the most controversial issue in the Seventh Directive was probably the issue of the legal approach versus the economic approach, it is very important to note the view of the Study Group.

The Study Group allowed two exceptions to the requirement of consolidation when the parent owns more than 50 percent of the voting stock: (1) the inclusion of the subsidiary has an immaterial effect on the total and (2) the inclusion would lead to misleading results.[18] However, the Study Group made it clear that subsidiaries in different industries were not to be excluded for that reason and that the stratification by industry was preferable to exclusion.[19] The Study Group was quite traditional and general in its recommended treatments for intercompany transactions, minority interests, and the difference between book value and fair market value at the date of purchase.[20] It concluded that it was not desirable to try to specify the detailed rules for consolidation, which could be left to the decision of national and international accounting organizations.[21] It avoided the foreign currency translation issue but recommended disclosure of the method chosen in the notes to the accounts.[22] It also mentioned the equity method of accounting for affiliated companies but considered the method still too controversial to be required.[23]

The Study Group memorandum could be labeled very general, nationalistic, traditional, relatively flexible, and noncontroversial. This is not surprising in the relatively short time that the issue was studied. The differences between the memorandum and the 1976 draft, in which a more economic control viewpoint was adopted by the EEC administrative staff trained more in law than in accounting, will be interesting.

THE 1976 DRAFT OF THE COMMISSION

The EEC has fourteen commissioners appointed for four-year terms; two each are appointed by the larger member states of France, West Germany, Britain, and Italy. Each remaining member

[17] Ibid.
[18] Ibid.
[19] Ibid., 2–3.
[20] Ibid., 3–4.
[21] Ibid., 3.
[22] Ibid., 5.
[23] Ibid.

state appoints one.[24] These fourteen commissioners are responsible for twenty-eight departments called either directorate generals or administrative offices.[25] The department responsible for the seventh directive was Directorate-General III (DG 3), Internal Markets and Industrial Affairs. Within DG 3, the work was done in Directorate D, Approximation of Laws, Freedom of Establishment and Freedom to Provide Service, and by its Section 2, Company Law, Industrial Democracy and Standards.[26] The staff of DG 3.D.2 ranged from two to four in the time period of the preparation of the Seventh Directive. Much of this period overlapped its work on the Fourth Directive. It is remarkable that DG 3.D.2 could handle as much work load as it did, since both the Fourth and Seventh Directives involved mammoth efforts.

As one might expect from the significance of company law in the EEC member states, the two top officials of DG 3.D.2 were lawyers.[27] The commission is not merely the administrative arm of the EEC, since its most important power is the right to initiate policy proposals. The Council of Ministers cannot introduce a Community Law unless it has received a proposal on the subject of such a law from the commissioner.[28]

A directive is not, in principle, immediately effective internally but creates obligations on the governments of member states that individuals and enterprises may cite before the courts of law.[29] The individuals have redress to a national court, the European Court, or to the commission.[30]

The 1976 Draft began with a preamble that contained some very revealing points:

Whereas the annual accounts of companies belonging to a group cannot by themselves give a true and fair view of their position;
Whereas groups of companies are in fact economic units in which all the member companies and undertakings are managed on a central and unified basis in the interest of the whole group, . . . it must become compulsory to draw up group accounts both in respect of companies heading a group and those which are in a position of dependency within a group;

---

[24] Ruth Barrington and John Cooney, *Inside the EEC: An Irish Guide* (Dublin: O'Brien Press, 1984), 43.
[25] Ibid., 45–46.
[26] *Directory of the Commission of the European Communities* (Luxembourg: Office for Publications of the European Communities, 1984), 25–26.
[27] Interview with member of staff of DG III, D2.
[28] Barrington and Cooney, *Inside the EEC*, 47.
[29] Price Waterhouse, *Doing Business in the European Communities*, 20.
[30] Ibid.

and

Whereas a number of general principles . . . must be laid down in order to ensure that items . . . can be readily compared.[31]

The first point showed a preference of the tradition of the United Kingdom for a true and fair view, rather than the continental orientation to the chart of accounts.[32] That the Fourth Directive also adopted the true and fair view approach should be noted.[33]

The second point stressed "managed on a central and unified basis" rather than the more than 50 percent ownership basis. Another way of looking at this is as an economic versus legal approach, or with tongue in cheek, West Germany versus everyone else. The third point involved compulsory creation of consolidated accounts, which seemed to give little room to maneuver. The fourth point concerning general principles meant that specific rules were to be promulgated.

The terms "dependent undertaking," "dominant undertaking," and "dominant influence" in Article 2 indicated that the more than 50 percent ownership test would not be the only test employed for consolidations. A dependency would also occur when an undertaking could appoint more than half of the members of the other undertaking's administrative, managerial, or supervisory body.[34] Article 3 required that the dominant undertaking exercised in practice its dominant influence to the effect that all such undertakings are managed on a central and unified basis by the dominant undertaking.[35] There was an assumption that an article 2 dependency situation led to management on a central and unified basis.[36] Article 4 went further and stated that even if no Article 2 relationship existed, a group existed if there were management on a central and unified basis.[37] If there were an ownership of 20 percent or more and one or more group undertakings were exercised in practice, a dominant influence on one or more other undertakings to the effect that all such undertakings were managed

[31] *Official Journal of the European Communities*, C14 Volume 22 (17 January 1979), 2–4.
[32] Christopher Nobes, *Internal Classification of Financial Reporting* (London, Sydney, and New York: Croom Helm and St. Martin's Press, 1984), 4–5.
[33] Price Waterhouse, *Handbook on the EEC Fourth Directive: The Impact on Company Accounts in the Nine Member States* (Belgium: Price Waterhouse, 1979), 4.
[34] *Official Journal*, 5.
[35] Ibid.
[36] Ibid.
[37] Ibid., 6.

on a central and unified basis, those dependent undertakings shall also form part of the group, and each is a group undertaking.[38]

Article 6.2(a) required parent companies to file consolidated subaccounts for their subsidiaries, although the parent was itself a subsidiary of a parent having a registered office in the EEC member states.[39] Article 6.2(b) required consolidated subgroup accounts for a parent that had its registered office outside the EEC.[40] Both proposals were the subjects of much controversy. Article 12.1(a) required that the values existing at the moment of the acquisition of the consolidated holding be used as the basis for consolidation.[41] Hence, a fair value approach was endorsed. Article 12.1(a) also specified that if the differences between book values and market values at acquisition were attributable to specific items, the differences were to be added to the relevant items. The unattributed amount was to be kept as a separate item.[42] Article 14.2(b) allowed intercompany profit on the sale of a fixed asset that had a limited useful life and had been the result of a transaction concluded at normal market conditions.[43] Article 15(d) mandated deferred taxation arising in consolidation to be recognized.[44] Article 16 required a write-off of goodwill over a maximum period of five years.[45] Article 18.1 gave member states the option to require consolidation on a pro rata basis if an undertaking were managed by a consortium of firms.[46]

There were many means to air differences in opinion as to the EEC draft. One was through the public newsletters of the large international accounting firms. For instance, Price Waterhouse had a very prompt reaction to the Commission Draft issued on April 29, 1976. The firm considered the economic concept to be foreign to eight of the nine member states.[47] That this could lead to consolidation when there is no ownership control, and nonconsolidation when there is ownership control but not central and unified management, was stressed.[48] There was opposition to the five-year maximum period for the write-off of goodwill since this

[38] Ibid.
[39] Ibid., 8.
[40] Ibid., 8–9.
[41] Ibid., 11–12.
[42] Ibid.
[43] Ibid., 13.
[44] Ibid., 14.
[45] Ibid.
[46] Ibid., 16.
[47] Price Waterhouse, *EEC Bulletin No. 23* (May 1976), 2.
[48] Ibid.

was one area where it might be wiser to take a less rigid approach.[49] The last sentence in the Price Waterhouse response to the 1976 Draft was quite apropos to the need to balance the national interests of the nine (and later ten, with Greece added to the EEC in 1981) member states: "It seems that much will depend on everybody's willingness to achieve a compromise between the economic and legal concepts of a group."[50]

The point of the controversy concerning the economic concept of control is important, especially in light of its alien nature to U.S. practice. Accountants dominate formulation of accounting rules in the United States, but lawyers, economists, and union officials may be at least as important as accountants in Europe when accounting rules are made. It is not necessarily a better or worse situation, but it is clearly a different situation.

THE 1977 ACTION OF THE ECONOMIC AND SOCIAL COMMITTEE

At the time of the Seventh Directive, the Council of the EEC had appointed 144 members, based on national lists to the Economic and Social Committee. This committee was created by the Treaty of Rome with advisory status basically to represent three main groups: employers, union members, and the general interest. Each national delegation reflects this tripartite composition,[51] and the selection process for the commission guarantees this balance.[52] The committee is helpful to both the Council and the Commission by forwarding its opinions to them before policy is set.[53] The Economic and Social Committee was requested by the EEC Council to deliver an opinion on the 1976 Draft of the Seventh Directive. The committee referred the matter to its section for Industry, Commerce, Crafts and Service, which in turn asked its Study Group on Company Law to draft its opinion.[54] The Study Group was comprised of thirteen members whose positions at the time were most impressive,[55] as were the positions of all the members in the 1984 index for the Economic and Social Committee.[56]

The report of the Study Group on Company Law raised some

[49] Ibid., 4.
[50] Ibid., 5.
[51] El-Agraa, *Economics*, 32.
[52] Barrington and Cooney, *Inside the EEC*, 22.
[53] El-Agraa, *Economics*, 32.
[54] Economic and Social Committee, *Report of the Section for Industry, Commerce, Crafts and Services on the Proposal for a Seventh Directive* . . . (Brussels: Economic and Social Committee, 1977), 1.
[55] Letter from the staff of the Economic and Social Committee.
[56] *Index* (Brussels: Economic and Social Committee, January 1984), 71 pp.

key points under the general comments section, one of which concerned exemptions for smaller companies because of cost of compliance and lack of expertise. A second one regarded the vagueness inherent in the terms "significant influence" and "dominant influence."[57] On this topic, the Study Group of the Economic and Social Committee was opposed to Article 6(2)(b) on the requirement of a company registered outside the EEC to consolidate holdings in the EEC.[58] There also was opposition to the mandatory write-off of goodwill and to the maximum period of five years.[59] The Study Group on Company Law also opposed the requirement for sales analysis by product and by geographical area as being prejudicial for smaller companies from a competition viewpoint.[60]

On February 24, 1977, the Economic and Social Committee gave its formal opinion, which was to adopt the commission draft with the comments forwarded from the Study Group on Company Law.[61] Four amendments were offered from the floor, and three were defeated.[62] The one that passed (thirty-nine for, twenty-seven against, and eight abstentions) dealt with Article 6(2)(a) of the 1976 Draft by the commission. It mandated consolidated subgroup accounts only when overall consolidated statements were not prepared.[63] The report referred to the opinions on consolidations by such organizations as the United Nations, the Organization for Economic Cooperation and Development, and the International Accounting Standards Committee, especially its Standard No. 3.[64]

The work of the Economic and Social Committee was completed relatively quickly and focused on the controversial areas. The very high caliber of the members of this body gave its opinion much weight; however, the role of this committee may be underrated by many.

In its August 1977 *EEC Bulletin,* Price Waterhouse noted the opinion of the Economic and Social Committee and other groups. The concerns of smaller companies were stressed as coming not only from the Committee but also from the Union of Industries

[57] Economic and Social Committee, *Report,* 3–4.
[58] Ibid., 21–22.
[59] Ibid., 18.
[60] Ibid., 21–22.
[61] Economic and Social Committee, *Opinion of the Economic and Social Committee on the Proposal for a Seventh Directive . . .* (Brussels: Economic and Social Committee, 1973), 1.
[62] Ibid., Appendix, 1–3.
[63] Ibid., Appendix, 3.
[64] Ibid., 3.

of the Economic Community (UNICE).[65] The committee's view of the requirement of firms not subject to the Fourth Directive to meet the requirements of the Seventh Directive was noted, as well as a similar position taken by the European Communities Committee of the House of Lords in the United Kingdom.[66] Although the Economic and Social Committee favored the economic approach, UNICE did not. The EEC Accountants' Study Group had proposed a compromise in which

> . . . through additional disclosure, one set of financial statements would give consolidated financial information on both an economic basis and a power of control basis, in those cases where the two results would not be the same.[67]

Opposition to the economic approach in the European Communities Committee in the House of Lords was noted.[68] Opposition to the five-year write-off of goodwill was nearly universal. A change in that proposed requirement in the Fourth Directive was hoped to lead to the same change in the Seventh Directive.[69]

THE 1978 REPORT OF THE EUROPEAN PARLIAMENT

The first direct election of the European Parliament occurred in 1979.[70] Before that, Parliament members were appointed by the nine national parliaments in the member countires.[71] There are no national sections, only European-level political groups.[72] Parliament must be expressly consulted by the commission on important matters and meets for one-week sittings seven or eight times a year. Parliamentary committees meet between sessions.[73] The president of the European Parliament referred the 1976 commission draft to the Legal Affairs Committee on May 25, 1976. Its report on May 17, 1978, had twenty-one opening points. The committee approved the concepts as well as central and unified management in points 2 and 3. In point 8 it endorsed subgroup reporting for non–EEC registered companies but permitted an alternative of

[65] Price Waterhouse, *EEC Bulletin No. 32*, 2.
[66] Ibid.
[67] Ibid.
[68] Ibid.
[69] Ibid.
[70] Barrington and Cooney, *Inside the EEC*, 52.
[71] Nancy L. Hoepli, ed., *The Common Market, The Reference Shelf*, vol. 46, no. 5 (New York: H. W. Wilson Company, 1975), 15:
[72] Ibid., 20.
[73] Ibid., 20–21.

worldwide consolidated accounting. In point 14 it endorsed a write-off of intangibles longer than five years.[74]

The Report of the Legal Affairs Committee broadened the concept of the group to include a horizontal group (consortium). In this situation, the central and unified management is exercised not by a single dominant undertaking but by all the undertakings forming the grouping.[75] The committee also wanted a more precise definition of deferred taxation,[76] and it concluded that the commission proposal would aid in comparing EEC companies and would protect the interests of shareholders, employees, and third parties.[77]

A short report of the Committee on Economic and Monetary Affairs of the European Parliament was included with the report of the Legal Affairs Committee. The Committee on Economic and Monetary Affairs seemed to endorse the legal concept in that clarity and ease of handling were enhanced by that concept.[78] It did, however, issue a strong endorsement of the consolidation of EEC holdings of companies headquartered outside the EEC, in that multinational companies must be brought under international surveillance.[79]

A debate on the report in the European Parliament was held on June 15, 1978, and the report was passed on the next day.[80] The discussant of the Legal Affairs Committee report also endorsed the report for his parliamentary group, the Christian Democrats.[81] The spokesman for the Socialist Group commented on the importance of involving workers employed with a company in the decision process of that company.[82] The spokesman for the European Conservative group endorsed the report. The commission representative responded to the views expressed in the report and modified the commission's position on Article 6[83] and most of the other amendments.[84] He defended the economic concept as being

[74] European Parliament, *Report . . . on the Proposal . . . for a Seventh Directive, . . .* Document 103/78, 5–7.
[75] Ibid., 26.
[76] Ibid., 31.
[77] Ibid., 36.
[78] Ibid., 38.
[79] Ibid., 39.
[80] *Debates of the European Parliament, Sitting of Friday, 16 June 1978*, 300.
[81] *Debates of the European Parliament, Sitting of Thursday, 15 June 1978*, 242–44.
[82] Ibid., 245.
[83] Ibid., 248.
[84] Ibid.

in line with the reality of business relationships in all the member states, not just a few.[85]

The input by the European Parliament was not, in the writer's opinion, in proportion to the length of time it held the 1976 draft. Since the Parliament is not nationalistic but political party oriented, national interests were primarily left to the next, and last, stage of the process. Obviously, accounting is much more a political issue in the EEC than in the United States.

The Price Waterhouse *EEC Bulletin* No. 37 of June 197 reported that the long wait was worthwhile in that subgroup consolidation was disapproved, worldwide reporting could replace EEC consolidation for a non–EEC dominant undertaking, and the amortization of goodwill could be longer than five years.[86] The view of the Economic and Monetary Committee on the legal concept was noted.[87]

THE 1979 COMMISSION DRAFT

The Fourth Directive had been approved by the EEC Council of Ministers on July 25, 1978,[88] and the second draft of the Seventh Directive was issued on January 17, 1979.[89] The most important change occurred in Article 6a in which subgroup consolidated accounts could be avoided by meeting six requirements.[90] Article 11.2 adopted the limits of two of the three size criteria of the Fourth Directive and allowed the member states to permit companies to file a group consolidated balance sheet in an abridged form.[91] Article 15d on deferred taxes gave companies the option of showing the cumulative amount in the balance sheet or in the notes to the accounts.[92] The same size test for abridged reporting was applied in Article 20a for the disclosure of financial commitments, sales by geographical areas, average number of employees, and the effect of accounting differences with the Fourth Directive.[93] The second draft of the commission was completed relatively promptly and did respond to the concerns as to subgroup consol-

[85] Ibid.
[86] Price Waterhouse, *EEC Bulletin No. 37* (June 1978), 8.
[87] Ibid.
[88] *Official Journal of the European Communities,* C 14 Volume 22, 2.
[89] Ibid., cover page.
[90] Ibid., 8.
[91] Ibid., 11.
[92] Ibid., 14.
[93] Ibid., 16–18.

idations and smaller groups. The deferred tax issue was sidestepped. The Commission remained firm, however, on its view of economic consolidation. Price Waterhouse *EEC Bulletin* No. 42 of March 1979 noted the continuation of the definition of a group, although the wording was changed from central and unified management to unified management, and of consolidations of EEC companies by dominant companies registered outside the EEC.[94]

THE 1983 DIRECTIVE

The last stage took from September 1978[95] to June 13, 1983,[96] and was comprised of a council working party of national representatives, the Committee of Permanent Representatives (Coreper), and the Council of Ministers.[97] The Commission was involved in the working party.[98] There were four readings, rather than the usual three, by the working party.[99] In this last stage, national interests played a most important role, especially in light of the 1966 Luxembourg compromise that made unanimity necessary for agreement when vital national interests are at stake.[100] When one considers the diversity of reporting requirements of the then ten EEC member states, it is no wonder that almost five years elapsed before the directive was passed. Sharon M. McKinnon noted three of these differences of requirements among the countries: (1) parents obliged to prepare consolidation accounts, (2) normal basis of consolidation, and (3) consolidation technique adopted. For instance, in the first difference, Denmark, Ireland, the Netherlands, and the United Kingdom required all parents; France (recommended) and Italy (requirement being introduced) focused on parents listed on a stock exchange; Belgium (if listed) and Germany (or if a parent is public company) stressed parents of large groups; Greece and Luxembourg set no requirements.[101]

The purpose of this paper was not to review the many specifics of the 1983 promulgation but to comment on the six stages of

[94] Price Waterhouse, *EEC Bulletin No. 42* (March 1979), 1.
[95] Ibid., 1.
[96] Commission of the European Communities, *Seventeenth General Report of the Activities of the European Communities* (Brussels: Office for Official Publications of the European Communities, 1984), 86.
[97] McKinnon, *Consolidated Accounts,* 25.
[98] Price Waterhouse, *Doing Business in the European Community,* 21.
[99] McKinnon, *Consolidated Accounts,* 27.
[100] Barrington and Cooney, *Inside the EEC,* 13.
[101] McKinnon, *Consolidated Accounts,* 16.

the approval process. As such, the discussion of the provisions of the 1983 directive is brief. Article 1 required consolidations in companies in which a majority voting interest or the power to appoint the majority of the board of directors was held.[102] The German situation was covered by requiring consolidation of an undertaking which has the contractual power to exercise dominant influence.[103] Article 5 was a concession to Luxembourg and granted an exemption for financial holding companies.[104] Article 11 modified the controversial consolidation of EEC holdings of non–EEC registered companies by giving an exemption if overall consolidation statements are issued, if the statements follow, or are equivalent to, the Fourth Directive, and if the statements are audited.[105] Article 20 permitted pooling accounting if at least 90 percent of the consideration was in stock.[106] Article 31 adopted the goodwill amortization rules of the Fourth Directive, which permitted a maximum write-off period of more than five years, as long as that period does not exceed the useful economic life of goodwill.[107] Negative goodwill was covered in Article 31, which allowed a transfer to the profit and loss accounts only in two limited situations.[108] Article 40 gave the member states until January 1, 1988, to put into effect the laws, regulations, and administrative provisions for the Seventh Directive and until January 1, 1990, to require the first application of consolidated accounts.[109]

The last stage was by far the most nationalistic of the stages of development of the Seventh Directive. Without a doubt, the expression of national interests is needed to cover such controversial issues as economic control. One must be impressed with the way the final draft covered all the bases to please the various countries. One is less impressed with the time it took to achieve this accord and with the time that the Seventh Directive was mandated to be in effect.

[102] *Seventh Council Directive Concerning Consolidated Accounts*, as reprinted in Price Waterhouse *EEC Bulletin* (July 1983), 29.
[103] McKinnon, *Consolidated Accounts*, 34.
[104] Ibid., 46.
[105] *Seventh Directive*, 31.
[106] Ibid., 32.
[107] Ibid., 19, 32.
[108] Ibid., 32.
[109] Ibid., 34.

CONCLUSIONS

The result of the Seventh Directive is quite impressive, as is the fact that this was accomplished with a small staff in DG3.D.2. Although there might be little or no additional disclosures for U.K. companies, this is certainly not true for Greek, Luxembourgian, French, and Italian companies. The goal of harmonization must be tempered by the fact that different member states have different concepts, practices, and laws to control relationships. The use of optional requirements by member states helps greatly in this area. Harmonization of different control situations might have led to similar accounting for dissimilar events. Clearly, time and means available were adequate for interest groups to make known their views.

In some areas there were apparent inefficiencies. The first stage might have been the place to introduce more nationalistic concerns into the memorandum from the EEC Accountant's Study Group. The commission would probably have benefitted greatly from this input. The second stage, the EEC first draft, was perhaps more lawyer oriented than accounting oriented. While this was necessary considering the complexities of the number of member states, more consideration to problems of accounting implementations would have saved much controversy. The third stage of the Economic and Social Committee opinion was, to the writer, done extremely well and quickly. The fourth stage of the opinion of the European Parliament took too long, even considering that the Fourth Directive was not yet promulgated. The European Parliament setting of political parties, rather than national parties, resulted in a delay before national interests came to play. The fifth stage, the 1979 EEC second draft, was done quickly and was fairly responsive to the opinions of the Economic and Social Committee and the European Parliament. The last stage was lengthy but necessarily so, since national interests had yet to be presented effectively, all states had to agree, and considerable differences of opinion were present. The inclusion of Spain and Portugal, and perhaps others, make this stage more and more difficult if unanimity is to be kept.

What does this Seventh Directive mean to U.S. accountants? Clearly, uniformity for consolidated accounts is not, and will not, be present, since member states have some time to change their company laws and have, even then, significant options. It may be worth examining how many instances of economic control exist in the United States, where this issue has not been rigorously examined from a consolidation approach, although the equity approach does touch on the economic control concept. The Seventh Directive might be usefully studied from the viewpoint of public versus private-sector control of the financial accounting rules body. The Seventh Directive and its background are important for many U.S. accountants.

[19]

SOFT-TRANSFORMATIONS OF ACCOUNTING RULES OF THE 4th DIRECTIVE IN GERMANY[1]

Dieter ORDELHEIDE

1 - PROBLEM AND BACKGROUND

National accounting rules can be regarded as elements of an economy's organizational structure. As such, they tend to resist international harmonization endeavors. Speaking with PARSONS, they form a part of a "boundary maintaining system"[2].

That national legal systems show a tendency towards self-preservation is by itself not astonishing. Interesting questions in this context, however, are :

— which accounting rules are resisting a change,
— which are the reasons therefore and
— by which mechanisms alterations are prevented.

From a scientific point of view the harmonization of the European accounting rules is an attractive field-experiment for studying the resistance to change in respect of the internationalization of accounting provisions. I would like to start by showing briefly some of the means of defence that have been used against the attempt to harmonize European accounting rules. Fig. 1 makes clear that a lot of obstacles have to be moved out of the way before a change is successful.

---

(1) Paper presented at the STUTTGART meeting of the EAA – April 1989.

(2) Cf. PARSONS, T. : The Social System, 1951 (here : 1964 edition, p. 482).

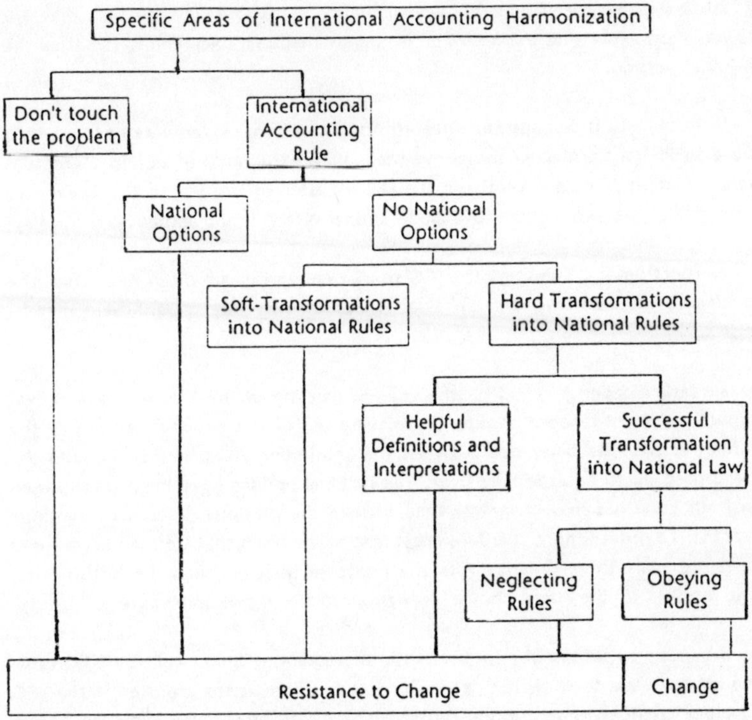

Figure 1 : Mechanisms of Resistance to International Accounting Harmonization

— **Omitting Problems** : The 4th Directive has not tried to regulate or has not regulated many important accounting problems. Examples are accounting for long-term-contracts, leasing, new financial instruments or foreign currency translation, although accounting principles for these problems have been developed and are applied in some countries.

— **National Options** : The 4th Directive contains a great number of national options which can be and have been used by the individual member countries to maintain their traditional accounting practices.

— **Soft-Transformations** : They concern rules for which the 4th Directive does not state national options. Soft-Transformations are provisions of the 4th Directive that have been transformed into national law in such a way that accounting according to the new national law makes results possible which do not comply with the intentions of the Council of the European Communities. Soft-Transformations thus allow keeping up traditional national accounting practices even in those areas for which international agreements do not provide national options. The opposite of this are "Hard-Transformations". Here the international rule becomes a national one either by literal implementation in national law or by a different formulation expressing the intention of the international rule even better than the original version.

— **Helpful Definitions and Interpretations** : These concern regulations too, which have been transformed in the above mentioned hard way but obtain a different interpretation of central terms. In the FRG an attempt is made in this fashion to circumvent the prohibition to include special direct selling expenses.

— **Neglecting the Rules** : In the FRG smaller enterprises are often neglecting the disclosure requirements. This behavior is facilitated by weak punishment mechanisms.

In an earlier paper(1) – held on the London meeting of the EAA – I have shown how changes have been avoided by making use of the national options of the 4th Directive. The difference between the accounting rules in the FRG and the UK turned up to be especially large. The national options have been transformed in both countries in such a way that most of the previous differences continue to exist. To put it simply, the differences lead to the result that German accounting rules are more in accordance with the prudence principle than the British ones. This applies to the profit shown as well as to the distributable profit.

In this paper, I would like to deal with a mechanism that I call "Soft-Transformations". I want to show how and why Soft-Transformations are used in the FRG to block changes in accounting possibilities induced by the 4th Directive. I limit my analysis to :
— rules determining the amount of profit [General principle ; Items to be included ; Valuation principles ; Deferred taxes]
— the FRG and there particularly to
— the accounting of Public Limited Companies (Stock Corporations).

2 - SOFT-TRANSFORMATIONS

In a first step I have compared :
— the former law,
— the 4th Directive and
— the new law
for those accounting rules for which the 4th Directive does not provide national options. This comparison leads to 4 classes of rules [see Tab. 1].

(1) Cf. ORDELHEIDE, D. : The Transformation of the 4. EEC-D's Rules of Profit Calculation in EEC Member States, Paper held on the annual congress of the EAA in London 1987.

	no change old law = new law	change old law ≠ new law
Hard-Transformation 4th Dir. = new law	no problem (nop)	successful harmonization of rules (sh)
Soft-Transformation 4th Dir. ≠ new law	resistance to harmonization of rules (rh)	new problem (nep)

Table 1 : Classification of the success of harmonization

For the **no problem-rules**, previous German law, provision of the 4th Directive and new Accounting Directives Law (BIRILIG) are identical or nearly identical. This is true for a large number of rules, for example :

— the item by item valuation principle and the going concern concept,
— the systematic depreciation of fixed assets which are subject to depletion,
— the obligation to write down current assets to the quoted or market price or appropriate value, or
— the requirement to include liabilities and to accrue uncertain liabilities.

Most of these rules are internationally not in dispute. Therefore, I will neither deal with them in the following nor include them in the list of rules analysed (see Tab. 2).

An exceptional case are those valuation rules of tax law which are applicable to the financial statement only for the reason that their recognition for tax purposes requires the same treatment be accorded to the items in question in the commercial financial statement (Tab. 2, Row 8). This authoritative basis of tax accounts for the financial statement plays a considerable role in the FRG. Due to separate settlements of the 4th directive (Art. 35 (1d), Art. 39 (1e)) this tradition could be maintained. Because of surviving national tax sovereignty those separate settlements obtain the character of national options.

The **new problem-rules** are the opposite. These are rules where the old law has been incompatible with the 4th Directive and changed in the course of the transformation. Notably the new rules do not comply with the 4th Directive either. On the one hand I have classified under this heading the provisions for pension

4

promises, because the stipulation of the 4th Directive is unclear : Art. 20 of the 4th Directive suggests a requirement whereas Art. 43 (7) suggests an option. Up to now the German law held an option to accrue for pension promises. According to the new law there exists a requirement to accrue for new pension promises. If stress is laid on Art. 20 and one thus agrees that the 4th Directive contains a requirement, a successful harmonization [sh] has been achieved.

On the other hand I have considered here those cases in which the tax accounts form an authoritative basis for valuation in the financial statement. It has already been mentioned above that due to separate settlements of the 4th Directive valuation principles of tax law are applicable to the financial statement as well. The German legislator has used these separate settlements to strengthen and clarify the authoritative basis which tax accounts have for the financial statement in this point [§ 6 (3) EStG; § 5 (1) EStG 1990]. In this fashion the Articles 35 (1d) and 39 (1e) become kind of a trojan horse out of which national accounting practices intrude into the financial statement and thus withstand harmonization attempts.

Those harmonization efforts are considered successful which changed the previous law in accordance with the 4th Directive [sh-rules].

— This applies to the requirement to capitalize intangible fixed assets acquired for a consideration [Tab. 2 Row 3]. Up to now this was debatable due to an unprecise formulation of 153 (3) of the old Stock Corporation Law (AktG). On the occasion of the transformation the German legislator has now put that point straight.

— Further this proves true for the consistency concept [Tab. 2 Row 5]. The previous German law did not require the consistency of the valuation methods. Nevertheless, changes in the method of valuation and considerable effects on the results had to be reported in the notes. In the process of the transformation of Art. 31 (1b) of the 4th Directive, it has been tried to weaken this provision by a Soft-Transformation [a permissive provision]. At first glance this attempt seems to have been successful since the wording of the first draft that "the valuation methods... must be retained" was reformulated to "...should be retained" in later versions. (1) This, however, was not successful at last. The formulation of § 252 (1) No. 6, stating that "the valuation methods... should be retained", has to be interpreted as "must be retained". (2) The formulation "should" has only been chosen to express that exceptions are possible. This, however, had already been provided for in the 4th Directive.

(1) Cf. Comment of the Deutscher Steuerberaterverband e.V. of Sept. 10th, 1985, in : Anlage 1 zum Stenographischen Protokoll der 18. und 19. Sitzung des Rechtsausschusses des Deutschen Bundestags, Unterausschuss "Bilanzrichtliniengesetz", am 23. und 24. September 1985, pp. 103-104.

(2) Cf. BIENER, H./BERNEKE, W. : Bilanzrichtliniengesetz, Düsseldorf 1986, p. 91.

— Moreover a partial success has been achieved concerning the requirement to write back a depreciation if the reasons for the depreciation do no longer exist [Tab. 2, Row 9]. There exists, however, no requirement to reinstate original values if this would lead to a tax disadvantage.

As yet a major number of rules has not been changed [rh-rules]. This is obvious, however, only for one rule [Tab. 2, Row 2]. Art. 2 (5) of the 4th Directive specifies that even clear provisions must be departed from if their application is incompatible with a true and fair view. According to German law this would be inadmissible. [1] Should such a case obtain, the balance sheet and the profit and loss account would nevertheless have to be prepared in compliance with that specific rule. The true and fair view can only be achieved by additional explanatory comments in the notes. A transformation akin to that of Section 228 (5) of Schedule 4 of the CA 1985 in Britain, according to which provisions can be departed from in order to give a true and fair view, does not exist in German law. Thus a case like that of the british Wedgewood plc, where the audit opinion stated that the accounts give a true and fair view of the state of affairs of the company, although they did not follow SSAP No. 20 in that unrealised exchange gains were not reflected in the profit and loss account in 1984, [2] is inadmissible in Germany.

The situation is less obvious for other rules which have been assigned to the class rh in Table 2 [Rows 1, 7, 10, 11]. This is typical for Soft-Transformations. First the formulation of the international rule is changed while being transformed into national law. The interpretation of this altered definition is controversial. Then for each rule of that kind more or less numerous commentators of the law show up deeming an interpretation adequate or at least applicable which is in the sense of the former traditional way of accounting. Enterprises can then refer to these commentators and are thus practically enabled to maintain their previous accounting habits. In the following part of my paper I am going to show this procedure for the specific rules (see table 2).

True and fair view : separation-thesis [Tab. 2, Row 1]

The requirement that the accounting be in compliance with the principle of the true and fair view reads in the original formulation [4th Directive Art. 2 (3)(4)] :

"The annual accounts shall give a true and fair view of the company's assets, liabilities, financial position and profit or loss.

---

[1] In this sense : Justification of the governmental proposal, BR-Drucks. 61/82, p. 76 : The general principle as laid down in § 264 (2) sentence 1 HGB "does not take precedence over the legal provisions in that sense that it permits the form and contents of the financial statements to be determined in deviation from these rules."

[2] Cf. HOFFMANN, K.-J. : "True and fair view" aus englischer Sicht, Frankfurt am Main 1989, p. 72.

	AktG 1965	4th Directive	HGB 1985	class
General Principle				
1. true and fair view, separation thesis	—	Art. 2 (3) (4) no	§ 264 (2) disputed	rh
2. true and fair view, deviation from individual rules	—	Art. 2 (4) compulsory	§ 264 (2) not stated	rh
Items to be Included				
3. intangible assets acquired for a consideration	§ 153 (3) compulsory/ optional : disputed	Art. 9, 10 compulsory	§ 264 (1) compulsory	sh
4. provisions for pension promises (only new ones)	BGH optional	Art. 20, 43 (7) compulsory/ optional : disputed	Art. 28 EGHGB compulsory	nep/ sh
Valuation				
5. consistency concept	— optional	Art. 31 (b) compulsory	§ 252 (1) 6 compulsory	sh
6. minimum value of manufacturing cost	§ 153 (2) ; GOB variable costs	Art. 35 (3a) materials and direct costs	§ 255 (2) disputed	rh
7. Selling expenses as part of manufacturing cost	§ 154 (2) special direct costs	Art. 39 (2) prohibited	§ 255 (2) disputed	rh
8. Acceptance of tax allowed depreciation	§ 154 (2) § 155 (3, 2) optional	Art. 35 (1d) Art. 39 (1e) optional	§ 254 279 (2), 281 optional	nop/ nep
9. Requirement to reinstate original values (without tax consequence)	§ 154 (2) § 155 (4) optional	Art. 35 (1 c/dd) & Art. 39 (1 d, e) compulsory	§ 280 compulsory	sh
Deferred taxes				
10. deferred taxes considered as assets	no	Art. 43 (11) compulsory, within total amount	§ 274 (2) optional	rh
11. deferred taxes considered as uncertain liabilities (not tax accruals)	no	Art. 43 (11) unclear	§ 274 (1) disputed	rh

Table 2 : Success of the transformation ot the rules of the 4th Directive.

Where the application of the provisions of this Directive would not be sufficient to give a true and fair view within the meaning of paragraph 3, additional information must be given".

This became in German law [§ 264 (2) HGB] :

"The financial statements of the company must, in compliance with required accounting principles, present a true and fair view of the net worth, financial position and results of the company. If special circumstances result in the financial statements not showing a true and fair view within the meaning of sentence 1, then additional disclosures are required in the notes."

On the one hand this wording is interpreted in accordance with the 4th Directive in the sense that the true and fair view principle is valid likewise for balance sheet and profit and loss account as far as no specific legal rule precludes this. Options, margins of judgement and legal gaps have to be interpreted in respect of the true and fair view. (1) Other commentators are advocating the so-called separation or uncoupling thesis. (2) According to their opinion the true and fair view basically has a bearing on the notes only whereas balance sheet and profit and loss account have to be set up in accordance with the individual rules and the German GAAP [see above : "...in compliance..."]. Since judges of the German supreme fiscal court - the BFH - are among these commentators and as they are the ones who finally determine what is to be understood as accounting principle in Germany, a corporation draws up its financial statement quite correctly if it refers to these commentators and makes use of the separation thesis.

Minimum value of manufacturing cost [Tab 2, Row 6]

Art. 35 (3) of the 4th Directive defines manufacturing or production costs as follows :

"The production costs shall be calculated by adding to the purchasing price of the raw materials and consumables the costs directly attributable to the product in question.
A reasonable portion of the costs which are only indirectly attributable to the product in question may be added into the production costs to the extent that they relate to the period of production."

(1) Cf. BIENER, H. : Die Rechnungslegung der GmbH nach dem Regierungsentwurf eines BIRILIG, in : GmbHR 1982, p. 56 ; ORDELHEIDE, D./HARTLE, J. : Rechnungslegung und Gewinnermittlung von Kapitalgesellschaften nach dem Bilanzrichtlinien-Gesetz, in : GmbHR 1986, pp. 10-13 ; BUDDE, W.D./KARIG, K.P. : in : Beck'scher Bilanzkommentar, München 1986, § 264 Anm. 25 ff. ; BUDDE, W.D./FOERSCHLE, G. : Das Verhältnis des "True and fair view" zu den Grundsätzen ordnungsmässiger Buchführung und zu den Einzelvorschriften, in : MELLWIG, W./MOXTER, A./ORDELHEIDE, D. (eds.) : Einzelabschluss und Konzernabschluss, Wiesbaden 1988, pp. 39-42.

(2) Cf. MOXTER, A. : Bilanzlehre, Bd. 2 : Einführung in das neue Bilanzrecht, 3rd ed., Wiesbaden 1988, pp. 67 ff. : BEISSE, H. : Die Generalnorm des neuen Bilanzrechts und ihre steuerliche Bedeutung, in : MELLWIG, W./MOXTER, A./ORDELHEIDE, D. (eds.) : Handels - und Steuerbilanz, Wiesbaden 1989.

The corresponding rule [§ 255 (2) HGB] of the German Accounting Directives Law reads :

In the manufacturing cost "shall be included the cost of materials, production cost and special costs of production. In determining manufacturing costs, appropriate portions of materials overheads, necessary production overheads and depreciation of fixed assets may be included..."

In the discussion of this rule, various boundaries have been detected :

— the direct costs in the sense of cost accounting. These comprise the values of the goods consumed in production which can directly be assigned to the item in question.
— the so-called "commercial accounting direct costs". (1) They consist of two parts :
= cost components like costs of materials, productive wages and special costs of production whose inclusion is mandatory regardless of the way in which they have been registered, and
= other costs like costs of supplies which are only considered if actually registered individually.
— the variable costs as sum of direct costs and variable overhead.(2)

The details of this discussion are of no particular interest for the point surveyed here. It only matters that the previous accounting practices, which regarded the variable costs as the minimum value of manufacturing costs, is still deemed adequate.

Deferred Taxes [Tab. 2, Row 10, 11]

The 4th Directive requires the accounting for deferred taxes. This follows indirectly from Art. 43 (1) No. 11 :

"...the notes on the accounts must set out information in respect of the following matters at least :
...the difference between the tax charged for the financial year and for earlier financial years and the amount of tax payable in respect of those years, provided that this difference is material for purposes of future taxation. This amount may also be disclosed in the balance sheet as a cumulative amount under a separate item with an appropriate heading."

(1) Cf. PANKOW, M./SCHMIDT-WENDT, D. : in : Beck'scher Bilanzkommentar, München 1986, § 255, Anm. 525 ; MOXTER, A. : Aktivierungspflichtige Herstellungskosten in Handels - und Steuerbilanz, in : Betriebs-Berater 1988, p. 942.
(2) Cf. ORDELHEIDE, D./HARTLE, J. (FN 1 p. 8), p. 39 ; KNOP, W./KÜTING, K. : in: KÜTING, K./WEBER, C.-P. (ed.) : Handbuch der Rechnungslegung, 2nd ed., 1987, p. 690.

In the course of the transformation into German law, the rule was reformulated as follows [§ 274 HGB] :

"(1) If the taxation expense relating to the financial year or earlier financial years is too low because taxable income under the tax regulations is lower than the results shown in the financial statements, and if such lower tax expense of the financial year or earlier years will probably be equalized in later financial years, an accrual shall be set up pursuant to § 249, paragraph (1), sentence 1, in the amount of the probable tax charge of the later years and shall be shown separately in the balance sheet or in the notes. The accrual shall be released as soon as the higher tax charge occurs or is no longer likely to arise.

(2) If the taxation expense relating to the financial year or earlier financial years is too high because taxable income under the tax regulations is higher than the results shown in the financial statements, and if the excessive tax charge of the financial year or earlier financial years will probably be equalized in later financial years, a prepaid expense may be shown as an accounting convenience on the assets side of the balance sheet in the amount of the probable tax saving in the following years. This item is to be shown separately with an appropriate description and explained in the notes. If such an item is taken up, profits may only be distributed if, after the distribution, the freely available revenue reserves plus retained profits less accumulated losses brought forward at least equal the amount capitalized. The amount shall be eliminated as soon as the tax saving occurs or is no longer likely to arise."

This provision has led to an extensive and very controversial discussion as deferred taxes were alien to the former law. (1) The discussion is of interest only insofar as the previous accounting rule is a possible interpretation of the new § 274. The former rule held an obligation to accrue for future tax liabilities, while a matching of tax charges to periods was prohibited. This old rule is still applicable because § 274 is interpreted in such a manner that the reasons leading to a capitalization of deferred taxes need not to be regarded even before deferred tax assets are deducted from liabilities for deferred taxes. Furthermore, § 274 is understood to hold a requirement to take into account only those reasons for deferred taxes which actually lead to future tax payments. Because of this, the following reasons do not lead to deferred taxes :

— Writing up assets subject to depletion in the commercial financial statement only.
— Capitalization of start-up and business expansion expenses which is inadmissible for tax purposes.
— Paid interest is considered part of the manufacturing costs in the commercial financial statement alone.

(1) Cf. LASER, H. : Latente Steuern, in : CASTAN, E./HEYMANN, G./MÜLLER, E./ORDELHEIDE, D./SCHEFFLER, E. (eds.) : Beck'sches Handbuch der Rechnungslegung, München 1987, B 235.

This explains why many German companies do not show deferred taxes but only accrue for future tax payments which have become due in the previous period. The former accounting habit can be continued.

Selling Expenses as Component of Manufacturing Costs [Tab. 2, Row 7]

The selling expenses are an exception. The wording of Art. 39 (2) sentence 3 has been transformed literally into German law. Furthermore, the chairman of the Law Commission of the Deutscher Bundestag (German Parliament) has expressly stated during the hearings that the capitalization of any selling expenses is prohibited, including the special direct selling expenses as well - doubtless a hard transformation. This is interpreted in the same way by the majority of the commentators.

Some commentators, however, are taking pains to interpret cost components, formerly always regarded as selling expenses, differently - as manufacturing costs.(1) Expenses incurred to prepare and acquire orders concerning long-term production are defined as manufacturing costs in order to evade the prohibition to capitalize selling expenses. This makes clear that in case neither national options nor Soft-Transformations are able to prevent a change, further mechanisms exist which serve the same purpose. The mechanisms used in this case may be called **"helpful definitions and interpretations"**.

3 - REASONS FOR HARD AND SOFT-TRANSFORMATIONS

Why has only part of the rules listed in Table 2 been transformed in a hard and others in a soft way? What are the reasons for certain traditional accounting rules showing a tendency towards self-preservation? The opposition against the change demanded by the 4th Directive can be interpreted as the result of a collective national decision-making process. Rules considerably decreasing the expected utility of the relevant groups are transformed not at all or only in a soft way. The other rules are transformed in a hard way.

This attempt of an explanation raises a lot of questions. Which are the relevant groups? How do the new provisions influence expected utility? Are there conflicting interests among the groups? Luckily, the situation is easier in the case analysed here, since a considerable part of the results of the transformation can be explained by an intervening variable. With respect to this, the interests of the groups concerned are parallel. Thus the connections between accounting rules and effects on expected utility can be shown quite easily. This intervening variable

(1) Cf. SELCHER, W.: Probleme der Unter - und der Obergrenze von Herstellungskosten, in: Betriebs-Berater 1986, pp. 2298 ff.; FOERSCHLE, G.: Bilanzierung sogenannter Sondereinzelkosten des Vertriebes aus handelsrechtlicher Sicht, in: ZfbF-Ergänzungsheft 1/1987, pp. 95 ff.; SARX, M.: Ausgewählte Einzelprobleme der Bilanzierung, in: MELLWIG, W./MOXTER, A./ORDELHEIDE, D. (eds.): Handels - und Steuerbilanz, Wiesbaden 1989

is the risk of the tax load being increased by the transformation. Modifications of accounting rules increasing the probability of an additional tax load are evaded by Soft-Transformations. On the contrary, new rules possibly leading to a tax reduction become transformed in a hard way.

Maintaining or reducing the tax load is beneficial to all members participating in a firm. The "cake" which can be distributed to them as income is at least not reduced in size. The obvious conflict with the exchequer did not need to be regarded in this particular case. The German Bundesregierung as well as the Bundestag had declared to transform the 4th Directive in a way avoiding an additional tax burden.[1]

The tax risk does not comprise all effects on utility. Additional intervening variables thus have played a role in the discussion concerning the transformation. Examples are particularly the effects on the amount of equity capital disclosed and the distributable profit, as well as on the accounting discretion of the managers. In case of a conflict with the aim of a tax reduction, however, these explanatory variables are of minor importance. This is due to a number of reasons:

— First, a reduction of the tax burden directly increases the cash flow. The effect in the FRG is considerable, due to an average tax rate of 63,33 % for profits retained.[2]

— Secondly, not all of the accounting rules listed in table 2 which increase the disclosed equity capital are unanimously agreed upon by the individuals participating in a company, as these rules regularly increase the distributable profit too. In case of a conflict, the argument of a tax reduction is of greater weight. This applies likewise to discretionary accounting.

— Furthermore, the effects of these rules on the amount of equity capital shown is of minor importance, as other possibilities to increase equity capital have been created. On the one hand, the transitional provisions to the new law enable all enterprises to release hidden reserves without impact on the taxable profit. On the other hand, the argument of an insufficient equity capital plays a role especially for those corporations which make use of international capital markets. In an international comparison, the relative amount of equity capital shown by German firms is quite low. Credit risk estimations of international capital markets, however, are based on consolidated financial statements. As they are neither determining the tax payments nor the distributable profit in the FRG, all accounting measures can be used here to increase the amount of equity capital disclosed,

(1) Cf. Justification of the governmental proposal of the Accounting Directives Law: BR-Drucksache 10/317, p. 68; cf. 2nd and 3rd parliamentary consultation of the Accounting Directives Law, in: BIENER, H./BERNECKE, W.: Bilanzrichtliniengesetz, Düsseldorf 1986, pp. 780 f.

(2) Cf. MELLWIG, W.: Investition und Besteuerung, Wiesbaden 1985, p. 293.

regardless of tax or dividend arguments. This is made possible by a number of national options contained in the 4th and 7th Directive which have been made use of in Germany.

Again, this argument applies likewise to discretionary accounting. The reduction of the available margin through the transformation of the rules reducing the tax burden - especially the requirement to accrue pension obligations [Tab 2, Row 4] - is compensated by new rules like the option of an expense equalization accrual according to § 249 (2) or the option to capitalize deferred taxes. The extent of this compensation depends on the specific situation of the corporation.

In the following I would like to discuss the importance of the tax-relief argument and the influence of other reasons with references to the individual provisions listed in Table 2 :

In the UK the true and fair view principle allows accounting not complying with German GAAP. Particularly the prudence principle may be violated.(1)

Hence the opinion has been advanced - especially by judges of the supreme fiscal court(2) - that the commercial financial statements can no longer form an authoritative basis for the tax accounts if the true and fair view principle is transformed in compliance with the general principle of the 4th Directive. Tax legislation unimpaired by the prudence principle governing commercial accounting could develop in a way which bears a considerable risk of an increasing tax burden.

Furthermore, the idea of an overriding general principle which takes precedence over individual rules is alien to German legal principles. According to the German opinion, the general principle derives from the specific individual rules. In case of doubt, the principle "lex specialis overrides lex generalis" applies in the first instance.

The implementation of the requirement to capitalize intangible fixed assets acquired for a consideration did not encounter opposition.

— First of all this is explained by the fact that according to the former law the option of the commercial law was already interpreted for tax purposes as a requirement to capitalize intangible assets. By taking over the requirement of the 4th Directive the tax load was thus not increased.

(1) Cf. ORDELHEIDE, D. : The Transformation of the 4. EEC-D's Rules of Profit Calculation in EEC Member States, Paper held on the annual congress of the EAA in London 1987; HOFFMANN, K.-J. : "True and fair view" aus englischer Sicht, Frankfurt am Main 1989, pp. 62-63, 76-77.

(2) Cf. BEISSE, H. : Die Generalnorm des neuen Bilanzrechts und ihre steuerliche Bedeutung, in : MELLWIG, W./MOXTER, A./ORDELHEIDE, D. (eds.) : Handels - und Steuerbilanz, Wiesbaden 1989.

— Secondly, the aim of increasing the disclosed equity capital did not stand opposite to the transformation of the requirement to include these items.

— Finally, acquired intangible assets are regularly considered in management accounting; thus transformation made both accounting systems parallel.

There existed a conflict between the aims of reducing the tax risk and increasing the amount of equity capital disclosed - at least partly - in connection with the transformation of the requirement to accrue pension promises :

— According to the old law increases in accruals for pensions were not considered for tax purposes because commercial law held only an option. By implementing a requirement to accrue pension promises, increases in them became tax deductible for the first time.

— Opposite to this stood the reduction of the amount of equity capital shown. This did not prove true, however, for the large number of those corporations which had accrued pension promises for sake of the prudence concept, altough they were not accepted for tax purposes. The above mentioned reasons for the priority of the tax risk added to this. The economic incentive of considerable tax reliefs has obviously been of greater importance than the influence on the equity capital of those corporations which had not yet accrued pensions.

— The decision to state a requirement to accrue pension promises was additionally promoted by a special event. In the course of the transformation of the 4th Directive, a large German group of companies ran into trouble serious enough to endanger the corporate pensions of the employees, unless a solidarity fund of the German industry had ensured them. Because the problem was so serious, the German enterprises were charged considerable extraordinary payments into this solidarity fund. This led many parties concerned to demand an improvement of corporate precautions against this risk by requiring pension promises to be accrued.

Due to the tax risk there was no opposition against the following three rules [Tab 2, Row 5-7]. They became transformed either literally, like the **consistency concept** or the prohibition to include **selling expenses**, or even move concrete in substance, like the definition of **manufacturing cost**. Nevertheless there has been and continues to be considerable resistance to the general prohibition to include selling expenses. A strong tax argument, making an evasion of the precise provision of the 4th Directive possible, was missing in this case, however. Therefore, the opposition against a change of previous accounting practices makes use here of "helpful definitions and interpretations".

Pains are taken especially to define the special direct selling expenses of long-term contracts as manufacturing costs. The reasons for this are the large losses which would have to be shown by firms of this branch of industry if the costs of acquiring and preparing orders could not be capitalized, although at the moment the order is placed it can be expected to render a profit.

The particular way in which Art. 35 (1d) and Art. 39 (1e) [Tab. 2, Row 8], as well as the requirement to reinstate original values, have influenced the Accounting Directives Law can again be explained by tax considerations. The addition to § 6 (3) of the income tax law [§ 5(1) sentence 2, EStG 1990] in connection with §§ 254, 279 (2), 281 HGB directly makes the authoritative basis of the commercial financial statements for the tax accounts complete and more precise. Indirectly it serves the purpose of decreasing the tax risk. Due to the authoritative principle, different valuations resulting from the transformation of the 4th Directive - eg. the requirement to write up assets if the reasons for earlier depreciations no longer exist - might otherwise have had an influence on the tax load.

The Soft-Transformation of the provision concerning deferred taxes allows maintaining previous accounting practices which only permitted accruals for future tax payments. This kind of transformation can be explained by the prudence principle which dominates German accounting rules. Balancing accruals for uncertain liabilities against a fictitious tax credit [deferred tax asset] is incompatible with this principle. This is clearly expressed by § 274 HGB as well. Liabilities for deferred taxes have to be set up as an accrual for uncertain liabilities according to § 249 (1) HGB, whereas deferred tax assets are rated as an accounting convenience. There is no requirement to capitalise them. Furthermore, the classification as an accounting convenience has the effect that using it would signal indigence.

4 - SUMMARY

Certain national accounting rules resist international harmonization requirements. Among the most important mechanisms preventing a change are the omission of problems and national options. These mechanisms are effective during the formulation of the international rule. Beyond that there are further mechanisms which go into action when the international rule is transformed into a national one and when the national rule is finally applied :

— Soft-Transformations, and
— helpful definitions and interpretations.

It has been shown that both mechanisms have been used in the course of the transformation of the 4th Directive into German accounting law in order to maintain traditional accounting.

Furthermore I have shown that the risk of a possible increase in tax burden as a consequence of the transformation served as a gate-keeper :

— rules increasing the risk were transformed softly ;
— new rules decreasing the tax risk have been transformed in the hard way.

Even rules without a bearing on the tax load of German firms have encountered opposition for various reasons, such as

— the aim of avoiding incorrect signalling of a loss [special direct selling expenses] or
— the prudence principle [deferred taxes].

[20]

Accounting in Europe

Harmonization of accounting standards

A view from the European community

K. Van Hulle
EC Commission and K. U. Leuven

CONTEXT OF THE HARMONIZATION

Harmonization of accounting standards in the EC is part of the company law harmonization programme. This programme should contribute to further the establishment by companies of branches and subsidiaries in other Member States. Since the adoption of the White Paper on the completion of the internal market, other priorities have been added such as the promotion of cross-border co-operation between companies from different Member States. More specifically, one could also argue that the harmonization of accounting standards should also contribute to bringing about a European capital market.

There can be no doubt that a true internal market can only function with a minimum amount of financial transparency. It is therefore essential to look at the harmonization from a European angle. Or, to say it in other words, it is not enough that the national market could function without certain disclosure rules – because there are other information channels – to extrapolate this situation to the level of the Community.

Harmonization does not necessarily mean uniformity. In the Community, we want to achieve as far as possible equivalence and comparability of financial information. Therefore, the rules are often minimum rules and it is not uncommon to have options for Member States and/or for companies.

Harmonization takes place through Directives. A Directive is a legal

Address for correspondence
Commission of the European Communities, Rue de la Loi 200, B-1049 Brussels, Belgique.

instrument addressed to the Member States which must transpose its provisions into national law within a certain period of time. A Directive is adopted by the Council of Ministers with a qualified majority. One *disadvantage* of a Directive is that Member States must still take some action before the rules of the Directive become part of national law. Under the supervision of the European Court of Justice, the Commission must see to it that the Directives are implemented in time and that the implementing legislation is and remains in conformity with the Directives. An *advantage* of a Directive is the flexibility which it gives to Member States in the implementation process. Member States can choose the ways and means to implement the Directive. This allows them to introduce the Community rules into their national law in full respect of their national traditions.

ACHIEVEMENTS

Accounting harmonization in the EC started with the Fourth Directive of 25 July 1978 on the annual accounts of limited liability companies (O. J. Nr. L 222 of 14 August 1979). This Directive applies to some 3 million limited liability companies. It requires these companies to prepare annual accounts which must show a true and fair view of the company's assets, liabilities, financial position and profit or loss. The balance sheet and the profit and loss account must be drawn up in accordance with the layouts prescribed by the Directive. The valuation rules in the Directive are based on the principle of purchase price or production cost. Member States may allow the application of alternative valuation methods such as replacement cost, inflation accounting and periodic revaluation. The notes on the accounts and the annual report must contain at least the information prescribed by the Directive. The accounts must be audited by a qualified professional. They must be published together with the annual report and the audit report. The Directive also contains a number of exemptions which Member States may introduce in favour of small and medium-sized companies. Size criteria for the definition of small and medium-sized companies are included in the Directive. They are based upon the amount of net turnover, the balance sheet total and the average number of persons employed during the financial year. The thresholds were adapted by a Directive of 8 November 1990 (O. J. Nr. L 317 of 16 November 1990) in the light of economic and monetary developments in the Community. This Directive also increased the derogations which Member States may provide for small and medium-sized companies.

The Fourth Directive has now been implemented by all Member States. Recent surveys conducted by FEE (Fédération des experts-comptables européens) have shown that the quality of financial reporting in the EC has considerably improved with the implementation of the Directive and that the comparability of accounts has increased, at least in those areas which are specifically covered by the Directive.

The Fourth Directive has been the basis for a number of other accounting Directives which have been adopted by the Council of Ministers. There is first of all the Seventh Directive of 13 June 1983 on consolidated accounts (O. J. Nr. L 193 of 18 July 1983). This Directive introduces a requirement to prepare consolidated accounts and a consolidated annual report for those undertakings (parent undertakings) which have the legal power to control another undertaking (subsidiary undertaking). In addition, Member States may also require consolidation where a parent undertaking controls in fact a subsidiary undertaking on the basis of a minority participating interest or where several undertakings are managed on a unified basis (horizontal group). Exemptions may be provided where the parent undertaking is not a limited liability company, for small groups, for certain financial holding companies and – under certain conditions – for intermediate holding companies. If the ultimate parent of a group is established outside the Community, the intermediate holding company situated in the Community may be exempted from the obligation to draw up consolidated accounts for its subgroup on the condition that the ultimate parent of the group publishes in the Member State where the intermediate holding company is situated consolidated accounts which are prepared in a manner which is at least *equivalent* with consolidated accounts prepared under the Seventh Directive. In close consultation with experts from the Member States, the Commission has tried to define the concept of equivalence, which is also relevant for other accounting Directives. The Seventh Directive also deals with the preparation of the consolidated accounts. For the layout of the consolidated accounts and the valuation rules, reference is made to the relevant provisions of the Fourth Directive. The Directive allows the application of the pooling method in the case of a pooling of interests and the proportional consolidation for joint ventures. For associated undertakings, the equity method must be applied. The consolidated accounts must be audited by a qualified professional. They must be published together with the annual report and the audit report.

All Member States, with the exception of Ireland, have implemented the Seventh Directive. Consolidation is new for most Member States. Because consolidated accounts are not used as a basis for profit distribution and because they do not usually serve for the determination of taxable profit, there is a certain tendency – at least in some Member States – to move away from a strict interpretation of the prudence principle in the consolidated accounts.

The annual accounts and the consolidated accounts must be audited by a qualified professional who satisfies the conditions of the Eighth Directive of 10 April 1984 on the minimum qualifications of the statutory auditors

(O. J. Nr. L 126 of 12 May 1984). As the statutory audit has been introduced in the public interest, the auditors must at least be competent and independent. The Eighth Directive contains a number of provisions which concern the professional qualification of the auditor (examination of professional competence, practical training, etc.). On the issue of independence, the Eighth Directive does not contain detailed rules. Some rules on independence are incorporated in the modified proposal for a Fifth Directive on the structure of the public company which has not been adopted yet. As a result of the so-called 'Mutual Recognition Directive', auditors which have been approved in one Member State will be able to practise throughout the Community, subject to an adaption period not exceeding three years or to an aptitude test.

The Eighth Directive has been implemented in all Member States, with the exception of Italy and the Netherlands. It will contribute to the development of a highly qualified accounting profession in the Community.

Special rules have been elaborated for banks and insurance companies. The Directive of 8 December 1986 on the annual accounts and consolidated accounts of banks and other financial institutions (O. J. Nr. L 372 of 31 December 1986) largely refers to the Fourth Directive. It contains only those rules which were found necessary in order to take account of the particular characteristics of credit institutions. Similarly, the Directive of 19 December 1991 on the annual accounts and consolidated accounts of insurance companies deals only with the particularities of the insurance industry. Both Directives allow important derogations from the historical cost convention. Higher market values may be applied to certain current investments in the case of banks and to all investments in the case of insurance companies.

The specific situation of branches is dealt with in two separate Directives. The Directive of 13 February 1989 (O. J. Nr. L 44 of 16 February 1989) deals with the disclosure obligations of branches of credit institutions while the Eleventh Directive of 21 December 1989 (O. J. Nr. L 395 of 30 December 1989) concerns the disclosure obligations of branches of limited liability companies in general. As a rule, Member States may no longer require the publication by a branch of accounts covering its own activities, where the branch has been set up by a company from another Member State, on the condition that the branch discloses certain information about the foreign company, including its accounts. However, pending subsequent further co-ordination, Member States may still require branches of credit institutions to publish certain information on their activities in order to assess their importance. If the branch has been set up by a company from a third country, the accounts of the company which are published by the branch must have been drawn up in accordance with the accounting Directives or in a manner which is at least equivalent thereto.

The concept of equivalence is the same as the similar wording in the Seventh Directive for groups with an ultimate parent situated outside the Community.

With a Directive of 8 November 1990 (O. J. Nr. L 317 of 16 November 1990), the scope of application of the Fourth and Seventh Directives has been extended to those partnerships and unlimited companies where all unlimited members are established as limited liability companies. Member States have different possibilities to deal with this complex structure which exists primarily in Germany under the name of 'GmbH & Co KG'. These different treatments reflect differences in the legal environment.

Finally, to conclude this picture, it may be useful to indicate that it has not been possible so far to introduce a rule which would allow all companies to draw up and to publish their accounts in ecus. A proposal to that effect was rejected by Member States because they feared that companies for which the ecu does not constitute a functional currency might still use the ecu as the reporting currency if this could improve their results. Therefore, the Directive of 8 November 1990, which also deals with the exemptions for small and medium-sized companies, allows companies to publish their accounts in ecus only in addition to the publication in the national currency.

MAIN CHARACTERISTICS OF THE HARMONIZATION

In order to understand the nature and the extent of the harmonization of accounting standards in the EC, it might be useful to recall the main characteristics of the harmonization.

1. Company law approach

All limited liability companies must disclose financial information in the interest of shareholders, creditors, employees and other third parties. The disclosure obligation is very much linked to the limited liability. Because of this approach, the financial reporting requirements are not directed solely or even primarily towards the investors. In addition, there are no specific rules for listed companies, which require more or different financial information to be disclosed. The only exception is the requirement for listed companies to publish a statement of sources and uses of funds.

2. Equivalence and comparability

The accounting Directives contain a number of important options for Member States and/or for companies. The options reflect the different attitudes towards accounting and financial reporting in the Member States. They are justified because the harmonization does not aim at the development of uniform accounting rules in the EC. In order to establish comparability, additional information will often have to be provided for in the notes on the accounts. Although the rules are not the same, Member States have accepted to recognize mutually the accounts prepared on the basis of the Accounting Directives, without further additions.

3. Accounting standards are part of the law

As the harmonization takes place through Directives, Member States must transpose the provisions of the Directives into national law. This has important consequences. Respect of the standards may be enforced through the normal mechanisms of the legal system. In addition, the national rules must be interpreted in the light of the Directive upon which they are based. Finally, accounting standards developed by a national accounting standards board must be in conformity both with the law and with the Directives.

4. Accounting standards are not set by the accounting profession

The Accounting Directives are the result of a complex political process which involves all parties which have an interest in financial reporting. The proposals are made by the Commission. They are submitted for consultation to the Economic and Social Committee and to the European Parliament and they are adopted by the Council of Ministers in co-operation with the European Parliament on the basis of a qualified majority vote. The accounting profession will intervene at various stages of this process by giving its opinion on particular points or by preparing a first draft.

5. Multilingual and multicultural process

All experts participating in the decision-making process have the opportunity of expressing themselves in their own language. There is no predominance of any one of the nine official languages. As a result, the cultural identity of each of the Member States is fully respected. The Directives are also published in all official languages of the Community.

RECENT DEVELOPMENTS

In January 1990, the Commission organized a conference in Brussels on the future of the harmonization of accounting standards in the EC. Experts from the various competent ministries of the Member States, representatives of European organizations of the main users and preparers of accounts, of the accounting profession and academics, as well as representatives from national accounting standards setting bodies, attended the Conference. The Commission wanted to receive some advice on future steps to be taken in the accounting field. On the basis of the discussions at the Conference, a number of important decisions have been taken.

1. No reduction of the options in the Fourth Directive

It was generally agreed that it was premature to reduce the options in the Fourth Directive. The options reflect real differences between the Member States. Their existence does not prevent comparability. These reactions came somewhat as a surprise because IASC had just decided to reduce the options in IAS.

2. Continuation of the harmonization

A survey of accounts published on the basis of the Fourth Directive conducted by FEE had shown that the quality of financial reporting had considerably increased with the implementation of the Fourth Directive and that comparability of accounts had improved at least on those issues which had been specifically dealt with in the Fourth Directive. However, many issues had not been addressed by the Fourth Directive: foreign currency translation, leasing, deferred taxation, government grants, long-term contracts, etc. In addition, there was a serious risk that the harmonization level would diminish as a result of new and sometimes divergent accounting standards issued by national bodies. Therefore, virtually all participants agreed that the harmonization efforts should continue. On the other hand, many people stressed the need for more flexibility in the harmonization process. It takes a long time to negotiate a Directive and it is equally difficult to amend a Directive. There is a need to react more quickly to new developments. It might therefore be useful to explore the possibility of further progress by way of recommendation rather than by adopting new Directives. The fact that all Member States were late with the implementation of the Fourth Directive and that the implementing legislation was still rather new also explain the reluctance of some participants to embark upon a route of new Community and thus national legislation.

3. Creation of an Accounting Advisory Forum

A clear message which came out of the Conference was the need which the parties with an interest in financial reporting felt to be more closely associated with the initiatives of the Commission in the accounting field. The Commission therefore decided to set up a new advisory body which has now been named the Accounting Advisory Forum and which should advise the Commission on technical solutions for problems which have not been dealt with in the Accounting Directives and provide guidance on the position to be taken in international accounting harmonization debates. The Forum should also provide a platform for discussions between users and preparers and national standards setting bodies on accounting issues and developments. In a way, the Forum mirrors the Contact Committee on the Accounting Directives which was set up by the Fourth Directive and which is composed of government experts. The members of the Forum do not as such represent a national government. They have been asked by the Commission to be a member of the Forum in a personal capacity. The Forum is presided over by the Commission. It has twenty-two members from the accounting standards setting bodies of the Member States, the European organizations of preparers of accounts (UNICE, Eurochambres, UEAPME), the European organizations of users of accounts (Banking Federation, Federation of Stock Exchanges, Federation of Financial Analysts, Confederation of Trade-unions, Federation of Insurers), the European Federation of Accountants and the European Accounting Association. It has not been easy to limit the membership of the Forum. It was also difficult to identify an accounting standards setting body for each Member State. This was and is notably the case for Germany and Luxemburg.

The Forum has met twice since its creation. It has discussed three topics which had been identified as major lacunae in the Fourth Directive: foreign currency translation, government grants and leasing. These are all difficult subjects. *Foreign currency translation* is particularly difficult because of its fiscal consequences. It looks as if it will be impossible at this stage to agree on a solution which would allow for comparability between the three methods which have been identified for individual accounts. For consolidated accounts, there is broad agreement about the closing rate/ net investment approach for non-integrated foreign operations and about the temporal method for integrated foreign operations. Accounting for *government grants* is a less important topic. If the investment which has benefited from the grant is shown on a net basis, i.e. under deduction of the grant received, the notes must contain sufficient information to allow for comparability with companies applying the gross method. *Accounting for lease contracts* is a highly controversial subject. The distinction between a finance lease and an operational lease is not always evident. In addition, most contracts are construed in such a way that there are virtually no finance leases left. Therefore, the question can be raised whether the distinction serves a useful purpose.

The meetings of the Forum are prepared on the basis of working documents which are discussed in small working groups. There is a lot of technical input from FEE.

From the first meetings of the Forum, it has already become clear that it will be difficult in the EC to agree on a benchmark or a fortiori on one single accounting solution. It is evident that the coexistence of different solutions does not make it easy to compare accounts. But we must be realistic. If we can achieve progress by identifying the main solutions and allowing for comparability through additional disclosures in the notes, we will have made considerable progress.

It is the intention to publish the work of the Forum. The Commission will have to decide which status it will give to conclusions arrived at in the Forum. The decision will be made on a case by case basis in close consultation with the members of the Forum and of the Contact Committee. If progress can be achieved without new legislation at Community level, there might be a case for not initiating new legislation. Of course, the Commission can also decide to incorporate a proposal from the Forum into a recommendation.

THE COMMUNITY AND THE INTERNATIONAL SCENE

Prior to the January 1990 Conference, a lot of discussion took place on whether there should be European standards, in addition to national standards and international standards. This debate was not a very useful one. There is no 'Fortress Europe' in accounting. More than any trading bloc in the world, the Community is interested in what is happening outside its area of competence. On the other hand, the Community as such has not been very much involved in the international harmonization debate, outside intergovernmental bodies such as the OECD and the UN. Therefore, the particularities of the Member States of the EC are not sufficiently reflected in international accounting standards. This is the main reason why these standards are hardly applied at all by companies in the Community.

At the Conference, several participants stressed the need for a continued international perspective in the Community harmonization. In order to be informed about international developments, the Commission has accepted the invitation from IASC to participate as an observer in the work of IASC both at the level of the Board and at the level of the Improvements Steering Committee which redrafts the IAS within the context of the Comparability project. In addition, on a proposal from the Commission, the Forum has set up a working group which will examine the exposure drafts issued by the Board of IASC as part of its Comparability project. In this context, it is important to stress that most IAS do not conflict with the EC Accounting Directives. But, because the Directives contain options for Member States, it may well be that a particular option is not any more allowed by an IAS. The fact that there is no conflict with an EC Accounting Directive does not preclude a conflict between the standard and the national law of a Member State. The reduction of options in the IAS is therefore likely to create problems for a number of Member States which had fought very hard to have the option included in a Directive.

Of course, on the European continent, other important developments have taken place. The agreement between the EC and EFTA to build a *European Economic Area* by 1 January 1993 will also have consequences for accounting developments in the EFTA countries (Austria, Finland, Ireland, Liechtenstein, Norway, Sweden and Switzerland). These countries have agreed to bring their legislation into conformity with the EC Accounting Directives. Another consequence is that these countries will be closely associated with the work of the Community in the accounting field.

The *Eastern European countries* are also engaged in an accounting reform. Accounting in a centrally planned economy is virtually incomparable with accounting in a market economy. In order to make the transition possible, there is an urgent need for an accounting framework and an accounting profession. Because these countries are very interested in a closer co-operation with the Community and because their basic legal structure is very similar to that of most continental European countries, several of them have decided to base their accounting reform upon the EC Accounting Directives. As a result, the harmonization will be extended to Eastern Europe as well.

THE FUTURE

It is always difficult and even dangerous to try to predict the future. On the basis of current information, there are three areas where I expect some developments in the near future.

1. Adaptation of the decision-making process

When the White Paper on the completion of the internal market was agreed upon, it was clear that the realization of an internal market by 31 December 1992 would not be possible without some institutional changes. These changes were adopted in 1986 with the Single European Act. Among those changes, it was also agreed to extend the Commission's executive powers. Technical adaptations of existing Community legislation should be possible without having to go through the normal procedure for changes in a Directive. The Commission is now examining to what extent such a simplified procedure could also be introduced in the accounting field. Unless the Accounting Directives are adapted to changing circumstances, there is a risk that accounting standards in the Community will remain cast in stone. This would be unrealistic and a bad service to interested parties.

2. Mutual recognition of accounts

I have already explained that we have a system of mutual recognition of accounts within the Community. We do mutually recognize the accounts of companies from different Member States because we believe that – although the rules are not exactly the same – there is broadly speaking equivalence between the accounts of a French and a Dutch company or between the accounts of a German and an English company. Member States are not even allowed to require additional information as long as the accounts have been prepared in accordance with the Accounting Directives. We would like to extend this concept of mutual recognition to our main trading partners. Formal negotiations would require a mandate from the Council of Ministers. This is now being examined. Of course, this is not an easy subject. It is very difficult to admit that the same objective can be obtained with less stringent rules. Theoretically, there are not limits to disclosure. Many things are interesting to know, but are they really necessary? Maybe some parties have an interest in complex accounting rules. There are also differences in legal tradition and culture which might militate against mutual recognition. Anyway, there is a strong feeling in the Community that there is some potential here, which should be further explored. In this respect, it should be stressed that reconciliation is not a good answer to overcome differences in accounting treatment. If a German company publishes a profit of 100 in Germany and has to disclose (after reconciliation) a profit of 1000 in the US, the only result is confusion for everybody concerned.

3. International harmonization

The IASC has done excellent work. Its standards are, however, not enforceable. In order to make companies apply these standards, there will have to be some government intervention unless companies should decide out of their own free will to apply IAS. This is unlikely unless there is a benefit to be gained. This is why IASC and IOSCO (International Organization of Securities Commissions) have joined hands in order to facilitate multinational securities offerings. If companies engaged in a multinational securities offering were able to present accounts which are prepared in accordance with IAS or which have been reconciled to IAS instead of having to comply with the local standards of each country where the offer is made, important progress would have been made. However, because of different traditions, it will remain difficult to find the right middle way between over- and under-regulation.

For the Community the execution of this project will not remain without difficulties. It will require changes in both Community and national law. In order to be successful, more account will have to be taken of the particular situation in the Community with its distinction between annual accounts and consolidated accounts and its linkage between accounting and taxation. If the IAS were limited to consolidated accounts, it might be easier to make progress.

CONCLUSION

With the implementation of the Fourth, Seventh and Eighth Directives, accounting has become an important matter in all Member States of the Community. But, in the same way as all animals are equal but some animals are more equal than others, some Member States attach more importance to accounting than others. This is also the reason why the development of a conceptual framework for the Community is not a realistic proposition in the immediate future. There is clearly a conflict between those who – for conceptual reasons – want to change their accounting system and those who – for selfish reasons – believe that accounting harmonization was finished in 1978. It is only through regular contacts within the Contact Committee and within the Forum that we will be able to channel the various positions so as to ensure that we can make progress on points where it is felt that a solution provided for in an existing Directive has become obsolete because of changed circumstances or because of another insight in the matter.

NOTE

The author is Principal Administrator and Head of Accounting at the EC Commission (Directorate-General XV 'Financial Institutions and Company Law') and also Professor of Accounting Law at the KU Leuven.

The views expressed in this article are attributable only to the author.

European Accounting Review 1993, **2**, 387–396

Harmonization of accounting standards in the EC

Is it the beginning or is it the end?

K. Van Hulle
EC Commission and KU Leuven

WHAT IS HARMONIZATION?

It is fair to say that accounting standards still differ quite extensively from country to country. It is also interesting to see how proud people are about their own accounting rules. In fact, they may not like them, but they still believe that they are so much better than those which exist in other countries. This is the challenge of harmonization.

This challenge can be taken up in different ways. One way is the development of uniform rules. Because the objective of harmonization is the comparability of accounts, some people believe that it is necessary that all entities concerned apply the same rules. Such an approach is not very different from standard setting in a homogeneous environment. Another way is the one followed in the EC. It is believed that it is not necessary to develop uniform rules.

Options are perfectly acceptable as long as they can be considered equivalent and are supplemented by appropriate disclosures in the notes. This approach is based upon the establishment of a modus vivendi. Within certain limits, the remaining differences are mutually recognized.

A third approach is the one advocated by the IASC. Options are not totally ruled out. They are, however, labelled as good ones (preferred) and bad ones (alternative). Those undertakings which apply the alternative treatment must reconcile to the preferred method. The IASC approach is somewhat between the first and the second approach described above. It is however closer to the first approach because the ultimate objective is the abolition of all accounting options.

Address for Correspondence
Commission of the European Communities, Rue de la Loi 200, B–1049 Brussels, Belgique.

HOW TO HARMONIZE?

Harmonization of accounting standards is not the privilege of the EC Many organizations are active in the world in this field: the United Nations (UN), the Organization for Economic Co-operation and Development (OECD), the International Accounting Standards Committee (IASC) and the EC.

Some people believe that these organizations are not really doing a good job. Other suggestions have therefore been made. One is the Smith Kline Beecham option as presented by its chief financial officer, Mr Hugh Collum, at the World Congress of Accountants in Washington, DC (11–14 October 1992). In his view there are only two major stock exchanges in the world: London and New York. The accounting standard-setting bodies of the UK and the US should therefore get together and develop *the* accounting standards. The rest of the world should merely follow their lead.

Another suggestion was advanced by Daimler-Benz. It was stated by its chief financial officer, Mr Gerhard Liener, when he announced the listing of the shares of Daimler-Benz at the New York Stock Exchange before the end of 1993. I quote from his speech (30 March 1993): 'During the last few decades the English language has become the world language without a resolution of the UN or any other institution. It just happened. Well, something very similar is happening in international accounting. The Anglo-Saxon principles are gaining more and more ground and thus getting nearer and nearer to become the world's accounting language.' The expression 'Anglo-Saxon' might be misleading in this case. As used by Mr Liener it clearly does not include the UK. The option by Daimler-Benz is clearly an option for US GAAP.

So far, for the latest newcomers on the accounting harmonization scene!

Let us, however, return to the organizations which I have mentioned before. The United Nations have established an Intergovernmental Working Group of Experts on Standards of Accounting and Reporting (ISAR). This is the only international body in which the developing countries and the formerly centrally planned economies meet with representatives from the developed countries in order to discuss questions of harmonization and financial reporting. ISAR has developed a number of conclusions on accounting and financial reporting. It also publishes a yearly *Review on International Accounting and Reporting Issues*, as a result of its annual sessions. ISAR is not a standard-setting body.

The OECD have also set up a Working Group on Accounting Standards. As with the UN, the OECD Working Group came about within the context of the work of the organization on multinational enterprises (which are referred to as transnational corporations in the UN language).

In the OECD Accounting Working Group, government experts from the developed world discuss accounting subjects. The group has developed a number of clarifications of the accounting terms in the disclosure chapter of the *Guidelines on Multinational Enterprises.*

It has also addressed a number of accounting topics which are particularly relevant to accounting standard setters of the member countries, such as consolidation, intangibles, leasing, financial instruments, foreign currency translation, etc. The Working Group is not an accounting standard setting body.

The IASC is a private organization representing the accounting profession. Although it has tried to broaden its base (by including financial analysts as members of the Board and by inviting the FASB and the EC Commission to sit on the Board in an observer capacity) and to open the debate by setting up a consultative committee, it remains the only accounting standard-setting body at international level which is so strongly dominated by the accounting profession. The IASC has developed a number of International Accounting Standards. It has been asked by the International Organization of Securities Commissions (IOSCO) to come up with a set of standards which could be accepted by all major stock exchanges in the world, in order to facilitate multinational securities offerings. A number of multinational companies (for instance, SAS) prepare their accounts in conformity with International Accounting Standards.

Some countries (for instance, Zimbabwe) have adopted all the International Accounting Standards and made them into national standards. Although the IASC is an accounting standard-setting body, its standards are not mandatory and compliance is purely voluntary.

In the EC, accounting harmonization is part of the harmonization of company law. It should contribute to the creation of a truly internal market between the twelve Member States. The instrument used in the harmonization process is the directive. It is a legal instrument adopted by the Council of Ministers after a proposal from the Commission. It is addressed to the Member States which must transpose the directive into national law within a given period of time.

I will not describe the harmonization programme in detail. It deals with both annual accounts and consolidated accounts and contains special rules for financial reporting by banks and by insurance companies. An important feature of the harmonization in the EC is that the accounting standards which are included in the directives are incorporated into the law of each Member State. This should render their enforcement easier. Some people have criticized this legal approach as too static. As a lawyer, I disagree, of course, because the law can be drafted in such a way that there is room for interpretation. In addition, the law can be changed relatively easily, especially if the rules are not included in an Act of

Parliament but in a government decree. The use of the law as a means of standard setting can also be an interesting mechanism against too frequent (and sometimes unnecessary) changes.

WHAT SHOULD BE HARMONIZED?

There is no general agreement on what should be harmonized: the annual accounts, the consolidated accounts, the accounts of all entities, the accounts of all companies, the accounts of listed companies, the accounts of large companies, etc. In the UN and the OECD, there is an understanding that the discussions deal only with multinational companies. In the IASC, things are less clear. Some Board members believe that the IAS apply to both annual accounts and consolidated accounts and that they are valid for all types of companies, small and large, listed and non-listed. There is, however, no agreement, although the main focus seems to be on listed companies given the pressure by IOSCO.

In the EC, the directives apply principally to limited liability companies. There is no distinction between listed and non-listed companies. For SMEs, Member States may introduce accounting exemptions. These concern the amount of information which must be disclosed and the audit requirement. The harmonization deals with both annual accounts and consolidated accounts. Small groups may be exempted from the obligation to prepare consolidated accounts.

EXPERIENCES IN THE EC WITH HARMONIZATION OF ACCOUNTING STANDARDS

I think that most people would agree with me that the quality of financial reporting in the EC has considerably improved with the implementation of the accounting directives. This was one of the conclusions of the surveys on the annual accounts published on the basis of the Fourth Directive, produced by the European Federation of Accountants (FEE). It would be difficult to imagine an internal market in which companies would compete on unequal terms. A minimum of financial transparency seems necessary. This presupposes that financial information on the main actors in the economy (i.e. limited liability companies) is readily available. This was the first objective of the harmonization programme. All limited liability companies in the EC (some 3 million) must disclose annual accounts. Although this principle was already embodied in the First Company Law Directive of 1968 and subsequently confirmed in the Fourth Directive of 1978, it is still not standing practice.

Indeed, more than 90 per cent of German limited liability companies refuse to publish their accounts. This is a major political issue which is the subject of an infringement procedure introduced by the Commission against Germany. We hope that this matter can be settled in the very near future. Disclosure is one thing, but the content of the disclosure is another thing. People tend to forget that most Member States of the EC did not have any detailed accounting rules prior to the adoption of the Fourth Directive. It is therefore not difficult to say that things have changed profoundly since the implementation of the Fourth Directive. Accounting has become something serious in all Member States of the EC.

If one leaves out the adoption of the Seventh Directive on consolidated accounts and the sectoral directives on banks and insurance companies, one must admit that nothing has happened since 1978. This is all the more strange because most Member States have used the implementation of the Fourth Directive as an opportunity to set up an accounting standards setting-body in order to ensure that the accounting rules could be adapted at regular intervals to changing economic circumstances. The lack of dynamism at EC level could prove very dangerous. Indeed, as long as the directives are not amended, Member States must comply with them. New standards at national level can therefore be issued only within the limits set by the EC accounting directives. The absence of new common rules for subjects not dealt with in the accounting directives and the development of standards at national level on these matters could also result in disharmonization. Of course, this lack of progress at EC level is not limited to the accounting field. It seems to be our fate that we make real progress in European integration only when we are faced with a threat from outside. I would tend to argue that this threat is already there.

Based upon our experience, we have developed a harmonization model which allows for mutual recognition on the basis of minimum rules combined with options. This permits our Member States to take account of local particularities. International harmonization, notably through IASC, is less respectful of local particularities. In that context, options are bad, methods are categorized as good or as bad and costly reconciliations are imposed. Another 'threat' comes from the US, where very detailed rules determine the financial reporting behaviour of companies. This is very different from the less regulatory approach which some of the EC Member States would prefer. The lack of progress at national or at EC level has already led several major EC companies to turn to US GAAP. Some companies go as far as to state that their accounts are prepared in conformity with US GAAP without any further reference to the respect of their own national law. Other companies include a reconciliation to US GAAP in their annual report. And still other companies will prepare their own mix of accounting rules, inspired by US GAAP or by IAS. In Switzerland this is sometimes referred at as 'IAS light'. It is certainly true that some of these companies are listed in New York and must therefore conform to US GAAP. It is also a fact that the FASB and the SEC are very active in the accounting field and that the quality of the standards which they develop is impressive. But, could it be the hidden agenda of our Member States that the largest companies in the EC apply US GAAP in the absence of equivalent national or EC standards?

There is not only a lack of progress at EC level, there are also many problems with the transposition of the accounting directives into national law. On many points there are doubts whether the directives have been correctly implemented. Some of the problems have been settled informally. Others remain.

Some examples: the non-transposition of the true and fair view override, the possibility of revaluing intangible assets (such as brands), the non-depreciation of certain fixed assets, the deduction of goodwill from reserves in the annual accounts, the amortization of goodwill through reserves in the consolidated accounts, the deduction of acquired own shares from reserves, the treatment of prior year adjustments and changes in accounting policies (transit through reserves instead of through the profit and loss account), the non-respect of the group definition in the Seventh Directive, the incorrect exclusion of certain subsidiaries from full consolidation, etc. This is only a short list of some important infringements. The list is however much longer, unfortunately. As the internal market project is almost finished now, there is more time to examine the implementing legislation more closely. A systematic analysis of national legislation should help us to obtain a clearer picture on the problem areas. This is of course a delicate matter. Not everybody will be prepared to help the Commission carrying out this task, as this examination will inevitably force the experts to put their finger on the sore points of their national accounting legislation.

However, we cannot escape this responsibility. It is a question of credibility and of fairness towards other Member States. We cannot exclude the possibility that the European Court of Justice will have to deal with some of these infringements on the occasion of a preliminary ruling on a question put to the Court by a national court.

In this respect, I can only regret that the practice which existed before, whereby national officials who are responsible for the drafting of the implementing legislation would contact their colleagues in the Commission in order to discuss the draft prior to the adoption of the legislation, no longer exists as systematically as it used to. We therefore welcome wholeheartedly the initiative by many of the new applicant Member States to discuss their draft legislation with us. This is even more important for them because they have not been involved in the negotiation of the directives.

Lack of dynamism at EC level, problems of incorrect implementation, the bleak picture is not yet complete. More and more people complain about the deterioration of the quality of financial information in Europe. The most incredible things happen. I will give the example of the true and fair view override. Some companies in the UK interpret this override in a rather personal manner. I quote from the accounting policies in the annual report 1992 of George Wimpey (construction company):

> Investments held as current assets are stated at market value at the balance sheet date and the difference between cost and market value is taken to the profit and loss account.

This treatment is a departure from UK accounting rules which stipulate that unrealized profits be credited to a revaluation reserve. In the opinion of the directors, the treatment adopted is necessary to present a 'true and fair view'.

Or let us take an example from France. I quote from the notes to the 1991 consolidated financial statements in the annual report of Cap Gemini Sogeti:

> When the acquisition of companies allows the group to obtain significant positions in specific markets, the excess of purchase cost over the fair value of assets acquired is allocated to the market share acquired. Such market share is valued at the date of acquisition in relation to objective economic data with reference to activity and profitability indicators.

This solves the problem of goodwill, doesn't it? And valuation at market value solves the problem of depreciation.

Let there be no misunderstanding. Although my examples come from the UK and from France, I could certainly give you other examples from other Member States. The common thrust of these examples is that companies no longer stick to the accounting conventions and that, apparently, nobody calls them to order. This is not likely to increase confidence in investors.

EC companies which are listed in New York sometimes also refuse to give in Europe the information which they disclose in the US. This is certainly not acceptable. We have dealt with this problem in the EC context where all shareholders must be treated equally, but we do not yet have a similar requirement for companies which are listed outside the EC.

PERSPECTIVES

What are we going to do about this? What are our options?

a) *We could stop all further harmonization efforts in the EC.* We have now achieved a certain level of harmonization. We can leave further developments in the hands of Member States or others.

   I think that this would be unfortunate. We would quickly lose the harmony which came out of the accounting directives. And let us not forget, unless the directives are amended, Member States and national standard-setting bodies will still have to comply with them.

b) *We could leave everything to IASC.* After all, they have the experts. Unfortunately, things are not that easy. We have already experienced in the EC that IAS are not directly transposable in most of our Member States, because of the linkage between accounting and taxation which is totally overlooked by IASC. In addition, some Member States would argue that IASC does not sufficiently respect the prudence principle. Although the Commission is only an observer on the Board of IASC, we already face criticism from certain Member States because 'we act without a mandate'. It is true that the positions which are taken by representatives of the accounting profession of the EC Member States which are members of the Board of IASC are not the same as the official positions taken by the government representatives of these Member States around the Brussels negotiation table. This is unfortunate, but it is due to the fact that the accounting profession does not officially represent the Member States concerned.

c) *We could also leave the work to the Americans.* So many companies in the EC are attracted by US GAAP. Why make their lives difficult? Give them what they want. Well, there may be some disagreement about this. Some of our Member States would certainly argue that they could do a better job than the Americans. But, after all, Europe cannot always leave the initiative to the Americans. From an accounting point of view, it is, however, interesting to see that German accounting practice is closer to US GAAP than to UK GAAP. And there is mutual recognition of accounts between the UK and Germany and not between the US and Germany.

d) *We could also become a more active player in the harmonization debate.* This was the view of Member States, national accounting standard-setting bodies and users and preparers at the Commission's 1990 conference on the future of accounting harmonization in the EC. Most people present at that conference were of the view that EC harmonization should continue, although not necessarily with new directives. As a result of this conference, the Commission has set up the Accounting Advisory Forum which should advise the Commission on further steps to be taken in order to improve the existing level of harmonization. Members of the Forum are the national accounting standard-setting bodies, the European organizations representing the main users and preparers (including the accounting profession) and last but not least the EAA. One of the problems with the Forum is that so many organizations want to participate that we have already reached the number of about sixty people who attend the meetings. This makes a real debate difficult. Some interesting things have come out of the work of the Forum:

- there is large preference for a *pragmatic approach* rather than an approach based upon a conceptual framework (although some members of the Forum would love to discuss the fundamentals of accounting);
- there *does not* seem to be a majority in favour of a *distinction* between *annual and consolidated accounts*;
- there is great *reluctance* to embark upon the road towards *reconciliation*: limited comparability is preferred over absolute comparability.

The Forum is still young. There are problems. The Commission will have to show that the efforts of the Forum are not bound to disappear into the drawers of professional harmonizers.

It is in this context that academics can help. Although there has already been a lot of research on harmonization in the EC, many questions still remain unanswered:

- Is harmonization of accounting standards in the EC really necessary or is it a mere luxury or pastime for government and other experts?
- What are the benefits of harmonization? Are the accounts published in other Member States consulted on a regular basis? Are they comparable?
- To what extent is harmonization necessary? For all companies? For large companies? For listed companies?
- What does comparability mean? Is absolute comparability possible or desirable?
- Does reconciliation make sense?
- On a broader international level: is it true that capital markets need harmonization of accounting standards?
- Are options so bad? Is it necessary to rule out accounting methods just for the sake of uniformity?
- Is it logical to stigmatize an accounting method as 'not the preferred one' but still to allow the method?
- What are the common features of European accounting? So far, there still is no book on European accounting. Most research concentrates on the differences.
- Can there be progress in harmonization by distinguishing between individual accounts and consolidated accounts? How far can such a distinction sensibly go?
- Are multinational companies prepared to reconcile with IAS and to accept the IASC as the standard setter of the world?
- Is it at all possible to make progress in the EC without a European

accounting standards-setting body or a European watchdog for the financial markets such as the SEC?
What are the prerequisites (objective and not political) for a mutual recognition of accounts between the EC and the US or between the EC and Japan?

These are a few suggestions for further research on harmonization. When I have all the answers to these questions, I will be better equipped to advise on whether harmonization in the EC is finished or should continue. Meanwhile, I would suggest that we adopt a pragmatic approach. Unless the EC invests more time and effort in the harmonization of accounting standards, Europe will continue to be absent from the international accounting debate. As long as some Member States continue to quarrel about whether the harmonization is completed or whether the EC has any role to play in this debate, the initiative will come from outside and, rather than contribute in shaping the rules, our role will be limited to reacting to things which have already been decided. It is unfortunate that we spend so much effort and money in defending our national achievements and developing standards by ourselves rather than sitting together and combining our efforts.

For the moment, there is no alternative to the Accounting Advisory Forum. Its functioning can be improved. A more active participation from national accounting standards-setting bodies would be desirable. The Commission is not equipped nor does it have the ambition to take over the role of an active standard setter in the accounting field.

The objective is not to develop European standards for the sake of doing so. But, if we believe that we have a role to play, we must combine our scarce resources so as to be able to influence the international debate. Harmonization is so difficult because it requires modesty and respect for the achievements of the others. We are fortunate in Europe to be as different as we are. This is our common heritage. Why don't we use it?

NOTE

This is a slightly amended version of the paper presented at the 16th Annual Conference of the European Accounting Association in Turku (29 April 1993).

The author is Principal Administrator and Head of Accounting at the EC Commission (Directorate-General XV 'Financial Institutions and Company Law') and also Professor of Accounting Law at the KU Leuven.

The views expressed in this article are attributable only to the author.

[22]

Accounting and Business Research, Vol. 24, No. 93, pp. 35–48, 1993

The True and Fair View Requirement: Impact on and of the Fourth Directive

Christopher Nobes*

Abstract—The overriding British legal requirement for financial reporting of giving 'a true and fair view' (TFV) has been exported to continental Europe via the European Community's (EC) Fourth Directive on Company Law. This paper considers accounting rules in continental Europe before this process, and traces the gradual acceptance of the predominance of TFV in the drafting of the Directive after UK accession to the EC. The signifiers used in different European languages in the various drafts of the Directive are examined. It is noted that all (eight) other versions contain only one adjective (generally equivalent to 'faithful') rather than true *and* fair. The origins of the Dutch *getrouw*, the French *fidèle*, etc. are looked into. As the Directive evolved, and particularly as it was implemented in the twelve EC states, greater linguistic variety emerged, such that five countries changed the wording from the original Directive and two others qualified the wording. Whether this affects what TFV signifies is investigated. Countries can also be divided into several groups with respect to the effects of having the TFV in law. The extremes appear to be the UK and Germany.

This paper traces the development of the true and fair view (TFV) requirement in the Fourth Directive, and then the relevant effects of this element of the Directive on the laws and practices in EC member states.

In the context of the UK, Walton (1991) suggests that we should follow Saussure (1919) and distinguish between the signifier and the signified when examining the TFV. The signifiers are the words 'give a true and fair view', whereas the signified is the underlying idea. What is signified by a particular signifier can change. For example, in order to give a TFV it might, over time, become necessary (i) to disclose transfers from reserves, or (ii) to present consolidated accounts of a holding company, or (iii) to capitalise certain leases, or (iv) to include current value information.

*The author is Coopers & Lybrand Professor of Accounting, University of Reading. He is grateful for advice on earlier drafts from David Alexander (University of Hull), John Bowen-Walsh (Institute of Chartered Accountants in Ireland), Walther Busse von Colbe (Ruhr Universität-Bochum), Octavio Gastambide Fernandes (Câmara dos Revisores Oficias de Contas, Lisbon), Maria Leonor Fernandes Ferreira (Technical University of Lisbon), Steve Goldberg (Purdue University), John Hegarty and Saskia Slomp (FEE, Brussels), Karel Van Hulle (EC Commission), Horst Kaminski (Institut der Wirtschaftsprüfer, Düsseldorf), P. Lepidas (SOL, Athens), Dieter Ordelheide (Goethe Universität, Frankfurt), Bob Parker (University of Exeter), Alan Roberts (University of Reading), Fulvia Rocchi (Università degli Studi di Venezia), Brian Rutherford (University of Kent), Jean-Claude Scheid (INTEC, Paris), Antonio Socías Salvá (Universitat de les Illes Balears), George Tridimas (University of Reading), Peter van der Zanden (Ernst & Young, Eindhoven), Peter Walton (LSE), Geoff Whittington (University of Cambridge), Stefano Zambon (Università degli Studi di Padova), Steve Zeff (Rice University), and two anonymous referees.

It is suggested here that, when studying the TFV, a third dimension is necessary: the effects. There are particularly two types of effect: (i) any adjustments (designed to promote a TFV) to detailed accounting rules at the stage of national implementation of the EC Directives (called here 'direct effects'), and (ii) any continuing effects of the existence of the legal requirement for TFV on directors, auditors and rule-makers (called here 'indirect effects').

This paper examines the signifier in English; in all the other language versions of the EC Fourth Directive; and in the legal implementations in the twelve EC member states. Then there are preliminary observations concerning the signified and the effects throughout the EC.

Source of True and Fair

It will be suggested below that the origins of the concept of the predominance of the 'true and fair view' (TFV) are British, although the signifiers used in other European languages are, in general, not literal translations of this. The TFV wording (see Table 1) appeared first in British law in the Companies Act 1947 and was then consolidated into the 1948 Act (Parker, 1989, pp. 20–1). The previous British legal requirement (e.g. Companies Act 1900, S. 23) was that 'a true and correct view' should be given but this was changed after advice from the accountancy profession that 'correct' was too precise a word to reflect the practice of accounting and auditing (Walker, 1984; Rutherford, 1985). Other combinations of 'full', 'fair', 'true' and 'correct' had been used in nineteenth century laws. The change of signifier in 1947 may have had no effect on what was signified.

Table 1
General Purpose Requirements in UK law, German law and the Fourth Directive

1948 Companies Act (S. 149)	1. Every balance sheet of a company shall give a true and fair view of the state of affairs of the company . . . and every profit and loss account [etc.]. 3. . . . the [detailed] requirements of [the 8th Schedule] shall be without prejudice. . . . to the general requirements of subsection (1) . . .
1965 *Aktiengesetz* (§ 149)	1. The annual financial statements shall conform to proper bookkeeping principles. They shall be clear and well set out and give the surest possible insight of the company's financial position and its operating results pursuant to the valuation provisions.
1971 Draft (Art. 2)	1. The annual accounts shall comprise the balance sheet, the profit and loss account and the notes on the accounts. These documents shall constitute a composite whole. 2. The annual accounts shall conform to the principles of regular and proper accounting. 3. They shall be drawn up clearly and, in the context of the provisions regarding the valuation of assets and liabilities and the lay-out of accounts, shall reflect as accurately as possible the company's assets, liabilities, financial position and results.
1974 Draft (Art. 2)	1. (as 1971 Draft) 2. The annual accounts shall give a true and fair view of the company's assets, liabilities, financial position and results. 3. They shall be drawn up clearly and in conformity with the provisions of this Directive.
1978 Final (Art. 2)	1. (as 1971 Draft) 2. They shall be drawn up clearly and in conformity with the provisions of this Directive. 3. The annual accounts shall give a true and fair view of the company' assets, liabilities, financial position and profit or loss. 4. Where the application of the provisions of this Directive would not be sufficient to give a true and fair view within the meaning of paragraph 3, additional information must be given. 5. Where in exceptional cases the application of a provision of this Directive is incompatible with the obligation laid down in paragraph 3, that provision must be departed from in order to give a true and fair view within the meaning of paragraph 3. Any such departure must be disclosed in the notes on the accounts together with an explanation of the reasons for it and a statement of its effect on the assets, liabilities, financial position and profit or loss. The Member States may define the exceptional cases in question and lay down the relevant special rules.

The meaning of TFV (what is signified by it) has been discussed elsewhere from several points of view (e.g. Chastney, 1975; Flint, 1982; Rutherford, 1985; Harris, 1987; Lyas, 1992). What is signified by TFV has been acknowledged by lawyers in the UK as changeable because it is related to prevailing accepted accounting practices (Hoffman and Arden, 1983; Arden, 1993). As for effects, it was the absence of rules rather than the presence of the TFV that was traditionally important in the UK. Hopwood (1990) suggests that the TFV became particularly important to Britain only when seen as a means of countering legalism in the 1971 draft of the Fourth Directive. Parker and Nobes (1991) make the related point that the TFV seems to have been increasingly useful to the British profession as accounting rules became more codified in standards (from 1970) and in law (from 1981). The signified and the effects of TFV for British directors and auditors are noted later.

Incidentally, that the same signifier (and similar signifieds) can have different indirect effects (i.e. those not written into the detail of the law) may be illustrated by comparing the UK and Australia. What is signified by TFV in the UK and Australia is probably very similar in terms of how things should be valued and measured and what things should be disclosed (e.g. Parker, 1991a). However, the legal imposition of TFV in Britain is an overriding one (see Table 1), but in Australia TFV overrides neither law nor standards. The Australian Corporations Act 1989 (amended 1991) provides only that the directors shall 'add such information and explanation as will give a true and fair view' (S. 299 (1))

(Miller, 1993; Parker, 1994). In the US, a different signifier is used, but here the indirect effect is also clearly different from that in the UK: US financial statements are required to 'present fairly *in conformity with* generally accepted accounting principles'.[1]

In summary, in terms of indirect effects, the TFV may be used by standard setters, directors or auditors in the UK, Australia and the US. However, only in the UK can it also be used to override the law or standards.

For the present purpose, the distinguishing features of TFV in EC Directives are taken as being (i) the implication of an underlying reality, the portrayal of which is more important than any particular rules of practice, and, therefore, (ii) the requirement for the rules to be broken if this is necessary in order to portray the reality.

Impact on the Directive

The work on the *avant projet* for the Fourth Directive began in 1965 under the chairmanship of Dr. Elmendorff.[2] Elmendorff's committee, which first met in 1966, comprised professional accounting experts from the six countries that were then members of the EC. It was to be expected that a German would chair such a project, because the Germans had the most developed company law on accounting in the EC, in particular their public companies Act, the *Aktiengesetz* (AktG) of 1965.

German law, in common with the rules of most continental countries had no explicit or implicit requirement for TFV. The relevant section of the AktG (§ 149) is reprinted in Table 1. It requires that the surest possible insight (*einen möglichst sicheren Einblick*) is to be achieved but only as far as is possible in accordance with the valuation provisions of the Act. This implies that overvaluation is not acceptable but that undervaluation is.[3] Clarity is also mentioned but truth and fairness are not. In France, the requirement was *regularité et sincerité*;[4] in Italy, *chiarezza e precisione* and *evidenza e verità*[5] (see Ferrero, 1991 for more details). The main purpose[6] of these words seems not to signify 'fair' in its sense of 'not misleading', and the rules certainly did not require departures from the detail of the regulations on this basis.

The Elmendorff Committee delivered a draft of the Fourth Directive to the EC Commission in 1968 (and a draft of the Seventh in 1969). The Committee last met in 1970. The first draft of the Fourth Directive was published by the Commission in 1971. The general purpose clause (Article 2, paragraphs 2 and 3) bore a strong resemblance to that in the AktG, as Table 1 shows. Here, again, fairness did not feature, and 'accuracy' was to be subject to the provisions of the Directive. The requirement to use 'principles of regular and proper accounting' would have been familiar to German lawyers or auditors but not to those of all other EC countries.

January 1973 saw the arrival of the UK, Ireland and Denmark in the Community. Denmark had little accounting law; it had accepted Anglo-American influences since World War II but had no TFV or similar requirement (Christiansen, 1992, p. 104). The UK and Ireland also had little law on how to do accounting, but they did have the legal predominance of 'true and fair'. Negotiation led to many changes in the Directive, some of which are discussed by Nobes (1983). In particular, as Table 1 shows, the TFV requirement was to be found in the second published draft (1974) of the Directive. It has been confirmed[7] by the secretary to the Elmendorff Committee and by the EC Commission that it was the UK's accession to the EC that began this process. The requirement to use principles of regular and proper accounting was changed to a requirement to conform to the provisions of the Directive.

The only continental EC country which was an exception to the lack of TFV was the Netherlands, where the Annual Accounts of Enterprises Act 1970 contained the overriding requirement that accounts should enable a sound insight and should be shown faithfully and systematically (see Table 2 and Appendix 1). It has been suggested elsewhere that Dutch accounting should be seen as having more in common with Anglo-Saxon than with continental accounting (e.g. Parker, 1991b). The word for 'faithful' (*getrouw*) may also mean fair, as discussed below. It seems that the prior lack of such a provision in Dutch accounting law was due more to the sparseness of law than to any point of

[1]Emphasis added. See Zeff (1992) for an analysis of this case. David Alexander has pointed out that perhaps unpromulgated GAAP could override promulgated GAAP, but it seems unlikely that the SEC would accept this since the SEC gives 'substantial authoritative support' to the FASB in Accounting Series Release 150 of 1973. Also Statement on Auditing Standards 69 puts fairness into the framework of GAAP. This is despite the AICPA Code of Professional Conduct (Rule 203, Interpretation 203-1) which warns against allowing a literal interpretation of a rule to result in misleading financial statements.

[2]Dr. Elmendorff was trained as a business economist and then a Wirtschaftsprüfer. He was founder of one of the larger German accountancy firms, now Wollert-Elmendorff Deutsche Industrietreuhand GmbH.

[3]That is, in addition to the general international requirement for prudence and the unusually strong German version of this (e.g. Gray, 1980), the AktG requires not the most accurate or the most fair but the most sure/safe insight.

[4]In accordance with the rules and in good faith.

[5]Clarity and preciseness; obviousness and truth (Civil Code, Arts. 2423 and 2217).

[6]The Tribunale di Milano (23.12.1968) held that it meant mainly giving information to all interested parties.

[7]Conversation with Horst Kaminski (1.3.1993), and letter from Karel Van Hulle, Head of Company Law Section of the EC Commission (11.1.1993).

Table 2
The Origins and Spread of True and Fair (for translations see Appendix I)

1	2	3	4	5
Country	*Words in Law before Directive (first appearance)*	*Words in Directive*	*Implementation of Directive*	*Words in Law if Different from Directive*
UK	a true and fair view (1947)	a true and fair view	1981	—
Ireland	a true and fair view (1963)		1986	—
Netherlands	1. geeft een zodanig inzicht dat een verantwoord oordeel kan worden gevormd ... 2. geeft getrouw en stelselmatig (1970)	een getrouw beeld	1983	1. (as in 1970) 2. geeft getrouw, duidelijk en stelselmatig
Denmark	—	et pålideligt billede	1981	et retvisende billede
France	—	une image fidèle (een getrouw beeld in Flemish)	1983	—
Luxembourg			1984	—
Belgium			1985	—
Germany	—	ein den tatsächlichen Verhältnissen entsprechendes Bild	1985	Unter Beachtung der Grundsätze ordnungsmässiger Buchführung (then, as Directive)
Greece	—	ten pragmatiki ikona	1986	—
Spain	—	una imagen fiel	1989	la imagen fiel ... de conformidad con las disposiciones legales
Portugal	—	uma imagem fiel	1989	uma imagem verdadeira e apropriada (1989 plan)
Italy	—	un quadro fedele	1991	rappresentare in modo veritiero e corretto

philosophy or practice. Although Dutch *accounting* law had no TFV requirement before 1970, the Registeraccountants Act (Auditing Law) of 1962 required the auditor to testify to faithfulness (*getrouwheid*). In accounting and auditing practice, '*getrouw*' also has a long history, as explained in the following section.

The influence of the *Groupe d'Etudes* should be mentioned here. This committee of EC accountancy bodies had been formed at the request of the EC Commission in order to advise on matters such as Directives.[8] The Elmendorff Committee was a predecessor. Representatives from the UK, Ireland and Denmark joined fully when their countries acceded to the EC in 1973. However, before this, the *Groupe d'Etudes* had already come to the view[9] that the TFV was the right accounting philosophy. This may seem curious, but the UK already had observer status at the *Groupe d'Etudes*. Also, although it has been sometimes impossible to persuade, for example, the German government to agree with certain Anglo-Saxon accounting ideas, it has been easier to achieve consensus with the German accountancy profession, often represented by partners from German offices of multinational accounting firms.[10] The Economic and Social

[8]At the beginning of 1987, a new body, the *Fédération des Experts Comptables Européens* (FEE), took over this role and that of the *Union Européenne des Experts Comptables, Economiques et Financiers* (UEC).

[9]Published opinion in June 1972.

[10]The author uses first hand accounts or personal experience of over a decade's membership of *Groupe* and *FEE* committees. His memory is confirmed by the *FEE* Secretary General (letter from John Hegarty, 19.11.1992), and by Karel Van Hulle of the EC Commission (letter of 11.1.1993).

Committee (ECOSOC) of the EC is required to give opinions on draft Directives. In February 1973, it suggested that 'faithful picture' should replace 'accuracy' in Article 2.3 of the 1970 draft. However, the *Groupe d'Etudes* and the ECOSOC did not propose the predominance of TFV over rules.

The 1974 draft of the Directive contained requirements both to give a TFV and to comply with the provisions of the Directive. However, the draft did not deal with cases where the two requirements might conflict. One interpretation of this is that use of the provisions would automatically lead to a TFV, so that the specific TFV requirement related to matters on which there were no provisions or to cases where there was a need to give extra information. As will be explained, this is the German view, and by implication, it is also now the view in the US and Australia, as already noted. This interpretation was not acceptable to the profession in countries like the UK, where it is argued that the TFV is the ultimate objective, which implies the need in certain circumstances to override other legal provisions (e.g. Tweedie, 1983). For example, from this standpoint, the practice in some continental countries of writing off assets for accounting purposes in order to take advantage of generous tax depreciation might be legally sanctioned but should not be permitted in accounts because it would not give a true and fair view.

This full-blooded version of the significance of TFV (discussed further later) triumphed in the 1978 adopted version of the Directive, as shown in Table 1. At the formal level, this could be seen as a victory for Anglo-Saxon accounting philosophy. Its effects on practice are more complex, as will be seen later.

Language in the Directive

Rutherford (1983) sets out the signifiers analogous to TFV in the versions of the Directive in six languages. Table 2 (column 3) in this paper shows the signifiers in all the languages as prepared by the EC Commission in the 1978 adopted Directive (and subsequently for Greece, Spain and Portugal). It seems possible to classify these as in Figure 1, using literal translations of the adjectives involved. On this basis, eight[11] languages have a unitary wording and only English has a dual wording (i.e. true *and* fair).

Whether the English 'true and fair' signifies a dual concept or a portmanteau is investigated elsewhere by Walker (1984), Nobes and Parker (1991a) and Parker and Nobes (1991). These last two papers conclude that UK financial directors of large companies see TFV as unitary. However,

Figure 1
'True and Fair' Signifiers in the Directive

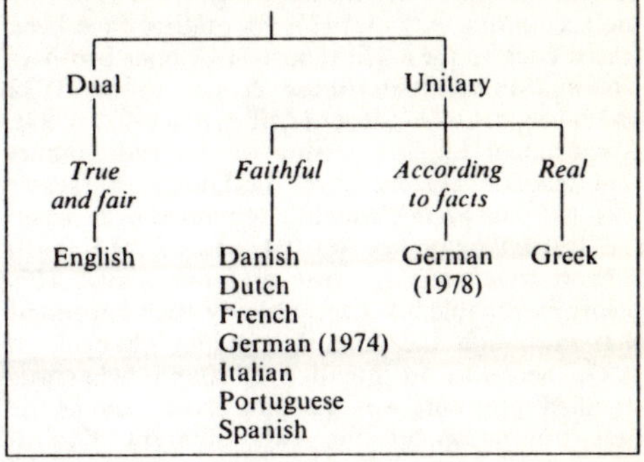

their auditors see it as dual: approximately, 'truth' is taken to mean that the accounts are in accordance with facts, and 'fairness' that they are not misleading.

What is the origin of the unitary signifier? Column 2 of Table 2 shows any analogous wording in laws before the Fourth Directive. It has been suggested above that only the UK, Ireland and the Netherlands had 'true and fair' or its analogue. Given that all the other versions use a unitary signifier, can it be maintained that English is the source? As shown in the next paragraph, it seems that Britain is the main source of the idea that there is an underlying TFV, the presentation of which should override rules. However, we need to look elsewhere for the source of the predominant type of signifier.

Given (i) that, even in the Netherlands, earlier law did not actually refer to the '*getrouw beeld*' of the Directive, (ii) that the draft Fourth Directive had no TFV requirement until *after* the UK and Ireland had joined the EC, and (iii) the confirmation from the Elmendorff Committee, the case for British origins seems certain. Parker (1989) certainly regards the TFV as a British export to the Commonwealth and then the EC. The Spanish also acknowledge a British origin (Socías, 1991, p. 38), as do the Germans (Busse von Colbe, 1984, p. 121) and the French (CNCC, 1984). Further, as will be noted later, the Italian Ministerial Commentary on their 1991 law specifically refers to the British version as the original. Nevertheless, Ordelheide (1993) points out that the exact formulation of the Fourth Directive was an EC matter, and that the resulting TFV sections in all EC laws sweep away previous provisions, including the British. In particular, all official language versions are formally equal, and none is to be seen as the original.

Given the clear British origins of the overriding nature of the TFV, the source of the majority

[11]Van Hulle (1993, p. 100) is wrong to state that Portuguese has a dual signifier in the Directive. This is so for the Portuguese law but not for the Portuguese versions of the Directives.

unitary signifier needs to be investigated in more detail. The Dutch word '*getrouw*' had been evident outside the law before the auditing Act of 1962 and the accounting Act of 1970. Its origins have been traced back to the audit report of Cooper Brothers Co. and Price, Waterhouse & Co. in the 1932 annual report of Unilever (Zeff *et al.*, 1992, p. 99). The original English version of the audit report said 'true and correct view'; the Dutch translation was '*getrouw beeld*', which it remained even when the British Companies Act 1947 caused the English version to change to 'true and fair view'. This seems reasonable, as it has already been suggested that, although the English signifier changed in 1947, there was no intention to change what was signified. Not only was '*getrouw beeld*' seen as the best translation of the two different English phrases, but also of the American 'present fairly' (Zeff *et al.*, 1992, p. 101). However, as noted earlier, the US 'present fairly' has a noticeably different significance from the British 'give a true and fair view', and Zeff (1990) argues elsewhere that the best English signifier for the Dutch '*getrouw beeld*' is given by the British phrase not the American.

The French signifier '*image fidèle*', which has a clear echo in the later Italian '*quadro fedele*' or Spanish '*imagen fiel*', can be traced back in the accounting literature to 1920 (Chaveneau, 1920). It seems that a draft French law of 1921 would have required balance sheets to give '*une image aussi fidèle que possible*' (Pasqualini, 1992, p. 37). The word '*fidèle*' in this context can be traced back further to a law in Berne of 1860 and the Swiss Commercial Code of 1863 (Pasqualini, 1992, p. 37).[12] It seems that this French expression was 'the leading one' in the commission.[13] The unitary wording '*fidèle*', like any other adjective, has layers of meaning. At one level, it could imply 'faithful' as in 'faithful representation' (e.g. IASC's Conceptual Framework, para. 33). At another level, it could signify preparation of the accounts 'in good faith'. However, the French governmental body in charge of the *plan comptable* suggested that '*image fidèle*' was a bad translation of TFV, without offering an alternative (CNCC, 1984).

The German signifier in the 1974 draft of the Directive fitted neatly with all these continental equivalents (i.e. *einen getreuen Einblick*). '*Einblick*' had been the word in the 1965 AktG. However, the final version of the Directive moves away from both adjective and noun to '*ein den tatsächlichen Verhadeltnissen entsprechendes Bild*' (see Appendix 1 for translation). Incidentally, in all other languages the Directive's signifiers for TFV in 1978 are the same as those in 1974.

It is clear that the use of a unitary signifier tells us little about what is signified. This will be examined further in the later section on language in the EC laws.

A Note on Language in the Seventh Directive

The Seventh Directive concerns consolidated accounts. As noted above, an early draft was prepared by the Elmendorff Committee in 1969, but a draft was not published by the Commission until 1976 nor adopted by the Council until 1983. The Seventh Directive applies many of the provisions of the Fourth to group accounts and specifically demands that:

> Consolidated accounts shall give a true and fair view of the assets, liabilities, financial position and profit or loss of the undertakings included therein taken as a whole. (Article 16(3))

The rest of Article 16 contains the overriding TFV provisions as in Article 2 of the Fourth Directive (see Table 1).

The Seventh Directive uses the same signifiers in all languages for TFV as the Fourth Directive had done. For example, despite the fact that Denmark had before 1983 already implemented signifiers different from the Danish version of the Fourth Directive (see next section, and Table 2), the Danish version of the Seventh Directive uses the same signifiers as the Fourth. One interesting point is that the 1976 German draft of the Seventh Directive used the '*einen getreuen Einblick*' wording (as in the 1974 draft of the Fourth Directive), whereas the 1978 draft and the 1983 final versions used the longer wording of the 1978 final version of the Fourth Directive (see Table 2).

Impact of the Directive

The Fourth Directive took many years to implement, as Table 2 (column 4) shows. Some countries anticipated the content and then made subsequent legal adjustments (such as Belgium); others were quick off the mark (such as the relative newcomers, Denmark and the UK); some were slow (such as founder EC member, Italy) or had joined the EC after the adoption of the Directive (Greece, Spain and Portugal). The laws come into force on dates after those shown in Table 2. In the case of the last country, Italy, this means usually implementation for 31.12.1993 year ends. The more general effects of the Fourth Directive are examined elsewhere (e.g. Gray and Coenenberg, 1984). This section examines the TFV specifically.

The implementation of the TFV requirement shows the ability of countries to impose their own culture on what, to some of them, was an alien

[12]I am particularly grateful to Alan Roberts for the historical references in this paragraph.

[13]Letter from K. Van Hulle of 11.1.1993, and conversation with H. Kaminski of 1.3.1993.

concept. This expresses itself in the signifiers, the signified and the effects.

Signifiers and the Signified

When it comes to implementations of the laws in the member states, several further linguistic complications are added to those of the previous section, as column 5 of Table 2 shows. In seven cases (for the five exceptions, see below), the national laws implementing the Directive follow the words in the Directive as prepared in Brussels. The Belgian law implements both the French and the Dutch signifiers from the Directive. The Luxembourg law implements the French. The lengthy wording in the German law follows from the Directive as adopted in Brussels rather than being a subsequent invention of the German parliament. However, as discussed later, even in the German case (and the Spanish) important words were *added*.

The five departures from the Directive's signifiers will now be examined. The Dutch revised earlier legal wordings rather than exactly following the Directive. The 1970 Law was amended by adding the word '*duidelijk*' (clearly) from Art. 2.2 of the Directive. Other national implementations also contain the clarity requirement. The Dutch also retained the fundamental requirement of giving a sound insight, and it is this requirement which is the overriding one. The Danes substituted '*retvisende*' for the Directive's '*pålideligt*', moving from 'faithful' towards 'right-looking' or 'not misleading', which seems close to 'fair'.

In the case of Italian, the Directive used the word '*fedele*' (consistent with the Dutch/French), but this was rejected by the drafters of the Italian law. The train of linguistic events is somewhat complex. The 1942 Civil Code allows departure from the legal valuation rules for *speciali ragioni* (special reasons).[14] This ambiguous provision did not lead in practice to major departures, even for inflation accounting in the 1970s. However, in the revaluation law of 1983 (so-called Visentini-bis; 72/1983, Art. 9), *speciali ragioni* were defined as those where departure from legal rules was necessary in order to give *un quadro fedele*. As mentioned earlier, these Italian words had first appeared in published form in Article 2 of the draft EC Directive in 1974.

When it came to the drafting of the Italian law to implement the Fourth Directive (Decreto Legislativo n. 127/1991), the words '*quadro fedele*' were deliberately not used, perhaps because they already had the above particular usage in Italian law. In the *Relazione Ministeriale* (Ministerial Commentary) to the new law, it was stated that '*rappresentare in modo veritiero e corretto*' had been adopted because '*sembra costituire la più esatta traduzione dell'espressione* true and fair view *dalla quale trae origine la norma della Direttiva*'.[15]

Despite this attempt to match the English, '*veritiero e corretto*' seems nearer to the abandoned British phrase 'true and correct' (although it has already been noted that the Dutch translation of 'true and fair' was the same as that for 'true and correct'). The word '*corretto*', in a law in a Roman law country, appears to mean[16] 'in accordance with legal rules'. The Ministerial Commentary states that '*veritiero*' requires that the preparers of the accounts '*operino correttamente le stime*' (make correct valuation estimates); so '*veritiero*' rests partially on '*corretto*'. In combination, '*veritiero e corretto*' does not seem intended to signify what is understood in the UK by 'true and fair'.

The Spanish moved from 'a faithful picture' to 'the faithful picture' as discussed below. The *Plan General de Contabilidad*[17] notes that *la imagen fiel* deals with the double concept of lack of bias and objectivity, and there is also a reference to truth.[18] The Portuguese have the Directive's '*imagem fiel*' in the Commercial Code but departed from this in the *Plano Oficial de Contabilidade* in an attempt to translate the English original. The resulting '*verdadeira e apropriada*' seems the most literal of all the versions.

In terms of a classification of the signifiers in laws, four out of twelve countries have a dual expression, as shown in Figure 2. However, this superficial classification disguises the fact that:

(i) a dual signifier can have a more unitary meaning (e.g. in Italy, '*veritiero*' is defined partly in terms of '*correttamente*'), and by contrast

(ii) a single adjective (e.g. *fidèle* or *fiel*) can have layers of meaning.

There is a further linguistic point. In most translations, the indefinite article is used, leading to the conclusion (e.g. Flint, 1982; *Mémento Pratique Lefebvre*, 1992, 355, 3, 3) that a number of different financial statements could give *a* true and fair view of any particular state of affairs or profit or loss.

[14] '*Se speciali ragioni richiedono una deroga alle norme di questo articolo, gli ammistratori e il collegio sindacale devono indicare e giustificare le singole deroghe nelle loro relazioni all'assemblea*' (Art. 2425).

[15] 'It seems to represent the most exact translation of the phrase *true and fair view* from which the original rule in the Directive derives'.

[16] I am grateful to several Italian colleagues for help in this area. For an earlier reference confirming this, see Colombo (1977) who says that the correct valuation will follow only if and when there is conformity with the rules of the law (p. 19).

[17] General accounting plan of 1990, parts 1, 4 and 5 of which are obligatory for Spanish companies. *La imagen fiel* is dealt with in part 1.

[18] '*la doble noción de imparcialidad y objetividad*' and '*un tercero podría formarse sobre "la verdadera"*' (para. 10).

Figure 2
'True and Fair' Signifiers in National Rules

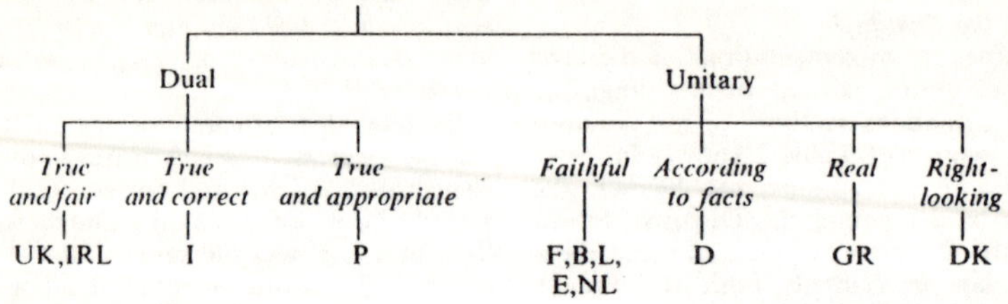

The exceptions are:

(i) *Italian Law*. Although the Italian Directive had '*un quadro fedele*', the law rephrases the requirement in such a way that no article is used.

(ii) *Spanish Law*. Although the Spanish Directive had '*una imagen fiel*', the Spanish Law substitutes '*la imagen fiel*', which is also followed in audit reports.[19] It has been suggested that this is an attempt to imply precision in the law.[20]

(iii) *Dutch Law*. As Table 2 shows, the law departs from the Directive in a way that avoids using an article.

(iv) *Greek Directive and Law*. In Greek, *the* real picture is to be presented. This may have appeared to the Greek draftsmen to make linguistic sense because, although there could be several reasonable/faithful pictures, it might have been thought that there can only be one *real* picture (however philosophically unsound that might be).

Conclusion on What is Signified

The section immediately above has to some extent considered what is signified by TFV. It seems clear that, although changes in rules and practice effect TFV, it must be intended to have an existence independent of rules or general practice. Otherwise, the Fourth Directive's requirements in Article 2.4 and 2.5 for extra information or departure from rules would not make sense. A further example is Article 14 of the Seventh Directive, which requires exclusion of dissimilar subsidiaries from consolidation when inclusion would not give a TFV.

Ordelheide (1993) suggests that, in cases of conflict, the ultimate meaning of TFV in any (or all) EC jurisdictions can now only be decided by the European Court, which may construe a meaning quite different from that intended by the inventors of the source phrase. One can certainly agree with Ordelheide that the UK meaning may not be legally relevant elsewhere. However, given that what is signified by TFV is related to practice (i.e. to what the readers of accounts expect to see), and given that practice is clearly different in different EC countries, it is hard to see that a Court could arrive at the view that TFV meant the same thing in each EC country. Bird (1984) concurs that different signifieds are likely to arise, as does Van Hulle (1993). Ordelheide has suggested[21] that, in practice, the Court would set out a broad enough meaning that different countries could fit their different interpretations into it. Van Hulle (1993) also provides a gloss on this by suggesting that, even though accounts may give a TFV in their state of origin:

> in order to be true and fair for readers in another Member State, some further explanations are no doubt required. This is the reason why the Accounting Directives require in many instances further information in the notes to the Accounts.

However, it seems implausible that a Danish company could be taken to task for not making disclosures that might specifically help a Greek reader. Presumably, also, Van Hulle did not intend the apparent implication that this was the only or the main reason for further disclosures.

Effects

As noted earlier, it seems possible to distinguish between (i) any direct effects on detailed accounting rules that may have accompanied the implementation of the TFV, and (ii) the continuing indirect effects of the legal imposition of the TFV requirement. With respect to the overriding nature of the TFV, the idea that departure from a specific provision of the law should rest upon the opinion of standard setters, directors or auditors is hard

[19] E.g. the audit report of Arthur Andersen on CEPSA's 1991 accounts. Interestingly, the company's English translation of the report refers to '*a true and fair view*'.

[20] F. Grau, Company Secretary of CEPSA in Brussels on December 3, 1992.

[21] Notes from discussion with Dieter Ordelheide at EIASM Conference in Edinburgh, 18 June 1993.

to accept, even for English lawyers (Tweedie and Kellas, 1987), let alone for those in a civil law framework. The national stances towards the implementation of the Directive may be classified into three main types:

(i) Continued dominance of TFV. In the UK and Ireland, the continued primacy of the TFV has been used both by standard setters and by directors and auditors to enable commercial circumstances of various sorts to prevail over specific legal considerations (Parker and Nobes, 1991). The primacy of TFV has been used by the standard setters to override the details of the law in several cases. For example:

(a) SSAP 9 (Stocks and Work in Progress, para. 39 and Appendix 3, para. 12) suggests that LIFO should not normally be used because it will not give a true and fair view, whereas the Fourth Directive (Art. 40) and the British law specifically allow it (Companies Act 1985, Schedule 4).
(b) SSAP 19 (Investment Properties) requires investment buildings not to be depreciated whereas the Fourth Directive and, therefore, the British law require all fixed assets with limited useful lives to be depreciated (Companies Act 1985, Schedule 4).
(c) Other cases where 'true and fair' has been used may not override the detail of the law but address conflicts in it. For example, SSAP 20 (Foreign Currency Translation) requires the taking to income of gains on unsettled long-term foreign currency loans. This is not 'prudent', which is a mandatory principle in the Directive, and therefore the gains are not distributable. However, the Directive (Article 31.2) and the British law do allow departures from the basic principles for accounting. SSAP 20 claims that, in this case, the accruals convention (also a mandatory principle in the Directive) should override prudence in order to give a TFV.

The EC Contact Committee has concluded that the TFV override can only be used in cases relating to individual companies rather than to general circumstances (EC, 1990). This would be a problem for the UK at least for point (b) above.[22] However, the conclusions of the Contact Committee have no direct authority, and Alexander (1993) suggests that the Committee's conclusion is clearly invalid in terms of the Fourth Directive, given that Article 2.5 allows member states to define the exceptional circumstances and lay down the relevant special rules. This seems correct, despite Van Hulle's (1993) suggestion that Article 2.5 was designed to restrict flexibility not to increase it. To take the UK as illustration, according to the British Companies Act 1985 (as amended in 1989), the Accounting Standards Board can be interpreted as being delegated with the setting of accounting standards on behalf of the member state, so a standard could define departures (though only for exceptional cases).

A further aspect of the indirect effects of TFV concerns whether departure from legal provisions is to be seen as a last resort to be used only when even extra information is insufficient. This seems to be the view of the Contact Committee (EC, 1990). However, it is not the view of UK standard setters (e.g. Tweedie and Kellas, 1987, p. 93). The Companies Act 1989 amended the TFV section to move the law more towards the standard setters' view.[23]

Cases where UK directors have not complied with law in the name of TFV include, for example, non-consolidation of subsidiaries or departure from formats of financial statements. Cases of non-compliance with standards include the base stock method of inventory valuation and non-revaluation of investment properties (Parker and Nobes, 1991, p. 355).

In the Netherlands, the primacy of 'sound insight' and 'faithful' also continues (see Table 2). These concepts are used by the *Raad voor de Jaarverslaggeving* (RJ, Council for Annual Reporting; see Parker, 1991b or Zeff *et al.*, 1992) when producing *Richtlijnen* (Guidelines), and by directors and auditors when interpreting the law and Guidelines or in areas where there is no such guidance. However, since the Netherlands has a Civil Code system, the RJ would not feel able to set Guidelines which overrode law. Countries other than the UK and Ireland interpret the 'special circumstances' of Article 2.5 of the Directive (see Table 1) in a way that would not allow general departures to be formulated.

(ii) Enthusiastic change. In some countries, the implementation of the Fourth Directive was used as a means of changing accounting in an implicitly Anglo-Saxon direction. Governments (including stock market regulators) may have already been moving in this direction as capital markets expanded and international capital flows grew. Denmark, for example, was first to implement the Directive, included many options and seems closer in line with the UK and the Netherlands now than before the Directive. In the case of France, it has been suggested that the *image fidèle* requirement had the direct effect of undermining the strength of tax-based rules (Pham, 1984), though the relationship between tax and accounting is complex

[22] It may not be a problem for point (a) because SSAP 9 is merely narrowing down options allowed by the Directive, nor for point (c) where there is a conflict in the Directive.

[23] 'If in special circumstances [in the case of any company,] compliance with any of those provisions is inconsistent with the requirements to give a true and fair view [even if additional information were provided in accordance with sub-section (4)], the directors shall depart from that provision . . .' S. 226 of the 1985 Act as amended; bracketed parts deleted in 1989.

(Standish, 1991). The undermining is only obvious in the regulations relating to consolidated accounts (where tax is not relevant) which result from the implementation of the Seventh Directive. Moves in the direction of Anglo-Saxon accounting had already been made by many large French groups, and such a process suited the Stock Exchange regulatory body, the Commission des Opérations de Bourse. Article 29 of the Seventh Directive is relevant here. It allows that:

> . . . a member state may require or permit the use in the consolidated accounts of other methods of valuation [than the parent's] in accordance with the [Fourth Directive]. (Article 29.2).
>
> Where assets to be included in consolidated accounts have been the subject of exceptional value adjustments solely for tax purposes, they shall be incorporated in the consolidated accounts only after those adjustments have been eliminated. A member state may, however, require or permit [no] elimination, . . . provided [disclosure]. (Article 29.5).

No member states have *required* the 'other methods' of Article 29.2, but all except Portugal and Greece have allowed them. In no member state is there a requirement not to permit the eliminations of Article 29.5. The result of this combination of provisions is that companies in most member states have greater room for manoeuvre in group accounts than in individual accounts.

In the case of France, group accounts can move, and for many groups have moved, away from former tax-based rules towards several 'substance over form' and accruals accounting features, such as the capitalisation of leases, the recognition of deferred taxation, and the recognition of unsettled gains on currency amounts (Scheid and Walton, 1992).

The authoritative *Mémento Pratique Francis Lefebvre* (1992) suggests that the effects in France of the legal requirement to give *une image fidèle* should be in those areas where the rules do not exist or where they are not sufficiently detailed. A further point is that the French implementation of the Directive's Article 2.4 (see Table 1) requires the extra information to be given '*dans l'annexe*' (in the Notes), whereas the Directive and, for example, the UK law do not specify where, allowing for the financial statements themselves to contain the extra information.

To some extent, the moves away from tax-based and legal form accounting are reflected in Spain. Indeed, it has been suggested that the arrival of the TFV led to a 'thorough accounting transformation' (Casanovas, 1992). One specific example is that substance over form has been addressed in the area of leasing. The 1989 law implementing the Fourth Directive requires finance leases to be capitalised. However, because this might appear to be 'untrue' in law even if 'fair' in substance, the 1990 *Plan General de Contabilidad* requires the leases capitalised to be shown as intangible assets (i.e. the *rights* to use the assets), whereas in other capitalising countries they would be included as tangible assets.

Despite some changes, Spain has nevertheless put *imagen fiel* firmly into the context of legal provisions. The Commercial Code (Book 1, ch. III, section 2, Art. 34,2) states:

> The annual accounts must be drafted with clarity and show the true and fair view of the net assets, financial situation and net profit or loss of the business, in conformity with the legal provisions.

The last five words are not in the Directive, nor in the laws of most member states[24] (see the further German exception below). The 1990 *Plan General de Contabilidad* also states (Part 1, Accounting Principles, para. 1) that:

> The application of the accounting principles included in the following sections should mean that annual accounts, drafted with clarity, will show the true and fair view of the net assets, financial situation and net profit or loss of the business.

This makes it even clearer in Spain than in France that, although the TFV seems to have affected specific rules, this does not imply that individual companies and auditors have much freedom to apply it.

In Portugal, too, the implementation of the Fourth Directive saw the official *Comissão de Normalização Contabilística* using words in the plan (see Table 2) that were designed[25] to establish a legal basis to allow movement away from tax rules in certain cases. The plan also requires substance over form (Principle 4f). The combination of these requirements has led to uncertainty in Portugal, for example about the need and legality of revaluations in times of price instability (Fernandes Ferreira, 1992).

The FEE Survey (FEE, 1991) of published accounts shows (from a fairly small sample)[26] the following on the subject of departures from legal provisions in order to give a true and fair view:

> In 10 instances departures from provisions of the national legislation for that reason are reported: in Belgium, Denmark (three), France (two), Ireland, Luxembourg (two) and the United Kingdom. In seven of those 10 cases

[24] The Luxembourg law of 1984 does not include these words, but the official guidance on audit reports from the Institut des Réviseurs d'Entreprises does.

[25] Letter of 9.2.1993 from Sen. Fernandes of the Câmara dos Revisores Oficias de Contas.

[26] 341 Companies from nine EC countries.

the reason for the departure was explained in the accounts (p. 27).

FEE (1992) examines this in more detail, showing that the UK and Irish departures were caused by compliance with standards, and three of the other five were departures from formats. It should be noted that a German example does not appear. For Spain, Italy and Portugal, the Directive was not in force for the accounts surveyed.

(iii) Specific rules continue to override general rules. In Germany, which seems to be an extreme example of this case, it is assumed that compliance with the legal provisions will normally ensure that a TFV is given.[27] In particular, the *Bilanzrichtlinien-Gesetz* of 1985, which implemented the Fourth, Seventh and Eighth Directives, is the only EC implementation which does not specifically require the true and fair view to override legal provisions in exceptional cases (i.e. it does not implement Article 2.5; see Table 1). The German law uses the words from the Directive but, like the Spanish, precedes them with words which might be translated approximately as 'in compliance with accepted accounting principles' (see Table 2). This helps to rob the TFV of its significance. There are some legal requirements which have been seen as inimical to TFV (von Wysocki, 1984). There are even legal views (cited by Ordelheide, 1990, p. 8) that the TFV refers only to the notes to the accounts, and has no effect in interpreting the detailed rules or for filling gaps in rules relating to the financial statements. Certainly, as in France, the German rules require the extra information called for by Article 2.4 of the Directive to be presented in the notes (*im Anhang*).

It is suggested that German tradition would have had to have been overturned in order to allow TFV to override specific rules (Otte, 1990). Unlike France, there have been few direct effects caused by the legislators making changes designed to reflect commercial substance. This is not, of course, intended to be a criticism of Germany: like the UK, Germany has found its own way of continuing with its traditions despite the Directive. Ordelheide (1990) suggests that national accounting rules tend to resist attempts at harmonisation.

One feature of German accounting that may be seen as a counter-example is the option (§308, HGB) to depart from certain tax-based rules in the preparation of group accounts. A minority of large German groups take advantage of this (Treuarbeit, 1990).

Italy seems to be a further example within this third category of country. Firstly, unlike the cases of France and Spain, no amendments were made to legal accounting principles specifically in order to allow 'substance' to override 'form', apart from the compulsory content of the Directives themselves. Certainly, the drafters of *principi contabili*[28] would not expect to be able to override the law. Indeed, the implementation of the Directives may cause accounting practices of some large listed groups to move *away* from a number of 'substance-based' practices, in that previously the accounts of listed companies followed *principi contabili* and IASC standards, which are close to UK/US rules. Secondly, the Ministerial Commentary on the 1991 Law notes that, although it is not possible to specify the exceptional circumstances which would require the rules to be departed from, these would be '*casi veramente eccezionali*'. This suggests extreme rarity or, in practice, that '*veritiero e corretto*' is the same as being in conformity with the rules. Thirdly, the auditors of listed companies were previously required by Presidential Decree to check that accounts followed correct accounting principles[29] but these words were removed in 1991.

Nevertheless, the legal amendments of 1991 do require far more information than most Italian companies were giving. Also, it is possible that some reduction in the influence of tax law will arise as a result of the testing of '*veritiero e corretto*' in the courts.

Continuum of Effects of TFV

From the above discussion it seems possible to suggest that EC countries can be seen as on a continuum with respect to the effects of the TFV. Starting from the most strong, five different positions may be identified (example of countries are given):

Case I — TFV is used by directors/auditors in interpreting the law and standards or where there is no law or standard, and sometimes to override the law or standards. TFV can also be used by standard-setters to make rules that override details of the law. (UK, Ireland).

Case II — TFV (and 'insight') is used by directors/auditors as the basic principle in interpreting the law and (non-governmental) guidelines. It can be used by them to override guidelines and, potentially, in exceptional cases, the law. It is also used by guideline-setters to make rules but not to override the law. (The Netherlands).

[27] A minute of the EC Council states that this may normally be taken to be the case (Council R 1961/78 [ES93] 18.7.1978, No. 2).

[28] 'Accounting principles' as published by a joint committee of the Italian professional bodies: Dottori Commercialisti and Ragionieri.

[29] Decreto Presidente della Repubblica No. 136, 31.3.1975: '*secondo corretti principi contabili*'.

Table 3
Summary of Some Relationships between TFV Signifier, Signified and Effects

1. Same signified but different signifiers (e.g. probably little change in 1947 to what the British law signified despite the wording change from 'true and correct' to 'true and fair').
2. Apparently similar signifiers with different signifieds (e.g. the different signifieds of the apparently similar signifiers in the UK and Portugal or in the Netherlands and Spain).
3. Same signifier but changing signified (e.g. changing signified of TFV in the UK, as lease capitalisation became standard practice).
4. Same signifier and similar signified but different indirect effects of having TFV in law (e.g. same words in UK and Australia with similar meaning in terms of acceptable or necessary accounting practices for most transactions, but quite different legal status).
5. Same signifier but changing effect of having TFV in law (e.g. the increasing practical importance of having TFV in British law from 1970 to date).
6. Signifiers intended to be the same by the EC Commission but with different effects (e.g. continuum of decreasing significance of TFV in UK, France, Germany).
7. Same non-English signifier to translate three different English signifiers (e.g. the use by the Dutch of *getrouw beeld* to translate 'true and correct view', 'true and fair view' and 'present fairly').
8. Same English signifier represented at different times by more than one signifier in another language (e.g. German signifiers of 1974 and 1978; and changing Danish, Portuguese and Italian signifiers from Directive to national rules).

Case III The arrival of TFV was used by lawmakers to allow some change towards 'substance' rather than 'form'. It may be used by directors/auditors when there are no governmental requirements, or to interpret requirements and, in principle, to override them in exceptional cases. (France, Spain).

Case IV TFV may be used by directors/auditors to interpret government requirements or in cases where there are no requirements. In very exceptional cases, which in practice will probably not arise, it could be used to depart from the law. (Italy).

Case V It is unresolved whether TFV relates only to notes or whether it might be usable by directors/auditors to interpret government requirements or in cases where there are no requirements. It is clear, however, that TFV cannot be used to depart from the law. (Germany).

Summary and conclusion

The legal requirement for annual accounts to give a true and fair view uses different signifiers, implies different signifieds and has different effects from time to time and from place to place. A summary of the diversity of the relationships between signifier, signified and effects is shown in Table 3, in each case with examples drawn from this paper.

The non-English signifiers at TFV's first official EC appearance in the 1974 versions of the Directive (or later versions for Greek, Spanish and Portuguese) all involve one adjective only (generally corresponding to 'faithful'). The French and Dutch signifiers have decades of history in the context of accounting. By the time the Directive had been implemented into laws, six out of ten non-English-speaking countries had departed from the Directive's original words, apparently in some cases in an attempt to get closer to the English. Further diversity is likely as the Fourth Directive spreads to the European Economic Area and to Eastern Europe, giving rise to signifiers in Swedish, Finnish, Polish,[30] etc.

The reason why the signified changes over time, and presumably from place to place, is because the TFV is connected to practice, although intended to be an independent concept.

In the UK there was little effect in having TFV in law while there were no detailed laws or even standards. However, as regulation increased from the 1970s, so directors and auditors found TFV useful for special cases. At a similar time, the perceived UK need to counter EC-based regulation of accounting, which also involved rules alien to

[30]A Polish ministerial decree of 15.1.1991 requires a true and fair view in the context of the regulations. The words used are '*rzetelny i jasny obraz*', which seem to be literally translated from English. However, an Act, which has higher authority, was passed in October 1991 requiring correctness and honesty (*prawidlowosc* and *rzetelnosc*), which seems to be drawn from interwar Polish legislation. I am grateful to Marek Schroeder of Birmingham University for this information.

UK practices, gave prominence to the TFV as an argument to be used by the UK profession and by the UK government in Brussels.

Except in Ireland and the Netherlands, there was no analogy to the overriding British TFV requirements elsewhere in Europe. This position has been maintained in practice by Germany, at least for the content of the financial statements themselves. Other EC countries fall between these two extremes, in some cases with the arrival of the TFV being accompanied by significant changes in the accounting rules in the direction of Anglo-Saxon practices. In particular, in some countries (e.g. France and Spain) it seems to have been used by regulators as a philosophy to accompany reform of the rules. However, although the detailed rules have changed, the continuing indirect effects for directors, auditors and rule-makers of the fact that there is a TFV legal requirement is small in these countries.

In some countries, then, the TFV legal requirement has moved from non-existence to existence without effects; in others from non-existence to existence with small direct effects on rules and marginal indirect effects. Paradoxically, in terms of the usefulness of the TFV legal provision to directors, auditors and non-governmental rule-makers, perhaps the greatest *change* in effects from 1970 to date has been in the UK.

References

Accountancy (1990), 'Doubts about UK Practice', November, p. 11.

Alexander, D. (1993), 'A European True and Fair View?', *European Accounting Review*, Vol. 2, No. 1.

Alexander, D. and S. Archer (1992), *The European Accounting Guide*, Academic Press.

Bird, P. (1984), 'What is "A True and Fair View"?', *Journal of Business Law*, November.

Busse von Colbe, W. (1984), 'A True and Fair View: A German Perspective', in Gray and Coenenberg (1984).

Casanovas, I. (1992), 'Spain and the Process of Harmonization with EC Accounting Regulations', in J. A. Gonzalo, *Accounting in Spain*, Asociación Española de Contabilidad y Administración de Empresas, p. 169.

Chastney, J. G. (1975), *True and Fair View—History, Meaning and the Impact of the Fourth Directive*, Institute of Chartered Accountants in England and Wales.

Chaveneau, J. (1920), 'Les bilans—Etablissement et vérifications aux points de vue commercial, industriel et fiscal', *Librairie Arthur Rousseau*, cited in G. Haddou, 'Fiscalité et Comptabilité; Evolution Législative depuis 1920', *Revue Francaise de la Comptabilité*, July-August 1991.

Christiansen, M. (1992), 'Denmark' in Alexander and Archer (1992).

CNCC (1984), cited in Rutherford (1989) as *Assises Nationales du Commissariat aux Comptes, Documents du Travail*, Compagnie Nationale des Commissaires aux Comptes.

Colombo, G. E. (1977), 'La Disciplina Italiana della Revisione', *Rivista dei Dottori Commercialisti*, January-February.

EC (1990), *Accounting Harmonisation in the EC. Problems of Applying the Fourth Directive*, Commission; commented on in *Accountancy* (1990).

FEE (1991), *European Survey of Published Accounts*, Routledge.

FEE (1992), *Analysis of European Accounting and Disclosure Practices*, Routledge.

Fernandes Ferreira, R. (1992), 'Free Valuations of Tangible Fixed Assets', paper presented at the EAA Conference, Madrid.

Ferrero, G. (1991), *I Complementari principi della 'Chiarezza', della 'Verita' e della 'Correttezza' nella Redazione del Bilancio d'Esercizio*, Giuffrè Editore.

Flint, D. (1982), *A True and Fair View in Company Accounts*, Institute of Chartered Accountants of Scotland.

Gray, S. J. (1980), 'The Impact of International Accounting Differences from a Security-Analysis Perspective: Some European Evidence', *Journal of Accounting Research*, Spring.

Gray, S. J. and A. G. Coenenberg (1984), *EEC Accounting Harmonization*, North Holland.

Harris, N. G. E. (1987), 'Fairness in Financial Reporting', *Journal of Applied Philosophy*, Vol. 4, No. 1.

Hoffman, L. and M. Arden (1983), 'Counsel's Opinion on True and Fair', *Accountancy*, November 1983.

Hopwood, A. G. (1990), 'Ambiguity, Knowledge and Territorial Claims: Some Observations on the Doctrine of Substance over Form: A Review Essay', *British Accounting Review*, March, p. 84.

Lyas, C. (1992), 'Accounting and Language', in M. Mumford and K. V. Peasnell (eds.), *Philosophical Perspectives on Accounting*, Routledge.

Miller, M. C. (1993), 'Financial Reporting in Australia', in T. E. Cooke and R. H. Parker (eds.), *Financial Reporting in the West Pacific Rim*, Routledge.

Nobes, C. W. (1983), 'The Origins of the Harmonising Provisions of the 1980 and 1981 Companies Acts', *Accounting and Business Research*, Winter.

Nobes, C. W. (1989), *Interpreting European Financial Statements*, Butterworths.

Nobes, C. W. and R. H. Parker (1991a), 'True and Fair: a Survey of UK Financial Directors', *Journal of Business Finance and Accounting*, Spring.

Nobes, C. W. and R. H. Parker (1991b), *Comparative International Accounting*, Prentice Hall.

Nobes, C. W. and S. Zambon (1991), 'Piano, Piano: Italy Implements the Directives', *Accountancy*, July.

Ordelheide, D. (1990), 'Soft-Transformations of Accounting Rules of the Fourth Directive in Germany', *Les Cahiers internationaux de la Comptabilité*, Editions Comptables Malesherbes.

Ordelheide, D. (1993), 'True and Fair View—A European and a German Perspective', *European Accounting Review*, Vol. 2, No. 1.

Otte, H-H. (1990), 'Harmonisierte Europäische Rechnungslegung', *Zeitschrift für Betriebswirtschaft*, No. 42.

Parker, R. H. (1989), 'Importing and Exporting Accounting: the British Experience' in A. G. Hopwood (ed.), *International Pressures for Accounting Change*, Prentice Hall.

Parker, R. H. (1991a), 'Financial Reporting in the UK and Australia', ch. 7 in Nobes and Parker (1991b).

Parker, R. H. (1991b), 'Financial Reporting in the Netherlands', ch. 10 in Nobes and Parker (1991b).

Parker, R. H. (1994), 'Debating True and Fair in Australia: An Exercise in Deharmonisation?', *Journal of Accounting, Auditing and Taxation*, forthcoming.

Parker, R. H. and C. W. Nobes (1991), 'Auditors' View of True and Fair', *Accounting and Business Research*, Autumn.

Pasqualini, F. (1992), *Le Principe de l'Image Fidèle en Droit Comptable*, Litec.

Pham, D. (1984), 'France' in Gray and Coenenberg (1984).

Rutherford, B. A. (1983), 'Spoilt Beauty: The True and Fair View Doctrine in Translation', *AUTA Review*, Spring.

Rutherford, B. A. (1985), 'The True and Fair View Doctrine: A Search for Explication', *Journal of Business Finance and Accounting*, Vol. 12, No. 4.

Rutherford, B. A. (1989), 'The True and Fair Doctrine: Some Recent Developments', in G. Macdonald and B. A. Rutherford, *Accounts, Accounting and Accountability*, Van Nostrand.

Saussure, F. de (1919), *Cours de Linguistique Générale*, Payot: Lausanne, translated as *Course in General Linguistics*, Philosophical Library: New York, 1959.

Scheid, J.-C. and P. Walton (1992), 'France' in Alexander and Archer (1992).

Socías, A. (1991), *La Normalización Contable en el Reino Unido, Francia, Alemania y España*, Asociación Española de Contabilidad y Administración de Empresas.

Standish, P. E. M. (1991), 'Financial Reporting in France', ch. 8 in Nobes and Parker (1991b).

Treuarbeit (1990), *Konzernabschlüsse '89*, IDW-Verlag.

Tweedie, D. P. (1983), 'True and Fair Rules', *Accountant's Magazine*, November.

Tweedie, D. P. and J. Kellas (1987), 'Off-Balance Sheet Financing', *Accountancy*, April.

Van Hulle, K. (1983), 'Truth and Untruth about True and Fair', *European Accounting Review*, Vol. 2, No. 1.

Von Wysocki, K. (1984), 'Germany' in Gray and Coenenberg (1984).

Walker, R. G. (1984), *A True and Fair View and the Reporting Obligations of Directors and Auditors*, National Companies and Securities Commission, Melbourne.

Walton, P. (1991), *The True and Fair View: A Shifting Concept*, Occasional Research Paper No. 7, Chartered Association of Certified Accountants.

Zeff, S. A. (1990), 'The English Language Equivalent of Geeft een Getrouw Beeld', *De Accountant*, October 1990, p. 83.

Zeff, S. A. (1992), 'Arthur Andersen & Co. and the Two-part Opinion in the Auditor's Report: 1946–1962', *Contemporary Accounting Research*.

Zeff, S. A., F. van der Wel and K. Camfferman (1992), *Company Financial Reporting: A Historical and Comparative Study of the Dutch Regulatory Process*, North Holland.

Appendix I

Translations of Words in Table 2 and Elsewhere

Netherlands	geeft een zodanig inzicht dat een verantwoord oordeel kan worden gevormd	presents an insight such that a well-founded opinion can be formed
	geeft getrouw, duidelijk en stelselmatig	presents faithfully, clearly and consistently (over time)
	een getrouw beeld geven	present a faithful picture
Denmark	et pålideligt billede	a faithful picture
	et retvisende billede	a right-looking picture
Germany	(unter Beachtung der Grundsätze ordnungsmässiger Buchführung) ein den tatsächlichen Verhältnissen entsprechendes Bild	(in compliance with accepted accounting principles) a picture in accordance with the facts
France	une image fidèle	a faithful picture
Greece	ten pragmatiki ikona	the real picture
Spain	una (la) imagen fiel ... (de conformidad con las disposiciones legales)	a (the) faithful picture ... (in conformity with the legal provisions)
Portugal	uma imagem fiel	a loyal view
	uma imagem verdadeira e apropriada	a true and appropriate view
Italy	un quadro fedele	a faithful picture
	rappresentare in modo veritiero e corretto	presents in a true and correct way

[23]

Accounting and Business Research, Vol. 24, No. 96, pp. 319-333, 1994

European Rule-making in Accounting: The Seventh Directive as a Case Study

Graham Diggle and Christopher Nobes*

Abstract—This paper analyses EC rule-making, using the Seventh Directive as a case study. Three stages of a Directive's life are identified, with different key players taking the lead. The paper analyses the evolution of the Seventh Directive up to its adoption in 1983, looking at 19 key features. The adopted Directive is close to previous UK consolidation practices, but investigation shows that, from its origins in the late 1960s to the published drafts of the late 1970s, it showed clear German parentage. The coalition of forces leading to the major changes from German to UK practices is examined.

Introduction

The Seventh Directive on company law, concerning consolidated accounts, was adopted by the EC[1] Council in 1983, after many preceding drafts (see Table 1 for detailed references). The purpose of this paper is to propose a framework for understanding the setting of Directives, to analyse the evolution of the Seventh Directive and to suggest why, in this case, particular national influences seem to have dominated. The paper does not in general follow the Directive into subsequent member state laws. This is a large and different task, which has been carried out in detail by the Fédération des Experts Comptables Européens (FEE) (1993).

The background to the Seventh Directive is that the Fourth Directive (on annual accounts of individual companies) had been adopted in 1978. Nobes (1983) traces its development, noting particularly the influences from the German Public Companies Act (*Aktiengesetz*) of 1965. The Elmendorff Committee, which had completed the *avant projet* for the Fourth Directive in 1968, delivered[2] a memorandum on group accounting to the EC Commission in 1970. Just as the *Aktiengesetz* (AktG) stamped much of the Fourth Directive with its character, one would expect to see substantial influence of German legislation in the Seventh Directive: Dr. Elmendorff came from Germany, which had the EC's most developed company law at the time; and the UK was not then a member of the EC. However, a reading of the eventual Seventh Directive does not give the impression of German origins. One would rather have the impression of Anglo-Saxon[3] sources for most of its provisions.

This paper first examines rule-making in accounting, considering EC Directives in particular. The evolution of the Seventh Directive is then used as a case study. Finally, conclusions are offered about the nature and effects of the forces operating on the rule-making system.

Rule-making in accounting

A number of papers have examined the process of national standard-setting. For example, Watts and Zimmerman (1978) examine lobbying behaviour in a US context (and that paper prompts many reactions); Mumford (1979) notes a cycle in the degree of interest in and the solutions proposed for inflation accounting in the UK; Hope and Briggs (1982) and Hope and Gray (1982) examine UK policy-making in two controversial areas; Laughlin and Puxty (1983) explore the politics of

---

*The authors are, respectively, senior lecturer in accounting at Oxford Brookes University and Coopers & Lybrand Professor of Accounting at the University of Reading. They are grateful, for comments on earlier drafts, to Adolf Coenenberg (Universität Augsburg), Dieter Ordelheide (Goethe Universität, Frankfurt), Bob Parker (University of Exeter), Alan Roberts (University of Reading), Peter Wessel (Moret Ernst & Young, Eindhoven) and two referees. Correspondence should be addressed to Professor C. Nobes, Department of Economics, Faculty of Letters and Social Sciences, University of Reading, P.O. Box 218, Whiteknights, Reading RG6 2AA.

[1]EC is used in this paper to mean 'European Communities'. Despite the fact that the EC became a constituent part of the European Union in 1993, the programme of Directives and such organs as the Commission remain EC not pan-EU matters.

[2]This was confirmed to the authors on 1.3.1993 by Herr Horst Kaminski of the Institut der Wirtschaftsprüfer, who had been secretary to the Elmendorff Committee. For more details on the Committee, see Nobes (1993).

[3]'Anglo-Saxon' is used here as a label for countries where accounting has traditionally been seen as a professional (not a governmental) field, where fairness is the objective, where tax rules are less influential, where conservatism is constrained by matching, where the pressures for disclosure overcome secrecy, where consolidation has a long history. Approximately, this means English-speaking countries, with a few others, such as the Netherlands and Denmark. The expression 'continental' is used here to denote the alternative system.

Table 1
Chronology

1965	Aktiengesetz
1968	Elmendorff *avant projet* of the Fourth Directive
1969	Publizitätsgesetz
1970/71	Elmendorff memorandum on consolidated accounts as draft of additions to Fourth Directive (XIV/533/71)
1971	First draft of the Fourth Directive
1973	UK, Ireland and Denmark join the EC
1973	Commission's note on consolidation (XI/669/73)
1974	Second draft of Fourth Directive
1974	Groupe d'Etudes comment on Commission's 1973 note (GEEC-6DSA-17774)
1976	First draft of Seventh Directive[a]
1977	Comments by Economic and Social Committee on draft Seventh Directive[b]
1978	European Parliament comments on draft Seventh Directive[c]
1978	Fourth Directive adopted
1978	Second draft of Seventh Directive[d] (issued in January 1979)
1983	Seventh Directive adopted[e]

References
[a]*Bulletin of the European Communities*, Supplement 9/76.
[b]*Official Journal of the European Communites*, 75, 26.3.1977.
[c]*Official Journal of the European Communities*, 163, 10.7.1978
[d]COM (78) 703 final.
[e]*Official Journal of the European Communities*, 18 July 1983 (DJ, 1983, L193).

standard-setting; Nobes (1992) examines the political forces in the case of the UK goodwill debate. There has also been some analysis of the process of *international* standard-setting (e.g. Wallace, 1990). However, little seems to have been written about the forces at work in accounting rule-making at the European Community level.

Laughlin and Puxty (1983) note that some writers believe that accounting rule-making is or should be a technical activity and others believe that it is or should be a political activity. In the context of the EC's harmonisation programme, it is particularly obvious that political pressures are at work, given that the final negotiations on Directives are conducted by representatives of the governments of member states. Furthermore, there has never been any pretence that a coherent conceptual framework should be used in this context or that one is even implicit. Nevertheless, particularly in the drafting stages, lawyers and accountants are heavily involved, and the Directives have technical as well as political input.

Hope and Gray (1982) examine the literature relating to the modelling of the political decision-making process. They suggest that one might begin with Dahl's (1961) pluralist approach in which 'an attempt is made to study specific outcomes in order to determine who . . . prevails in decision-making' (Polsby, 1963, p. 113). They note that Lukes (1974) criticises this as one-dimensional in that it leaves out the ways in which power can be used to ensure that the potential issues are not decided or not even considered. However, Hope and Gray (p. 536) conclude that, for analysis of an accounting issue that has been settled after observable conflicts on key issues, the one-dimensional pluralist approach is the most suitable. Following these ideas, the interested parties, the key issues and the eventual decisions are identified in order to illuminate the rule-making process in the case of the Seventh Directive.

The various stages of the Seventh Directive's progress can be charted:

Stage I: Avant Projet

As has been mentioned, a memorandum on the subject of EC rules on consolidation was prepared in 1970 by a committee of professional accountants, chaired by a German. At that date, there were only six members of the EC (see the dates in Table 2). A version of this memorandum was issued by the Commission in 1971 in the context of the recently published first draft of the Fourth Directive (see Table 1 for chronology and references). The memorandum was presented in terms of new draft Articles 50 to 57 to be added to the Fourth Directive to cover group accounting. This had several German features (to be explained further later):

(i) definition of the group based on central control;
(ii) requirement to comply with the provisions of the law but no requirement to give a true and fair view;
(iii) uniform formats;
(iv) the group accounts should maintain the valuation bases of the constituent individual accounts;

Table 2
Members of the EC, with Dates of Joining

Anglo-Saxon accounting*	*Continental* accounting*
Netherlands (1957)	France (1957)
UK (1973)	W. Germany (1957)
Ireland (1973)	Italy (1957)
Denmark (1973)	Belgium (1957)
	Luxembourg (1957)
	Greece (1980)
	Spain (1986)
	Portugal (1986)

*see footnote 3

(v) no goodwill to be recognised;
(vi) no consolidation of associates or joint ventures.

Following this, in 1973, the Commission produced a note on the co-ordination of laws on consolidation, proposing a Directive on the subject. The Groupe d'Etudes (a body representing EC professional accountants, which had its origins in the Elmendorff Committee) commented on this in 1974 (again, see Table 1 for references). By this time, the EC had been enlarged by the accession of the UK, Ireland and Denmark.

Given that EC countries might be seen as divided into two quite different groups (see Table 2) with respect to accounting (e.g. Nair and Frank, 1980; Nobes, 1992), one might expect the consensus of professional accountants in the EC to have changed from 1970 to 1974 as a result of the influx of 'Anglo-Saxon' countries in 1973. Indeed, the Group d'Etudes in its 1974 comments made several Anglo-Saxon suggestions:

(i) the Directive should be as general as possible and only lay down basic rules, leaving the details for national and international accounting organisations (one notes that the International Accounting Standards Committee had been formed in 1973);
(ii) the objective of the consolidated accounts should be to give a true and fair view;
(iii) consolidation should be based on ownership of more than 50% of voting rights;
(iv) the possibility of excluding dissimilar subsidiaries;
(v) uniform group accounting policies;
(vi) goodwill should be recognised;
(vii) permission to use the equity method for associated companies and proportional consolidation for joint ventures.

This remarkable change in the consensus professional view needs further explanation, which is attempted in the concluding section of this paper.

Stage II: Published Drafts of the Directive

The second main element of the process is the published drafts of a Directive. In the case of the Seventh Directive, there were drafts in 1976 and 1978. The drafting is controlled by Commission staff, predominantly lawyers from codified law countries.[4] This would lead one to expect a sympathy with the approach of German law, which was so evident in the Fourth Directive (Nobes, 1983). As the paper will show, the 1976 and 1978 drafts were indeed close to the consolidation provisions of the *Aktiengesetz* and largely ignored the Anglo-Saxon suggestions of the 1974 Groupe d'Etudes paper.

Stage III: Government Negotiations

The final stage in the evolution of a Directive is the negotiation in the committees of the Council of Ministers. Here full rein can be given to political pressures. One would expect to see the effects of nationalism, lobbying by preparers of accounts, concerns by governments over tax revenues and competitiveness, etc. As will be shown, in the case of the Seventh Directive, the really major changes from German practices occurred at this stage (i.e. after 1978). To some extent, as usual, the addition of options enabled international agreement, but there was also a coalition of forces in favour of movement towards Anglo-Saxon accounting.

Plan of the Argument Below

Before drawing conclusions on the political processes at work, this paper examines the evolution of the Directive in 19 major areas (see Appendix 1) under five main headings:

- Scope of consolidation
- Preparation of consolidated accounts
- Consolidation methods
- Goodwill
- Size exemptions

In general, from now on, three documents are considered: the AktG of 1965, the First Draft of 1976 and the adopted Directive of 1983. Another

[4]For most of this period, Hermann Niessen was in charge of company law. More recently, Gisbert Wolff has succeeded him. Both are German lawyers. Their subordinate, Karel van Hulle (now head of accounting), is a Belgian lawyer.

document of some relevance is the amended proposal of 1978, which was prepared by the Commission after the content of the Fourth Directive was settled and after consideration of the First Draft of the Seventh Directive by the Economic and Social Committee and the European Parliament (for details, see Vangermeersch, 1985). The 1978 amendments (see Appendix 2) are referred to below where appropriate. Table 1's chronology also covers these documents.

Scope of consolidation

The AktG had required consolidated accounts to be prepared, but the scope of group accounting was very different from that envisaged by the EC legislation. Under the AktG (§329), only groups with AGs and KGaAs as parent companies had to prepare consolidated accounts; foreign subsidiaries could be excluded from consolidation; and no reference was made to associated companies (with the implication from §153 AktG that these were to be carried in the group accounts at historical cost). The first of these issues (i.e. who must prepare consolidated accounts) saw an expansion in the Implementation Act for the AktG[5] by the inclusion of GmbH companies with AG or KGaA subsidiaries. Also, the *Publizitätsgesetz* (PublG) of 1969 extended the requirements of the AktG to all groups, independent of legal form, that were above certain size criteria.[6]

The first eight Articles of the First Draft (Supplement 9/76 Group Accounts: Proposal for a Seventh Directive) announce a still broader scope. Consolidated accounts, according to this First Draft, are to be prepared wherever a group *contains* a GmbH, an AG or a KGaA (or equivalent companies, e.g. UK public or private limited companies) whether as a parent or a subsidiary, and all group undertakings are to be consolidated regardless of their domicile (First Draft, Article 6 (1) (a) and (b)). Anti-avoidance is one of the motivations at work here: it would be all too easy to circumvent the purpose of the Directive by placing an unincorporated enterprise at the head of the group (Supplement 9/76, p. 23). Eventually there is an option to narrow this scope to groups with parents of the relevant legal form—as will be made clear below.

Definitions of Parent

The definitions of parent and subsidiary company that had been used in member states appeared to fall into two types. The Explanatory Memorandum (Supplement 9/76, p. 20) accompanying the First Draft divides them into:

(i) A very general definition that rests on the idea of a group of legally independent units which operate as a single economic unit. (It is significant that this type is described as pertaining in one member state, which is not named.)

(ii) A much more concrete and precise kind of definition, e.g. ownership of the majority of shares or control of a majority of the voting rights.

The first of the two cases is illustrated by the AktG, under which the evidence of uniform direction ('*einheitliche Leitung*') was the criterion for whether consolidated accounts were prepared or not:

> If the combine [*sic*] enterprises of a combine are under the uniform direction of a stock corporation ... the board of management of the head association ... shall prepare ... a consolidated balance sheet and a consolidated profit and loss statement ... (AktG §329, translation: Mueller and Galbraith, 1976).

The AktG (§§16–18) contains several criteria for determining the existence of uniform direction, including (a) the existence of a control contract, (b) integration of one company into the other,[7] or (c) (rebuttably) majority ownership of the shares (not the voting rights).

In the Explanatory Memorandum quoted above, the EC authors make it plain that a choice has to be made between the two types of group definition: the former (i.e. (i) above) has the advantage of greater flexibility and it reaches to the heart of the idea of the group. It is selected for the First Draft.

Therefore the Commission developed, in these early stages, a general and comprehensive definition of the group. It did so by stating what a subsidiary is (one which may be subject to the controlling influence of another—Art. (2)(1)), and that this relationship may be presumed in certain circumstances (ownership of the majority of subscribed capital, control of the majority of voting rights, or the power to appoint the majority of the board of directors). However, as in the AktG, the touchstone of the definition of the group is 'uniform direction'. The exercise of uniform direction over two or more undertakings defines them as a group. A parent-subsidiary relationship as described above allows us to presume uniform direction, but uniform direction may exist even where there is no evidence of the criteria for a parent-subsidiary relationship.

[5]§28 of the *Einführungsgesetz zum AktG*.

[6]Undertakings coming above two of the three criteria: balance sheet total of DM 125 m, sales of DM 250 m and over 5,000 employees.

[7]The AktG §18(1) says '*eingegliedert ist*'.

The wording '*einheitliche Leitung*' also appears in the German version of Articles 3 and 4 of the First Draft and is used in the commentary to the draft (Supplement 9/76, p. 21). As noted, it is its flexibility that commends this definition to the EC legislators; a single test which excludes majority shareholdings where no control is intended, but includes minority shareholdings where actual control is exercised. By contrast, a legalistic definition of all specific circumstances under which a group would be held to exist would also have the disadvantage of requiring precise circumstances for exceptions, which can lead to abuse as the authors of the First Draft point out (Supplement 9/76, p. 21).

In the final version of the Seventh Directive (hereafter called 'the Directive'), the Commission seems to have made an about-face on this issue, notwithstanding their earlier defence of the general and flexible clause. Article 1 of the final version gives a series of definitions of the narrow, legalistic type rejected earlier; a majority of voting rights (Art. 1(1)(a)); the right to appoint or remove the majority of the board (Art. 1(1)(b)); and control of a company through a contractual agreement (Art. 1(1)(c)). This necessitates the allowing of a number of exceptions (Art. 13; see later). In addition, 'and pending subsequent co-ordination', actual exercise of a dominant influence or the management of two or more companies on a unified basis may be grounds for requiring consolidated accounts if member states so wish (Art. 1(2)(b)). Far from setting the tenor of this aspect of the law, the German concept of the group has been relegated to an option that is subject to future revision.

Legal Form of Parent

On the issue of the legal form of the parent, the Directive (Art. 4(2)) allows a member state to choose whether to require consolidation if (i) the parent is a limited company (AG, KGaA or GmbH, in the case of Germany) or (ii) the group *contains* such a company. The former was (and is) the British position. The latter had been the German and the First Draft's position (Art. 6(1)(a)).

No Parent

A further case is where there is no parent undertaking at all: two or more formally unconnected undertakings may be managed on a unified basis as a result of legal arrangements or overlapping management. The AktG (§329) refers to group undertakings under unified management. However, according to the AktG (§18(2)), *einheitliche Leitung* could exist without a parent. The resulting group would be called a '*Gleichordnungskonzern*'.

Similarly, the First Draft (Arts. 4(1) and 7(1)) requires the preparation of group accounts by any limited company in such a case: undertakings that do not stand in a parent-subsidiary relationship to one another also form a group if they are under unified management. This case of the 'horizontal group' is specifically mentioned in the commentary (Explanatory Memorandum, p. 22). The Directive (Art. 12) *allows* a member state to require this 'horizontal' consolidation, presumably for the protection of lenders or employees in the 'group'.

Sub-group Consolidation

Another topic where German origins may be detected is 'sub-group consolidation'. The AktG (§330(1)) requires AG and KGaA parents to produce group accounts even if they are themselves subsidiaries. However, there is an exemption for those sub-groups included in a higher consolidation using German law (even if the higher consolidation is performed by an ultimate parent outside Germany).[8] In effect, this meant that sub-group consolidation was not common because few AGs or KGaAs were subsidiaries of parents falling outside of the AktG or PublG.[9] Likewise, the First Draft (Art. 6(2)(a)) requires all companies of the relevant legal form[10] which are parents to prepare accounts for their sub-group. Article 6(2)(b) also requires partial consolidation where the ultimate parent company has its domicile outside the EC, and relates to all EC-domiciled parents at the top of their 'family trees' within the EC.

The First Draft would have had an effect dramatically wider than that of the AktG. This is because the First Draft has no sub-group exemptions and because it extends the consolidation requirement to all sub-groups headed by all types of limited company (e.g. in the German context, to GmbHs which are the vast majority[11] of limited companies).

There seems to be no German or British precedent for this. The EC Commission justified these demands as being necessary for the protection of all interest groups connected with the subsidiary companies:

> Why, in other cases, is the drawing up of consolidated accounts for a sub-group still thought necessary when consolidated accounts are already available for the group as a whole? The Commission considers that sub-group accounts play a useful part in

[8]Any such foreign group accounts must be published in the *Bundesanzeiger* and audited by a Wirtschaftsprüfer (§330(2)).

[9]There were only about 2,000 AGs and very few KGaAs in 1983. Very large GmbHs came under the rules of the *Publizitätsgesetz* of 1969, which approximately applied AktG rules. There was a large incentive for subsidiaries to avoid audit and publication rules by being GmbHs.

[10]The Article also requires other (non limited-company) parents to prepare sub-group accounts if the group includes a limited company, but only if the sub-group is not included in a higher consolidation.

[11]There were about 260,000 GmbHs in 1983.

> supplementing the information already given in the group accounts and add to the protection of the various parties having an interest in dependent group companies required to draw up such accounts. The shareholders and the creditors obtain a better view of their company's position ... This information cannot be evaluated without these other two documents. The situation might arise, for example, where the sub-group accounts showed a profit while the group accounts showed a loss. Both sets of information are important for shareholders in dependent group companies (Supplement 9/76, pp. 23, 24).

The rationale is extended to the protection of other interest groups (including regional or state interests in the case of some important subsidiary groups) and the importance of the principle is underlined to the extent that no exceptions to this rule are envisaged. One could also detect a mistrust of preparers in the comment:

> There is some danger of group accounts, and in particular those of large groups with a large number of operations in different countries, becoming a jumble in which a great deal of important information is lost (Supplement 9/76, p. 24).

In the final version of the Directive, the scope clause (Article 1) continues to include all EC-domiciled parent companies—a definition that would include parents which are themselves subsidiaries of other companies. However, the full force of this began to be diluted in the 1978 amended proposal by adding exemptions (see Appendix 2). In the final Directive, exemptions from the preparation of group accounts must in general[12] be made available to subsidiary companies that are wholly or 90% owned by parents domiciled in the EC (Article 7). For other subsidiary companies, sub-group accounts can be dispensed with so long as these are not requested by the shareholders (Article 8). As a member state option, subsidiaries of non-EC parents may also be exempted, provided these prepare accounts in conformity with the provisions of the Seventh Directive or are equivalent to such accounts (Seventh Directive, Article 11), whatever 'equivalent' may eventually be held to mean (FEE, 1993, ch. 4). This last provision was originally introduced in the 1978 revised draft, although in that draft an EC auditor had to verify the compliance or equivalence. In effect, sub-group consolidation has been eliminated in the adopted Directive, except where it is required as a protection of the interests of the minority shareholders or in certain cases where the ultimate parent is outside the EC.

[12]Under certain conditions, e.g. that the sub-group is included in a higher consolidation.

Legal Form of Subsidiaries

It should be noted that, although a member state may choose to require only parent *companies* to prepare group accounts, the required scope of consolidation clearly goes beyond subsidiary companies to cover all *undertakings* (i.e. including unlimited companies and unincorporated entities). This was clear from the AktG §329 (as quoted above). It may also be found in the First Draft (Art. 1, etc.) and in the Directive (Art. 1, etc.). This is different from previous British legal precedent (Companies Act 1948) or accounting standard (SSAP 14) which are drafted in terms of subsidiary *companies*. An explanatory point here is that unlimited entities are of greater economic significance in Germany than in the UK (Macharzina and Langer, 1991).

Foreign Subsidiaries

The AktG §329(2) allows foreign subsidiaries to be excluded from consolidation, which would have relieved the group from the difficulties of non-uniform accounting policies and of currency translation. However, even from the 1970 Elmendorff proposals, this permissive exclusion is abandoned in the context of international rules. Foreign subsidiaries are specifically to be included according to the First Draft (Art. 6) and the Directive (Art. 3).

Dissimilar Activities

The issue of exclusion of undertakings on the grounds of different activities was similarly reviewed and revised. In the First Draft, no such exclusion was to be possible:

> A diversity of activities within a group is not in itself a valid reason for permitting undertakings to be excluded from consolidation. An individual company may also undertake different activities and will not be prevented from drawing up annual accounts. Some of the difficulties which might arise in such cases with regard to consolidation may be avoided by inserting special headings in the accounts with appropriate entries in the notes to the accounts, or by effecting a consolidation in terms of the different kinds of activity (Supplement 9/76, p. 26).

No exact version of such an exclusion existed in the AktG either, although §329(2) required the exclusion of a subsidiary from consolidation if it would impair the value of the disclosures in the consolidated financial statements. The 1978 revised draft *permits* the exclusion of subsidiaries that have very different activities from the rest of the group (Art. 10A). Article 14 of the Directive instead *requires* exclusion of subsidiaries from the consolidated accounts if, because of their different activities, their inclusion would impair the true and fair view given by the group accounts.

This is clearly a version of the then prevailing Anglo-Saxon idea whereby particularly financial subsidiaries were routinely treated by the equity method in group accounts. This practice was overturned by SFAS 94 in the US (1987) and the subsequent IAS 27. This change of mind occurred *after* the Directive was adopted. It is ironic, therefore, that the UK standard setters have had to try to circumvent the implementation in the Companies Act 1989 of Article 14 of the Directive by stating (in FRS 2, para. 25 of 1992) that this exclusion of subsidiaries on the grounds of 'true and fair' is exceptional.

Excludable Subsidiaries

Other *permitted* exclusions change across the documents. The AktG (§329(2)) allows immaterial subsidiaries to be excluded, as does the First Draft (Art. 10). The Directive (Art. 13) allows exclusions where the subsidiary is immaterial; where there are severe long-term restrictions on management; where the information necessary would involve disproportionate expense or undue delay; or where the shares are held exclusively with a view to resale. This extensive list goes beyond German precedent but is very similar to the permitted exclusions of the British Companies Act 1948 or the required exclusions of the British SSAP 14 (see Appendix 1).

Preparation of consolidated accounts

Other changes from the First Draft revise positions that otherwise would have given the Directive a German flavour.

Accounting Date

AktG (§331(3)) requires group companies to have the same accounting date or to prepare, and have audited, special accounting statements covering the period of the consolidated accounts (i.e. not just interim statements). This strict requirement is carried through to Article 14 (1)(e) of the First Draft, including the requirement to have any special accounts audited. The insistence on a common accounting date and accounting policies is justified by the EC legislators by the fact that a company with dominant influence over others would be in a position to insist on these matters (Supplement 9/76, p. 29). In the final Directive, Article 27(3) permits a group company to have a balance sheet date up to three months before that of the consolidated accounts. A greater difference in time would necessitate only interim accounts for the intervening period to be drawn up, and there is no mention of audit in this context. This is more in line with Anglo-Saxon practice of the period (e.g. SSAP 14, para. 18).

Accounting Policies

The AktG, the 1971 draft of the Fourth Directive and the *avant projet* for the Seventh Directive do not contain a 'true and fair view' requirement. However, this changes by the 1974 version of the Fourth Directive and by the First Draft of the Seventh Directive (Art. 9). In these two documents, the true and fair view requirement has a status equal with the requirement to comply with the provisions of the Directive. However, by 1978, in the adopted version of the Fourth Directive and in the European Parliament amended version of the Seventh Directive, the true and fair view is required to override[13] other provisions, although not the scope of the group.[14] This is obviously a move in the UK direction.

As to uniform group accounting policies, the AktG §331(1) requires consolidated accounts to take up the values as they appear in the single entity accounts, except when they are not in accordance with German principles[15] (§336 (3)). The First Draft's Article 15 also requires the same values to be consolidated as they appear in the single entity accounts. This is presumably a measure to prevent manipulation and also aids readers of both the single entity accounts and consolidated statements to gauge the impact of the former on the latter. However, in order to ensure a coherent view of the results and financial position of the group, as if from the standpoint of a single economic entity, the First Draft includes the additional provision that all group companies use the same valuation methods (Art. 15(b) and (c)). That is, the German emphasis on transparency has been supplemented by the need to show a true and fair view of the group. The Explanatory Memorandum makes this explicit: 'The group accounts can only give the desired true and fair view ('*getreuen Einblick*')[16] where the items contained therein are valued on an identical or at least comparable basis' (Supplement 9/76, p. 29).

In the final version of the Directive, Article 29(2) requires the consolidating company to use the same valuation methods in the group accounts as in its own accounts (although member states may

[13]For a detailed examination of the wordings and strengths of the true and fair requirement in EC countries, see Nobes (1993).

[14]The true and fair requirement in the Seventh Directive relates to the undertakings included in the group accounts not to which undertakings shall be included.

[15]The values must be in accordance with *Grundsätze ordnungsmässiger Buchführung*, which are not fully codified.

[16]The 1976 draft of the Seventh Directive, like the 1974 draft of the Fourth Directive, contains the words '*einen getreuen Einblick*'. These words are replaced in the final versions of both Directives (1978 and 1983, respectively) by the longer wording now familiar in German law (see Nobes, 1993 for more detail).

prescribe or allow the use of different valuation methods, provided these are disclosed). Assets and liabilities of group companies using different rules must be revalued according to group valuation methods. The elimination of inter-company profit can, according to Article 26 of the Seventh Directive, be limited to the group's share of those profits rather than the total. This is not the case in the AktG (§331(2)) or in the First Draft (Art. 14). There seems to be neither German nor British (nor US)[17] precedent for this.

Consolidation methods

Acquisitions and Mergers

In the AktG, only full consolidation is dealt with. By contrast, the First Draft, in Articles 12 and 18, describes full and proportional consolidation. The Seventh Directive describes three methods in Articles 19, 20 and 32, having added the pooling of interests method. This takes account of the range of European practice.

The method of full consolidation described in the First Draft (Art. 12) is Anglo-Saxon. The Explanatory Memorandum (p. 27) discusses the choice that had to be made in this respect:

> In one Member State, consolidation is normally carried out on the basis of the net assets of the undertaking to be consolidated as it stands at the end of each financial year. Under this method, the reserves formed by the undertaking to be consolidated during its group membership will disappear into the consolidation differences and will not be shown under the group reserves in the group accounts. The consolidation differences will therefore change every year according to the movement of the reserves held in the undertaking to be consolidated.

This describes the predominant practice[18] in Germany on the basis of AktG 1965 (§331) (Beeny, 1975, p. 29), and is contrasted with the Anglo-Saxon method, leading as the latter does to a fuller presentation of movements on group reserves instead of hiding transfers to and from reserves in the 'difference on consolidation'. Since the results before and after acquisition are thereby strongly differentiated, the clarity of the picture of the group's financial position and the results of its activity is enhanced. Article 19 of the Seventh Directive retains this method. The treatment of goodwill resulting from this calculation is considered in the next subsection.

Merger accounting for situations in which the acquiring company has issued shares as consideration for its controlling participation in another company is not described as a separate technique in the AktG. Beeny (1975, p. 30), however, points out that the then normal German acquisition method of consolidation approximates to what in the UK would be called the merger method: shares issued as consideration were recorded at their nominal value as were the shares transferred to the 'acquiring' company, the assets and liabilities were transferred at their book values rather than fair values and there was no distinction between pre- and post-acquisition profits in calculating the difference on consolidation. Despite (or perhaps because of) this similarity, there was no separate mention of merger accounting in the AktG.

In the First Draft, there is also no mention of merger accounting. This is not surprising, given this German background, the lack of use of the method in most of continental Europe and the fact that it was of uncertain legality in the UK and Ireland in 1976.[19] However, the method was made legal in the Companies Act 1981 in the UK, although it has not been made legal in Ireland. After the 1981 Act, the UK's Accounting Standards Committee issued ED 31 on the subject of merger accounting in 1982. The UK put pressure on the EC to include merger accounting as an option in the Directive, and this resulted in Article 20, which is a member state option.

Associates and Joint Ventures

As mentioned earlier, the AktG did not recognise a particular treatment for associates or joint ventures, which were therefore to be treated as investments. However, in the First Draft (Art. 17) and the Directive (Art. 33), the equity method is demanded for associates and allowed for joint ventures. Proportional consolidation is the member state optional alternative for joint ventures. This is consistent with UK practice of the time, and that of several other member states. The definition of an associate in the Directive (and the First Draft) is broadly in line with the UK's (i.e. based on significant influence, generally holdings of between 20% and 50%). Previous French precedent was holdings of $33\frac{1}{3}$% to 50%; Dutch precedent, 25% to 50%. In the 1970s, most other EC countries did not have rules on group accounting or did not allow the equity method.

[17] ARB 51 requires complete elimination.

[18] We are grateful to Dieter Ordelheide for pointing out that one interpretation of the capital consolidation method was that the initial consolidation difference was not subsequently changed, but reserves were adjusted. This was called the '*modifizierte anglo-amerikanische Methode*' (see Busse von Colbe and Ordelheide, 1976, pp. 98 ff.).

[19] The illegality concerns the issue of shares at par, without the creation of a share premium account. This was suspected to be illegal, but was not clearly so until the 1980 tax case of Shearer v. Bercain.

Goodwill

Calculation

The precise calculation of goodwill is also an issue where the evolution can be followed. On this subject, the AktG referred only to individual accounts. Goodwill could not be recognised as a specific asset, but individual assets acquired when acquiring an enterprise could be held at inflated values:

> If . . . the consideration paid for the acquisition of an enterprise exceeds the values of the individual assets of the enterprise at the date of the acquisition, then the difference may be included in the captions of fixed and financial assets. The amount must be shown separately and amortised by depreciations of at least one fifth in each subsequent fiscal year. (AktG §153 (5); translation: Mueller and Galbraith, 1976.)

Such increased values would be taken through to group accounts. However, the prohibition on recognising goodwill as a separate asset was not removed for the group accounts. Consequently, where the parent had bought the shares of a company for more than the book value of its net assets, a consolidation difference was shown in the group balance sheet, as discussed earlier.

By contrast, Article 12 of the First Draft states that, up to a point, the consolidation difference at the date of acquisition must be allocated to the related asset and liability captions:

> Differences arising from compensation shall be entered directly against the relevant items in the group consolidated balance sheet. Any balance not so attributable shall be shown as a separate item with an appropriate heading.

One could read from this that 'fair values' of assets were generally to be the end result, with goodwill as the excess.

However, this mixture of the German feature of starting with book values and the Anglo-Saxon features of acquisition date and fair values was abandoned. Consequently, in Article 19(1) of the final Directive, there is an option between: (a) initial use of book values at the date of first consolidation followed by allocation to items whose 'value' is above or below their book values, and (b) initial use of (fair) 'values' of identifiable assets and liabilities at the date of acquisition.

Subsequent Treatment

Article 16 of the First Draft envisaged that any residual difference on consolidation should be posted to a special caption (goodwill) and written off over a period not exceeding five years. Although not specifically stated, depreciation through the profit and loss account is presumed to be the requirement. The amortisation period is the same as that for the revalued assets in §153(5) AktG, quoted above. The revised 1978 version of the draft is more flexible (see Appendix 2), and Article 30(1) of the final Directive provides for goodwill to be amortised over a period of up to five years or longer up to its useful economic life (as according to Article 37 of the Fourth Directive). In addition, Article 30(2) allows direct deduction from reserves. Each of these changes is a move away from the AktG.

Size exemptions

The AktG, which applied to AGs and KGaAs, did not contain exemptions from its rules based on size criteria. However, the *Publizitätsgesetz* of 1969 had applied many of the rules of the AktG to other types of company (principally GmbHs)[20] above certain size criteria.[21] This idea of exempting smaller companies from certain provisions was absorbed into the Fourth and Seventh Directives, based on the same type of criteria (i.e. balance sheet total, net turnover and average number of employees), though at much lower size levels.

In the Directives there are two such sets of thresholds[22] and therefore three size categories of company or group (small, medium and large). The Seventh Directive refers to the appropriate Articles in the Fourth Directive to establish the exact size criteria. The exemptions in the First Draft of the Seventh Directive are as follows:

Small groups: exempt from audit (Art. 23); abbreviated format for balance sheet publication (Art. 24).

Medium and small groups: abbreviated format for profit and loss account publication (Art. 11).

These are somewhat extended in the 1978 amended proposal (see Appendix 2). In the final Directive, none of the exemptions appears specifically. Instead, there is a member state option to exempt small and medium groups from the preparation (and, therefore, obviously from audit) of group accounts (Art. 6). This is a very broad exemption, of which *all* member states have taken some advantage (FEE, 1993). Clearly, the German idea of reducing burdens for smaller companies was retained in the Directive (and indeed has been exported to the UK).

---

[20]However, those GmbHs with AG or KGaA subsidiaries would already have been covered.

[21]See footnote 6.

[22]The two-of-three rule is kept. The size criteria in the 1974 draft are, for small companies: balance sheet total of Ecu 100,000; sales of Ecu 200,000; and 20 employees. For medium companies: Ecu 1m; Ecu 2m; and 100 employees. By the final Directive of 1978, the criteria for small companies are Ecu 1m; Ecu 2m; and 50 employees. For medium companies: Ecu 4m; Ecu 8m and 250 employees.

Conclusions

The Start Point and the Direction of Movement

It is clear from the analysis above that the German 1965 *Aktiengesetz* was an important model for the first published draft of the Seventh Directive. It is also clear that there are increasing differences from the AktG as one moves to the First Draft, then to the 1978 amended proposal, and then to the final Directive.

This prompts the question of whether a particular direction of movement can be discerned. In the period of evolution of the Directive (late 1960s to 1983), the countries in the EC with the most detailed rules on group accounting, apart from Germany, were the UK and Ireland.[23] The British Companies Act 1947 (consolidated as the 1948 Act) contained instructions to prepare group accounts and a number of detailed provisions. SSAP 1 of 1971 regulated accounting for associates; SSAP 14 of 1978 contained basic rules for the preparation of group accounts; ED 3 of 1971 and ED 31 of 1982 had dealt with acquisition accounting and merger accounting; and ED 30 of 1982 proposed rules on goodwill. All the while, very extensive 'generally accepted practice' was in operation.

The first three columns of Appendix 1 show, for 19 main features of the Directive, how most of the provisions gradually moved away from the AktG. It can be seen that, in the following 14 cases, the final Directive was closer to UK rules or practice (column 4 of Appendix 1) than to the AktG. Mostly, this results from substituting UK rules for German rules, but in a few cases by adding a UK option to German rules. In all these instances, the Directive led to changes to German law. The 14 cases (using the numbering of Appendix 1) are:

1. Definition of parent.
2. Legal form of parent company.
3. Groups with no parent company
6. Foreign subsidiaries included.
7. Dissimilar subsidiaries excluded.
8. Permitted exclusions.
10. True and fair view override.
11. Uniform policies required.
13. Merger accounting allowed.
14. Equity method required for associates.
15. Joint ventures to be equity accounted or proportionally consolidated.
16. Date of goodwill calculation.
17. Use of fair values.
18. Choice of goodwill treatment.

[23]Similar Irish laws followed the British Companies Act 1948. Standard-setting was carried out jointly for the UK and Ireland from 1970 to 1990 by the Accounting Standards Committee and its predecessor.

An International Coalition

The remarkably broad front over which the changes in the Directive took place, mainly from 1979, suggest a substantial coalition in the EC in favour of the Anglo-Saxon methods.[24] It was noted in the early part of this paper that in Stage I of the process (the *avant projet*) a similar change to professional consensus had occurred much earlier, by 1974. An explanation for this shift is proposed now.

In the 1970s, the countries with experience of group accounting for most groups over many decades were the UK, Ireland and the Netherlands.[25] Denmark had introduced consolidation requirements in 1973 (Christiansen, 1992). All these countries were heavily influenced by multinational companies, multinational accounting firms and US practice. France, through the efforts of the Commission des Opérations de Bourse (founded in 1967), was encouraging the development of consolidation in the 1970s and was also influenced by the practices of New York and London (Standish, 1991; Scheid and Walton, 1992). It is suggested that professional accountants from at least the five countries referred to in this paragraph were sufficiently persuasive by the time of the Groupe d'Etudes' memorandum of 1974 to overcome the earlier German-based consensus of the original six countries. Further clues to this move are that:

(i) For most EC countries, a typical professional representative on the Groupe d'Etudes and other similar bodies is a partner in a large accountancy firm, with strong Anglo-American influences.

(ii) German and other civil law country representatives were comparatively relaxed about changes away from the AktG in the field of consolidation because such changes have no effect on either taxation or distributable profit, which are the key issues in German accounting. Further, there was no long tradition to defend, since German consolidation practices dated only from after 1965 when the AktG came into force.

From 1974 onwards the coalition built further, as will be explained, so that by Stage III (governmental negotiations) it was very powerful. The International Accounting Standards Committee

[24]'Anglo-Saxon' is defined in footnote 3. 'Anglo-Saxon methods' refer here to the broad consensus that the fair view demands the production of consolidated accounts and that these should include foreign subsidiaries, equity accounted associates, fair valued assets of subsidiaries, etc.

[25]The UK and Ireland have already been discussed. Reference for extensive consolidation practice in the Netherlands includes Zeff et al. (1992).

containing four EC states[26] as permanent board members had, in 1976, issued its consolidation standard (IAS 3) which was consistent with UK practice. In its 1977 opinion[27] on the First Draft, the EC's Economic and Social Committee noted the publication of IAS 3 and encouraged the Commission to establish maximum conformity between international and European rules. The Italian governmental regulatory body for listed companies (CONSOB) had also called for the use of international accounting standards for group accounts in 1981. The Groupe d'Etudes had also issued several documents[28] in favour of the moves shown in Appendix 1. By contrast, Greece, Spain and Portugal, where consolidation was rare or non-existent in the 1970s, did not join the EC until 1980, 1986 and 1986, respectively. By the end of the 1970s, the scene was set for a major move towards UK group accounting.

Changes Stage by Stage

A suggested explanation for the change to professional consensus in Stage I has been given above. In Stage II, the Commission largely ignored this change and drafted a Directive clearly based on the AktG. Again, it has already been suggested that this is not surprising given the control by lawyers from a civil law tradition, who were basically supplementing the Fourth Directive, which had a clear German feel. Some changes were made in the second (1978) draft of the Directive; the major ones (those in Appendix 2, except for the first one) being consequential on the amendments agreed in the adopted version of the Fourth Directive of the same year. However, most of the major changes occur after 1978, once the Directive entered Stage III (negotiations in the Council of Ministers). Incidentally, the 1971 memorandum proposed eight Articles; the First Draft contained 21 Articles; the 1978 draft added eight further Articles;[29] and the adopted Directive contained 51 Articles. The increase after 1978 was largely due to extra options, exemptions and transitional provisions.

As suggested above, the international context of Stage III (the period from 1979 to 1983) would have supported a move from German to Anglo-Saxon consolidation techniques. Further, the German governmental negotiators would have been less concerned with changes required by the Seventh Directive than with the Fourth for the same reasons as suggested for professionals as in (ii) above: the lack of relevance of group accounts for the calculations of tax and distribution of profit, and the lack of a long tradition of group accounting in Germany. Indeed, the subsequent German implementation of the Seventh Directive chose to take several of the Directive's Anglo-Saxon options into law.[30] Incidentally, the final Council of Ministers negotiations were carried out in the first half of 1983 when Germany held the presidency of the Council.

By contrast, the prevailing UK opinion was that the really important financial statements were the group accounts. One continental European governmental negotiator has commented that generally the UK negotiators adopted 'a rather uncompromising manner as though no other text than that of the British Companies Act could ever qualify for inclusion in the Directive'.[31] It was also possible to use the conclusions of IAS 3 (agreed by a committee with a large EC presence, as noted earlier) as persuasive argument for change from the published drafts of the Directive.

Political Players

Three main players have been identified as being particularly associated with the three stages: respectively, professional accountants at the *avant projet* stage, Commission lawyers at the published draft stage, and governmental negotiators leading up to the adoption of the Directive. However, each group was involved in more than its own stage. For example: (i) it was the Commission that requested the initial professional memoranda and set their terms of reference; (ii) the profession commented on the published drafts in Stage II and on many private drafts in Stage III; (iii) certain members of the profession were involved in Stage III as governmental advisers or even delegates;[32] (iv) governmental pressures would have been brought to bear on the Commission at all stages; and (v) the Commission would have defended its ideas in Stage III.

The fundamental objectives of these main players may be as follows. The professional accountants would be keen to ensure that the Directive

[26]France, West Germany, Netherlands, UK-and-Ireland. The UK and Ireland were jointly represented on the board of the IASC by nominees of the Consultative Committee of Accountancy Bodies.

[27]*Official Journal* of the EC, C75/1977, p.6.

[28]See, for example, a remark on this in the Commission's Explanatory Memorandum preceding the 1978 amended proposal.

[29]The 1978 draft retained the numbering of 1976, so new Articles were inserted as '17A', etc.

[30]For example, the German 1985 *Bilanzrichtliniengesetz* changes German law by not requiring horizontal consolidation and by exempting groups not headed by a limited company. There are also options to use the Anglo-Saxon version of fair value accounting and to depart from the parent's valuation rules in the group accounts (see FEE, 1993).

[31]Peter Wessel, one of the Dutch negotiators on the Fourth and Seventh Directives, suggests this in a letter of 1 November 1993.

[32]For example, Paul Rutteman of Arthur Young (as it was then) extensively advised the UK governmental negotiators; and Peter Wessel of Moret Limperg was appointed as a temporary special governmental delegate.

would continue to allow their own preferred national practices, and they might have an evangelical wish to see such practices spread throughout Europe. The Commission staff aim for, and are largely judged on, the successful adoption of Directives and the subsequent co-ordination of laws. They will favour legalistic solutions and have little interest in economic conceptual frameworks. Governmental negotiators will be alert to policy considerations such as taxation and international competitiveness, though the former may be of little significance in this particular case. Governments will also respond to strong lobby groups, e.g. the accountancy profession in the UK or industrialists in Germany. These groups will be aiming to preserve the status quo, to maintain flexibility, to minimise costs, and so forth. One powerful example of the influence of corporate lobbyists is the inclusion of special Articles in the Seventh Directive that enable the unique consolidation practices of Unilever and Royal Dutch Shell to continue (Articles 12 and 15). Other lobbyists who might work through the Economic and Social Council, among other routes, would include unions and analysts who would be interested in better quality information and more disclosures.

In summary, what became the Seventh Directive was first drafted in the late 1960s by a committee chaired by a German (with no UK member). Throughout the whole period until 1983, the Commission employee responsible for the Directive was a German lawyer. The final Council of Ministers' negotiations in the first half of 1983 were conducted while Germany was presiding. Nevertheless, although the earliest memoranda and the First Draft were close to the AktG, the Directive itself was far removed; most of the change having occurred in the Council stage from 1979. This is connected with the building of a coalition of opinion in favour of change, which had formed in professional groups by 1974 and more generally by 1979. This paper has proposed a model of EC rule-making and has examined the evolution of the Seventh Directive in detail for the first time.

Appendix 1: Evolution of consolidation rules

AktG	First Draft	Seventh Directive	UK practice (before 1983)
Scope			
1. Definition of Parent: Uniform direction (§329), evidenced by controlling influence, control contract, complete integration, or (rebuttably) majority ownership of equity (§§16–18).	Uniform direction (Arts. 3 and 4). Controlling influence may be exercised (Art. 2(1)). Presumed where: Majority of voting rights (Art. 2(2)(a)). Right to appoint majority of board (Art. 2(2)(b)). Actual exercise of control (Art. 2(2)(c)).	Majority of votes (Art. 1(1)(a)), or right to appoint majority of board (Art. 1(1)(b)), or right to exercise dominant influence over board (Art. 1(1)(c)), OR* has exercised dominant influence over board (Art. 1(1)(d)(aa)), or control agreement (Art. 1(d)(bb)), OR* actual exercise of dominant influence (Art. 1(2)(a)), OR* uniform direction (Art. 1(2)(b)).	Majority of the equity (1948 Act, S. 154), or controls the composition of the board (1948 Act, S. 154), *but* exclusion if not controlled (SSAP 14, para. 21).
2. Groups with AGs and KGaAs as parents (§329). Also, groups containing such companies (EG AktG, §28), and other large groups (PublG).	Groups containing AGs, KGaAs, or GmbHs (Art. 6(1)(a)).	Parent undertaking is an AG, KGaA or GmbH OR* where group contains such a company (Art. 4(1) and (2)).	Parent is limited company (1948 Act, S. 150(1))

3. Uniform direction requires horizontal consolidation (§§18(2) and 329).	Unified management requires horizontal consolidation (Art. 4(1)).	Horizontal consolidation is a member state option (Art. 12).	No consolidation if no parent.
4. Sub-group consolidation only where ultimate parent does not produce group accounts per AktG (§330).	All limited company parents must produce group accounts even if consolidated themselves (Art. 6(2)(b)).†	Not required unless requested by shareholders (Art. 8) OR* in certain cases if ultimate parent is outside EC (Art. 11).	Not required if the company is a wholly owned subsidiary of another British company (1948 Act, S. 150(2)(a)).
5. Subsidiary undertakings (§330).	Subsidiary undertakings (Art. 2).	Subsidiary undertakings (Art. 1).	Subsidiary companies (1948 Act, S. 154).
6. Foreign subsidiaries could be excluded (§329).	Domestic and foreign subsidiaries to be consolidated (Art. 6(1)(b)).	Domestic and foreign subsidiaries to be consolidated (Art. 3(1)).	Domestic and foreign subsidiary companies to be consolidated (1948 Act, S. 150(1)).
7. Exclusion required if value of disclosures impaired (§329).	No exclusion.†	Exclusion required if subsidiaries are so different as to impair the true and fair view (Art. 14).	Exclusion required if subsidiaries are so dissimilar as to be misleading (SSAP 14, para. 21).
8. Exclusion permitted where immaterial (§329).	Exclusion permitted where immaterial (Art. 10).†	Exclusion permitted where immaterial, severe long-term restrictions, expense or delay, shares held for resale (Art. 13).	Exclusion permitted where impractical, immaterial, expense or delay, misleading or harmful, very different (1948 Act, S. 150(2)(b). Exclusion required where so dissimilar to be misleading, not controlled, severe restrictions, temporary control (SSAP 14, para. 21).
Preparation of consolidated accounts			
9. Same date for group companies, or special accounts to group date (§331(3)).	Same date for group companies, or special accounts to group date *and* audit (Art. 14(1)(e)).	Same date for group companies OR* date within 3 months prior to group date, or interim accounts (Art. 27(3)).	Same date unless good reasons then make adjustments and disclose (1948 Act, S. 153(1)).
Accounting values/policies			
10. Proper principles. As sure a view as possible according to the valuation rules (§149).	True and fair view (Art. 9(2)).†	True and fair view overrides (Art. 16).	True and fair view overrides (1948 Act, S. 149).

(*continued on next page*)

11. Same values as in single entity accounts, but not uniform policies (§331(1)).	Same values as in single entity accounts and uniform policies (Art. 15).	Uniform policies, therefore revaluations where necessary (Art. 29).	Uniform policies (therefore adjustment where necessary) or, in exceptional cases, disclosure and numerical reconciliation (SSAP 14 para. 16).
12. Elimination of 100% of intra-group profit (§331(2)).	As AktG (Art. 14).	As Draft, OR* elimination of only group's share (Art. 26).	No rule, but general practice to eliminate fully.
Consolidation methods			
13. Full consolidation (§331).	Acquisition method (Art. 12).	Acquisition method (Art. 19) OR* merger accounting (Art. 20).	Acquisition method or merger accounting (general practice, e.g. ED 31).
14. Associates at cost (§153).	Equity method (Art. 17).	Equity method (Art. 33).	Equity method (SSAP 1).
15. Joint ventures at cost (§153).	Equity method OR* proportional consolidation (Art. 18).	As Draft (Art. 32).	Equity method or proportional consolidation (SSAP 1, para. 10).
Goodwill			
16. Difference on consolidation calculated each year (§331).	Goodwill calculated at time of acquisition (Art. 12).	Goodwill calculated at time of first consolidation or at acquisition (Art. 19).	Goodwill calculated at acquisition (general practice, e.g. ED 30).
17. Difference calculated using book values (§331(1)).	Goodwill calculated using book values then allocated to individual net assets as far as possible (Art. 12).	Goodwill calculated starting with book values at first consolidation OR* using fair values at acquisition. (Art. 19).	Goodwill calculated using fair values (general practice, e.g. ED 30).
18. Difference not amortised.	Goodwill amortised over up to 5 years (Art. 16.).†	Goodwill amortised against profit over up to 5 years or longer, OR* immediately written off against reserves (Art. 30).	Goodwill immediately written off against reserves or amortised over useful life (general practice; e.g. ED 30).
Size exemptions			
19. AktG extended by Publizitätsgesetz but only to large undertakings.	Size exemptions for audit and formats (Arts. 11, 23, 24).†	Size exemptions a member state option for the preparation of group accounts (Art. 6).	No size exemptions.

*OR denotes a member state option.
†A change from the 1976 position first appears in the 1978 version.

Appendix 2

Important Changes in the 1978 Amended Proposal for the Seventh Directive (same Article numbers as 1976 Draft)

Art. 6(2). Sub-group consolidated accounts may be dispensed with provided a parent at a higher level has produced consolidated accounts in conformity with the Seventh Directive. Any minority shareholders must approve.

Art. 9(4 and 5). Where application of the rules would not lead to a true and fair view, additional information must be provided or, in exceptional cases, the rules must be departed from.

Art. 16. Member states may authorise a write-off period for goodwill on acquisition of greater length than the five years of the First Draft, provided the expected useful life of this asset is not exceeded.

Art. 24. Small groups to be exempted from publishing a profit and loss account and directors' report. Medium groups can publish an abbreviated balance sheet and notes.

References

Beeny, J. H. (1975), *European Financial Reporting—Germany* (London: ICAEW).

Busse von Colbe, W. and Ordelheide, D. (1976), *Konzernabschlüsse*, 2nd ed. (Wiesbaden: Gabler).

Christiansen, M. (1992), 'Denmark' in Alexander, D. and Archer, S., *The European Accounting Guide* (London: Academic Press).

Dahl, R. A. (1961), *Who Governs? Democracy and Power in an American City* (Yale University Press).

FEE (1993), *Seventh Directive Options and their Implementation* (London: Routledge).

Hope, T. and Briggs J. (1982), 'Accounting Policy Making—Some Lessons from the Deferred Taxation Debate', *Accounting and Business Research*, Spring.

Hope, T. and Gray, R. (1982), 'Power and Policy Making: The Development of an R & D Standard', *Journal of Business Finance and Accounting*, Winter.

Laughlin, R. C. and Puxty, A. G. (1983), 'Accounting Regulation: An Alternative Perspective', *Journal of Business Finance and Accounting*, Autumn.

Lukes, S. (1974), *Power: A Radical View* (Macmillan).

Macharzina, K. and Langer, K. (1991), 'Financial Reporting in Germany', Ch. 9 in Nobes, C. W. and Parker, R. H., *Comparative International Accounting* (Hemel Hempstead: Prentice Hall).

Mueller, R. and Galbraith, E. G. (1976), *The German Stock Corporation Law* (Frankfurt: Knapp).

Mumford, M. (1979), 'The End of a Familiar Inflation Accounting Cycle', *Accounting and Business Research*, Spring.

Nair, R. D. and Frank, W. G. (1980), 'The Impact of Disclosure and Measurement Practices on International Accounting Classifications', *Accounting Review*, July.

Nobes, C. W. (1983), 'The Origins of the Accounting Provisions of the 1980 and 1981 Companies Acts', *Accounting and Business Research*, Winter.

Nobes, C. W. (1992), 'A Political History of Goodwill in the UK: An Ilustration of Cyclical Standard Setting', *Abacus*, Vol. 28, No. 2.

Nobes, C. W. (1993), 'The True and Fair View: Impact on and of the Fourth Directive', *Accounting and Business Research*, Winter.

Polsby, N. W. (1963), *Community Power and Politcal Theory* (New Haven: Yale University Press).

Scheid, J.-C. and Walton, P. (1992), 'France' in Alexander, D. and Archer S., *The European Accounting Guide* (London: Academic Press).

Standish, P. E. M. (1991), 'Financial Reporting in France' in Nobes, C. W. and Parker, R. H., *Comparative International Accounting* (Hemel Hempstead: Prentice Hall).

Vangermeersch, R. (1985), 'The Route of the Seventh Directive of the EEC on Consolidated Accounts—Slow, Steady, Studied and Successful', *International Journal of Accounting*, Spring.

Wallace, R. S. O. (1990), 'Survival Strategies of a Global Organization: The Case of the International Accounting Standards Committee', *Accounting Horizons*, June.

Watts, R. and Zimmerman, J. (1978), 'Towards a Positive Theory of the Determination of Accounting Standards', *Accounting Review*, January.

Zeff, S. A., van der Wel, F. and Camfferman, K. (1992), *Company Financial Reporting* (Amsterdam: North Holland), Ch. 2.

Part IV
Official Material

[24]

Preface to Statements of International Accounting Standards

This Preface is issued to set out the objectives and operating procedures of the International Accounting Standards Committee (IASC) and to explain the scope and authority of the Statements of International Accounting Standards. The Preface was approved in November 1982 for publication in January 1983 and supersedes the Preface published in January 1975 (amended March 1978). The approved text of this Preface is that published by the International Accounting Standards Committee in the English language.

1. The International Accounting Standards Committee (IASC) came into existence on 29 June 1973 as a result of an agreement by accountancy bodies in Australia, Canada, France, Germany, Japan, Mexico, the Netherlands, the United Kingdom and Ireland, and the United States of America. A revised Agreement and Constitution were signed in November 1982. The business of IASC is conducted by a Board comprising representatives of up to thirteen countries and up to four organisations having an interest in financial reporting.

The Objectives

2. The objectives of IASC as set out in its Constitution are:

'(a) to formulate and publish in the public interest accounting standards to be observed in the presentation of financial statements and to promote their worldwide acceptance and observance, and

(b) to work generally for the improvement and harmonisation of regulations, accounting standards and procedures relating to the presentation of financial statements.'

3. The relationship between IASC and the International Federation of Accountants (IFAC) is confirmed by the Mutual Commitments into which they have entered. The membership of IASC (which is the same as that of IFAC) acknowledges in the revised Agreement that IASC has full and complete autonomy in the setting and issue of International Accounting Standards.

4. The members agree to support the objectives of IASC by undertaking the following obligations:

'to support the work of IASC by publishing in their respective countries every International Accounting Standard approved for issue by the Board of IASC and by using their best endeavours:

(i) to ensure that published financial statements comply with International Accounting Standards in all material respects and disclose the fact of such compliance;

(ii) to persuade governments and standard-setting bodies that published financial statements should comply with International Accounting Standards in all material respects;

(iii) to persuade authorities controlling securities markets and the industrial and business community that published financial statements should comply with International Accounting Standards in all material respects and disclose the fact of such compliance;

(iv) to ensure that the auditors satisfy themselves that the financial statements comply with International Accounting Standards in all material respects;

(v) to foster acceptance and observance of International Accounting Standards internationally.'

Published Financial Statements

5. The term 'financial statements' used in paragraphs 2 and 4 covers balance sheets, income statements or profit and loss accounts, statements of changes in financial position, notes and other statements and explanatory material which are identified as being part of the financial statements. Usually, financial statements are made available or published once each year and are the subject of a report by an auditor. International Accounting Standards apply to such financial statements of any commercial, industrial, or business enterprise.

6. The management of such an enterprise may prepare financial statements for its own use in a number of different ways best suited for internal management purposes. When financial statements are issued to other persons, such as shareholders, creditors, employees, and the public at large, they should conform to International Accounting Standards.

7. The responsibility for the preparation of financial statements and for adequate disclosure is that of the management of the enterprise. The auditor's responsibility is to form his opinion and to report on the financial statements.

Accounting Standards

8. Within each country, local regulations govern, to a greater or lesser degree, the issue of financial statements. Such local regulations include accounting standards which are promulgated by the regulatory bodies and/or the professional accountancy bodies in the countries concerned.

9. Prior to the formation of IASC there were frequently differences of form and content between the published accounting standards of most countries. IASC takes cognisance of exposure drafts, or of accounting standards already issued on each subject, and in the light of such knowledge produces an International Accounting Standard for worldwide acceptance. One of the objects of IASC is to harmonise as far as possible the diverse accounting standards and accounting policies of different countries.

10. In carrying out this task of adaptation of existing standards, and in formulating International Accounting Standards on new subjects, IASC concentrates on essentials. It therefore endeavours not to make the International Accounting Standards so complex that they cannot be applied effectively on a worldwide basis. International Accounting Standards issued by IASC are constantly reviewed to take into account the current position and the need for updating.

11. International Accounting Standards promulgated by IASC do not override the local regulations, referred to in paragraph 8 above, governing the issue of financial statements in a particular country. The obligations undertaken by the members of IASC, as explained in this Preface, provide that where International Accounting Standards are complied with in all material respects, this fact should be disclosed. Where local regulations require deviation from International Accounting Standards, the local members of IASC endeavour to persuade the relevant authorities of the benefits of harmonisation with International Accounting Standards.

The Scope of the Standards

12. Any limitation of the applicability of specific International Accounting Standards is made clear in the statements of those standards. International Accounting Standards are not intended to apply to immaterial items. An International Accounting Standard applies from a date specified in the standard and unless indicated to the contrary is not retroactive.

Working Procedure – Exposure Drafts and Standards

13. The agreed working procedure is to select certain subjects for detailed study by Steering Committees. As a result of this work an exposure draft is

prepared on a particular subject for consideration by the Board. If approved by at least two-thirds of the Board, the exposure draft is addressed to accountancy bodies and to governments, securities markets, regulatory and other agencies and other interested parties. Adequate time is allowed for consideration and comment on each exposure draft.

14. Since the formation of the Consultative Group in 1981, their views are taken into account at each major decision-making stage.

15. The comments and suggestions received as a result of this exposure are then examined by the Board and the exposure draft is revised as necessary. Provided that the revised draft is approved by at least three-quarters of the Board, it is issued as an International Accounting Standard and becomes operative from a date stated in the standard.

16. At some stage in the above process, the IASC Board may decide that, in order to promote discussion of a topic, or to allow adequate time for points of view to be put forward, a discussion paper should be issued. A discussion paper requires approval by a simple majority of the Board.

Voting

17. For the purpose of voting referred to in paragraphs 13 to 16 above, each country and each organisation represented on the Board has one vote.

Language

18. The approved text of any exposure draft or standard is that published by IASC in the English language. Members are responsible, under the authority of the Board, for preparing translations of exposure drafts and standards so that, where appropriate, such translations may be issued in the languages of their own countries. These translations indicate the name of the accountancy body that prepared the translation and that it is a translation of the approved text.

The Authority attaching to the Standards

19. Standing alone, neither the IASC nor the accountancy profession has the power to enforce international agreement or to require compliance with International Accounting Standards. The success of IASC's efforts is dependent upon the recognition and support for its work from many different interested groups acting within the limits of their own jurisdiction. In most countries of the world, the accounting profession has a prestige and standing which is of great significance in these efforts.

Conclusion

20. The members of IASC believe that the adoption in their countries of International Accounting Standards together with disclosure of compliance will over the years have a significant impact. The quality of financial statements will be improved and there will be an increasing degree of comparability. The credibility and consequently the usefulness of financial statements will be enhanced throughout the world.

Introduction

Purpose and Status

1. This framework sets out the concepts that underlie the preparation and presentation of financial statements for external users. The purpose of the framework is to:

(a) assist the Board of IASC in the development of future International Accounting Standards and in its review of existing International Accounting Standards;

(b) assist the Board of IASC in promoting harmonisation of regulations, accounting standards and procedures relating to the presentation of financial statements by providing a basis for reducing the number of alternative accounting treatments permitted by International Accounting Standards;

(c) assist national standard-setting bodies in developing national standards;

(d) assist preparers of financial statements in applying International Accounting Standards and in dealing with topics that have yet to form the subject of an International Accounting Standard;

(e) assist auditors in forming an opinion as to whether financial statements conform with International Accounting Standards;

(f) assist users of financial statements in interpreting the information contained in financial statements prepared in conformity with International Accounting Standards; and

(g) provide those who are interested in the work of IASC with information about its approach to the formulation of International Accounting Standards.

2. This framework is not an International Accounting Standard and hence does not define standards for any particular measurement or disclosure issue. Nothing in this framework overrides any specific International Accounting Standard.

3. The Board of IASC recognises that in a limited number of cases there may be a conflict between the framework and an International

Accounting Standard. In those cases where there is a conflict, the requirements of the International Accounting Standard prevail over those of the framework. As, however, the Board of IASC will be guided by the framework in the development of future Standards and in its review of existing Standards, the number of cases of conflict between the framework and International Accounting Standards will diminish through time.

4. The framework will be revised from time to time on the basis of the Board's experience of working with it.

Scope

5. The framework deals with:

(a) the objective of financial statements;

(b) the qualitative characteristics that determine the usefulness of information in financial statements;

(c) the definition, recognition and measurement of the elements from which financial statements are constructed; and

(d) concepts of capital and capital maintenance.

6. The framework is concerned with general purpose financial statements (hereafter referred to as "financial statements") including consolidated financial statements. Such financial statements are prepared and presented at least annually and are directed toward the common information needs of a wide range of users. Some of these users may require, and have the power to obtain, information in addition to that contained in the financial statements. Many users, however, have to rely on the financial statements as their major source of financial information and such financial statements should, therefore, be prepared and presented with their needs in view. Special purpose financial reports, for example, prospectuses and computations prepared for taxation purposes, are outside the scope of this framework. Nevertheless, the framework may be applied in the preparation of such special purpose reports where their requirements permit.

7. Financial statements form part of the process of financial reporting. A complete set of financial statements normally includes a balance sheet, an income statement, a statement of changes in financial position (which may be presented in a variety of ways, for example, as a statement of cash flows or a statement of funds flow), and those notes and other statements and explanatory material that are an integral part of the financial statements. They may also include supplementary schedules and information based on or derived from, and expected to be read with, such statements. Such

schedules and supplementary information may deal, for example, with financial information about industrial and geographical segments and disclosures about the effects of changing prices. Financial statements do not, however, include such items as reports by directors, statements by the chairman, discussion and analysis by management and similar items that may be included in a financial or annual report.

8. The framework applies to the financial statements of all commercial, industrial and business reporting enterprises, whether in the public or the private sectors. A reporting enterprise is an enterprise for which there are users who rely on the financial statements as their major source of financial information about the enterprise.

Users and Their Information Needs

9. The users of financial statements include present and potential investors, employees, lenders, suppliers and other trade creditors, customers, governments and their agencies and the public. They use financial statements in order to satisfy some of their different needs for information. These needs include the following:

(a) *Investors*. The providers of risk capital and their advisers are concerned with the risk inherent in, and return provided by, their investments. They need information to help them determine whether they should buy, hold or sell. Shareholders are also interested in information which enables them to assess the ability of the enterprise to pay dividends.

(b) *Employees*. Employees and their representative groups are interested in information about the stability and profitability of their employers. They are also interested in information which enables them to assess the ability of the enterprise to provide remuneration, retirement benefits and employment opportunities.

(c) *Lenders*. Lenders are interested in information that enables them to determine whether their loans, and the interest attaching to them, will be paid when due.

(d) *Suppliers and other trade creditors*. Suppliers and other creditors are interested in information that enables them to determine whether amounts owing to them will be paid when due. Trade creditors are likely to be interested in an enterprise over a shorter period than lenders unless they are dependent upon the continuation of the enterprise as a major customer.

(e) *Customers*. Customers have an interest in information about the continuance of an enterprise, especially when they have a long-term involvement with, or are dependent on, the enterprise.

(f) *Governments and their agencies*. Governments and their agencies are interested in the allocation of resources and, therefore, the activities of enterprises. They also require information in order to regulate the activities of enterprises, determine taxation policies and as the basis for national income and similar statistics.

(g) *Public*. Enterprises affect members of the public in a variety of ways. For example, enterprises may make a substantial contribution to the local economy in many ways including the number of people they employ and their patronage of local suppliers. Financial statements may assist the public by providing information about the trends and recent developments in the prosperity of the enterprise and the range of its activities.

10. While all of the information needs of these users cannot be met by financial statements, there are needs which are common to all users. As investors are providers of risk capital to the enterprise, the provision of financial statements that meet their needs will also meet most of the needs of other users that financial statements can satisfy.

11. The management of an enterprise has the primary responsibility for the preparation and presentation of the financial statements of the enterprise. Management is also interested in the information contained in the financial statements even though it has access to additional management and financial information that helps it carry out its planning, decision-making and control responsibilities. Management has the ability to determine the form and content of such additional information in order to meet its own needs. The reporting of such information, however, is beyond the scope of this framework. Nevertheless, published financial statements are based on the information used by management about the financial position, performance and changes in financial position of the enterprise.

Framework

The Objective of Financial Statements

12. The objective of financial statements is to provide information about the financial position, performance and changes in financial position of an enterprise that is useful to a wide range of users in making economic decisions.

13. Financial statements prepared for this purpose meet the common needs of most users. However, financial statements do not provide all the information that users may need to make economic decisions since they largely portray the financial effects of past events and do not necessarily provide non-financial information.

14. Financial statements also show the results of the stewardship of management, or the accountability of management for the resources entrusted to it. Those users who wish to assess the stewardship or accountability of management do so in order that they may make economic decisions; these decisions may include, for example, whether to hold or sell their investment in the enterprise or whether to reappoint or replace the management.

Financial Position, Performance and Changes in Financial Position

15. The economic decisions that are taken by users of financial statements require an evaluation of the ability of an enterprise to generate cash and cash equivalents and of the timing and certainty of their generation. This ability ultimately determines, for example, the capacity of an enterprise to pay its employees and suppliers, meet interest payments, repay loans and make distributions to its owners. Users are better able to evaluate this ability to generate cash and cash equivalents if they are provided with information that focuses on the financial position, performance and changes in financial position of an enterprise.

16. The financial position of an enterprise is affected by the economic resources it controls, its financial structure, its liquidity and solvency, and its capacity to adapt to changes in the environment in which it operates. Information about the economic resources controlled by the enterprise and its capacity in the past to modify these resources is useful in predicting the ability of the enterprise to generate cash and cash equivalents in the future. Information about financial structure is useful in predicting future borrowing needs and how future profits and cash flows will be distributed among those with an interest in the enterprise; it is also useful in predicting

how successful the enterprise is likely to be in raising further finance. Information about liquidity and solvency is useful in predicting the ability of the enterprise to meet its financial commitments as they fall due. Liquidity refers to the availability of cash in the near future after taking account of financial commitments over this period. Solvency refers to the availability of cash over the longer term to meet financial commitments as they fall due.

17. Information about the performance of an enterprise, in particular its profitability, is required in order to assess potential changes in the economic resources that it is likely to control in the future. Information about variability of performance is important in this respect. Information about performance is useful in predicting the capacity of the enterprise to generate cash flows from its existing resource base. It is also useful in forming judgements about the effectiveness with which the enterprise might employ additional resources.

18. Information concerning changes in the financial position of an enterprise is useful in order to assess its investing, financing and operating activities during the reporting period. This information is useful in providing the user with a basis to assess the ability of the enterprise to generate cash and cash equivalents and the needs of the enterprise to utilise those cash flows. In constructing a statement of changes in financial position, funds can be defined in various ways, such as all financial resources, working capital, liquid assets or cash. No attempt is made in this framework to specify a definition of funds.

19. Information about financial position is primarily provided in a balance sheet. Information about performance is primarily provided in an income statement. Information about changes in financial position is provided in the financial statements by means of a separate statement.

20. The component parts of the financial statements interrelate because they reflect different aspects of the same transactions or other events. Although each statement provides information that is different from the others, none is likely to serve only a single purpose or provide all the information necessary for particular needs of users. For example, an income statement provides an incomplete picture of performance unless it is used in conjunction with the balance sheet and the statement of changes in financial position.

Notes and Supplementary Schedules

21. The financial statements also contain notes and supplementary schedules and other information. For example, they may contain additional information that is relevant to the needs of users about the items in the balance sheet and income statement. They may include disclosures about

Framework

the risks and uncertainties affecting the enterprise and any resources and obligations not recognised in the balance sheet (such as mineral reserves). Information about geographical and industry segments and the effect on the enterprise of changing prices may also be provided in the form of supplementary information.

Underlying Assumptions

Accrual Basis

22. In order to meet their objectives, financial statements are prepared on the accrual basis of accounting. Under this basis, the effects of transactions and other events are recognised when they occur (and not as cash or its equivalent is received or paid) and they are recorded in the accounting records and reported in the financial statements of the periods to which they relate. Financial statements prepared on the accrual basis inform users not only of past transactions involving the payment and receipt of cash but also of obligations to pay cash in the future and of resources that represent cash to be received in the future. Hence, they provide the type of information about past transactions and other events that is most useful to users in making economic decisions.

Going Concern

23. The financial statements are normally prepared on the assumption that an enterprise is a going concern and will continue in operation for the foreseeable future. Hence, it is assumed that the enterprise has neither the intention nor the need to liquidate or curtail materially the scale of its operations; if such an intention or need exists, the financial statements may have to be prepared on a different basis and, if so, the basis used is disclosed.

Framework

Qualitative Characteristics of Financial Statements

24. Qualitative characteristics are the attributes that make the information provided in financial statements useful to users. The four principal qualitative characteristics are understandability, relevance, reliability and comparability.

Understandability

25. An essential quality of the information provided in financial statements is that it is readily understandable by users. For this purpose, users are assumed to have a reasonable knowledge of business and economic activities and accounting and a willingness to study the information with reasonable diligence. However, information about complex matters that should be included in the financial statements because of its relevance to the economic decision-making needs of users should not be excluded merely on the grounds that it may be too difficult for certain users to understand.

Relevance

26. To be useful, information must be relevant to the decision-making needs of users. Information has the quality of relevance when it influences the economic decisions of users by helping them evaluate past, present or future events or confirming, or correcting, their past evaluations.

27. The predictive and confirmatory roles of information are interrelated. For example, information about the current level and structure of asset holdings has value to users when they endeavour to predict the ability of the enterprise to take advantage of opportunities and its ability to react to adverse situations. The same information plays a confirmatory role in respect of past predictions about, for example, the way in which the enterprise would be structured or the outcome of planned operations.

28. Information about financial position and past performance is frequently used as the basis for predicting future financial position and performance and other matters in which users are directly interested, such as dividend and wage payments, security price movements and the ability of the enterprise to meet its commitments as they fall due. To have predictive value, information need not be in the form of an explicit forecast. The ability to make predictions from financial statements is enhanced, however, by the manner in which information on past transactions and events is displayed. For example, the predictive value of the income statement is enhanced if

unusual, abnormal and infrequent items of income or expense are separately disclosed.

Materiality

29. The relevance of information is affected by its nature and materiality. In some cases, the nature of information alone is sufficient to determine its relevance. For example, the reporting of a new segment may affect the assessment of the risks and opportunities facing the enterprise irrespective of the materiality of the results achieved by the new segment in the reporting period. In other cases, both the nature and materiality are important, for example, the amounts of inventories held in each of the main categories that are appropriate to the business.

30. Information is material if its omission or misstatement could influence the economic decisions of users taken on the basis of the financial statements. Materiality depends on the size of the item or error judged in the particular circumstances of its omission or misstatement. Thus, materiality provides a threshold or cut-off point rather than being a primary qualitative characteristic which information must have if it is to be useful.

Reliability

31. To be useful, information must also be reliable. Information has the quality of reliability when it is free from material error and bias and can be depended upon by users to represent faithfully that which it either purports to represent or could reasonably be expected to represent.

32. Information may be relevant but so unreliable in nature or representation that its recognition may be potentially misleading. For example, if the validity and amount of a claim for damages under a legal action are disputed, it may be inappropriate for the enterprise to recognise the full amount of the claim in the balance sheet, although it may be appropriate to disclose the amount and circumstances of the claim.

Faithful Representation

33. To be reliable, information must represent faithfully the transactions and other events it either purports to represent or could reasonably be expected to represent. Thus, for example, a balance sheet should represent faithfully the transactions and other events that result in assets, liabilities and equity of the enterprise at the reporting date which meet the recognition criteria.

34. Most financial information is subject to some risk of being less than a faithful representation of that which it purports to portray. This is not due to bias, but rather to inherent difficulties either in identifying the

transactions and other events to be measured or in devising and applying measurement and presentation techniques that can convey messages that correspond with those transactions and events. In certain cases, the measurement of the financial effects of items could be so uncertain that enterprises generally would not recognise them in the financial statements; for example, although most enterprises generate goodwill internally over time, it is usually difficult to identify or measure that goodwill reliably. In other cases, however, it may be relevant to recognise items and to disclose the risk of error surrounding their recognition and measurement.

Substance Over Form

35. If information is to represent faithfully the transactions and other events that it purports to represent, it is necessary that they are accounted for and presented in accordance with their substance and economic reality and not merely their legal form. The substance of transactions or other events is not always consistent with that which is apparent from their legal or contrived form. For example, an enterprise may dispose of an asset to another party in such a way that the documentation purports to pass legal ownership to that party; nevertheless, agreements may exist that ensure that the enterprise continues to enjoy the future economic benefits embodied in the asset. In such circumstances, the reporting of a sale would not represent faithfully the transaction entered into (if indeed there was a transaction).

Neutrality

36. To be reliable, the information contained in financial statements must be neutral, that is, free from bias. Financial statements are not neutral if, by the selection or presentation of information, they influence the making of a decision or judgement in order to achieve a predetermined result or outcome.

Prudence

37. The preparers of financial statements do, however, have to contend with the uncertainties that inevitably surround many events and circumstances, such as the collectability of doubtful receivables, the probable useful life of plant and equipment and the number of warranty claims that may occur. Such uncertainties are recognised by the disclosure of their nature and extent and by the exercise of prudence in the preparation of the financial statements. Prudence is the inclusion of a degree of caution in the exercise of the judgements needed in making the estimates required under conditions of uncertainty, such that assets or income are not overstated and liabilities or expenses are not understated. However, the exercise of prudence does not allow, for example, the creation of hidden reserves or excessive provisions, the deliberate understatement of assets or income, or the deliberate overstatement of liabilities or expenses, because

the financial statements would not be neutral and, therefore, not have the quality of reliability.

Completeness

38. To be reliable, the information in financial statements must be complete within the bounds of materiality and cost. An omission can cause information to be false or misleading and thus unreliable and deficient in terms of its relevance.

Comparability

39. Users must be able to compare the financial statements of an enterprise through time in order to identify trends in its financial position and performance. Users must also be able to compare the financial statements of different enterprises in order to evaluate their relative financial position, performance and changes in financial position. Hence, the measurement and display of the financial effect of like transactions and other events must be carried out in a consistent way throughout an enterprise and over time for that enterprise and in a consistent way for different enterprises.

40. An important implication of the qualitative characteristic of comparability is that users be informed of the accounting policies employed in the preparation of the financial statements, any changes in those policies and the effects of such changes. Users need to be able to identify differences between the accounting policies for like transactions and other events used by the same enterprise from period to period and by different enterprises. Compliance with International Accounting Standards, including the disclosure of the accounting policies used by the enterprise, helps to achieve comparability.

41. The need for comparability should not be confused with mere uniformity and should not be allowed to become an impediment to the introduction of improved accounting standards. It is not appropriate for an enterprise to continue accounting in the same manner for a transaction or other event if the policy adopted is not in keeping with the qualitative characteristics of relevance and reliability. It is also inappropriate for an enterprise to leave its accounting policies unchanged when more relevant and reliable alternatives exist.

42. Because users wish to compare the financial position, performance and changes in financial position of an enterprise over time, it is important that the financial statements show corresponding information for the preceding periods.

Constraints on Relevant and Reliable Information

Timeliness

43. If there is undue delay in the reporting of information it may lose its relevance. Management may need to balance the relative merits of timely reporting and the provision of reliable information. To provide information on a timely basis it may often be necessary to report before all aspects of a transaction or other event are known, thus impairing reliability. Conversely, if reporting is delayed until all aspects are known, the information may be highly reliable but of little use to users who have had to make decisions in the interim. In achieving a balance between relevance and reliability, the overriding consideration is how best to satisfy the economic decision-making needs of users.

Balance between Benefit and Cost

44. The balance between benefit and cost is a pervasive constraint rather than a qualitative characteristic. The benefits derived from information should exceed the cost of providing it. The evaluation of benefits and costs is, however, substantially a judgmental process. Furthermore, the costs do not necessarily fall on those users who enjoy the benefits. Benefits may also be enjoyed by users other than those for whom the information is prepared; for example, the provision of further information to lenders may reduce the borrowing costs of an enterprise. For these reasons, it is difficult to apply a cost-benefit test in any particular case. Nevertheless, standard-setters in particular, as well as the preparers and users of financial statements, should be aware of this constraint.

Balance between Qualitative Characteristics

45. In practice a balancing, or trade-off, between qualitative characteristics is often necessary. Generally the aim is to achieve an appropriate balance among the characteristics in order to meet the objective of financial statements. The relative importance of the characteristics in different cases is a matter of professional judgment.

True and Fair View/Fair Presentation

46. Financial statements are frequently described as showing a true and fair view of, or as presenting fairly, the financial position, performance and changes in financial position of an enterprise. Although this framework does not deal directly with such concepts, the application of the principal qualitative characteristics and of appropriate accounting standards normally results in financial statements that convey what is generally understood as a true and fair view of, or as presenting fairly such information.

The Elements of Financial Statements

47. Financial statements portray the financial effects of transactions and other events by grouping them into broad classes according to their economic characteristics. These broad classes are termed the elements of financial statements. The elements directly related to the measurement of financial position in the balance sheet are assets, liabilities and equity. The elements directly related to the measurement of performance in the income statement are income and expenses. The statement of changes in financial position usually reflects income statement elements and changes in balance sheet elements; accordingly, this framework identifies no elements that are unique to this statement.

48. The presentation of these elements in the balance sheet and the income statement involves a process of sub-classification. For example, assets and liabilities may be classified by their nature or function in the business of the enterprise in order to display information in the manner most useful to users for purposes of making economic decisions.

Financial Position

49. The elements directly related to the measurement of financial position are assets, liabilities and equity. These are defined as follows:

(a) An *asset* is a resource controlled by the enterprise as a result of past events and from which future economic benefits are expected to flow to the enterprise.

(b) A *liability* is a present obligation of the enterprise arising from past events, the settlement of which is expected to result in an outflow from the enterprise of resources embodying economic benefits.

(c) *Equity* is the residual interest in the assets of the enterprise after deducting all its liabilities.

50. The definitions of an asset and a liability identify their essential features but do not attempt to specify the criteria that need to be met before they are recognised in the balance sheet. Thus, the definitions embrace items that are not recognised as assets or liabilities in the balance sheet because they do not satisfy the criteria for recognition discussed in paragraphs 82 to 98. In particular, the expectation that future economic benefits will flow to or from an enterprise must be sufficiently certain to meet

the probability criterion in paragraph 83 before an asset or liability is recognised.

51. In assessing whether an item meets the definition of an asset, liability or equity, attention needs to be given to its underlying substance and economic reality and not merely its legal form. Thus, for example, in the case of finance leases, the substance and economic reality are that the lessee acquires the economic benefits of the use of the leased asset for the major part of its useful life in return for entering into an obligation to pay for that right an amount approximating to the fair value of the asset and the related finance charge. Hence, the finance lease gives rise to items that satisfy the definition of an asset and a liability and are recognised as such in the lessee's balance sheet.

52. Balance sheets drawn up in accordance with current International Accounting Standards may include items that do not satisfy the definitions of an asset or liability and are not shown as part of equity. The definitions set out in paragraph 48 will, however, underlie future reviews of existing International Accounting Standards and the formulation of further Standards.

Assets

53. The future economic benefit embodied in an asset is the potential to contribute, directly or indirectly, to the flow of cash and cash equivalents to the enterprise. The potential may be a productive one that is part of the operating activities of the enterprise. It may also take the form of convertibility into cash or cash equivalents or a capability to reduce cash outflows, such as when an alternative manufacturing process lowers the costs of production.

54. An enterprise usually employs its assets to produce goods or services capable of satisfying the wants or needs of customers; because these goods or services can satisfy these wants or needs, customers are prepared to pay for them and hence contribute to the cash flow of the enterprise. Cash itself renders a service to the enterprise because of its command over other resources.

55. The future economic benefits embodied in an asset may flow to the enterprise in a number of ways. For example, an asset may be:

(a) used singly or in combination with other assets in the production of goods or services to be sold by the enterprise;

(b) exchanged for other assets;

(c) used to settle a liability; or

(d) distributed to the owners of the enterprise.

56. Many assets, for example, property, plant and equipment, have a physical form. However, physical form is not essential to the existence of an asset; hence patents and copyrights, for example, are assets if future economic benefits are expected to flow from them to the enterprise and if they are controlled by the enterprise.

57. Many assets, for example, receivables and property, are associated with legal rights, including the right of ownership. In determining the existence of an asset, the right of ownership is not essential; thus, for example, property held on a lease is an asset if the enterprise controls the benefits which are expected to flow from the property. Although the capacity of an enterprise to control benefits is usually the result of legal rights, an item may nonetheless satisfy the definition of an asset even when there is no legal control. For example, know-how obtained from a development activity may meet the definition of an asset when, by keeping that know-how secret, an enterprise controls the benefits that are expected to flow from it.

58. The assets of an enterprise result from past transactions or other past events. Enterprises normally obtain assets by purchasing or producing them, but other transactions or events may generate assets; examples include property received by an enterprise from government as part of a programme to encourage economic growth in an area and the discovery of mineral deposits. Transactions or events expected to occur in the future do not in themselves give rise to assets; hence, for example, an intention to purchase inventory does not, of itself, meet the definition of an asset.

59. There is a close association between incurring expenditure and generating assets but the two do not necessarily coincide. Hence, when an enterprise incurs expenditure, this may provide evidence that future economic benefits were sought but is not conclusive proof that an item satisfying the definition of an asset has been obtained. Similarly the absence of a related expenditure does not preclude an item from satisfying the definition of an asset and thus becoming a candidate for recognition in the balance sheet; for example, items that have been donated to the enterprise may satisfy the definition of an asset.

Liabilities

60. An essential characteristic of a liability is that the enterprise has a present obligation. An obligation is a duty or responsibility to act or perform in a certain way. Obligations may be legally enforceable as a consequence

of a binding contract or statutory requirement. This is normally the case, for example, with amounts payable for goods and services received. Obligations also arise, however, from normal business practice, custom and a desire to maintain good business relations or act in an equitable manner. If, for example, an enterprise decides as a matter of policy to rectify faults in its products even when these become apparent after the warranty period has expired, the amounts that are expected to be expended in respect of goods already sold are liabilities.

61. A distinction needs to be drawn between a present obligation and a future commitment. A decision by the management of an enterprise to acquire assets in the future does not, of itself, give rise to a present obligation. An obligation normally arises only when the asset is delivered or the enterprise enters into an irrevocable agreement to acquire the asset. In the latter case, the irrevocable nature of the agreement means that the economic consequences of failing to honour the obligation, for example, because of the existence of a substantial penalty, leave the enterprise with little, if any, discretion to avoid the outflow of resources to another party.

62. The settlement of a present obligation usually involves the enterprise giving up resources embodying economic benefits in order to satisfy the claim of the other party. Settlement of a present obligation may occur in a number of ways, for example, by:

(a) payment of cash;

(b) transfer of other assets;

(c) provision of services;

(d) replacement of that obligation with another obligation; or

(e) conversion of the obligation to equity.

An obligation may also be extinguished by other means, such as a creditor waiving or forfeiting its rights.

63. Liabilities result from past transactions or other past events. Thus, for example, the acquisition of goods and the use of services give rise to trade payables (unless paid for in advance or on delivery) and the receipt of a bank loan results in an obligation to repay the loan. An enterprise may also recognise future rebates based on annual purchases by customers as liabilities; in this case, the sale of the goods in the past is the transaction that gives rise to the liability.

64. Some liabilities can be measured only by using a substantial degree of estimation. Some enterprises describe these liabilities as provisions. In some countries, such provisions are not regarded as liabilities because the concept of a liability is defined narrowly so as to include only amounts that can be established without the need to make estimates. The definition of a liability in paragraph 49 follows a broader approach. Thus, when a provision involves a present obligation and satisfies the rest of the definition, it is a liability even if the amount has to be estimated. Examples include provisions for payments to be made under existing warranties and provisions to cover pension obligations.

Equity

65. Although equity is defined in paragraph 49 as a residual, it may be sub-classified in the balance sheet. For example, in a corporate enterprise, funds contributed by shareholders, retained earnings, reserves representing appropriations of retained earnings and reserves representing capital maintenance adjustments may be shown separately. Such classifications can be relevant to the decision-making needs of the users of financial statements when they indicate legal or other restrictions on the ability of the enterprise to distribute or otherwise apply its equity. They may also reflect the fact that parties with ownership interests in an enterprise have differing rights in relation to the receipt of dividends or the repayment of capital.

66. The creation of reserves is sometimes required by statute or other law in order to give the enterprise and its creditors an added measure of protection from the effects of losses. Other reserves may be established if national tax law grants exemptions from, or reductions in, taxation liabilities when transfers to such reserves are made. The existence and size of these legal, statutory and tax reserves is information that can be relevant to the decision-making needs of users. Transfers to such reserves are appropriations of retained earnings rather than expenses.

67. The amount at which equity is shown in the balance sheet is dependent on the measurement of assets and liabilities. Normally, the aggregate amount of equity only by coincidence corresponds with the aggregate market value of the shares of the enterprise or the sum that could be raised by disposing of either the net assets on a piecemeal basis or the enterprise as a whole on a going concern basis.

68. Commercial, industrial and business activities are often undertaken by means of enterprises such as sole proprietorships, partnerships and trusts and various types of government business undertakings. The legal and regulatory framework for such enterprises is often different from that applying to corporate enterprises. For example, there may be few, if any,

restrictions on the distribution to owners or other beneficiaries of amounts included in equity. Nevertheless, the definition of equity and the other aspects of this framework that deal with equity are appropriate for such enterprises.

Performance

69. Profit is frequently used as a measure of performance or as the basis for other measures, such as return on investment or earnings per share. The elements directly related to the measurement of profit are income and expenses. The recognition and measurement of income and expenses, and hence profit, depends in part on the concepts of capital and capital maintenance used by the enterprise in preparing its financial statements. These concepts are discussed in paragraphs 102 to 110.

70. The elements of income and expenses are defined as follows:

(a) *Income* is increases in economic benefits during the accounting period in the form of inflows or enhancements of assets or decreases of liabilities that result in increases in equity, other than those relating to contributions from equity participants.

(b) *Expenses* are decreases in economic benefits during the accounting period in the form of outflows or depletions of assets or incurrences of liabilities that result in decreases in equity, other than those relating to distributions to equity participants.

71. The definitions of income and expenses identify their essential features but do not attempt to specify the criteria that would need to be met before they are recognised in the income statement. Criteria for the recognition of income and expenses are discussed in paragraphs 82 to 98.

72. Income and expenses may be presented in the income statement in different ways so as to provide information that is relevant for economic decision-making. For example, it is common practice to distinguish between those items of income and expenses that arise in the course of the ordinary activities of the enterprise and those that do not. This distinction is made on the basis that the source of an item is relevant in evaluating the ability of the enterprise to generate cash and cash equivalents in the future; for example, incidental activities such as the disposal of a long-term investment are unlikely to recur on a regular basis. When distinguishing between items in this way consideration needs to be given to the nature of the enterprise and its operations. Items that arise from the ordinary activities of one enterprise may be unusual in respect of another.

73. Distinguishing between items of income and expense and combining them in different ways also permits several measures of enterprise performance to be displayed. These have differing degrees of inclusiveness. For example, the income statement could display gross margin, profit from ordinary activities before taxation, profit from ordinary activities after taxation, and net profit.

Income

74. The definition of income encompasses both revenue and gains. Revenue arises in the course of the ordinary activities of an enterprise and is referred to by a variety of different names including sales, fees, interest, dividends, royalties and rent.

75. Gains represent other items that meet the definition of income and may, or may not, arise in the course of the ordinary activities of an enterprise. Gains represent increases in economic benefits and as such are no different in nature from revenue. Hence, they are not regarded as constituting a separate element in this framework.

76. Gains include, for example, those arising on the disposal of non-current assets. The definition of income also includes unrealised gains; for example, those arising on the revaluation of marketable securities and those resulting from increases in the carrying amount of long term assets. When gains are recognised in the income statements, they are usually displayed separately because knowledge of them is useful for the purpose of making economic decisions. Gains are often reported net of related expenses.

77. Various kinds of assets may be received or enhanced by income; examples include cash, receivables and goods and services received in exchange for goods and services supplied. Income may also result from the settlement of liabilities. For example, an enterprise may provide goods and services to a lender in settlement of an obligation to repay an outstanding loan.

Expenses

78. The definition of expenses encompasses losses as well as those expenses that arise in the course of the ordinary activities of the enterprise. Expenses that arise in the course of the ordinary activities of the enterprise include, for example, cost of sales, wages and depreciation. They usually take the form of an outflow or depletion of assets such as cash and cash equivalents, inventory, property, plant and equipment.

79. Losses represent other items that meet the definition of expenses and may, or may not, arise in the course of the ordinary activities of the enterprise. Losses represent decreases in economic benefits and as such they are no different in nature from other expenses. Hence, they are not regarded as a separate element in this framework.

80. Losses include, for example, those resulting from disasters such as fire and flood, as well as those arising on the disposal of non-current assets. The definition of expenses also includes unrealised losses, for example, those arising from the effects of increases in the rate of exchange for a foreign currency in respect of the borrowings of an enterprise in that currency. When losses are recognised in the income statement, they are usually displayed separately because knowledge of them is useful for the purpose of making economic decisions. Losses are often reported net of related income.

Capital Maintenance Adjustments

81. The revaluation or restatement of assets and liabilities gives rise to increases or decreases in equity. While these increases or decreases meet the definition of income and expenses, they are not included in the income statement under certain concepts of capital maintenance. Instead these items are included in equity as capital maintenance adjustments or revaluation reserves. These concepts of capital maintenance are discussed in paragraphs 102 to 110 of this framework.

Recognition of the Elements of Financial Statements

82. Recognition is the process of incorporating in the balance sheet or income statement an item that meets the definition of an element and satisfies the criteria for recognition set out in paragraph 83. It involves the depiction of the item in words and by a monetary amount and the inclusion of that amount in the balance sheet or income statement totals. Items that satisfy the recognition criteria should be recognised in the balance sheet or income statement. The failure to recognise such items is not rectified by disclosure of the accounting policies used nor by notes or explanatory material.

83. An item that meets the definition of an element should be recognised if:

(a) it is probable that any future economic benefit associated with the item will flow to or from the enterprise; and

(b) the item has a cost or value that can be measured with reliability.

84. In assessing whether an item meets these criteria and therefore qualifies for recognition in the financial statements, regard needs to be given to the materiality considerations discussed in paragraphs 29 and 30. The interrelationship between the elements means that an item that meets the definition and recognition criteria for a particular element, for example, an asset, automatically requires the recognition of another element, for example, income or a liability.

The Probability of Future Economic Benefit

85. The concept of probability is used in the recognition criteria to refer to the degree of uncertainty that the future economic benefits associated with the item will flow to or from the enterprise. The concept is in keeping with the uncertainty that characterises the environment in which an enterprise operates. Assessments of the degree of uncertainty attaching to the flow of future economic benefits are made on the basis of the evidence available when the financial statements are prepared. For example, when it is probable that a receivable owed by a enterprise will be paid, it is then justifiable, in the absence of any evidence to the contrary, to recognise the receivable as an asset. For a large population of receivables, however, some degree of non-payment is normally considered probable; hence an expense representing the expected reduction in economic benefits is recognised.

Reliability of Measurement

86. The second criterion for the recognition of an item is that it possesses a cost or value that can be measured with reliability as discussed in paragraphs 31 to 38 of this framework. In many cases, cost or value must be estimated; the use of reasonable estimates is an essential part of the preparation of financial statements and does not undermine their reliability. When, however, a reasonable estimate cannot be made the item is not recognised in the balance sheet or income statement. For example, the expected proceeds from a lawsuit may meet the definitions of both an asset and income as well as the probability criterion for recognition; however, if it is not possible for the claim to be measured reliably, it should not be recognised as an asset or as income; the existence of the claim, however, would be disclosed in the notes, explanatory material or supplementary schedules.

87. An item that, at a particular point in time, fails to meet the recognition criteria in paragraph 83 may qualify for recognition at a later date as a result of subsequent circumstances or events.

88. An item that possesses the essential characteristics of an element but fails to meet the criteria for recognition may nonetheless warrant disclosure in the notes, explanatory material or in supplementary schedules. This is appropriate when knowledge of the item is considered to be relevant to the evaluation of the financial position, performance and changes in financial position of an enterprise by the users of financial statements.

Recognition of Assets

89. An asset is recognised in the balance sheet when it is probable that the future economic benefits will flow to the enterprise and the asset has a cost or value that can be measured reliably.

90. An asset is not recognised in the balance sheet when expenditure has been incurred for which it is considered improbable that economic benefits will flow to the enterprise beyond the current accounting period. Instead such a transaction results in the recognition of an expense in the income statement. This treatment does not imply either that the intention of management in incurring expenditure was other than to generate future economic benefits for the enterprise or that management was misguided. The only implication is that the degree of certainty that economic benefits will flow to the enterprise beyond the current accounting period is insufficient to warrant the recognition of an asset.

Recognition of Liabilities

91. A liability is recognised in the balance sheet when it is probable that an outflow of resources embodying economic benefits will result from the settlement of a present obligation and the amount at which the settlement will take place can be measured reliably. In practice, obligations under contracts that are equally proportionately unperformed (for example, liabilities for inventory ordered but not yet received) are generally not recognised as liabilities in the financial statements. However, such obligations may meet the definition of liabilities and, provided the recognition criteria are met in the particular circumstances, may qualify for recognition. In such circumstances, recognition of liabilities entails recognition of related assets or expenses.

Recognition of Income

92. Income is recognised in the income statement when an increase in future economic benefits related to an increase in an asset or a decrease of a liability has arisen that can be measured reliably. This means, in effect, that recognition of income occurs simultaneously with the recognition of increases in assets or decreases in liabilities (for example, the net increase in assets arising on a sale of goods or services or the decrease in liabilities arising from the waiver of a debt payable).

93. The procedures normally adopted in practice for recognising income, for example, the requirement that revenue should be earned, are applications of the recognition criteria in this framework. Such procedures are generally directed at restricting the recognition as income to those items that can be measured reliably and have a sufficient degree of certainty.

Recognition of Expenses

94. Expenses are recognised in the income statement when a decrease in future economic benefits related to a decrease in an asset or an increase of a liability has arisen that can be measured reliably. This means, in effect, that recognition of expenses occurs simultaneously with the recognition of an increase in liabilities or a decrease in assets (for example, the accrual of employee entitlements or the depreciation of equipment).

95. Expenses are recognised in the income statement on the basis of a direct association between the costs incurred and the earning of specific items of income. This process, commonly referred to as the matching of costs with revenues, involves the simultaneous or combined recognition of revenues and expenses that result directly and jointly from the same transactions or other events; for example, the various components of expense making up the cost of goods sold are recognised at the same time as the income derived from the sale of the goods. However, the application

of the matching concept under this framework does not allow the recognition of items in the balance sheet which do not meet the definition of assets or liabilities.

96. When economic benefits are expected to arise over several accounting periods and the association with income can only be broadly or indirectly determined, expenses are recognised in the income statement on the basis of systematic and rational allocation procedures. This is often necessary in recognising the expenses associated with the using up of assets such as property, plant, equipment, goodwill, patents and trademarks; in such cases the expense is referred to as depreciation or amortisation. These allocation procedures are intended to recognise expenses in the accounting periods in which the economic benefits associated with these items are consumed or expire.

97. An expense is recognised immediately in the income statement when an expenditure produces no future economic benefits or when, and to the extent that, future economic benefits do not qualify, or cease to qualify, for recognition in the balance sheet as an asset.

98. An expense is also recognised in the income statement in those cases when a liability is incurred without the recognition of an asset, as when a liability under a product warranty arises.

Measurement of the Elements of Financial Statements

99. Measurement is the process of determining the monetary amounts at which the elements of the financial statements are to be recognised and carried in the balance sheet and income statement. This involves the selection of the particular basis of measurement.

100. A number of different measurement bases are employed to different degrees and in varying combinations in financial statements. They include the following:

(a) *Historical cost*. Assets are recorded at the amount of cash or cash equivalents paid or the fair value of the consideration given to acquire them at the time of their acquisition. Liabilities are recorded at the amount of proceeds received in exchange for the obligation, or in some circumstances (for example, income taxes), at the amounts of cash or cash equivalents expected to be paid to satisfy the liability in the normal course of business.

(b) *Current cost*. Assets are carried at the amount of cash or cash equivalents that would have to be paid if the same or an equivalent asset was acquired currently. Liabilities are carried at the undiscounted amount of cash or cash equivalents that would be required to settle the obligation currently.

(c) *Realisable (settlement) value*. Assets are carried at the amount of cash or cash equivalents that could currently be obtained by selling the asset in an orderly disposal. Liabilities are carried at their settlement values; that is, the undiscounted amounts of cash or cash equivalents expected to be paid to satisfy the liabilities in the normal course of business.

(d) *Present value*. Assets are carried at the present discounted value of the future net cash inflows that the item is expected to generate in the normal course of business. Liabilities are carried at the present discounted value of the future net cash outflows that are expected to be required to settle the liabilities in the normal course of business.

Framework

101. The measurement basis most commonly adopted by enterprises in preparing their financial statements is historical cost. This is usually combined with other measurement bases. For example, inventories are usually carried at the lower of cost and net realisable value, marketable securities may be carried at market value and pension liabilities are carried at their present value. Furthermore, some enterprises use the current cost basis as a response to the inability of the historical cost accounting model to deal with the effects of changing prices of non-monetary assets.

Concepts of Capital and Capital Maintenance

Concepts of Capital

102. A financial concept of capital is adopted by most enterprises in preparing their financial statements. Under a financial concept of capital, such as invested money or invested purchasing power, capital is synonymous with the net assets or equity of the enterprise. Under a physical concept of capital, such as operating capability, capital is regarded as the productive capacity of the enterprise based on, for example, units of output per day.

103. The selection of the appropriate concept of capital by an enterprise should be based on the needs of the users of its financial statements. Thus, a financial concept of capital should be adopted if the users of financial statements are primarily concerned with the maintenance of nominal invested capital or the purchasing power of invested capital. If, however, the main concern of users is with the operating capability of the enterprise, a physical concept of capital should be used. The concept chosen indicates the goal to be attained in determining profit, even though there may be some measurement difficulties in making the concept operational.

Concepts of Capital Maintenance and the Determination of Profit

104. The concepts of capital in paragraph 102 give rise to the following concepts of capital maintenance:

(a) *Financial capital maintenance.* Under this concept a profit is earned only if the financial (or money) amount of the net assets at the end of the period exceeds the financial (or money) amount of net assets at the beginning of the period, after excluding any distributions to, and contributions from, owners during the period. Financial capital maintenance can be measured in either nominal monetary units or units of constant purchasing power.

(b) *Physical capital maintenance.* Under this concept a profit is earned only if the physical productive capacity (or operating capability) of the enterprise (or the resources or funds needed to achieve that capacity) at the end of the period exceeds the physical productive capacity at the beginning of the period, after excluding any distributions to, and contributions from, owners during the period.

Framework

105. The concept of capital maintenance is concerned with how an enterprise defines the capital that it seeks to maintain. It provides the linkage between the concepts of capital and the concepts of profit because it provides the point of reference by which profit is measured; it is a prerequisite for distinguishing between an enterprise's return on capital and its return of capital; only inflows of assets in excess of amounts needed to maintain capital may be regarded as profit and therefore as a return on capital. Hence, profit is the residual amount that remains after expenses (including capital maintenance adjustments, where appropriate) have been deducted from income. If expenses exceed income the residual amount is a net loss.

106. The physical capital maintenance concept requires the adoption of the current cost basis of measurement. The financial capital maintenance concept, however, does not require the use of a particular basis of measurement. Selection of the basis under this concept is dependent on the type of financial capital that the enterprise is seeking to maintain.

107. The principal difference between the two concepts of capital maintenance is the treatment of the effects of changes in the prices of assets and liabilities of the enterprise. In general terms, an enterprise has maintained its capital if it has as much capital at the end of the period as it had at the beginning of the period. Any amount over and above that required to maintain the capital at the beginning of the period is profit.

108. Under the concept of financial capital maintenance where capital is defined in terms of nominal monetary units, profit represents the increase in nominal money capital over the period. Thus, increases in the prices of assets held over the period, conventionally referred to as holding gains, are, conceptually, profits. They may not be recognised as such, however, until the assets are disposed of in an exchange transaction. When the concept of financial capital maintenance is defined in terms of constant purchasing power units, profit represents the increase in invested purchasing power over the period. Thus, only that part of the increase in the prices of assets that exceeds the increase in the general level of prices is regarded as profit. The rest of the increase is treated as a capital maintenance adjustment and, hence, as part of equity.

109. Under the concept of physical capital maintenance when capital is defined in terms of the physical productive capacity, profit represents the increase in that capital over the period. All price changes affecting the assets and liabilities of the enterprise are viewed as changes in the measurement of the physical productive capacity of the enterprise; hence, they are treated as capital maintenance adjustments that are part of equity and not as profit.

110. The selection of the measurement bases and concept of capital maintenance will determine the accounting model used in the preparation of the financial statements. Different accounting models exhibit different degrees of relevance and reliability and, as in other areas, management must seek a balance between relevance and reliability. This framework is applicable to a range of accounting models and provides guidance on preparing and presenting the financial statements constructed under the chosen model. At the present time, it is not the intention of the Board of IASC to prescribe a particular model other than in exceptional circumstances, such as for those enterprises reporting in the currency of a hyperinflationary economy. This intention will, however, be reviewed in the light of world developments.

[26]

OFFICIAL TEXT OF THE FOURTH DIRECTIVE

FOURTH COUNCIL DIRECTIVE

of 25 July 1978

based on Article 54 (3) (g) of the Treaty on the annual accounts of certain types of companies

(78/660/EEC)

THE COUNCIL OF THE EUROPEAN COMMUNITIES,

Having regard to the Treaty establishing the European Economic Community, and in particular Article 54 (3) (g) thereof,

Having regard to the proposal from the Commission,

Having regard to the opinion of the European Parliament(1),

Having regard to the opinion of the Economic and Social Committee (2),

Whereas the coordination of national provisions concerning the presentation and content of annual accounts and annual reports, the valuation methods used therein and their publication in respect of certain companies with limited liability is of special importance for the protection of members and third parties;

Whereas simultaneous coordination is necessary in these fields for these forms of company because, on the one hand, these companies' activities frequently extend beyond the frontiers of their national territories and, on the other, they offer no safeguards to third parties beyond the amounts of their net assets; whereas, moreover the necessity for and the urgency of such coordination have been recognized and confirmed by Article 2 (1) (f) of Directive 68/151/EEC(3);

Whereas it is necessary, moreover, to establish in the Community minimum equivalent legal requirements as regards the extent of the financial information that should be made available to the public by companies that are in competition with one another;

Whereas annual accounts must give a true and fair view of a company's assets and liabilities, financial position and profit or loss; whereas to this end a mandatory layout must be prescribed for the balance sheet and the profit and loss account and whereas the minimum content of the notes on the accounts and the annual report must be laid down; whereas, however, derogations may be granted for certain companies of minor economic or social importance;

Whereas the different methods for the valuation of assets and liabilities must be coordinated to the extent necessary to ensure that annual accounts disclose comparable and equivalent information;

Whereas the annual accounts of all companies to which this Directive applies must be published in accordance with Directive 68/151/EEC; whereas, however, certain derogations may likewise be granted in this area for small and medium-sized companies;

Whereas annual accounts must be audited by authorized persons whose minimum qualifications will be the subject of subsequent coordination; whereas only small companies may be relieved of this audit obligation;

Whereas, when a company belongs to a group, it is desirable that group accounts giving a true and fair view of the activities of the group as a whole be published; whereas,

(1) OJ No C 129, 11.12.1972, p. 38.

(2) OJ No C 39, 7.6.1973, p. 31.

(3) OJ No L 65, 14.3.1968, p. 8.

OFFICIAL TEXT OF THE FOURTH DIRECTIVE

however, pending the entry into force of a Council Directive on consolidated accounts, derogations from certain provisions of this Directive are necessary;
Whereas, in order to meet the difficulties arising from the present position regarding legislation in certain Member States, the period allowed for the implementation of certain provisions of this Directive must be longer than the period generally laid down in such cases,

HAS ADOPTED THIS DIRECTIVE:

Article 1

1. The coordination measures prescribed by this Directive shall apply to the laws, regulations and administrative provisions of the Member States relating to the following types of companies:
– in Germany:
die Aktiengesellschaft, die Kommanditgesellschaft auf Aktien, die Gesellschaft mit beschränkter Haftung;
– in Belgium:
la société anonyme/de naamloze vennootschap, la société en commandite par actions/de commanditaire vennootschap op aandelen, la société de personnes à responsabilité limitée/de personenvennootschap met beperkte aansprakelijkheid;
– in Denmark:
aktieselskaber, kommanditaktieselskaber, anpartsselskaber;
– in France:
la société anonyme, la société en commandite par actions, la société à responsabilité limitée;
– in Greece:
anonymos eteria, eterorrythmos kata metochas eteria, eteria periorismenis efthinis
– in Ireland:
public companies limited by shares or by guarantee, private companies limited by shares or by guarantee;
– in Italy:
la società per azioni, la società in accomandita per azioni, la società a responsabilità limitata;
– in Luxembourg:
la société anonyme, la société en commandite par actions, la société à responsabilité limitée;
– in the Netherlands:
de naamloze vennootschap, de besloten vennootschap met beperkte aansprakelijkheid;
– in the United Kingdom:
public companies limited by shares or by guarantee, private companies limited by shares or by guarantee.
2. Pending subsequent coordination, the Member States need not apply the provisions of this Directive to banks and other financial institutions or to insurance companies.

OFFICIAL TEXT OF THE FOURTH DIRECTIVE

SECTION 1

General provisions

Article 2

1. The annual accounts shall comprise the balance sheet, the profit and loss account and the notes on the accounts. These documents shall constitute a composite whole.
2. They shall be drawn up clearly and in accordance with the provisions of this Directive.
3. The annual accounts shall give a true and fair view of the company's assets, liabilities, financial position and profit or loss.
4. Where the application of the provisions of this Directive would not be sufficient to give a true and fair view within the meaning of paragraph 3, additional information must be given.
5. Where in exceptional cases the application of a provision of this Directive is incompatible with the obligation laid down in paragraph 3, that provision must be departed from in order to give a true and fair view within the meaning of paragraph 3. Any such departure must be disclosed in the notes on the accounts together with an explanation of the reasons for it and a statement of its effect on the assets, liabilities, financial position and profit or loss. The Member States may define the exceptional cases in question and lay down the relevant special rules.
6. The Member States may authorize or require the disclosure in the annual accounts of other information as well as that which must be disclosed in accordance with this Directive.

SECTION 2

General provisions concerning the balance sheet and the profit and loss account

Article 3

The layout of the balance sheet and of the profit and loss account, particularly as regards the form adopted for their presentation, may not be changed from one financial year to the next. Departures from this principle shall be permitted in exceptional cases. Any such departure mut be disclosed in the notes on the accounts together with an explanation of the reasons therefor.

Article 4

1. In the balance sheet and in the profit and loss account the items prescribed in Articles 9, 10 and 23 to 26 must be shown separately in the order indicated. A more detailed subdivision of the items shall be authorized provided that the layouts are complied with. New items may be added provided that their contents are not covered by any of the items prescribed by the layouts. Such subdivision or new items may be required by the Member States.
2. The layout, nomenclature and terminology of items in the balance sheet and profit and loss account that are preceded by Arabic numerals must be adapted where the special nature of an undertaking so requires. Such adaptations may be required by the Member States of undertakings forming part of a particular economic sector.
3. The balance sheet and profit and loss account items that are preceded by Arabic

OFFICIAL TEXT OF THE FOURTH DIRECTIVE

numerals may be combined where:

(a) they are immaterial in amount for the purposes of Article 2 (3);or

(b) such combination makes for greater clarity, provided that the items so combined are dealt with separately in the notes on the accounts. Such combination may be required by the Member States.

4. In respect of each balance sheet and profit and loss account item the figure relating to the corresponding item for the preceding financial year must be shown. The Member States may provide that, where these figures are not comparable, the figure for the preceding financial year must be adjusted. In any case, non-comparability and any adjustment of the figures must be disclosed in the notes on the accounts, with relevant comments.

5. Save where there is a corresponding item for the preceding financial year within the meaning of paragraph 4, a balance sheet or profit and loss account item for which there is no amount shall not be shown.

Article 5

1. By way of derogation from Article 4 (1) and (2), the Member States may prescribe special layouts for the annual accounts of investment companies and of financial holding companies provided that these layouts give a view of these companies equivalent to that provided for in Article 2 (3).

2. For the purposes of this Directive, 'investment companies' shall mean only:

(a) those companies the sole object of which is to invest their funds in various securities, real property and other assets with the sole aim of spreading investment risks and giving their shareholders the benefit of the results of the management of their assets;

(b) those companies associated with investment companies with fixed capital if the sole object of the companies so associated is to acquire fully paid shares issued by those investment companies without prejudice to the provisions of Article 20 (1) (h) of Directive 77/91/EEC.

3. For the purposes of this Directive, 'financial holding companies' shall mean only those companies the sole object of which is to acquire holdings in other undertakings, and to manage such holdings and turn them to profit, without involving themselves directly or indirectly in the management of those undertakings, the aforegoing without prejudice to their rights as shareholders. The limitations imposed on the activities of these companies must be such that compliance with them can be supervised by an administrative or judicial authority.

Article 6

The Member States may authorize or require adaptation of the layout of the balance sheet and profit and loss account in order to include the appropriation of profit or the treatment of loss.

Article 7

Any set-off between asset and liability items, or between income and expenditure items, shall be prohibited.

OFFICIAL TEXT OF THE FOURTH DIRECTIVE

SECTION 3

Layout of the balance sheet

Article 8

For the presentation of the balance sheet, the Member States shall prescribe one or both of the layouts prescribed by Articles 9 and 10. If a Member State prescribes both, it may allow companies to choose between them.

Article 9

Assets

A. Subscribed capital unpaid
of which there has been called
(unless national law provides that called-up capital be shown under 'Liabilities'. In that case, the part of the capital called but not yet paid must appear as an asset either under A or under D (II) (5)).

B. Formation expenses
as defined by national law, and in so far as national law permits their being shown as an asset. National law may also provide for formation expenses to be shown as the first item under 'Intangible assets'.

C. Fixed assets

I. *Intangible assets*

1. Costs of research and development, in so far as national law permits their being shown as assets.
2. Concessions, patents, licences, trade marks and similar rights and assets, if they were:
   (a) acquired for valuable consideration and need not be shown under C (I) (3); or
   (b) created by the undertaking itself, in so far as national law permits their being shown as assets.
3. Goodwill, to the extent that it was acquired for valuable consideration.
4. Payments on account.

II. *Tangible assets*

1. Land and buildings.
2. Plant and machinery.
3. Other fixtures and fittings, tools and equipment.
4. Payments on account and tangible assets in course of construction.

III. *Financial assets*

1. Shares in affiliated undertakings.
2. Loans to affiliated undertakings.
3. Participating interests.
4. Loans to undertakings with which the company is linked by virtue of participating interests.
5. Investments held as fixed assets.
6. Other loans.
7. Own shares (with an indication of their nominal value or, in the absence of a nominal value, their accounting par value) to the extent that national law permits their being shown in the balance sheet.

OFFICIAL TEXT OF THE FOURTH DIRECTIVE

D. Current assets
- I. *Stocks*
  1. Raw materials and consumables.
  2. Work in progress.
  3. Finished good and goods for resale.
  4. Payments on account.
- II. *Debtors*

  (Amounts becoming due and payable after more than one year must be shown separately for each item).
  1. Trade debtors.
  2. Amounts owed by affiliated undertakings.
  3. Amounts owed by undertakings with which the company is linked by virtue of participating interests.
  4. Other debtors.
  5. Subscribed capital called but not paid (unless national law provides that called-up capital be shown as an asset under A).
  6. Prepayments and accrued income (unless national law provides for such items to be shown as an asset under E).
- III. *Investments*
  1. Shares in affiliated undertakings.
  2. Own shares (with an indication of their nominal value or, in the absence of a nominal value, their accounting par value) to the extent that national law permits their being shown in the balance sheet.
  3. Other investments.
- IV. *Cash at bank and in hand*

E. Prepayments and accrued income
(unless national law provides for such items to be shown as an asset under D (II) (6)).

F. Loss for the financial year
(unless national law provides for it to be shown under A (VI) under 'Liabilities').

Liabilities

A. Capital and reserves
- I. *Subscribed capital*

  (unless national law provides for called-up capital to be shown under this item. In that case, the amounts of subscribed capital and paid-up capital must be shown separately).
- II. *Share premium account*
- III. *Revaluation reserve*
- IV. *Reserves*
  1. Legal reserve, in so far as national law requires such a reserve.
  2. Reserve for own shares, in so far as national law requires such a reserve, without prejudice to Article 22 (1) (b) of Directive 77/91/EEC.
  3. Reserves provided for by the articles of association.
  4. Other reserves.
- V. *Profit or loss brought forward*
- VI. *Profit or loss for the financial year.*

  (unless national law requires that this item be shown under F under 'Assets' or under E under 'Liabilities').

OFFICIAL TEXT OF THE FOURTH DIRECTIVE

B. Provisions for liabilities and charges
   1. Provisions for pensions and similar obligations.
   2. Provisions for taxation.
   3. Other provisions.

C. Creditors
(Amounts becoming due and payable within one year and amounts becoming due and payable after more than one year must be shown separately for each item and for the aggregate of these items.)
1. Debenture loans, showing convertible loans separately.
2. Amounts owed to credit institutions.
3. Payments received on account of orders in so far as they are not shown separately as deductions from stocks.
4. Trade creditors.
5. Bills of exchange payable.
6. Amounts owed to affiliated undertakings.
7. Amounts owed to undertakings with which the company is linked by virtue of participating interests.
8. Other creditors including tax and social security.
9. Accruals and deferred income (unless national law provides for such items to be shown under D under 'Liabilities').

D. Accruals and deferred income
(unless national law provides for such items to be shown under C (9) under 'Liabilities').

E. Profit for the financial year
(unless national law provides for it to be shown under A (VI) under 'Liabilities').

Article 10

A. Subscribed capital unpaid
of which there has been called
(unless national law provides that called-up capital be shown under L. In that case, the part of the capital called but not yet paid must appear either under A or under D (II) (5)).

B. Formation expenses
as defined by national law, and in so far as national law permits their being shown as an asset. National law may also provide for formation expenses to be shown as the first item under 'Intangible assets'.

C. Fixed assets
   I. *Intangible assets*
   1. Costs of research and development, in so far as national law permits their being shown as assets.
   2. Concessions, patents, licences, trade marks and similar rights and assets, if they were:
      (a) acquired for valuable consideration and need not be shown under C (I) (3); or
      (b) created by the undertaking itself, in so far as national law permits their being shown as assets.
   3. Goodwill, to the extent that it was acquired for valuable consideration.
   4. Payments on account.

OFFICIAL TEXT OF THE FOURTH DIRECTIVE

II. *Tangible assets*
  1. Land and buildings.
  2. Plant and machinery.
  3. Other fixtures and fittings, tools and equipment.
  4. Payments on account and tangible assets in course of construction.

III. *Financial assets*
  1. Shares in affiliated undertakings.
  2. Loans to affiliated undertakings.
  3. Participating interests.
  4. Loans to undertakings with which the company is linked by virtue of participating interests.
  5. Investments held as fixed assets.
  6. Other loans.
  7. Own shares (with an indication of their nominal value or, in the absence of a nominal value, their accounting par value) to the extent that national law permits their being shown in the balance sheet.

D. Current assets

I. *Stocks*
  1. Raw materials and consumables.
  2. Work in progress.
  3. Finished goods and goods for resale.
  4. Payments on account.

II. *Debtors*

(Amounts becoming due and payable after more than one year must be shown separately for each item.)
  1. Trade debtors.
  2. Amounts owed by affiliated undertakings.
  3. Amounts owed by undertakings with which the company is linked by virtue of participating interests.
  4. Other debtors.
  5. Subscribed capital called but not paid (unless national law provides that called-up capital be shown under A).
  6. Prepayments and accrued income (unless national law provides that such items be shown under E).

III. *Investments*
  1. Shares in affiliated undertakings.
  2. Own shares (with an indication of their nominal value or, in the absence of a nominal value, their accounting par value) to the extent that national law permits their being shown in the balance sheet.
  3. Other investments.

IV. *Cash at bank and in hand*

E. Prepayments and accrued income

(unless national law provides for such items to be shown under D (II) (6)).

F. Creditors: amounts becoming due and payable within one year.
  1. Debenture loans, showing convertible loans separately.
  2. Amounts owed to credit institutions.
  3. Payments received on account of orders in so far as they are not shown separately as deductions from stocks.

4. Trade creditors.
5. Bills of exchange payable.
6. Amounts owed to affiliated undertakings.
7. Amounts owed to undertakings with which the company is linked by virtue of participating interests.
8. Other creditors including tax and social security.
9. Accruals and deferred income (unless national law provides for such items to be shown under K).

G. Net current assets/liabilities (taking into account prepayments and accrued income when shown under E and accruals and deferred income when shown under K).

H. Total assets less current liabilities

I. Creditors: amounts becoming due and payable after more than one year.
1. Debenture loans, showing convertible loans separately.
2. Amounts owed to credit institutions.
3. Payments received on account of orders in so far as they are not shown separately as deductions from stocks.
4. Trade creditors.
5. Bills of exchange payable.
6. Amounts owed to affiliated undertakings.
7. Amounts owed to undertakings with which the company is linked by virtue of participating interests.
8. Other creditors including tax and social security.
9. Accruals and deferred income (unless national law provides for such items to be shown under K).

J. Provisions for liabilities and charges
1. Provisions for pensions and similar obligations.
2. Provisions for taxation.
3. Other provisions.

K. Accruals and deferred income
(unless national law provides for such items to be shown under F (9) or I (9) or both).

L. Capital and reserves

I. *Subscribed capital*
(unless national law provides for called-up capital to be shown under this item. In that case, the amounts of subscribed capital and paid-up capital must be shown separately).

II. *Share premium account*

III. *Revaluation reserve*

IV. *Reserves*
1. Legal reserve, in so far as national law requires such a reserve.
2. Reserve for own shares, in so far as national law requires such a reserve, without prejudice to Article 22 (1) (b) of Directive 77/91/EEC.
3. Reserves provided for by the articles of association.
4. Other reserves.

V. *Profit or loss brought forward*

VI. *Profit or loss for the financial year*

Article 11

The Member States may permit companies which on their balance sheet dates do not

exceed the limits of two of the three following criteria:
- balance sheet total: 1 000 000 EUA,
- net turnover: 2 000 000 EUA,
- average number of employees during the financial year: 50

to draw up abridged balance sheets showing only those items preceded by letters and roman numerals in Articles 9 and 10, disclosing separately the information required in brackets in D (II) under 'Assets' and C under 'Liabilities' in Article 9 and in D (II) in Article 10, but in total for each.

Article 12

1. Where on its balance sheet date, a company exceeds or ceases to exceed the limits of two of the three criteria indicated in Article 11, that fact shall affect the application of the derogation provided for in that Article only if it occurs in two consecutive financial years.
2. For the purposes of translation into national currencies, the amounts in European units of account specified in Article 11 may be increased by not more than 10 %.
3. The balance sheet total referred to in Article 11 shall consist of the assets in A to E under 'Assets' in the layout prescribed in Article 9 or those in A to E in the layout prescribed in Article 10.

Article 13

1. Where an asset or liability relates to more than one layout item, its relationship to other items must be disclosed either under the item where it appears or in the notes on the accounts, if such disclosure is essential to the comprehension of the annual accounts.
2. Own shares and shares in affiliated undertakings may be shown only under the items prescribed for that purpose.

Article 14

All commitments by way of guarantee of any kind must, if there is no obligation to show them as liabilities, be clearly set out at the foot of the balance sheet or in the notes on the accounts, and a distinction made between the various types of guarantee which national law recognizes; specific disclosure must be made of any valuable security which has been provided. Commitments of this kind existing in respect of affiliated undertakings must be shown separately.

SECTION 4

Special provisions relating to certain balance sheet items

Article 15

1. Whether particular assets are to be shown as fixed assets or current assets shall depend upon the purpose for which they are intended.
2. Fixed assets shall comprise those assets which are intended for use on a continuing basis for the purposes of the undertaking's activities.
3. (a) Movements in the various fixed asset items shall be shown in the balance sheet or in the notes on the accounts. To this end there shall be shown separately, starting with the purchase price or production cost, for each fixed asset item, on the one hand, the additions, disposals and transfers during the financial year and, on

the other, the cumulative value adjustments at the balance sheet date and the rectifications made during the financial year to the value adjustments of previous financial years. Value adjustments shall be shown either in the balance sheet, as clear deductions from the relevant items, or in the notes on the accounts.

(b) If, when annual accounts are drawn up in accordance with this Directive for the first time, the purchase price or production cost of a fixed asset cannot be determined without undue expense or delay, the residual value at the beginning of the financial year may be treated as the purchase price or production cost. Any application of this provision must be disclosed in the notes on the accounts.

(c) Where Article 33 is applied, the movements in the various fixed asset items referred to in subparagraph (a) of this paragraph shall be shown starting with the purchase price or production cost resulting from revaluation.

4. Paragraph 3 (a) and (b) shall apply to the presentation of 'Formation expenses'.

Article 16

Rights to immovables and other similar rights as defined by national law must be shown under 'Land and buildings'.

Article 17

For the purposes of this Directive 'participating interest' shall mean rights in the capital of other undertakings, whether or not represented by certificates, which, by creating a durable link with those undertakings, are intended to contribute to the company's activities. The holding of part of the capital of another company shall be presumed to constitute a participating interest where it exceeds a percentage fixed by the Member States which may not exceed 20 %.

Article 18

Expenditure incurred during the financial year but relating to a subsequent financial year, together with any income which, though relating to the financial year in question, is not due until after its expiry must be shown under 'Prepayments and accrued income'. The Member States may, however, provide that such income shall be included in 'Debtors'. Where such income is material, it must be disclosed in the notes on the accounts.

Article 19

Value adjustments shall comprise all adjustments intended to take account of reductions in the values of individual assets established at the balance sheet date whether that reduction is final or not.

Article 20

1. Provisions for liabilities and charges are intended to cover losses or debts the nature of which is clearly defined and which at the date of the balance sheet are either likely to be incurred, or certain to be incurred but uncertain as to amount or as to the date on which they will arise.

2. The Member States may also authorize the creation of provisions intended to cover charges which have their origin in the financial year under review or in a previous financial year, the nature of which is clearly defined and which at the date of the balance sheet are either likely to be incurred, or certain to be incurred but uncertain as to amount

OFFICIAL TEXT OF THE FOURTH DIRECTIVE

or as to the date on which they will arise.

3. Provisions for liabilities and charges may not be used to adjust the values of assets.

Article 21

Income receivable before the balance sheet date but relating to a subsequent financial year, together with any charges which, though relating to the financial year in question, will be paid only in the course of a subsequent financial year, must be shown under 'Accruals and deferred income'. The Member States may, however, provide that such charges shall be included in 'Creditors'. Where such charges are material, they must be disclosed in the notes on the accounts.

SECTION 5

Layout of the profit and loss account

Article 22

For the presentation of the profit and loss account, the Member States shall prescribe one or more of the layouts provided for in Articles 23 to 26. If a Member State prescribes more than one layout, it may allow companies to choose from among them.

Article 23

1. Net turnover.
2. Variation in stocks of finished goods and in work in progress.
3. Work performed by the undertaking for its own purposes and capitalized.
4. Other operating income.
5. (a) Raw materials and consumables.
   (b) Other external charges.
6. Staff costs:
   (a) wages and salaries;
   (b) social security costs, with a separate indication of those relating to pensions.
7. (a) Value adjustments in respect of formation expenses and of tangible and intangible fixed assets.
   (b) Value adjustments in respect of current assets, to the extent that they exceed the amount of value adjustments which are normal in the undertaking concerned.
8. Other operating charges.
9. Income from participating interests, with a separate indication of that derived from affiliated undertakings.
10. Income from other investments and loans forming part of the fixed assets, with a separate indication of that derived from affiliated undertakings.
11. Other interest receivable and similar income, with a separate indication of that derived from affiliated undertakings.
12. Value adjustments in respect of financial assets and of investments held as current assets.
13. Interest payable and similar charges, with a separate indication of those concerning affiliated undertakings.
14. Tax on profit or loss on ordinary activities.
15. Profit or loss on ordinary activities after taxation.

16. Extraordinary income.
17. Extraordinary charges.
18. Extraordinary profit or loss.
19. Tax on extraordinary profit or loss.
20. Other taxes not shown under the above items.
21. Profit or loss for the financial year.

Article 24

A. Charges

1. Reduction in stocks of finished goods and in work in progress:
2. (a) raw materials and consumables;
   (b) other external charges.
3. Staff costs:
   (a) wages and salaries;
   (b) social security costs, with a separate indication of those relating to pensions.
4. (a) Value adjustments in respect of formation expenses and of tangible and intangible fixed assets.
   (b) Value adjustments in respect of current assets, to the extent that they exceed the amount of value adjustments which are normal in the undertaking concerned.
5. Other operating charges.
6. Value adjustments in respect of financial assets and of investments held as current assets.
7. Interest payable and similar charges, with a separate indication of those concerning affiliated undertakings.
8. Tax on profit or loss on ordinary activities.
9. Profit or loss on ordinary activities after taxation.
10. Extraordinary charges.
11. Tax on extraordinary profit or loss.
12. Other taxes not shown under the above items.
13. Profit or loss for the financial year.

B. Income

1. Net turnover.
2. Increase in stocks of finished goods and in work in progress.
3. Work performed by the undertaking for its own purposes and capitalized.
4. Other operating income.
5. Income from participating interests, with a separate indication of that derived from affiliated undertakings.
6. Income from other investments and loans forming part of the fixed assets, with a separate indication of that derived from affiliated undertakings.
7. Other interest receivable and similar income, with a separate indication of that derived from affiliated undertakings.
8. Profit or loss on ordinary activities after taxation.
9. Extraordinary income.
10. Profit or loss for the financial year.

Article 25

1. Net turnover.

OFFICIAL TEXT OF THE FOURTH DIRECTIVE

2. Cost of sales (including value adjustments).
3. Gross profit or loss.
4. Distribution costs (including value adjustments).
5. Administrative expenses (including value adjustments).
6. Other operating income.
7. Income from participating interests, with a separate indication of that derived from affiliated undertakings.
8. Income from other investments and loans forming part of the fixed assets, with a separate indication of that derived from affiliated undertakings.
9. Other interest receivable and similar income, with a separate indication of that derived from affiliated undertakings.
10. Value adjustments in respect of financial assets and of investments held as current assets.
11. Interest payable and similar charges, with a separate indication of those concerning affiliated undertakings.
12. Tax on profit or loss on ordinary activities.
13. Profit or loss on ordinary activities after taxation.
14. Extraordinary income.
15. Extraordinary charges.
16. Extraordinary profit or loss.
17. Tax on extraordinary profit or loss.
18. Other taxes not shown under the above items.
19. Profit or loss for the financial year.

Article 26

A. Charges

1. Cost of sales (including value adjustments).
2. Distribution costs (including value adjustments).
3. Administrative expenses (including value adjustments).
4. Value adjustments in respect of financial assets and of investments held as current assets.
5. Interest payable and similar charges, with a separate indication of those concerning affiliated undertakings.
6. Tax on profit or loss on ordinary activities.
7. Profit or loss on ordinary activities after taxation.
8. Extraordinary charges.
9. Tax on extraordinary profit or loss.
10. Other taxes not shown under the above items.
11. Profit or loss for the financial year.

B. Income

1. Net turnover.
2. Other operating income.
3. Income from participating interests, with a separate indication of that derived from affiliated undertakings.
4. Income from other investments and loans forming part of the fixed assets, with a separate indication of that derived from affiliated undertakings.
5. Other interest receivable and similar income, with a separate indication of that derived from affiliated undertakings.

OFFICIAL TEXT OF THE FOURTH DIRECTIVE

6. Profit or loss on ordinary activities after taxation.
7. Extraordinary income.
8. Profit or loss for the financial year.

Article 27

The Member States may permit companies which on their balance sheet dates do not exceed the limits of two of the three following criteria:

– balance sheet total: 4 million EUA,
– net turnover: 8 million EUA,
– average number of employees during the financial year: 250.

to adopt layouts different from those prescribed in Articles 23 to 26 within the following limits:

(a) in Article 23: 1 to 5 inclusive may be combined under one item called 'Gross profit or loss';
(b) in Article 24: A (1), A (2) and B (1) to B (4) inclusive may be combined under one item called 'Gross profit or loss';
(c) in Article 25: (1), (2), (3) and (6) may be combined under one item called 'Gross profit or loss';
(d) in Article 26, A (1), B (1) and B (2) may be combined under one item called 'Gross profit or loss'.

Article 12 shall apply.

SECTION 6

Special provisions relating to certain items in the profit and loss account

Article 28

The net turnover shall comprise the amounts derived from the sale of products and the provision of services falling within the company's ordinary activities, after deduction of sales rebates and of value added tax and other taxes directly linked to the turnover.

Article 29

1. Income and charges that arise otherwise than in the course of the company's ordinary activities must be shown under 'Extraordinary income and extraordinary charges'.
2. Unless the income and charges referred to in paragraph 1 are immaterial for the assessment of the results, explanations of their amount and nature must be given in the notes on the accounts. The same shall apply to income and charges relating to another financial year.

Article 30

The Member States may permit taxes on the profit or loss on ordinary activities and taxes on the extraordinary profit or loss to be shown in total as one item in the profit and loss account before 'Other taxes not shown under the above items'. In that case, 'Profit or loss on ordinary activities after taxation' shall be omitted from the layouts prescribed in Articles 23 to 26.

Where this derogation is applied, companies must disclose in the notes on the accounts the extent to which the taxes on the profit or loss affect the profit or loss on ordinary activities and the 'Extraordinary profit or loss'.

SECTION 7

Valuation rules

Article 31

1. The Member States shall ensure that the items shown in the annual accounts are valued in accordance with the following general principles:
(a) the company must be presumed to be carrying on its business as a going concern;
(b) the methods of valuation must be applied consistently from one financial year to another;
(c) valuation must be made on a prudent basis, and in particular:
(aa) only profits made at the balance sheet date may be included,
(bb) account must be taken of all foreseeable liabilities and potential losses arising in the course of the financial year concerned or of a previous one, even if such liabilities or losses become apparent only between the date of the balance sheet and the date on which it is drawn up,
(cc) account must be taken of all depreciation, whether the result of the financial year is a loss or a profit;
(d) account must be taken of income and charges relating to the financial year, irrespective of the date of receipt or payment of such income or charges;
(e) the components of asset and liability items must be valued separately;
(f) the opening balance sheet for each financial year must correspond to the closing balance sheet for the preceding financial year.

2. Departures from these general principles shall be permitted in exceptional cases. Any such departures must be disclosed in the notes on the accounts and the reasons for them given together with an assessment of their effect on the assets, liabilities, financial position and profit or loss.

Article 32

The items shown in the annual accounts shall be valued in accordance with Articles 34 to 42, which are based on the principle of purchase price or production cost.

Article 33

1. The Member States may declare to the Commission that they reserve the power, by way of derogation from Article 32 and pending subsequent coordination, to permit or require in respect of all companies or any classes of companies:
(a) valuation by the replacement value method for tangible fixed assets with limited useful economic lives and for stocks;
(b) valuation by methods other than that provided for in (a) which are designed to take account of inflation for the items shown in annual accounts, including capital and reserves;
(c) revaluation of tangible fixed assets and financial fixed assets.

Where national law provides for valuation methods as indicated in (a), (b) and (c), it must define their content and limits and the rules for their application.

The application of any such method, the balance sheet and profit and loss account items concerned and the method by which the values shown are calculated shall be disclosed in the notes on the accounts.

2. (a) Where paragraph 1 is applied, the amount of the difference between valuation

by the method used and valuation in accordance with the general rule laid down in Article 32 must be entered in the revaluation reserve under 'Liabilities'. The treatment of this item for taxation purposes must be explained either in the balance sheet or in the notes on the accounts.

For purposes of the application of the last subparagraph of paragraph 1, companies shall, whenever the amount of the reserve has been changed in the course of the financial year, publish in the notes on the accounts *inter alia* a table showing:

– the amount of the revaluation reserve at the beginning of the financial year,
– the revaluation differences transferred to the revaluation reserve during the financial year,
– the amounts capitalized or otherwise transferred from the revaluation reserve during the financial year, the nature of any such transfer being disclosed,
– the amount of the revaluation reserve at the end of the financial year.

(b) The revaluation reserve may be capitalized in whole or in part at any time.

(c) The revaluation reserve must be reduced to the extent that the amounts transferred thereto are no longer necessary for the implementation of the valuation method used and the achievement of its purpose.

The Member States may lay down rules governing the application of the revaluation reserve, provided that transfers to the profit and loss account from the revaluation reserve may be made only to the extent that the amounts tranferred have been entered as charges in the profit and loss account or reflect increases in value which have been actually realized. These amounts must be disclosed separately in the profit and loss account. No part of the revaluation reserve may be distributed, either directly or indirectly, unless it represents gains actually realized.

(d) Save as provided under (b) en (c) the revaluation reserve may not be reduced.

3. Value adjustments shall be calculated each year on the basis of the value adopted for the financial year in question, save that by way of derogation from Articles 4 and 22, the Member States may permit or require that only the amount of the value adjustments arising as a result of the application of the general rule laid down in Article 32 be shown under the relevant items in the layouts prescribed in Articles 23 to 26 and that the difference arising as a result of the valuation method adopted under this Article be shown separately in the layouts. Furthermore, Article 34 to 42 shall apply *mutatis mutandis*.

4. Where paragraph 1 is applied, the following must be disclosed, either in the balance sheet or in the notes on the accounts, separately for each balance sheet item as provided for in the layouts prescribed in Articles 9 and 10, except for stocks, either:

(a) the amount at the balance sheet date of the valuation made in accordance with the general rule laid down in Article 32 and the amount of the cumulative value adjustments; or

(b) the amount at the balance sheet date of the difference between the valuation made in accordance with this Article and that resulting from the application of Article 32 and, where appropriate, the cumulative amount of the additional value adjustments.

5. Without prejudice to Article 52 the Council shall, on a proposal from the Commission and within seven years of the notification of this Directive, examine and, where necessary, amend this Article in the light of economic and monetary trends in the Community.

OFFICIAL TEXT OF THE FOURTH DIRECTIVE

Article 34

1. (a) Where national law authorizes the inclusion of formation expenses under 'Assets', they must be written off within a maximum period of five years.
   (b) In so far as formation expenses have not been completely written off, no distribution of profits shall take place unless the amount of the reserves available for distribution and profits brought forward is at least equal to that of the expenses not written off.
2. The amounts entered under 'Formation expenses' must be explained in the notes on the accounts.

Article 35

1. (a) Fixed assets must be valued at purchase price or production cost, without prejudice to (b) and (c) below.
   (b) The purchase price or production cost of fixed assets with limited useful economic lives must be reduced by value adjustments calculated to write off the value of such assets systematically over their useful economic lives.
   (c) (aa) Value adjustments may be made in respect of financial fixed assets, so that they are valued at the lower figure to be attributed to them at the balance sheet date.
   (bb) Value adjustments must be made in respect of fixed assets, whether their useful economic lives are limited or not, so that they are valued at the lower figure to be attributed to them at the balance sheet date if it is expected that the reduction in their value will be permanent.
   (cc) The value adjustments referred to in (aa) and (bb) must be charged to the profit and loss account and disclosed separately in the notes on the accounts if they have not been shown separately in the profit and loss account.
   (dd) Valuation at the lower of the values provided for in (aa) and (bb) may not be continued if the reasons for which the value adjustments were made have ceased to apply.
   (d) If fixed assets are the subject of exceptional value adjustments for taxation purposes alone, the amount of the adjustments and the reasons for making them shall be indicated in the notes on the accounts.
2. The purchase price shall be calculated by adding to the price paid the expenses incidental thereto.
3. (a) The production cost shall be calculated by adding to the purchasing price of the raw materials and consumables the costs directly attributable to the product in question.
   (b) A reasonable proportion of the costs which are only indirectly attributable to the product in question may be added into the production costs to the extent that they relate to the period of production.
4. Interest on capital borrowed to finance the production of fixed assets may be included in the production costs to the extent that it relates to the period of production. In that event, the inclusion of such interest under 'Assets' must be disclosed in the notes on the accounts.

Article 36

By way of derogation from Article 35 (1) (c) (cc), the Member States may allow investment companies within the meaning of Article 5 (2) to set off value adjustments to investments directly against 'Capital and reserves'. The amounts in question must be shown separately under 'Liabilities' in the balance sheet.

Article 37

1. Article 34 shall apply to costs of research and development. In exceptional cases, however, the Member States may permit derogations from Article 34 (1) (a). In that case, they may also provide for derogations from Article 34 (1) (b). Such derogations and the reasons for them must be disclosed in the notes on the accounts.
2. Article 34 (1) (a) shall apply to goodwill. The Member States may, however, permit companies to write goodwill off systematically over a limited period exceeding five years provided that this period does not exceed the useful economic life of the asset and is disclosed in the notes on the accounts together with the supporting reasons therefore.

Article 38

Tangible fixed assets, raw materials and consumables which are constantly being replaced and the overall value of which is of secondary importance to the undertaking may be shown under 'Assets' at a fixed quantity and value, if the quantity, value and composition thereof do not vary materially.

Article 39

1. (a) Current assets must be valued at purchase price or production cost, without prejudice to (b) and (c) below.
   (b) Value adjustments shall be made in respect of current assets with a view to showing them at the lower market value or, in particular circumstances, another lower value to be attributed to them at the balance sheet date.
   (c) The Member States may permit exceptional value adjustments where, on the basis of a reasonable commercial assessment, these are necessary if the valuation of these items is not to be modified in the near future because of fluctuations in value. The amount of these value adjustments must be disclosed separately in the profit and loss account or in the notes on the accounts.
   (d) Valuation at the lower value provided for in (b) and (c) may not be continued if the reasons for which the value adjustments were made have ceased to apply.
   (e) If current assets are the subject of exceptional value adjustments for taxation purposes alone, the amount of the adjustments and the reasons for making them must be disclosed in the notes on the accounts.
2. The definitions of purchase price and of production cost given in Article 35 (2) and (3) shall apply. The Member States may also apply Article 35 (4). Distribution costs may not be included in production costs.

Article 40

1. The Member States may permit the purchase price or production cost of stocks of goods of the same category and all fungible items including investments to be calculated either on the basis of weighted average prices or by the 'first in, first out' (FIFO) method, the 'last in, first out' (LIFO) method, or some similar method.
2. Where the value shown in the balance sheet, following application of the methods of calculation specified in paragraph 1, differs materially, at the balance sheet date, from the value on the basis of the last known market value prior to the balance sheet

date, the amount of that difference must be disclosed in total by category in the notes on the accounts.

Article 41
1. Where the amount repayable on account of any debt is greater than the amount received, the difference may be shown as an asset. It must be shown separately in the balance sheet or in the notes on the accounts.
2. The amount of this difference must be written off by a reasonable amount each year and completely written off no later than the time of repayment of the debt.

Article 42
Provisions for liabilities and charges may not exceed in amount the sums which are necessary.
The provisions shown in the balance sheet under 'Other provisions' must be disclosed in the notes on the accounts if they are material.

SECTION 8

Contents of the notes on the accounts

Article 43
1. In addition to the information required under other provisions of this Directive, the notes on the accounts must set out information in respect of the following matters at least:

(1) the valuation methods applied to the various items in the annual accounts, and the methods employed in calculating the value adjustments. For items included in the annual accounts which are or were originally expressed in foreign currency, the bases of conversion used to express them in local currency must be disclosed;

(2) the name and registered office of each of the undertakings in which the company, either itself or through a person acting in his own name but on the company's behalf, holds at least a percentage of the capital which the Member States cannot fix at more than 20 %, showing the proportion of the capital held, the amount of capital and reserves, and the profit or loss for the latest financial year of the undertaking concerned for which accounts have been adopted. This information may be omitted where for the purposes of Article 2 (3) it is of negligible importance only. The information concerning capital and reserves and the profit or loss may also be omitted where the undertaking concerned does not publish its balance sheet and less than 50 % of its capital is held (directly or indirectly) by the company;

(3) the number and the nominal value or, in the absence of a nominal value, the accounting par value of the shares subscribed during the financial year within the limits of an authorized capital, without prejudice as far as the amount of this capital is concerned to Article 2 (1)(e) of Directive 68/151/EEC of to Article 2 (c) or Directive 77/91/EEC;

(4) where there is more than one class of shares, the number and the nominal value

or, in the absence of a nominal value, the accounting par value for each class;

(5) the existence of any participation certificates, convertible debentures or similar securities or rights, with an indication of their number and the rights they confer;

(6) Amounts owed by the company becoming due and payable after more than five years as well as the company's entire debts covered by valuable security furnished by the company with an indication of the nature and form of the security. This information must be disclosed separately for each creditors item, as provided for in the layouts prescribed in Articles 9 and 10;

(7) the total amount of any financial commitments that are not included in the balance sheet, in so far as this information is of assistance in assessing the financial position. Any commitments concerning pensions and affiliated undertakings must be disclosed separately;

(8) the net turnover within the meaning of Article 28, broken down by categories of activity and into geographical markets in so far as, taking account of the manner in which the sale of products and the provision of services falling within the company's ordinary activities are organized, these categories and markets differ substantially from one another;

(9) the average number of persons employed during the financial year, broken down by categories and, if they are not disclosed separately in the profit and loss account, the staff costs relating to the financial year, broken down as provided for in Article 23 (6);

(10) the extent to which the calculation of the profit or loss for the financial year has been affected by a valuation of the items which, by way of derogation from the principles enunciated in Articles 31 and 34 to 42, was made in the financial year in question or in an earlier financial year with a view to obtaining tax relief. Where the influence of such a valuation on future tax charges is material, details must be disclosed;

(11) the difference between the tax charged for the financial year and for earlier financial years and the amount of tax payable in respect of those years, provided that this difference is material for purposes of future taxation. This amount may also be disclosed in the balance sheet as a cumulative amount under a separate item with an appropriate heading;

(12) the amount of the emoluments granted in respect of the financial year to the members of the administrative, managerial and supervisory bodies by reason of their responsibilities, and any commitments arising or entered into in respect of retirement pensions for former members of those bodies, with an indication of the total for each category;

(13) the amount of advances and credits granted to the members of the administrative, managerial and supervisory bodies, with indications of the interest rates, main conditions and any amounts repaid, as well as commitments entered into on their behalf by way of guarantees of any kind, with an indication of the total for each category.

2. Pending subsequent coordination, the Member States need not apply paragraph 1 (2) to financial holding companies within the meaning of Article 5 (3).

Article 44

The Member States may permit the companies referred to in Article 11 to draw up abridged notes on their accounts without the information required in Article 43 (1) (5) to

OFFICIAL TEXT OF THE FOURTH DIRECTIVE

(12). However, the notes must disclose the information specified in Article 43 (1) (6) in total for all the items concerned.
Article 12 shall apply.

Article 45

1. The Member States may allow the disclosures prescribed in Article 43 (1) (2):
(a) to take the form of a statement deposited in accordance with Article 3 (1) and (2) of Directive 68/151/EEC; this must be disclosed in the notes on the accounts;
(b) to be omitted when their nature is such that they would be seriously prejudicial to any of the undertakings to which Article 43 (1) (2) relates. The Member States may make such omissions subject to prior administrative or judicial authorization. Any such omission must be disclosed in the notes on the accounts.

2. Paragraph 1 (b) shall also apply to the information prescribed by Article 43 (1) (8). The Member States may permit the companies referred to in Article 27 to omit the disclosures prescribed by Article 43 (1) (8). Article 12 shall apply.

SECTION 9

Contents of the annual report

Article 46

1. The annual report must include at least a fair review of the development of the company's business and of its position.
2. The report shall also give an indication of:
(a) any important events that have occurred since the end of the financial year;
(b) the company's likely future development;
(c) activities in the field of research and development;
(d) the information concerning acquisitions of own shares prescribed by Article 22 (2) of Directive 77/91/EEC.

SECTION 10

Publication

Article 47

1. The annual accounts, duly approved, and the annual report, together with the opinion submitted by the person responsible for auditing the accounts, shall be published as laid down by the laws of each Member State in accordance with Article 3 of Directive 68/151/EEC.
The laws of a Member State may, however, permit the annual report not to be published as stipulated above. In that case, it shall be made available to the public at the company's registered office in the Member State concerned. It must be possible to obtain a copy of all or part of any such report free of charge upon request.
2. By way of derogation from paragraph 1, the Member States may permit the companies referred to in Article 11 to publish:
(a) abridged balance sheets showing only those items preceded by letters and roman numerals in Articles 9 and 10, disclosing separately the information required in

OFFICIAL TEXT OF THE FOURTH DIRECTIVE

brackets in D (II) under 'Assets' and C under 'Liabilities' in Article 9 and in D (II) in Article 10, but in total for all the items concerned; and

(b) abridged notes on their accounts without the explanations required in Article 43 (1) (5) to (12). However, the notes must disclose the information specified in Article 43 (1) (6) in total for all the items concerned.

Article 12 shall apply.

In addition, the Member States may relieve such companies from the obligation to publish their profit and loss accounts and annual reports and the opinions of the persons responsible for auditing the accounts.

3. The Member States may permit the companies mentioned in Article 27 to publish:

(a) abridged balance sheets showing only those items preceded by letters and roman numerals in Articles 9 and 10 disclosing separately, either in the balance sheet or in the notes on the accounts:
   - C (I) (3), C (II) (1), (2), (3) and (4), C (III) (1), (2), (3), (4) and (7), D (II) (2), (3) and (6) and D (III) (1) and (2) under 'Assets' and C (1), (2), (6), (7) and (9) under 'Liabilities' in Article 9,
   - C (I) (3), C (II) (1), (2), (3) and (4), C (III) (1), (2), (3), (4) and (7), D (II) (2), (3) and (6), D (III) (1) and (2), F (1), (2), (6), (7) and (9) and (I) (1), (2), (6), (7) and (9) in Article 10,
   - the information required in brackets in D (II) under 'Assets' and C under 'Liabilities' in Article 9, in total for all the items concerned and separately for D (II) (2) and (3) under 'Assets' and C (1), (2), (6), (7) and (9) under 'Liabilities',
   - the information required in brackets in D (II) in Article 10, in total for all the items concerned, and separately for D (II) (2) and (3);

(b) abridged notes on their accounts without the information required in Article 43 (1) (5), (6), (8), (10) and (11). However, the notes on the accounts must give the information specified in Article 43 (1) (6) in total for all the items concerned.

This paragraph shall be without prejudice to paragraph 1 in so far as it relates to the profit and loss account, the annual report and the opinion of the person responsible for auditing the accounts.

Article 12 shall apply.

Article 48

Whenever the annual accounts and the annual report are published in full, they must be reproduced in the form and text on the basis of which the person responsible for auditing the accounts has drawn up his opinion. They must be accompanied by the full text of his report. If the person responsible for auditing the accounts has made any qualifications or refused to report upon the accounts, that fact must be disclosed and the reasons given.

Article 49

If the annual accounts are not published in full, it must be indicated that the version published is abridged and reference must be made to the register in which the accounts have been filed in accordance with Article 47 (1). Where such filing has not yet been effected, the fact must be disclosed. The report issued by the person responsible for auditing the accounts may not accompany this publication, but it must be disclosed whether the report was issued with or without qualification, or was refused.

OFFICIAL TEXT OF THE FOURTH DIRECTIVE

Article 50

The following must be published together with the annual accounts, and in like manner:

– the proposed appropriation of the profit or treatment of the loss,

– the appropriation of the profit or treatment of the loss,

where these items do not appear in the annual accounts.

SECTION 11

Auditing

Article 51

1. (a) Companies must have their annual accounts audited by one or more persons authorized by national law to audit accounts.

(b) The person or persons responsible for auditing the accounts must also verify that the annual report is consistent with the annual accounts for the same financial year.

2. The Member States may relieve the companies referred to in Article 11 from the obligation impose by paragraph 1.

Article 12 shall apply.

3. Where the exemption provided for in paragraph 2 is granted the Member States shall introduce appropriate sanctions into their laws for cases in which the annual accounts or the annual reports of such companies are not drawn up in accordance with the requirements of this Directive.

SECTION 12

Final provisions

Article 52

1. A Contact Committee shall be set up under the auspices of the Commission. Its function shall be:

(a) to facilitate, without prejudice to the provisions of Articles 169 and 170 of the Treaty, harmonized application of this Directive through regular meetings dealing in particular with practical problems arising in connection with its application;

(b) to advise the Commission, if necessary, on additions or amendments to this Directive.

2. The Contact Committee shall be composed of representatives of the Member States and representatives of the Commission. The chairman shall be a representative of the Commission. The Commission shall provide the secretariat.

3. The Committee shall be convened by the chairman either on his own initiative or at the request of one of its members.

Article 53

1. For the purposes of this Directive, the European unit of account shall be that defined by Commission Decision No 3289/75/ECSC of 18 December 1975(1). The equivalent in national currency shall be caculated initially at the rate obtaining on the date of

(1) OJ No L327, 19.12.1975, p. 4.

adoption of this Directive.
2. Every five years the Council, acting on a proposal from the Commission, shall examine and, if need be, revise the amounts expressed in European units of account in this Directive, in the light of economic and monetary trends in the Community.

Article 54
This Directive shall not affect laws in the Member States requiring that the annual accounts of companies not falling within their jurisdiction be filed in a register in which branches of such companies are listed.

Article 55
1. The Member States shall bring into force the laws, regulations and administrative provisions necessary for them to comply with this Directive within two years of its notification. They shall forthwith inform the Commission thereof.
2. The Member States may stipulate that the provisions referred to in paragraph 1 shall no apply until 18 months after the end of the period provided for in that paragraph. That period of 18 months may, however, be five years:
(a) in the case of unregistered companies in the United Kingdom and Ireland;
(b) for purposes of the application of Articles 9 and 10 and Articles 23 to 26 concerning the layouts for the balance sheet and the profit and loss account, where a Member State has brought other layouts for these documents into force not more than three years before the notification of this Directive;
(c) for purposes of the application of this Directive as regards the calculation and disclosure in balance sheets of depreciation relating to assets covered by the asset items mentioned in Article 9, C (II) (2) and (3), and Article 10, C (II) (2) and (3);
(d) for purposes of the application of Article 47 (1) of this Directive except as regards companies already under an obligation of publication under Article 2 (1) (f) of Directive 68/151/EEC. In this case the second subparagraph of Article 47 (1) of this Directive shall apply to the annual accounts and to the opinion drawn up by the person responsible for auditing the accounts;
(e) for purposes of the application of Article 51 (1) of this Directive.
Furthermore, this period of 18 months may be extended to eight years for companies the principal object of which is shipping and which are already in existence on the entry into force of the provisions referred to in paragraph 1.
3. The Member States shall ensure that they communicate to the Commission the texts of the main provisions of national law which they adopt in the field covered by this Directive.

Article 56
The obligation to show in the annual accounts the items prescribed by Articles 9, 10 and 23 to 26 which relate to affiliated undertakings, and the obligation to provide information concerning these undertakings in accordance with Article 13 (2), 14 or 43 (1) (7), shall enter into force at the same time as a Council Directive on consolidated accounts.

Article 57
1. Until the entry into force of a Council Directive on consolidated accounts, and without prejudice to the provisions of Directives 68/151/EEC and 77/91/EEC, the Member States need not apply to the dependent companies of any group governed by their

national laws the provisions of this Directive concerning the content, auditing and publication of the annual accounts of such dependent companies where the following conditions are fulfilled:

(a) the dominant company must be subject to the laws of a Member State;
(b) all shareholders or members of the dependent company must have declared their agreement to the exemption from such obligation; this declaration must be made in respect of every financial year;
(c) the dominant company must have declared that it guarantees the commitments entered into by the dependent company;
(d) the declarations referred to in (b) and (c) must be published by the dependent company in accordance with the first subparagraph of Article 47 (1);
(e) the annual accounts of the dependent company must be consolidated in the group's annual accounts;
(f) the exemption concerning the preparation, auditing and publication of the annual accounts of the dependent company must be disclosed in the notes on the group's annual accounts.

2. Articles 47 and 51 shall apply to the group's annual accounts.
3. Articles 2 to 46 shall apply as far as possible to the group's annual accounts.

Article 58

1. Until the entry into force of a Council Directive on consolidated accounts, and without prejudice to the provisions of Directive 77/91/EEC, the Member States need not apply to the dominant companies of groups governed by their national laws the provisions of this Directive concerning the auditing and publication of the profit and loss accounts of such dominant companies where the following conditions are fulfilled:

(a) this exemption must be published by the dominant company in accordance with Article 47 (1);
(b) the annual accounts of the dominant company must be consolidated in the group's annual accounts;
(c) the exemption concerning the auditing and publication of the profit and loss account of the dominant company must be mentioned in the notes on the group's annual accounts;
(d) the profit or loss of the dominant company, determined in accordance with the principles of this Directive, must be shown in the balance sheet of the dominant company.

2. Articles 47 and 51 shall apply to the group's annual accounts.
3. Articles 2 to 46 shall apply as far as possible to the group's annual accounts.

Article 59

Pending subsequent coordination, the Member States may permit the valuation of holdings in affiliated undertakings by the equity method provided the following conditions are fulfilled:

(a) the use of this method of valuation must be disclosed in the notes on the accounts of a company having such holdings;
(b) the amount of any differences existing when such holdings were acquired between their purchase price and the percentage of the capital which they represent, including the affiliated undertaking's reserves, profit and loss and profits and losses brought forward, must be shown separately in the balance sheet or in the notes on

the accounts of a company having such holdings;

(c) the purchase price of these holdings shall be increased or reduced in the balance sheet of a company having such holdings by the profits or losses realized by the affiliated undertaking according to the percentage of capital held;

(d) the amounts specified in subparagraph (c) shall be shown each year in the profit and loss account of a company having such holdings as a separate item with an appropriate heading;

(e) when an affiliated undertaking distributes dividends to a company having such holdings, their book values shall be reduced accordingly;

(f) when the amounts shown in the profit and loss account in accordance with subparagraph (d) exceed the amounts of dividends already received or the payment of which can be claimed, the amount of the differences must be placed in a reserve which cannot be distributed to shareholders.

Article 60

Pending subsequent coordination, the Member States may prescribe that investments in which investment companies within the meaning of Article 5 (2) have invested their funds shall be valued on the basis of their market value.

In that case, the Member States may also waive the obligation on investment companies with variable capital to show separately the value adjustments referred to in Article 36.

Article 61

Until the entry into force of a Council Directive on consolidated accounts, the Member States need not apply to the dominant companies of groups governed by their national laws the provisions of Article 43 (1) (2) concerning the amount of capital and reserves and the profits and losses of the undertakings concerned if the annual accounts of such undertakings are consolidated into the group's annual accounts or if the holdings in those undertakings are valued by the equity method.

Article 62

This Directive is addressed to the Member States.

Done at Brussels, 25 July 1978.

For the Council

The President

K. von DOHNANYI

[27]

OFFICIAL TEXT OF THE SEVENTH DIRECTIVE

SEVENTH COUNCIL DIRECTIVE
of 13 June 1983
based on the Article 54 (3) (g) of the Treaty on consolidated accounts

(83/349/EEC)

THE COUNCIL OF THE EUROPEAN COMMUNITIES,

Having regard to the Treaty establishing the European Economic Community, and in particular Article 54 (3) (g) thereof,

Having regard to the proposal from the Commission([1]),

Having regard to the opinion of the European Parliament([2]),

Having regard to the opinion of the Economic and Social Committee([3]),

Whereas on 25 July 1978 the Council adopted Directive 78/660/EEC([4]) on the coordination of national legislation governing the annual accounts of certain types of companies; whereas many companies are members of bodies of undertakings; whereas consolidated accounts must be drawn up so that financial information concerning such bodies of undertakings may be conveyed to members and third parties; whereas national legislation governing consolidated accounts must therefore be coordinated in order to achieve the objectives of comparability and equivalence in the information which companies must publish within the Community;

Whereas in the determination of the conditions for consolidation, account must be taken not only of cases in which the power of control is based on a majority of voting rights but also of those in which it is based on agreements, where these are permitted; whereas, furthermore, Member States in which the possibility occurs must be permitted to cover cases in which in certain circumstances control has been effectively exercised on the basis of a minority holding; whereas the Member States must be permitted to cover the case of bodies of undertakings in which the undertakings exist on an equal footing with each other;

Whereas the aim of coordinating the legislation governing consolidated accounts is to protect the interests subsisting in companies with share capital; whereas such protection implies the principle of the preparation of consolidated accounts where such a company is a member of a body of undertakings, and that such accounts must be drawn up at least where such a company is a parent undertaking; whereas, furthermore, the cause of full information also requires that a subsidiary undertaking which is itself a parent undertaking draw up consolidated accounts; whereas, nevertheless, such a parent undertaking may, and, in certain circumstances, must be exempted from the obligation to draw up such consolidated accounts provided that its members and third parties are sufficiently protected;

Whereas, for bodies of undertakings not exceeding a certain size, exemption from the obligation to prepare consolidated accounts may be justified; whereas, accordingly, maximum limits must be set for such exemptions; whereas it follows therefrom that the Member States may either provide that it is sufficient to exceed the limit of one only of

---

([1]) OJ No C121, 2.6.1976, p. 2.
([2]) OJ No C163, 10.7.1978, p. 60.
([3]) OJ No C 75, 26.3.1977, p. 5.
([4]) OJ No L222, 14.8.1978, p. 11. See appendix 2.

OFFICIAL TEXT OF THE SEVENTH DIRECTIVE

the three criteria for the exemption not to apply or adopt limits lower than those prescribed in the Directive;

Whereas consolidated accounts must give a true and fair view of the assets and liabilities, the financial position and the profit and loss of all the undertakings consolidated taken as a whole; whereas, therefore, consolidation should in principle include all of those undertakings; whereas such consolidation requires the full incorporation of the assets and liabilities and of the income and expenditure of those undertakings and the separate disclosure of the interests of persons outwith such bodies; whereas, however, the necessary corrections must be made to eliminate the effects of the financial relations between the undertakings consolidated;

Whereas a number of principles relating to the preparation of consolidated accounts and valuation in the context of such accounts must be laid down in order to ensure that items are disclosed consistently, and may readily be compared not only as regards the methods used in their valuation but also as regards the periods covered by the accounts;

Whereas participating interests in the capital of undertakings over which undertakings included in a consolidation exercise significant influence must be included in consolidated accounts by means of the equity method;

Whereas the notes on consolidated accounts must give details of the undertakings to be consolidated;

Whereas certain derogations originally provided for on a transitional basis in Directive 78/660/EEC may be continued subject to review at a later date,

HAS ADOPTED THIS DIRECTIVE:

SECTION 1

Conditions for the preparation of consolidated accounts

Article 1

1. A Member State shall require any undertaking governed by its national law to draw up consolidated accounts and a consolidated annual report if that undertaking (a parent undertaking):

(a) has a majority of the shareholders' or members' voting rights in another undertaking (a subsidiary undertaking); or

(b) has the right to appoint or remove a majority of the members of the administrative, management or supervisory body of another undertaking (a subsidiary undertaking) and is at the same time a shareholder in or member of that undertaking; or

(c) has the right to exercise a dominant influence over an undertaking (a subsidiary undertaking) of which it is a shareholder or member, pursuant to a contract entered into with that undertaking or to a provision in its memorandum or articles of association, where the law governing that subsidiary undertaking permits its being subject to such contracts or provisions. A Member State need not prescribe that a parent undertaking must be a shareholder in or member of its subsidiary undertaking. Those Member States the laws of which do not provide for such contracts or clauses shall not be required to apply this provision; or

(d) is a shareholder in or member of an undertaking; and

(aa) a majority of the members of the administrative, management or supervisory bodies of that undertaking (a subsidiary undertaking) who have held office during the financial year, during the preceding financial year and up to the time when the consolidated accounts are drawn up, have been appointed solely as a result of the exercise of its voting rights; or

(bb) controls alone, pursuant to an agreement with other shareholders in or members of that undertaking (a subsidiary undertaking), a majority of shareholders' or members' voting rights in that undertaking. The Member States may introduce more detailed provisions concerning the form and contents of such agreements.

The Member States shall prescribe at least the arrangements referred to in (bb) above.

They may make the application of (aa) above dependent upon the holding's representing 20 % or more of the shareholders' or members' voting rights.

However, (aa) above shall not apply where another undertaking has the rights referred to in subparagraphs (a), (b) or (c) above with regard to that subsidiary undertaking.

2. Apart from the cases mentioned in paragraph 1 above and pending subsequent co-ordination, the Member States may require any undertaking governed by their national law to draw up consolidated accounts and a consolidated annual report if that undertaking (a parent undertaking) holds a participating interest as defined in Article 17 of Directive 78/660/EEC in another undertaking (a subsidiary undertaking), and:

(a) it actually exercises a dominant influence over it; or

(b) it and the subsidiary undertaking are managed on a unified basis by the parent undertaking.

Article 2

1. For the purposes of Article 1 (1) (a), (b) and (d), the voting rights and the rights of appointment and removal of any other subsidiary undertaking as well as those of any person acting in his own name but on behalf of the parent undertaking or of another subsidiary undertaking must be added to those of the parent undertaking.

2. For the purposes of Article 1 (1) (a), (b) and (d), the rights mentioned in paragraph 1 above must be reduced by the rights:

(a) attaching to shares held on behalf of a person who is neither the parent undertaking nor a subsidiary thereof; or

(b) attaching to shares held by way of security, provided that the rights in question are exercised in accordance with the instructions received, or held in connection with the granting of loans as part of normal business activities, provided that the voting rights are exercised in the interests of the person providing the security.

3. For the purposes of Article 1 (1) (a) and (d), the total of the shareholders' or members' voting rights in the subsidiary undertaking must be reduced by the voting rights attaching to the shares held by that undertaking itself by a subsidiary undertaking of that undertaking or by a person acting in his own name but on behalf of those undertakings.

Article 3

1. Without prejudice to Articles 13, 14 and 15, a parent undertaking and all of its subsidiary undertakings shall be undertakings to be consolidated regardless of where the registered offices of such subsidiary undertakings are situated.

2. For the purposes of paragraph 1 above, any subsidiary undertaking of a subsidiary undertaking shall be considered a subsidiary undertaking of the parent undertaking which is the parent of the undertakings to be consolidated.

OFFICIAL TEXT OF THE SEVENTH DIRECTIVE

Article 4

1. For the purposes of this Directive, a parent undertaking and all of its subsidiary undertakings shall be undertakings to be consolidated where either the parent undertaking or one or more subsidiary undertakings is established as one of the following types of company:

(a) *in Germany:*
die Aktiengesellschaft, die Kommanditgesellschaft auf Aktien, die Gesellschaft mit beschränkter Haftung;

(b) *in Belgium:*
la société anonyme/de naamloze vennootschap – la société en commandite par actions / de commanditaire vennootschap op aandelen – la société de personnes à responsabilité limitée / de personenvennootschap met beperkte aansprakelijkheid;

(c) *in Denmark:*
aktieselskaber, kommanditaktieselskaber, anpartsselskaber;

(d) *in France:*
la société anonyme, la société en commandite par actions, la société à responsabilité limitée;

(e) *in Greece:*
anonymos eteria, eterorrythmos kata metochas eteria, eteria periorismenis efthinis;

(f) *in Ireland:*
public companies limited by shares or by guarantee, private companies limited by shares or by guarantee;

(g) *in Italy:*
la società per azioni, la società in accomandita per azioni, la società a responsabilità limitata;

(h) *in Luxembourg:*
la société anonyme, la société en commandite par actions, la société à responsabilité limitée;

(i) *in the Netherlands:*
de naamloze vennootschap, de besloten vennootschap met beperkte aansprakelijkheid;

(j) *in the United Kingdom:*
public companies limited by shares or by guarantee, private companies limited by shares or by guarantee.

2. A Member State may, however, grant exemption from the obligation imposed in Article 1 (1) where the parent undertaking is not established as one of the types of company listed in paragraph 1 above.

Article 5

1. A Member State may grant exemption from the obligation imposed in Article 1 (1) where the parent undertaking is a financial holding company as defined in Article 5 (3) of Directive 78/660/EEC, and:

(a) it has not intervened during the financial year, directly or indirectly, in the management of a subsidiary undertaking;

(b) it has not exercised the voting rights attaching to its participating interest in respect of the appointment of a member of a subsidiary undertaking's administrative, management or supervisory bodies during the financial year or the five preceding financial years or, where the exercise of voting rights was necessary for the operation of

OFFICIAL TEXT OF THE SEVENTH DIRECTIVE

the administrative, management or supervisory bodies of the subsidiary undertaking, no shareholder in or member of the parent undertaking with majority voting rights or member of the administrative, management or supervisory bodies of that undertaking or of a member thereof with majority voting rights is a member of the administrative, management or supervisory bodies of the subsidiary undertaking and the members of those bodies so appointed have fulfilled their functions without any interference or influence on the part of the parent undertaking or of any of its subsidiary undertakings;

(c) it has made loans only to undertakings in which it holds participating interests. Where such loans have been made to other parties, they must have been repaid by the end of the previous financial year; and

(d) the exemption is granted by an administrative authority after fulfilment of the above conditions has been checked.

2. (a) Where a financial holding company has been exempted, Article 43 (2) of Directive 78/660/EEC shall not apply to its annual accounts with respect to any majority holdings in subsidiary undertakings as from the date provided for in Article 49 (2).

(b) The disclosures in respect of such majority holdings provided for in point 2 of Article 43 (1) of Directive 78/660/EEC may be omitted when their nature is such that they would be seriously prejudicial to the company, to its shareholders or members or to one of its subsidiaries. A Member State may make such omissions subject to prior administrative or judicial authorization. Any such omission must be disclosed in the notes on the accounts.

Article 6

1. Without prejudice to Articles 4 (2) and 5, a Member State may provide for an exemption from the obligation imposed in Article 1 (1) if as at the balance sheet date of a parent undertaking the undertakings to be consolidated do not together, on the basis of their latest annual accounts, exceed the limits of two of the three criteria laid down in Article 27 of Directive 78/660/EEC.

2. A Member State may require or permit that the set-off referred to in Article 19 (1) and the elimination referred to in Article 26 (1) (a) and (b) be not effected when the aforementioned limits are calculated. In that case, the limits for the balance sheet total and net turnover criteria shall be increased by 20 %.

3. Article 12 of Directive 78/660/EEC shall apply to the above criteria.

4. This Article shall not apply where one of the undertakings to be consolidated is a company the securities of which have been admitted to official listing on a stock exchange established in a Member State.

5. For 10 years after the date referred to in Article 49 (2), the Member States may multiply the criteria expressed in ECU by up to 2,5 and may increase the average number of persons employed during the financial year to a maximum of 500.

Article 7

1. Notwithstanding Articles 4 (2), 5 and 6, a Member State shall exempt from the obligation imposed in Article 1 (1) any parent undertaking governed by its national law which is also a subsidiary undertaking if its own parent undertaking is governed by the law of a Member State in the following two cases;

(a) where that parent undertaking holds all of the shares in the exempted undertaking.

The shares in that undertaking held by members of its administrative, management of supervisory bodies pursuant to an obligation in law or in the memorandum or acticles of association shall be ignored for this purpose; or

(b) where that parent undertaking holds 90 % or more of the shares in the exempted undertaking and the remaining shareholders in or members of that undertaking have approved the exemption.

In so far as the laws of a Member State prescribe consolidation in this case at the time of the adoption of this Directive, that Member State need not apply this provision for 10 years after the date referred to in Article 49 (2).

2. Exemption shall be conditional upon compliance with all of the following conditions:

(a) the exempted undertaking and, without prejudice to Articles 13, 14 and 15, all of its subsidiary undertakings must be consolidated in the accounts of a larger body of undertakings, the parent undertaking of which is governed by the law of a Member State;

(b) (aa) the consolidated accounts referred to in (a) above and the consolidated annual report of the larger body of undertakings must be drawn up by the parent undertaking of that body and audited, according to the law of the Member State by which the parent undertaking of that larger body of undertakings is governed, in accordance with this Directive;

(bb) the consolidated accounts referred to in (a) above and the consolidated annual report referred to in (aa) above, the report by the person responsible for auditing those accounts and, where appropriate, the appendix referred to in Article 9 must be published for the exempted undertaking in the manner prescribed by the law of the Member State governing that undertaking in accordance with Article 38. That Member State may require that those documents be published in its official language and that the translation be certified;

(c) the notes on the annual accounts of the exempted undertaking must disclose:

(aa) the name and registered office of the parent undertaking that draws up the consolidated accounts referred to in (a) above; and

(bb) the exemption from the obligation to draw up consolidated accounts and a consolidated annual report.

3. A Member State need not, however, apply this Article to companies the securities of which have been admitted to official listing on a stock exchange established in a Member State.

Article 8

1. In cases not covered by Article 7 (1), a Member State may, without prejudice to Articles 4 (2), 5 and 6, exempt from the obligation imposed in Article 1 (1) any parent undertaking governed by its national law which is also a subsidiary undertaking, the parent undertaking of which is governed by the law of a Member State, provided that all the conditions set out in Article 7 (2) are fulfilled and that the shareholders in or members of the exempted undertaking who own a minimum proportion of the subscribed capital of that undertaking have not requested the preparation of consolidated accounts at least six months before the end of the financial year. The Member States may fix that proportion at not more than 10 % for public limited liability companies and for limited partnerships with share capital, and at not more than 20 % for undertakings of other types.

2. A Member State may not make it a condition for this exemption that the parent

OFFICIAL TEXT OF THE SEVENTH DIRECTIVE

undertaking which prepared the consolidated accounts described in Article 7 (2) (a) must also be governed by its national law.

3. A Member State may not make exemption subject to conditions concerning the preparation and auditing of the consolidated accounts referred to in Article 7 (2) (a).

Article 9

1. A Member State may make the exemptions provided for in Articles 7 and 8 dependent upon the disclosure of additional information, in accordance with this Directive, in the consolidated accounts referred to in Article 7 (2) (a), or in an appendix thereto, if that information is required of undertakings governed by the national law of that Member State which are obliged to prepare consolidated accounts and are in the same circumstances.

2. A Member State may also make exemption dependent upon the disclosure, in the notes on the consolidated accounts referred to in Article 7 (2) (a), or in the annual accounts of the exempted undertaking, of all or some of the following information regarding the body of undertakings, the parent undertaking of which it is exempting from the obligation to draw up consolidated accounts:

– the amount of the fixed assets,
– the net turnover,
– the profit or loss for the financial year and the amount of the capital and reserves,
– the average number of persons employed during the financial year.

Article 10

Articles 7 to 9 shall not affect any Member State's legislation on the drawing up of consolidated accounts or consolidated annual reports in so far as those documents are required:

– for the information of employees or their representatives, or
– by an administrative or judicial authority for its own purposes.

Article 11

1. Without prejudice to Articles 4 (2), 5 and 6, a Member State may exempt from the obligation imposed in Article 1 (1) any parent undertaking governed by its national law which is also a subsidiary undertaking of a parent undertaking not governed by the law of a Member State, if all of the following conditions are fulfilled:

(a) the exempted undertaking and, without prejudice to Articles 13, 14 and 15, all of its subsidiary undertakings must be consolidated in the accounts of a larger body of undertakings;

(b) the consolidated accounts referred to in (a) above and, where appropriate, the consolidated annual report must be drawn up in accordance with this Directive or in a manner equivalent to consolidated accounts and consolidated annual reports drawn up in accordance with this Directive;

(c) the consolidated accounts referred to in (a) above must have been audited by one or more persons authorized to audit accounts under the national law governing the undertaking which drew them up.

2. Articles 7 (2) (b) (bb) and (c) and 8 to 10 shall apply.

3. A Member State may provide for exemptions under this Article only if it provides for the same exemptions under Articles 7 to 10.

OFFICIAL TEXT OF THE SEVENTH DIRECTIVE

Article 12

1. Without prejudice to Articles 1 to 10, a Member State may require any undertaking governed by its national law to draw up consolidated accounts and a consolidated annual report if:

(a) that undertaking and one or more other undertakings with which it is not connected, as described in Article 1 (1) or (2), are managed on a unified basis pursuant to a contract concluded with that undertaking or provisions in the memorandum or articles of association of those undertakings; or

(b) the administrative, management or supervisory bodies of that undertaking and of one or more other undertakings with which it is not connected, as described in Article 1 (1) or (2), consist for the major part of the same persons in office during the financial year and until the consolidated accounts are drawn up.

2. Where paragraph 1 above is applied, undertakings related as defined in that paragraph together with all of their subsidiary undertakings shall be undertakings to be consolidated, as defined in this Directive, where one or more of those undertakings is established as one of the types of company listed in Article 4.

3. Articles 3, 4 (2), 5, 6, 13 to 28, 29 (1), (3), (4) and (5), 30 to 38 and 39 (2) shall apply to the consolidated accounts and the consolidated annual report covered by this Article, references to parent undertakings being understood to refer to all the undertakings specified in paragraph 1 above. Without prejudice to Article 19 (2), however, the items 'capital', 'share premium account', 'revaluation reserve', 'reserves', 'profit or loss brought forward', and 'profit or loss for the financial year' to be included in the consolidated accounts shall be the aggregate amounts attributable to each of the undertakings specified in paragraph 1.

Article 13

1. An undertaking need not be included in consolidated accounts where it is not material for the purposes of Article 16 (3).

2. Where two or more undertakings satisfy the requirements of paragraph 1 above, they must nevertheless be included in consolidated accounts if, as a whole, they are material for the purposes of Article 16 (3).

3. In addition, an undertaking need not be included in consolidated accounts where:

(a) severe long-term restrictions substantially hinder:

   (aa) the parent undertaking in the exercise of its rights over the assets or management of that undertaking; or

   (bb) the exercise of unified management of that undertaking where it is in one of the relationships defined in Article 12 (1); or

(b) the information necessary for the preparation of consolidated accounts in accordance with this Directive cannot be obtained without disproportionate expense or undue delay; or

(c) the shares of that undertaking are held exclusively with a view to their subsequent resale.

Article 14

1. Where the activities of one or more undertakings to be consolidated are so different that their inclusion in the consolidated accounts would be incompatible with the obligation imposed in Article 16 (3), such undertakings must, without prejudice to Article 33 of this Directive, be excluded from the consolidation.

2. Paragraph 1 above shall not be applicable merely by virtue of the fact that the undertakings to be consolidated are partly industrial, partly commercial, and partly provide services, or because such undertakings carry on industrial or commercial activities involving different products or provide different services.
3. Any application of paragraph 1 above and the reasons therefor must be disclosed in the notes on the accounts. Where the annual or consolidated accounts of the undertakings thus excluded from the consolidation are not published in the same Member State in accordance with Directive 68/151/EEC(1), they must be attached to the consolidated accounts or made available to the public. In the latter case it must be possible to obtain a copy of such documents upon request. The price of such a copy must not exceed its administrative cost.

Article 15

1. A Member State may, for the purposes of Article 16 (3), permit the omission from consolidated accounts of any parent undertaking not carrying on any industrial or commercial activity which holds shares in a subsidiary undertaking on the basis of a joint arrangement with one or more undertakings not included in the consolidated accounts.
2. The annual accounts of the parent undertaking shall be attached to the consolidated accounts.
3. Where use is made of this derogation, either Article 59 of Directive 78/660/EEC shall apply to the parent undertaking's annual accounts or the information which would have resulted from its application must be given in the notes on those accounts.

SECTION 2

The preparation of consolidated accounts

Article 16

1. Consolidated accounts shall comprise the consolidated balance sheet, the consolidated profit-and-loss account and the notes on the accounts. These documents shall constitute a composite whole.
2. Consolidated accounts shall be drawn up clearly and in accordance with this Directive.
3. Consolidated accounts shall give a true and fair view of the assets, liabilities, financial position and profit or loss of the undertakings included therein taken as a whole.
4. Where the application of the provisions of this Directive would not be sufficient to give a true and fair view within the meaning of paragraph 3 above, additional information must be given.
5. Where, in exeptional cases, the application of a provision of Articles 17 to 35 and 39 is incompatible with the obligation imposed in paragraph 3 above, that provision must be departed from in order to give a true and fair view within the meaning of paragraph 3. Any such departure must be disclosed in the notes on the accounts together with an explanation of the reasons for it and a statement of its effect on the assets, liabilities,

(1) OJ No L65, 14.3.1968, p. 8.
See page 360 of this book.

financial position and profit or loss. The Member States may define the exceptional cases in question and lay down the relevant special rules.

6. A Member State may require or permit the disclosure in the consolidated accounts of other information as well as that which must be disclosed in accordance with this Directive.

Article 17

1. Articles 3 to 10, 13 to 26 and 28 to 30 of Directive 78/660/EEC shall apply in respect of the layout of consolidated accounts, without prejudice to the provisions of this Directive and taking account of the essential adjustments resulting from the particular characteristics of consolidated accounts as compared with annual accounts.

2. Where there are special circumstances which would entail undue expense a Member State may permit stocks to be combined in the consolidated accounts.

Article 18

The assets and liabilities of undertakings included in a consolidation shall be incorporated in full in the consolidated balance sheet.

Article 19

1. The book values of shares in the capital of undertakings included in a consolidation shall be set off against the proportion which they represent of the capital and reserves of those undertakings:

(a) That set-off shall be effected on the basis of book values as at the date as at which such undertakings are included in the consolidations for the first time. Differences arising from such set-offs shall as far as possible be entered directly against those items in the consolidated balance sheet which have values above or below their book values.

(b) A Member State may require or permit set-offs on the basis of the values of identifiable assets and liabilities as at the date of acquisition of the shares or, in the event of acquisition in two or more stages, as at the date on which the undertaking became a subsidiary.

(c) Any difference remaining after the application of (a) or resulting from the application of (b) shall be shown as a separate item in the consolidated balance sheet with an appropriate heading. That item, the methods used and any significant changes in relation to the preceding financial year must be explained in the notes on the accounts. Where the offsetting of positive and negative differences is authorized by a Member State, a breakdown of such differences must also be given in the notes on the accounts.

2. However, paragraph 1 above shall not apply to shares in the capital of the parent undertaking held either by that undertaking itself or by another undertaking included in the consolidation. In the consolidated accounts such shares shall be treated as own shares in accordance with Directive 78/660/EEC.

Article 20

1. A Member State may require or permit the book values of shares held in the capital of an undertaking included in the consolidation to be set off against the corresponding percentage of capital only, provided that:

(a) the shares held represent at least 90 % of the nominal value or, in the absence of a nominal value, of the accounting par value of the shares of that undertaking other than shares of the kind described in Article 29 (2) (a) of Directive 77/91/EEC(1);

(b) the proportion referred to in (a) above has been attained pursuant to an arrangement providing for the issue of shares by an undertaking included in the consolidation; and

(c) the arrangement referred to in (b) above did not include a cash payment exceeding 10 % of the nominal value or, in the absence of a nominal value, of the accounting par value of the shares issued.

2. Any difference arising under paragraph 1 above shall be added to or deducted from consolidated reserves as appropriate.

3. The application of the method described in paragraph 1 above, the resulting movement in reserves and the names and registered offices of the undertakings concerned shall be disclosed in the notes on the accounts.

Article 21

The amount attributable to shares in subsidiary undertakings included in the consolidation held by persons other than the undertakings included in the consolidation shall be shown in the consolidated balance sheet as a separate item with an appropriate heading.

Article 22

The income and expenditure of undertakings included in a consolidation shall be incorporated in full in the consolidated profit-and-loss account.

Article 23

The amount of any profit or loss attributable to shares in subsidiary undertakings included in the consolidation held by persons other than the undertakings included in the consolidation shall be shown in the consolidated profit-and-loss account as a separate item with an appropriate heading.

Article 24

Consolidated accounts shall be drawn up in accordance with the principles enunciated in Articles 25 to 28.

Article 25

1. The methods of consolidation must be applied consistently from one financial year to another.

2. Derogations from the provisions of paragraph 1 above shall be permitted in exceptional cases. Any such derogations must be disclosed in the notes on the accounts and the reasons for them given together with an assessment of their effect on the assets, liabilities, financial position and profit or loss of the undertakings included in the consolidation taken as a whole.

---

(1) OJ No L26, 31.1.1977, p. 1.
See page 361 of this book.

OFFICIAL TEXT OF THE SEVENTH DIRECTIVE

Article 26

1. Consolidated accounts shall show the assets, liabilities, financial positions and profits or losses of the undertakings included in a consolidation as if the latter were a single undertaking. In particular:

(a) debts and claims between the undertakings included in a consolidation shall be eliminated from the consolidated accounts;

(b) income and expenditure relating to transactions between the undertakings included in a consolidation shall be eliminated from the consolidated accounts;

(c) where profits and losses resulting from transactions between the undertakings included in a consolidation are included in the book values of assets, they shall be eliminated from the consolidated accounts. Pending subsequent coordination, however, a Member State may allow the eliminations mentioned above to be effected in proportion to the percentage of the capital held by the parent undertaking in each of the subsidiary undertakings included in the consolidation.

2. A Member State may permit derogations from the provisions of paragraph 1 (c) above where a transaction has been concluded according to normal market conditions and where the elimination of the profit or loss would entail undue expense. Any such derogations must be disclosed and where the effect on the assets, liabilities, financial position and profit or loss of the undertakings, included in the consolidation, taken as a whole, is material, that fact must be disclosed in the notes on the consolidated accounts.

3. Derogations from the provisions of paragraph 1 (a), (b) or (c) above shall be permitted where the amounts concerned are not material for the purposes of Article 16 (3).

Article 27

1. Consolidated accounts must be drawn up as at the same date as the annual accounts of the parent undertaking.

2. A Member State may, however, require or permit consolidated accounts to be drawn up as at another date in order to take account of the balance sheet dates of the largest number or the most important of the undertakings included in the consolidation. Where use is made of this derogation that fact shall be disclosed in the notes on the consolidated accounts together with the reasons therefor. In addition, account must be taken or disclosure made of important events concerning the assets and liabilities, the financial position or the profit or loss of an undertaking included in a consolidation which have occurred between that undertaking's balance sheet date and the consolidated balance sheet date.

3. Where an undertaking's balance sheet date precedes the consolidated balance sheet date by more than three months, that undertaking shall be consolidated on the basis of interim accounts drawn up as at the consolidated balance sheet date.

Article 28

If the composition of the undertakings included in a consolidation has changed significantly in the course of a financial year, the consolidated accounts must include information which makes the comparison of successive sets of consolidated accounts meaningful. Where such a change is a major one, a Member State may require or permit this obligation to be fulfilled by the preparation of an adjusted opening balance sheet and an adjusted profit-and-loss account.

OFFICIAL TEXT OF THE SEVENTH DIRECTIVE

Article 29

1. Assets and liabilities to be included in consolidated accounts shall be valued according to uniform methods and in accordance with Articles 31 to 42 and 60 of Directive 78/660/EEC.

2. (a) An undertaking which draws up consolidated accounts must apply the same methods of valuation as in its annual accounts. However, a Member State may require or permit the use in consolidated accounts of other methods of valuation in accordance with the abovementioned Articles of Directive 78/660/EEC.
   (b) Where use is made of this derogation that fact shall be disclosed in the notes on the consolidated accounts and the reasons therefor given.

3. Where assets and liabilities to be included in consolidated accounts have been valued by undertakings included in the consolidation by methods differing from those used for the consolidation, they must be revalued in accordance with the methods used for the consolidation, unless the results of such revaluation are not material for the purposes of Article 16 (3). Departures from this principle shall be permitted in exeptional cases. Any such departures shall be disclosed in the notes on the consolidated accounts and the reasons for them given.

4. Account shall be taken in the consolidated balance sheet and in the consolidated profit-and-loss account of any difference arising on consolidation between the tax chargeable for the financial year and for preceding financial years and the amount of tax paid or payable in respect of those years, provided that it is probable that an actual charge to tax will arise within the foreseable future for one of the undertakings included in the consolidation.

5. Where assets to be included in consolidated accounts have been the subject of exceptional valuc adjustments solely for tax purposes, they shall be incorporated in the consolidated accounts only after those adjustments have been eliminated. A Member State may, however, require or permit that such assets be incorporated in the consolidated accounts without the elimination of the adjustments, provided that their amounts, together with the reasons for them, are disclosed in the notes on the consolidated accounts.

Article 30

1. A separate item as defined in Article 19 (1) (c) which corresponds to a positive consolidation difference shall be dealt with in accordance with the rules laid down in Directive 78/660/EEC for the item 'goodwill'.

2. A Member State may permit a positive consolidation difference to be immediately and clearly deducted from reserves.

Article 31

An amount shown as a separate item, as defined in Article 19 (1) (c), which corresponds to a negative consolidation difference may be transferred to the consolidated profit-and-loss account only:

(a) where that difference corresponds to the expectation at the date of acquisition of unfavourable future results in that undertaking, or to the expectation of costs which that undertaking would incur, in so far as such an expectation materializes; or
(b) in so far as such a difference corresponds to a realized gain.

OFFICIAL TEXT OF THE SEVENTH DIRECTIVE

Article 32

1. Where an undertaking included in a consolidation manages another undertaking jointly with one or more undertakings not included in that consolidation, a Member State may require or permit the inclusion of that other undertaking in the consolidated accounts in proportion to the rights in its capital held by the undertaking included in the consolidation.

2. Articles 13 to 31 shall apply *mutatis mutandis* to the proportional consolidation referred to in paragraph 1 above.

3. Where this Article is applied, Article 33 shall not apply if the undertaking proportionally consolidated is an associated undertaking as defined in Article 33.

Article 33

1. Where an undertaking included in a consolidation exercises a significant influence over the operating and financial policy of an undertaking not included in the consolidation (an associated undertaking) in which it holds a participating interest, as defined in Article 17 of Directive 78/660/EEC, that participating interest shall be shown in the consolidated balance sheet as a separate item with an appropriate heading. An undertaking shall be presumed to exercise a significant influence over another undertaking where it has 20 % or more of the shareholders' or members' voting rights in that undertaking. Article 2 shall apply.

2. When this Article is applied for the first time to a participating interest covered by paragraph' 1 above, that participating interest shall be shown in the consolidated balance sheet either:

(a) at its book value calculated in accordance with the valuation rules laid down in Directive 78/660/EEC. The difference between that value and the amount corresponding to the proportion of capital and reserves represented by that participating interest shall be disclosed separately in the consolidated balance sheet or in the notes on the accounts. That difference shall be calculated as at the date as at which that method is used for the first time; or

(b) at an amount corresponding to the proportion of the associated undertaking's capital and reserves represented by that participating interest. The difference between that amount and the book value calculated in accordance with the valuation rules laid down in Directive 78/660/EEC shall be disclosed separately in the consolidated balance sheet or in the notes on the accounts. That difference shall be calculated as at the date as at which that method is used for the first time.

(c) A Member State may prescribe the application of one or other of (a) and (b) above. The consolidated balance sheet or the notes on the accounts must indicate whether (a) or (b) has been used.

(d) In addition, for the purposes of (a) and (b) above, a Member State may require or permit the calculation of the difference as at the date of acquisition of the shares, or where they were acquired in two or more stages, as at the date on which the undertaking became an associated undertaking.

3. Where an associated undertaking's assets or liabilities have been valued by methods other than those used for consolidation in accordance with Article 29 (2), they may, for the purpose of calculating the difference referred to in paragraph 2 (a) or (b) above, be revalued by the methods used for consolidation. Where such revaluation has not been carried out that fact must be disclosed in the notes on the accounts. A Member State may require such revaluation.

OFFICIAL TEXT OF THE SEVENTH DIRECTIVE

4. The book value referred to in paragraph 2 (a) above, or the amount corresponding to the proportion of the associated undertaking's capital and reserves referred to in paragraph 2 (b) above, shall be increased or reduced by the amount of any variation which has taken place during the financial year in the proportion of the associated undertaking's capital and reserves represented by that participating interest; it shall be reduced by the amount of the dividends relating to that participating interest.
5. In so far as the positive difference referred to in paragraph 2 (a) or (b) above cannot be related to any category of assets or liabilities it shall be dealt with in accordance with Articles 30 and 39 (3).
6. The proportion of the profit or loss of the associated undertakings attributable to such participating interests shall be shown in the consolidated profit- and-loss account as a separate item under an appropriate heading.
7. The eliminations referred to in Article 26 (1) (c) shall be effected in so far as the facts are known or can be ascertained. Article 26 (2) and (3) shall apply.
8. Where an associated undertaking draws up consolidated accounts, the foregoing provisions shall apply to the capital and reserves shown in such consolidated accounts.
9. This Article need not be applied where the participating interest in the capital of the associated undertaking is not material for the purposes of Article 16 (3).

Article 34

In addition to the information required under other provisions of this Directive, the notes on the accounts must set out information in respect of the following matters at least:

1. The valuation methods applied to the various items in the consolidated accounts, and the methods employed in calculating the value adjustments. For items included in the consolidated accounts which are or were originally expressed in foreign currency the bases of conversion used to express them in the currency in which the consolidated accounts are drawn up must be disclosed.
2. (a) The names and registered offices of the undertakings included in the consolidation; the proportion of the capital held in undertakings included in the consolidation, other than the parent undertaking, by the undertakings included in the consolidation or by persons acting in their own names but on behalf of those undertakings; which of the conditions referred to in Articles 1 and 12 (1) following application of Article 2 has formed the basis on which the consolidation has been carried out. The latter disclosure may, however, be omitted where consolidation has been carried out on the basis of Article 1 (1) (a) and where the proportion of the capital and the proportion of the voting rights held are the same.
   (b) The same information must be given in respect of undertakings excluded from a consolidation pursuant to Articles 13 and 14 and, without prejudice to Article 14 (3), an explanation must be given for the exclusion of the undertakings referred to in Article 13.
3. (a) The names and registered offices of undertakings associated with an undertaking included in the consolidation as described in Article 33 (1) and the proportion of their capital held by undertakings included in the consolidation or by persons acting in their own names but on behalf of those undertakings.
   (b) The same information must be given in respect of the associated undertakings referred to in Article 33 (9), together with the reasons for applying that provision.
4. The names and registered offices of undertakings proportionally consolidated pur-

suant to Article 32, the factors on which joint management is based, and the proportion of their capital held by the undertakings included in the consolidation or by persons acting in their own names but on behalf of those undertakings.

5. The name and registered office of each of the undertakings, other than those referred to in paragraphs 2, 3 and 4 above, in which undertakings included in the consolidation and those excluded pursuant to Article 14, either themselves or through persons acting in their own names but on behalf of those undertakings, hold at least a percentage of the capital which the Member States cannot fix at more than 20 %, showing the proportion of the capital held, the amount of the capital and reserves, and the profit or loss for the latest financial year of the undertaking concerned for which accounts have been adopted. This information may be omitted where, for the purposes of Article 16 (3), it is of negligible importance only. The information concerning capital and reserves and the profit or loss may also be omitted where the undertaking concerned does not publish its balance sheet and where less than 50 % of its capital is held (directly or indirectly) by the abovementioned undertakings.
6. The total amount shown as owed in the consolidated balance sheet and becoming due and payable after more than five years, as well as the total amount shown as owed in the consolidated balance sheet and covered by valuable security furnished by undertakings included in the consolidation, with an indication of the nature and form of the security.
7. The total amount of any financial commitments that are not included in the consolidated balance sheet, in so far as this information is of assistance in assessing the financial position of the undertakings included in the consolidation taken as a whole. Any commitments concerning pensions and affiliated undertakings which are not included in the consolidation must be disclosed separately.
8. The consolidated net turnover as defined in Article 28 of Directive 78/660/EEC, broken down by categories of activity and into geographical markets in so far as, taking account of the manner in which the sale of products and the provision of services falling within the ordinary activities of the undertakings included in the consolidation taken as a whole are organized, these categories and markets differ substantially from one another.
9. (a) The average number of persons employed during the financial year by undertakings included in the consolidation broken down by categories and, if they are not disclosed separately in the consolidated profit-and-loss account, the staff costs relating to the financial year.
   (b) The average number of persons employed during the financial year by undertakings to which Article 32 has been applied shall be disclosed separately.
10. The extent to which the calculation of the consolidated profit or loss for the financial year has been affected by a valuation of the items which, by way of derogation from the principles enunciated in Articles 31 and 34 to 42 of Directive 78/660/EEC and in Article 29 (5) of this Directive, was made in the financial year in question or in an earlier financial year with a view to obtaining tax relief. Where the influence of such a valuation on the future tax charges of the undertakings included in the consolidation taken as a whole is material, details must be disclosed.
11. The difference between the tax charged to the consolidated profit-and-loss account for the financial year and to those for earlier financial years and the amount of tax payable in respect of those years, provided that this difference is material for the purposes of future taxation. This amount may also be disclosed in the balance sheet

OFFICIAL TEXT OF THE SEVENTH DIRECTIVE

as a cumulative amount under a separate item with an appropriate heading.

12. The amount of the emoluments granted in respect of the financial year to the members of the administrative, managerial and supervisory bodies of the parent undertaking by reason of their responsibilities in the parent undertaking and its subsidiary undertakings, and any commitments arising or entered into under the same conditions in respect of retirement pensions for former members of those bodies, with an indication of the total for each category. A Member State may require that emoluments granted by reason of responsibilities assumed in undertakings linked as described in Article 32 or 33 shall also be included with the information specified in the first sentence.
13. The amount of advances and credits granted to the members of the administrative, managerial and supervisory bodies of the parent undertaking by that undertaking or by one of its subsidiary undertakings, with indications of the interest rates, main conditions and any amounts repaid, as well as commitments entered into on their behalf by way of guarantee of any kind with an indication of the total for each category. A Member State may require that advances and credits granted by undertakings linked as described in Article 32 or 33 shall also be included with the information specified in the first sentence.

Article 35

1. A Member State may allow the disclosures prescribed in Article 34 (2), (3), (4) and (5):

(a) to take the form of a statement deposited in accordance with Article 3 (1) and (2) of Directive 68/151/EEC; this must be disclosed in the notes on the accounts;

(b) to be omitted when their nature is such that they would be seriously prejudicial to any of the undertakings affected by these provisions. A Member State may make such omissions subject to prior administrative or judicial authorization. Any such omission must be disclosed in the notes on the accounts.

2. Paragraph 1 (b) shall also apply to the information prescribed in Article 34 (8).

SECTION 3

The consolidated annual report

Article 36

1. The consolidated annual report must include at least a fair review of the development of business and the position of the undertakings included in the consolidation taken as a whole.

2. In respect of those undertakings, the report shall also give an indication of:

(a) any important events that have occurred since the end of the financial year;

(b) the likely future development of those undertakings taken as a whole;

(c) the activities of those undertakings taken as a whole in the field of research and development;

(d) the number and nominal value or, in the absence of a nominal value, the accounting par value of all of the parent undertaking's shares held by that undertaking itself, by subsidiary undertakings of that undertaking or by a person acting in his own name but on behalf of those undertakings. A Member State may require or permit the disclosure of these particulars in the notes on the accounts.

OFFICIAL TEXT OF THE SEVENTH DIRECTIVE

SECTION 4

The auditing of consolidated accounts

Article 37

1. An undertaking which draws up consolidated accounts must have them audited by one or more persons authorized to audit accounts under the laws of the Member State which govern that undertaking.
2. The person or persons responsible for auditing the consolidated accounts must also verify that the consolidated annual report is consistent with the consolidated accounts for the same financial year.

SECTION 5

The publication of consolidated accounts

Article 38

1. Consolidated accounts, duly approved, and the consolidated annual report, together with the opinion submitted by the person responsible for auditing the consolidated accounts, shall be published for the undertaking which drew up the consolidated accounts as laid down by the laws of the Member State which govern it in accordance with Article 3 of Directive 68/151/EEC.
2. The second subparagraph of Article 47 (1) of Directive 78/660/EEC shall apply with respect to the consolidated annual report.
3. The following shall be substituted for the second subparagraph of Article 47 (1) of Directive 78/660/EEC: 'It must be possible to obtain a copy of all or part of any such report upon request. The price of such a copy must not exceed its administrative cost'.
4. However, where the undertaking which drew up the consolidated accounts is not established as one of the types of company listed in Article 4 and is not required by its national law to publish the documents referred to in paragraph 1 in the same manner as prescribed in Article 3 of Directive 68/151/EEC, it must at least make them available to the public at its head office. It must be possible to obtain a copy of such documents upon request. The price of such a copy must not exceed its administrative cost.
5. Articles 48 and 49 of Directive 78/660/EEC shall apply.
6. The Member States shall provide for appropriate sanctions for failure to comply with the publication obligations imposed in this Article.

SECTION 6

Transitional and final provisions

Article 39

1. When, for the first time consolidated accounts are drawn up in accordance with this Directive for a body of undertakings which was already connected, as described in Article 1 (1), before application of the provisions referred to in Article 49 (1), a Member State may require or permit that, for the purposes of Article 19 (1), account be taken of the book value of a holding and the proportion of the capital and reserves that it represents as at a date before or the same as that of the first consolidation.

2. Paragraph 1 above shall apply *mutatis mutandis* to the valuation for the purposes of Article 33 (2) of a holding, or of the proportion of capital and reserves that it represents, in the capital of an undertaking associated with an undertaking included in the consolidation, and to the proportional consolidation referred to in Article 32.
3. Where the separate item defined in Article 19 (1) corresponds to a positive consolidation difference which arose before the date of the first consolidated accounts drawn up in accordance with this Directive, a Member State may:
(a) for the purposes of Article 30 (1), permit the calculation of the limited period of more than five years provided for in Article 32 (2) of Directive 78/660/EEC as from the date of the first consolidated accounts drawn up in accordance with this Directive; and
(b) for the purposes of Article 30 (2), permit the deduction to be made from reserves as at the date of the first consolidated accounts drawn up in accordance with this Directive.

Article 40

1. Until expiry of the deadline imposed for the application in national law of the Directives supplementing Directive 78/660/EEC as regards the harmonization of the rules governing the annual accounts of banks and other financial institutions and insurance undertakings, a Member State may derogate from the provisions of this Directive concerning the layout of consolidated accounts, the methods of valuing the items included in those accounts and the information to be given in the notes on the accounts:
(a) with regard to any undertaking to be consolidated which is a bank, another financial institution or an insurance undertaking;
(b) where the undertakings to be consolidated comprise principally banks, financial institutions or insurance undertakings.
They may also derogate from Article 6, but only in so far as the limits and criteria to be applied to the above undertakings are concerned.
2. In so far as a Member State has not required all undertakings which are banks, other financial institutions or insurance undertakings to draw up consolidated accounts before implementation of the provisions referred to in Article 49 (1), it may, until its national law implements one of the Directives mentioned in paragraph 1 above, but not in respect of financial years ending after 1993:
(a) suspend the application of the obligation imposed in Article 1 (1) with respect to any of the above undertakings which is a parent undertaking. That fact must be disclosed in the annual accounts of the parent undertaking and the information prescribed in point 2 of Article 43 (1) of Directive 78/660/EEC must be given for all subsidiary undertakings;
(b) where consolidated accounts are drawn up and without prejudice to Article 33, permit the omission from the consolidation of any of the above undertakings which is a subsidiary undertaking. The information prescribed in Article 34 (2) must be given in the notes on the accounts in respect of any such subsidiary undertaking.
3. In the cases referred to in paragraph 2 (b) above, the annual or consolidated accounts of the subsidiary undertaking must, in so far as their publication is compulsory, be attached to the consolidated accounts or, in the absence of consolidated accounts, to the annual accounts of the parent undertaking or be made available to the public. In the latter case it must be possible to obtain a copy of such documents upon request. The price of such a copy must not exceed its administrative cost.

OFFICIAL TEXT OF THE SEVENTH DIRECTIVE

Article 41
1. Undertakings which are connected as described in Article 1 (1) (a), (b) and (d) (bb), and those other undertakings which are similarly connected with one of the aforementioned undertakings, shall be affiliated undertakings for the purposes of this Directive and of Directive 78/660/EEC.
2. Where a Member State prescribes the preparation of consolidated accounts pursuant to Article 1 (1) (c), (d) (aa) or (2) or Article 12 (1), the undertakings which are connected as described in those Articles and those other undertakings which are connected similarly, or are connected as described in paragraph 1 above to one of the aforementioned undertakings, shall be affiliated undertakings as defined in paragraph 1.
3. Even where a Member State does not prescribe the preparation of consolidated accounts pursuant to Article 1 (1) (c), (d) (aa) or (2) or Article 12 (1), it may apply paragraph 2 of this Article.
4. Articles 2 and 3 (2) shall apply.
5. When a Member State applies Article 4 (2), it may exclude from the application of paragraph 1 above affiliated undertakings which are parent undertakings and which by virtue of their legal form are not required by that Member State to draw up consolidated accounts in accordance with the provisions of this Directive, as well as parent undertakings with a similar legal form.

Article 42
The following shall be substituted for Article 56 of Directive 78/660/EEC:
'Article 56
1. The obligation to show in annual accounts the items prescribed by Articles 9, 10 and 23 to 26 which relate to affiliated undertakings, as defined by Article 41 of Directive 83/349/EEC, and the obligation to provide information concerning these undertakings in accordance with Articles 13 (2), and 14 and point 7 of Article 43 (1) shall enter into force on the date fixed in Article 49 (2) of that Directive.
2. The notes on the accounts must also disclose:
(a) the name and registered office of the undertaking which draws up the consolidated accounts of the largest body of undertakings of which the company forms part as a subsidiary undertaking;
(b) the name and registered office of the undertaking which draws up the consolidated accounts of the smallest body of undertakings of which the company forms part as a subsidiary undertaking and which is also included in the body of undertakings referred to in (a) above;
(c) the place where copies of the consolidated accounts referred to in (a) and (b) above may be obtained provided that they are available.'

Article 43
The following shall be substituted for Article 57 of Directive 78/660/EEC:
'Article 57
Notwithstanding the provisions of Directives 68/151/EEC and 77/91/EEC, a Member State need not apply the provisions of this Directive concerning the content, auditing and publication of annual accounts to companies governed by their national laws which are subsidiary undertakings, as defined in Directive 83/349/EEC, where the following conditions are fulfilled:
(a) the parent undertaking must be subject to the laws of a Member State;

(b) all shareholders or members of the subsidiary undertaking must have declared their agreement to the exemption from such obligation; this declaration must be made in respect of every financial year;
(c) the parent undertaking must have declared that it guarantees the commitments entered into by the subsidiary undertaking;
(d) the declarations referred to in (b) and (c) must be published by the subsidiary undertaking as laid down by the laws of the Member State in accordance with Article 3 of Directive 68/151/EEC;
(e) the subsidiary undertaking must be included in the consolidated accounts drawn op by the parent undertaking in accordance with Directive 83/349/EEC;
(f) the above exemption must be disclosed in the notes on the consolidated accounts drawn up by the parent undertaking;
(g) the consolidated accounts referred to in (e), the consolidated annual report, and the report by the person responsible for auditing those accounts must be published for the subsidiary undertaking as laid down by the laws of the Member State in accordance with Article 3 of Directive 68/151/EEC.'

Article 44
The following shall be substituted for Article 58 of Directive 78/660/EEC:
'Article 58
A Member State need not apply the provisions of this Directive concerning the auditing and publication of the profit-and-loss account to companies governed by their national laws which are parent undertakings for the purposes of Directive 83/349/EEC where the following conditions are fulfilled:
(a) the parent undertaking must draw up consolidated accounts in accordance with Directive 83/349/EEC and be included in the consolidated accounts;
(b) the above exemption must be disclosed in the notes on the annual accounts of the parent undertaking;
(c) the above exemption must be disclosed in the notes on the consolidated accounts drawn up by the parent undertaking;
(d) the profit or loss of the parent company, determined in accordance with this Directive, must be shown in the balance sheet of the parent company.'

Article 45
The following shall be substituted for Article 59 of Directive 78/660/EEC:
'Article 59
1. A Member State may require or permit that participating interests, as defined in Article 17, in the capital of undertakings over the operating and financial policies of which significant influence is exercised, be shown in the balance sheet in accordance with paragraphs 2 to 9 below, as sub-items of the items "shares in affiliated undertakings" or "participating interests", as the case may be. An undertaking shall be presumed to exercise a significant influence over another undertaking where it has 20 % or more of the shareholders' or members' voting rights in that undertaking. Article 2 of Directive 83/349/EEC shall apply.
2. When this Article is first applied to a participating interest covered by paragraph 1, it shall be shown in the balance sheet either:
(a) at its book value calculated in accordance with Articles 31 to 42. The difference between that value and the amount corresponding to the proportion of capital and

OFFICIAL TEXT OF THE SEVENTH DIRECTIVE

reserves represented by the participating interest shall be disclosed separately in the balance sheet or in the notes on the accounts. That difference shall be calculated as at the date as at which the method is applied for the first time; or

(b) at the amount corresponding to the proportion of the capital and reserves represented by the participating interest. The difference between that amount and the book value calculated in accordance with Articles 31 to 42 shall be disclosed separately in the balance sheet or in the notes on the accounts. That difference shall be calculated as at the date as at which the method is applied for the first time.

(c) A Member State may prescribe the application of one or other of the above paragraphs. The balance sheet or the notes on the accounts must indicate whether (a) or (b) above has been used.

(d) In addition, when applying (a) and (b) above, a Member State may require or permit calculation of the difference as at the date of acquisition of the participating interest referred to in paragraph 1 or, where the acquisition took place in two or more stages, as at the date as at which the holding became a participating interest within the meaning of paragraph 1 above.

3. Where the assets or liabilities of an undertaking in which a participating interest within the meaning of paragraph 1 above is held have been valued by methods other than those used by the company drawing up the annual accounts, they may, for the purpose of calculating the difference referred to in paragraph 2 (a) or (b) above, be revalued by the methods used by the company drawing up the annual accounts. Disclosure must be made in the notes on the accounts where such revaluation has not been carried out. A Member State may require such revaluation.

4. The book value referred to in paragraph 2 (a) above, or the amount corresponding to the proportion of capital and reserves referred to in paragraph 2 (b) above, shall be increased or reduced by the amount of the variation which has taken place during the financial year in the proportion of capital and reserves represented by that participating interest; it shall be reduced by the amount of the dividends relating to the participating interest.

5. In so far as a positive difference covered by paragraph 2 (a) or (b) above cannot be related to any category of asset or liability, it shall be dealt with in accordance with the rules applicable to the item "goodwill".

6. (a) The proportion of the profit or loss attributable to participating interests within the meaning of paragraph 1 above shall be shown in the profit-and-loss account as a separate item with an appropriate heading.

(b) Where that amount exceeds the amount of dividends already received or the payment of which can be claimed, the amount of the difference must be placed in a reserve which cannot be distributed to shareholders.

(c) A Member State may require or permit that the proportion of the profit or loss attributable to the participating interests referred to in paragraph 1 above be shown in the profit-and-loss account only to the extent of the amount corresponding to dividends already received or the payment of which can be claimed.

7. The eliminations referred to in Article 26 (1) (c) of Directive 83/349/EEC shall be effected in so far as the facts are known or can be ascertained. Article 26 (2) and (3) of that Directive shall apply.

8. Where an undertaking in which a participating interest within the meaning of paragraph 1 above is held draws up consolidated accounts, the foregoing paragraphs shall apply to the capital and reserves shown in such consolidated accounts.

9. This Article need not be applied where a participating interest as defined in paragraph 1 is not material for the purposes of Article 2 (3).'

Article 46

The following shall be substituted for Article 61 of Directive 78/660/EEC:

'Article 61

A Member State need not apply the provisions of point 2 of Article 43 (1) of this Directive concerning the amount of capital and reserves and profits and losses of the undertakings concerned to companies governed by their national laws which are parent undertakings for the purposes of Directive 83/349/EEC:

(a) where the undertakings concerned are included in consolidated accounts drawn up by that parent undertaking, or in the consolidated accounts of a larger body of undertakings as referred to in Article 7 (2) of Directive 83/349/EEC; or

(b) where the holdings in the undertakings concerned have been dealt with by the parent undertaking in its annual accounts in accordance with Article 59, or in the consolidated accounts drawn up by that parent undertaking in accordance with Article 33 of Directive 83/349/EEC.'

Article 47

The Contact Committee set up pursuant to Article 52 of Directive 78/660/EEC shall also:

(a) facilitate, without prejudice to Articles 169 and 170 of the Treaty, harmonized application of this Directive through regular meetings dealing, in particular, with practical problems arising in connection with its application;

(b) advise the Commission, if necessary, on additions or amendments to this Directive.

Article 48

This Directive shall not affect laws in the Member States requiring that consolidated accounts in which undertakings not falling within their jurisdiction are included be filed in a register in which branches of such undertakings are listed.

Article 49

1. The Member States shall bring into force the laws, regulations and administrative provisions necessary for them to comply with this Directive before 1 January 1988. They shall forthwith inform the Commission thereof.

2. A Member State may provide that the provisions referred to in paragraph 1 above shall first apply to consolidated accounts for financial years beginning on 1 January 1990 or during the calendar year 1990.

3. The Member States shall ensure that they communicate to the Commission the texts of the main provisions of national law which they adopt in the field covered by this Directive.

Article 50

1. Five years after the date referred to in Article 49 (2), the Council, acting on a proposal from the Commission, shall examine and if need be revise Articles 1 (1) (d) (second subparagraph), 4 (2), 5, 6, 7 (1), 12, 43 and 44 in the light of the experience acquired in applying this Directive, the aims of this Directive and the economic and monetary situation at the time.

OFFICIAL TEXT OF THE SEVENTH DIRECTIVE

2. Paragraph 1 above shall not affect Article 53 (2) of Directive 78/660/EEC.

Article 51
This Directive is addressed to the Member States.
Done at Luxembourg, 13 June 1983.
For the Council
The President
H. TIETMEYER

FIRST COUNCIL DIRECTIVE
(68/151/EEC)

Article 3

1. In each Member State a file shall be opened in a central register, commercial register or companies register, for each of the companies registered therein.

2. All documents and particulars which must be disclosed in pursuance of Article 2 shall be kept in the file or entered in the register; the subject-matter of the entries in the register must in every case appear in the file.

3. A copy of the whole or any part of the documents or particulars referred to in Article 2 must be obtainable by application in writing at a price not exceeding the administrative cost thereof.

Copies supplied shall be certified as 'true copies', unless the applicant dispenses with such certification.

4. Disclosure of the documents and particulars referred to in paragraph (2) shall be effected by publication in the National Gazette appointed for that purpose by the Member State, either of the full or partial text, or by means of a reference to the document which has been deposited in the file or entered in the register.

5. The documents and particulars may be relied on by the company as against third parties only after they have been published in accordance with paragraph (4), unless the company proves that the third parties had knowledge thereof. However, with regard to transactions taking place before the sixteenth day following the publication, the documents and particulars shall not be relied on as against third parties who prove that it was impossible for them to have had knowledge thereof.

6. Member States shall take the necessary measures to avoid any discrepancy between what is disclosed by publication in the press and what appears in the register or file.

However, in cases of discrepancy, the text published in the press may not be relied on as against third parties; the latter may nevertheless rely thereon, unless the company proves that they had knowledge of the texts deposited in the file or entered in the register.

7. Third parties may, moreover, always rely on any documents and particulars in respect of which the disclosure formalities have not yet been completed, save where non-disclosure causes them not to have effect.

SECOND COUNCIL DIRECTIVE
(77/91/EEC)

Article 22

1. Where the laws of a Member State permit a company to acquire its own shares, either itself or through a person acting on his own name but on the company's behalf, they shall make the holding of these shares at all times subject to at least the following conditions:

a. among the rights attaching to the shares, the right to vote attaching to the company's own shares shall in any event be suspended;

b. if the shares are included among the assets shown in the balance-sheet, a reserve of the same amount, unavailable for distribution, shall be included among the liabilities.

2. Where the laws of a Member State permit a company to acquire its own shares, either itself or through a person acting in his own name but on the company's behalf, they shall require the annual report to state at least;

a. the reasons for acquisitions made during the financial year;

b. the number and nominal value or, in the absence of a nominal value, the accountable part of the shares acquired and disposed of during the financial year and the proportion of the subscribed capital which they represent;

c. in the case of acquisition or disposal for a value, the consideration for the shares;

d. the number and nominal value or, in the absence of a nominal value, the accountable part of all the shares acquired and held by the company and the proportion of the subscribed capital which they represent.

Name Index